This book must be returned immediately it is asked for by the Librarian,
and in any case by the last date
stamped below.

SWANSEA UNIVERSITY COLLEGE LIBRARY

The Irish Co-operative Movement

The Irish Co-operative Movement
Its History and Development

Patrick Bolger

INSTITUTE OF PUBLIC ADMINISTRATION
DUBLIN

© Patrick Bolger 1977

Published by Institute of Public Administration
59 Lansdowne Road, Dublin 4, Ireland

ISBNs
0 902173 75 8 hard covers
0 902173 76 6 paperback

Set in 10 on 12 point Plantin by Koningsveld & Zoon (I) Ltd.

Printed in the Republic of Ireland by Cahill (1976) Ltd.,
East Wall Road, Dublin 3

*For Kate first of all
but, in no way less,
for everyone else*

Contents

ILLUSTRATIONS

Foreword

by Patrick Kelly, Director-General,
Irish Agricultural Organisation Society Limited

The Irish Agricultural Organisation Society Ltd (IAOS) is now in its eighty-third year, serving as the central organisation of the agricultural co-operative movement, for the whole of Ireland up to 1922 and subsequently for the Republic of Ireland. In 1922 the Ulster Committee of the IAOS was established as an autonomous Organisation Society for Northern Ireland — The Ulster Agricultural Organisation Society Ltd (UAOS). The principal reason for this division of function was political and a direct result of the establishment of separate governments in Dublin and Belfast. Pat Bolger has now woven, with great expertise, a fascinating story out of the tangled threads of Irish political, social and economic history, as he traces the development of the Irish agricultural co-operative movement from its tentative, hesitant beginnings in the eighteen eighties to its predominant position in the Irish business world of today. His book, a comprehensive and detailed account of agricultural co-operation in Ireland, remedies the serious neglect of one of the most significant developments of the 'Ireland of the new Century'.

In his many articles, Pat Bolger has shown that he is a shrewd observer of the agricultural community. He reveals the same characteristic in his history of Irish co-operation. While he is at all times critically objective in relating the practices, the reader is left in no doubt of his enthusiasm for the fundamental principles.

It has been said that "there is properly no history, only biography". In this respect the chapters of the book which establish the ideological link between the great social and economic reformers of the eighteenth and nineteenth centuries and the early pioneers of the Irish agricultural co-operative movement are fascinating. The pen pictures of Robert Owen, William Thompson and the Rochdale Pioneers are vividly descriptive and illuminating. Pat Bolger indicates how each in his own way advanced the cause of social justice and equitable dealing for the great mass of the people. The Irish rural population of the nineteenth century was as socially insignificant as the working classes of the cities and towns of industrial England. The influence of Michael Davitt and the Land League in teaching "an oppressed and subservient people the art of working together" was later acknowledged by the founder of Irish agricultural co-operation, Sir Horace Plunkett, as significant in helping Irish farmers to realise that self-help through mutual help was not just an empty slogan.

It is a little sad to reflect that the names of the men who had the foresight, courage and ability to lead the farmers of Ireland into the business world of vested interest at the turn of the twentieth century, should be almost forgotten in Ireland. Sir Horace Plunkett, Father Tom Finlay, George Russell (AE), R.A. Anderson — men of diverse political and religious views — are shown to have had a single-minded conviction of the importance of the co-operative movement for Irish farmers. Their contribution to the development of the social and economic fabric of the country is worthy of far greater recognition than has been accorded so far.

Pat Bolger's history is not just a continuous methodical record of dates, facts and figures, although these are present. It is not merely biographical sketches of the outstanding personalities, although these are important. The story essentially relates the achievements of ordinary people whose motivation in many cases was "little more than an ill-defined desire for rural improvement". However inarticulate ordinary farmers may have been, their actions bore the stamp of conviction. Many of them pledged their farms so that finance would be available to start co-operatives for the benefit of the communities in which they lived.

Pat Bolger observes that, in the past, co-operation was increasingly threatened by competition between the societies. Now that so many co-operatives are large-scale business enterprises, there is the urgent task of unifying and welding their efforts so that co-operative coordination, rather than co-operative competition, will prevail. This is no easy task.

The primary purpose of agricultural co-operatives is to provide effective and efficient business services to farmers. This can only be done by well-supported, well-managed and well-coordinated co-operatives, controlled by farmers and operating in their interests. The integration of business efficiency with democratic control becomes increasingly complex with the growth in the size of co-operatives. Continuous programmes of education and training are necessary, reinforced by up-to-date methods of communicating information, so that the members may exercise control in an enlightened, constructive and responsible manner.

Acknowledgements

I wish to thank all those who helped me with this book — they really are too numerous to mention! I have a list of over 1,300 people who helped me directly but there are a great many more who assisted *them*. Even a listing of helpful organisations would make a formidable text. Special thanks, however, must go to the IAOS, UAOS, IAWS, CWS, Co-operative Union and their counterpart organisations, as well as individual co-operative societies and co-operators in many lands. My colleagues in the county development team system and former colleagues in the agricultural advisory and allied services gave me a superb local research and information 'network'. State departments and offices, state-sponsored bodies, business enterprises and voluntary organisations all responded and corresponded admirably, often, I fear, at great inconvenience but with much enthusiasm, retrieving and researching old files. Librarians and archivists were everywhere most helpful, as were scholars in universities and other educational and research institutions, public officials, editors, journalists and local historians. A special commendation is due to Mr E. MacIntyre and his staff in Donegal County Library who not only bore the burden of procuring hundreds of books and rare texts but voluntarily gave much spare time to seeking additional sources.

I should like to name the people who entrusted me with rare books, personal papers, photographs and other cherished items, but many of them asked me not to, for fear, as one expressed it, of becoming an open target for future researchers! Yet, I will risk praising Seamus O'Raghallaigh for his persistent encouragement and his long-term loan of loads of key books and papers long since out-of-print: as sources of reference always at hand, they made my task immeasurably easier. Tom Broderick and later Leonard Roarty and Bill Walsh took on an unfair share of the night meetings, which are part of our development work, to allow me time to write. My very special thanks also to Rosemary Canning for an excellent job of typing. Outside my own family, she was the one most immediately and constantly afflicted while this book was in the making. Many experts, organisational, scientific and historical, as well as some who regard themselves as ordinary readers, have read part or all of my scripts, revealed inaccuracies and made helpful suggestions. From the time I submitted the first drafts, the publisher's help has been most valuable — I am particularly grateful to James O'Donnell, Jonathan Williams and staff.

In writing this book I have experienced real co-operation, and much of the value of the volume must be credited to those who helped me. The mistakes remain my own.

Patrick Bolger
Lifford, County Donegal
9 December 1976

Author to Reader

Co-operation is, of course, *the* basic social process. Whenever we work together or aid or facilitate each other, even at the most trivial task, we are 'co-operating'. When, however, we speak of the co-operative movement, we conceive of a more formal organisation of people with similar ideals, consciously working together for common aims and guided by a set of principles which distinguishes their activity from other forms of human endeavour.

The modern formal co-operative movement dates from 1844 when twenty-eight poor weavers of Rochdale came together with a capital of £1 each to open a small retail shop. They adopted a set of rules which were later to become enshrined as the Rochdale Principles and which today effectively guide the philosophy and conduct of co-operative societies all over the world.

A co-operative society has been defined as "an association for the purposes of joint trading, originating among the weak and conducted always in an unselfish spirit, on such terms that all who are prepared to assume the duties of membership may share in its rewards in proportion to the degree in which they make use of their association."[1] This classical definition might well be qualified, but it has enough validity and general application to carry us through our history of the formal co-operative movement in Ireland from its early nineteenth-century British origins when the emerging movements of co-operation and trade unionism were practically indistinguishable.

In Britain the two movements maintained close ties, with the result that British co-operation grew up as a movement of artisans and thrifty middle-class workers mainly occupied in the consumer retail business. There was no such cohesion in Ireland, and the failure of co-operators and trade unionists to come together is still a perplexing Irish phenomenon. During the forty years following Rochdale, when the British movement was undergoing considerable expansion, there was little co-operative progress in Ireland. When modern Irish co-operation did emerge, it did so as an almost exclusively agricultural movement — and as such it has remained.

The history of the Irish co-operative movement from 1890 is essentially a story of many ordinary people in small local groups doing things, some of them exceptional, but most of which, if viewed individually, would appear commonplace and pedestrian. However, these small individual efforts, added together, are invested with considerable glory.

1 C.R. Fay, *Co-operation at Home and Abroad* (London: P.S. King & Son, 1908), p.5.

To document the full story of Irish co-operative endeavour is a little like trying to write the local history of Ireland. A catalogue of local happenings tends to monotony unless the incidents are properly related and placed in a suitable framework. On the other hand, the framework on its own is as bare as a structurally complete but still empty house, and a brief recounting of the bald 'national' facts of co-operative history would convey little of the life and colour of the movement. Co-operation by its very nature is something of a hidden phenomenon: the co-operative realities may be so closely entwined and accepted in daily life that we cannot appreciate their true significance. One must try to place oneself, as AE recommended, "on the outside of a crowd to best measure its greatness and force."[2]

The Irish have been too preoccupied with their political and military history. The country's social history is still largely untouched, particularly the intimate history of local communities; too often local historians concentrate on the remote past, to the neglect of what has happened within the last 100 years. It is a pity that local social history is not written within the period of living memory while the facts are still retrievable. Even though modern Irish co-operative history dates back less than four generations, it was repeatedly brought home to me that I had begun my researches at least thirty years too late. I earnestly urge every co-coperative society to start writing its own local history now, so that the wealth of local lore can be recorded and preserved before it is too late.[3] I hope that this book provides the broad background against which local recall and the old records, minute books and correspondence of local societies become more significant.

I have written of many events in terms which imply that these were momentous happenings, even though they do not appear as such either in the perspective of national public opinion at the time when they occurred or in the context of the conventional wisdom of today. The lack of publicity for the co-operative movement is a theme which is elaborated in later chapters.

I may be accused of exaggeration. I may indeed prove blameworthy in many instances because of my failure to relate certain co-operative ventures to concurrent political and military events, or in my social record because I presume too much or too little of the reader's knowledge of other aspects of Irish history. Otherwise, I am unrepentant and remain unconvinced that many of the so-called 'victories' in the military and political fields are significantly more important than the modest co-operative achievements recorded here. An assessment of the Irish agricultural co-operative movement must always take account of the fact that nearly every co-operative society in the early days (and to a somewhat lesser extent even to this day) was founded by a handful of people, mostly of unexceptional abilities and often with little more than an ill-defined desire for rural

---

2 G.W. Russell, "The Building up of a Rural Civilisation", an address to the IAOS Annual General Meeting, 1909.
3 My researches have indicated that this folklore is still extant but, for obvious reasons, it could not be included in this volume.

improvement. Theirs was the task of recruiting some dozens or hundreds of unenthusiastic and reluctant farmers in order to establish a workable business association.

This history has much that is heroic, but also aspects that are shameful and depressing. There are insights into soul-destroying poverty, gombeenism, degradation, sloth and pusillanimity. Happily, however, the persistence and cheerfulness of the people in the co-operative movement is never submerged.

Chapter One

Robert Owen:
The Father of Co-operation

Robert Owen was born in 1771, the son of a craftsman saddler in the village of Newtown, Montgomeryshire, Wales. His father was also the village postmaster. He was to grow to manhood in a period which has been described as the worst in the history of English labour.[1] The old pastoral England of villages and rural crafts,[2] where life had changed little since the Middle Ages, was rapidly disappearing.

From about the middle of the eighteenth century, there was an accumulation of wealth from trading at home and profits (some would say plunder) abroad. The rising wealthy class had money to invest. The small farms of the yeoman peasantry were bought up, the common fields of villages were fenced off and farming was reorganised with improved implements and methods. The traditions of cottage industry and village self-sufficiency were also under attack. In 1733 the flying shuttle was invented. Soon afterwards, out of necessity, came the spinning jenny to enable the spinners to keep up with the weavers. Thereafter, the power loom, the steam engine and other kinds of power machinery came into use. The cottagers and the village craftsmen had no money to buy the new machines nor, indeed, any place to put them. Factories were built and towns to house the workers sprang up around them.

These were the dark satanic mills of England's Industrial Revolution. In some factories, the labour of men was replaced by that of women and children, some of them no more than eight or nine years old, working twelve, fourteen and even sixteen hours a day under pitiable conditions.[3] Men, slaving for starvation wages, were often kept to their tasks by threats and blows.[4] The Combination Laws of 1799 and 1800 prevented workers from 'combining' or uniting to seek better wages or conditions.

1 Thorold Rogers, *Six Centuries of Work and Wages* (London: Unwin, 1923), p.492.
2 "A spinning wheel was to be found in every cottage and farmhouse in the kingdom, a loom in every village": Arnold Toynbee, *Industrial Revolution* (Newton Abbot: David and Charles, 1969).
3 Many of these were pauper children from towns, notably London, who were apprenticed *en masse*, through the parish authorities, to factory owners who agreed to house, feed and employ them. "It was often agreed by the parish authorities, in order to get rid of imbeciles, that one idiot should be taken by the millowner with every twenty sane children. The fate of those idiots has never been disclosed": Gibbins, *Industrial History of England*, cited by Catherine Webb (ed.), *Industrial Co-operation* (Manchester: Co-operative Union Ltd., 1904).
4 In the opening pages of his book, *A Century of Co-operation* (Manchester: Co-operative

4

Robert Owen is commonly regarded as the Father of Co-operation. It is a debatable title, since conscious co-operation,[5] often with a considerable formal organisational structure, had existed in many countries outside Britain long before his time. However, it is readily agreed that Owen was a central figure in the evolution of the early formal movement. The structures and principles of the British (or Rochdale) system were eventually accepted as the organisational basis of the co-operative movement throughout the world. We cannot disregard the influence of the times in which he lived, nor can we lightly dismiss the contribution of the many remarkable men who were his followers or intimate associates.[6]

Robert Owen's genius had a distinctly practical bent. At the age of nine he started work in a neighbour's shop in Newtown; later he worked in various stores in London and Manchester. At nineteen he went into manufacturing, first as a partner making 'mules' for spinning mills, and afterwards as a proprietor producing fine cotton yarn. His versatile talents and shrewd business acumen made success look easy and, by the age of forty-five, he was worth an estimated quarter of a million pounds.

In 1799, when Owen was twenty-eight, he got to know David Dale, owner of the great cotton mills at New Lanark on the Clyde. With the forceful combination of business alacrity and romantic gallantry which characterised his life-style, Owen purchased Dale's mills and married his daughter, Ann Caroline.

At New Lanark, Owen added to his already extensive knowledge of cotton spinning, conceiving of many technical and organisational changes for improving the business. He also was confronted immediately with the seamier side of the business — the physical and moral degradation of the factory system:

> He found at New Lanark that the population lived in idleness, in poverty and in almost every kind of crime; consequently in debt, out of health and in misery. There were five hundred children employed, chiefly received from workhouses and charities in Edinburgh at six, seven, or eight years of age. Though these children were comparatively well cared for in a properly managed boarding-house, they had to work from 6 a.m. to 7 p.m., so that when their apprenticeship was over about the age of fifteen, they were prematurely worn out, and seem as a rule to have drifted to Glasgow and Edinburgh to swell the lower ranks of labour or fall victims to vice.[7]

Union Ltd., 1944), Professor G.D.H. Cole gives a good account of the various pressures on the manufacturers themselves, especially those who had entered manufacturing with limited capital, showing their behaviour, if no less deplorable, at least more understandable.

5   For a discussion on the distinction of conscious and unconscious co-operation, see F. Hall and W.P. Watkins, *Co-operation* (Manchester: Co-operative Union Ltd., 1937), p.13 et seq.

6   To mention but two at this stage, Dr William King of Brighton and William Thompson of Rosscarberry, County Cork.

7   Catherine Webb (ed.), *Industrial Co-operation* (Manchester: Co-operative Union Ltd., 10th edition 1926), p.48.

Although Dale was by no means the worst employer, he was, like most ordinary men, comparatively helpless when faced with such conditions. It takes a man of rare ability and courage to effect even minor improvements under a system of socio-economic regression.

Robert Owen set about a thoroughgoing reformation. He reduced working hours and increased wages, built new houses for the workers and improved old ones. Instead of being wholly at work in the mills, the children spent much of the day in excellently equipped schools. Owen had some novel ideas about the education of children[8] and a number of his associates were later to have religious scruples about some of his methods and 'godless' instruction. He started a shop to sell goods to the workers at low prices, cultivated land for the supply of vegetables, and even acquired a large house with extensive and well-kept grounds which he threw open for the recreation and edification of the workers. When the mills had to be closed because of war or slackness in trade, he continued to pay the workers their wages. In spite of such extravagance, or more likely because of it, the mills continued to make good profits and the philanthropic Owen acquired a world-wide reputation. Many famous people, including a Russian Grand Duke, came to visit the New Lanark community.

Owen was loud in his denunciation of excess profits. He believed that capital ought to be content with a modest dividend and that all surplus should be applied for the benefit of the workers. He campaigned ceaselessly for better working conditions and was largely responsible for the passing of the Factory Act of 1819. Although the Act conceded far less than Owen had sought,[9] it was a start. It was followed five years later by the repeal of the Combination Laws, and in due course by the Ten Hour Act of 1847 and other important Acts in the eighteen seventies.

Owen's detestation of capitalism increased with every shameful individual experience. Although a mild-mannered man, he was driven to savage verbal onslaughts on those who continued to abuse and underpay their workers. He was particularly enraged by the cynical disdain with which local 'conspiracies' of mill-owners and politicians ignored even the few legal rights which the workers had. His fury inevitably extended to those in responsible positions who allegedly stood by and watched injustice happen.

In 1817 Owen denounced organised religion. All established religions and religious sects were, he said, the "great repulsive powers of society".

8   "The children were never to be beaten, or even to hear a harsh word, but were to be taught the inseparable connection which exists between the interest and happiness of each individual and the interest and happiness of every other individual." ibid., p.49. The source of Owen's educational ideas was probably the teachings of the French philosopher, Jean-Jacques Rousseau (1712-78).

9   It applied only to cotton mills, instead of to all textile trades. It fixed the minimum employment age at nine instead of ten and the working day at twelve hours for under sixteens instead of the ten-and-a-half hour day for under eighteens as Owen had urged. It fixed no limit at all for workers over sixteen years. The legislators also refused Owen's pleas for the abolition of night work for children, for compulsory education and for the appointment of factory inspectors.

They "materially injured the finest qualities", and while any of them prevailed they would be a "permanent obstacle to the peace, progress in knowledge, charity and love and happiness of the human race."[10] Obviously no great believer in original sin, he berated the churches for preaching the "doctrine of human responsibility for evil and therefore blamed men for being evil instead of recognising that the sources of evil lay in the bad environment to which men were subjected."[11]

Owen's total condemnation of organised religion was, to say the least, a tactical error. It created powerful enemies, hardened existing attitudes and branded him as an atheist. This distracted attention from the extreme social and spiritual malaise which he had hoped to cure. Owen stoutly denied that he was either "an atheist or an infidel". He held that it was impossible to know or understand God but yet he believed in Him: God was an intelligence and power far beyond the faculties of humanity to comprehend and it was arrogant of churchmen to define and interpret Him rigidly.

It was unfortunate that Owen should commit himself to an open confrontation. A shrewder (though possibly less honest) man, whilst retaining his own personal beliefs, might have continued to participate in some form of orthodox religious practice and from that position of 'respectability' might have directed his attack more accurately. In his autobiography, Owen admits that there is an element of truth in all religions.[12] His global attack on all organised religion may well have been an excess, brought on, ironically, by strong compelling forces in his character and environment — his conceit of his own ability and judgement, his benevolent enthusiasm and that feeling of frustration so cogently expressed some years later by the Christian Socialists.[13]

The Christian Socialists, while utterly repudiating Owen's extreme "doctrine of circumstances" and the philosophy of atheistic socialism being propounded by Owenites in Britain and by Fourier, St Simon and Cabet abroad, were appalled by the condition of society under the fashionable capitalistic philosophy of the Industrial Revolution with its terrible twins — the doctrines of free competition and *laissez faire*. No less distressing than the degeneration of the working classes were the ineffectual 'ministrations' of the churches.

---

10 Quotations are from Owen's autobiography, *Life of Robert Owen. With Selections from His Writings and Correspondence* (London: Frank Cass, 1968).

11 G.D.H. Cole, *A Century of Co-operation* (Manchester: Co-operative Union Ltd., 1944), p.19.

12 "This essence is the spirit of pure, undefiled, universal love and charity for man applied to daily practice in voice, manner and act, and of love for that energy and power which composes, decomposes and recomposes perpetually the elements of the universe and which is called God."

13 Frederick Denison Maurice, John Malcolm Ludlow, Edward Vansittart Neale, Charles Kingsley and Thomas Hughes. Maurice, their acknowledged leader, was a clergyman and Professor of Moral Philosophy in Cambridge. Kingsley, another cleric, was their great popular exponent both as preacher and writer of pamphlets, novels and verse (*Yeast, Alton Locke*). Hughes is perhaps best remembered as the author of *Tom Brown's Schooldays*. Neale, Ludlow and Hughes were tireless workers in the cause of co-operation and were to exercise a profound influence on the Irish co-operative movement.

There were, of course, splendid examples of the benevolence and self-sacrifice of individuals here and there ... But speaking broadly, the religious bodies at their best stood for personal piety, and the hope of salvation for individual believers; at their worst they represented mere dull formalities and conventionalities, defence of property, class privileges and theological shibboleths, with opposition to every form of progress and enlightenment.[14]

The Christian Socialists saw clearly that, while the pretended religion was Christianity, the new industrial society was avowedly based on the principle of selfishness, the very antithesis of Christian brotherhood. It was scandalous that, in so far as the present life was concerned, Christianity should be relegated to the "subservient office of healing here and there some wound inflicted by its triumphant rival."[15]

Owen's conflict with organised religion was of considerable significance. Many of his followers were confirmed atheists, so the early co-operative movement readily acquired an atheistic label. It was a convenient tag to try to discredit those who, like the Rochdale Pioneers, sought to effect a genuine improvement in the condition of the working class. Members of this class, in their turn, especially those who were superstitious or prone to religious scruples, could frequently be deterred from joining a co-operative led by atheists and heretics. The atheistic connotation still lingers about the co-operative movement. Its 'godless' origins, the apparently narrow distinctions between co-operativism and the aberrant forms of communism and socialism, the perversion of the co-operative ideal in totalitarian régimes, and the enthusiasm shown by various left-wing elements for their own particular concepts of co-operation — all continue to provide reactionary capitalists and exploiters with varying degrees of polemical advantage.[16]

In spite of his views on religion, Owen was respected as an employer whose positive achievements could not be gainsaid. Many of his fellow manufacturers were glad to be associated with so powerful a public figure, particularly in his representations to the government to remit the import duty on cotton. There was also the dilemma of the Poor Law Rate. It was permissible for the factory owners to exploit the workers, but something had to be done about the destitute and the unemployed. At the end of the Napoleonic War, when prices slumped, the cost of parish relief [17] was felt more heavily than before and Owen's claim that he had found a way to relieve rates and taxes commanded a sympathetic hearing.

14 C.Webb, op.cit., p.72.
15 ibid., p.72.
16 Horace Plunkett, founder of the modern Irish co-operative movement, was condemned as a dreadful socialist and atheist — and a Protestant one at that! The accusation of godlessness levelled at Rev T.A. Finlay SJ betrayed both parochial and sectarian prejudices. In the estimation of certain merchants of Dungloe, he was a Northerner and an Orange priest.
17 Which under the Speenhamland system was tied to the price of bread. See Cole, op. cit., p.10.

Following the success of his New Lanark experiment, Owen sought to extend the field of social improvement. He began to have increasingly fanciful visions of a 'new moral world'. He urged that the parish and the state, instead of doling out relief, should subscribe capital for the establishment of 'villages of co-operation' in which the workers, the poor and the unemployed could provide for their own needs. Some of these villages would be industrial (like New Lanark), others agricultural, and many would combine both industrial and agricultural activity. What each settlement did not consume, it should exchange with others. Owen conceived that, once his ideas were acted upon, their success would be so remarkable that Britain and the rest of the world would soon be covered by self-governing villages of co-operation which, joined in association, would provide every nation with simple but equitable government. This was to be his new moral world,[18] based on the principles of co-operation and brotherly love, which he believed would rapidly supersede the immoral world of competition and exploitation and usher in the millennium of universal benevolence and peace.

It was all a bit much for the mill-owners and politicians of England, so Owen set off to try out his ideas in the unspoiled atmosphere of the USA. There he addressed the President and the full Congress and undertook a nation-wide lecture tour. In 1825 he bought out a settlement belonging to a sect of German religious emigrants, the Rappites, at New Harmony, Indiana, and proceeded to set up a village of co-operation. This New Harmony colony survived for a great number of years but gradually lost much of its communal character. Back in Britain, Owen established another commune in 1826 at Orbiston near Glasgow and a further one at Ralahine, County Clare in 1831. Both were short-lived, not because of any intrinsic deficiency, but because the land was sold over their heads and the colonists were evicted. His last attempt was Queenwood, or Harmony Hall, at East Tytherly in Hampshire. Here, between 1839 and 1846, the last act in the Owenite drama was played. Its failure can be attributed in some measure to Owen's insistence on the virtues of 'spade husbandry' and the ideal of providing work for men instead of for horses and machines.[19] The failure of Queenwood represented the collapse of the Owenite movement as a vital force in British life, but there was an important element of continuity. Among those who recouped part of their money were James Smithies, George Healey, John Garside and John Collier, who, like many others of the Rochdale Pioneers, were active Owenites.

The decade from 1824 was a period of great political excitement: the repeal of the Combination Acts in 1824, Catholic emancipation with Daniel O'Connell in 1829, and the Reform Act of 1832, which somewhat extended the franchise.[20] There was a tremendously rapid growth of trade unionism

18 Also the title of a weekly co-operative newspaper published between 1834 and 1845.
19 For a fuller discussion of the possible causes of the failure of the communes, see Hall and Watkins, op.cit., p.65.
20 The Reform Act was disappointing for Owen and his followers since it did not extend the franchise below the middle classes. It increased the electorate from about 440,000 to 725,000. The second Reform Act of 1867 brought the number of voters to approximately 2,250,000.

and co-operation which went almost unnoticed in the public press. Some 250 co-operative societies were formed between 1826 and 1835, most of them small distributive stores set up by working men who hoped, by trading in groceries, provisions and clothing, to give themselves a better living and enough capital for bigger co-operative schemes. New trade unions were being founded all over industrial England. Existing unions, which up to 1824 had to disguise themselves as benefit societies, were coming into the open.

In 1829 John Doherty organised cotton spinners into the Grand General Union of the United Kingdom (including Northern Ireland). He then tried to organise all British trades into a National Association of United Trades for the Protection of Labour, which was the immediate precursor of the still more ambitious Grand National Consolidated Trades Union of 1833. Doherty's GNCTU was purely a trade union body, but he zealously advocated the idea of co-operation, especially co-operative self-employment, whenever the workers became organised.

Doherty (1799-1854), an ardent Owenite and Roman Catholic, was born in Buncrana, County Donegal. In 1814 he was working in a cotton mill in Larne, County Antrim. Five years later he became recognised leader of the Manchester Cotton Spinners Union. The structure of this union is said to have closely resembled the military organisation of the United Irishmen. In 1819 Doherty was jailed for two years "for conspiring with others to intimidate persons from working at Messrs. Ewart & Company's cotton factory." In 1831 he started his famous weekly newspaper, *Voice of the People*. In contrast to many industrial workers of his time, Doherty approved and defended the use of machinery in industry.

The association of co-operation and trade unionism was so close that, in many industrial towns, the leadership and membership of both the local co-operative society and the local trade union were practically identical. The rules and objectives of both brotherhoods reflected Owenite teaching. Many of the trade unionist workers who established co-operative shops did so not only to provide themselves with goods at reasonable prices but also to capitalise villages of co-operation with their profits. Many of them were displaced agricultural workers and village craftsmen who hated the new industrial state and who longed to get back to the land. It became a common occurrence for trade unionists on strike, especially in trades which did not require too much capital or expensive machinery, to set up co-operative workshops and strike out in opposition to their employers, often disposing of some of their production through the local co-operative shop. The first known co-op in Rochdale (not to be confused with the later more famous Co-op store) was a co-operative workshop founded by striking flannel weavers in 1830.[21] Co-operators and trade unionists had little difficulty in recognising their common interest, so that at national and local level the two movements sought to achieve the greatest possible solidarity.

21 The earliest co-operative ventures into manufacturing in Britain were mostly of the type where charitable persons subscribed the initial capital to build a co-operative corn mill (for the use of the poor) which they hoped would become self-sustaining thereafter. There are

Although he was the chief inspiration of the Grand National Consolidated Trades Union, Robert Owen did not become a member at its foundation. He joined only in 1834 when the whole structure of trade unionism was imperilled by the arrest of the six Dorchester labourers, now immortalised as the Tolpuddle Martyrs. His efforts were in vain. Growing militancy by the government and employers, widespread lockouts and a series of unsuccessful strikes broke the national grouping of the GNCTU before it had time to consolidate. After 1834, Chartism displaced Owenism as the predominant working-class gospel. Instead of the gentle Robert Owen, a militant Irishman and Chartist, Feargus O'Connor, became the revered leader of the miners and factory workers.

Feargus Edward O'Connor, the son of Irish Nationalist politician, Roger O'Connor, was born in Cork about 1796. His family claimed descent from Roderick O'Connor, the last High King of Ireland. Admitted to the Irish Bar in 1830, O'Connor was elected MP for Cork in 1832, as a follower of Daniel O'Connell, with whom he soon quarrelled and parted company. In England he became the most prominent leader of the Chartist movement.[22]

The Chartists sought a political rather than an economic co-operative solution to the workers' ills, and maintained, with considerable justification, that no improvement of working-class conditions could be achieved except through a Parliament elected by universal suffrage. Although O'Connor and his followers did essay a few attempts at instituting co-operative-type land settlements for workers (somewhat on the lines of Owen's villages of co-operation), these were very much peripheral activities. For the most part, the Chartists were disdainful of the efforts of benevolent gentlemen like Owen and, although they acknowledged and defended the workers' efforts towards economic self-help, their obsession was with the political solution. This they pursued with a degree of militancy which sometimes resulted in violence. One is tempted here to draw comparisons, however tenuous, between the Owenite/Chartist relationship of this period and the position which obtained half-a-century later in Ireland, when English-born Horace Plunkett was seeking support for his co-operatives and was being accused of "drawing a red herring across the path of Home Rule".

Owen spent the last thirteen years of his life in comparative retirement. However, even in old age, he retained a lively interest in the progress of the co-operative movement, showing particular sympathy with the work of the Christian Socialists for whom he had to some extent prepared the way. In

reports of such mills being established at Wolverhampton (c.1767) and Hull (1795). It was fairly common for charitably disposed persons to finance shops, some of which acquired a sort of co-operative structure. Owen envisaged that much of the initial capital for villages of co-operation would be provided by the state, the local authorities and private subscriptions. It was Dr William King of Brighton, who took the more realistic view that co-operative enterprises were unlikely to be financed other than by the co-operators themselves, who sought to guide the movement in this direction.

22 For a fuller account of O'Connor's career, see J.W. Boyle (ed.), *Leaders and Workers* (Cork: Mercier Press, 1963). There is some evidence to suggest that about 1848 the Chartists in England had an agreement with the Fenians to keep the Army busy on the home front in the event of a rebellion in Ireland.

1858, he collapsed while addressing a congress of the Social Science Association in Liverpool, and died shortly afterwards, on 17 November, in his home town of Newtown. He was buried there in the grave of his parents. There also, in 1902, a memorial was unveiled and an address given by his biographer and last survivor of his 'social missionaries', the veteran co-operator, George Jacob Holyoake.

Robert Owen was Britain's first socialist and was acclaimed, by common consent, as the Father of Co-operation, but as Holyoake explained:

> Robert Owen no more constructed Co-operation than did George Stephenson the railway system, which a thousand exigencies have suggested and a thousand brains matured. Yet, as Stephenson made locomotion possible, so Owen set men's minds on the track of co-operation, and time and need, failure and gain, faith and thought, and the good sense and devotion of multitudes have made it what it is.[23]

Robert Owen

23 George Jacob Holyoake, *History of Co-operation*, Volume 1, 1875, p.70.

Chapter Two

Ralahine

Robert Owen visited Ireland in 1823 and received an almost royal welcome. At a large meeting held in the Rotunda, at which he expounded his ideas on mutual co-operation and the new moral world, the Lord Mayor of Dublin presided; also on the platform were the Archbishop of Dublin, Dr Murray, the Duke of Leinster,[1] Lord Meath and Lord Cloncurry. Socialism in those days was still the "fad of the rich instead of the faith of the poor."[2] Further meetings led to the foundation of the Hibernian Philanthropic Society. Despite a budget of over £2,600, the Society was ineffectual and short-lived but Owen's ideas still fascinated one man who had sat attentively throughout the meetings. This was John Scott Vandaleur, an Irish landlord with two estates in County Clare; a forebear had been an excise officer in Clare in the seventeenth century and Vandaleur himself was a former high sheriff of the county. One of the estates, comprising 700 acres, was tenanted, but the other, of 618 acres, at Ralahine near Bunratty, on the back road from Limerick to Ennis, was farmed in progressive fashion by Vandaleur himself, who lived there in a fine mansion close by the ruined castle of the McNamaras.

Back home in Clare, Vandaleur enthused about the possibility of forming a village of co-operation on the lines outlined by Owen. He argued that a measure of mutual co-operation would lead to much better productivity and improved relations between landlord and worker, but his family remained unimpressed. They felt that the tenant and labouring classes would have to be kept in control and any concession of sharing could only lead to worse trouble. Vandaleur doubted if things could be much worse, for the countryside of Clare was in a very unsettled state. Murders and agrarian outrages were nightly affairs, as the Terry Alts and the Whiteboys wreaked vengeance on the property or persons of offending landlords.

Yet Vandaleur still cherished his proposed co-operative solution and about 1830 proceeded to lay the foundation of his co-operative village by building a row of comfortable stone cottages, a dormitory for single women and another for single men, a store, a school, a large dining room and a

---

1 Augustus Frederick FitzGerald, third Duke of Leinster, nephew of Lord Edward FitzGerald.
2 James Connolly, *Labour in Ireland* (Dublin and London: Maunsel & Company Limited, 1917), vol. I, p.129.

meeting room. By 1830 the agrarian trouble had become serious enough for Clare magistrates to beg Dublin Castle to help them suppress the armed bands of peasants who were trying to terrorise landlords into reducing rents and increasing wages.[3] Vandaleur commanded some measure of respect as a humane employer but his relationship with his workers was not improved by his steward, Daniel Hastings, who "showed much harshness to the labourers under his control and raised their indignation by a number of petty yet stinging acts of oppression."[4] The measure of this indignation was revealed in April 1831 when the labourers met at midnight in a wood near the estate to decide who should kill the steward. The selected assassin, without compunction, shot Hastings to death in the presence of his young wife.

Thoroughly frightened, Vandaleur's wife and their five children took refuge in Limerick, leaving armed police to guard the mansion. Vandaleur himself embarked for Manchester. He had maintained contact with Owen through visits and correspondence and had learned much of the co-operative movement in Britain. In Manchester he saw Edward Thomas Craig, editor of the *Lancashire Co-operator*, one of the many co-operative journals encouraged by Owen which were appearing at that time. Craig had studied the principles of co-operative colonisation and Vandaleur persuaded him to come to Ireland to organise a co-operative system at Ralahine, tactfully omitting to mention the disturbed state of the country or the murder of the steward — "from a desire", Craig recounted later, "not to discourage me". Still, young Craig was not the type to look for security and a pension. He was "a convinced Socialist, a bit of a Puritan and full of the intellectual excitement of an age which was still seeking to reconcile the worker with the machine. He had ideas on everything from sanitation to beehives. Like Owen, his socialism was paternalistic (the poor would have to be led and educated), but his kindness and patience were heroic."[5]

In the spring of 1831, Craig arrived in Ralahine and found matters in an unpromising state. The labourers were surly, suspicious and moody. Craig's arrival tended to make them worse since they were inclined to look on him as a spy. He had also to endure the "vulgar jests and coarse humour" of the servants of the Big House. Even Vandaleur's own family were "distinctly cool" and, apart from the enthusiastic Vandaleur himself, poor Craig did not

---

3 One retrograde clause of the Catholic Emancipation Act 1829 was the disfranchisement of the forty-shilling freeholders, allegedly because of their defiance of the landlords in electing Daniel O'Connell MP for Clare in 1828. These smallholders (with land valuation less than forty shillings) were very much at the mercy of the landlords. Their tiny farms, often no more than half an acre, were unable to support a family. They depended on the landlord to hire them as labourers and were often in arrears of rent. If they failed to vote as their landlord wished, labour was no longer given and rent was demanded. At the Clare election they came out in open defiance to vote for O'Connell — from the Burren to Loop Head, from the cliffs of Moher to the banks of the Shannon — and during the week of the election some 30,000 persons were camped in the streets of Ennis. Said one, "The landlord may take my cow, my pig, my home, even my body, but he has no power over my soul." The 1829 Act raised the franchise to a £10 valuation.

4 Catherine Webb, op. cit., p.61. A more sadistic act of oppression was the denial of drinking water on hot summer days to the workers in the harvest fields.

5 Michael Viney, "The Commune of Clare", a series of articles in *The Irish Times*, May 1966.

have many friends. The news reaching Ralahine from other parts of Ireland was not reassuring. There was famine in Mayo. At a 'tithe auction' in Bunclody, County Wexford, police shot and killed thirteen people who objected violently to the seizure of their goods. Similar trouble in Skibbereen claimed thirty lives, and at Carrickshock, County Kilkenny, eleven policemen were battered to death. Elsewhere the activities of the secret societies — Blackfeet, Whitefeet, Terry Alts, Ribbonmen and others — continued unabated. In one year there were 196 murders. Craig, however, was not one to be discouraged easily and by the end of the year had earned himself considerable respect.

Edward Thomas Craig

In November there was a special meeting of all the labourers, artisans and servants on the estate and some others from outside. Vandaleur explained that he was convinced that only through the system of mutual co-operation devised by Robert Owen could they hope to establish respectful rapport between landlord and worker. He outlined his plans to the assembled company and was accorded polite applause. The company then proceeded to elect by ballot the members of the new Ralahine Agricultural and Manufacturing Co-operative Association.[6]

Fifty-two members were elected; even Craig's membership was put to the vote. However, the democratic process did not extend to Vandaleur who was self-appointed president and reserved the right to choose the secretary, treasurer and storekeeper. Vandaleur did not intend to lose any money by the new arrangement. An agreement was drawn up between him and three trustees on behalf of the Association for a year's rental of the land: 320 barrels of wheat, 240 of barley, 50 of oats and various other items such as 30 cwts of pork and 70 cwts of beef — a total nominal value of about £700. The livestock (valued at £1,500), farm implements and effects

---

6 A comprehensive account of the Ralahine commune is given in Ronald G. Garnett, *Co-operation and the Owenite Socialist Communities in Britain* (Manchester: Manchester University Press, 1972).

would still belong to the landlord until the Association had made enough money to pay for them. Meanwhile, "interest upon the capital value thereof" was to be paid at 6 per cent. per annum. This would amount to another £200.

The declared objectives of the Association were:

i) The acquisition of a common capital
ii) The mutual assurance of its members against the evils of poverty, sickness, infirmity and old age
iii) The attainment of a greater share of the comforts of life thàn the working class now possess
iv) The mental and moral improvement of its adult members
v) The education of their children.

A long list of rules was drawn up, providing for all the details of government and conduct of the members. The wages were fixed at eight pence (8d) per day for a labouring man and five pence for a woman, these being the ordinary wages of the country.[7] The wages were to be spent at the store for such articles as were kept there or were produced by the Society:

> No member was to be expected to perform any service or work but such as was agreeable to his or her feelings, and such as they were able to perform, but power was given to a general meeting to expel any useless member. Each individual was given perfect liberty of conscience and freedom in the expression of opinions and in religious worship.[8]

The working day was fixed at twelve hours in summer and from dawn to dusk in winter, with an hour's break for dinner. Other rules included a total prohibition of spirituous liquor, tobacco and snuff and a ban on gambling of all kinds. These regulations were consistent with the concern of landlords to promote habits of temperance and thrift in their tenantry, if not in themselves! Craig, the Owenite socialist, could rationalise them in precise economic terms: "The distillation of alcohol from grain is an improvident waste of capital and labour." There was also, strangely enough, a ban on the use of nicknames, presumably for the sake of social harmony in the confines of the commune. As an incentive, the agreement provided that if a profit was made after the first year's working, the wages would be raised to 10d a day for men and 6d a day for women.

When all the rules had been explained and the voting carried out, the Association consisted of fifty-two people: 7 married couples, 21 bachelors, 5 single women and 12 orphaned children. Of these, only eighteen were able-bodied men. One of the first families admitted was a widow with six children, three of whom were under working age; another child was a

---

7 The secretary (Craig), storekeeper, smiths, joiners and few other skilled workers were to get something more, the excess being borne by Vandaleur.
8 Catherine Webb, op. cit., p.62.

hunchback and the woman herself was haggard, careworn, and deemed only fit to look after poultry. Not a very promising community, but Vandaleur and Craig concluded that it would make the experiment all the more authentic because the Association contained an average cross-section of the rural population.

The members found the communal living a bit hard to get used to — men in one dormitory, women in another, and married couples in the new cottages. The children, whose food, clothing and education were financed from the common fund, lived mostly in the new school and the dormitory above it. "There is a vast waste of productive labour", wrote Craig, "to say nothing of irritation, in requiring a healthy woman to devote all her time to the nursing and care of children, the preparation of meals and the drudgery incident to the management of the individual, isolated homes of the working classes."

New Harmony was working in Indiana, Owen was propounding villages of co-operation in Britain, and Charles Fourier was still planning *phalansteries*[9] in France, but the people of Ralahine found it all very strange. Even the poor old woman with the six orphans wept bitterly when her wretched cabin was demolished.[10]

Money, as always, created difficulties. Craig hoped that the commune would work on an internal system of mutual credit and reward, and all dealings with the outside world in buying and selling would be done by the community itself. But the Ralahine labourers were used to having money in their fists and were poorly versed in the new economic theory. Craig introduced a system of labour notes — pieces of stiff cardboard printed with their value, such as, "eight pence for one day's labour". The members were doubtful of them at first, but the treasurer's readiness to exchange them for coin for outside spending quickly solved the problem. Most of the notes were traded at the Association's own store, which gratified Craig's concept of self-sufficiency:

> It made the worker's operations independent of the outside ordinary currency. It gave the members full control over their own resources and prompted them to habits of prudence and economy.

Prices were fixed. Milk was a penny a quart, beef and mutton 4d a pound and the labourer could take all the vegetables or fruit his family could eat for a shilling a week.

The Ralahine community got down to work. Half of the 618 acres were earmarked for tillage, and some twenty acres of scrub had to be reclaimed

9 Agricultural-industrial communities of about 1,800 people holding property in a common complex, not unlike the modern Israeli *kibbutzim*.

10 Michael Viney, in his *Irish Times* articles, offers the following ironic comment: "Some of the most comprehensive communes in the world today are run by capitalists for private gain. America and Italy can both offer examples of industrial complexes in which a worker lives in a company house, travels on a company bus, eats in the company canteen, sends his children to the company school and is insured and finally buried by the company. And the 'organisation man' in a capitalist commune doesn't even have the privilege of helping to elect the company board who decide his daily duties."

and trenched for potatoes. Peat had to be cut and saved on the sixty-three-acre bog. There were not enough labourers and, in the first uneasy months of the new order, no new applicants for membership arrived. Those outside saw the commune as a new type of workhouse and nobody called except a few tramps and beggars. However, things were going well. The people were better fed and cared for than they had ever been, and working conditions, without the ministrations of the steward, were extremely pleasant. The workers willingly settled down to work and displayed hitherto unsuspected signs of ingenuity and skill. The committee (subject to election every six months) met every night to allocate the next day's work, and each morning the members found their duties written on slates hung up in the common room. Gradually the word got out that something good was happening 'abroad at Vandaleur's' and there was a steady trickle of applications from neighbours wishing to join the community. New members were chosen for their promise of "health, vigour and powers of endurance" and, by harvest time 1832, the association totalled eighty-one, including twenty-three children. The commune built six new cottages for newcomers and newly-weds. Marriage within the commune in no way affected membership, but if someone wanted to marry an outsider their admission into the community had to be put to a vote. A teacher in the school lost her place because her prospective husband was not acceptable.

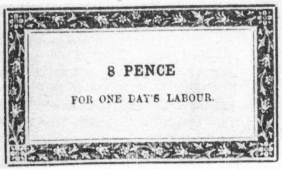

A Ralahine 'labour note'

Outside there was still trouble and turmoil: agrarian outrages continued and localised famine and destitution caused great hardship; Daniel O'Connell was gathering political strength to press for Repeal; there was a cholera epidemic in Clare. Ralahine, however, was a hive of industry and a haven of peace. Good food, good housing and Craig's well-designed sanitary system kept the people free from sickness and the fever raging outside. The sickness fund, to which members contributed a halfpenny of every shilling they earned, grew steadily without any significant pay-outs.

The first mowing machine in Ireland was introduced by the Ralahine Agricultural and Manufacturing Co-operative Association. The acceptance was significant, for at that time machinery was regarded as the enemy of human labour, and workers in Ralahine had previously smashed a loom on which Vandaleur hoped to weave linen. Craig was still conscious of the possibility of weaving linen from the commune's flax and had his eye on a nearby lake as a source of water and power for any manufacturing enterprise. With the arrival of the mowing machine, both he and Vandaleur hastened to reassure the workers of the commune and the county at large.

Vandaleur's "Address to the Agricultural Labourers of Clare"[11] reveals much that was admirable in the Irish landlord who, in the brief references which historians make, is often summarily dismissed as a gambler and a dilettante socialist. It shows him as a man of good sense, intellectually engaged in Owenite philosophy. "This machine of ours", he wrote,

> is one of the first machines ever given to the working classes to lighten their labour and at the same time increase their comforts. It does not benefit any one person among us exclusively or throw any individual out of employment . . . Tell the owners of land that if they wish to use machinery beneficially they should form you into societies, where it cannot injure you, but where you would have an interest in using and protecting it.

Some unusual machinery was already in use in Ralahine. Potatoes were washed in a large rotating 'squirrel cage', steamed in a boiler and transported in a truck on rails to the dining hall. Like Vandaleur, Craig had none of Owen's prejudices against agricultural machinery nor any illusions about the physical or moral superiority of 'spade husbandry'. Already he was thinking of a large steam-digger, the forerunner of the modern tractor rotovator.

The 1832 harvest was good. Vandaleur got his rental of corn and there was plenty to spare.[12] The orchard abounded with fruit and, despite the best efforts of the members and their children who could eat all they wished, two cartloads of apples and pears rotted for want of consumers. Craig vowed that this would not happen again and began planning for a market and for planting more fruit trees along the hedgerows. Even the potatoes grown on the new land (which formerly had been "scarcely equal to the feeding of a goat") were larger and more plentiful than those grown elsewhere. The harvest festival was a marvellous spectacle. The last load of wheat was decorated with garlands and flowers, and the members, in colourful procession, marched round the boundaries of the commune. At their head was E.T. Craig, mounted on a grey pony and wearing a silken sash with the legend in gold letters, "Each for ALL". At length they drew

11 Addresses, written mostly in ornate prose, were a popular vehicle for contemporary reformers. 'Martin Doyle' (Rev William Hickey), who founded Ireland's first agricultural school in Carrick-on-Bannow in 1821, was about this time in Boolavogue, County Wexford, delivering his "Address to the Landlords of Ireland", "Address to the Small Farmers of County Wexford", and many others.

12 Cormac Ó Gráda, in his paper "The Owenite Community at Ralahine, County Clare, 1831-33: A Reassessment" (*Irish Economic and Social History*, I (1974), 36-48), endorses the opinion of previous commentators that the commodity rental was excessive. Dr Ó Gráda substantiates this in the light of present insights into pre-Famine crop yields and suggests that a bad season could have put the commune in some difficulty if Vandaleur insisted on his full "commodity bundle".

up before the great door of the mansion where Vandaleur, surrounded by his family, gave them a rousing speech. Cheering their president, they went off to dance and make merry. That night they ate the first bread made from the wheat of Ralahine.

In the big seventy-acre field where Boyle Vandaleur, John Scott's father, used to exercise his stud, the Association grew a fine crop of potatoes in 1832 and followed that autumn with a sowing of winter wheat. Some time afterwards a hunted fox crossed the millcourse, cut through the orchard and sped away across the field. In a matter of seconds the fox would have been followed by huntsmen galloping over the tender braird when, "By a sudden impulse", writes Craig, "the members of the farmyard closed the gates and brought the huntsmen abruptly to bay and thereby put a stop to the chase for the day. The horsemen were astonished at the presumption of the men of the new system." This incident exemplifies what their commune meant to the workers of Ralahine. At that time many a peasant had his face split open with a hunting crop — not for closing gates, but for failing to open them quickly enough for the hunting gentry.

All was going well and would have continued so if Vandaleur had followed the same rules as the Ralahine Association imposed on its members. But suddenly disaster struck. William Pare, friend and colleague of Robert Owen,[13] takes up the story:

> I crossed from England to Ireland in the month of October 1833, in company with the proprietor, to visit and examine the colony of Ralahine, then in the third year of its existence, with the special view of acquiring knowledge, derived from practical experience, to aid me and my co-trustees in carrying out the design of my lately deceased friend Thompson as propounded in his will. At the urgent request of Mr Vandaleur I visited Ralahine first and remained a guest in his mansion sufficiently long to enable me to make a complete and searching investigation of the affairs of the association he had founded . . . After-wards on my way back to England I doubled through Limerick to deliver a promised lecture on the 'Equitable Labour Exchange Bazaars' then flourishing in England . . . and on this occasion I again and for the last time met Mr Vandaleur, who seemed in high spirits. Judge then of my surprise on arriving home early in November — filled with delight at the great good I had seen effected at Ralahine and with gratitude to its excellent founder — to find heading one of the columns of a Dublin newspaper the words, 'Flight of John Scott Vandaleur'. This other-wise respectable and really amiable man was addicted to the damning vice, unknown until then to me, as to many of his friends. This was the vice of gambling.[14]

In Ralahine, Craig was staring at the same headline in surprise and

13 Later, in 1869, Pare was mainly responsible for the first of the National Co-operative Congresses which led to the founding of the Co-operative Union.

14 William Pare, *Co-operative Agriculture in Ireland* (London: Longmans Green, 1870), now out-of-print.

shock. Only a few days previously Vandaleur had driven from Ralahine in the family carriage. He had called on Craig to give him some business papers and to present him with a fine double-barrelled gun. He had seemed "somewhat strange, distracted and unusually reserved" but had said nothing out of the ordinary. The newspaper headline was the first intimation to Craig and the family in the Big House that Vandaleur had gambled all he possessed and lost. Realising his desperate predicament, he boarded ship for America and would never again return to Ralahine.

That night from the cottages came the wild agonised keening of the Gael:

> The way in which the people received the intelligence was painful and distressing in the extreme. Upon its confirmation I heard women, and stout men even, grieving piteously and bewailing their loss as if the dearest friend or relative had been snatched from them by sudden death. As the room occupied by myself and Mrs Craig was above the cottages of two of the married members the wailing of the people in the night had a sad and heartrending effect . . . I arose next morning with many grey hairs.

The commune was shown no mercy. A distant relative of Vandaleur, a Limerick banker, obtained a fiat in bankruptcy against him which would protect the interests of the family at the expense of the co-operative. The agreement between Vandaleur and the Association was not accepted and the sheriff moved in to seize stock and implements. "There was neither means at hand, nor time", said Craig,

> to avert the evil impending. The members were held to be common labourers with no rights or claims for improvements, as all they had created and added to the estate belonged to the landlord. Legally they were right. It was robbery, nevertheless. We had paid our rent but were remorselessly evicted. We had no remedy.[15]

Craig's immediate problem was to meet the worth of the labour notes still held by the members. Every member had saved something and there was about £25 worth of notes still to be cashed.

> Unfortunately, like the so-called Bank of England, we had issued tokens of 'promises to pay on demand' without having wealth, gold or deposits to meet these promises or tokens. This was a serious error both in principle and practice, and fell on me as another heavy penalty in relying on Mr Vandaleur to keep faith with those who had accepted the notes and to discharge his obligations. There was now what may be termed a run on the bank, my resources were soon exhausted and then panic fear affected those who had not got their notes cashed.[16]

15 E. T. Craig, *An Irish Commune: History of Ralahine* (Dublin: Martin Lester, new edition, 1919), out-of-print.
16 ibid.

The dairymaid and her herdsman husband had saved £5 worth of notes; Craig had to sell Vandaleur's gun to honour these. He then borrowed to meet the rest until every single note was redeemed.

The members of the commune met for the last time on 23 November 1833 and placed on record a declaration of "The contentment, peace and happiness they had experienced for two years under the arrangements introduced by Mr Vandaleur and Mr Craig and which through no fault of the Association was now at an end."

With the project in ruins, Craig returned to England. There he became engaged in another co-operative venture in Norfolk which again left him "shipwrecked and penniless". But Craig was persistent. The Ralahine experiment had attracted much interest among English co-operators and, up to his death in 1894, he was known and respected as "Mr Craig of Ralahine". In his later days, through old age and illness, he was in somewhat straitened circumstances, but the Co-operative Union raised a fund to provide him with an annuity, which then passed to his widow until her death in 1897.

Vandaleur was never heard of again and his wife[17] died within ten years of his disappearance. His three daughters died of tuberculosis and his elder son was drowned. Only the younger son survived — Arthur, who was three when his father fled; he fought in the Crimean War and mortgaged the Ralahine estate to pay his father's debts. One way or another the Vandaleur family held on to the ownership of Ralahine until well into the present century, allowing the estate to be run by a succession of lessees. The first of these was Pierce Creagh who in 1866 sold his interest to a Clareman, William Halpin. In 1885 the then Mrs Vandaleur coveted the improvements carried out by Halpin and forced him to quit. The last occupant of the Big House was a Mr Stoney who operated a successful dairy farm at Ralahine up to 1920; some of his labourers lived in the cottages built by Vandaleur.

With the implementation of the Land Act in the nineteen twenties, Ralahine was divided into medium-sized holdings of about seventy acres each. Some of the present owners are direct descendants of commune members. The historic seventy-acre wheat field where the 'communists' stopped the hunt is now in ten-acre pastures, the sixty-three acres of bog are entirely cut away and the wood where the labourers plotted the murder of Hastings has likewise disappeared. The fine old mansion was levelled during the nineteen forties.

It may be argued that Ralahine has little relevance to modern co-operative developments in Ireland. It was to a great extent a paternalistic experiment, imposed from above with limited democratic control. Perhaps the labourers were lucky. They had the resources of land, capital and management 'forced' upon them. The modern co-operative ideal of awaiting the members' initiative, providing capital from their own nonexistent resources, and of committing management to the conscious and informed dynamics of the democratic community would have been as

17 Formerly Emily Molony of Kiltanon, County Clare.

unrealistic then as entrusting the running of a modern household to a family of orphaned children. The Ralahine commune was a success for its members but was undone by the legal system of land tenure and the attitudes towards land ownership; indeed, the Irish obsession with land ownership, but apparently small regard for productivity, is a recurring theme in this narrative. It is chastening to reflect on how little things have changed. In many ways (certainly without a great deal of capital) the problem of securing co-operative trust in communal ownership and the working of land remains as intractable as ever.[18] The Ralahine experiment can still be regarded as an outstanding example of co-operative success because of the devotion of its management, its meticulous economic and social planning, and its scrupulous implementation of the democratic principle. It succeeded in what it attempted to do, and in a very short time.

Yet, it is ironic, in a country where political and military events are commemorated at every crossroads, that the story of one of Ireland's greatest social experiments remains practically unknown — no signpost or plaque denotes its location.

What might Ralahine have done if it had been given a chance? Craig could rightly claim that the system, even where only partly applied, had "effected what neither the Government, the soldier, the priest nor the political economist could accomplish... Socialism could induce poor ignorant Irish peasants to live in peace and harmony with each other."

Later, James Connolly was to select Ralahine as a social blueprint for a new Ireland:

> And when Ireland does emerge into complete control of her own destinies she must seek the happiness of her people in the extension on a national basis of the social arrangements of Ralahine.[19]

George William Russell (AE), in his preface to the edited version of Craig's history of the commune, [20] writes with great feeling of missed opportunity and regret:

> When John Scott Vandaleur gambled at his club he gambled away not merely his own property, but what may well have been a happier destiny for his country. It is inconceivable that if the community founded at Ralahine had developed as it began, it would not have affected the rest of Ireland. It might have saved us many years of tragic history and instead of beginning our agricultural co-operation long after Denmark, Germany and France, we might have been the pioneer nation.

18 See Viney, op.cit. His third article (*The Irish Times*, 25 May 1966) compares the Ralahine experiment with the attempts at a co-operative land ownership for sheep farming by Father James McDyer in Glencolumbkille. There is a section on Farming Societies in Chapter 24.
19 James Connolly, *Labour in Ireland* (Dublin and London: Maunsel & Company Limited, 1917), vol. I, p.141.
20 See note 15 above.

Chapter Three

William Thompson

Ralahine attracted many visitors in its short-lived heyday. Lord Wallscourt[1] was so impressed that he put some of the commune's concepts into practice on his own estate. Joseph Cox, a young solicitor's clerk in London, threw up his job and walked from London to Liverpool and then from Dublin to Ralahine to join the community. James Redmond Barry from Glandore, County Cork, who advanced the £5 on Vandaleur's gun, came too.[2] Yet the most colourful visitor of all was Barry's friend and neighbour, William Thompson, whose bust adorns the Lenin Museum in Hibernsky Street, Prague.[3] He is generally regarded as the finest intellect to be associated with the Owenite movement and has been hailed as "the most eminent founder of scientific socialism".[4]

Thompson, of the Protestant ascendancy and absentee landlord class, was born in Cork in 1775. His father, Alderman John Thompson, was a former Lord Mayor of Cork as well as high sheriff of the county. When his father died in 1814, Thompson inherited a prosperous merchant business including a fleet of trading vessels and an estate of some 1,500 acres near Rosscarbery, County Cork.[5] However, the heir had little interest in making money. His concern, like that of his contemporary Wolfe Tone, was with that large and respectable class, the men of no property.[6]

Whenever he was home from his extensive travels, Thompson lived mostly in his fine house in Patrick Street, Cork. He was a charming, kindly man and a brilliant conversationalist, yet had a matchless talent for satire and an apparently effortless ability to antagonise people. The grandson of a

1   Otherwise Mr Blake of Ardfry, Loughrea, County Galway (the title is now extinct). Years later he wrote to Craig: "It answers much beyond my hopes, in as much as it identifies the workmen with the success of the farm, besides giving me full liberty to travel on the continent for a year at a time; and upon my return I have always found that the farm had prospered more than when I was present."

2   For an account of this benevolent landlord and middleman (1798-1879), see *Utopia in Glandore*, a booklet by Rev James Coombes, (Tipperary: Muintir na Tíre, 1970).

3   'Hibernsky' commemorates the Irish Franciscans who had a friary in Prague in the seventeenth and eighteenth centuries.

4   Dr Anton Menger (?-1906), famous Austrian economist, jurist and sociologist, in *Das Recht auf den Vollen Arbeitstrag* (Right to the Whole Produce of Labour). See W.P. Ryan, *The Irish Labour Movement* (Dublin: Talbot Press, 1919).

5   Townlands of Clounkeen, Three Gneeves, Carhogarriff, Corran, Tullig and Cooladreen.

6   See Patrick Lynch, "William Thompson and the Socialist Tradition", a Thomas Davis Lecture, RTE, in J.W. Boyle (ed.), *Leaders and Workers* (Cork: Mercier Press, 1963).

Protestant divine, he professed himself an atheist and dispraised churches and clergymen of all denominations. Religions, he claimed, were doubly bad — they were oppressive and irrational. They were used by the rich to perpetuate their wealth and power and were a dangerous mixture of wisdom and folly, truth and fable — an enormous mass of puerile dogmas, visions and dreams — regulations made by able barbarians for a barbarous state of society.[7]

These opinions did little to endear Thompson to the clergy and he managed to make himself equally unpopular with the prosperous laity. He outraged the men of property by his revolutionary ideas on the distribution of wealth, by his generosity to his tenants and by his concern for the poor. He particularly affronted the Protestant gentry by his support for Christopher Hely-Hutchinson and the cause of Catholic emancipation, especially at the elections of 1812 and 1826.

Thompson was a disciple and life-long friend of Bentham, the English utilitarian. In the early nineteenth century, David Ricardo, classical economist of the free-trade school, was propounding the idea that the value of a commodity was the value of the labour which produced it. Thompson agreed, but contended that the labourer was entitled to the full value of his labour, which under the capitalist system he never got because he was invariably paid the lowest wages possible; the rest of the product went to the capitalist in profit and interest. Nobody explained this situation and its economic implications more clearly and it was this tenet of the right of the worker to the full product of his labour[8] which marked Thompson as the original founder of 'scientific socialism' — a fact acknowledged, though not overgenerously, by Karl Marx when he published *Das Kapital* in 1867.

William Thompson lived his life with the guilty feeling that he was a parasite. He was living on rent, the produce of the efforts of others. He tried to make up for it, seeking, in his own words, to raise himself to "an equality of usefulness with the productive classes." In Rosscarberry he gave leases on generous terms, built cottages, supplied ploughs, harrows, agricultural implements and even household furniture. He experimented with the modern scientific agriculture of his time, bringing in better rotations, new methods and new crops.[9] His Catholic tenants may have been shocked by many of his views — he railed about the excessive number of church holidays which kept tenants from their farm work, describing Saints Peter and Paul as "two of the greatest vagabonds" — but they judged him on his actions and remembered him for his unbounded

7 See R.K.P. Pankhurst, *William Thompson* (London: Watts & Co., 1954), chapter 13.
8 More specifically, the global right of 'Organised Labour' to the collective product, acknowledging that it was impossible even then to determine the exact extent of the individual worker's produce in an interdependent production process. Thompson visualised a just measure of "distribution according to need". It was implicit in his thinking that the young, aged, sick and disabled should be willingly accorded the full essentials of subsistence.
9 He introduced new root crops, beet and mangel-wurzel, and distributed seed to local farmers. One of his friends, Joseph Johnston, a chemist of Youghal, invented a new method of extracting sugar from potatoes. There is also a possibility that Thompson may have helped to devise the new method of cooking potatoes used in Ralahine.

kindness.[10] One thing they remarked on particularly was his personal frugality; men of his class usually ate and drank heavily while the poor went hungry. For the last seventeen years of his life he neither drank nor smoked and his diet was largely vegetarian.

Thompson's castigations were not confined to the clergy. He commented scathingly on doctors for the worthlessness of many of their remedies, their vested interest in sickness and their scant interest in positively promoting good health. Laziness he deplored, whether in the workers or the idle rich. On the other hand, he had a special abhorrence of lawyers because they were so perniciously busy in their oppressive exactions and the interminable and costly processes of the law. Unlike Robert Owen, he was under no illusions about the chances of enlisting the rich to help the poor.[11] In 1822 he wrote:

> No high sounding moral maxims influence or can influence the rich as a body. A few individuals may rise above the impulses of their class . . . but the rich as a class, like all other classes in every community, must obey the influence of the peculiar circumstances in which they are placed, must acquire the inclinations and the characters, good or bad, which spring out of the state of things surrounding them from their birth.

In 1824 Thompson published an enormous book entitled *An Inquiry into the Principles of the Distribution of Wealth most conducive to Human Happiness, applied to the newly proposed System of Voluntary Equality of Wealth*, which soon established him as the outstanding theoretician of the co-operative movement. Robert Owen was so impressed that he helped distribute the book at his own expense and took a large number of copies with him to America. *En voyage* he read from it to fellow passengers and, when he arrived, read extracts and distributed copies to vast audiences, including many distinguished Americans. John Minter Morgan pronounced it "the most able work upon Political Economy since Adam Smith's *Wealth of Nations*."[12] Thompson directed his appeals to the masses, and not to the wealthy and scholarly few. For him, if not for others of his time, co-operation was a faith for the poor, not a fad for the rich.

Thompson also expressed strong opinions on education. He was a leading member of the Cork Institution and of the Philosophical, Scientific and Literary Society. He saw the Cork Institution as a foundation to provide, at low cost, a liberal education for the children of the middle class, many of whom were denied schooling because boarding schools were

10 In 1817, he was declared a bankrupt, principally through a dispute with his sisters over a charge in their favour, made on the estate by their father in 1808. His fortunes must have improved considerably in later years, however, for he was able to travel widely and subscribe generously to many causes.

11 However, on deeper acquaintance with Owen, he became convinced that Owen's object in "courting or seeming to court" the patronage of the despots of Europe was merely to have "intercourse with the minds of his fellow creatures under their control" (Pankhurst, op. cit., p.23).

12 John Minter Morgan, *The Revolt of the Bees* (1826), pp.18, 81.

charging from £40 to £100 per annum.[13] Thompson's idea was that the period when the teenager was too old for primary school, and too young for business, should be used for education, which the Institution should provide at a cost of not more than £10 per child. In a series of letters to the *Cork Southern Reporter*, which he later published in pamphlet form (*Practical Education for the South of Ireland*), he exposed the ways in which the Institution was being mismanaged and its government endowment misused.[14] Only £300 a year was being spent on lecturers instead of the mandatory £900. An annual subsidy of £900 for agriculture was not publicly advertised and had mysteriously disappeared; £200 yearly went to the employment of a superintendent who did nothing, and a further £300 per annum was spent on a library which was never open to the public but was reserved for a privileged few who rarely used it. Few attended the Institution's lectures on agriculture, allegedly because the Cork farmers were not interested in hearing about the "sandy turnip and barley soil of Norfolk".

> His particular interest was the social sciences, economics and the philosophy of history but he also wanted the people to read literature so as to cultivate their taste. His test of education was utility, and so he sometimes ridiculed the time spent on the study of dead languages. He was appalled by the neglect in a commercial city, such as Cork, of a systematic study of the social sciences and practical economics. His quest was for a means of combining human happiness with an industrial age. To do this hè sought a better understanding of economic forces and of their impact on political and social relationships.[15]

Thompson was also concerned about the role of women in society, particularly their legal rights. He was an early and vigorous advocate of women's liberation, birth control and family planning. In 1825 he published *Appeal of One Half of the Human Race, Women, against the Pretensions of the Other Half, Men.*[16] His collaborator in this work was Anna Wheeler, youngest daughter of the famous Protestant divine, Archbishop Doyle, and godchild of Henry Grattan. At the age of fifteen Anna Doyle was married off to nineteen-year-old Francis Massey Wheeler, grandson of the second Baron Massey who had succeeded to the family estate of Ballywire at Lizard Connell in County Limerick and who had "conceived a passion for Anna Doyle on seeing her at the races." The marriage was disastrous: "the master of the house [Francis] spent half his days lounging in the stables or on horseback and every evening drank himself into a stupor." Anna, an intellectual who had been reared in an

13 At that period a shopkeeper with a net income of £300 to £400 per annum would be deemed comfortably well-off.
14 Pankhurst, op. cit., pp.10-14.
15 Lynch, op. cit., p.13.
16 An unabridged reprint of the 1825 London edition was made by Source Book Press (New York) in 1970.

atmosphere of great refinement, did not take kindly to her treatment, and, eventually, after twelve years and six children, fled with her daughters to her uncle, Sir John Doyle, then Governor of Guernsey. There, in the splendid grandeur of Government House, the talented Anna became a prominent social figure. She was in her element in urbane cosmopolitan society. She visited London and Dublin and later made her way to Caen where, in the centre of a Saint-Simonian circle, she was acclaimed the 'Goddess of Reason' and the most gifted woman of the age.

Anna met William Thompson at the home of their mutual friend, Jeremy Bentham, and their names are often linked in the records of the co-operative movement. In the dedication of his *Appeal*, Thompson acknowledges that part of the book was the exclusive product of Mrs Wheeler's mind and pen, the remainder being their joint property. Thompson, whilst applauding Mary Wollstonecraft for her book, *Vindication of the Rights of Women* (1772), regarded the views expressed by her as "too narrow". Anna Wheeler's, in contrast, he found "totally free of prejudice". With characteristic indignation and unanswerable logic, he berated a society where a woman had no legal rights, got no education and was bound by either the absolute authority of her father or an oppressive one-sided 'contract' of marriage. A husband had the legal right to imprison his wife and to chastise her "with a stick no thicker than his thumb".

Thompson viewed the ill-treatment of women as another deplorable but typical symptom of the 'morality' of the hypocrites who justified the abuse of wealth and the oppression of the working classes. To him, a code of morals which was rigidly legalistic and took no cognisance of the social and economic environment of the time was nonsense: there could be no moral justification for hanging a hungry man for stealing food. An ardent opponent of marriage, he resented the one-sided contract which left a married woman totally dependent on her husband for sexual pleasure but imposed no such restriction on the married man; adultery by a wife was legally forbidden and subject to the severest penalties, "only short of death", but an adulterous husband was not answerable to the law. In prophetic asides, he foresaw the time when sexual intercourse outside marriage would be accepted whenever it did not entail "an imprudent increase in numbers" or occasion any harm to the participants. In a typical shaft against the unequal condition of women, he queries,

Were such the order of nature, that in the human race, as in the eagle tribe and amongst some other animals, the female had been formed the stronger animal, what would man have thought of women's justice, had she deprived him of political rights?

In 1830 Thompson published[17] his most important work on co-operation, *Practical Directions for the Speedy and Economic Establishment*

17 In 1827 he had published another magnum opus, *Labour Rewarded — or How to Secure to Labour the Whole Product of Its Exertions.*

*of Communities, on the Principle of Mutual Co-operation, United Possessions,
Equality of Exertions and of the Means of Enjoyment.*[18] Here he was no
longer theorising but was covering every aspect of the arrangements in the
minutest detail. The following is a précis of some 'directions' for the
establishment of a co-operative community at Rosscarberry:

> The community . . . would consist of some 2,000 members. Land
> would be taken at the rate of one acre for every individual. If a start
> were made with 200 adult members, 52 workers would be required for
> gardening and agriculture, 66 for building and furnishing, 59 for
> textile manufactures, and 23 for miscellaneous work, baking,
> shoemaking, milling, store-keeping and teaching. Full freedom could
> not appear at once; it would have to be deferred until the community
> was safely established. In the initial period, members must work
> 'diligently' at whatever tasks might be allotted to them by the
> managers, though after the first year the community should be fully
> controlled by elected committees. Each committee would superintend
> its particular department . . .
>
> 'The milk of the cows on the land and the bread and potatoes made
> and prepared by the members and purchased out of their funds' would
> be the only food available for the first 200 days. Capital expenditure
> would have to be restricted to procure stock, machinery and raw
> materials. Necessities would have to be produced before luxuries; no
> new clothes could be distributed until six months after work began.
> Even after the first year members must not consume 'more than three-
> fourths of their annual produce' . . .
>
> As soon as the first 200 members had paid their deposits and an
> equal sum had been subscribed in shares, measures would be taken to
> commence operations . . .
>
> A Treasurer, Thomas Lyons, had already been appointed and, 'to
> accommodate subscribers', he was taking deposits in weekly
> instalments. M'Carthy, the Librarian of the Cork Mechanics'
> Institution, would also receive deposits and as soon as £50 was
> collected it would be deposited in the National Provincial Bank.[19]

Thompson died on 28 March 1833, before the Cork co-operative
community could get under way. At the insistence of his nephew (and
expected heir), Mr White of Bantry, the parson reluctantly agreed to burial
in consecrated ground and in accordance with the Anglican rites. When the
will was read after the funeral, Parson J.T. Jones was dismayed and
enraged to hear that it forbade any priest, Christian, Mohammedan or
Hindu, to meddle with Thompson's remains. Thompson had bequeathed

18 Thompson, on a visit to Ralahine, presented a copy of his *Practical Directions* to E.T.
Craig. He also sent a copy to another friend, Dr William King, founder of the Brighton
Co-operative Trading Association. King was at that time taking steps to establish a
commune modelled on the Orbiston community (see p.9).
19 Pankhurst, op. cit., pp.137–38.

his body for medical research "to aid in conquering the foolish and frequently most mischievous prejudice against the public examination of corpses." The skeleton was to be transferred to the first co-operative community successfully established in Britain or Ireland.[20]

The most upsetting aspect of Thompson's will was the disposal of his property. He set aside £4,000 to discharge any claims against the estate. He gave an annuity of £100 to Anna Wheeler, and bequeathed the residue to the co-operative movement.[21] This caused consternation. White, the heir apparent, who had wrangled so hard for his uncle's interment, got nothing. The relatives contested the will and sought to have it set aside on the plea that the testator was not of sound mind; but, despite Thompson's colourful eccentricities, this was no easy task. Alternatively, they pleaded that the aims of the will "distinctly showed an intention to abolish marriage" and, therefore, should not be recognised. The case dragged on for more than twenty-five years. The co-operative movement lacked the money and perhaps the determination to contest the case to full effect and in the end the chief beneficiaries were the lawyers, those "perniciously busy" gentlemen so bitterly scolded by Thompson. Nothing is known of the final settlement except that some of the land was in the possession of Thompson's sister, Mrs Sarah Dorman, in 1852; the records, along with the will itself, were burned during the conflagration in the Four Courts, Dublin, which marked the outbreak of the Civil War in 1922.

It is a pity that Thompson deferred putting his theory of co-operation into practice,[22] and a tragedy that Rosscarberry was not ready to carry on the work so successfully undertaken and so abruptly terminated at Ralahine. There is added poignancy in reflecting that much of the delay was attributable to that ardent co-operator, Robert Owen, who at the time was postulating that a sum of up to £250,000 was necessary to establish a successful commune. Thompson overspent his time on meticulous budgeting and, up to his death, was still keenly observing the practical details of the Ralahine experiment and awaiting the financial accounts of the second full year of the commune's work, to confirm his own computation that success was possible on an initial capital of £5,000 to £6,000. It must be conceded, however, that, although Thompson could have readily launched his own commune at Rosscarberry, he was still unable, despite all his researches, to suggest how a body of wage-earning workers without the help of a benevolent landlord or other benefactor could raise the amount of capital necessary to undertake a successful

20 Dr Daniel Donovan (father of Dr Daniel Donovan, author of *Sketches in Carbery*, Dublin: 1876), the local physician, later asserted that the body had been bequeathed to him on condition that he strung up the bones and sent them as a memento of love to Mrs Wheeler: "there were most minute particulars as to the preparation of the skeleton and how the ribs were to be tipped with silver so that it might present a fashionable appearance." (Pankhurst, op. cit., pp.184-85).

21 By a codicil on 9 March 1833 John Jagoe of Bantry was appointed executor and the trustees were to include Anna Wheeler, John Minter Morgan, John Finch, Henry McCormac and John Scott Vandaleur.

22 See F. Hall and W.P. Watkins, *Co-operation* (Manchester: Co-operative Union Ltd., 1937), pp.52-56.

co-operative development. He undoubtedly wasted further time in pondering this question — the answer to which was shortly to be supplied by the workers themselves.

Chapter Four

The Rochdale Pioneers

The great beauty of co-operation is that it may
be begun without any capital at all. A man wants
nothing but his wages and an honest companion.
(Dr William King)

Rochdale is a fairly large industrial town some ten miles north of
Manchester. Hereabout the Roch river meets the Spodden and the
Rochdale Canal has flowed through the town since 1798. In the days of the
industrial revolution the canal was a very important waterway connecting
on the one hand, via the Aire and Calder, with the Humber mouth and the
trade of Europe; and on the other with Manchester, the Mersey, Liverpool
and the new world of America. The once-busy canal now lies idle and the
central part of it has been covered in.

In the middle of Rochdale stands a statue of John Bright (1811-89),
statesman, orator, millowner and prototype of Victorian radicalism. Bright
is not widely remembered today but there are few who have not heard some
reference to his famous declamation — "The Angel of Death has been
abroad throughout the land. You may almost hear the beating of his
wings."[1]

In another part of the town is a quaint-looking shop, refurbished in
recent times with meticulous care to look exactly as it did in the middle of
the nineteenth century.[2] Here in a ground-floor warehouse on the evening
of 21 December 1844 "A few poor weavers, out of employ, nearly out of
food and quite out of heart with the social state", opened a shop to sell
simple provisions and so wrote themselves into the economic and social
history of England and the world. It was, however, a timid and fretful start.

A few of the co-operators had clandestinely assembled to witness their
own denouement; and there they stood in that dismal lower room of
the warehouse, like the conspirators under Guy Fawkes in the
Parliamentary cellars, debating on whom should devolve the temerity
of taking down the shutters and displaying their humble preparations.

---

1 In a speech in the House of Commons on 23 February 1855 during a debate on the
   Crimean War. Bright abhorred trade unionism and factory legislation but encouraged
   co-operation "as a means of making wages go further and encouraging thrift".
2 Officially opened as a co-operative museum by Ben Jones of Bournemouth, well-known
   veteran co-operator, on 11 April 1931.

One did not like to do it, and another did not like to be seen in the shop when it was done; however, having gone so far there was no choice but to go further and at length one bold fellow, utterly reckless of consequences, rushed at the shutters and in a few minutes Toad Lane was in a titter. Lancashire has its gamins as well as Paris. The 'doffers' are the gamins of Rochdale. The 'doffers' are lads of from ten to fifteen who take off full bobbins from the spindles and put on empty ones. On the night when our Store was opened the 'doffers' came out strong in Toad Lane — peeping with ridiculous impertinence round the corner, ventilating their opinion at the top of their voices, or standing before the door inspecting, with pertinacious insolence, the scant arrangements of butter and oatmeal; at length they exclaimed in a chorus, 'Aye the owd weavers' shop is opened at last'.[3]

The Toad Lane Shop

What was there about these twenty-eight poor weavers,[4] and their co-operative Rochdale Equitable Pioneers Society, that they should be so well remembered? There were hundreds of co-operative ventures established before their time, many of which were very much alike in their humble beginnings. The ideals of the Pioneers were similar to those which had inspired hundreds before them:

The objects and plans of this Society are to form arrangements for the pecuniary benefit and the improvement of the social and domestic condition of its members by raising a sufficient amount of capital in shares of one pound each, to bring into operation the following plans

---

3 George Jacob Holyoake, *Self Help by the People: History of Co-operation in Rochdale*, published 1858 (first written as a series of articles in the *Daily News*, 1855).

4 Not all of them were poor, not all were weavers, and there is some doubt about their original number. Leading member Charles Howarth was a warper in a cotton mill. James Smithies and Joseph Smith were woolsorters. There were two John Kershaws, one a collier, the other a warehouseman, George Healy (hatter), David Brooks (block printer), John Garside (cabinet-maker), John Collier (engineer), John Bent (tailor), John Scowcroft (hawker), James Tweedsdale (clogger), James Wilkinson (shoemaker). James Daly, a Northern Irishman and secretary of the Society, was a joiner. Flannel weavers formed the largest group, which included William Cooper, James Standring, James Manock, James Maden, John Lord, Ben Ludman, Charles Barnish and the three Ashworths, George, Sam and Miles. See *A Century of Co-operation*, op.cit., p.402 et seq.

and arrangements:

1. The establishment of a Store for the sale of provisions, clothing, etc.;
2. The building, purchasing or erecting [of] a number of houses in which those members desiring to assist each other in improving their domestic and social conditions may reside;
3. To commence the manufacture of such articles as the society may determine upon for the employment of such members as may be without employment or who may be suffering in consequence of repeated reductions in their wages;
4. As a further benefit and security to the members of their Society, the Society shall purchase or rent an estate or estates of land, which shall be cultivated by the members who may be out of employment, or whose labour may be badly remunerated;
5. That as soon as practicable, this Society shall proceed to arrange the powers of production, distribution, education and government; or in other words, to establish a self-supporting home colony of united interests, or assist other Societies in establishing such colonies;
6. That, for the promotion of sobriety, a temperance hotel be opened in one of the Society's houses as soon as convenient.[5]

At first sight, these objects may seem a remarkable hotch-potch. However, they reflect much of the experience of previous co-operative experiments, and the Owenite ideal of a new moral (and economic) world is strongly in evidence.[6] A frequent first step towards a more formal co-operation was the collective purchase of a bag of meal. On payday a few poor men would combine to buy and divide a bag of flour, saving them each a few pennies. The Rochdale Pioneers co-operated informally in this way, while preparing their bigger venture, by raising a weekly subscription of 2d (later 3d) per man. At length, with a formidable capital of £28, they were in business in a store which they rented for £10 a year. The fame of the Rochdale Pioneers arises not in what they did, but in the way in which they did it.

★ ★ ★

The folklore has it that Charlie Howarth was lying awake in the middle of

---

5 The objects were not numbered in the original script.
6 Even the sixth object had deep roots in co-operative tradition. As strong advocates of temperance (and its helpful effects on cash trading), the Rochdale Pioneers were not teetotallers (a few perhaps were) and in fact held many of their early meetings in either the 'Weavers Arms' or the 'Labour and Health' beerhouse. Speculation on this point arose from their refusal to sell liquor in their store and the fact that at an early stage they planned a temperance hotel, which however never materialised. There was a great upsurge in the temperance movement in Britain at the time and in Ireland an obscure Franciscan priest, Theobald Matthew, from a little friary in the back lanes of Cork, was leading a great temperance society. So successful was he in his campaign against drunkenness and its consequent evils that it was a news item of international interest that at the summer assizes in Cork in 1844 only one prisoner appeared for trial. The tradition of sobriety, linked with an equally strong tradition of hospitality, generosity and light-hearted good fellowship, has persisted very strongly in the co-operative ethic.

the night thinking about how best to do business in the shop they were going to start. If their prices were too low, they would incur the wrath of the private traders and the 'truckers' who were influential and strong enough to break up the shop. Although the Truck Act of 1831 had made it unlawful for employers to pay wages in kind or to 'tie' workers to a particular shop, workers were forced to buy their provisions at the 'tommy shop' run by the owner, manager, or perhaps foreman, of the works. Prices in these 'truck shops' were high and the goods were of poor quality and frequently adulterated. A favourite trick was mixing flour with white china clay. Howarth was thinking also of the difficult business of book-keeping, trading with members and non-members,[7] and the equitable distribution of profits or surpluses. Suddenly he struck on the idea of a dividend on purchases. They would charge regular prices, but divide the trading surplus between members in accordance with the amounts of their purchases from the store.

The story may be true, but what is much more certain is that Howarth was not the first to think of it.[8] What made Howarth and his band of Equitable Pioneers famous was not the concept of dividend on purchases, which had been known and used for some time; rather it was a combination of ideas, none of them individually new, but which, cumulatively, produced an essentially new system. These ideas, incorporated in the rules of the Rochdale Equitable Pioneer Society, were:

1. Democratic control
2. Open membership
3. Fixed or limited return on capital subscribed
4. Dividend on purchases
5. Trading strictly on a cash basis; no credit
6. Selling only pure and unadulterated goods
7. Provision for the education of the members
8. Political and religious neutrality.

There were other ideas and working techniques[9] which for a time were regarded as essential elements, but the above eight represent the major distinguishing features of the true co-operative. These Rochdale principles, first assembled for the guidance of a small consumer co-operative in Lancashire, went on to gain universal acceptance and have been adopted, with modifications, in most countries as the basic ideological structure for a

---

7 The only form of registration open to the Rochdale Pioneers was under the Friendly Societies Acts of 1829 and 1834. These forbade trading with non-members, the purchase of land or the investment of funds other than in government securities. The Society was registered on 15 August 1844.
8 Alexander Campbell, Owenite missionary and 'father' of Scottish co-operation, expounded it to the Glasgow Baking Society in 1822. Another Scottish society, Lennoxtown, claimed to have paid a dividend on purchases as early as 1812.
9 Including the equality of both sexes in membership rights, the need for regular and frequent meetings, the proper keeping and auditing of accounts and the presentation of balance sheets to the members. These continue to be incorporated in the rules of nearly all modern co-operative societies.

wide variety of co-operative activities. The rules pertaining to cash trading and dealing in only "pure unadulterated goods" were very important in the days of the Pioneers. They have since been replaced by the accepted set of co-operative principles but are still deeply enshrined in the co-operative consciousness as promoting a spirit of self-reliance and thrift, and a policy of quality and honest value in co-operative goods.

The original Rochdale principles are elaborated in the set of six co-operative principles approved by the International Co-operative Alliance Congress in Vienna in 1966:

1. Membership of a co-operative society should be voluntary and available without artificial restriction on any social, political, racial or religious discrimination, to all persons who can make use of its services and are willing to accept the responsibilities of membership.
2. Co-operative societies are democratic organisations. Their affairs should be administered by persons, elected or appointed, in a manner agreed by the members and accountable to them. Members of primary societies should enjoy equal rights of voting (one member, one vote) and participation in decisions affecting their societies. In other than primary societies, the administration should be conducted on a democratic basis in a suitable form.
3. Share capital should receive only a strictly limited rate of interest, if any.
4. Surplus or savings, if any, arising out of the operations of a society, belong to the members of that society and should be distributed in such a manner as would avoid one member gaining at the expense of others. This may be done by decision of the members as follows:
    (a) by provision for development of the business of the co-operative;
    (b) by provision of common services;
    (c) by distribution among the members in proportion to their transactions with the society.
5. All co-operative societies should make provision for the education of their members, officers and employees and of the general public, in the principles and techniques of co-operation, both economic and democratic.
6. All co-operative organisations, in order to best serve the interests of their members and the communities, should actively co-operate in every practical way with other co-operatives at local, national and international levels.

In Rochdale both the men and the principles stood the test. They started their shop with a meagre supply of the barest essentials. After paying for alterations, fixtures and wooden forms for sitting on, they spent £16 11s 11d on groceries:

	£	s	d
Butter (28 lbs)	2	1	1
Sugar (56 lbs)	1	14	0
Flour (6 cwts)	11	0	6
Oatmeal (1 sack)	1	7	0
Tallow candles (24)		9	4
Total Cost	£16	11	11

At first, the store opened only two nights a week and the committee met weekly in the 'Weavers Arms'. The early takings were very small. By the end of the first quarter (31 March 1845), however, it was possible to pay a dividend of 3d in the £ on all groceries bought by members. It was also decided to pay the shopmen, Sam Ashworth and Willie Cooper, at the rate of 3d per hour. In the first full year of trading the turnover was only £710, but share capital rose from the original £28 to £181 and the Pioneers were able to show a surplus of £22 on the year's trade. They plodded on doggedly, making a small profit every year. From early in 1845 the store opened every evening but it was not until 1851, when membership reached 600 and sales £13,000, that they were able to stay open all day. By 1860 there were 3,450 members, a turnover of £152,000 and a trading surplus for the year of £15,906. In 1973 the Equitable Pioneers Society flourished with membership over 52,000 and sales topping £5 million. In 1956, Miss Gracie Fields, famous singer and former mill girl, came back to her native Rochdale to visit the old Toad Lane store and, amid scenes of some emotion, to officially open a major reconstruction of the Society's central block, Pioneer House, now streamlined into a modern supermarket.

The Rochdale Pioneers

The Pioneers were tough men, starting business in very hard times. Between 1836 and 1849 there were two years of serious economic crisis (1837 and 1847), nine years of depression, one fair year and only two years of reasonably good trade and employment. The Pioneers were lucky: they opened their store in the 'fair' year, 1844. They had only ten days of it left but it was followed by the only two years which could be described as good.

Otherwise the Toad Lane store, despite the grit of its founders and the excellence of its principles, might have gone the way of so many others. Even so, success in the 'hungry forties' called for enthusiasm and sound business sense. It also demanded a certain obduracy and many heartbreaking decisions. Some of the rules were tough but they were absolutely necessary for survival. It must have been exceedingly difficult to refuse all credit to fellow members who were temporarily destitute or out of work. Even principle 6, "Selling only pure and unadulterated goods", created certain problems for the early Pioneers. Pure, unadulterated food was selling in the store at a fair price, but when a member was down to his last few pennies, he had often to turn to the "badger"[10] for credit or else buy the stale loaf or the underweight, adulterated stone of meal.

One consequence of the rules, and the vital one, was that the Society survived. The other less fortunate one was that the appeal of co-operation was to great extent limited to those whose livelihood was relatively more secure — those who had steadier, better paid jobs and some savings to tide them over the rough patches.

> Co-operation became perforce a movement mainly of the better off and thriftier sections of the working class; nor has it ever wholly escaped this limitation, though with rising standards of life and developing social services, the range of its appeal has become very much wider than it used to be. In the early days there were many who could not become co-operators because in bad times they depended on credit, and in good times they were still tied to the tradesman whose advances they were paying off or to whom they felt an obligation because their credit had not been cut off when times were bad. Co-operative loyalty is one thing but there is another loyalty which often pulled men and women the opposite way.[11]

Modern co-operators, however hard their own experiences and however much they read of the early days, can hardly hope to get more than a partial understanding of the terrible conditions under which the early Pioneers worked. A quotation from Freidrich Engels's *The Condition of the Working Classes in England in 1844* is pertinent. He was then living in Manchester as a representative of a German firm engaged in the cotton trade:[12]

> In a word we must confess that in the workmen's dwellings of Manchester, no cleanliness, no convenience and consequently no comfortable family life is possible; that in such dwellings only a physically degenerate race, robbed of all humanity, degraded, reduced

10 A shopkeeper who gave credit and covered the risk of defaulters by charging high prices for adulterated goods to those in his debt.
11 *A Century of Co-operation*, p.9.
12 Those who may suspect Engels's account as that of a socialist agitator, should turn to the sober official reports of Edwin Chadwick and his collaborators, *The Sanitary Condition of the Labouring Population* and *The State of Large Towns and Populous Districts* or the evidence given before the Royal Commission on the Health of Towns (1844).

morally and physically to bestiality, could feel comforted and at home . . .

The habitual food of the individual working man naturally varies according to his wages. The better paid workers, especially those in whose families every member is able to earn something, have good food as long as this state of things lasts; meat daily, and bacon and cheese for supper. Where wages are less, meat is used only two or three times a week, and the proportion of bread and potatoes increases. Descending gradually, we find the animal food reduced to a small piece of bacon cut up with the potatoes; lower still even this disappears and there remain only bread, cheese, porridge and potatoes, until, on the lowest rung of the ladder, among the Irish, potatoes form the sole food.

If the social and economic state of the worker co-operators was grim, their legal position was equally so. Prior to 1852 a co-operative society was at best regarded in law as only a private partnership. Hence,

1 Every member was responsible to the last penny of his property for its debts.
2. Any member who could get possession of the property of the society was practically at liberty to keep it.
3. If the society had more than twenty-five members, it was strictly speaking an illegal company,[13] unless it undertook the heavy expense of registering as a joint stock company.
4. As an illegal company, it had no legal redress against the public at large.
5. There were no legal means of enforcing honesty on the part of the leading members.
6. There was no security for savings invested in the common enterprise.
7. There was no means of compelling obedience to the society's rules.

It would be hard to see how co-operative societies could make progress under such restraints. They didn't, and hundreds of them went to the wall. The wonderful thing was that so many were formed and managed to survive. The Rochdale Pioneers, half of them Owenites (with a reputation for atheism), the remainder Chartists (with a reputation for violence), Corn Law Repealers, factory reformers and what have you, were a rare band.

A new group were on the horizon to take up where the Owenites and Chartists had faltered and henceforth made most of the running for co-operation and reform: a band of scholarly men, faithful Christians, zealous churchgoers — the Christian Socialists — who were soon to gather a great following and render an inestimable service to the working classes by securing changes in the law. The Christian Socialists were directly

13 This may perhaps account for some of the difficulty in identifying the twenty-eight poor weavers with a similar number who reputedly were the founder members of the Rochdale Society of Equitable Pioneers.

responsible for the passing of the Industrial and Provident Societies Acts of 1852 and 1862. The first of these protected the property of the societies and gave binding force to their rules; the latter one gave the most valued privilege of all — limited liability — circumscribing the liability of members to the amount of their shares.

Even against the intimidating odds, the Rochdale Pioneers Society grew rapidly. In 1846 it established a butcher's shop, and a year later opened a drapery department, selling cloth made by some of the members. In 1850 a wholesale department was set up and the Rochdale Co-operative Corn Mill was founded. Some of these ventures faltered but were taken up successfully by other societies. The Pioneers never acquired their "estate of land", but other co-operators nearby did so.[14] When the Pioneers undertook the building of houses for their members in 1868, the notion of community living had receded. Houses were built to provide sound dwellings at reasonable rents rather than for the object of mutual improvement through living together, as envisaged in the original aims.

Although the major success of the Rochdale Society was in the retail trade, setting the pattern of the British co-operative movement of the future, the Pioneers effected something more than a novel experiment in shop-keeping. Their scheme was a shrewd blending of idealism with immediate and practical utility, as veteran co-operator George Jacob Holyoake wrote of them:

> They took their affairs into their own hands, and what is more to the purpose, they kept them in their own hands.

---

14 Jumbo Farm near Oldham, famous in connection with the founding of the Co-operative Wholesale Society (CWS), was founded in 1851 and survived for a full ten years after the more ambitious agrarian schemes of Robert Owen and Feargus O'Connor had failed.

Chapter Five

The Land for the People

Some fifteen miles north-east of Rochdale the village of Baxenden is now incorporated in the town of Accrington, which in turn was absorbed in 1974 in the new Borough of Hyndburn. In the eighteen fifties Baxenden was a small hamlet, one of a number of small villages usually grouped around cotton mills in an area of developing industry on the level country by the river Hyndburn.

In Stellfoxes Victoria Mill, Baxenden, on 8 March 1857, a distressing but not uncommon industrial accident occurred. An eleven-year-old child worker had his arm badly mangled in a machine. The arm had to be amputated and the chances of the boy's survival were slim. There were no anaesthetics safe to use on one so young and so badly injured, but he was tough and survived. He was developing a talent for survival. He had struggled for life when he was born in Ireland, amid hunger and pestilence, on 25 March in the famine year of 1846. He survived eviction when his family was thrown on the roadside. He survived the hazardous journey to England and the anxious and hungry period of resettlement. As a 'foreign' child among strangers, he had endured the grinding ten-hour workdays in the mill, to help his father's earnings.

The boy was Michael Davitt. He never became directly involved in the co-operative movement but his work was to have a profound influence on it. It is difficult to imagine how, without reference to Davitt's story, one could adequately portray the agrarian and political background against which the new Irish co-operative movement was launched in the last decade of the nineteenth century.

Out of hospital with an empty sleeve, young Davitt could find no work. Very soon there would be no jobs for many others, for Lancashire was to feel the effects of the cotton famine caused by the American Civil War. The Southern cotton-growing confederate states were in conflict with the federal government and exports of cotton were seriously hampered.[1] Since he could not work, Michael Davitt went to school. After a few years he had

---

1   In Rochdale too there was much distress. In 1862 the Pioneers had a drop in membership of four hundred, in capital of £4,500 and in sales of £35,000. During the years of the 'Famine' the Society paid out £22,000 and its stability was an important factor in helping the town to weather the storm. Rochdale was also fortunate in having a woollen industry which began to benefit from the cotton shortage. By 1864 the Pioneers Society's sales were back to the previous record figure (£175,000).

mastered the rudiments and preferred to do his reading elsewhere. He got himself a job as a newsboy and doubled as a printer's devil. A young, active, literate Irishman with few employment opportunities and a fair sense of grievance, it is not surprising to find him in 1865 in the ranks of the Fenian Brotherhood. Davitt's secretarial services were appreciated and within three years he was organising secretary of the Irish Republican Brotherhood for England and Scotland. His physical handicap did not prevent him from playing an active military role. In 1867 he was chosen to command the force that was ordered to attack Chester Castle and seize its store of arms. The assailants were betrayed by an informer but Davitt displayed remarkable ingenuity and resourcefulness in getting his men away safely. Undeterred by the failure of the 1867 Rising, he continued to make preparations for a renewed struggle but on 14 May 1870, near Paddington Station, he was apprehended by a London policeman. He was charged with treason and felony (sending firearms to Ireland) and convicted on the evidence of an informer. Davitt served seven harsh years of a fifteen-year sentence in the cells and stonebreaking yards of Dartmoor before Isaac Butt and the Amnesty Association secured his release on ticket-of-leave.[2]

After a short period in the United States visiting his mother and consulting with Fenian leaders, Davitt made his debut in the Irish political arena. On 19 April 1879, at the small village of Irishtown outside Claremorris in his native Mayo, Davitt mounted the platform to address a meeting of some 7,000 people. In an electrifying speech he denounced rack-renting and eviction, called for the abolition of the landlord system and the establishment of a peasant proprietary. The crowd echoed his words with a mighty roar: "Down with landlordism — the land for the People!"

One result of this Irishtown meeting was that the local landlord[3] ceased his threat of eviction and reduced rents by 25 per cent. Other meetings were to follow and, in Westport in June, Davitt was joined on the platform by Charles Stewart Parnell,[4] who told 8,000 cheering tenants to resist eviction and "keep a firm grip of [their] homesteads". In the twenty-seven years of Davitt's exile, Ireland had seen many changes, but few of them for the better.

Most of the land still belonged to some 10,000 landlords, whose relationships with their tenants were unhappy: there was constant conflict on the matter of land tenure and rents. Although rents varied considerably

---

2   A description of Davitt's prison experience is given in his *Leaves from a Prison Diary*. He spent several months in solitary confinement in a tiny cell. There was hardly any light and in hot weather, to avoid suffocation, he had to lie full length on the cell floor and inhale air under the cell door. At other times he was made to pound putrifying bones to make bonemeal fertiliser or harnessed to a dray like an animal to haul rocks from the prison quarry. Davitt's account, however, contains no expression of bitterness or self-pity.

3   Canon Geoffrey Burke, who on the death of his father inherited his estate and became a small landlord — "a kindly and not ungenerous man, but he had the landlord's notions about landlord rights..." See E.A. D'Alton, *History of Ireland* (London: Gresham Publishing Company, 1910) Vol. III, p.277.

4   Parnell was elected MP for Meath in 1875. After the death of Isaac Butt in 1879, Parnell became the acknowledged leader of the Irish Party in 1880.

from landlord to landlord and from one part of the country to another, there is little doubt that in many places they were excessive and sometimes ruinous. The prime landlord was frequently unknown to his tenants: he was often an English nobleman who held title to a vast area of land on which he gave leases in perpetuity involving parcels of several thousand acres. In many cases further sublettings were made, so that as many as five devolutions existed between the original landowner and the man who took annual letting of conacre. A major inequity of this system was that sometimes the ultimate tiller of the soil had his crops constrained because of a dispute between two landlords.

One of the provisions of the Penal Laws enacted in the latter years of the seventeenth century was that Catholic tenants should pay a rent equivalent to two-thirds of the gross annual output of the land.[5] This enactment had set a target which, although it could rarely be met and had been greatly ameliorated over the years, nevertheless had a profound influence on the level of rents for almost the whole remaining period of the landlord/tenant system. The profitability of tillage during the period of the Napoleonic wars, which enabled farmers' sons with little or no capital to rent land and start farming on their own account, induced many landlords to increase their revenue by permitting more tenants on the land and matching rents to the demand for land. A population growth of 2 per cent. per annum during this period ensured that the demand for land persisted long after the boom had finished. In the slump after the battle of Waterloo, many landlords found their estates subdivided and congested to an extent which made it impossible to carry out land improvements or to adopt pastoral farming, which by then was relatively more profitable. Although many tenants could not pay and others paid tardily, the landlords maintained the level of rents and in some cases increased them in the hope that economic stringency would relieve the congestion and enable the farming system to adapt to current economic trends. They sometimes evicted non-paying tenants to enable them to farm cattle and sheep on their own account or to let the land in adequate acreages to graziers. Yet wholesale evictions were rarely undertaken, so many non-paying tenants were left in possession for lengthy periods. This inability of landlords to regulate tenancies, coupled with a rise in rural population, ensured that the system of land congestion and uneconomic husbandry persisted in many areas, and sometimes even increased, in the face of all economic dictates. The inexorable rise in population, with ever-increasing numbers seeking subsistence from a restricted acreage, inevitably precipitated the Great Famine of 1845-47. It is well to remember, however, that the Famine (often regarded as a discrete phenomenon) was in fact no more than a tragic telescoping of an economic and social process which was already well under way.[6]

The excessive population growth in the decades before the Famine was a

5 In the early eighteenth century, English tenants were paying an estimated one-third of their gross output in rents. See G. Sigerson, *History of the Land Tenures and Land Classes of Ireland* (London: Longman, Green, Reader and Dyer, 1871), p.173.

6 See Raymond D. Crotty, *Irish Agricultural Production — Its Volume and Structure* (Cork: Cork University Press, 1966), chapter 2 *passim*.

biological carry-over from the period prior to 1815 and could not be immediately arrested. Long before the Famine, however, the classic checks on economic deprivation were beginning to operate. The predominantly Catholic ethic discountenanced most forms of voluntary birth control, but by 1830 the birth-rate had been greatly reduced by the expedients of later and fewer marriages. This trend accelerated and the crude birth-rate fell from 6.0 per 1,000 population in 1830 to 3.8 per 1,000 in 1844. Although there are no figures for the period prior to 1841, it is very likely that the death-rate also increased in the thirty years before the Famine.

Emigration was a major factor of economic and social adjustment and an accelerating pattern was well developed from 1815 onwards. From 1780 to 1815 the average annual rate of emigration to North America was 4,000 but it increased to 33,000 per annum from 1815 to 1845. In the census year of 1841 the total emigration to Britain and elsewhere from 1 January to 7 July was calculated to average 2,500 per week — the equivalent of 130,000 per annum. It was merely a matter of time before the population of Ireland would have started to decline.

The Famine, in a very drastic and cruel way, effected the reduction in rural population which could have cleared the ground for a better farming system,[7] making it easier for agriculture to adapt to more extensive (as opposed to intensive) forms of husbandry. In many areas this actually happened and the economic condition of the farmers improved over the next twenty years. In all too many instances, however, the old problem of landlord/tenant conflict intruded again to negate the benefits which might have been gained by better farming.

At any period in Irish history there were very few really good landlords of the kindly and paternalistic kind typified in nineteenth-century England — men who took a real interest in their estates, carried out improvements and charged reasonable rents. The Famine had to a great extent a disimproving effect on the calibre of Irish landlords. With thousands of tenants starving, dying or emigrating, there was a considerable reduction in the amount of money which could be collected in rents. Consequently, a great number of landlords, including many of the more merciful ones who had contributed to famine relief, found themselves in financial difficulties. The Encumbered Estates Act of 1849 was passed to enable bankrupt landlords to sell their estates through a Court of Commissioners. Sharman Crawford,[8] MP for Rochdale, had introduced Land Bills in 1848 and 1850

---

7 Acknowledging the constraints of landlord ownership and a system which regarded land primarily as a source of profit rather than a source of sustenance, as under the previous Brehon system. Effectively, what had happened in the years just before the Famine was that a large proportion of the population was forced to seek sustenance from approximately one million acres of potatoes. There is little doubt that, under a different system, the twenty million acres of Irish land could have provided an abundance of food for a population of eight million or more, even allowing for drastic crop failures.

8 William Sharman Crawford (1781-1861), Sheriff of County Down, 1811; MP for Dundalk, 1835-37; Chartist supporter and MP for Rochdale 1841-52. He procured the formation of the Tenant Right Association in Ulster in 1846. As early as 1835, Sharman Crawford had introduced a Bill on similar lines but the representatives of the Irish landlords totally opposed its very moderate measures. Only two MPs supported it, one of them William Smith O'Brien.

to improve the tenants' rights, but Irish landlords were so desperate to evict non-paying tenants and increase rents to repair their shattered fortunes, that his Bills got little hearing. British statesmen of both parties believed that if the bankrupt landlords were replaced by solvent ones, the tenants would no longer be harassed and there would be no further need for legislative interference on the question of Irish land. Their special hope was that Englishmen with money would buy these encumbered estates and establish a similar relationship of mutual help and forbearance as existed between landlord and tenant in England.

Few Englishmen came, but instead there was a major transfer of landownership to a meaner class of Irishman. The 'gombeen-man', the Irish species of dishonest shopkeeper, produce-buyer, money-lender and usurer, had long preyed on the impoverished rural community. His activities were particularly notorious during periods of famine (and localised famines were a frequent occurrence long before the nation-wide catastrophe of the eighteen forties) when many families traded their livestock and personal possessions at grave financial disadvantage in order to obtain food or the passage money for emigration. The Encumbered Estates Act gave the gombeen-man an opportunity to invest his famine profits in land. Some of these unscrupulous dealers had social ambitions to enhance their status *vis-à-vis* the aristocracy and were bent on making more money. They had little care for their unfortunate tenants and the net effect of the 1849 Act was to set up a meaner and more ruthless class of tyrant landlord than the absentee.

Between 1849 and 1879 some five million acres, approximately one quarter of the land of Ireland, changed hands under the Encumbered Estates Act.[9] Some 90,000 tenants are known to have been evicted in 1849 and in 1850 the total had gone up to 104,000. Although the proximate cause of eviction was invariably given as non-payment of rent, it is believed that many of these evictions and those in subsequent years had their origin in shop debts.[10]

When Michael Davitt returned to Mayo in 1879, he found a rural landscape of miserable tenant shacks and ostentatious mansions. The countryside was essentially the same as that described by a French visitor in 1839: "The traveller in Ireland meets only magnificent castles or miserable hovels but no edifice holding a middle rank between the palaces of the great and the cabins of the lowly; there are only the rich and the poor."[11] Davitt found little difference between the hovels he had left and those he found on his return, except that they were fewer in number. The repeal of the Corn Laws in 1846 was beginning to have its effect; Britain was benefiting from cheaper grain, but in Ireland tillage was declining.

9   See F.S.L. Lyons, *Ireland Since the Famine* (London: Weidenfeld and Nicolson, 1971), Part I, section 4 *passim*.
10 See Barbara Lewis Solow, *The Land Question and the Irish Economy 1870-1903* (Cambridge, Mass: Harvard University Press, 1971).
11 Gustave de Beaumont, *Ireland, Social, Political and Religious*, edited by W.C. Taylor (London: 1839) cited by R.D. Collison Black, *Economic Thought and the Irish Question 1817-1870* (Cambridge: Cambridge University Press, 1960).

Store cattle were more profitable and landlords were keen to clear their estates of 'potato-and-oat patch' tenants to make way for the grazing bullock. Evictions multiplied and so did agrarian outrages.[12]

"No edifice holding a middle rank . . . "

Gladstone's Land Act of 1870 offered some hope. The Ulster custom[13] was given the force of law where it existed; and where it didn't, as in most of the country, the tenant was given increased security in his holding. This was to be done in two ways. First, the tenant was entitled to compensation for improvements carried out during his tenancy; secondly, tenants evicted for reasons other than non-payment of rent would have to be financially compensated for the dislodgment. In this, Gladstone hoped to deter landlords from unjust evictions by "cutting their hands on the sharp edge of pecuniary damages." Also, largely at John Bright's insistence, tenants were to be allowed to borrow from the state two-thirds of the cost of their holdings, repaying their debt by 5 per cent. annuities spread over thirty-five years.[14] The Act, if honestly administered, would have done something to improve the lot of the tenants; but the landlords, by various devices, managed to defeat nearly all of its provisions. Very few peasant proprietors were created; few of the smaller tenants had any substantial cash income and fewer still, short of utterly depriving themselves, were able to save the required one-third of the purchase price. Furthermore, few tenants were strong enough to challenge landlords' decisions in the courts, so rack-renting and evictions continued with little or no compensation or redress. The Ballot Act of 1872 introduced secret instead of open voting, but this new item of political freedom had not yet found an effective use. The one definite effect of the 1870 Land Act was that landlords' improvements, which hitherto had benefited some larger tenant farmers in the better farming areas, now all but ceased.

12 In 1877 there were 1,323 evictions; in 1878 1,749 and in 1879 2,667. See D'Alton, op.cit., Vol. III, p.273.
13 By custom, but not by law, tenants in Ulster had always been left undisturbed as long as they paid their rent. They were also allowed to sell the goodwill (tenant right) of their holding to anyone whom the landlord accepted as a suitable tenant.
14 This is the same John Bright mentioned in Chapter Four. Some of the clauses of the 1870 Land Act came to be popularly known as the 'Bright Clauses'.

The tenant farmers in England and their parliamentary representatives were constantly perplexed by the Irish outcry about rack-renting. Statistics indicated that the average per acre rent in Ireland was, by English standards, eminently reasonable. Sir Richard Griffith's valuation had been carried out between 1853 and 1865. This valuation figure was deemed to be a fair rent. As applied to farm land, it was based on a modest estimate of the ability of each particular holding to produce certain standard crops and livestock,[15] the income from which was estimated from the average prices obtaining in forty market towns in Ireland during the years 1849, 1850 and 1851. From this was deducted the costs of production, including labour, depreciation, repairs, insurance, rates and taxes and a 5 per cent. allowance for tenant capital. The result, after these deductions, would be the net annual value of the holding — a figure which a tenant would be willing to offer a landlord for rent. Of course, the intention of the valuation was not to calculate fair rents but to provide an assessment for local taxes. The valuations arrived at were certainly not excessive and liberal allowance was made for labour and other farm costs. The yield estimates were conservative and it would have been difficult to pick three years in which produce prices were lower than 1849 to 1851. By 1865 prices for crops had increased by between fifty and sixty per cent. and by about eighty per cent. for animal products.[16]

We will see how subsequent events in the eighteen eighties demonstrated the general acceptance by tenants that the Griffith valuation provided a fair figure for rent. Meanwhile, the perplexity of English observers was heightened by the fact that, while Davitt and Parnell were initiating their nation-wide land agitation against rack-renting, the overall figure for Irish rents was within the limits of Griffith's now outdated valuation.[17] The evidence was that only fourteen per cent. of Irish landlords were charging rents in excess of the Griffith valuation and that in some areas rents were too low.[18] In consequence, it was stated that the tenants took things easy and farmed less diligently than those on nearby estates where rents were higher.

It is undoubtedly true that, in many parts of Ireland in the eighteen seventies, farmers, particularly those tenanting reasonable acreages, had numerous problems but rent was not a major one. It is equally true that in the poorer land areas the ultimate rents (i.e., at or near the end of the sub-letting scale) paid by smallholders were sometimes double or treble the rent per acre paid in more fertile areas. Even where they were ostensibly modest, the rents exacted for poor quality land were still disproportionate to the productivity of the soil. The Englishman's concept of a fair rent presumed a reasonable acreage of well-used farmland, well-fenced and drained, with adequate farm buildings and equipment and farmed to a high standard of husbandry. He had little comprehension of the chaotic

15 The eight products were wheat, oats, barley, flax, butter, beef, mutton and pork.
16 Solow, op. cit., p.61.
17 It was intended under the Act of 1852 that a revaluation be made at not less than fourteen-year intervals but funds were never provided for any revision.
18 See Solow, op. cit., p.46 et seq.

conditions obtaining in Ireland. Overall average figures conveyed little because of the wide range and variation in the rents charged. Quoted figures could mean little in a situation where rents were frequently raised or lowered at the landlord's whim;[19] nor could the exact 'rent' be readily computed in money terms to allow for the labour services provided to the landlord, the arbitrary fines imposed by him for some real or supposed misdemeanours in husbandry and the various exactions and bribes which had sometimes to be paid in order to acquire or retain a tenancy. Sir Richard Griffith's scrupulous computation could not have anticipated the often disastrous deterioration in soil fertility or the declining working capital resources and husbandry standards of individual tenants. Neither could his averaging of produce prices at the forty market centres take cognisance of the actual prices paid in remote areas to the primary producer by the gombeen-man. Griffith's prices, based on an immediate post-famine 'low', were at the best of times probably no lower than those received by many smallholders in the clutches of the gombeen-man; certainly after the farm price slump of 1879, a rent equivalent to the Griffith valuation provided very little leeway for many such tenants. Thus rents, which under normal conditions would be fair and reasonable, became rack-rents. Adding to these the number of rents which were blatantly excessive in even the best trading circumstance, it is understandable that by the end of the eighteen seventies the great majority of tenant farmers were led to identify rack-renting as the major cause of their troubles.

The eighteen seventies saw a crisis in industry following the ending of the world-wide industrial boom. In the middle of the decade, British manufacturers flooded the Irish market and native industry suffered. Even before that, local industries in the remoter areas, like the west, were feeling the pinch. Industrial activity in smaller towns was often extensive: breweries, distilleries, ropeworks, tanneries, together with numerous craft enterprises, weavers, tailors, seamstresses, hatters, nailmakers, blacksmiths and shoemakers. The coming of the railways opened up the country to the mass-produced British product, often inferior but invariably cheaper than the small-scale or handcrafted, homemade article.

The crisis in industry coincided with a crisis in agriculture. Up to 1877 agriculture had been reasonably prosperous. Then followed three bad harvests in a row. The output of the main agricultural crops, measured in fixed prices, fell from £36.5 million in 1876 to £22.7 million in 1879. Valued in market prices, output fell even more sharply, because, contrary to the usual experience, low yield did not result in higher prices. In this case the reverse happened, and the disastrous combination of declining output and falling prices ensued. Such were the effects of the transoceanic steamship and the opening up of new agricultural lands overseas.[20]

19 The former often because of tenants' improvements, supposedly demonstrating the ability to pay more; the latter (less frequent) for some exceptional personal service or as a concession aimed at getting some rent from a particularly distressed tenant who for some reason could not readily be evicted.
20 See L.M. Cullen, *An Economic History of Ireland* (London: B.T. Batsford Ltd., 1972), p.138.

In the latter half of 1879 it rained on average two days out of every three and crops of hay, corn and turf were ruined. Inevitably the potatoes were blighted and yields averaged only 26 cwts per acre, 6 cwts lower than in 1861, which was the worst potato year since the Famine. The winter of 1879-80 was a time of near starvation for the smallholder. In the district of Belmullet, County Mayo, one in every three people was getting outdoor relief; in the Strokestown poor law union of County Roscommon the figure was sixty per cent. of total population. Relief measures, such as the Mansion House Fund, were set up to alleviate hunger in the west.[21] It is ironic that the main food which prevented total starvation was the yellow meal, ground from American maize, which was making Irish grain-growing unprofitable. Another factor contributing to the general distress was that the migrant agricultural workers from the western seaboard found little work in Britain because of the bad harvest; they returned home with hardly any money to tide the family over until the next season.

In circumstances such as these, resentment against landlords ran high, even against moderate landlords whose rental exactions could be a cause, but clearly not the *major* cause, of tenant distress. Even a modest half year's rent in a single payment became an almost intolerable burden. The gombeen merchant, who in most cases was a far more ruthless exploiter of the peasantry, was not slow to cover his own misdeeds by blaming the landlord entirely for the impoverished condition of the people. The gombeen-man who was also a landlord explained convincingly that the rents he charged were extremely modest (at least by comparison with some notorious landlords in a nearby county) and if they were still onerous, there was a ready and plausible explanation for this too. He, the gombeen-man, had bought the land initially to save his people from eviction or from swingeing rent increases contemplated by the previous owners. This he had effected at an exorbitant cost, and was still committed to enormous repayments and various other outrageous taxes and levies to which as a native (sometimes Catholic or Nationalist) landowner he was unfairly subjected. The gombeen-man's rents were as low as they possibly could be and at least people could be thankful that they were not committed to the mercies of tyrant landlords. The real trouble, said the gombeen-man, was the ruinous state of the economy and the lack of money in circulation — a situation which could hardly be otherwise when all the dissolute and absentee landlords were bleeding the people and squandering the nation's wealth abroad.

The story was convincingly told. There were few among the unlettered tenantry who could identify the falsities and half-truths. The explanation often gained ready credence because rack-renting landlords did exist; as did landlords who carried out evictions. They may have been few and far between but the news of their inhumanity travelled fast and the horrifying stories of their savage deeds made them very proximate in the peasant

21 In the United States the *New York Herald* also formed a relief committee and sought Parnell's co-operation, which he refused, alleging that much of the relief money subscribed in 1847 had gone, not for the relief of the starving people, but into the pockets of the landlords.

mind. Also the psychological transference which tends to create an overall impression of a profession or class in accordance with the reputation gained by some of its less worthy members, led people unfairly to impute, if not the actions, at least the motives, of the few to the many and to brand all landlords as unfeeling tyrants.

Resentment against the landlord was always a powder keg awaiting only the torch of an economic recession to bring about an explosion of agrarian violence. Chapter Two documented the widespread disorder in Clare and elsewhere, rightly attributed to the inequities of the system and landlord oppression, but sparked to blazing fury by the economic situation brought about by the post-Napoleonic slump. In the late eighteen seventies, after a period of comparative prosperity, Ireland was again in the grip of a severe economic recession, and by 1879 the countryside was primed to erupt into mindless agrarian savagery.

Onto this troubled scene strode Davitt and Parnell, both born in the famine year of 1846, one in a whitewashed cabin in Straide, County Mayo, and the other in the stately mansion of Avondale, County Wicklow. Parnell was of the gentry and the landlord class. His great-grandfather, Sir John Parnell, was a former Chancellor of the Exchequer.

All through the summer Davitt held meetings. When Parliament rose, Parnell came to his support and during August and September the cry of 'The Land for the People' echoed from many platforms throughout Ireland. In August Davitt held a county convention in Castlebar and founded the National Land League of Mayo to protect tenants and fight landlordism. He urged Parnell to turn this into a national organisation with a central body in Dublin and branches throughout the land. On 21 October 1879, at a meeting in the Imperial Hotel, Sackville Street, Dublin, the Irish National Land League was founded, with Parnell as president and Davitt as secretary.[22] The League had two main objectives:

i) In the short term, to protect tenants from rack-renting and unjust evictions.
ii) In the longer term, to make them owners of their own farms.

As the League developed its campaign during the next two years, it assumed the character of a great mass movement, based primarily on moral force, which would finally shatter the power of landlordism in Ireland. Brilliantly led by a handful of men — many of them, like Davitt, Fenians or ex-Fenians — the League was soon giving the people not only protection, but a new feeling of self-respect. Much of its early work was concerned with bringing relief to the starving and destitute families who had been evicted, but from the beginning it organised public demonstrations to deter landlords from evicting. It was also quick to mobilise public opinion against landlords who evicted and against any man who dared to take a farm from which a former tenant had been wrongly evicted.

22 There were actually three joint secretaries: Davitt, Thomas Brennan and A.J. Kettle.

At a meeting in Ennis in September 1880, Parnell instructed his listeners in a new technique, which in time was destined to provide an effective, non-violent strategy for oppressed peoples everywhere. Soon, also, it would add a new word to the English language:

> Before the month was out this advice was acted upon in the case of Captain Boycott in Mayo, who dwelt near Ballinrobe, on the picturesque shores of Lough Mask. As agent to the Earl of Erne, he refused to accept the rents offered by the tenants, standing out for the full amounts due and then issuing processes of ejectment. The tenants retaliated by attacking the process-server and driving him into the shelter of Lough Mask House. But further, partly by persuasion, principally by terror and threats, they got Captain Boycott's servants and labourers to leave him. No one would save his crops, no one would drive his car, the smith would not shoe his horses, the laundress would not wash for him, the grocer would not supply him with goods; even the post-boy was warned not to deliver his letters. The Ulster Orangemen came to the rescue, and fifty of them, escorted by police and military with two field-pieces, came to Lough Mask. They saved the Captain's crops valued at £350, but at an estimated cost to the State and to the Orange Society of £3,500; and when they left, Lough Mask House became vacant, for Captain Boycott fled to England. The genial and witty parish priest of the Lough Mask district, Father John O'Malley, suggested to his friend, Mr Redpath, an American journalist, perplexed for a suitable word, that boycott was a better word than ostracise, the latter being too difficult to be understood by the people.[23]

This was effective economic war. It forced Gladstone, who returned to power in 1880, to look again at the Irish Question and to introduce his Land Act of 1881. This new Act was the first significant measure of relief for the Irish tenant farmer. It gave him 'the three Fs' — fair rent, fixity of tenure and free sale — and set up the Land Commission with machinery for fixing judicial rents. This resulted in applicants having their rents reduced by an average of 20 per cent.[24] However, the Commission could not hope to settle quickly the thousands of cases before it and the Act had excluded more than half the tenants who had holdings of over one acre — the most hard-hit being the 150,000 leaseholders and the 130,000 occupiers who were in arrears with their rents.

In 1886 the Land League introduced its own brand of negotiating machinery — the so-called Plan of Campaign.[25] On estates where rents were excessive, the League advised tenants to lodge with trustees what was agreed as a reasonable rent. The League accepted the Griffith valuation as

23 D'Alton, op. cit., p.287.
24 Another Act in 1887 authorised the Land Commission to review reductions already sanctioned, and by 1888 the average reductions granted were 28 per cent.
25 Meanwhile the Ashbourne Act of 1885 had made a further small concession in making available £5 million to tenants, at 4 per cent, to purchase their holdings.

the figure representing a fair rent; this was the sum that was agreed locally and offered in most cases. It was a good tactical move : the valuation was by now a very reasonable rent for any solvent tenant. It provided a readily available and uniform basis for making rent offers in the nation-wide campaign and its use precluded objections from landlords that the tenants' demands were arbitrary or grossly unreasonable. The rents were to be offered to the landlord, not singly, but in bulk; if he refused then, he was to be paid nothing until he came to terms. Instead, the money was to be used to help any tenant who was evicted.

In 1886 and subsequent years the Plan of Campaign was put into operation on about 120 Irish landlord estates. The intransigence and bitter resistance of the landlords often resulted in outbreaks of violence. These outbursts, although they scarcely matched the savagery of some of the Land League's earlier essays in resisting evictions, drew condemnation from many sources. A rescript from Pope Leo XIII in April 1888 condemned the Plan and the system of boycotting and pointedly warned some of the Irish clergy, who had become embroiled, to stand clear. The bloody riots of the Campaign days must, however, be viewed in the context of the times.[26] Violence was then a common ingredient of Irish peasant life. Faction fights, with lead-weighted blackthorn sticks (shillelaghs) between rival local groups, were a common occurrence. These battles were sometimes encouraged by landlords. Wagers were laid by profligate landlords and other 'sporting' gentlemen, who sometimes also championed outstandingly skilful stickfighters and 'bullymen', under a system of patronage similar to that operated by plantation owners in the southern states of the USA for their 'fighting niggers'.

Irish landlords and their agents, with few exceptions, were not men to grant concessions easily or graciously — least of all under pressure from 'inferiors'. Whatever the character of nineteenth-century Anglo-Irish landlords, many of them still retained links, however tenuous, with an original nobility; and whatever else they might be, they were rarely cowards. "They were often hard and unjust", wrote Lysaght, "but they seldom showed the white feather!"[27] Indeed, it was proven courage that down the years had helped perpetuate the tyrant landlords' grip on their tenantry. It was a foolhardy peasant who would singly confront one of these reckless horsemen and skilled swordsmen, especially those who were trigger-happy and ready to construe the slightest lack of obeisance as a mortal insult. Although by 1880 the old-style, hard-riding, swashbuckling landlord was a rarity,[28] his exploits were well remembered and the process

26 At Mitchelstown, County Cork on 9 September 1887, the police, having failed to bludgeon their way to a Land League platform by the use of batons and clubbed carbines, retired to their barracks and opened fire on the large crowd, killing three men and wounding several others. The enraged crowd stormed the barracks with stones, sticks and every kind of weapon. They would have wrecked the building and killed the twenty policemen were it not for the intervention of John Dillon, the main speaker, and the local clergy. Also on the platform that day was Thomas P. Gill. (See p.79).
27 E.E. Lysaght, *Sir Horace Plunkett* (Dublin & London: Maunsel & Co. Ltd., 1916), p.34.
28 A stylised but essentially authentic portrayal of the association between a sporting landlord and a champion stick-fighter is given in the stage play "The King of Friday's Men" by M.J. Molloy.

of psychological transference still operated to invest all landlords· with something of his qualities. The Plan of Campaign may have brought great violence but in its essentially non-violent confrontation with the landlord, it represented a considerable moral advance on the previous situation, in which the only confrontation with a tyrant was done with a blunderbuss from behind a hedge!

The landlords had no answer to this solidarity. If they retaliated by eviction, the weapon of the 'boycott' was used. The Land Acts of 1891, 1896 and 1903 gave bigger concessions and provided monies[29] so that tenants could buy out their farms over a long period by annual payments to the Land Commission, which were considerably smaller than the former rents. Although at the turn of the century only a minority of farmers had actually purchased their holdings, the teeth of landlordism had effectively been drawn and Davitt had advanced a good distance towards the achievement of his ambition of 'The Land for the People'.

Parnell was the charismatic national leader without whose influence and political expertise the Irish National Land League might never have been a potent force. Like so many agrarian organisations before and after, it might have flared briefly only to dwindle in local isolation and die. Davitt was not lacking in personal charm or eloquence but he played his role as a practical man of the people. Untiringly he built up the grassroot organisational structures which, so often in the past, loquacious political leaders at national level had tended to neglect. His administrative skill and personal attention held the Land League together in circumstances where the tenants might have been outmanoeuvred, or else pushed into impulsive violence. Davitt was at heart a militant Fenian and fairly extreme agrarian socialist. His philosophy and ideals were essentially those of the Irish revolutionary thinker James Fintan Lalor (1807-50), who held that all title to land derived ultimately from the people and that private ownership of land should be conditional, not absolute. He was also deeply influenced by the American reformer, Henry George, a personal friend.[30]

The success of the Land League was, for Davitt, a very limited victory. He felt that peasant proprietorship would not remove the evils inherent in private ownership of land. In particular, it would do little to benefit the smaller farmers, the agricultural labourers, or any of the working classes.

As a parliamentary politician,[31] Davitt was decidedly inept and his subsequent political career up to his untimely death in 1906 does him little credit. Yet he was the first man to steer Irish politics in a new and fruitful direction. He deflected the militants from their policy of futile

---

29 The 1891 Act provided £30 million; the Balfour Act of 1896 gave more generous terms of repayment, and the Wyndham Act of 1903 gave an additional £100 million for land purchase and £12 million as a bonus to the selling landlords.

30 Henry George (1839-97), popularly known as 'Single Tax' George because of his advocacy of the system of simplified taxation. He was the author of many works, including *Our Land and Social Policy* (1871), *Progress and Poverty* (1880) and *The Irish Land Question* (1881).

31 On entering Parliament in 1892 he thought of himself as entering the "Parliamentary Penitentiary". When, after his dramatic protest against the Boer War, he walked out of the House of Commons never to re-enter, he did so shouting "I leave this House with greater pleasure than I ever entered it, convinced that no just cause will ever find support here unless it is backed up by force."

insurrectionism, shook the Nationalist Party out of its preoccupation with sterile constitutional argument and directed it to constructive agrarian reform. It is to his credit that in so doing, this angry and rigid patriot often submerged his own cherished personal ideals for the sake of unity.

Davitt himself was not destined to play any direct role in the Irish co-operative movement. His later years were largely devoted to advancing the Labour movement in Britain. He believed that national independence could be won for Ireland only with the support of the British working classes. He did effective organisational work back in his old boyhood area of Lancashire and campaigned on behalf of Labour Party candidates there and in many other parts of Britain. He had little direct contact with the co-operative movement either in Britain or at home; indeed, his view of the Irish movement was less than kindly. Yet, more than any man of his time, he had paved the way for the Irish co-operator. He taught a large, oppressed and subservient section of the Irish people the art of working together. Horace Plunkett, recognised founder father of the Irish co-operative movement, generously acknowledged that but for the work of Davitt among the peasant farmers, Irish co-operation would have had to face a much more uphill task.[32]

At the time when Plunkett was experiencing his first co-operative success in Drumcollogher in 1889, Parnell was at the height of his glory. He had emerged heroically from the Pigott forgery case. Everywhere he went in Britain or Ireland he was greeted with scenes of the wildest enthusiasm. In July 1889 he was made a freeman of the city of Edinburgh and many national bodies were rushing to accord him their highest honours. Within two short years, however, his party was shattered and Parnell was dead. The fall of this great national hero was to create a political situation which would impede the progress of the new co-operative movement, drastically in its early years and with greater or lesser intensity for almost the first thirty years of its existence. For the co-operators there was the added poignancy that Parnell was a powerful leader who might readily have espoused the co-operative cause. He had expressed considerable interest and it is reported that Plunkett had an appointment to meet him on the matter. Parnell failed to keep the appointment; it was the day on which the news of the divorce scandal broke.

Following the excitement of the Land League and the Plan of Campaign, political attention focussed on Home Rule. National morale was high and the overwhelming nationalist sentiment was that 'even good government is no substitute for self-government'. One can only speculate on what might have happened had a measure of political freedom been conceded by 1890. The problems of 'economic freedom' and economic development might have retained the interest of the politicians. Given consensus on economic aims by their leadership, the newly liberated tenants, and indeed all the Irish people, could have made progress in tackling the country's economic

32 See G.D.H. Cole, *A Century of Co-operation* (Manchester: Co-operative Union Ltd., 1944), p.242.

problems. Then a peasant proprietorship might have generated rural prosperity. Instead there was agronomic stagnation.[33] As it happened, the downfall of Parnell made it easy for reactionary Unionists in Britain and Ireland to withhold any political concessions, while Irish nationalists, now in two opposing camps, relapsed once more into sterile constitutional bickering with little sympathy between them other than a tacit agreement that nothing good could happen in Ireland (or, indeed, be allowed to happen) until it was given Home Rule.

33 Some striking similarities and contrasts between the land struggle in Ireland and that in New Zealand, the evolution of various tenure systems and their economic effects, can be found in J.B. Condliffe, *New Zealand in the Making* (London: Allen & Unwin, revised edition 1959).

Chapter Six

Plunkett and Company

"Who is Mr Plunkett, anyway?"

"Just another =:!/&?+ Honourable like myself — b-b-but his father was Lord Dunsany, and so he c-c-couldn't help it."

The Honourable Alexis Roche, brother of Lord Fermoy, had a speech impediment but an excellent vocabulary and a salty turn of phrase.

It was the autumn of 1889 in Doneraile, County Cork. Robin Anderson, Clerk of the Petty Sessions, had been installed as sub-agent to Lord Castletown, with a modest salary and a free house on the estate. It was fair progress, but with a wife and infant son it would be difficult enough on £200 a year to move a step higher on the social scale and live with modest graciousness — to hunt and shoot a little and once in a while give a small dinner party.

"P-P-Plunkett", said Roche, "is the strangest b-b-being you ever met. In f-f-fact h-e-e is like n-n-nothing on earth."

A few days later, Anderson was to meet this strange Mr Plunkett and judge for himself.

The Honourable Horace Curzon Plunkett looked small beside the commanding figure of Roche — a thin spare man in his middle thirties with a prominent nose and kindly eyes. At close range he was not so small, maybe 5′10″ or so, but with that slight stoop and frail appearance that often go with chronic ill-health. Alexis Roche could relate that, despite his apparent frailty, Plunkett was a very tough cowboy indeed. They had ridden the ranges of Wyoming together for ten years. In October 1879 Roche, his brother Edmond, and a few other young bloods had set up a ranch in the Powder River Valley in north Wyoming. Plunkett had come along for the sake of his health. He was a weak, consumptive youth[1] who seemed to have little to contribute but his share of the money. But far from being a passenger, Plunkett became the shrewd operator who would lead the group on to fortune.

Plunkett was a man of remarkable energy. He loved horses and the rough outdoor life, though he often complained, as in his days at Dunsany, that he would have enjoyed riding better if he had a bit more meat on his bones. The rough cowhands of Wyoming at first scoffed at his physique and bristled at his aristocratic ways and his primness in matters relating to

---

1 Tuberculosis had already carried off his mother, younger brother and sister.

women and alcohol, but they found it hard to feel animosity towards a man of raw courage. Whether it was a savage horse, a crazy Indian or a gun-happy cowboy, Plunkett faced them all with the same calm, white-faced determination.

Roche remembered the round-up of 1885. They were due to cross the high mountains when word came that 500 Indians, starving after a hard winter, had broken out of their reservation and were slaughtering the ranchers' cattle. An Indian war might break out at any moment. The rivers were running high and the storms were not yet over. "I must go", said Plunkett. "I am paid to look after the cattle on the other side and can't flee like the Biblical hireling."[2] He went alone and reported that the Indians were indeed hungry but not immediately looking for a fight. The cowboys took his word for it.

Alexis Roche had returned to Ireland to marry his sweetheart, Lucy Maude Goschen, in the spring of 1889. Plunkett came home about Christmas every year, returning to Wyoming in the early spring. For him there were no romantic attachments. Since the autumn of 1887 he had been increasingly drawn back home by family responsibilities. His eldest brother, Randall, had died of tuberculosis on Christmas Day 1883. The second brother, John William, was clever but somewhat erratic and not much of a businessman. Their father, the old Admiral,[3] was eighty years of age, in poor health, and always begging Horace to stay at home and look after the estates, collieries and other commercial interests in Ireland and England. In 1884 Plunkett's brother-in-law died and he conscientiously undertook to manage his sister Mary's affairs. After 1887, Plunkett, who had prospered and had widespread business interests in the United States, had managed only one brief visit back to Cheyenne, in 1888. His father died suddenly on 22 February 1889 while Plunkett was in Ireland but not in Dunsany.

Plunkett was now a very busy man. He had recently been to see the colliery and steamship company in Newcastle which his father had left him, the boatbuilding yard in Romsey,[4] and his property at Beguidly in Wales, where he rode about on a pony inspecting the farms. He was detained, too, by friends who took advantage of his business ability. He was now in Doneraile to see his friends, Alex Roche and Barney Fitzpatrick.[5] There was also business in view — but not private personal business, of which he had already more than enough: he wanted the people to start a co-operative society.

2   As well as participating in land deals, Plunkett also took on assignments for other ranchers.
3   Edward Plunkett, sixteenth Baron Dunsany, born 1808, married Anne Constance Dutton, daughter of Lord Sherbourne, in 1846. He was then a Commander in the Royal Navy and was made an Admiral in 1877. They had four sons, Randall, John, Horace and Reginald, and three daughters, Mary, Constance and Julia. Their mother died of consumption at the age of forty in 1858, when Horace Plunkett was not quite four years old.
4   There he attended the workmen's annual dinner and gave them a bonus of a shilling in the pound on the year's profits.
5   Bernard Edward Barnaby Fitzpatrick, second Baron Castletown (Anderson's employer), who had succeeded to the title in 1883 and had estates at Granston Manor, Abbeyleix and Doneraile Court.

Plunkett, Roche and Anderson walked and talked. Anderson was hearing many strange new ideas and was struggling to cope with Plunkett's West British accent and rapid sequence of thought:

> Most of what he said was Greek to me and I was honest enough to say so. Plunkett saw how raw and ignorant of the world I was, but it only made him the more patient with me and the more earnest in expounding his strange new doctrine ... Apparently his idea was to induce people TO COMBINE FOR BUSINESS PURPOSES AND THEREBY TO HELP THEMSELVES WHILE THEY HELPED ONE ANOTHER. AND IT WAS TO BE DONE WITHOUT INJURY TO PROPERTY OR PERSON. IN SHORT, WEALTH WAS NOT TO BE TAKEN FROM ONE CLASS TO ENRICH ANOTHER, BUT ACTUALLY TO BE *CREATED*, BY THRIFT, BY HONEST DEALING AND BY THE LOYALTY OF THE PARTICIPANTS IN PARTNERSHIP ONE WITH ANOTHER ... All this had sounded most attractive, but it seemed rather Utopian. However, I had said I would take a hand in the game and I was in for it now, so I determined to do my best.[6]

For a year or more Plunkett had travelled through Ireland visiting friends and holding meetings to try and interest people in co-operation. Roche remembered the young Plunkett, just out of Oxford[7] and home to act as agent for his father, when he started the Dunsany Co-operative Society. It was just a small shop selling groceries and providing a local market for eggs and butter. The shareholders were the country folk, Dunsany's tenants and labourers, the steward and Horace Plunkett himself. Plunkett worked in the shop before they could afford a manager, weighing provisions and fumbling with paper and string to tie up parcels for old women, until they begged him to desist and let them do it properly themselves. There had been a letter in *The Times* insinuating that the old Admiral, Plunkett's father, had "started the store out of the small savings of his servants to get his own goods cheap".

Back in Doneraile, Plunkett was pleading for support to launch another venture. Roche couldn't refuse, Barney Fitzpatrick[8] proved enthusiastic, Anderson was committed, and a decision was reached to establish forthwith a co-operative shop on the Dunsany (and Rochdale) model, but somewhat larger. They acquired a substantial shop in the main street and stocked it with goods mainly supplied by the English Co-operative

6 R.A. Anderson, *With Horace Plunkett in Ireland* (London: Macmillan, 1935), pp. 3, 4. The capitals are mine. Although professedly ignorant of co-operation, Anderson had some organisational experience, having been connected with an unsuccessful attempt to establish a creamery at nearby Churchtown as early as 1884. See *Cork Examiner*, 17 March, 1884.

7 Plunkett graduated from University College, Oxford in 1878 with a BA and a Second in Modern History.

8 Who designated himself on his personal notepaper as "Mac Giolla Phadraig", in support of the Gaelic League.

Wholesale Society which by this time had established a number of depots in Ireland, including one in Limerick. The CWS also supplied the manager, a gentleman who was to become the object of considerable local amusement. "A spick-and-span individual", said Anderson, "but quite inefficient, because he did not understand the people, nor they him." It is interesting to note that Anderson, himself more than a little Anglo-Irish,[9] described the unfortunate manager as a "Saxon".

Thus, the Doneraile Co-operative Society had an inauspicious start. Even the acquisition of their shop was to prove a matter of immediate controversy. In October 1895 the London correspondent of the *Irish News* reported on an anonymous circular, widely distributed and delivered to all MPs in the House of Commons, alleging that Plunkett had planted his first co-operative store in the house of an evicted tenant. The charge was less than accurate. There had been no eviction, but the previous unsuccessful occupant had been advised of his growing arrears of rent and encouraged to relinquish his tenancy. In fact, a number of houses in Doneraile, with similar histories, were offered for sale at the same time. Part of the lot was purchased by local merchants who incurred no censure whatever. Although the incident occasioned bad publicity for Plunkett, the venture at Doneraile was hardly affected at all.

The committee of Doneraile Co-op (duly affiliated to the Co-operative Union in Manchester) decided that its store should stock everything from a needle to an anchor and supply all the requirements of both gentry and proletariat. Anderson, the secretary, thought it was ambitious for Doneraile but majority opinion prevailed. They started a bakery, even though there was already an excellent baker in the village. The co-operative bread was good, but somehow lacked the quality of that baked by Mickey the Fairy, the village baker. The co-operative baker, almost certainly in frustration, went on a spree and the bakery project folded.

The store carried on through ups and downs. The 'Saxon' manager was exchanged for an energetic young native who kept the store going for several years, but gradually the co-operative aspect disappeared and it ultimately became a proprietary concern. Despite its ultimate failure as a co-operative, it had conferred considerable benefits. It made local traders sit up, improve their shops and greatly reduce their exorbitant prices. It also doubtlessly helped to create the co-operative climate for the Doneraile Agricultural Bank (a credit society modelled on the Raiffeisen societies of Germany) founded in Doneraile in 1894, and the first of its type in Ireland. By this time Anderson had bigger fish to fry and was deeply engaged in the national movement. He was committed to the strange new doctrine of co-operation and entirely captivated by Plunkett:

A great admiration, almost amounting to awe, was inspired in me for

9 Robert Andrew Anderson was born on 26 June 1860 at Mount Corbett, Buttevant, County Cork, of a Scots father and a Canadian mother. Andrew Anderson, an ex-Army officer, purchased the Mount Corbett estate and came to live in Ireland in 1851. Anderson's great-grandfather had been a doctor at the battle of Culloden, on the side of Bonnie Prince Charlie.

this frail but fearless and outspoken man, who habitually lived an abstemious, almost ascetic life, drinking but rarely and then sparingly, smoking scarcely at all. He was horrified at the way I could drink whiskies and soda and he rather frowned on my beloved pipe . . .

All the same, I think he gave me more of his confidence than he gave to any other man and trusted me implicitly. I think I can say truthfully, that I never once let him down . . .

How did he win this affection, this fine fidelity? Not by flattery, nor the temptation of reward. I can only answer for myself. He shamed me into it. He set the example of hard work, of an invincible belief in his policy. He denied himself all the pleasures and enjoyments of his class and worked like a slave at his great task.

He was always fair and often magnificently generous yet never effusive. Though he deeply attracted, there were times when he temporarily almost repelled one. Perfectly charming and delightfully simple, in his many moods of gentle confidence, yet for some little *bêtise*, some apparently harmless solecism, he would become suddenly and severely aloof. He was always very much alone with himself except when he entertained his numerous friends at his hospitable home at Kilteragh. There his hospitality was unbounded and he entertained lavishly any who were in the least interested in his work, as well as many others whose chief attraction was the cuisine and the excellent cellar.[10]

R.A. Anderson

The editor of the *Skibbereen Eagle* once described Anderson as "Plunkett's Man Friday". Their last parting was on the platform of the little railway station at Weybridge, Surrey towards the end of 1931:

As the train left I saw his frail little figure, hatless, waving his last

10 Anderson, op. cit., pp. 11, 282.

farewell to me and seeming to urge me onward, to persevere.

*   *   *

There is no precise record as to where or when Horace Plunkett first came into contact with the co-operative movement. He himself records[11] that his first inspiration came from "my study of the co-operative principle under such leaders as Holyoake, Vansittart Neale, Tom Hughes and Alfred Marshall." However, it seems that he had little personal contact with the British co-operators until he attended the Co-operative Congress at Ipswich in 1889. There he met Beatrice Potter and Sidney Webb.[12]

Plunkett left Eton in 1872 and, having spent a period with a tutor in Brighton, entered University College Oxford in 1874, just before his twentieth birthday.[13] In later years, when he came to know more of Oxford, he felt that he had made small use of his opportunities. It was a period of great change and sweeping social reforms: the Education Act (1870), the legalisation of trade unions (1871), the secret ballot (1872), another Provident Societies Act (1876) and the Factories and Workshops Act of 1878. In Ireland there was the first Land Act and the disestablishment of the Irish Church. The social conscience of the time was pervasive. In his old age Plunkett wrote:

> It was at this period of my life that I took a strange, somewhat vague idealism. That either the English or the Irish social economy, in which I had been brought up, would endure, I did not believe. In some ways it all seemed wrong. I underrated the conservatism of the English and had not read enough of their treatment of Ireland in the past to realise the impossibility of their understanding the conditions on which their domination of that country could be accepted. But I knew a little about the Industrial Revolution and saw what was bound to happen . . . I would try and anticipate it in Ireland.[14]

When he returned to Dunsany to act as agent and estate manager,[15] he found some of his tenants also catching the spirit of the times and expecting a transference of land to themselves. Their action went no

11 In the foreword to *Agricultural Co-operation in Ireland,* a survey by the Horace Plunkett Foundation (London: George Routledge & Sons Ltd., 1931).

12 For a concise account of this remarkable couple (from 1929, Lord and Lady Passfield), see Arnold Bonner, *British Co-operation* (Manchester: Co-operative Union Ltd., revised edition 1970), p. 513.

13 He was born on the 24 October 1854, in the home of his mother's family, the Jacobean mansion of Sherborne in Gloucestershire. In 1860, two years after his mother's death, the family settled in Dunsany Castle, County Meath, the ancestral seat.

14 M. Digby, *Horace Plunkett: An Anglo-American Irishman* (Oxford: Blackwell, 1949), p.17.

15 Until the threat of tuberculosis compelled him to seek a change of climate in Wyoming, he lived a cheerful bachelor life at Dunsany, alone with his domestic staff including the butler Reid, "a black Northern Protestant who used to curse the Papists with terrible curses and live with them in perfect amity. He waited at dinner with the ends of his trousers tucked into his boots and when he thought that guests had stayed too long he would open the door and thrust his head round it, 'Does any of yes want your yokes?" (Digby, p. 19).

further than threatening letters, which Plunkett ignored; but his democratic instincts (still heavily overlaid with paternalism) were nevertheless stirring him to lead and serve his people. He felt that the landlord classes should make some move towards bridging the 'cultural divide' and participate more in the social life, the sports and amusements of their tenants, as he aptly stated it — "with money and thought". He was distressed by the tenants' economic condition. The people were extremely poor and badly supplied with the necessities of life. In rural areas the shopping facilities were poor. The rich did most of their shopping in the larger towns, even in London, and thus the standards of service in rural Ireland suffered and prices were exorbitantly high.

> . . . dirty meal mouldering in rotten bins, a few loaves for those whose style of living demands scientifically whitened bread, a few jars of peppermint or sugarstick, and a heap somewhere of rapidly fermenting dried fruit . . . a few clay pipes lolling their heads against the window sashes as a sign that even luxuries are supplied . . . wasps and flies, who if it were not for the profusion of cobwebs would hold undisputed possession of the store.[16]

Save only the cat in the window, the picture was complete. Conditions were similar to those in Rochdale a half century earlier and prompted the formation of Dunsany Co-operative Society.

On his return to Ireland Plunkett also recommended the formation of a Co-operative Store Organisation Society, with its headquarters in Dublin, to coordinate the business of the retail store co-operatives throughout the country. The first of these stores had been founded at Inchicore, Dublin in 1859, but in striking contrast to the rapid growth of co-operatives in industrial England, progress was painfully slow. In 1888 there were only ten co-operatives, with a total membership of 1,127 and a turnover of not quite £35,000 per annum.[17] In July of that year there was an Irish Exhibition in London and, at the prompting of Plunkett, Ernest Hart, a director of the Exhibition, invited the southern section of the Co-operative Union to organise a conference to discuss the possibility of extending the co-operative movement in Ireland:

> The invitation was cordially accepted and on August 1 a large gathering of Southern co-operators, with a sprinkling of Irish visitors, was held under the chairmanship of Lord Aberdeen. A paper read by Mr Benjamin Jones, then Hon. Secretary of the Southern Section, urged that steps should be taken to teach the principles of co-operation to the Irish workers as a means of making their labour more productive, and of increasing the amount of labour required, and suggested that co-operative effort in Ireland should begin with production, promising the help of English co-operators in this work.

16 H. Plunkett, an article in *Nineteenth Century* magazine, September 1888.
17 C. Webb, *Industrial Co-operation,* p. 147.

The proposals were enthusiastically taken up by the conference, and a committee appointed to form a propagandist association.[18]

Members of this committee were Edward Vansittart Neale, the Christian Socialist who had spent forty years and a fortune in unselfish service to co-operation, and George Jacob Holyoake, friend and biographer of Robert Owen. An Irish Co-operative Aid Association was formed, funds were raised and the Association made contact with everyone known to have influence .in Ireland. Soon people in every parish in Ireland received literature by post, explaining the co-operative movement and its possibilities.

By this time Plunkett realised that a British-style co-operative in retailing, wholesaling or manufacturing consumer goods would not suffice. Such societies had an undoubted role[19] but if the co-operative movement was to make headway, it must apply itself to Ireland's major activity — peasant farming:

> The Irish peasant was emerging slowly from the pit of the famine years and from the successive bad harvests of the middle eighties. The drain of population to America, deplorable to those who wanted to see a compact, self-conscious Irish nation, had relieved the worst pressure of population on the land, and with the newly won security of tenure came for the first time the opportunity to farm more carefully, to save and to improve. But it was not enough to have liberated the peasant from the grasping or unscrupulous landlord. Steamships and railways had opened the American Continent and food from overseas was competing with Irish produce in the English market. The cattle trade was fairly prosperous but it was for the rich graziers of Meath rather than for the little dairy farms of the south and west. Irish butter, made by primitive methods on the farm, passed haphazard through fairs and village grocers to the dealers in the ports and, after crude blending, reaching the English market in no state to compete with the best product of other countries. The Irish egg, untested and ungraded, was a form of small change, passing over the counter in payment for flour or porter or even postage stamps. The Irish peasant, strengthened in his dealings with his landlord, was helpless in the hands of traders with a world market at call.[20]

Butter was a traditional Irish export: as far back as 1641 it was the third most important. French markets, and especially Flanders, were an outlet for Irish butter in the seventeen seventies and eighties; in the seventeen thirties French vessels putting into Cork loaded beef and salted butter for

18 ibid.,p.147.
19 Store societies were also proving extraordinarily difficult to establish because of opposition from the gombeen-men, who were shopkeepers, publicans, moneylenders and produce-buyers all in one. Their grip on the people, and their influence in politics and the churches, was for the time being too strong to break.
20 Margaret Digby, op. cit., p.51.

the colonies. In the eighteenth century it had become an established custom for dairy farmers in the Munster counties to rent dairy herds from middlemen. By 1800 there was a growing market in Britain to feed an increasing industrial population. The low prices and marketing difficulties encountered by Irish butter producers in the eighteen eighties seemed at first sight to be strongly against the run of play. The USA could be blamed for cheap grain, but not for cheap butter. France, Germany and Russia were taking an increasing interest in supplying food to Britain, but one look at the British butter market identified Denmark as the major competitor.

Following a disastrous war with Germany, in 1865 Denmark set about reorganising her agriculture. Instead of trying to compete as a grain exporter, she used home-grown tillage crops and imported grain to develop large-scale intensive farmyard enterprises — dairying, pigs and poultry — on her smallholdings. By maintaining a high proportion of tillage, Denmark was able to score heavily over Ireland in year-round dairying. Well-fed cows ensured ample exports of fresh butter in winter and summer. The cream separator, a device for separating milk from cream by centrifugal spin, had been invented in Sweden and the Danes were not slow to realise its possibilities. Largely because of the influence of Bishop Grundtvig and his Folk High Schools, the Danes were already well advanced in co-operative organisation and by 1890 had some 600 co-operative creameries.[21] These were able to produce butter of a consistently high quality.

In Ireland production methods were still primitive and the marketing system, if such it could be called, was deplorable. The following is a contemporary account[22] of operating methods employed by the travelling butter buyers who in many areas provided the traditional outlet for the sale of farm butter:

> The publican at the crossroads will give a place in his house to the butter-buyer to put up his scales. Perhaps it is in the stables he would get it, and even if it is, doubtless it is in the public-house he will pay for the butter. The men of the parish will collect around him with the week's butter. He will welcome them, he will praise the butter, he will praise the women, he will give the highest price to each of them. He will find no fault with greasy butter, nor with ribbed butter, nor with butter not properly washed from buttermilk nor with smoky butter. He will stand them a drink at his own cost — the open-handed man — and he will take leave of them at the shop counter, where they will have another drink or two as a compliment to the publican who gave them the use of his house. Indeed it would grieve you to talk to the fools going home after that, half drunk, praising the buyer who gave them

---

21 By 1900 Danish co-operative creameries numbered 942 and this figure doubled by the mid-nineteen thirties.

22 From a prize-winning essay by Fear na dTri mBo (Patrick O'Shea, Glengarriff) in the Munster Feis, Cork, 1902, translated from the Gaelic by Mary Spring Rice. See IAOS Annual Report, 1902-03-04, p. 191.

all 'top prices' and none of them thinking that they all got the price of the smoky butter. I saw with my own eyes this work going on in two parishes, this year, and I need not say there was no co-operation or society among the farmers there. If there were, they could communicate with merchants in London or Liverpool who would take their butter. They would be told that grease is not butter and that buttermilk never took the place of salt. They would be taught to dress up their butter neatly in clean vessels made of hard wood, and those who would be sensible enough to do that would get a different 'top price' from what they got from the jobber who used to buy the butter in the public house.

A firkin[23] of Irish homemade butter arriving on the British market would frequently contain layers of butters of varying ages, flavours, colours and textures, not to mention aromas. It was not surprising that the Danes, the Swedes and the French, with co-operative organisations, machinery and scientific methods, had practically beaten Ireland out of the British butter market by 1890.

In Ireland the adoption of the cream separator was a slow process.[24] The machine was demonstrated at the Royal Agricultural Show in Clonmel in 1880. One of the earliest purchasers was Dr Nulty, Bishop of Meath, who had a separator set up in the dairy of Navan convent. Two separators were reported in County Limerick in 1881, one for Mr E. Russell and the other for Mr H. Croker, the well-known racehorse owner who also kept an extensive dairy herd. A factory system with power churning but without separators was established in Dungannon, County Tyrone, as early as 1800 but it survived for only a short time. Possibly the first creamery (with separators) to serve a number of farmers was the Midleton Dairy Company, County Cork, promoted and planned by Penrose Fitzgerald, which started operations in 1882. Canon Richard Bagot of Kildare, an ardent agriculturalist, was largely responsible for the creamery established at Hospital, County Limerick in 1884 and one at Galbally in the same county shortly afterwards. Thereafter progress accelerated, particularly from 1887 onwards. Some of the more enterprising clergymen in the dairying districts of the south were advocating the formation of creameries, usually in the form of farmers, joint-stock companies, but the major shareholders were often butter buyers and merchant investors. With the separator and power-driven barrel churn, these creameries were turning out an article superior to the average farm butter, and with much less trouble for the farmer's wife. Plunkett saw the 'industrialisation' of butter production as inevitable but also recognised the danger of the process falling into the grasp of middlemen. If this were allowed to happen, the

23 A small wooden cask, strictly a volume measurement — nine gallons —, but in the butter trade varying sizes of firkins developed holding anything from 56 lbs to 100 lbs of butter. See James S. Donnelly, "Cork Market: Its Role in the Nineteenth-Century Irish Butter Trade", in *Studia Hibernica*, No. 11, 1971.
24 See a series of articles by John Blount in *Irish Farming World*, 15 January - 19 February 1892.

farmer who produced milk, the most perishable of all farm products, would be even more helpless than before.

The English co-operative movement could provide very little technical assistance. Following the failure of the agricultural communes, such as Queenwood, co-operation in Britain had become almost exclusively 'industrial' in retailing, wholesaling and manufacturing. There were even a few co-operative ventures in shipping and coalmining, but very little in farming.[25] However the English were very willing to help, and a deputation from the English Co-operative Aid Association visited Ireland. On their return to London, they reported that the expense and labour of successful organisation was more than could be borne by the voluntary organisation. Thereupon the Co-operative Union, at the insistence of its generous patron member, E.V. Neale, agreed to form an Irish section.[26] J.C. Grey, of the Co-operative Union, came to Ireland to help. He and Plunkett attended the Co-operative Congress in Ipswich[27] towards the end of 1889 and reported on conditions in Ireland. Nevertheless the gulf between the characters and circumstances of the two countries was so great that, apart from some welcome money from England to assist the propaganda effort, fruitful collaboration proved impossible.

The hard work had to be done in Ireland and it fell entirely on Plunkett and the newly recruited R.A. Anderson to do it, with whatever voluntary help they could get. The difficulties proved almost insuperable. It is reported that Plunkett held forty meetings before he succeeded in organising a single co-operative. Meanwhile in 1889, W.L. Stokes, the representative of the Co-operative Wholesale Society in Limerick, and Robert Gibson, a butter merchant,[28] had succeeded, under the advice and guidance of the Co-operative Union, in establishing Ireland's first co-operative creamery at Drumcollogher in west Limerick. The Co-operative Union provided "a model code of rules and an admirable constitution" for this co-operative which was to provide the constitutional basis for subsequent creamery co-operatives. After about two years the Drumcollogher Society faltered as a result of poor management, but it prospered long enough to provide a model and showpiece and to "enable Horace Plunkett to hitch on to it his more ambitious programme".

Plunkett found it hard to establish a rapport with farmers and prospective co-operators. He was an Anglo-Irish, Protestant landlord,

25 In 1867 Edward Owen Greening set up the Agricultural and Horticultural Association with the object of selling farmers' requirements by methods already worked out in consumer and wholesale co-op stores. In 1869 a group of farmers in Cumberland formed their own society for the supply of fertilisers and feedingstuffs of tested quality: the Aspatria Co-operative Society is still extant. See M. Digby & A. Gorst, *Agricultural Co-operation in the United Kingdom* (Oxford: Blackwell, 1957).

26 On the formation of the section, the Irish Aid Association was dissolved. Plunkett was elected chairman of the Irish sectional board and shortly afterwards R.A. Anderson was appointed secretary.

27 Plunkett stayed at the White Horse Hotel immortalised by Dickens in *The Pickwick Papers*.

28 Gibson was something of a 'character', a butter merchant and an esoteric Buddhist. He read the *Grocers Review*, the *Grocers Gazette* and the *Light of Asia* without discrimination. He also professed to a hatred of drink.

offering no prizes but a harsh programme of self-help. Worst of all, in a loquacious country and in an age of oratory, he was a poor public speaker. He could attract and hold the loyalty of the few but could not draw crowds. "The only trouble with you", said the blunt Bishop O'Dwyer of Limerick, "is that you won't use the wrong word when you can't remember the right one!" To help overcome these difficulties, Plunkett had enlisted the help of a golden-tongued Nationalist MP, Mulhallen Marum,[29] a great personal friend who spoke with him at many public meetings. Unfortunately, Marum dropped dead one Sunday morning after attending Mass in Listowel. Plunkett and Anderson soldiered on. There was an abortive attempt to build a creamery close to the walls of Kilcooley Abbey, County Tipperary, the home of Plunkett's widowed sister, Mary Ponsonby, but 1890 passed without a single co-operative creamery being added to the solitary total of Drumcollogher. Thereafter the tide turned. The first breakthrough was at Ballyhahill near Lord Monteagle's house at Mount Trenchard, Foynes, County Limerick, and by the end of 1891 fifteen more creamery societies were established.[30]

Meanwhile Anderson travelled the length and breadth of Ireland by train, sidecar, horseback and bicycle, holding meetings in all kinds of buildings and addressing all manner of suspicious and sometimes hostile audiences. He recalls that in one month he slept in thirty different places, sometimes on the seat of a night train with no covering but his frieze overcoat and no pillow but his wallet of papers. He was attacked by the *Skibbereen Eagle*, whose editor described Plunkett as a "monster in human form" and called on him to "cease his hellish work". A more serious threat was posed by the coopers of Miltown Malbay, County Clare, whose livelihood of making firkins was threatened and who had their drawing knives ready to "cut the livers" out of Anderson had he not escaped in the guardsvan of the West Clare Railway. At a meeting arranged for the Courthouse in Ennistymon, the only attender was the Clerk of the Petty Sessions who opened the door with some trepidation. "T'was a pity you came here", he said, "and this the best butter market in West Clare."

There is a well-recounted incident from County Limerick of Anderson attending a meeting to form a co-operative creamery when a local solicitor (probably Patrick Liston) sprang to his feet and declared, "Rathkeale is a Nationalist town — Nationalist to the backbone — and any pound of butter made in Rathkeale will be made in accordance with Irish, Nationalist principles, or it will not be made at all."

The most fantastic episode of all, however, must surely be that related by Anderson concerning a certain Daniel B——, a farmer who claimed direct descent from the Emperor Nero! In those early days, disused cornmills were the bane of the organiser's existence. Every man who had

29 Marum was the hero of a famous escapade in which he rode a hunter up and down the marble steps of St Canice's Cathedral in Kilkenny.
30 Among the earliest ones were Glin, Shanagolden, Bulgaden, Castlemahon, Ardagh, Glenwilliam, Clouncagh, Granagh and Feenagh in County Limerick; Liscarroll and Lombardstown, County Cork; Glen of Aherlow, County Tipperary, and Muckalee, County Kilkenny.

such a mill was anxious to have it taken over and equipped as a creamery. The virtues of the mill were extolled with all the persuasiveness of a house agent with an outstanding property — an excellent building and unfailing supply of water for power, washing and cooling and, not least, for the disposal of creamery effluent. It was always located at the "centre of the natural fall of the country." Dan B——, a farmer from near Kilrush, had such a mill and, with a view to favouring its selection as a creamery, undertook a modest business entertainment. It would have been churlish to refuse, so Anderson and friends found themselves in the parlour of Dan's big farmhouse. The feast was one of rude Celtic abundance: a large homecured ham, a pair of geese, a pair of ducks, two legs of mutton (roast and boiled), some chickens and ample dishes of cabbage and potatoes. Dan whetted a huge knife with his scythe stone and set Anderson to carve. There was a gallon of whiskey, a half stone of lump sugar and all the necessary equipment for making punch. They sat back from the meal about four o'clock to drink the jar of John Quinn's whiskey and hear the elaborate detail of Dan B——'s ancestry.

The Emperor Nero was reputedly such a hard man for the drink and the women that he developed a "hobnail liver" (cirrhosis) and lost his taste for all his amusements. On the advice of a small slave boy from Clare, Nero retired to Mutton Island near Kilkee to eat nothing but carrageen moss and drink plain seawater until his insides were purified and his health entirely restored.

> 'An' when he got well he took a liking to the whiskey an' the salty mutton an' also to the Clare girls. He left the little boy go back to his people with enough money to buy out their farm. These Imperors had some kind of a plan for marrin' — quite regular accordin' to the laws of those days — so many wives as they cared for or could keep. An' didn't Nairo spot a very likely girl of the B——'s. An' didn't he marry her! And here am I, now, a workin' farmer and a proud descendant from that illustrious (but some people say, infamous) Imperor!'

Horace Curzon Plunkett, descended from a former Deputy Governor of Ireland and numbering amongst his ancestral kinsmen such notables as Shane O'Neill and Blessed Oliver Plunkett, could hardly lay claim to a more illustrious pedigree.

But the aspects of the occasion which tickled Anderson the most, and which he recounted on every convivial occasion, were the gallon of whiskey, half-stone of lump sugar and Dan B——'s immortal instructions to his wife — "Bridget, be *continually* bringing hot water!"

Chapter Seven

Irish Agricultural Organisation Society

Plunkett's brief visit to the United States in 1889 was cut even shorter by a cable telling him that his only surviving brother, John William, was seriously ill with typhoid in Naples. The attack was fortunately short-lived and when the fever broke, Horace took his convalescent brother for a short trip to Egypt.[1] An unfortunate result of this journey was that Plunkett contracted a type of recurrent dysentery. Soon afterwards he had a hunting accident which left him with a broken hip.[2] This temporarily limited his mobility but did not divert him from his purpose. Plunkett talked co-operation to everyone — to his "sporting friends at the Horse Show and to bewildered dinner parties at the Castle", to Lord Yerburg and Henry Wolff, to the Duchess of Hamilton, to Vaughan Nash, the future secretary of the Development Commission, to Lady Aberdeen, Lord Zetland and many others. "I mean", he said, "to get to know all the useful men in Ireland." He pondered this resolution and added ruefully, "It may not give me a very large acquaintance."

His doctrine of co-operation was attracting many useful converts. Notable among these was an energetic, middle-aged Jesuit priest recommended by Bishop O'Dwyer as "the ablest man in Ireland". If this was an exaggeration, it was by no means an outrageous one; the Rev Thomas Aloysius Finlay was indeed a remarkable and very able man.

As a student at the Gregorian College in Rome, Finlay had witnessed the stirring events of the first Vatican Council and Garibaldi's entry into the city. With Rome in confusion, he had to spend the years from 1871 to 1873 at Maria Laach in Germany. He was impressed by the new agricultural policies of the Prussian government and also by the Raiffeisen system of credit banks which he studied in great detail — a lesson in practical economics which he was later to put to practical use in Ireland. Finlay was

Finlay

---

1 On the return voyage he met Mrs Laurence Oliphant, a grand-daughter of Robert Owen. She was coming from Haifa where her husband was attempting to found a colony of Jews and a new religion.

2 This injury kept him from riding ever afterwards — a sad limitation for an enthusiastic horseman. About this time he was greatly interested in silage-making and had a fine hunter which he named Silo. Another colt with a doubtful foreleg he facetiously named Tripod.

69

ordained a priest in 1880 and in 1883 was nominated to one of the fellowships in the Royal University and appointed Professor of Metaphysics at the Catholic University College, a position which he held until 1900.[3]

The Reverend T.A. Finlay

Another distinguished cleric who quickly espoused the co-operative cause was the Bishop of Raphoe, Most Rev Patrick (later Cardinal) O'Donnell. At the time of his consecration in 1888 he was, at thirty-two, the youngest Catholic bishop in the world. He was born at Kilraine near Glenties.[4] Such was his scholarly achievement that on his ordination in 1880 he was made Professor of Theology at Maynooth. He would go on to be Cardinal Archbishop of Armagh. He was openly political and an ardent nationalist. A native Irish speaker, O'Donnell was famous for his bilingual pastorals, his active organising of Gaelic cultural events and his absorbing interest in scientific agriculture.

One of Plunkett's earliest helpers was Lord Monteagle of Brandon who lived at Mount Trenchard, Foynes. Thomas Spring Rice, second Baron Monteagle, was held in such high regard and affection that his patronage was of inestimable value in making the new co-operative movement 'respectable'. The family was one of the oldest and most influential in the land (it was Monteagle's father, the first Baron, who as Chancellor of the Exchequer had been responsible for the introduction of the penny post in Britain in 1839). Monteagle himself, born in 1849, was a quiet, self-effacing man who probably won more co-operative followers than anyone of his time. The gentry followed him because he was at least their peer, and the lowly looked up to him as a generous landlord.

3 Father Finlay became Professor of Political Economy in 1901 and, when the Royal University ended in 1909, was immediately appointed to the same Chair in the New National University of Ireland. When he resigned in 1930, he could claim that he had never missed a lecture in forty-seven years.

4 A quiet townland destined also to be the birthplace of a well-known latter-day co-operator, Rev James McDyer, parish priest of Glencolumbkille.

Under Monteagle's influence, another powerful Limerick family was enlisted to Plunkett's aid. Edward William O'Brien was a stern but well-respected man. A wealthy Protestant landowner, O'Brien was an establishment figure, but like his famous father, William Smith O'Brien, very much 'his own man'. He organised and established a flourishing co-operative creamery at Ardagh which was to remain a model of co-operative efficiency for many years. O'Brien was married twice. His first marriage was to Lord Monteagle's sister, and their only son Dermod was destined to give valuable and life-long service to the co-operative cause.

Across in County Tipperary another individualistic member of the Irish gentry, Arthur Moore, of Mooresfort, was speedily organising a co-operative creamery in the Glen of Aherlow. In the early eighteenth century the Moores of Ballymoney were captains of industry in the linen trade and pillars of the Orange establishment. As a young man Moore had leanings towards the priesthood but, when his father died in 1869, he left the seminary at Ushaw to look after the family estate and other business interests. He also entered politics and was elected MP for Derry at a by-election in 1879. There was some consternation when the Orangemen of Derry discovered that this Moore was both a Papist and a Home-Ruler. This amazing blunder was rectified at the general election of 1880 but Moore stood also for Clonmel, was elected and remained MP until his death in 1904. He inherited an immense fortune from his father, made money himself, but spent nearly everything on philanthropic works of various kinds. In 1879 he was made a papal count for his services to the church. His financial contribution to the Irish co-operative movement was exceedingly great and, were it not for his untimely death at fifty-five, he would very likely have had a considerable impact as a national co-operative leader when the basic structures of co-operation were established.

Through his talks and writings, Plunkett was becoming well-known. Early in 1891 the governor of the Bank of Ireland offered him a directorship. He refused because of his commitment to his co-operative work, regretting the valuable commercial training he could have gained. In May of that year, the Chief Secretary, Arthur Balfour,[5] invited him to become one of the first members of the Congested Districts Board, a component of Balfour's Land Bill then fighting its way through parliament. This Board's objective would be the relief of distress in the overcrowded western counties and the development of the district's resources. Plunkett readily accepted the offer and, after consulting with fellow prospective members and suggesting amendments to the Act, set off with characteristic haste[6] to the United States to investigate the possibility of emigration for western congests. Before departing, he had his first meeting with John Dillon, the Irish Nationalist leader who had been prominent in the Plan of Campaign. Plunkett tried to interest him in the co-operative movement and the Congested Districts Board, but Dillon, shopkeeper as well as politician, was somewhat reserved.

5 Irreverently known as Daddy-Long-Legs or more commonly as Bloody Balfour.
6 The Dunsany family motto was *festina lente* — "hasten slowly"!

Meanwhile the volunteer co-operators, Anderson, Monteagle, Stokes, Gibson and others, were crying out for help. Development of creameries was growing apace and success was bringing new problems:

> There was a cry for advice on methods of organisation . . . there was a demand for technical advice on creamery engineering, on the testing of milk for purity and butter-fat content, even on farm management, which it was beyond their scope to give. There was the problem of supplying fuel and salt and boxwood and the even greater problem of marketing co-operative creamery butter so that one creamery should not compete with another and none should be helpless in the hands of the wholesalers.[7]

Plunkett, who from the beginning had recognised the need for a central organising body, now saw it as an urgent necessity. He tried repeatedly but unsuccessfully to interest the Royal Dublin Society. The more cynical of his friends quipped that the RDS was merely "the Kildare Street Club daubed with cowdung" and unlikely to interest itself in the problems of five-cow tenant farmers in west Limerick. For organisational help, he sought a better understanding with the Co-operative Union but detected a "narrow selfishness" in the British movement and could establish a rapport only with the Christian Socialists, Neale, Ludlow and Hughes. This was not enough to swing the Irish section to a generous participation. "Tom Hughes", he wrote, "stands up manfully for the higher ideals, but he, dear old man, is too outspoken."

Anderson, now a full-time salaried organiser, was despatched to Sweden at Plunkett's expense, accredited by letters from the Duchess of Hamilton, to study organised dairy and modern creamery techniques over a six-week period.[8] In March 1891, a conference of dairy co-operative societies was held in Newcastle West, County Limerick. This was followed by a further conference in June at Limerick; delegates from fifteen societies attended and discussed business for an entire day. "Not a word except business", wrote Plunkett gleefully. "The affair was unique in the industrial history of Ireland."

The intention was to form an agency for the joint marketing of creamery products. There were numerous petty obstacles and it took many meetings and a personal financial guarantee from Plunkett to get the Irish Co-operative Agency Society into being in 1893.[9] There were then some thirty creamery societies with a turnover of about £150,000. An interesting account of the early days of the Agency Society is found in one of the first information leaflets published by the co-operators:[10]

7 Digby, op. cit., p.63.
8 For an account of his adventures, see his book, *With Horace Plunkett in Ireland*, p.47 et seq. He was attacked by fleas, wrestled unsuccessfully with a large female attendant in a public bath-house, lost his trousers on a train and, on a more formal occasion, was graciously entertained by King Oscar.
9 Plunkett was elected president and Stokes appointed manager.
10 *Trade Federation*, IAOS Leaflet No. 60, 1902.

The agency was established by sixteen dairy societies who took shares in it proportionate to the amount of their trade. The capital thus raised amounted in cash to £137. The societies bound themselves to sell all their butter through the agency at a commission of 2½ per cent., for which they were indemnified against bad debts. They selected a committee of management and established the headquarters of the Agency at Manchester, the greatest centre of butter distribution in the north-west of England. A series of misfortunes followed, and unsatisfactory management resulted in two law suits in which the Agency lost all its capital; the societies wavered in their allegiance to the federation, and some broke their agreements and refused to consign their produce. Prospects looked black enough, but the Committee stood grimly to their guns . . . The societies, by their refusal to consign, forced it from its original position of a commission agency and obliged it in brisk markets to purchase its supplies at firm prices, just like any competing firm of butter merchants, and only when its prices were equal to, or higher than, those obtainable elsewhere did it 'get the preference'. In dull markets the creameries made it their 'dumping ground' for butter which they could not sell elsewhere. Frequently butter refused by its competitors was thrust upon the Agency for sale, and in such quantities (and sometimes, too, of such bad quality) that the low prices which had to be accepted were quoted against the Agency in comparison with those that some societies, more fortunate than the rest, had realised elsewhere.

However, the Agency Society[11] persevered and even made a small profit every year after 1897. At the turn of the century it was one of the largest shippers of butter in Ireland. For a short period in 1896 it carried on a department for supplying its federated societies with fertilisers, seeds and implements, and for the marketing of barley,[12] but early in 1897 it was decided to form a separate federation for this purpose, the Irish Co-operative Agricultural Agency. This Agency was short-lived, and its functions were taken over by the comprehensive Wholesale Federation, IAWS Ltd., founded later that year.

Meanwhile in 1893, Plunkett, who realised that a trading agency was not going to solve all the problems, was gathering together his co-operators. By the spring of 1894 he was ready. He gave a dinner for the press and on 18 April the meeting to found the Irish Agricultural Organisation Society was attended by some 250 people, representative of all sides of Irish life. Plunkett took the chair and addressed the meeting for more than an hour. No-one was restless: for once in his life Plunkett was making a good speech. The theme

11 Known by its full title, Irish Co-operative Agency Society Ltd., or by the initials ICASL. In 1971 that name was changed to Irish Co-operative Society Ltd.
12 A store was rented at Templemore, County Tipperary, where the barley was received from the societies, inspected, classified and sold through a broker in Dublin. A bad harvest meant that very little grain was suitable for malting, and large importations of grain pulled down prices. See IAOS Annual Report 1897.

was "Better Farming, Better Business, Better Living,"[13] and Plunkett stated the objectives of the new society:

> To improve the condition of the agricultural population of Ireland by teaching the methods and principles of co-operation as applicable to farming and the allied industries; to promote industrial organisation for any purpose which may appear beneficial; and generally to counsel and advise those engaged in agricultural pursuits . . . To bring to the help of those whose life is passed in the quiet of the field the experience which belongs to wider opportunities of observation and a larger acquaintance with commercial and industrial affairs.

They would take up the work which had already made rapid progress.[14] Perhaps they had been unconsciously imitating Denmark and Sweden in dairy development. Now, to extend the movement, they might find themselves consciously imitating co-operative methods employed in France, Germany, Italy or Russia. Co-operative societies were the best channel for agricultural education, and the government would find their help invaluable. But self-help was better than state aid. The society would be essentially propagandist but non-political: "The more business you introduce into politics and the less politics you introduce into business, the better for both." Finally, members should be prepared for months, perhaps years, of apparently fruitless but beneficial toil. In a storming finish, Plunkett quoted Houghton's famous lines:

> If what seemed afar so grand
> Turn to nothing in your hand,
> On again, the virtue lies
> In the struggle, not the prize.

The applause was thunderous and prolonged. It waned only to break again, drowning the first words of Lord Cloncurry's formal motion,[15] which he repeated:

> That this meeting having heard the principles of the Irish Agricultural Organisation Society hereby approves of the same and resolves that immediate steps be taken to carry them into practical effect.

James Byrne from Castletownroche was quickly on his feet to second the resolution. On this high note of enthusiasm. Plunkett declared the meeting ended and announced the first ordinary general meeting to be held on 10

13 The actual slogan was probably not composed until some time later. In 1905 Plunkett suggested it to the US President, Theodore Roosevelt, as the motto for his rural life policy. Roosevelt said, "Bully, Horace, I'll megaphone that all over the country."
14 See *Report of Inaugural Meeting*, IAOS pamphlet, 1896.
15 The choice of Lord Cloncurry as proposer was appropriate. His grandfather, a former Lord Cloncurry, similarly named Valentine Lawless, had graced the platform in this same building for Robert Owen's meeting in 1823.

May. It was a shrewd piece of stage-management — any attempt at further business would be anti-climactic. Besides, everyone knew that the election of a committee was a delicate matter best deferred so that, in their selection, conflicting parties, creeds and classes could be carefully if unostentatiously balanced. Plunkett, exhausted but elated, left by the night mail for London feeling that he had started "an industrial revolution".

★   ★   ★

Horace Plunkett was elected president of the IAOS. He had been returned as Unionist MP for South Dublin in 1892. During that year, despite other activities, he managed a brief election campaign. He spent nights preparing 'impromptu' election speeches but, for all his careful rehearsal, invariably delivered them badly. However, his growing popularity was such that he easily topped the poll.[16] Plunkett would prove to be an odd type of Unionist, but he held the seat until 1900.

The vice-president of the Society was the Right Honourable Christopher Talbot Reddington, the Resident Commissioner for National Education. His presence on the committee indicated a measure of official approval for the new movement and its educational objectives, but Reddington was also an ardent co-operator in his own right. He lived at Kilcornan, Oranmore, County Galway and was president of the Agricultural Bank founded at Oranmore in 1899.

The Bishop of Raphoe was there, together with Lord Monteagle and Count Arthur Moore. Father Tom Finlay could be seen, before the proceedings started, in animated conversation with Christopher Digges La Touche, managing director of Guinness's.

James Byrne, of Wallstown Castle, Castletownroche (near Doneraile), was also present. Besides being a farmer, a land valuer and a breeder of shorthorn cattle, he was also a coroner. Byrne was a solid nationalist whose presence on the IAOS committee legitimated the co-operative movement in the eyes of many strong farmers of his ilk. He spoke in a low voice through his thick beard and those who were hard of hearing (like Plunkett), or who were not fully attuned to his Cork accent, often failed to catch the drift of what he said. However, he had no difficulty communicating with Major John Alexander of Milford, County Carlow, another enthusiastic breeder of pedigree shorthorns, or with Gerald Dease of Celbridge, County Kildare.

Dease was a tall, slim, white-haired man of sixty-three, with a trim moustache and an alert military bearing. Since 1887 he had been colonel commanding the fourth battalion of the Royal Irish Fusiliers. The Dease family was one of the most prominent, wealthy and highly respected Catholic landlord families in the midlands and Dease's paternal grandmother was a Plunkett of the Fingal family. From 1880, Colonel Dease was

---

16 Plunkett, 4,371; Ffrench-Mullen 2,261; Esmonde 1,452. Something of Plunkett's local popularity is reflected in the reception accorded to him on his return to Dunsany. Near Dunshaughlin he was met by a large crowd of people who unyoked the horses and hauled his carriage all the way to Dunsany Castle.

chamberlain to successive Lords Lieutenant until his death in 1903. A charming, hospitable man, much given to entertaining and gracious living, Dease was nevertheless a tireless worker, an excellent farmer and an enthusiastic organiser. He was never destined to achieve spectacular co-operative success — County Kildare, like other counties within the Pale, was not to prove fruitful co-operative ground — but his efforts and influence were of immense value to the movement.

Jamie (later Sir James) Musgrave of Belfast was five years older than Dease. He was born in Antrim in 1826 (his father had been imprisoned in 1798 for his connection with the United Irishmen). The family subsequently moved to Belfast where Musgrave founded a firm of ironmongers and patent stove-makers. The venture succeeded and he became a very wealthy man. He was appointed chairman of the Belfast Harbour Commissioners and under his guidance great improvements were carried out on the harbour and the docks — the Musgrave Channel is named after him. A shrewd Protestant businessman, Musgrave was also a benevolent patron of innumerable charities and other good causes. He founded the Chair of Pathology at Queen's University. Plunkett chose him as the most influential name to represent the northern co-operators.

The Nationalist MP members, John Redmond and Thomas Sexton, never attended meetings but it was useful to have their names on the committee. George F. Stewart, with an address at 6 Leinster Street Dublin, was also a member of this first IAOS committee. Michael Joseph Cleary, the dapper veterinary surgeon from Mullingar, was to have been a member of the first committee but at the last moment he stood down because, as a Catholic and a Parnellite, he would have upset the delicate balance of representation. He chose instead to be honorary auditor to the Society until he became a full committee member in 1896.

Chapter Eight

The Recess Committee and the Department of Agriculture and Technical Instruction

Plunkett continued to be dogged by ill-health.[1] In his spartan life in Wyoming he had tried (perhaps too hard) to build up his frail body. Now, back in Ireland, he was desperately anxious to be strong and healthy. He rose early, worked himself to exhaustion and then worried about his lack of stamina. He took short trips abroad to rest, but the inaction left him miserable.[2] He wrote incessantly, directing the co-operative effort, formulating new ideas, submitting outlines and also soliciting drafts of co-operative publications. His absences through illness and his preoccupation with co-operatives made some of the Unionist electors of South Dublin feel that he was neglecting them and their local problems. Parliament was dissolved in June 1895 and Plunkett had to seek re-election. Despite an attack of shingles, he conducted a vigorous campaign and was returned with an increased majority.

On 27 August Plunkett wrote a letter to the papers, "a proposal affecting the general welfare of Ireland". Treading (as always) on dangerous political ground, he submitted that, since Home Rule was in abeyance as long as the existing Unionist government was in power,[3] the Irish should not dissipate their energies by fighting about it, but for the time being should unite for the purpose of promoting useful legislation that all parties were substantially agreed upon. He cited two items: a Board of Agriculture for Ireland and a Technical Education Bill, and then made what he called a "crude, informal

---

1 There is considerable evidence that throughout his life he was in almost constant physical pain. Lady Fingall recalls in her memoirs that he probably had more surgical operations than any man alive.

2 In the winter of 1893-94 he spent six weeks in South Africa as the guest of Cecil Rhodes. Later in 1894 he was in Germany with the Monteagles. Early the next year he was so weak that he was compelled to take a complete rest in Bournemouth followed by a month in Egypt.

3 Final results of the July general election were: Unionists 411, Liberals 177, Nationalists 70 and Parnellites 12. This gave the Unionists a majority of 152, the largest obtained at any election since 1832.

and unconventional" proposal that the various party leaders should each nominate a few MPs to form the nucleus of a committee. They should then co-opt by unanimous agreement representatives of the agricultural, industrial, commercial and professional interests North and South.

> ... we Unionists, without abating one jot of our Unionism, and the Nationalists, without abating one jot of their Nationalism, can each show our faith in the cause for which we have fought so bitterly and so long, by sinking our party differences for our country's good ...

The press was initially favourable to the proposal, but later began to change. John Redmond, the Parnellite leader, and Justin McCarthy, leader of the larger Nationalist anti-Parnellite faction, both astute politicians, winced at Plunkett's tactless exposé of the facts on Home Rule. After a lengthy newspaper correspondence in which he stated his party's position, Redmond was able to accept Plunkett's invitation to join the committee. McCarthy persisted in his refusal, maintaining that this was just another Unionist ploy to find a substitute for Home Rule. Plunkett was saddened at McCarthy's rigidity. Although an imperialist by upbringing and outlook, Plunkett was no longer shocked at the prospect of Home Rule. His foreign travels and his appreciation of economic realities confirmed his (and Grattan's) concept of the relationship of the two islands — "the sea divides but the ocean unites". He could no more conceive of an isolated, independent Ireland than he could of an Achill Republic, but in his growing understanding of the Irish culture and temperament he was beginning to see a grain of truth in Campbell-Bannerman's dictum that good government was no substitute for self-government.[4]

The failure to gain representation from the largest political party in the country could have proved a death blow, but support for Plunkett's idea grew, possibly because so many people were growing weary of the sterile quibblings of politicians. The all-party conference was first known as the Round Table and then the Recess Committee.[5] The committee comprised MPs John Redmond, John Parnell, William Field, Richard Dane and Sir Thomas Lee. The co-opted public figures included R.F. McCoy (Lord Mayor of Dublin), Rev Monsignor Gerald Molloy, Mr Justice Ross, The Earl of Mayo, The O'Connor Don, Sir John Arnott, V.B. Dillon, C. Litton Falkiner, H. Brougham Leech, Joseph Kenny, Joseph Meade, Thomas Andrews and Thomas Sinclair. A number of co-operators were on the committee: T.A. Finlay, Lord Monteagle and Count Arthur Moore. James Musgrave from Belfast, another co-operator, was appointed chairman of a

4 Plunkett had committed his first offence against party discipline during the introduction of Gladstone's Home Rule Bill in 1892 when he refused to support Balfour's amendment which proposed excluding Irish representation from the Imperial Parliament. This brought him under Unionist suspicion and did not make him any more popular with the Nationalists. The single-minded Davitt, who was impatient to forge ahead from a 'land' victory to the political victory of Home Rule, regarded Plunkett's co-operative schemes as a childish and irritating distraction, at least for the time being.

5 So called because many of those taking part were MPs and most meetings had to be held during the Parliamentary recess.

special consultative committee for Ulster.[6] Plunkett was made chairman and T.P. Gill secretary of the committee.

Thomas P. Gill was one of the ablest of the talented people Plunkett had enlisted to his aid. Two years younger than Plunkett, he came of a strongly nationalist Catholic family from Nenagh, County Tipperary. A graduate of Trinity College Dublin, Gill had won distinction as a journalist in London and New York. When he returned to Ireland in 1851, he was elected MP for South Louth and soon found himself in the thick of the Land War. He was one of the organisers of the Plan of Campaign and, when Dillon and O'Brien were imprisoned, became, with Redmond and Clancy, one of its leaders. A man of great organisational ability, a linguist, orator and talented journalist, he had a shrewd understanding of the Irish people and the workings of the Irish mind. At the time of the Parnell split, he was a diligent intermediary in the Boulogne negotiations which sought to reconcile the Parnellites and anti-Parnellites within the party. His objectivity and calm detachment in debate earned him the sobriquet 'Neutral Gill'. R.A. Anderson conceded that Gill was a man of immense personal magnetism and charm, but still an enigma:

> I had been accustomed to look at things squarely. When one tried to look at T.P. the vision was all oblique. George Russell [AE] was asked to explain him once and he said — I have devised two mottoes for T.P. one is 'the longest way round is the shortest way home' and the other is like unto it — 'The means are more important than the end.' Both or either fitted T.P. as did his well-groomed skin.[7]

George W. Russell (AE)

6   The members were Thomas Andrews, James Dempsey, Sir Daniel Dixon, Sir W.Q. Ewart, John Fagan, Maurice FitzGerald (Queen's University, Belfast), Rev R.R. Kane, Robert McGeagh, R.J. McConnell, Alex Robb, Thomas Roe, Thomas Sinclair and John F. Small.
7   *With Horace Plunkett in Ireland*, pp.102-03.

From the first Conference, held in the Mansion House in September 1895, matters proceeded with commendable speed. The appointed committee met three times in the autumn of 1895, adjourned and resumed its sessions early in 1896. A great deal of research was done in the intervening months. Plunkett was no impecunious do-gooder; he had made a lot of money in the United States[8] and was not averse to spending it to Ireland's advantage. Largely at his own expense, he despatched investigators to study and report on agricultural departments, technical instruction and co-operation in half the countries of Europe. Gill was sent to Denmark and France. Michael Mulhall, an eminent statistician, was commissioned to visit Belgium, Holland, Bavaria, Württemberg, Austria, Hungary and Switzerland. The committee also received valuable submissions from Monsieur E. Tisserand, the French Director-General of Agriculture, a man who, in Plunkett's estimation, was "probably the greatest living authority on State-aid to Agriculture."[9]

At home, R.A. Anderson, with Arnold Graves, secretary of the Technical Instruction Association, and T.W. Rolleston, secretary of the Irish Industries Association, undertook to review the economic condition of the country and the available resources awaiting development. The Northern section (the consultative committee for Ulster) held its meetings in Belfast, and Plunkett flitted busily back and forth urging the speedy collation of the research with a view to an early report. The committee was an unofficial one and had to work without the secretarial service and civil service support available to a Royal Commission, but Plunkett recruited an excellent staff. The material was collected, condensed, clarified and collated skilfully and with remarkable speed.

On the first day of August 1896, Plunkett was able to forward the unanimously agreed report to Gerald W. Balfour, Chief Secretary,[10] requesting him to submit it to the Lord Lieutenant of Ireland. It was a remarkable document which even today makes fascinating reading. It begins:

> We have in Ireland a poor country, practically without manufactures — except for the linen and ship-building of the North and the brewing and distilling of Dublin — dependent upon agriculture with its soil imperfectly tilled, its area under cultivation decreasing, and a diminishing population without industrial habits or technical skill.

8   He amassed a considerable fortune in land speculation, acquiring large areas of virgin prairie which, after fencing and irrigation, he resold very profitably in suitably sized ranches. Plunkett was one of the pioneers of 'feed-lot' development, linking grass ranches in the uplands with what he called 'fatteries' in the corn-growing lowland plains. He also had extensive holdings in railways, electric light companies, meat packing, cold storage and other industrial projects. In 1884 he even contemplated the establishment of a stock exchange in Cheyenne. It was not, however, an entirely one-sided success story. He had to weather heavy losses because of droughts, prairie fires, market slumps and poor performances by some of his managers.

9   Letter to the Chief Secretary, G.W. Balfour, as foreword to the *Report of the Recess Committee.*

10 Brother of Arthur (Bloody) Balfour, former Chief Secretary, Unionist leader in the House of Commons and the then Chief Secretary.

It proceeded to 418 pages of tightly-written, lucid script in five well-defined sections:

Part I Past action of the state in Ireland and its effect upon the economy and the habits of the people.

Part II The immediately available resources of Ireland (agricultural and industrial) and the possibilities of development.

Part III How resources were being developed in other countries through the action of (a) the people themselves; (b) the state.

Part IV How similar methods might be adopted with profit in Ireland.

Recommendations for the promotion of:
(a) Agriculture:
 (i) by organisation amongst the people
 (ii) by diffusion of expert information
 (iii) by representation of agricultural public opinion in the administration.

(b) Industry:
 (i) by the fostering and introduction of industries
 (ii) by the representation of industrial public opinion in the administration.

(c) The promotion of both *Agriculture* and *Industry* by practical education.

Part V The constitution of the new proposed Department of Agriculture and Industries.[11]

The Report analysed every aspect of the Irish economy and every development proposal, from daffodil growing in Cork to consideration of the forty-three different categories of cottage industries flourishing in the province of Moscow. The script teems with suggestions and recommendations. Possibly the best précis and appraisal is that of Margaret Digby:

The document itself bore throughout the impress of Plunkett's maturing thought. It described the existing economic position of Ireland and surveyed the unused or half-used potentialities. It reviewed the measures taken in Europe to promote agriculture and rural industries, fisheries and forestry. It offered a series of proposals for

---

11 *Report of the Recess Committee*, on the establishment of a Department of Agriculture and Industries for Ireland (Dublin: Browne and Nolan, 1896). It was also published in Belfast by W. Mullan and Son and in London by T. Fisher Unwin.

adapting these methods to Irish conditions. In agriculture there must be organisation of the people themselves, since no government could deal direct with the individual. Voluntary organisations, so long as they did not trade, should be subsidised by the State. In fisheries and industry the government might have to take direct action. There should be travelling instructors, model plots, experiment stations and laboratories. A consultative Council on Agriculture should be constituted, its members partly elected, partly appointed. Co-operative banking should be developed.

Technical, or as the Report preferred to call it, 'practical' education, should be greatly improved and should extend from the primary school to the University. The professional status of the agricultural technician and industrialist should be revised. Finally, there should be set up in Ireland a new Department of Agriculture and Industries, absorbing such existing bodies as the Congested Districts Board, the Fisheries and Veterinary Department and some sections of the Board of Education, in charge of a Minister responsible to Parliament, assisted by an appointed Agricultural Board and advised by the Consultative Council of Agriculture. The Committee, it was stated in conclusion, placed their reliance on individual and combined effort rather than on State aid, and in asking for the latter insisted that it should be granted in such a manner as to evoke and supplement the former.[12]

The Report had a tremendous impact. Plunkett had effectively taken an important Irish issue outside the British Parliament and had united his countrymen in a clear-cut demand for a considerable measure of Irish control in a specific sector. Although many Irish nationalists persisted in seeing it as a distraction, shrewd English politicians saw it as a more subtle approach than the blanket demand for total Home Rule at once, and much more difficult to oppose. Press comment both in England and Ireland was almost entirely favourable.[13] The Report's reception in government circles was somewhat colder — not surprising in view of its hard-hitting comments on government's past performance,[14] in which every attributed shortcoming was verified by meticulous references to impeccable sources — mostly English authors and official reports.

Plunkett did everything possible to ensure that his Report would not be pigeon-holed and suffer the common fate of so many previous Royal Commission Reports. He stirred up correspondence in the newspapers and

12 Margaret Digby, op. cit., pp.78-79.
13 "The Editors were not only favourable to this Report", said Plunkett, "some of them have actually read it!"
14 "It struck at all her industries, not excepting agriculture. It forced the population into entire dependence on the land and reduced the country to an economic condition involving periodical famines. The more energetic elements of the population were driven to emigrate, carrying their skill with them to foreign countries, and of those who remained behind the spirit and habits of the larger portion were subjected to the influence of the Penal Code. It was not to be wondered at that we at length came to have a population devoid of the industrial spirit." (*Report*, p.5). The statements in this short paragraph were supported by no fewer than five lengthy footnotes quoting authoritative sources.

in 1898 persuaded a Mr Dalziel, a millionaire businessman who among other ventures controlled a news agency, to buy the *Dublin Daily Express,* a diehard Unionist paper then on its last legs. The deal was that Plunkett and his co-operative friends would take over the editorial function with T.P. Gill as the titular editor. The paper appeared under new management in June 1898. Although it celebrated its re-emergence with a scoop, chartering a tug to take the visiting Guglielmo Marconi ten miles out in Dublin Bay to send the first ever press report (on a yacht race) by wireless telegraphy, the paper never made money and towards the end of 1899 Dalziel sold out to Lord Ardilaun and the *Express* reverted to its extreme Unionist bias. However, it had served Plunkett well as a daily (and increasingly popular) organ advocating the plans of the Recess Committee, preaching co-operation and urgently pressing for a new Department of Agriculture.

The machinery of government in Ireland at the turn of the century was a bewildering hotch-potch of departments, boards and offices. No single department was charged with overall responsibility for the development of agriculture or industry. Bits and pieces of administrative responsibility were allocated to different bodies from time to time in a seemingly haphazard fashion. Some departments, for instance those dealing with finance and defence, were little more than branches of United Kingdom ministries. Several, including those dealing with law and order, the police and the prisons, came under the direct control of the Executive[15] (or as it was (un)popularly known, Dublin Castle). A few boards, such as the Congested Districts Board, had varying degrees of autonomy, but in practice were usually susceptible to Executive pressure, especially on financial matters.[16]

The administration of agricultural affairs was particularly complicated. The Board of Works dealt with arterial drainage and land improvement. Agricultural instruction was administered by the National Board of Education but technical instruction was controlled by the Science and Art Department of South Kensington; the Irish branch of the UK Science and Art Department looked after the Botanic Gardens and the College of Science. The collection of agricultural statistics was shared by the Land Commission, the Fisheries Board and the Registrar General; the Veterinary Department of the Privy Council retained responsibility for statistics relating to animal diseases and livestock exports. The Land Commission conducted agricultural experiments and helped the Congested Districts Board carry out agricultural schemes. Fishery developers looked to the Fisheries Board, the Board of Works or the Congested Districts Board,

15 The Executive of 'Irish government' consisted of the Lord Lieutenant and the Chief Secretary (both politicians), the Under-Secretary (a civil servant), and their advisors. The Lord Lieutenant was the *de facto* head but had come to assume a role similar to the constitutional monarch, acting generally on the advice of the Chief Secretary who undertook chief responsibility for the administration. The Lord Lieutenant rarely left Dublin and the Vice-regal Lodge where he led the social life of the city with levees, soirées, grand balls and numerous receptions. The Chief Secretary had to spend a great deal of time in London where he piloted through Parliament legislation pertaining to Ireland, answered parliamentary questions and controlled the London branch of his own department. The responsibility for routine administration fell largely on the Dublin-based Under-Secretary.
16 Frequently, also, the Chief Secretary was chairman or president of a Board.

depending on the nature and location of the proposed developments. Although civil servants made it a point of honour to act independently of each other and were well-informed on the extent of their jurisdiction, the farmers, fishermen and most of their public representatives were extremely bewildered.

In April 1897 Gerald Balfour, Chief Secretary, introduced the Agriculture and Industries (Ireland) Bill, generously acknowledging that it was based on the *Report of the Recess Committee*.[17] The Queen's speech at the opening of Parliament had promised a Board of Agriculture for Ireland. A month later Arthur Balfour had to introduce his Irish Local Government Bill and this necessitated the withdrawal of the Agricultural and Industries Bill.[18] Plunkett chafed at this delay and the Irish co-operators were anxious lest this new hope for Ireland might never materialise. From the time of the publication of the *Report*, the IAOS had been busy. Well-attended district conferences were held all over the country; an abbreviated version of the *Report of the Recess Committee* was considered and its recommendations endorsed, usually unanimously. The IAOS officials were at pains to point out that, whilst they campaigned ardently for the legislation, co-operative societies should remember that the new Department of itself would not work miracles. The co-operative movement could benefit considerably from suitable state aid but only when co-operators made the maximum effort themselves. Anderson was fearful of the wild expectations sometimes encountered:

> I think at that time of expectation we had aroused an enthusiasm for co-operation which almost reached its peak. Of course the new Department was popularly endowed, in advance, with almost magical powers. It could, in the minds of the people, almost transmute mud into gold. One had to be eternally throwing cold water on these fanciful ideas and reminding the farmers that the hard and narrow road to success depended ever so much more on themselves than on the State. To a people alternately coerced and spoonfed, our admonitions were very unpalatable. Constantly I was met with the query 'What is this new Department going to do, at all, unless it puts more money in our pockets?'[19]

It was not until the Local Government Act of 1898 was safely passed that Gerald Balfour was able to come back, this time with a redrafted Agricultural and Technical Instruction Bill which had its first reading in the House of Commons on 9 May 1899. Balfour sought to push it through quickly before the summer recess. Plunkett was unable to be in the House. He had broken his hip, for the second time, when his bicycle had skidded on a wet road in Knightsbridge. By the second reading, on 6 July, it was obvious

17 Publication of the *Report* had brought Plunkett instant public recognition. He was appointed an Irish Privy Councillor.
18 On the grounds that the structure of the new Department, with its Board and Council, could not be legislated until the structure of local government was first decided.
19 *With Horace Plunkett in Ireland*, p.98.

that Balfour was becoming increasingly intolerant of criticism. Suggestions and amendments put forward by Redmond, Davitt, Moore and Dillon[20] got short shrift and the Bill was through the House by the end of July. Lord Ashbourne guided it speedily through the House of Lords and soon it was written in the Statue Book as "An Act establishing a Department of Agriculture and other Industries and Technical Instruction in Ireland and for other purposes connected therewith."

The new Department would have a President (the Chief Secretary) and a Vice-President, assisted by a Secretary and two Assistant Secretaries together with a number of inspectors, instructors, officers and servants. It was agreed that in practice the direction of the Department's affairs would be left to the Vice-President. Plunkett was appointed Vice-President and took up his post on 2 November 1899. The broad functions designated for the Department under the Act were those "of aiding, improving and developing the agriculture, fisheries and other industries of Ireland in so far as may be proper to such a Department and in such a manner as to stimulate and strengthen the self-reliance of the people." Several pieces of administration, which had previously been scattered amongst various boards and offices, were brought together and the work of the new Department was organised in six different branches. Two important bodies were the Council of Agriculture and the Board of Agriculture. The role of the Board was very similar to that of the board of directors of a company. It consisted of fourteen members, including the president and the vice-president of the Department. It discussed and advised on policy and organisation and had the power to veto expenditure from the Department's endowment fund.

The Council of Agriculture was a significant innovation and, had it lived up to Plunkett's early hopes, could have advanced the evolution of democracy in Ireland by at least three generations. Sociologists will observe in Plunkett's many pronouncements on co-operative development and state aid how remarkably close he was to articulating the modern concepts of community development. His terms of reference for the state department to apply state aid "in such a manner as to stimulate and strengthen the self-reliance of the People" was just one step short of the full community development idea of a "union of people and government", which had to await the establishment of the United Nations Organisation for its precise articulation and promulgation in the nineteen fifties.

If Plunkett was close in theory, he contrived to be as least as close in practice. In the Council of Agriculture he conceived of bringing the people (through their elected representatives) close to government — giving them a consultative and advisory role in policy-making. The Council, elected triennially and built on the newly established local government system, consisted of 104 members. Of these, sixty-eight were elected by county

20 It was during this debate that Balfour levelled the famous taunt at Dillon that he was "willing to wound, yet afraid to strike." Balfour's technique consisted mainly of challenging objectors to put themselves on record as opposing the Bill — "this measure of great and far-reaching import to the material interests of Ireland" — so they would be seen in Ireland as delaying the speedy institution of the new Department. Possibly because of this, the Bill encountered little serious opposition in the House.

councils and thirty-four were nominated by the Department.[21] Considerable strength and status accrued to the Council through its statutory right to elect eight members of the fourteen-member Agricultural Board. The Council, with the county councils and urban councils, elected the majority of the twenty-three members of the Board of Technical Instruction, which advised the Department on education and technical training. Although the Department was not legally bound to accept the advice of the Council, its recommendations, especially if backed by a strong majority, could not easily be ignored.

Horace Plunkett in his De Dion Bouton,
reputedly the first motor car in Ireland.

The Department, together with its elected Council of Agriculture and appointed Boards of Agriculture and Technical Instruction, was a unique experiment in constitutional machinery, for which Plunkett deserves most of the credit. He staked the success of the system on its hoped-for ability to evoke and fortify the self-reliance, enterprise and responsibility of the people to practise the processes of democracy at every level. He put it succinctly to an early meeting of the Council:

> The principle involves local initiation, local contribution, local administration, with central supervision and control. Consistent with this beautiful formula, we go down to a district and tell the people that they must think out a scheme, pay a large part of its cost, and then work it out largely themselves. At the same time, the moment they propose to do anything wrong, we immediately pull them up with a letter written, of course, in the politest officialese.

21 The President and Vice-President were *ex-officio* members.

Plunkett had worked very hard as a member of the Congested Districts Board. He made several visits to the remote west[22] where he saw the struggle of the people "in all its naked hopelessness". But the *modus operandi* of the Board never aroused him to great enthusiasm. Every dictate of his economic training and business mind checked and cross-checked to the same inevitable conclusion: so *many* people could not be sustained by so *few* resources. When, with honest pragmatism (and characteristic tactlessness), he enunciated the most likely reliefs — assisted emigration, land division and consolidation, smaller families, and communal farming and fishing — he found few supporters and offended many people. In turn, his own finely-drawn moral sensibilities were repelled by the thinly disguised philanthropy and paternalism of methods by which Congested District Board grants and 'handouts' were sought and received. Deputations of politicians, clergy and gentry invariably extolled visions of fields which would overflow with produce, seas which would teem with fish, and craftsmen who would disgorge manufactures as from an endless cornucopia, if only they were given a chance. Plunkett's queries about technical feasibility, capital requirements, profit margins, marketing systems, or the eventuality of such developments, were felt to be not only prosaic, pedestrian and penny-pinching, but an insult to the national spirit and aspirations of the people.

Now, however, with a co-operative movement growing stronger by the day, aided and abetted by a benevolent state department, designed to enhance the enterprise and industry of a likeable, resourceful people, there would be hope for the west and the rest of the country in the dawning of a new rural civilisation. The Congested Districts Board could be reorganised, for many of its institutions were practical and good. Plunkett and his technical and administrative staff elatedly took over the group of Georgian houses at the top of Merrion Street, Dublin, and in early April 1900 the new Department of Agriculture and Technical Instruction for Ireland was under way.[23]

Plunkett was forty-five. Behind him he had ten years of ranching and business in America. For twelve years he had successfully managed the Dunsany family estate. He had almost nine years service on the Congested Districts Board and eight as a member of Parliament. Yet his proudest achievement was in creating a rapidly expanding co-operative movement. He was concerned about the limitations of his frail constitution but trusted that his experience, enthusiasm and willpower would carry him through. For he had won the opportunity which so few men achieve, of being entrusted to carry out a policy which he himself had conceived and long and ardently advocated.

---

22 Including a number of voyages with the yacht *Granuaile* and later the *Helga*.
23 The Department was allocated a capital sum of approximately £200,000 and an annual endowment of £166,000. An additional sum was voted by Parliament in the ordinary civil service estimates for salaries and expenses. The work was allocated and organised between six different branches: agricultural, technical instruction, fisheries, statistics and intelligence, veterinary, and accounts.

Chapter Nine

Ireland in the New Century

Land of distraction! Where for ages past
All has been tumult — never rest or calm.
(W. Hazlitt Roberts)[1]

Much has been written in historical retrospect of the early years of the new century in Ireland. One writer has conceived of the period 1891 to 1916 as "a sort of crease in time, a featureless valley between the commanding chain of the Rising and the solitary enigmatic peak of Parnell."[2] We have James Joyce's picture of Dublin as "the centre of paralysis", squalid and shabby genteel. George Moore, in his *Salve Atque Vale*, has his own impish interpretation of the first decade. Others saw Dublin from their varying perspectives as a hotbed of revolution or as the grand centre of the Irish cultural renaissance. For many of the Ascendancy it offered repeated confirmation of the unfitness of the native Irish for self-government.

The Gaelic Athletic Association, building on the ground cleared by the Land League, was seeking to replace the servile mentality of a 'grateful tenantry' with a new spirit of Gaelic manliness and freedom. With aims at once scholarly and nationalistic, Douglas Hyde and his Gaelic League were working to revive the Irish language and, through it, bring an ignorant Ireland back to its ancient culture. Yeats and his circle of poets, playwrights and novelists wanted to create an audience of Irish men and women who knew the history of their country. The Irish Text Society was publishing old Irish manuscripts, the Feis Ceoil was fostering Irish music, and the Irish Literary Theatre was getting under way.

Not much was known generally of the secret Irish Republican Brotherhood or of Connolly's Irish Socialist Republican Party. Churchmen and optimistic Christians would like to think it inconceivable that there should be support for such subversiveness in a Christian country. Somebody recalled the moral dilemma of the countrywoman and the fairies — it was against her religion to believe in them, but they were there! The working man heeded his Church and was loyal to its liturgy but was not entirely forgetful of an older dream. Deep in his oppressed soul was the need to hope that the ancient gods were not dead but sleeping

1 From a poetic tribute to Horace Plunkett entitled "Ireland's Friend" in the March 1900 issue of the *Agricultural Economist*, quoted in *The Irish Homestead*, 17 March 1900.
2 See Conor Cruise O'Brien (ed.), *The Shaping of Modern Ireland* (London: Routledge & " Kegan Paul, 1960), p.13.

under the high mountains. Some deed of matchless bravery and sacrifice by the living Irish would bring them awake to lead an avenging army of reincarnated warrior kings and heroes of the Gael to sweep the oppressors from the land. It was not at all incongruous that a devastating St Patrick should be foremost in their number. We might easily be persuaded that Clarke, Pearse, Connolly and Larkin were fools; it was a small-souled Christian who would brand them as villains. Very little was known or heard of the co-operative movement. Some provincial weeklies fulminated against it but in the national journals any reference to it was incidental and in small type.

Towns in Ireland had been largely a Norman innovation, and even several centuries later they still tended to be inhabited and ruled by a distinctive breed of Irishman. Since the horror of the Great Famine, town-dwellers had become increasingly introverted; even small towns had tended to weave an insubstantial web of ersatz metropolitanism to screen them from the realities of the rural hinterland. Those who had fled the fields and the stench of rotten potatoes were loth to look back past the city walls. The town-bred burgher preferred the rural idyll of cottages and scenery in summertime to any investigation of poverty and squalor greater than his own. For many it was preferable to be poor in a poor street than have milk, greens and bacon in windswept rural isolation and black benighted loneliness. There were murmurings of a new 'co-operation' down the country to help and protect the poor farmers and improve agricultural production. Very few town-dwellers were impressed: it was well-known that farmers were the prime culprits of high food prices and were poor only because they preferred to hoard money rather than accord themselves a decent living. This was the divisive myth that every limited urban experience and gombeen declamation appeared to substantiate.

Very few of the Dublin intelligentsia had ever actually *seen* a co-operative creamery. They had the word of George Russell, Father Tom Finlay, Edward Martyn, Emily Anderson, Susan Mitchell[3] and others in artistic circles that agricultural co-operation was happening. Plunkett was famous now, but in most people's eyes his fame was entirely political. To many he seemed an exotic, aristocratic, liberal Unionist who had won for Ireland her own Department of Agriculture and Technical Instruction, who supported the Gaelic League and the Gaelic Athletic Association, and who was agitating for a Catholic University — a man whose political honesty was causing dismay but touching heartstrings in every camp. The agricultural co-operative movement, of which little was known, was accepted as evidence of Plunkett's solid worth and his ability to gather hardworking, influential men behind him.

By the turn of the century, the number of co-operative societies had grown to 374 with a membership of 36,683.[4] Lord Monteagle of Brandon

3   Miss Anderson, sister of R.A. Anderson, was an art inspector under the South Kensington Art and Science Department. Miss Mitchell was a poet and a dynamic assistant editor of *The Irish Homestead*.

4   See IAOS Annual Report 1899. This is an extensive report of 106 pages and of particular interest, being the last report issued before the Department of Agriculture and Technical Instruction was set up.

took over as President of the IAOS when Plunkett went to the Department. This was a period of intense activity, with both bodies working in close harmony.

T. P. Gill's appointment as Secretary of the Department of Agriculture and Technical Instruction was a controversial one. Plunkett was determined to have the best staff possible, whatever their political beliefs. The appointment of Nationalists and Catholics would be looked on unfavourably by the government and Lord Lieutenant, and would outrage the Unionists who had elected Plunkett in South Dublin. Plunkett considered Gill to be the best man for the job but was torn by his affection and regard for R. A. Anderson. Anderson, a staunch Protestant and Unionist (married to a Catholic wife), was urged to apply for the post by his Unionist associates, but, conscious of Plunkett's possible preference for Gill and what he considered his own limited ability, refused to put himself forward. Anderson disliked and distrusted Gill and hoped that Plunkett might make a better choice, but if Plunkett asked him, he would find it hard to refuse. The deciding interview between Plunkett and Anderson speaks volumes for both. Plunkett offered, "You have only to ask me and the job is yours." Anderson challenged him to state frankly that he preferred Gill. Never good at expressing the depth and range of his thought, Plunkett contrived to be honest without being hurtful, to praise objectively without sounding patronising. The balance was in favour of Gill. "Nevertheless," he concluded, "you have only to ask me and the job is yours." Anderson shook his head and then permitted himself a broad and happy smile. All was understood, there was no need for words.[5]

For a feverish period following the launching of the Department, Plunkett worked a minimum of eighteen hours a day, but "after a time", he wrote, "the torrent of business made channels for itself and went on in a more orderly fashion."[6] He saw little of the IAOS but it too was running successfully. The Department helped to defray the cost of the technical instruction and within a year had taken over much of this work, "an

5 By his action, Anderson won himself the affection and regard of his fellow co-operators. He had turned down a highly remunerative public position (permanent and pensionable) and his colleagues were anxious not only to applaud his gesture but to offer some monetary consolation. An Anderson Testimonial Committee was formed and, on 5 June 1901, he was made the recipient of a handsome cash presentation accompanied by a magnificently silver-bound, bog-oak covered book, artistically inscribed with the compliments and list of subscribing societies. This book is retained in the lobby of The Plunkett House. Following pages of tightly inscribed lists of co-operative societies, some of which contributed sizeable sums to the presentation, there comes one entire page devoted to a letter from the secretary of a small co-operative bank in Connemara: "Gentlemen, I am directed by the Moycullen Agricultural Bank Committee to enclose £1 subscribed by them towards the Anderson Testimonial and to express their sincere regret that they could not more fittingly subscribe to such a deserving fund. Wishing it every success, I remain, Gentlemen, Your humble servant, C. Kenny." An equally touching letter is included from the Co-operative Credit Society in Clare Island, County Mayo.

6 "He indoctrinated the Press. He inspected the Cork butter market . . . the Munster Dairy School . . . the Museums and scientific institutions of Dublin which the Department was to take over. He went to Belfast . . . Queen's College . . . to England . . . Dublin College of Science. He studied red tape at the Treasury and listened to advice from all quarters; touring in the *Granuaile* . . . to see the Marine Laboratory in Ballinakill harbour and the progress of improvement on the Aran Islands . . . later he bought a yacht in unsuccessful pursuit of foreign trawlers fishing within the three mile limit." Digby, op. cit., pp.85-86.

enormous help", which enabled the IAOS to devote its own funds to direct organisational work. The Department also undertook to defray the costs of organising agricultural credit banks, which were non-trading societies. Some inhibitions were felt about asking for state money to help organise the scores of new creameries and store co-operatives which were mushrooming throughout the country; merchant interests regarded these as dangerous competitors. The IAOS had up to now been financed by the funds provided by Plunkett and donations from friends and well-wishers of the movement.[7] The organisation now sought to become more self-supporting by asking the co-operative societies for affiliation fees and subscriptions. The response was less than generous. This source provided only a small amount of the funds required and the organisation mainly relied on donations. A fund-raising mission to the United States in 1903 by Anderson, Father Tom Finlay and Father Jerry O'Donovan led, in Anderson's words, to "unbounded hospitality but few dollars". Unfortunately, too, as the Department took up some of the burden and as responsibility was shifted onto the co-operative societies, private subscriptions tended to fall off.

Horace Plunkett

On the political front, Plunkett was soon in trouble. He was not a good party man nor a good speaker, and attended the House infrequently. When he was there, he often intervened without notice to speak and vote against his own party, whenever he thought they were wrong.[8] He was willing to support the Nationalists in sensible proposals but frequently found that he

7   Many of the committee subscribed heavily and regularly. In 1897, Sir Henry Cochrane made a gift of £5,000 and in 1900 Plunkett's nephew, the young Lord Dunsany, later to achieve fame as a scholar and poet, subscribed £1,000. Samuel Figgis, a London business-man, made several offers to match the amounts subscribed by the societies. Of the northern co-operators, Mr and Mrs Harold Barbour were outstandingly generous over many years.
8   "As early as 1896 he spoke in favour of an amnesty for political prisoners with both front benches against him." (Digby, op. cit., p.88).

could not support their exaggerated claims.[9] He later ruefully compared himself to "a dog on a tennis court", trying to be helpful to both sides but appreciated by none. He might have survived in the Mother of Parliaments which he fondly believed was "indulgent of sincerity however ineloquent", but the bigots in his own constituency were unlikely to forgive him for his attitude to Home Rule and land purchase, his criticism of the Local Government Bill or his support for a Catholic university. He was offered a safe seat in South Derry, "to chuck South Dublin before South Dublin chucked him", but with the characteristic obstinacy which maddened his friends, turned it down, refusing as always to take the easy way. South Dublin went to the polls in pouring rain on 9 October 1900 and Plunkett was defeated by a narrow margin.

Plunkett thought of standing for an Ulster or even an English constituency but shortly afterwards was unexpectedly invited to stand in a by-election in Galway.[10] The experience was an unhappy one, as he recorded in his diary:

> A terrible day! I witnessed the political and religious intimidation, of which we had heard so much, enacted in all its completeness. Bullying, bribing, threatening, material and spiritual and so forth. Priests in the polling booths ... priests outside ... priests marching their parishioners to the polls like Salvation Army processions. Result, Colonel Lynch 1,247, self 472!

The loss of his seat in Parliament put Plunkett in a very difficult position. The vice-presidency of the Department was a ministerial post. Although the letter of the law made it possible for him to remain Vice-President, he could no longer attend Parliament. Thus he would no longer be able to promote the best interest of his Department, to explain his work, to reply to questions or to answer attacks.

There was widespread public support for Plunkett's retention. The Council of Agriculture, the Agricultural Board and the Board of Technical Instruction urged him to remain in office until the work of organising the Department was further advanced. At a banquet held in Plunkett's honour in the Rotunda, he was presented with a memorial signed by 20,000 influential people, mostly Nationalists, begging him to retain his position. Encouraged by the sympathetic audience, Plunkett made an excellent speech — thoughtful and witty — and the halting delivery was hardly noticed as nearly every sentence was greeted with encouraging, often thunderous, applause. He agreed to remain at the helm and, given such popularity, the government was happy that he should do so.

There were political changes too. The Parnell split was beginning to heal

9 In 1897 he refused to join Dillon in calling on Balfour to recall Parliament to deal with the 'famine' arising from a partial failure of the potato crop.

10 His opponent in this election was the Nationalist 'Colonel' Arthur Lynch, a Paris based journalist who was a figure of some controversy since, reputedly, he had fought for the Boers in South Africa. See *The Galway Express*, 23 November 1901.

and the opposing Nationalist factions had come together early in 1900 under the banner of the United Irish League and the leadership of John Redmond.[11] However, this improved Nationalist solidarity did little to enhance the position of Plunkett's Department or his co-operative movement. Since Plunkett was attractive to the Nationalist citizen — the man in the street — it was not tactical to oppose him too vigorously. The strategy was to give him exaggerated support for any proposals that seemed to be at variance with Unionist policy and thus edge him closer to the Home Rule camp. The enemies of co-operation — Unionist, Nationalist and opportunist — were gathering.

> Plunkett realised at an early stage that as his Co-operative Movement was beginning to be understood it was opposed by all interests who had hitherto preyed upon the farmer — railways, banks, gombeen men and tradesmen. Michael Davitt, the Land Leaguer, attacked it. Parish Priests consulted their members of Parliament and were told to give it no countenance. The IAOS was accused of concealed political objects. Even the parson at Kilmessan preached against the schemes of politicians under the guise of philanthropy, and Plunkett made a note, 'I must ask him if he really meant to go for me.'[12]

In the midst of this "hotch-potch of party politics, trade prejudices and economic ignorance", Plunkett increasingly felt the need to put his case cogently before the Irish people. Towards the end of 1902 he began to formulate his thoughts and experiences in a book, published in February 1904, entitled *Ireland in the New Century*.[13] The book called for a reappraisal of the Irish problem, not in political, but in economic and ultimately moral terms. Plunkett, a historian by training, reviewed the history of British misrule, as he had done so devastatingly in the report of the Recess Committee. He noted the political vacuum created by the fall of Parnell and the evolution of a policy (his own, though he did not claim it) of dealing with the justified economic grievances of Ireland through economic rather than political methods. Never a pure economist (the core of his thought was always ethical), Plunkett quickly proceeded to a discussion of human behaviour and his enduring conviction that the solution of the Irish question was to be found in the strengthening of the Irish character. For him, the building of character was the precedent to all material, social and cultural advancement. Lack of moral courage amongst the Irish made political leadership easy but it was, he said, "the quicksand of Irish life". The principal agencies which moulded public opinion and the Irish character were the political parties, the educational system and the Catholic church. Plunkett surveyed them all critically and, even though his criticism was muted, it hurt deeply.

11 Although there were further discords which led to the formation of the All-for-Ireland League under William O'Brien and Tim Healy, the United Irish League continued to dominate the Nationalist cause up to World War I.
12 Digby, op. cit., pp.100-01.
13 The book was published in London in 1904 by John Murray.

In the second half of the book, Plunkett recorded the positive achievements of the later days, telling with persuasive enthusiasm the story of the co-operative movement and the foundation of the Department, and looking hopefully to the day when the Irish would finally cease to depend solely for the restoration of Ireland on the government which had injured their country.

> Ireland must be recreated from within. The main work must be done in Ireland and the centre of interest must be Ireland. When Irishmen realise this truth, the splendid human power of their country, so much of which now runs idly or disastrously to waste, will be utilised; and we may then look with confidence for the foundation of a fabric of Irish prosperity, framed in constructive thought and laid enduringly in human character.

It was a book of considerable literary merit, containing many of Plunkett's wisest and wittiest epigrams: "Anglo-Irish history is for Englishmen to remember, for Irishmen to forget"; "The more business in politics and the less politics in business, the better for both"; "The work of tomorrow will largely consist of the impossible of today." Plunkett's description of a day in the life of the Vice-President of the Department and his dealings with the various deputations and office-seekers is in parts exceedingly funny. However, neither serious eloquence, literary power nor good humour could save Plunkett from the storm that was to come.

The first reviews, with the exception of the *Morning Post*, were all favourable, some even lavish, in their praise. Although Plunkett had hit the Unionists hardest of all, the *Belfast Newsletter* was not unduly annoyed: "It is to some extent controversial but it is needless to say that there is no bitterness of tone nor a trace of the party spirit in it." The attack came on the religious rather than the political front when the *Freeman's Journal* slated the book for its references to extravagant church building and the failure of the Catholic church effectually to promote the virtues of self-reliance, industry, temperance and thrift. Plunkett was accused of saying that religion weakened the character of the people. He had been warned by Anderson and many of his co-operator friends against the inclusion of some passages which could bear that interpretation, but with characteristic tactlessness chose to ignore the possibility of misinterpretation being used as a weapon against himself or the co-operative movement. He was offended by the suggestion that a foreword by one of his clerical friends, or even "the picture of a bishop", would render the book more palatable or at least less open to unfair attack. He scorned such subterfuges and was determined to tell the truth as he saw it, regardless of the consequences. Also, if his ideas were exceptionable, he was determined that he alone should bear the blame.

The *Freeman's Journal* attack was followed by a public outcry. Provincial newspapers piled on more virulent condemnation, and a succession of county councils and public bodies discussed resolutions calling for the banning or burning of "this filthy book". Cardinal Logue, in his pastoral letter, added to the condemnation with thinly veiled references to the "enemies of the Church". The official attitude of the Catholic hierarchy in those days was that any public criticism of the church, even where it had some justification, was imprudent and a cause of scandal to the faithful. Monsignor Michael O'Riordan, rector of the Irish College in Rome, composed a 500-page 'reply' to Plunkett which was published in 1905.[14]

It was generally accepted that Plunkett had been wrong. Only a small minority held the view that his error was tactical rather than doctrinal. Among them were a number of eminent churchmen who (in public) tactfully held their peace. Despite Plunkett's naive wish that all blame would accrue solely to him, the episode inevitably damaged the co-operative movement. Some prominent churchmen stood stoutly behind the national movement but there were many instances of enthusiastic curates restricting their co-operative activities by order of their immediate superiors. The 'atheistic' label, first associated with the early British co-operators, was again in evidence. Added to this were sly suggestions of political discrimination and religious sectarianism, which were particularly harmful at parish level where invariably the most prominent, active and best educated co-operators were Unionist and Protestant. There was a double-edged effect, for, in that climate of suspicion and rumour, Catholic farmers were less inclined to join "Protestant dominated" co-operatives, and co-operative officers who were Protestants tended to be inhibited in the exercise of their leadership.

Plunkett and the Department faced a similar problem when appointments and promotions were being made. Plunkett feared that his own 'promotion' to the peerage by King Edward VII in 1903 would damage him in the Nationalist and 'neo-Celtic' mind but, on the contrary, he was the recipient of congratulations and good wishes.[15]

Some felt, however, that Plunkett was less than fair when it came to appointments in his own Department. There was indeed a preponderance of non-Catholics in certain branches. However, many of these were established civil servants who had been transferred to the Department on its foundation; Plunkett had no part in their appointment. His policy was to get the best men, regardless of political or sectarian considerations. Experts were not plentiful in Ireland so Plunkett recruited many of them from Britain and further afield.[16] The calibre and qualifications of his senior appointees left little room for objection but the fact that many of them were

---

14 Rev M. O'Riordan, *Catholicity and Progress in Ireland* (London: Kegan Paul, Trench, Trubner & Co. Ltd., 1905).

15 For an account of the serio-comic incidents associated with the conferring of the KCVO, see Digby, op. cit., pp.99-100. The visit of the King was on the whole very favourably received in Nationalist circles. The contrast in public attitudes to private morality are also very interesting: the revulsion at Parnell's involvement with Mrs O'Shea was still remembered, but King Edward's blatant associations with Miss Lily Langtry and other notable ladies were looked upon indulgently as endearing evidence of forgiveable human weakness in one of such high station.

16 The post of head of the agricultural branch was first offered to a Canadian who declined. It was subsequently accepted by a Scot, Professor J.R. Campbell.

Scots and English made it difficult for them to identify with the common people.[17] Whatever the differences on other matters, the Catholic clergy defended Plunkett and outspokenly voiced their belief in his absolute integrity.[18]

Trouble was looming ahead for both the Department and the co-operative movement. In 1904 the IAOS had revised its rules in order to turn over control of the organisation to the member societies, of which there were now nearly 900 compared to sixty-three at the time the Society was founded in 1894. The new committee allowed for a president and vice-president with four representatives from each of the four provinces, four subscribers' representatives, four co-opted members and two represen-tatives from the Department of Agriculture and Technical Instruction. In addition to affiliation fees, which amounted to a mere £600 a year, societies were asked to contribute a special capitation contribution of 6d per member as well as ensuring that the affiliation fees were paid in full and on time. Affiliation fees for most societies were to be calculated at the rate of ten shillings for every £1,000 of trade. Yet the response was not great and the IAOS had to report in 1906 that the organisation was still "mainly dependent upon the Department of Agriculture for its income." A special Departmental grant for the organisation and supervision of credit societies, livestock insurance societies and home industries societies, came to an end in February 1906 and there was great concern as to where funds should be raised. Nugent Talbot Everard, newly appointed President of the IAOS, urged the movement to stand on its own feet:

> It is doubtful whether it would be practicable for any State Department to provide sufficient funds to maintain an effective central body for Co-operative organisation. One way only seems possible. There must be built up within the Movement trade federations for every class of society which by their operation will make the business of the individual society more profitable . . . a substantial proportion of the profits of which would be available for the upkeep of the central organising body.

In the Council of Agriculture there was some animosity between co-operators and anti-co-operators, and in May 1906 a resolution to continue financial support to the IAOS was strongly contested, but was carried. A scheme was agreed between the Department and the IAOS whereby the former would subsidise the general work of the Society for the year ending February 1907 to an extent not exceeding £3,700; the IAOS would have to fund the balance necessary to carry out the agreed

---

17 See Rev E. Cahill, *The Framework of a Christian State* (Dublin: Gill & Son, 1940), p.179.

18 Giving evidence before the Committee of Inquiry in 1906, Dr Kelly, Bishop of Ross, stated that the only consideration in appointments was to get the best possible personnel. He himself was party to a number of these appointments including those of a Scottish Presbyterian to train nuns in domestic economy and a Scotsman, Mr Duncan, to be manager of the Department farm at Clonakilty. Even Dr Clancy, Bishop of Elphin (who had a poor opinion of Plunkett's co-operative creameries), was satisfied that "the appoint-ments made of officials from England and Scotland were of the most satisfactory kind."

programme of work. Nevertheless, the position with regard to internal support deteriorated. Of a total income of some £4,100 in 1906, only £425 came from affiliation fees.[19]

The Liberal Party swept back to power with a landslide victory in the 1906 general election. Plunkett saw that his position as a junior minister (difficult because he had no seat in Parliament) would become untenable now that his party was out of office. He expected to be immediately replaced, but unexpectedly the Liberal government decided to retain him. At home and in Britain there were calls for his dismissal or resignation. In the House of Commons there were Liberal/Labour demands that "this man should be weeded out", and at home the new Chief Secretary, Bryce, was forced to set up an official inquiry into the affairs of the Department.[20] Anticipating criticism of the Department's help to co-operative societies, the IAOS urged all societies to pass formal resolutions expressing their opinion on the value of the work of the IAOS and the propriety of the Department giving assistance.

For once, the co-operative societies did not disappoint their parent organisation. Their response was an immediate avalanche of more than 100 strongly worded resolutions.[21] The inquiry also elicited a stream of favourable testimony from former Chief Secretaries, members of the staff, public representatives, bishops, businessmen and many others. The report of the inquiry vindicated Plunkett. Complaints against the Department had broken down for lack of evidence and the report was approving, even laudatory. One important finding for the co-operators was that

> There does not . . . appear to be any provision in the Act which precludes the Department from contributing out of its endowment to the funds of the Irish Agricultural Organisation Society. The question is entirely one of policy and seems to be particularly one on which the opinion of the Council of Agriculture should carry determining weight.

The report was not published until 1908 and, although the Council of Agriculture, noting the progress of the inquiry, had reaffirmed its decision to support the IAOS, the conditions for obtaining the Department's subsidy were becoming more onerous.

19 Department grants totalled £3,416 (some in respect of 1905) and there was an end-of year deficit of £122. A Department allocation of £10,000 was made in 1904 to be used as loan capital for co-operative credit societies (agricultural banks). The 1906 grant of £3,700 was the first comprehensive grant towards the running of the IAOS *in toto*.

20 Known subsequently as the Digby Inquiry, from the man whom Plunkett described as a "formal, stiff, honest official, Home Office, retired". On St Patrick's Day 1906, Plunkett made a brief entry in his diary: "St Paddy. And I was the only official snake, which St Paddy did not abolish from my office."

21 A number of these resolutions are included in an appendix to the IAOS Annual Report 1906. One of the most moving tributes was that of Townawilly Agricultural Bank, a small credit society in the Bluestack Mountains of Donegal: ". . . when our little Bank started a few years ago there were a number of us helplessly and hopelessly in the clutches of the gombeen man. Now he has not one of us, *agus go raibh se go deo mar sin. Ta suibhneas, sean agus solas againn o fuair muid amach as na cruba neamh-throcaireacha.*"

On 20 March 1907, the IAOS was confronted by a statement from the Department setting forth conditions of a joint scheme of work for 1907-08. (The conditions were very restrictive and Anderson regarded Gill, who was subject to the pressure of merchant interests in the Nationalist Party, as the villain of the piece.) The IAOS was required to confine its work to organisation and auditing only. Its organisers were not to give technical advice except with Departmental approval. Salary scales and the expenses and allowances of IAOS officials would be subject to the approval and scrutiny of the Department's representatives, who should also be afforded "every facility for examining the accounts of the IAOS as well as the reports, diaries and expenses sheets of the organisers." One provision was intended to give the Department a complete stranglehold on whole workings of the IAOS:

> The organisation of Co-operative Societies shall not be proceeded with except with the approval of one of the Department's representatives on the Executive Committee. One member of the Executive Committee of the IAOS together with one of the Department's representatives on that Committee shall constitute a Sub-Committee, which shall meet weekly or as often as necessary in order that it may inquire into and control the work of organisation carried on by the IAOS and the expenditure of its funds . . . The Sub-Committee shall be constituted if the Department's representative is present, but not otherwise. The attendance of a representative of the IAOS shall not be essential at the Sub-Committee meetings.

The Society had little option but to accept the conditions,[22] but, as Anderson wrote later, the arrangement almost killed the spirit of co-operative enthusiasm amongst the IAOS staff:

> I found it hard to control the frayed tempers of my small staff. The monthly expenses and diaries of the organisers, my own included, were subjected to rigorous examination and criticism, so that much of our time was taken up by explanations as to why a telegram rather than a letter was sent or why an organiser hired a car when there was a railway (but no suitable train!). The whole . . . staff flared up when it was discovered that an official at £1,000 a year salary and first class expenses had dogged the itinerary of one of our most trustworthy and zealous organisers whose humble pay was £250.

Attacks on Plunkett's position were renewed in the House; John Dillon was particularly aggressive.[23] Plunkett consulted with Augustine Birrell, who had replaced Bryce as Chief Secretary, and tendered his resignation on

22 The arrangement also necessitated the IAOS severing its direct connection with the co-operative weekly newspaper, *The Irish Homestead*. The paper had been very outspoken and the Society thought it desirable to free it from any, even indirect, support from government funds.
23 During a three-hour discussion in Parliament on Plunkett's position, 24 April 1907.

20 April 1907. Shortly afterwards he handed over the office to his successor, Thomas Wallace Russell.

Plunkett's departure, though long foreseen, was nevertheless an occasion of great sorrow. The public realised that a great man had been hounded. Newspapers reviewed his achievements and voiced their regret. Many who had clamoured for his resignation were now extravagant in their praise. Several politicians had a shrewd suspicion that they had been tricked — that Plunkett had lingered to provoke their wildest outbursts and had then timed his resignation to cause their maximum embarrassment. At the IAOS the sentiment was different but even more strongly felt. They welcomed Plunkett back to resume the presidency with a reception which he himself described as "worth a whole herd of fatted calves". He deplored the fact that expressions of regret and the flood of sympathetic letters were almost entirely directed at the person of Horace Plunkett, with little thought for the future of his cherished Department or his co-operative movement. He had a few cynical words of consolation from young Winston Churchill: "Popularity is a good thing to despise — when you have got it."

Plunkett's fears for the future were well-founded. Russell,[24] his successor, was an able politician but had come to hate the co-operative movement. He saw the IAOS as a conspiracy of conniving landlords, gentry, clergy and industrialists seeking to thwart the honest political resolution which would be their undoing. Led by Plunkett, they were using the country people for their own ends in an effort to preserve something of the old order. Whether or not Russell believed all this (and there are some who suspect that for all his political cunning he was basically naive), he became the willing instrument of the latent gombeenism which exerted its hidden influence in all political parties.

Early in December 1907 the IAOS was curtly informed that the subsidy from the Department would be £3,000 for 1908, £2,000 for 1909 and £1,000 for 1910, after which the Department's support would cease entirely. The Society's reaction was one of anxiety mixed with relief. Father Tom Finlay said that the withdrawal of state subsidy would make the Society more self-reliant. At the annual general meeting on 20 December, at which he handed over the presidency to Plunkett, Colonel Nugent T. Everard noted the unfortunate results of subsidy: a decline in support from the co-ops and from private sources, Departmental red tape, and increasing opposition from traders, who felt that public money should not be used to further the interests of farmers. He felt that the IAOS was facing a crisis but they should retain their independence. They had little alternative but to accept the subsidy for the remaining period — but when it was gone, good riddance!

24 Thomas Wallace Russell, the grandson of an evicted Scottish crofter, was born at Cupar, Fife, in 1841. He came as a boy to Donaghmore, County Tyrone, where he worked as a draper's assistant before going to Dublin. He was elected to Parliament as a Unionist and was appointed Parliamentary Secretary to the Local Government Board in 1895. He had a rabid hatred of landlordism and turned Liberal in 1900. Later he became a Home Ruler. Tim Healy describes him: "devoid of the geniality and humour of his race, he sported a bilious face and splenetic manners."

The independence came even quicker than anticipated. All the co-operators, who in Plunkett's time had been nominated by the Department to the Council of Agriculture, were summarily removed and replaced by nominees more amenable to Russell's way of thinking.[25] Hostility towards the IAOS grew and in the autumn of 1907 Russell seized an opportunity to withdraw all financial aid. This was the famous incident of the Rolleston Letter.

At the annual general meeting at which he was so enthusiastically welcomed back to resume the presidency of the IAOS, Plunkett made a wide-ranging, constructive speech, clearly defining the role of the IAOS and its relationships with the farmers of Ireland, the trading interests and the Department of Agriculture. The co-operators were unanimous in recommending that it be published and circulated to all co-operative societies. The Rev E.F. Campbell, who made the formal proposal, felt that it would do a great deal to clarify some issues which had been misrepresented, and also to "stir up the old spirit which they wanted to see stirred up amongst them again." On the following morning Plunkett was delighted to find that *The Irish Times* had published his speech in full, thus providing an instant print for immediate distribution. He asked his friend and former Departmental employee, the poet T.W. Rolleston, to send copies of the paper to some American friends. Rolleston did so immediately.

The trouble arose just one month later when the *Freeman's Journal* (20 January 1908) published a letter from John Redmond, enclosing the covering letter which Rolleston had sent to a prominent Irish-American businessman in St Louis, Missouri:

> Hollywood,
> Glenealy,
> Co Wicklow
> December 21, 1907

> Dear Mr——————
> Sir Horace Plunkett has asked me to send you a copy of the *Irish Times* containing a full report of his speech delivered yesterday on resuming the Presidency of the Irish Co-operative Organisation, and a leading article on same. You will see that this speech is a very important event, and means an attempt to organise the Irish Farmers to shake off the grip of the small country publican and gombeen man, who has hitherto controlled the Parliamentary representation of the country, and has used it, without scruple, to damage and weaken the movement for agricultural co-operation in which the only hope of Ireland ever attaining a sound economic position lies. I know that you have been

25 The co-operators had long been concerned about the type of candidates elected to county councils who might eventually find their way onto the Council of Agriculture. In 1907 A.J. Crichton of Sligo, asking that all candidates for county council elections should be requested to state their support or otherwise for the co-operative movement, remarked that there were men on the Council of Agriculture who "hadn't enough land to sod a lark".

interested in Sir Horace Plunkett's views, and in his work. He is anxious that his friends in America should not be misled by the misrepresentations which are sure to be directed against the policy inaugurated yesterday. No sort of attack on Home Rule or upon Home Rulers as such is dreamt of. It is only insisted that Irish farmers will not choose people who will use their power, as Dillon and the rest of the Parliamentarians have been doing, to crush the farmer's movement for the better organisation of his business. That organisation will take him out of the hands of the small country trader and relieve him from [sic] an intolerable tyranny. Every effort had been made to bring about reform without a clash with the parliamentary party but in vain.

The farmer must now choose between having representatives who will represent him, or who will, as now, represent nothing but the village trader. The greatest economic interest in Ireland, that of the land, cannot be longer prevented from asserting itself and stepping into its true position and influence.

I trust you and all your friends in St Louis of whom I entertain so many pleasant recollections from the World Fair period are well and flourishing.

Very truly yours,
T.W. Rolleston

Redmond claimed that Rolleston's letter was evidence of a conspiracy against the Irish Party, Plunkett being the chief conspirator. The *Freeman's Journal* published the correspondence under the heading "Secret Campaign in America". It admitted that many of its previous accusations against Plunkett had of necessity been based upon surmise; but now "this precious epistle of Mr T.W. Rolleston, written at the suggestion of Sir Horace Plunkett, furnishes direct proof that had hitherto been skilfully concealed."

The statesman-like Plunkett, balancing on a knife-edge of diplomacy to reconcile the IAOS and the Department, was appalled. He was well aware that to win American support for your cause, you had to state it bluntly, but he himself could never do this. He saw too many shades of grey and could not bear to bend the truth. Rolleston's undoing was his indiscretion in giving the facts in writing — so successfully that his letter was published in the American press. Plunkett denied all knowledge of the letter. Rolleston asserted: ". . . the responsibility for the St Lous letter is mine and mine alone. Sir Horace Plunkett never saw it and knew nothing whatever of its contents till he read it in the Press."

This public exoneration of Plunkett did little to appease the politicians. *The Irish Homestead*, now an independent organ, was engaged in the controversy at an early stage and the sharp pen of its editor, AE, was not conciliatory. He nailed down the facts and then went on to make a virulent attack on Dillon whom he described as the likely driving force and spinning tail of the torpedo of which Redmond was the "rather blunt nose".

Mr Rolleston began his now famous letter ... by saying Sir Horace had asked him to forward a report of his speech. Then Mr Rolleston made some comments of his own with which we personally agree but for which Mr Rolleston, not the IAOS, not Sir Horace is responsible ... Irish farmers are well aware the Mr Dillon has been for many years the deadliest enemy to agricultural co-operation in Ireland. He has never failed to avail himself of any chance which offered to oppose the work of the IAOS. He has denounced it in the country, in the Press and in Parliament. His anger has increased as he found his denunciations had not the slightest effect, and that sixty or seventy societies had sprung up in his own County of Mayo. We do not deny that Mr Dillon has rendered service to Ireland but he is one of those jealous and ungenerous friends who say to farmers: "If you take benefits from me, you must refuse them from those who are not my friends." He wants those he helps to be the enemies of his enemies, to espouse all his quarrels, to adopt all his narrow ideas and prejudices and to injure their own fortunes by refusing all benefits he is not the responsible agent for.

After a few more bouts of polemics, all hopes of reconciliation had disappeared. Despite all disclaimers, T.W. Russell kept referring to the letter as having been sent to the United States "by order of Sir Horace Plunkett". The work of the Department would be seriously endangered if the impression gained ground throughout the country that Departmental funds were being employed for "the partisan purposes of clearing Dillon and the Parliamentarians out."[26] He urged the Agricultural Board to give serious consideration to the matter and said that there were not many options open: Rolleston's communication was a letter opening a campaign against the national representatives of the country and the Board was subsidising an organisation whose name was used in that relationship. The only way to solve the difficulty was "to cut off the supplies and let these gentlemen proceed on their crusade if they wish but they must do it at their own risk."

The Council of Agriculture rescinded its previous resolutions and voted to withhold all financial aid to the IAOS after 1908. Father Finlay said that its action demonstrated the tyranny of a so-called democratic majority. Now the fight was really on and the co-operators were aroused to a new determination. The IAOS annual report for 1908 reported that the Department's action had raised the movement to an entirely new plane:

> Its friends rallied in its support. The movement is now progressing as it has not done for many years. The progress is too recent to express itself as yet in a greatly augmented business turnover. But careful readers of this report ... will be gratified with the signs of fresh strength and vigour ... while 1907 showed progress, 1908 marks a real revival.

26 T.W. Russell, Letter to the Editor, *Freeman's Journal*, 22 May 1908.

On 15 May 1908, Plunkett sent a lengthy circular letter to each co-operative society appealing for funds, and in his presidential address in November hammered home the necessity to make Irish co-operation a truly self-help movement. He insisted, however, that help should be given in the right spirit:

> I want you to regard the IAOS and the Department as two great Irish agencies of progress, neither of which can realise its full opportunity for good unless their attitude towards each other be helpful . . . At the time I expressed my opinion publicly upon the circumstance which gave rise to the decision and am quite prepared to let bygones be bygones. I am going to show you that in the interests of the country it is the duty of every supporter of the co-operative movement to adopt the same attitude.

This appeal was fairly successful: affiliation fees and special subscriptions from societies reached over £1,000 and a further £1,200 came from individual subscribers. Symbolising the new spirit of independence was the co-operators' gift to Plunkett of a large Georgian house, 84 Merrion Square, Dublin, to enable him to carry on his work.[27] The Plunkett House, as it was appropriately named, provided a new base for the IAOS and greatly enhanced the society's ability to render service to the movement.

However, this new spirit of determination was short-lived. The IAOS Annual Report for 1909 pointed out that, while dues and subscriptions from the societies had increased, many societies contributed very little, and others nothing at all. In 1910 the problem was eased by several large donations, but support was still short of what it should have been. There was a deficit of £416 for the financial year ending 31 December 1909. In 1910 this had risen to almost £1,500. Services had to be curtailed but overall a very good programme was implemented. From 1909 to 1913 the IAOS was dependent entirely on its own resources and was kept going only through the generosity of Plunkett and his friends.[28]

Despite the financial strictures, it was a period of considerable progress. The number of co-operatives grew from 881 in 1908 to 985 in 1913. The society's trade turnover increased from £2.2 million to £3.3 million. Unfortunately, there was no improvement in relations between the IAOS and the Department. Although Plunkett was generous in seeking reconciliation, Russell's attitude was implacable. Many of the Department's personnel became cynical towards the co-operative

27 The presentation was made on 22 November 1908. A brass plate in the entrance hall carries the inscription:

TO
HORACE PLUNKETT
This house was presented by his friends and fellow workers in recognition of his efforts for the well-being of his country, and as an aid to him in the further development of his work.

11 November 1908

28 In 1912, affiliation fees, societies' special subscriptions and fees earned by the audit department brought in approximately £3,000. Individual subscribers gave £2,300 and, in all, the deficit was only £120 on a £6,200 expenditure.

movement and traces of these attitudes were to persist for a long time.

For many years Plunkett had involved himself deeply with the problems of rural life in the United States and played a major role in formulating the policies adopted by President Theodore Roosevelt's Country Life Commission. He developed a great friendship with Roosevelt and they frequently conversed together in cowboy slang! As Roosevelt's tenure of office drew to a close in 1908, he decided to put his gratitude to Plunkett (already freely and generously acknowledged) in a more formal testament. This he did in a letter to the British Ambassador:

> . . . my interest did not reach the point of action until I began to follow what was being accomplished through the farmers' co-operative movement in Ireland. My old friend, Horace Plunkett . . . kept me informed of the Irish agricultural situation and of the movement for better living on the farms of Ireland. We Americans owe much to Ireland and to Plunkett in the work we have been trying to do in the United States, and before I leave the Presidency I want to acknowledge our debt and to send through you my thanks for the help we have had, and not only my thanks but the thanks of every man who knows what has been done and sees the need and sure results of this great movement to help the men and women who feed the nation and stand at the foundation of its greatness and its progress.

> Yours sincerely,
> Theodore Roosevelt

Plunkett felt justly aggrieved when the British authorities refused to publish the letter. He felt that at that decisive time it would have strengthened his position and power for good in Ireland.[29]

One of the notable achievements of this period was the establishment of the United Irishwomen (later known as the Irish Countrywomen's Association) in 1910. Plunkett had long been thinking of a women's organisation allied to the IAOS to further the third and most important of his trinity of ideals . . . 'Better Living'. There was a great need for an organisation of women to promote better housekeeping and cottage industries:

> Long ago we should, following the precedent of the Women's Co-operative Guild in Britain, have appealed to leading women within our movement to try and organise their sex for three purposes: firstly

29 In 1910 Plunkett recounted his experience of rural life in America in a book entitled *The Rural Life Problems of the United States* (New York: Macmillan, 1910). Pamphlets which he published about this period were *Noblesse Oblige* (1908) — a last invitation to the gentry to play their part in a new Ireland —, *Plain Talks to Irish Farmers* (1910) and *The Crisis in Irish Rural Progress* (1912). In July 1914 he published his famous appeal to the Ulster Carsonites, *A Better Way — an appeal to Ulster not to desert Ireland*. In a different vein he addressed the Royal Dublin Society on "Some Tendencies of Modern Medicine from a Lay Point of View", also published in pamphlet form.

to attend to women's business in the life of a community which no man, least of all an old bachelor like myself, can understand [laughter]; secondly, to see that the farmers attend better to the business of their organisation and make them as helpful to women and the household as they are to men on the farm; and thirdly, for Irish women to take up their rightful part in the building up of a rural civilisation in Ireland.[30]

Plunkett had frequently discussed the matter with Lady Fingall, with his cousin Emily Lawless, with the wives, sisters and daughters of prominent co-operators, and particularly with ladies in such useful organisations as the Women's National Health Association, the Irish Industries League and the Royal Irish Industries Association.

The major inspiration, however, came from the remarkable address entitled "The Building up of a Rural Civilisation", delivered by AE at the annual general meeting of the IAOS in December 1909. So profound was the impression made on the ladies attending, that they came out of the meeting to embark immediately on the organising work. Mrs Ellice Pilkington, sister of Sir Thomas Esmonde (member of the IAOS committee 1898-1906), was appointed first honorary organiser. Another Wexford woman, Mrs Harold Lett of Enniscorthy, formed the first branch at Bree[31] on 15 June 1910, and shortly afterwards was elected first President of the national organisation. The United Irishwomen was registered as a co-operative society and invited to hold its committee meetings in the Plunkett House. Shortly before Christmas 1910 Mrs Pilkington travelled to Dungloe, County Donegal, "heralded by a telegram from Fr Tom Finlay and carrying a passport in Irish from the President of the Gaelic League."[32] With the help of Patrick Gallagher of the Templecrone Co-operative, she organised a branch of the United Irishwomen in Dungloe with a membership of 200. Back in County Wexford, Mrs Pilkington organised four more branches at Davidstown, Oylegate, Glenbrien and Coolgreaney, before moving westward to form the first Munster branch at Kilkee, County Clare. The organisation of United Irishwomen was embarked on its "long and fruitful career of modest usefulness".

Financial relief came at last in 1913 when the Development Commission, which was already giving aid to comparable organisation societies in England and Scotland,[33] finally agreed to make an annual grant to the IAOS. This was generous — up to £4,000 per annum on the basis of £1

---

30 Presidential address to the annual general meeting, 29 November 1910.
31 This first guild at Bree was greatly helped by that remarkable co-operator, Frederick Johnson, officially known as Johnson Pasha, a Turkish-born Irishman living at Ballinapierse, Enniscorthy, and a founder member of Enniscorthy Co-operative Agricultural Society. Johnson was greatly interested in arts and crafts and was a skilled potter. He gave many lectures and demonstrations to the United Irishwomen and took a keen interest in their social and recreational activities — he was a very enthusiastic croquet player. Johnson Pasha was a member of the IAOS national committee from 1910 to 1915.
32 Douglas Hyde, later President of Ireland.
33 The English Agricultural Organisation Society (founded 1900) and the Scottish equivalent, SAOS (1905), were largely inspired by Plunkett and modelled on the IAOS.

from the Commission for every £1 subscribed by the co-operators themselves. The arrangement greatly relieved the financial problems but
perhaps even more important was the sympathetic interest shown by the
commissioners in the work of the IAOS. Vaughan Nash and A.D. Hall
were co-opted onto the national committee and a number of other
commissioners regularly attended IAOS meetings. The morale of the staff
improved immensely and Anderson noted, "a great peace seemed to fall
upon us".

The next seven years was a period of plenty, in which the co-operative
movement made its greatest impact. In a memorandum prepared for the
visit of the American Commission in 1913,[34] the IAOS expressed the view
that the hardest part of its work was done: ". . . rural Ireland is ready to be
completely organised. We believe that in less than 20 years even urban
Ireland will recognise how much it owed to this movement among the
farmers." The Irish co-operative movement was becoming the centre of
world-wide interest. Students from abroad were coming to study the
organisation and methods of the IAOS in the Plunkett House. The weekly
Irish Homestead was effectively preaching the doctrine of self-help,
pursuing, in AE's words, "the Golden Heresy of Truth". His writings and
practical advice on both technical and organisational matters proved
immensely useful to readers at home and abroad.

Regrettably, there was little improvement in relations between the
Department of Agriculture and the IAOS. Few on either side had
Plunkett's fine appreciation of the necessary complementarity of self-help
and state aid. Many of his colleagues believed that state aid was absolutely
subversive of the co-operative ideal and their theories were being proved
right. Everyone realised that little would be achieved while T.W. Russell
remained as Departmental Secretary,[35] but the comment of an American
visitor[36] in 1915 indicated that the problem was by no means peculiar to
Ireland:

> . . . for in America as well as in Ireland there is a lamentable failure of
> many state agricultural departments in working hand in hand with
> agricultural organisations of a co-operative nature; and we have the
> same milk-and-water brand of 'non-controversial' co-operation in
> contemplation of which farmers shed tears and traders rejoice . . . I
> have been told that the Department is in favour of cow testing and
> lime-burning associations, both harmless from the trader's stand
> point, and quite admirable in their way. But this idea savours too much
> of methods in certain parts of America, which have aimed to increase
> production but which until recently have neglected marketing and dis-
> tribution in a lamentable fashion. Says Carl S. Vrooman, Assistant
> Secretary of the United States Department of Agriculture, in this

34 American Commission on Agricultural Co-operation and Rural Credit in Europe.
35 Plunkett quipped: "I doubt whether under Mr Russell even *lime* will become a burning
question."
36 Charles A. Lyman, "An American Estimate of the IAOS", in *Better Business*, January
1916.

connection: 'So long as it was an army worm or a case of hog cholera that was hampering the farmers' progress, the colleges and the Department of Agriculture would attack the case with a tremendous flourish and beating of tom-toms. But when the pest happened to take the form of a railway, of a grain elevator, or a high rate of interest, then there seems to be an unwritten law that the buck and gag should be applied to all the economic experts in whose power it was to help the farmer fight the fight.'

However, the same observer was impressed by the work of the IAOS and its success in going it alone.

In the few short months I have been in Ireland I have been tremendously impressed with the degree of exactness which the IAOS has attained in its agricultural co-operative principles. Other countries have a greater measure of agricultural prosperity no doubt, for in many of them the necessity of the application of the co-operative principle is accepted by all classes, and by the officials of the Government. For historical reasons the Irish farmer has been slower to respond, considering the aid and counsel he has received from the IAOS, than have the Danish and Finnish farmers. In these other countries the growth of political representation has kept pace with the organisation of co-operative societies. But in the single minded, steadfast, and scientific way that the IAOS has steadily taught co-operation in the face of the poverty and lack of education of the farming class, in spite of the opposition of profiteers, gombeen men, traders, and politicians controlled by trading interests, this organisation body, in my estimation, stands without a peer.

The World War was a period of increasing prosperity for the Irish farmer, happily accompanied by great progress in agricultural co-operation. Many new societies were formed and the trade turnover of co-operatives rose from £3½ million in 1914 to over £14½ million in 1920, a figure not to be equalled until 1944. Even the expanded staff of the Society was still inadequate to deal with the increased activity. The methodical Anderson, working incessantly to perfect the business methods of the co-operators, was worried that much of the new development was "jerry built". Nevertheless the IAOS Annual Report for 1919 expressed satisfaction with the progress made: "Co-operation is now a reality to many to whom it had hitherto meant little more than a trade term." There had been a remarkable increase in affiliation fees and subscriptions,[37] which brought the movement closer to the realisation of the early pioneers' wish that the IAOS would become an independent, self-supporting society.

Even as early as 1913, Father Tom Finlay, a man never given to undue

---

37 Affiliation fees and subscriptions for 1920 totalled almost £9,000, approximately two-thirds of the total IAOS income for the year. The audit department had a revenue of £6,900 and was practically self-supporting.

optimism, was hopefully forecasting the achievement of the ideal of a co-operative commonwealth:

> We are warranted in anticipating that our movement will spread over a larger area and that the volume of its business will increase at a more rapid rate than it has done in the years of adversity . . .
>
> We might even venture on the hope that it will so largely permeate the economic life of the nation that we may see realised amongst us that ideal which is described as 'the co-operative commonwealth'.

Father Finlay's[38] address at the annual general meeting on 10 December 1913 emphasised once more the basic philosophy of the Irish co-operative movement:[39]

> The Co-operative Community . . . is one in which groups of humble men combine their efforts, and to some extent their resources, in order to secure for themselves those advantages in industry which the masters of capital derive from the organisation of labour, from the use of costly machinery, and from the economies of business when done on a large scale. With this difference, however, that the gains from the better methods are shared equitably amongst all who are engaged in the industry; they are not reserved for an individual who controls it, or for a body of shareholders who are not actively involved in its operation.

There were three important aspects in which the movement differed essentially from either capitalism or socialism:

1. *A wholly voluntary movement:*
   "It is not forced upon anyone by State Authority; it is not imposed by the vote of any majority . . . Our combination is free — free in each of its members, free in each of the societies established within the systems."

2. *Not hostile to any class:*
   "We make no war upon capital or capitalist. We aim at being capitalists ourselves, at amassing for the group which works co-operatively the capital necessary to the operations carried on for the common benefit. But with us *the individual and the society alike obtain capital by work not by plunder.* In doing so we concede the same right to everyone who chooses to enter the field of industry in which we are occupied. We do not bar competition, we encounter it . . . The idea of a war of classes is wholly alien to our

---

38 He was standing in for Plunkett who was in hospital in Battle Creek, Michigan.
39 For a later discussion, see Rev J. Newman, "Vocational Organisation and the Co-operative Movement", *Christus Rex* magazine, July 1958.

movement, which, of its nature, makes for social and economic peace."[40]

3. *The diffusion of property:*

    "Our co-operative combination, with its common fund of capital, its common marketing agencies and whatever else is held for the common service, has for its ultimate object *to enhance the wealth and increase the property of the individual*; by no means to use the individual to create property for community. Briefly: with us community of effort is directed to give property to the individual; with the socialist the effort of the individual would be directed to create property for the community."

---

40 Father Finlay's favourite dictum was: "A man cannot fight with himself. This is a feat which even an Irishman cannot encompass!"

Chapter Ten

After Plunkett

Horace Plunkett died at Weybridge, Surrey, in 1932, in a house which he had purchased in 1923. Whilst convalescing in a friend's home after a serious operation, he had accidentally come across the house which was structurally a smaller replica of his magnificent home at Kilteragh so savagely bombed and burned on successive nights in January of that year.[1] Plunkett had retired to England broken in body and spirit, his experiences in Ireland having followed the pattern of treatment accorded to many Irish patriots, as sadly expressed by Plunkett's cousin, the poet Emily Lawless, in the words of that tragic mother, Ireland:

> She said, "They gave me of their best
> They lived and gave their lives for me
> I tossed them to the howling waste
> And flung them to the raging sea."

Plunkett's dismay at the destruction wreaked on his co-operative movement by the burning of creameries by British forces and the appalling consequences of an economic slump was exacerbated by the Civil War and the terrible deaths of men he had come to know and admire. The shooting of Michael Collins and the execution of Erskine Childers caused him particular grief.

His physical condition had deteriorated to a point where he no longer hoped to be "even remotely healthy" ever again. He now looked merely for effective medication that might keep him alert enough to prolong his work. Up to a few months before his death, he was working incessantly in Ireland and abroad to advance the cause of co-operation and community development. He resigned his seat in the Senate but retained the presidency of the IAOS in order to help make it more solvent and efficient. He hired and

1   A party of armed men broke into the house in the early hours of 30 January and placed two landmines which badly damaged the house but did not destroy it. Raiders returned the following night and set fire to the house, burning it to a shell. The identity and motives of the culprits have never been discovered. It has been claimed that a general order had been issued by the Republicans for the burning of senators' houses. Plunkett had been nominated a senator by President Cosgrave in December 1922.

fired ruthlessly until he got the right men. He sought to establish the best possible relations with the new Free State government, and got on well with the young Minister of Agriculture, Patrick Hogan. In addition, Plunkett travelled extensively to learn about co-operative developments in the USA, South Africa, India, and to glean first-hand information in the co-operatively more advanced nations of Europe — Belgium, Holland and the Scandinavian countries. He was particularly concerned about the future of the movement in Northern Ireland, and in England worked incessantly to rebuild the agricultural co-operatives which had suffered when the Agricultural Organisation Society failed in 1924. He managed an odd visit to the theatre[2] and entertained a great deal. The Kilteragh visitor's book, salvaged after the bomb attack, continued to be inscribed with famous names. Plunkett was particularly keen to bring politicians together socially and gently to advance his own concepts of co-operation and good government. The Horace Plunkett Foundation, established as a trust for rural social development,[3] and endowed by Plunkett to the tune of £20,000, was now housed in London. Plunkett regularly consulted with the trustees to ensure that it worked effectively, frequently subscribing extra monies to finance small additions to projects, so as not to upset the overall budget.

Plunkett did all this while suffering considerable physical pain. For five years or more he was on a dosage of morphine which for a less strong character could only lead to addiction. The drug gave him horrible night-mares but he continued heroically balancing the dosage with the level of tolerable pain, increasing it only when not to do so would have meant giving up work altogether. He was not afraid to die, but with the same rest-less inquiring mind that characterised Robert Owen, he questioned the mysteries of life, death and the deity. Like Owen, he could find no comfort in formal religion but would have liked to be able to do so. Were it not for the remote possibility of being spared to do a little more work, he would gladly have chosen euthanasia;[4] his great fear was that he might get a stroke and not be able to die. His biographer Margaret Digby offers this appraisal: "It was no dread of the hereafter but sense of the unfulfilled present which haunted him, since for him, as for Kant, the temporal seemed insufficient to the demands of his nature."

He was given his wish of a full life of usefulness. On 17 March he noted sadly in his diary: "St Paddy. No one sent me a shamrock; nor did I see one on the streets. *Sic transit*." He spent the day at the Plunkett Foundation in Doughty Street seeing callers from the Women's Institutes, from India and from the Friends' relief service in the Welsh coalfields. His biographer adds the last simple report: "He died nine days later on March 26 1932, conscious and courteous to the last."

2 A London production of O'Casey's *The Plough and the Stars* brought back Easter Week 1916 too vividly for enjoyment.
3 On 10 January 1919.
4 "It is my misfortune that I began my life in the gloom of the Low Church certainty of eternal torture for the vast majority of the human race and never quite rose above a preference for extinction."

Plunkett had achieved world-wide fame. Dr W.G.S. Adams[5] recalls that during his visits to a number of universities in China in 1931, he was frequently approached by students eager to make the acquaintance of an intimate friend of a great man and to hear something more of Plunkett's rural philosophy. In Ireland, however, Plunkett was almost forgotten and had been hardly in the news since the days of the ill-fated Irish Convention. News of his death came as a brief, sad recall in an Ireland busily preparing to stage an international Eucharistic Congress. It brought a stab of remembrance to those co-operators who knew him. For others the passing of the years had only further blurred their confused placing of the different, famous Plunketts. Was this the Lord Plunkett — or the venerable Count Plunkett, first Sinn Féin MP for Roscommon — or the poet Joseph Mary Plunkett — but, no, wasn't he executed in 1916? And wasn't there something some years back about a Plunkett reported dead but not dead?[6]

*   *   *

The general public is always led to rank the importance of movements and events in proportion to the extent of publicity given to them by the mass media: giving people the kind of information and comment that they like to hear is sometimes a corrective if not always a beneficial influence on editorial policy. The history of the co-operative movement in the British Isles from the days of the Rochdale Pioneers is one in which only the most momentous co-operative happenings could evoke even a mention in the newspapers. Urban business interests always contrived to suppress any helpful publicity for the co-operators and to ensure that even the most exciting co-operative news, if reported at all, should be recounted in the dullest way possible. In the case of co-operative activities, this selectivity was exercised to a degree far in excess of that justified by the accepted dictum that the virtuous and the commonplace are less exciting news than the vicious and the unusual. By consistent downplaying, the co-operative movement was thus relegated in the public mind — a useful institution but of minor importance.

In Ireland, after a campaign of virulent attack which proved counter-productive, the commercial press settled down to the much more subtle expedient of damning the movement with faint praise. Within a decade it

5 Dr Adams first met Plunkett as a Department of Agriculture employee in 1905 and remained a life-long friend. With Sir A. Daniel Hall and Dermod O'Brien, he was one of the original trustees of the Horace Plunkett Foundation. In his introduction to Miss Digby's biography, Adams gives a concise but masterly evaluation of Plunkett's life and work.

6 In July 1919 Plunkett, with the help of a wealthy supporter, Dr James Ashe, founded the Irish Dominion Party in the hope of mustering moderates North and South to achieve Home Rule and dominion status and so retain national territorial unity. The proposal was denounced in turn by Carson and de Valera and the new political party was short-lived. Plunkett, seriously ill, retired in late December 1919 to Battle Creek Sanatorium, Michigan, refusing to see the horde of newspaper reporters who beset him in New York. One reporter, apparently in retaliation for an ungranted interview, reported Plunkett dead. Obituary notices appeared in American, British and Irish papers, causing considerable distress to Plunkett's friends. Plunkett himself was greatly amused, recalling the similar experience of Mark Twain.

was relatively unheard of, and if some of its more eminent leaders like Plunkett occasionally made the headlines, it was invariably in connection with their political activities or the affairs of state institutions like the Department of Agriculture.

By the early nineteen thirties, the co-operators, bereft of their own publicity organ *The Irish Homestead* (at best of limited circulation), were a forgotten band as far as the 'educated' newspaper reading public was concerned. By this time, however, they could hardly quibble about the lack of publicity, for nothing was happening in the movement. The Report of the Drew Commission,[7] published in 1924, had pinpointed many of its weaknesses: gross undercapitalisation and minimal share capital, which left the majority of its members with no real stake in the business; lack of co-operative loyalty and of 'binding rules' to effect it; lax business methods, account-keeping and stocktaking; and lack of education and training. It was felt that the IAOS had not done "all that it might and should have done to check slipshod work and discourage unsound practices, especially in matters of finance."[8] The fact that the membership of the IAOS committee had undergone little change for many years was criticised too. Eleven of the twenty-six members[9] had been continuously on the committee from 1912 to 1922 and others gave the impression of having been around for a very long time. The gradual infiltration of new blood was recommended.

Sir Henry Grattan-Bellew

7   The Commission on Agriculture, initiated by the Minister for Agriculture, Patrick Hogan, in November 1922, commonly known as the Drew Commission after its chairman, James P. Drew, Professor of Agriculture at University College, Dublin.
8   See Daniel Hoctor, *The Department's Story: A History of the Department of Agriculture* (Dublin: Institute of Public Administration, 1971), p.154.
    See also J.G. Knapp, *An Appraisement of Agricultural Co-operation in Ireland* (Dublin: Stationery Office, 1964), Pr. 7467, pp.26-29.
9   Plunkett, Finlay, Dean Barry (Sugarstown), N.T. Everard, Harold Barbour, T.W.W. Bennett, P.P. Maloney, A.J. Crichton, Monteagle, Dermod O'Brien and Rev T. Phelan. Robert Barton, who first came on the committee in 1910, had missed only one year's service (1917-18) in twelve years. Sir Henry Grattan Bellew was an old-timer who had made a comeback from 1914. Other prominent figures on the 1922 committee included Paddy (the Cope) Gallagher, Canon J.R. Willis, Alex Haslett, Lionel Smith-Gordon and Rev Michael O'Flanagan.

Continued government support did little to lift the movement out of the doldrums.[10] Harry Norman, littérateur, theosophist, and former music critic, and Charlie Riddell worked diligently as joint secretaries of the IAOS but the organisation missed the bulldozing energy of R. A. Anderson, now deeply immersed in rescuing the Irish Agricultural Wholesale Society. There were hopes of a great revival when Henry Kennedy was appointed secretary in July 1926.[11] The movement took on new life and hope. The IAOS was reorganised; its amended rules provided for a committee of fourteen, including president and vice-president, with ten of the twelve members elected by district, compared to the former committee of twenty-four, largely elected by province. This gave control of the IAOS more directly to the societies which were supporting it.

As a hard-headed economist and technologist, Kennedy saw that the co-operative business was 80 per cent. creamery and that Ireland's real economic potential lay in her grasslands. Consequently he felt that a build-up of the dairy sector must be the basis for strengthening the whole movement. Kennedy had a willing ally in his brother-in-law, Patrick Hogan, the Minister for Agriculture. The reorganisation of the dairy industry through the acquisition of proprietary creameries and the establishment of the Diary Disposal Company in 1927 demonstrated Kennedy's ability to plan and effect improvements on a grand scale. Although the rationalisation effected through the Dairy Disposal Company represented an intervention by the state which should never have been necessary, it was a major achievement which truthfully can be said to have saved the co-operative movement from disaster, if not extinction. Kennedy also succeeded in getting the government favourably disposed towards the expansion of the creamery industry into areas like the midlands which were not served. A number of new co-operative creameries[12] were established between 1927 and 1929. These new ventures were financed largely by loans from the Agricultural Credit Corporation — a body whose foundation in September 1927 was largely influenced by Kennedy's forceful pleadings and his masterly analyses of the capital needs of Irish agriculture.

Quick on the heels of this heartening success, however, came the dismal failure of the Irish Associated Creameries.[13] Although the collapse of the scheme was by no means Kennedy's fault, it highlighted the difference between his approach and R.A. Anderson's. Anderson would go to endless

10 The government's grant, averaging £4,000 per annum from 1922, was raised to £10,000 for the year 1926-27 and fixed at £8,500 for each of the four subsequent years.
11 Anderson and Lionel Smith-Gordon interviewed candidates for the post on 9 July but Kennedy's appointment was decided by majority vote of the IAOS committee on 14 July. Henry Felix Norman was retained as consultant and Charles Coates Riddell was given the post of assistant secretary.
12 Central creameries established were Scarriff, Askeaton, Donaghmore, Rathscanlon (1927); Annagelliffe, North Cork, Clonmel and Newcastle, Roscrea, Midlands, South Leitrim (1928); Slaney Valley (1929) and West Clare (1930). Some eighteen independent auxiliary creameries were also established during these years, serving areas in Counties Carlow, Cavan, Clare, Cork, Kildare, Kilkenny, Laois, Leitrim, Longford, Mayo, Offaly and Wexford.
13 Irish Associated Creameries Ltd. was the federation designed for the marketing of Irish creamery butter (see pp.218-20).

trouble to explain every facet of a scheme, illustrating his story with simple and earthy examples. Kennedy was not a man to suffer fools gladly. He could sometimes be impatient with those who did not see the 'obvious' as clearly and as quickly as he did. His imposing figure and sometimes peremptory address (which fronted a shy personality) did not invite familiarity, yet he was essentially a jovial character. His steel-trap mind, jumping ahead to logical decisions on key issues and ignoring the minutiae, often led him to believe that he had won understanding and agreement from his listeners when in fact he had not.

In 1931 the Horace Plunkett Foundation published a comprehensive study entitled *Agricultural Co-operation in Ireland*. Plunkett, in a foreword, introduced it as a volume written by expert but independent and impartial observers of facts relating to agricultural co-operation in Ireland.[14] It is a document of absorbing interest, to both the student of co-operation and the general reader, because of its detailed reports on individual societies (some of which have long since disappeared) in each county. Particularly valuable is the critical appraisal of the condition of the movement in general and the IAOS in particular. Fears were expressed that the Society had lost much of its original idealism and dynamism and was tending to concentrate on the creameries "almost to the exclusion of all other existing and possible forms of co-operation."[15] The study asserted that the philosophy and direction of the IAOS were or vital importance:

> Irish co-operation, at least as a national movement, has not its destiny in its own hands ... Any change which destroyed the unity and centralised authority of the movement or anything which brought to an end the traditions of idealism and social service in which the IAOS was founded and for which in world opinion it has always stood would be a heavy blow to co-operation in Ireland and elsewhere.

The major external danger feared was that the new Co-operative Act then being mooted, carrying new conditions on grants, might radically alter the whole moral and legal basis of the IAOS, its policy and its practical working. Such fears were well-grounded: the IAOS became less financially independent and the government grant of £8,500 constituted more than two-thirds of the Society's total income.[16] More insidious were the dangers from within. There were suggestions of autocratic and even indifferent attitudes on the part of some members of the IAOS staff and committee. It was regretted that the ordinary co-operative member did not cherish his

14 Dr J.G. Knapp, in *An Appraisement of Agricultural Co-operation in Ireland*, attributes authorship to Margaret Digby and describes the volume as providing "a bench mark and a valuable corrective to the misunderstanding of the position of co-operatives some thirty years ago."

15 This criticism was pithily summarised: "... nothing smaller than a cow can get into the door of the IAOS."

16 There was considerable criticism of the Registrar's Office and its failure to collaborate closely with the IAOS. Its laxity in dealing with delinquent societies was creating entanglements which militated against positive co-operative development in many areas. See *Agricultural Co-operation in Ireland*, pp.400-03.

Society and that the annual general meetings were not "large, enthusiastic and turbulent assemblies of co-operative democracy" with hotly contested elections to its committee. The education of members was a major worry.

> Co-operators are born but they can also be made. Co-operative education can be divided in three stages — the education of the public in co-operative principles, the education of the members in co-operative conduct and the education of the officials in co-operative technique. Much more needs to be done in Ireland on all these lines . . . The schools can instill the co-operative as well as any other civic principle. The comparative failure of the clergy and the teachers to come forward as co-operative leaders has already been noted and contrasted with the experience of other countries . . . The training of co-operative members is a matter for the movement itself and has been amply provided for in all countries where the movement is strong. That the training of officials may, and perhaps in preference should, be the work of the movement is shown by the success of numerous co-operative schools and colleges. In several countries, however, co-operation as a subject has been admitted to the curricula of ordinary scholastic bodies, usually those under state control, and co-operative courses form a definite part of the work of universities and technical high schools. In Ireland such provision is already made for the technical training of creamery managers, but it includes no instruction in co-operative objects or methods . . . For the stores manager no training at all is available . . . The credit society secretary is equally shut off from any instruction except such as he receives from an organiser or auditor. To attempt to run a business movement without trained officials is to put too great a strain on personal talents and goodwill.

R.A. Anderson was unanimously elected president at the annual general meeting of 1933, ten months after Plunkett's death.[17] Although he was still a very active man, the younger members of the committee looked on him as an old-timer.[18] When he spoke at length of the spirit and idealism of the movement, he was shown the deference politely accorded to old warriors recounting the fight and fire of the past.

In the depth of a world depression, the new generation of co-operators could be forgiven for thinking that it had all been very simple in

17 Anderson had previously refused the presidency when in 1923 Plunkett, living in England, had proposed to relinquish the post and had named Anderson as the co-worker whom he would like to succeed him. Father Finlay had long since convinced his colleagues that any office higher than vice-president would be inappropriate for him. On Anderson's refusal to accept the presidency, Finlay, also in vain, sought to step down and have Anderson made vice-president.
18 Particularly following the deaths in subsequent years of many of the founder fathers of the movement: Monteagle, James Timoney, A.J. Crichton, Rev J.G. Digges in 1933; AE, Archdeacon Phelan, Thomas Grattan Esmonde, Frank Barbour in 1935, and the enforced absence of Father Finlay through illness for most of the time from 1935 until his death in 1940 at the age of ninety-two — an age span just exceeding that of 'old Mr Craig of Ralahine' who died in 1894, the year the IAOS was founded!

Anderson's day when one could tackle a gombeen-man, a rogue politician or a disloyal member with one's bare hands; now what was needed was not highflown idealism but the practical mechanics of relief.

In 1931 a new community development movement emerged. The name adopted for the movement was Muintir na Tire (People of the Country) and its acknowledged founder and first chairman was Rev John M. Hayes, a Catholic curate from Cashel. Its objective was "to organise the different elements of rural life in Ireland into one body for the common good ... to promote the true welfare of Ireland, spiritual, cultural and material, based on a wider and better knowledge and practices of Christian social principles." The movement was conceived as a nation-wide system of parish guilds with members from all creeds, classes and occupations; the committee of each guild would be elected on a vocational basis. However, Hayes was loth to formulate a constitution or a fixed set of rules for the movement; formal rigidities were the antithesis of his concept of 'neighbourliness'. He trusted that sensible and humane 'rules' would evolve as the movement progressed. The evolution was a slow one: the earliest activity mainly consisted of a number of rural weeks[19] on the pattern of the French *semaines rurales*, and it was not until spring 1937 that the first parochial guild was formed in Tipperary parish. By 1940 there were over seventy guilds across the country, but none in Northern Ireland.

Muintir na Tire did much to alleviate the problem of organisational incest which had a multiplicity of Irish organisations pursuing their own limited aims with little reference to each other or to the broader environment. However, the very width of its spectrum and its lack of formal programmes meant that its aims were not fully understood. Co-operation was a central theme of the Muintir na Tire philosophy and its practice was advocated from every platform. Yet the exhortations were indeterminate. People were urged to 'co-operate' but there was little advice about how they could initiate specific co-operative projects. The large national executive committee of Muintir na Tire in its early decades included very few people with much practical knowledge or experience of formal co-operation. Most of the public knew nothing of co-operative history and theory and it is doubtful whether the early leaders of Muintir na Tire ever imbibed the teaching of the Rev Thomas A. Finlay.

Much of the failure may be attributed to Kennedy's diffidence and preoccupation with the technical improvement of the dairying sector. It was not that he was lacking in idealism — all the evidence of personal intimates is to the contrary. Yet he rarely gave expression to the higher ideals either in private or in public. In many respects his logic, reticence and emotional austerity resembled those of a learned and dedicated priest. Such attributes, however commendable, were not conducive to the building of a large, enthusiastic, sentient movement of co-operative democracy.

19 More exactly, three-day rural weekends. The first of these was held in 1934 at Mount St Joseph's, Roscrea, the Cistercian monastery which owed its foundation to the generosity of Count Arthur Moore of the Giving Hand.

Following the departure from office of his brother-in-law[20] on the change of government in 1932, Kennedy became politically isolated. Although cordial relationships persisted with the Department of Agriculture and the new minister, Kennedy clearly had less direct influence on the shaping of government policy. To him, government policy was all important. In the near-hopeless economic situation, he saw little virtue in undertaking any programme of co-operative development which did not have the wholehearted ideological and financial support of government. He wanted the major problems of production and marketing to be tackled. His concern for macro-economics, and his estimation that Ireland's co-operative movement had at least passed the embryonic stage, left him exceedingly reluctant to go back to the primitive co-operation of Dr William King or the Rochdale Pioneers, when a worker allegedly needed no capital at all, but just his wages and an honest companion.

With an annual budget of the order of £12,000, Kennedy was reluctant to deploy his scanty organisational resources except to those areas where the need was greatest. Given a suitable working arrangement with Muintir na Tíre, local primary co-operatives with modest objectives could have been established. A renewal of credit co-operation and the revival of village banks was mooted and Kennedy would have been happy to have had an enthusiastic response from Muintir na Tíre, but little was forthcoming. Kennedy was never one to waste time in flogging a dead horse or indeed to encumber his organisation with an additional reluctant one. His motto was that one job well done was better than several done badly.

Muintir na Tíre could have revitalised existing co-operative structures. Education in co-operation was badly lacking and organisational abuses were common. Many small co-ops had lost all semblance of co-operation — share capital and share registers were neglected, returns were not made, dividends not paid. Meetings, including the mandatory annual general meetings, if held at all, were badly attended and poorly conducted. Often there was hardly any communication with the ordinary members, committees remained unchanged for many years and frequently the authority and business responsibility devolved on the manager. Amazingly, Muintir na Tíre neglected what must surely have been seen as a prime requirement designed to give a thorough grounding in co-operative theory and practice to all its members. Consequently, whenever a handful of enthusiastic amateurs attempted to regularise the conduct of the local co-op, they were all too easily repelled by an entrenched committee or manager.

In many ways Henry Kennedy was as neglectful of organisation, promotion and control locally as was the genial Father (later Canon) Hayes.

20 Patrick Hogan, former Minister for Agriculture and still Dáil deputy for Galway, was killed in a car accident near his home in Kilrickle on 14 July 1936. In fact relations between Kennedy and Hogan were anything but cordial in the later days of Hogan's ministry. Hogan had a real affinity with Plunkett but consistently evaded his appeals for a public declaration in favour of co-operation and the 'three betters' (farming, business, living), pointing out that he was giving generous financial support to the IAOS — "I suggest that £10,000 a year is worth all the propaganda I could do."

A man of great intellectual ability, he presumed too much of the intelligence of others and of their concern to educate themselves. Anderson, with less brainpower but deeper perception, kept warning him that even the most elementary business procedures would need to be forcibly taught to many co-operative personnel. Kennedy consistently refused to devote time or money to what he considered to be the responsibility of the primary co-ops themselves and a matter of 'a good national school education'.

From the nineteen forties onwards there were many frustrating meetings between Kennedy and Michael J. Costello, the dynamic general manager of Comhlucht Siúicre Eireann Teo (the state-sponsored Irish Sugar Company). Costello would come in full of enthusiasm for co-operative schemes to serve the needs of his beet growers and of Irish farmers and workers in general. Kennedy parried all proposals on the grounds that the time was not yet ripe; they must wait until genuine demands came from the people themselves, when they could elicit the wholehearted support of government. He was continually disappointed that the farmers were failing to emerge as a well-organised progressive force in Irish life. As he gradually became aware of the extent of the shortcomings of the Irish educational system and what he deemed the minimal concern of successive governments for co-operative development, Kennedy forthrightly refused to paper over the cracks.

In the early decades of the century Ireland had acquired considerable international prestige for the excellence of its co-operative movement. There were many in later years who would like to pretend that, despite current difficulties, the co-operative movement still flourished. Kennedy would have no part of such pretence; to him the movement was moribund and largely unco-operative. He would not pretend to service adequately a movement which subscribed to its Organisation Society only a fraction of the agreed dues.[21] His distaste for 'political schemes', like rates remission and small-scale agricultural grants, designed to be available to every farmer voter, drew him into a tense relationship, if not outright conflict, with politicians and Department officials. He deplored the habit of dissipating money in small handouts which afforded no developmental improvement and only minimum relief to the individual farmer. He urged that in any national budget where there was, say, £2 million available to help the nation's half-million farmers, it should not be squandered on some trivial scheme; rather, the government should take its courage in its hands and

21 For many years the level of affiliation fees and special subscriptions was fixed as follows: Affiliation: 10/- per £1,000 turnover. Minimum 10/-, maximum £10, plus special subscriptions. *Creameries*: a deduction of 4d in the £ on milk payments during the peak month. *Agricultural and Miscellaneous Societies*: ¼d (one farthing) in the £ of trade turnover. *Credit Societies*: ½d (one halfpenny) per £ of loans issued during the year. In 1940 affiliation fees amounted to £1,822.2.0 for 409 societies, an average of £4.45 per society. This sum included £1,502.13.0 from the creamery societies, of which there were 219 with an average turnover of £33,612. These societies had a total turnover of £7,362,066 and paid £3,153.1.10 in special subscriptions. The eighty-five agricultural and miscellaneous societies paid £165.19.0 in affiliation fees, approximately half of their commitment. They paid £72.16.1 by way of special subscriptions, approximately *one-tenth* of the amount due on the basis of a farthing in the £ on a 1939 turnover of £674,735.

apply the monies, through the co-operative movement, to some worthwhile sectoral or even local development, such as creamery re-equipment or the establishment of co-operative pilot farms. The constant response to these recommendations was that Kennedy's co-operative movement lacked spirit and determination and did not inspire confidence in its ability to make success of such schemes.

Many politicians within the movement, including the now considerable number on the IAOS committee,[22] regretted that Kennedy did not create a groundswell of enthusiasm for co-operation and so give the movement more muscle in the political arena, but he steadfastly refused to play politics. He had little enthusiasm for any hare-brained proliferation of crossroads co-operatives (Munster had, in his opinion, already three times too many). Such a caper would be a dishonest imitation of the Department's much publicised pretensions to be doing wonderful things for the Irish farmer. The IAOS has little funds but it had a certain integrity which should not be put at risk in a window-dressing operation.

While he lived, R.A. Anderson kept the ideals of the movement to the forefront. He constantly fought for IAOS resources to service the small store societies.[23] He urged all societies to educate themselves, to live up to their co-operative ideals,[24] to make individual sacrifices to give them financial strength, to take their business in their own hands, and to avoid the intrusion of the state into their co-operative domain:

> Where that happens, co-operation is dead. Our people, unlike those of other countries, have ever displayed a strange tendency to allow others to do for them the things that they ought to do for themselves, completely ignoring the fact that those who do the work will exact payment in full for their services.[25]

Kennedy, on the other hand, subscribed more to Plunkett's belief in the possibility of reconciling self-help with state aid. He travelled extensively in Scandinavia and elsewhere observing technical developments, such as grassland manuring and silage-making, that would advance Irish agriculture and which the Department of Agriculture might promote.[26]

When Anderson died, on Christmas Day 1942, there was no strong figure left to uphold and expound the co-operative ideology in terms

22 More than half of the 1940 committee had strong party political affiliations. They included two senators, P.F. Baxter (Cavan) and Martin O'Dwyer (Herbertstown), and two deputies, Frank Carty (Sligo) and P.J. Gorry (Offaly).

23 As managing director of the IAWS, he saw the invaluable contribution being made by these societies locally, especially in poor, remote and non-creamery districts. With touching nostalgia he recalled "the small store societies which achieved the greatest things", like the wonderful day in Thurles in 1895 when five small store societies smashed the Manufacturers Alliance and brought a nation-wide reduction of 20 per cent. or more in the price of fertilisers to all farmers.

24 Whilst Anderson lived, one could be assured of a good measure of ideological exhortation in the Annual Reports of the IAOS. Thereafter they tended to be restricted to bare factual accounts of events and decisions.

25 IAOS Annual Report 1936, p.20.

26 He carefully monitored agricultural developments in Latvia, Lithuania and Estonia, small countries like Ireland which had gained their political independence about the same time.

comprehensible to the ordinary farmer. After Plunkett, the guidance of the IAOS had increasingly devolved from the president and committee to the secretary. Now Kennedy exerted almost total influence, and economic and technological considerations superseded social concerns. The IAOS and the rural societies communicated almost exclusively on technical and financial matters.

The principal objective of Kennedy's writings and public discourses was to reveal the economic potential of Irish agriculture and the technical and business arrangements necessary for its development. Co-operation was now less a social creed and more a business device. Father Edward Coyne, the new president,[27] had supported Father Hayes in the foundation of Muintir na Tíre. He had also laid the foundations of the work which led to the establishment of the Catholic Workers College in Dublin. Flanked by the respectable managing director of *The Catholic Standard*,[28] he became the ideological and spiritual figurehead of the movement. His presence lent an aura of dignity and solemnity to the proceedings of the IAOS, ensuring to some extent that members attended regularly and punctually. A city man, Coyne was at sea in discussions of technical matters and was especially perplexed by the agricultural allusions and colloquialisms of the rural members. He was nevertheless a good chairman and successfully maintained the bonds of co-operative fellowship woven by his more jovial Jesuit predecessor.

Father Coyne spoke and wrote a good deal on the social and spiritual values of co-operation. However, his learned writings were often too erudite for the ordinary farmer. Given a sympathetic audience, he could be a brilliant public speaker and gave many inspirational addresses.[29] Unfortunately, these speeches were rarely reported and did little to awaken public interest in co-operation, which was known vaguely as a social ideal but hardly at all as a working movement. Even in co-operative circles, there was now little left of the stirring public sentiment and emotion that gave life and colour to the early movement.

Although political issues still continued to evoke turbulent emotions and rousing public displays, the nineteen thirties and forties were essentially the era of the unsentimental establishment — a time of cold reason, following the artistic, cultural and patriotic fervour of the earlier decades. Ireland was materially subdued by economic depression and the attendant ills of poverty, disease and emigration. She was depressed by remorse and disillusionment. It was as if the Irish people, appalled by their fratricidal savagery in the Civil War, had taken refuge in a rather sombre penitential

27 Father Edward Coyne (1896-1958) was the eldest son of William P. Coyne, a Professor of Political Economy in the Royal University, who was chosen by Plunkett as head of the statistics and intelligence branch of the Department of Agriculture.
28 Patrick Francis Baxter (1892-1958), a senator and committee member from Cavan.
29 At the annual luncheon of the Agricultural Co-operative Association of England in May 1954 he made a remarkable speech, unfortunately unrecorded, which brought the co-operators to their feet in a standing ovation: "He charmed his audience so utterly that when all was over there were rows of distinguished British co-operative directors waiting by the door to shake his hand and thank him for the delight his speech had brought to the great annual occasion." See IAOS Annual Report 1955, p.10.

Church which, in its current emphasis, seemed more designed for the sinner than the zealot. In its immediate task of banking down the fires of violence and human passion, the Church inevitably appeared somewhat lacking in human feeling. After so much hatred, there was a clear need to see Love as a theological virtue — a reasoned Charity. Human emotions, even of the kindliest type, were seen as potentially dangerous and one was urged to a higher, abstracted, spiritual love. The tendency was to repress sentiment and emotion, rather than harness them by idealism for the vigorous pursuit of noble causes. Few adverted to the need for "education of the heart",[30] least of all, perhaps, pragmatic mathematicians like Eamon de Valera and Henry Kennedy.

Ever since *The Irish Homestead* had expired in 1922, co-operators had felt the need of a co-operative journal to keep in closer touch with each other. Towards the late nineteen thirties the need was becoming more and more urgent in view of the growing lack of cohesion in the movement. Thanks to Kennedy's preferential treatment, the creamery societies had gained some financial strength. Through amalgamation and attrition, their numbers had been reduced to about 200 and, although membership had been reduced by over 7,000 in the decade, both share capital and turnover had greatly increased. The improvement was particularly noticeable in the case of the larger societies, but there was a growing tendency for societies of all kinds to operate in competition rather than in co-operation. The continued failure to support and expand the co-operative wholesale IAWS was a major disappointment. A survey of societies in 1939 indicated that a co-operative magazine could be assured of a reasonable circulation and, after much discussion, the IAOS decided to proceed with the project. However, the Society stressed that the magazine should be issued as an independent publication; it would take no responsibility for the periodical's policy or publication. The outbreak of war postponed the appearance of the first issue of *Agricultural Ireland* until July 1941.[31]

With Kennedy as editor, the magazine seemed more intent on improving Irish farming practice than on strengthening the co-operative organisation. There was very little newsy chit-chat on the activities of co-operatives and co-operators and few of the inspirational stories of endeavour and achievement that had characterised AE's *Homestead*. Many of the issues consisted largely of unrelieved pages of closely printed articles on technical aspects of such subjects as grassland improvement and animal nutrition. Discussion often ranged beyond the technical competence of the average reader and invariably required his maximum dedication to adduce the salient proposals. Although *Agricultural Ireland* continued to retain a sizeable captive market amongst co-operative societies for a number of years, its circulation was never extensive and after 1948 it was rapidly

30 A favourite theme of the renowned Father Seamus O'Flynn, who at that time was conducting his famous sessions of speech therapy, poetry and drama in 'The Loft' in Cork. He effected almost miraculous cures of hundreds of persons suffering from speech and personality defects.

31 Registered as a co-operative society in the miscellaneous category, Agricultural Ireland Ltd. started with a membership of nineteen and a paid-up share capital of £25.

superseded by the more popular *Irish Farmers' Journal*. In 1963 *Agricultural Ireland* became *The Irish Farmer* and a statement on its cover designated it the "official journal of the Irish Agricultural Co-operative Movement". The change of name apparently did not lead to any drastic change in policy. There were a few items on co-operative business but the magazine still seemed intent on being a technical publication. Its readership dwindled and publication ceased shortly afterwards. Subsequent attempts were made by the IAOS to issue a regular quarterly, *Co-operative Review*, in handy booklet size. The first issues showed much promise but publication faltered because of understaffing and editorial difficulties.

Both Kennedy and Coyne were members of the Commission on Vocational Organisation, which was appointed by the government on 10 January 1939 and which produced its lengthy report on 4 November 1943. Inspired by the forward social thinking of the Taoiseach, Eamon de Valera, the Commission, under the chairmanship of the Most Rev Michael Browne, Bishop of Galway, set out to examine and report on:

(i) the practicability of developing functional or vocational organisation in the circumstances of this country

(ii) the means best calculated to promote such development

(iii) the rights and powers which should be conferred and the duties which should be imposed on functional or vocational bodies and, generally, the relations of such bodies to the Oireachtas and to the government

(iv) the legislative and administrative measures that would be required.

In many ways reminiscent of the format of the report of the Recess Committee of 1896, the Commission's report reviewed vocational organisation in many countries: Italy and Portugal, Sweden and New Zealand, Denmark and Finland, Britain, Belgium, Netherlands and France, Germany and Russia.[32] There followed a lengthy review of the extent of vocational organisation in Ireland, the organisational structures of the professions and the various bodies dealing with agriculture, trade and industry, transport, finance, services and public administration.

As might be expected of such an ambitious attempt to effect a radical restructuring of Irish society, it proved impossible to produce agreed detailed proposals or to estimate the costs of implementation. The hardworking Commission, however, did get a remarkable degree of unanimity on general principles and methods and was able to outline in detail the structure of six vocational representative bodies which should be joined in the National Vocational Assembly,[33] the supreme authority which would "harmonise the endeavours of each vocational group to secure industrial peace, social security and economic regulation."

32 Grouped thus on the basis of certain similarities.
33 See *Report of Commission on Vocational Organisation* (Dublin: Stationery Office, 1943).

The proceedings of the Commission appear to have been conducted harmoniously, and Kennedy, contrary to his usual procedure, did not produce a minority report. However, the report contained no advanced thinking on co-operation or industrial democracy. Elaboration of the differences and similarities between co-operation and vocational organisation,[34] on which one would naturally expect considerable discussion, was nowhere undertaken. Although the highest level of co-operation between the distinct elements in each vocational grouping (e.g., employers, workers, producers, processors, manufacturers, traders, and so on) was everywhere implied, there were few practical suggestions about how this co-operation was to be achieved, other than through a sublime degree of Christian charity and goodwill.

The Commission, both before and after publication of its report, provoked comment from influential commentators and newspaper correspondents. Some warned against the perversion of vocational and co-operative organisation which had taken place in countries under communist and fascist régimes. Others saw the Irish co-operative movement as a happy example of how the different concepts were successfully blended. Nobody within the movement saw much point in demurring publicly. Yet there was some private disquiet on the condition of Irish co-operation: it was socially anaemic because of its continued failure to have its members relate to each other as people. Co-operation was increasingly threatened by economic competition between societies, and although the movement was seen essentially as a vocational system in agriculture, there was all too little vocational cohesion between the disparate elements: farmers, farm labourers, managers, milk carters and co-operative workers. The Creamery Managers' Association increasingly tended to assume the character of a militant trade union. Milk suppliers were remote from their committees; creameries competed for milk supplies and were often at odds with each other and with the IAOS. As creamery societies grew in size, their employees showed a greater tendency to strike, and misunderstandings between management and suppliers increased. In 1935 some forty creamery societies in Munster broke away from the IAOS and formed their own organisation, the Irish Federated Creameries Union, which they registered as a trade union in 1939. The reason quoted for the formation of this body was that the IAOS had not been "sufficiently active and independent in protecting the interests of the creamery members."[35]

The fine concept of vocational organisation ended up as a resounding

34 Vocational groupings are based on an *identity of function* on the part of the members. Co-operation is based on a *common method* of doing business and can exist between members of different vocational groupings who have nothing in common except their interest in the co-operative system of enterprise. The *vocational* system can be visualised as a *vertical* form of organisation; co-operation as a *horizontal* form.

35 See *Report of Commission on Vocational Organisation*, p.131. Further lack of co-operative consciousness was displayed at a later date by the foundation of an organisation called the Irish Creamery Milk Suppliers' Association. However, ICMSA had wider aims than agitation for higher milk prices. Many of its members were suppliers to the Dairy Disposal Company and the Association dealt with the government on a wide range of agricultural matters.

flop — a political non-event. Politicians saw in it a threatened diminution of their powers and refused to give it any hearing.

A subsequent report, that of the Committee of Inquiry on Post-Emergency Agricultural Policy (1943), got a somewhat better reception and many of its findings undoubtedly influenced government policy in later years. Kennedy submitted a minority report, masterly in its technical content, but although it advocated the extension of co-operation and increased financial support from the government for the IAOS, it did so only in general terms, without the slightest suggestion of a plan or budget. A most astounding revelation came to light in another minority report, that of Mr J. Mahony and Professor E.J. Sheehy:[36] (the italics are mine)

> . . . we recommend that measures be adopted for the purpose of extending agricultural co-operation and of securing the marketing of agricultural produce in the most efficient manner, but as this aspect of agricultural development *has not been examined by the Committee*, we are not in a position to recommend specific measures by which marketing organisation can be improved and co-operation developed and extended.

Beneath the outer drabness of those middle years there were shining examples of heroism by individuals and small groups. Managers, committee members and individual co-operative enthusiasts struggled to overcome seemingly impossible odds and often put themselves at serious financial risk. The IAOS field staff bore the brunt of bitter criticism as well as the burden of continuous overwork. The parent body IAOS, with a certain air of martyrdom,[37] worked tremendously hard, though neither committee nor staff got much outside praise or encouragement. Societies weathered the storms with some loss of numbers but, having survived, began to grow. The table overleaf indicates the main features of progress over thirty years.

Thanks to Kennedy's special attention, the most notable feature in co-operative growth was the burgeoning turnover of the larger creamery societies, which grew at a much faster rate than their smaller counterparts or any other type of society. The five largest creamery societies — Mitchelstown, Ballyclough, Dungarvan, Killeshandra and Drinagh — increased their turnover from approximately £½m. in 1931, to £1½m. in 1941, to nearly £5m. in 1951, accounting for more than 20 per cent. of the total turnover of all creameries in 1951; approximately one-third of their turnover was for the sale of agricultural goods.[38]

36 See *Reports on Agricultural Policy* (Dublin: Stationery Office, 1943), P.7175, pp.99 et seq.
37 Coyne suggested that the IAOS performed a useful function as a "lightning conductor, or possibly better, the whipping boy, on whom, when tempers are short and nerves raw, blame can be visited." See *Studies*, Spring 1955.
38 Much of the spectacular growth of these societies is attributed to the business ability and leadership of their managers: Eamon Roche (Mitchelstown), P.J. Power (Ballyclough), E. Maher (Dungarvan), M. McNamara (Drinagh), J. Gannon and J. O'Neill (Killeshandra).

Co-operative Societies 1931 to 1961

	1931	1941	1951	1961
Creameries				
Number	272	214	193	186
Membership	59,092	51,402	50,271	50,727
Share Capital	£340,240	£417,085	£445,939	£547,736
Turnover	£4.68m	£8.24m	£23.79m	£41.66m
Agricultural Societies				
Number	180	82	69	73
Membership	22,081	17,680	21,125	19,092
Share Capital	£65,059	£62,239	£83,052	£90,997
Turnover	£610,287	£750,665	£1.80m	£3.54m
Miscellaneous Societies				
Number	34	20	24	44
Membership	18,893	15,771	21,630	24,908
Share Capital	£138,678	£175,657	£398,349	£759,386
Turnover	£683,564	£2.47m	£4.66m	£19.45m
Livestock Marts				
Number	—	—	—	26
Membership	—	—	—	13,424
Share Capital	—	—	—	£759,386
Turnover	—	—	—	£12.13m

Source: Derived from IAOS Annual Reports

It will be noted that the rapid growth of turnover was not matched by a comparable increase in share capital. The failure to get (indeed, in some cases, failure to seek) additional share capital during the period of rapid growth from World War II onwards had a number of damaging effects which further blurred the co-operative image, as Dr Knapp reported (see footnote 42):

> The need for co-operatives to build capital rapidly fastened on them the practice of holding profits in reserves and the over-depreciation of fixed assets. As a result, the practice of paying out bonus practically disappeared and since that time it has never been re-established. As a result many of the co-operatives today show very little more members' capital than when they were much smaller organisations.

Distribution of surplus in proportion to each member's trade with his society was a basic Rochdale principle. The modification at a later stage, which allowed for alternative uses of surplus (for the further development of business and to provide common services), did not alter the principle; in particular, it did not minimise the necessity of *democratic control* whereby the disposing of surplus must in every case be done by the conscious and informed *decision of the members*. It was true that on occasions 'dividend hunting' (demands by members for excessive dividends on purchases) had seriously threatened the development of the co-operative retail stores in Britain. It was equally true that the same malaise had sometimes afflicted small co-operative societies in Ireland. Often when the full extent of 'profit' was revealed, the members insisted on having it all, leaving no provision for the morrow.[39]

Hence the lack of co-operative education, often glossed over as an academic consideration, had a deleterious effect on the movement. Some of the so-called shrewder managers (with or without the connivance of their committees) sought to acquire capital by stealth (i.e., by deception of the members), excusing themselves on the grounds that they were doing so 'in the best interests of the society'. Ironically, the very lack of education, which was at the root of the problem, also provided the means by which the problem could be circumvented. It was possible, because of the noted reluctance of the ignorant to betray their ignorance, to present annual accounts in such a way that a minimum of information was revealed and the decisive figures were plausibly 'talked away'. Annual general meetings became exercises in subterfuge and deception. Many amusing stories are told of how accounts and balance sheets were represented and interpreted in amazing terminology for the befuddlement of member audiences.[40] One manager/secretary reportedly had a very successful technique of fixing attention on some minor item of account (postage, telephone, packaging) whilst unobtrusively transferring five figure sums to the society's reserves.

An equitable solution to the problem of 'surplus' distribution would have been the allocation of extra shareholding. This was rarely suggested since it was feared that members would insist on a pay-out. Also, the idea was not appealing because of the extra book-keeping that would be necessary.

Many annual general meetings, instead of being great co-operative occasions, were contrived to be exceedingly dull. The statutory notices were sent out but the ordinary members got little encouragement to attend. Although considerable time might be given to the discussion of trivia, the major items were often given short shrift. ("We have here the Auditor's report with accounts and balance sheet, copies of which are available. Would someone please propose and second their adoption?"). This chore was often effected within fifteen seconds, whereas the appointment of an additional storeman might often take an hour's discussion. An atmosphere of secrecy, absolutely subversive of the whole co-operative ideal, developed

39 Frequently, as in the case of creamery societies, where the annual surplus even remotely approached the figure required to pay an extra halfpenny per gallon for milk, the members took more than all. This had particularly serious consequences in situations where the 'bonus' failed to induce enhanced turnover or profitability or where accounted depreciation was not sufficient to meet the inflated cost of replacing plant and equipment.

40 A more dangerous expedient was the undervaluation or omission of stocks of goods from audit so as to show a small surplus.

about the affairs of many societies. The manager and committee might be left unhindered to capitalise the profits but, outside, the members and the general public talked uncharitably amongst themselves, until frequently the finances of the local co-operative were the subject of as much cynical conjecture as those of the Catholic Church, the Masonic Order, or the Gaelic Athletic Association.

Gradually, however, under the influence of improved education,[41] a new generation of young farmers emerged who were taking an increasing interest in the affairs of their co-operatives. The truly progressive societies, which formerly were sometimes less than forthcoming about their affairs, successfully absorbed this new blood and with better-educated committees were able to progress democratically. The more reactionary institutions were to find themselves increasingly under siege. Nevertheless, an element of secrecy persisted in the movement for a very long time. Joseph G. Knapp, writing in 1963, observed:

> There appears to be a high degree of secrecy in the operations of co-operatives. Few managers and committees take the members into their confidence and explain fully how their organisation is being run. The idea that well-informed members make the best members is little recognised.[42]

From 1931 to 1948 the IAOS received a grant from the government averaging about £7,000 per annum. The amounts collected by the Society in affiliation fees and subscriptions gradually increased from approximately £4,000 in 1931 to over £10,000 in 1948. In the latter year the government grant was fixed at a maximum of £11,000 under a new arrangement whereby £8,000 was given as a fixed grant and the remaining £3,000 was to be granted on a pro-rata basis, dependent on the amounts raised by the IAOS in affiliation fees and subscriptions. This was designed to give the Society a greater incentive and more flexibility and independence. The arrangement continued until 1962-63 (when the grant was increased to £12,000) and during the period there was a steady increase from affiliations and subscriptions. These totalled £22,535 for the year 1962.

For more than thirty years the system of calculating the contributions of societies to the IAOS had undergone no material change; although the six-fold increase looked impressive at first, on deeper analysis it indicated a still deplorably poor level of support. If all societies had paid up in accordance with prescribed scale in 1962, then the total contribution for that year should have been approximately £84,376, instead of the £23,535 actually subscribed. In other words, they paid only 23 per cent. of their full assessment. Even at this low level, there was immense variation in the way

41 A significant educational contribution was made through the young farmers' organisation, Macra na Feirme (founded in 1944), and in the south the extra-mural courses of adult education provided by University College Cork laid the foundations of a new era of business and farming progress.
42 Joseph G. Knapp, *An Appraisement of Agricultural Co-operation in Ireland* (Dublin: Stationery Office, 1964), P.7467, p.60.

the different societies subscribed:

	Percentage of full assessment paid
All Societies	23
Central Creameries	34
Agricultural Societies	18
Livestock Marts	46
Miscellaneous Societies	10

This lack of generosity is further highlighted in trade turnover. Altogether, the contribution of co-operatives in 1962 was at the rate of 0.036 per cent. of turnover, i.e., £36 for every £100,000. Here again there were enormous differences, not only between different types of societies but between individual societies within each category. Relatively speaking, the larger societies gave least of all:

	Percentage of Turnover (average)	Range
Central Creameries	0.049	0.013 to 0.110
Auxiliary Creameries	0.035	
Agricultural Societies	0.027	0.002 to 0.066
Miscellaneous Societies	0.009	0.004 to 0.045
(with £100,000+ turnover)		

When the central creamery societies were grouped according to size, the following interesting pattern emerged:

Central Creameries	Number	Percentage of Turnover Subscribed
Turnover £1,000,000 or over	7	0.039
Turnover £500,000 — £1,000,000	8	0.052
Turnover £300,000 — £500,000	20	0.047
Turnover £200,000 — £300,000	24	0.052
Turnover £100,000 — £200,000	48	0.057
Turnover less than £100,000	35	0.069

On many occasions it was postulated that the complex system of assessment led to much of the difficulty in securing an adequate contribution from the societies. It was suggested that a simpler system would be better understood and evoke a more generous response. The system was considerably simplified after the Knapp Report (1964) but a number of ill-defined areas still remain.[43] What simplification has been effected to date has not, unfortunately, caused a remarkable improvement in the level of payments. Although by 1972 the societies' contributions had risen to £120,000, this figure actually showed a marginal percentage

---

43 The committee still retains the discretion to determine maxima and minima contributions and to negotiate the level of contributions from co-operative livestock marts and other specialised societies.

reduction on turnover compared to that of a decade earlier, 0.035 per cent. compared to 0.036 in 1962, i.e., £35 per £100,000 turnover as against £36.

The agreed assessment figure for 1972 of one-eighth of a new penny per £ turnover (0.125 per cent., or £125 per £100,000 turnover) could not be regarded as an excessive burden on any type of society, particularly since it was now being levied on the turnover of two years beforehand, as opposed to the turnover of the previous year as heretofore. No information is available on the special arrangements made in that year regarding maxima or minima contributions or concessions to individual societies, but if we accept as reasonable an overall contribution at 0.10 per cent., the figure should approximate to £278,376 instead of the £119,107. In 1973 the IAOS received a total of £133,370 in contributions which was approximately £40 per £100,000 of 1971 turnover but less than £32 per £100,000 if set against the 1972 turnover of £420 million. In 1974 the scale of contribution was further raised to 0.16 per cent. Although the financial support given by societies to the IAOS is probably less than half of what is reasonably required to provide a satisfactory service, it is interesting to note that the 1973 total represents a contribution of approximately 84 pence per member compared to the sixpence farthing (2½ pence) per member subscribed in 1916. This thirty-three fold increase, however, looks less remarkable in the light of a seventy-fold increase in turnover (£6m. to £420m.). In that historic year of 1916, R.A. Anderson made an impassioned plea for societies to subscribe the halfpenny (½d) per £1 turnover that would give the IAOS the strength and independence it required. He believed that if the committees would only properly present the matter to their members, they would subscribe generously:

> No farmer, however poor in pocket, will feel, nor however poor in spirit, will grudge, this trifling subscription of one half-penny in the £ on the business he does with his society.

The halfpenny is still being sought and is still not forthcoming. It remains the most fundamental defect of the whole movement that inadequate funds mean that the IAOS provides a poor service, which in turn makes it exceedingly difficult to collect an adequate contribution from the societies.

Father Eddie Coyne died in May 1958.[44] The period of his presidency, in his own words, had been one of "intense and fruitful activity" in the co-operative movement. His place was taken by Owen Binchy, a solicitor from Rath Luirc, County Cork, who had been vice-president since the retirement of Sandy McGuckian in 1949. Binchy was destined to be the last of the 'long-term' presidents[45] and his six-year term of office

---

44 Within a short period about that time there were heavy losses in the co-operative ranks. Between 1957 and early 1959, Tim Lucey, Charlie Riddell, James Fant and P.F. Baxter died.

45 At a special general meeting following the annual general meeting on 5 May 1964, the rules were changed so that neither the president nor the vice-president should hold office for more than three consecutive years.

established a prosaic, businesslike efficiency in the conduct of IAOS meetings. Like a good solicitor, he read his brief and expedited the business quickly. Binchy was a devoted and full-time co-operator. At one time he was president of both the IAOS and the IAWS, chairman of the now major creamery and food processing co-operative, Golden Vale Food Products Ltd., and chairman of the committee of his local creamery society, Ballyagran, County Limerick. Not content to be a figurehead office-holder, he pursued the welfare of all these organisations through long unpaid hours of committee work and outside negotiations which left him very little time for what could have been a lucrative legal practice.

Throughout the outstandingly progressive period of the nineteen fifties Henry Kennedy continued to dominate the movement. When the post-war technical revolution in agriculture struck Ireland in 1950, Kennedy was sixty-two years old, the same age at which Anderson had undertaken the managership of the IAWS in 1922. Like Anderson, he was plunged into his period of greatest and most productive endeavour. He always worked long hours but did so now with increasing zest and satisfaction as he saw many of his plans beginning to take shape. His strategy, enforced in the hopeless days of economic depression, had been to build on the foundations of most strength and he had staked the survival of the smaller, weaker societies on the hope that a new co-operative development would emerge from the strength of the larger units. The outburst of federal activity in the early nineteen fifties (Miloko, Golden Vale, Clover Meats), and the growing strength of smaller groupings, suggested that his gamble was about to pay off. He continued to write and speak authoritatively on agricultural matters — now, indeed, with enhanced authority and influence,[46] for many of his recommendations on grassland and dairying improvement were being demonstrated and proven.

Unfortunately, Kennedy's eyesight, long strained by incessant reading, began to deteriorate rapidly; later he developed cataract in both eyes. For a time he continued to write and dictate but it was a constant frustration that he required the help of others, few of whom could interpret his thoughts and expedite his correspondence at the impossible speed which he desired. He could no longer indulge in night-long orgies of reading and writing. Eventually, in a condition of almost total blindness, he retired in May 1963. Relieved of the responsibility of office, he continued to exert an impressive influence on agricultural and co-operative affairs until his death on 5 February 1968.

Kennedy will long continue to be a controversial figure in the history of the Irish co-operative movement. He has frequently been described as a giant amongst pygmies and a man of outstanding ability and vision. Many will argue that his policy of saving and building the movement by preferential support of the stronger societies was the only sensible course in the circumstances — a policy, they say, which has now been vindicated.

46 Ironically, someone deeply impressed and influenced by Kennedy was James Dillon, TD, Minister for Agriculture, and son of John Dillon, the notoriously 'anti-co-operative' Nationalist MP in the early days of the movement.

Others criticise him and assert that his neglect of the small societies in the areas of greatest need, and his failure to use his undoubted influence to promote co-operative education and developments, delayed co-operative progress for more than a quarter of a century. Few will dispute the fact that Kennedy built a very strong creamery movement and maintained the IAOS as a respected central organisation. Nearly all are agreed on his outstanding intellectual ability and regret that he had not lived in better times and got the measure of support from his own co-operators and from others which would have enabled him to exercise his full potential.

In 1954 a National Co-operative Council was founded "to promote through education, publicity and other activities a wide interest in co-operative principles and their practical application in the economic and social life of Ireland." A number of its founders and early members were influential and under its enthusiastic chairman, Breandán Ó Cearbhaill, the Council did much useful work. Working closely with the Irish Countrywomen's Association and other enthusiastic groups and individuals, the Co-operative Council greatly influenced events leading up to the establishment of the credit union movement in 1958. In 1958, also, the Council was largely instrumental in having the Minister for Industry and Commerce set up a committee to examine the legal position of co-operatives. Unfortunately the committee's terms of reference were so restricted that its deliberations proved of little value.[47] Otherwise, the National Co-operative Council evoked little enthusiasm, is now poorly supported, and has had little or no success in its efforts to bring town and country together to give the Irish co-operative movement a broader base.

Early in 1963 the Minister for Agriculture, Patrick Smith, after consultations with the IAOS, invited the veteran American co-operative expert, Dr Joseph G. Knapp, to carry out "a general appraisement of the agricultural co-operative movement in Ireland and to make such recommendations as he might deem desirable with a view to further strengthening the movement and increasing its influence." Knapp, who was born in Colorado in 1900, had almost forty years experience[48] as a research worker and educationalist in the development of American farmer co-operatives. Since 1953 he had been administrator of the Farmer Co-operative Service of the US Department of Agriculture. Dr Knapp had previously visited Ireland in 1937 and had met many leading co-operators. He had maintained these contacts during the intervening years and was already well briefed on the history and structures of the Irish movement.

Dr Knapp arrived in Ireland in June 1963 and, after an intensive month of field work followed by an undoubtedly prodigious amount of work back

47 See *Report of Committee on Co-operative Societies* (Dublin: Stationery Office, 1963), Pr. 7411 *passim*. See also article by Breandán Ó Cearbhaill in *The Irish Times*, 5 August 1974.
48 Knapp is a name revered in the annals of American agriculture. Dr Seaman A. Knapp (no relation), head of the extension service of the US Federal Department of Agriculture, was described by Plunkett as "one of the ablest organisers of farm improvement I have ever met." (See Horace Plunkett, *The Rural Life Problem of the United States* (New York: The Macmillan Company, 1910), p.75.) Dr Joseph G. Knapp's father was one of the first agricultural county agents in the state of Colorado.

home in the US ("at night and over weekends as my official duties would permit"), he was able to dispatch his report to the Irish Department of Agriculture on 29 November 1963. Inspired no doubt by Knapp's speed and efficiency, the Department also acted fast, and despite the intervention of the Christmas holiday, the report[49] was printed and on the bookshelves before the end of January. In a concise and readable document, Knapp compressed a mass of pertinent facts and displayed a wealth of co-operative wisdom. A complete study of the document must be regarded as a mandatory exercise for every co-operative member and official, and for every student of the Irish co-operative movement. Following a masterly forty-page presentation of the history of the movement from 1889 to 1962, he devoted a further fifty pages to analysing the problems and opportunities of the movement with numerous observations and suggestions, ending with a single page of conclusions and a further two pages elaborating his four major recommendations.

It is ironic that many Irishman's first real intimation of the exciting history of the Irish co-operative movement should come from the brief account of an American agriculturalist, but my interviews and discussions with some thousands of people indicate that such has been the case. The previous works of Anderson and Digby seem to have been poorly publicised and little known even amongst co-operative members. Very few of the younger or middle-aged members had heard of *The Irish Homestead* and, as previously noted, their historical placing of the various Plunketts had been decidedly muddled. Discussions with the younger (and indeed many of the older) politicians and government officials also revealed that any understanding of the movement and its historical origins dates to their reading of Knapp.[50] Probably one of the best results accruing from the publication of the Knapp Report is that it presented and explained the movement for the first time to a wide public.

The Report, a model of American diplomatic politeness, nevertheless added up to a devastating indictment of the co-operative movement. It prompted the inevitable questions as to how co-operatives with so many defects could have survived, and how they would fare in the future?

> It is recognised that this catalogue of weaknesses tends to over-emphasise what is wrong rather than right in these organisations, and the question may properly be raised as to how co-operatives can continue to exist when there is so much improvement needed. Probably the answer lies in the fact that these organisations have operated in an environment where competition with other organisations has not been great and standards of performance of business in general have not been high. The co-operative organisations

49 Op. cit., footnote 42.
50 The author must himself confess to having successfully completed a degree course in Agriculture at an Irish university (1945-49) without becoming more than vaguely aware of the existence of an Irish co-operative movement. Even conceding his outstanding capacity for inattention as a student, this must surely say something for the extent of co-operative education and publicity at the time.

have been able to get by with a minimum of system and management and there has been no great demand for a change . . .

It is only when competition is beginning to come from the outside that people associated with agricultural development are realising the importance of improving the efficiency of co-operative associations.[51]

Knapp's four main recommendations[52] placed major emphasis on the strengthening of the IAOS and the reorganisation of the dairying industry which he saw as still the basic sector of the movement:

1. Steps should be undertaken to reinvigorate the IAOS to enable it to give leadership and provide the technical services necessary to help farmers build strong co-operative organisations. 'It is believed that this aim could be rapidly achieved if the Government were to provide the IAOS with a substantial grant — say £100,000 or even more.' The government should facilitate the reorganisation and ensure that it be carried out with dispatch without attempting to direct or manage the organisation.

2. The IAOS should be given full responsibility for working out general reorganisation plans for the dairy industry.

3. The government should take steps to 'co-operativise' the Dairy Disposal Company (which was still handling about 25 per cent. of the milk processed).

4. The IAOS should be encouraged to broaden its field of service to embrace more generally all types of agricultural co-operation,[53] '. . . give more attention to the pressing co-operative needs of -western farmers, and take steps to strengthen co-operative programmes for producers of all kinds of crops and livestock.'

Knapp also presented an organisation chart showing how the IAOS might be more effectively organised. It suggested that the professional staff be grouped into four operating divisions:

1. Business Administration Division
2. Engineering and Technical Services Division
3. Member and Public Relations Division
4. Field Service Division.

The work to be undertaken by each division was clearly defined. The

51 Op. cit., p.60.

52 Among his many minor recommendations and suggestions was one to change the name of the IAOS to something like the 'Agricultural Co-operative Service'. "The IAOS has had a brilliant history and some might hesitate to change its name because of the high respect held for it. However, the almost equally venerable California Fruit Growers' Exchange changed its name to Sunkist Growers in 1952 and it is now generally agreed within the co-operative that this was a desirable move."

53 The Report of the *Interdepartmental Committee on the Problems of Small Western Farms*, published in 1963, had stressed the need for a "comprehensive and well-knit co-operative system" in the west.

director in charge of each division would report to the secretary as the chief administrative officer. Above all, Knapp recommended the magic ingredients which legislation or organisation could not of themselves produce — enthusiasm, dynamism and vigour on the part of all concerned, and real co-operative leadership:

> There are a great many people associated with Irish agriculture who would respond to vigorous co-operative leadership. This was demonstrated in the days of Plunkett and it could be demonstrated again. The logical centre for expressing this leadership is the IAOS. However, to provide it the IAOS must develop a straight-forward militant attitude, based on research, education and effective service work. The IAOS must become a leader in vigorous new co-operative activity and not a custodian of old-fashioned principles and practices. It must recapture the spirit of the IAOS in its very early days when the IAOS was a driving force with principles which enlisted the interest of the best minds of Ireland. However, no one can give leadership to the IAOS, for leadership, like co-operation, must be earned.[54]

Shortly after the publication of the Knapp Report, the IAOS committee[55] held a number of meetings to examine it in detail. A memorandum on the report was prepared by the committee and circulated to all societies. This memorandum accepted the recommendations of the Report and set out in detail the manner in which it proposed to implement them. The Knapp Report and IAOS memorandum were discussed in great detail at the IAOS annual general meeting in Harcourt Street, Dublin, on 5 May 1964. The meeting was well attended[56] and evoked something of the "large enthusiastic and turbulent assemblies of co-operative democracy" of the movement's early years. The resolution proposing the acceptance of the Knapp recommendations and the IAOS plans for implementation was adopted unanimously and with much acclaim.

In 1963 Patrick Kelly had settled quietly into the post of IAOS secretary, a position which he had understudied through the accelerating activity of the previous decade.[57] The latter years had been hectic, but now as chief executive he was plunged into a period in which the co-operative movement would undergo the most frantic activity and most spectacular growth and development in all its history.

---

54 *An Appraisement*, p.105.
55 Still a committee of sixteen including president and vice-president. In 1964 the IAOS elected its first (and to date the only) lady committee member, Miss Sheila Hamilton.
56 A full attendance of the committee of sixteen, plus 375 delegates representing 140 co-operatives. In all, 333 co-operatives were affiliated to the IAOS in that year. Knapp had complained that, although annual general meetings were reasonably well attended, there were usually less than one-third of the societies represented.
57 Kelly, who joined the IAOS in 1942, became assistant secretary on the retirement of C.C. Riddell in 1953. He was succeeded as assistant secretary in 1963 by James C. Moloney.

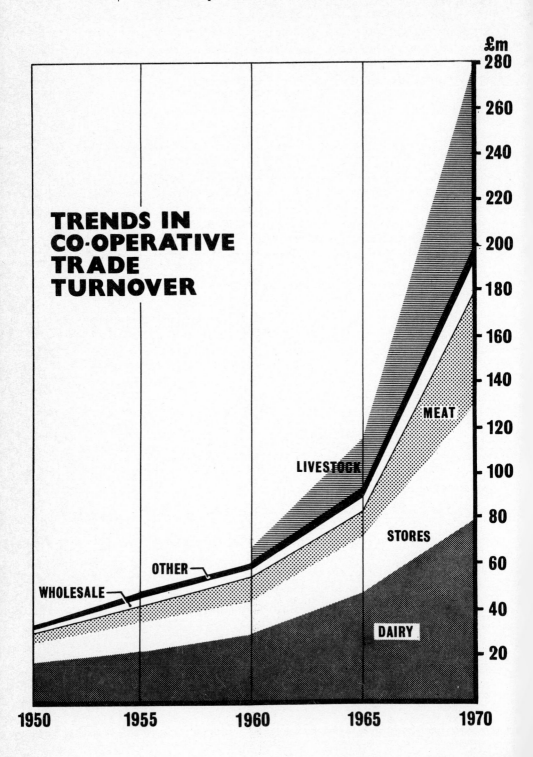

£m

TRENDS IN CO-OPERATIVE TRADE TURNOVER

MEAT

LIVESTOCK

STORES

OTHER

WHOLESALE

DAIRY

280
260
240
220
200
180
160
140
120
100
80
60
40
20

1950 1955 1960 1965 1970

Chapter Eleven

The Northern Co-operators

Ulstermen had long complained of their isolation from their co-operative colleagues in Dublin and the South. They felt that, despite the provincial representation provided for in the reorganisation of 1904, the northern societies were still not adequately serviced; the IAOS effort was too much centred on what the Ulster representatives called "the strong Munster creamery movement". It was proving difficult for the local advocates to persuade societies to send a sizeable sum of money every year "to a Society that they had never seen and was not doing them any good". As early as 1906 some Northerners[1] had called for the establishment of a separate branch of the IAOS in Belfast. The request was repeated at regular intervals.

At no time, however, was separation envisaged. On the contrary, every proposal was designed to achieve greater unity and solidarity — to help the ordinary co-operative member to participate more fully in the national movement with his Southern colleagues. It was necessary to establish better liaison between the agricultural movement of the IAOS and the consumer co-operatives affiliated to the British Co-operative Union, which were particularly strong in Ulster. Despite the fact that a number of these stores, including the Belfast Co-op,[2] made token subscriptions to the IAOS, an 'identity of interest' had not been established. The Ulster agriculturalists felt that, given the resources and personnel in a semi-autonomous northern organisation, they could negotiate better co-operation with the retail movement than any Dublin-based group.[3]

1 Notably Rev E.F. Campbell of Killyman, Rev J. Colhoun, dynamic president of the successful Dervock Poultry Society, and Hugh de Fellenberg Montgomery of Fivemiletown.
2 Belfast Co-operative Society Ltd, founded in May 1889 with 199 members, had by 1919 grown to a membership of over 21,300 and accounted for over £1 million of the £1.8 million turnover of the forty-eight retail co-operatives registered with the Co-operative Union in Ireland in that year. The majority of these societies were very small. Only three of them, Belfast, Enniscorthy and Lisburn, had a membership of over 1,000, whilst twenty-three had less than 200 members. Even in Cork the retail co-op had less than 700 members.
3 In 1914 a partial decentralisation was effected when a provincial office was set up in Dunmurray, County Antrim. This, however, was in line with the establishment of provincial offices at other centres and did not effectively alter the overall structure.

Above all, the northern co-operators who had steadfastly abjured political involvement, sought to alleviate the divisive effects, inevitable at local level, of the growing clamour for political separation.[4]

Plunkett had striven hard to achieve political reconciliation. As a loyal Briton, who in the interests of Europe's economy had constantly sought America's early intervention in the war, he had been appalled by the "foul treason" of Sir Roger Casement and the 1916 rebels. Of his old friend Constance Gore-Booth (Countess Markievicz) he noted in his diary, "She is deeply dyed in blood, but her motives were as noble as her methods were foul." He consulted with General Sir John Maxwell, Commander of the British Forces in Ireland, to help collect evidence of German participation in the insurrection; but when the military executions began, he pleaded with Maxwell for clemency for the leaders. It pained him beyond measure that it was the young poets, and labour leaders like Connolly — men of the highest motives and absolute sincerity — who were facing the firing squads.

Rev Edward Fitzharding Campbell

Plunkett sought to minimise the effects of the rebellion in three ways: by proving German complicity, by seeking relief for the grievances of the Irish workers and by urging clemency for the defeated.[5] His efforts were in vain. The Dublin employers proved as obdurate and unfeeling as ever. No German plot was uncovered and, as public sympathy grew with the continuing executions, Plunkett's ultra-loyal attitude and unequivocal condemnation of the rebellion alienated him from many of his best friends. He felt badly used by the government he had sought to help and refused to give evidence before the Royal Commission on the rebellion. When Chief Secretary Birrell resigned, he wrote of him with bitterness:[6] "He will have a great political funeral, as he has done the bidding of the Irish MPs for

4 Recommended background reading is M.W. Heslinga, *The Irish Border as a Cultural Divide* (Assen: Van Gorcum and Company, 1962).
5 As the executions continued, Plunkett was deeply grieved. He vainly tried to persuade the authorities to allow Connolly's widow to join her relatives in the United States and was incensed at their churlish refusal.
6 Plunkett rarely exceeded a limit of mild sarcasm, described by his friends as "a touch of horacic acid".

nine years. But more than any other living man he fomented this rebellion." Plunkett wrote to Carson[7] urging him to propose the disarming of the whole of Ireland.

Plunkett went to the United States[8] in December 1916 and renewed his efforts to involve that country in the European conflict — a process which required considerable pressure on the British government to forego coercion and grant an acceptable measure of Home Rule to Ireland. When America entered the War in April 1917, Plunkett, feeling that he had exerted a fruitful influence and had also done something to relieve Anglo-American and Anglo-Irish tensions, returned to Ireland. He found the Irish Question still at an impasse. Lloyd George, having guaranteed Ulster that it would not be taken over, had renewed his old offer to Redmond of immediate Home Rule for the twenty-six counties. When this was flatly refused, he seized on a tentative suggestion of Redmond's: a convention of all parties in Ireland to decide the future of the country. Plunkett saw it as a hopeful proposal and consulted with a wide variety of politicians and public figures to ensure that the convention at least got off the ground. Largely because of his efforts and the unwillingness of others to risk their reputations, Plunkett was given the awesome task of chairman. The Convention held its first meeting in Trinity College Dublin on 25 July 1917 and continued to meet until the spring of 1918. Yet, despite Plunkett's efforts, nothing was achieved and the Convention concluded its ill-fated sessions on 8 May 1918, having on at least one occasion come tantalisingly close to a settlement.[9] Ever since his famous appeal in 1914, Plunkett had spared no effort to persuade Ulster "not to desert Ireland". It was all in vain.

The events following the break-up of the Convention are too well-known to require repetition. They culminated with the Government of Ireland Act 1921 and the setting up of separate governments in Dublin and Belfast. This precipitated the need for the co-operators to establish separate organisation societies. The grant to the IAOS from the Development Commission would terminate at the end of the financial year, 31 March 1922. To the immense relief of Plunkett and the IAOS, the new Saorstat Minister for Agriculture, Patrick Hogan, agreed to support the organisation society with a government grant. There was a condition, however: monies granted had to be spent within the state. A promise of a

7   Plunkett had over the years developed an unlikely friendship with Carson, who was almost an exact contemporary. They could apparently discuss without acrimony everything from what Plunkett considered to be Carson's "awful responsibility as a promoter of anarchy" to the finer points of the game of hurling.

8   Throughout the summer and autumn of 1916 Plunkett was seriously ill with the effects of an X-ray burn inflicted by a careless surgeon. He was in constant, severe pain which could be relieved only by drugs. The fact that these drugs also delayed healing of the wound conflicted with his convictions and he urged to be allowed more pain and less medication. This illness compelled him to resign his membership of the Indian Industrial Commission. In December, however, he left for the USA with the burns still not completely healed.

9   A full chapter of Miss Digby's biography of Plunkett is devoted to a detailed account of the Convention, followed by a shorter chapter on subsequent events up to 1923, entitled "In Search of an Irish Settlement".

grant from the Belfast government by the new Minister for Agriculture, E.M. Archdale,[10] bore a similar condition. Both governments sought assurances that even funds subscribed by the co-operative societies themselves should be similarly spent within the respective areas.

After lengthy consideration and legal advice, the IAOS committee in Dublin decided that the only workable arrangement would be to provide an autonomous organisation society to operate in Northern Ireland. Accordingly, the Ulster Agricultural Organisation Society Ltd. was registered as a co-operative society on 14 October 1922, with a constitution identical to its parent body; it was designated to be "the officially recognised body for the organisation of Agricultural Co-operation in Northern Ireland." The first president of the UAOS, Harold Barbour, was elected at the preliminary meeting of the provisional committee on 23 October 1922. James Adams, previously secretary of the Ulster IAOS committee, was appointed secretary to the new Society. The committee elected a representative from each county: R.S.H. Noble (Antrim), George Blackwood (Armagh), Edward McGreevy (Down), W.H. West (Fermanagh), Alex Moore (Derry). Tyrone, as a large county with many co-operative societies, was accorded two representatives, Owen O'Doherty and Thomas Young.[11]

The decision to part company was taken reluctantly by both sides. For the IAOS it meant the loss of 141 societies[12] and some dedicated co-operators. Plunkett was particularly grieved by the departure of Harold Barbour, a youthful enthusiast whom he had thought of as his likely successor.[13]

The UAOS committee realised that an annual grant of £900 offered little hope of dynamic organisational development. Many also foresaw an uneasy coexistence with the Northern government and its Ministry of Agriculture. Although Archdale and his secretary, Dr J.S. Gordon, seemed sympathetic, and Harold Barbour's eldest brother, Sir Milne Barbour, was Minister for Finance, there were a number of officials who had joined the Northern Ministry of Agriculture from the Department of Agriculture and Technical Instruction and who were thought to be anything but favourably disposed to the co-operative movement. Barbour could rely on the friendship of some of the bigger and more enlightened industrialists, but they could offer only limited help. He also knew of the extent of the powerful opposition from trading interests and their political henchmen. The

10 A former President of Ballinamallard Co-operative Dairy Society, County Fermanagh, and a member of the IAOS committee for one year in 1899.
11 At the first general meeting held at the Society's offices, 16 Donegall Square, Belfast, on 8 November 1922, attended by delegates from some fifty co-operatives, the provisional committee was confirmed as the central committee. James Timoney and William Robert Thompson were elected subscribers' representatives and Patrick Cunningham, Samuel James Henry and Robert Rusk were co-opted.
12 Seventy-eight creameries, thirty-eight agricultural and twenty-five flax societies. Altogether these had a membership of 26,000, share capital of £163,000, loans of £117,000 and an annual turnover of £1.5 million.
13 Father Tom Finlay was by this time a sprightly seventy-four. R.A. Anderson was sixty-two. Harold Barbour was forty-eight and a highly successful businessman who had retained an extremely boyish appearance. This was a cause of some merriment when Barbour, on co-op visits with Anderson, was frequently treated as a schoolboy.

co-operative philosophy was no more acceptable to them than it was to the gombeen-men and hack politicians of the South. Particularly distressing was the prospect that the Unionist régime, recognising the simplest and crudest expedient for retaining power, would exploit sectarian differences. If they could keep the electorate voting on straight Unionist/Nationalist lines, they were assured of a permanent majority. Any movement which might fragment the political monolith, through promoting tolerance and independent thought, was unlikely to be looked on with favour.

The ability of the co-operative movement to bridge the sectarian divide was already well demonstrated. Committee members, painfully aware of their conflicting ideologies in other matters, did their co-operative business fairly and well: religion and politics were for the most part kept outside the door of the committee room. Sir Horace Plunkett was accepted as a great man. It was hard for the Ulster Unionist to reconcile Plunkett's political thought with his Protestantism and his patent 'loyalty' but they accepted him as a likeable character and a man apart.[14] His pragmatism in advising Ulstermen to "disinfect their politics with common sense" appealed directly to the dry northern humour, as had Father Tom Finlay's earlier suggestion to leave the 200-year-old quarrel between Dutchman (William) and Scotsman (James) to be settled between the two protagonists themselves — "That is", he said, "if too great a gulf do not now divide them."[15]

Few are now living who can recall co-operative meetings much earlier than the nineteen twenties. I quote but one assessment of several in a common vein:

> They were the worst of times — and the best of times. No doubt we had lots of enemies. No doubt we had our disagreements and our squabbles, often sore enough. But [spoken with great emotion] *nobody* ever had such friends.

Exalted feelings of good fellowship are of course not exclusive to the co-operative movement. They are to greater or lesser degree common to all collective action in a common cause. One cannot claim the 'co-operative feeling' as superior, but it is perhaps distinctive — even if the distinction is not easily definable. Much of this comradeship happily persists and today one can fairly claim that some (if not all) co-operative gatherings demonstrate a spirit of friendship — informal, tolerant, sympathetic and easygoing. The unique ability of the early co-operative movement to contain so many diverse elements is admirably demonstrated in the following report[16] of the annual general meeting of the Lowtherstown

14 Sir Henry Campbell-Bannerman, when challenged in the House of Commons to 'explain' Plunkett and to state to which party he belonged, reflected a moment before answering "He belongs to the Horace Plunkett category."

15 Finlay himself, the son of a Scots father and an Irish mother, is commonly claimed as an Ulster (Cavan) man. On entering his novitiate, he gave his place of birth as Lanesborough, County Roscommon. He was in fact born on a small island just north of Lough Ree. His father, William Finlay, was at that time an engineer on the Shannon drainage scheme. Father Tom always carefully explained "My father subsequently submerged the island."

16 *The Irish Homestead*, 18 March 1922.

Co-operative Agricultural Society, held at Irvinestown, County Fermanagh, on 23 February 1922.

> The meeting was followed by a concert and dance and the event brought together almost all the elements of the community. There was the farmer, labourer and artisan, the banker and humblest mill-worker, Hibernian and Orangeman, Freemasons, Sinn Féiners (Republicans and Free Staters) and Unionists, together with representatives of the many modern forces for the protection or terrorising of the individual, all vying with each other in the promotion of a happy and enjoyable evening.

The UAOS took over its Ulster territory at a time of great economic difficulty and set about rescuing many societies which were being forced towards liquidation by the post-war slump. Matters were not helped by a depletion of the experienced field staff. Two of their best men, McGowan and Magee, opted to work with the IAOS in Dublin. James Adams, the secretary, had been a good worker but was now fully occupied with administrative duties, so the burden of field work fell on Robert Bratton and the newly recruited James Johnston, who had attracted the attention of both Plunkett and Barbour as the efficient manager of a small creamery near Kesh, County Fermanagh.

The outlook was depressing and it was difficult for the Society to know where to start or how the meagre resources of men and money might be best deployed. It was decided that priority should be given to improving the business methods and organisation of existing societies, and to a moderate but well-directed educational programme.[17] The educational effort was accompanied by a practical piece of business calculated to evoke a ready response from almost every farmer member. This was an arrangement with the CIS (Co-operative Insurance Society Ltd.) whereby co-op members could effect workmen's compensation and other types of insurance.[18] In government and business circles there was an obvious determination to relegate the co-operative movement to a charitable and innocuous role. 'Co-operation' was to be liberally invoked in abstract terms over the whole field of daily chores but it must not be crystallised as a business philosophy. 'Co-operators' were useful in winning public acceptance for government schemes, but they should be discreetly redirected outside the mainstream of profitable business life.[19] It was a

17 In 1924 a major educational campaign was launched with the help of a grant-in-aid from the Plunkett Foundation.

18 Workmen's insurance was provided at 12/- (60 pence) per £100 wages, compared to the most favourable rate available elsewhere of 16/6d. A 10 h.p. motorcar, valued at £150, could be given full comprehensive insurance for £8.18.3, compared to £12.12.6 from other companies.

19 In 1924 the co-operative movement lent willing support to the government's Egg Marketing Act, the schemes for milk recording and the establishment of a government brand for Northern Ireland butter. Following the disastrous harvest of 1924, it sought government aid for distressed farmers, and the creameries helped overcome the turf shortage by providing coal at cost price.

strategy that was to prove eminently successful.

Intimations of future austerity were soon apparent. On 26 January 1924, a UAOS application for the renewal of its government grant (£1,200 in 1923) was refused on the following grounds:

1. There were sufficient creameries in the area
2. In view of the early introduction of legislation to improve egg marketing, it would not be wise at the present stage to undertake the organisation of any other form of co-operative society for the marketing of eggs
3. The Ministry would continue to give technical advice to the creameries
4. In the case of all other forms of co-operative societies, the Ministry would always be prepared to give technical advice and educational assistance.[20]

So much for the Rochdale Pioneers, Sir Horace Plunkett, AE, and all that had been written and expounded on the benefits of co-operation for eighty years. Harold Barbour and his colleagues were nonplussed and hardly knew how to reply to this extraordinary letter. They felt it displayed an astonishing ignorance of the whole *raison d'être* of the co-operative movement. Was this ignorance real or simulated?

The UAOS submission was short, polite and pragmatic: the starting of new creameries (if any) would be but a tiny part of the UAOS work. The major requirement was to improve marketing, book-keeping methods and the advice given to managers and committees on the day-to-day running of their business. Creameries had organisational rather than technical problems. The government's egg marketing legislation could not be fully effective without a thorough educational and organisational effort in each district, and this could be done better and more economically through local co-operative societies. The value of technical advice and educational assistance given by the Ministry of Agriculture was appreciated, but this advice and help, so necessary to co-operative societies, could best be provided by a voluntary organisation, namely the UAOS. The social and cultural benefits of co-operative self-help were mentioned, but not over-stressed. James Johnston, the newest member of the UAOS staff, sought a personal interview with the Ministry secretary, Dr J.S. Gordon. Gordon indicated that the decision to withdraw the grant had been taken with the approval of James Adams, the UAOS secretary, who in recent discussions with him had conveyed a very poor impression of the society — the co-operative societies were dilatory in subscribing money, and the organisation was superfluous and could not long survive. Gordon expressed surprise at Johnston's ignorance of the situation. The UAOS committee was even more surprised when Johnston reported to it. They strongly repudiated the suggestions on which the Ministry's decision was

20 See James Johnston, *Agricultural Co-operation in Northern Ireland* (London: Horace Plunkett Foundation, 1965), p.10.

based: the co-operatives were strongly and actively behind the UAOS; in a difficult year they had subscribed enough to secure the full amount of the grant (£1,200) on a £ for £ basis. The president and committee of the UAOS were determined to carry on the work. Dr Gordon said, however, that he could not now give way. The government could not be seen to be misinformed and questions in the House prompted the facile pronouncement that "the Ministry of Agriculture has been in close touch with that organisation [UAOS] and had always been and was still in entire sympathy with its objectives."

James Adams resigned as secretary in February and later joined the staff of the Ministry of Agriculture. The president and committee gratefully expressed their appreciation of the work Adams had done for the co-operative movement in Ulster during the previous twenty years. Robert Bratton had resigned a short time previously, having spent much of his last year of service winding up the affairs of the 'war casualties' amongst the agricultural and flax societies. The staff of the UAOS was thus reduced to two, James Johnston, the new secretary,[21] and his assistant, Miss McVicker. The UAOS asked the Development Commission in Britain to intervene but that body had no jurisdiction in Northern Ireland and could do little but state that it was giving financial support to the agricultural organisation societies in England, Scotland and Wales and acknowledge its appreciation of the work of the Irish movement:

> It is, of course, not a matter for the Development Commissioners to make any representations to the Northern Government upon the subject. They can only say that they are deeply interested in the future of a movement which they highly value and have consistently supported, and they would regard it as disastrous if that movement was to be suddenly crippled for want of resources.[22]

All efforts were in vain and the co-operators had to accept the Ministry's decision with deep disappointment. From that time onward, the UAOS was never in a financial position to employ sufficient staff to promote and foster a real co-operative movement. Application was made every year but the only support given was of the order of a few hundred pounds granted for special purposes such as the helping of Ministry campaigns. Thus the work of the UAOS organiser became more and more identified with that of the 'Ministry man' and the beneficiary farmer had little awareness of co-operation. There were unedifying instances of Ministry cheeseparing in the early nineteen thirties: the small grant of £700 was reduced to £600 in 1932 and £500 in 1933. James Johnston recalls that over a thirty-eight year period the total grants paid by the Northern Ireland govenment to the UAOS were less than the amount paid by the Free State government to the IAOS in *any one* of those years.[23]

21 He was appointed on 1 April 1924.
22 Memorandum from Development Commissioners, 14 July 1922.
23 Comparisons for 1955 showed that in that year government grants to the various organisation societies were: England £6,500, Wales £6,850, Scotland £17,000, Republic of

The trials and tribulations of the years following the withdrawal of government aid are well recounted in James Johnston's short history of the UAOS. Despite the appalling difficulties, useful work was done, much of it in the face of strong political and trade opposition. A market intelligence service was established in 1926 to keep societies informed of ruling butter and eggs prices on all the leading markets, and agreement was reached between forty-seven central creameries not to sell butter below an agreed price. The co-operators were also in conflict with the Ministry about the promotion of home sales of Northern Ireland butter. It seemed unreasonable to the co-operators to be spending a lot of money promoting Ulster butter on the British market, where it commanded only a poor price, while at home they were importing some 200,000 cwts of butter annually. They drew attention to the fact that the cattle population of Northern Ireland in 1925 was the lowest since 1865. Thanks to the co-operation of the giant Belfast Co-operative, which became the largest buyer of Northern Ireland creamery butter, the balance was redressed.

In 1928, when the price of bacon pigs became extremely low, a UAOS meeting in Enniskillen led to the establishment of a number of Pig Marketing Co-operative Associations. These 'farmers' associations' performed an inestimable service to the small farmers of west Ulster by providing alternative markets — shipping live pigs to leading English markets and exporting dead (bacon and pork) pigs to London.

Another tussle with vested trade interests which preyed on poorer parts of the province came in 1932 when, following widespread complaints of overcharging by the coal merchants of Derry, the co-operative societies in the area came together and registered a trading co-operative, the Agricultural Supply Association Ltd. Careful estimates were made of the total coal requirements of the group and Derry merchants were invited to quote. When no quotations were received, the Association made its own shipping arrangements and the various creamery and agricultural co-operatives collected their quotas of coal ex quay. Since practically all the societies in the north-west had participated, the financial impact was impressive and a year later the Derry merchants, who had stood so firmly together, were competing for the co-op contract. In subsequent years the Agricultural Supply Association, in conjunction with the IAWS Ltd. (who had branches in Derry and Belfast), effected a number of very successful joint purchasing schemes.[24]

In the early nineteen thirties the manufacture of butter was still largely in the hands of small Ulster farmers and their seventy-five creamery co-operatives — over fifty of them in Counties Tyrone and Fermanagh. Many felt that the Stormont government's reluctance to give aid to the butter industry in the severe period of depression was evidence of its lack of

Ireland £11,000 and Northern Ireland £250.

24 During the austere period of World War II and after, the willing co-operation of the societies, the IAWS and the Belfast Co-op ensured that co-ops could give an excellent service to their registered customers. Strict adherence to recommended prices and fairly liberal stocks of scarce goods had a considerable dampening effect on the blackmarketeering tendencies of some private merchants.

interest in the poorer (and less 'loyal') areas of the Northern Ireland state.[25] In 1934 the price of butter fell so low, as a result of foreign dumping, that many creameries were able to pay their farmer members no more than 2½d per gallon for milk. The position was becoming desperate and, following representations by the UAOS, the government introduced an equalisation scheme which guaranteed a price of 5d per gallon in summer and 6d per gallon in winter.[26] This scheme helped the small dairy farmers of Northern Ireland and had an interesting side-effect on the eastern side of the province: the establishment of a large proprietary firm, Armaghdown Creameries Ltd., in Newry. The principal shareholders in this company were Charles H. Nolan of Dublin and Louis Roche of Cork. They had creamery interests in County Cork, which had a reduced trade following the formation of the Dairy Disposal Board. They now came north to avail of the opportunities provided by the equalisation scheme, reportedly at the invitation of Sir Basil Brooke, then Minister for Agriculture, who had previously refused licences to both Killyman and Fane Valley Co-ops to establish in Loughbrickland.[27]

A happier development came four years later in County Down with the formation of a new type of co-operative, the Mourne Sheep-breeding Association. The Mourne mountain district had long had a reputation for good healthy sheep, which made excellent breeding stock and secured a correspondingly good price, but the rapid development of motor lorry transport meant that sheep from other areas were being offered at the autumn sales by dealers who presented and even advertised them as "Mourne bred". The registration and marking of genuine, approved Mourne flocks, which was carried out by the Association with the co-operation of the Ministry of Agriculture, helped to overcome the problem and won still better prices for the County Down breeders.

The same year of 1938 ended on a very sad note. Just two days before Christmas, Harold Barbour, still a youthful sixty-four, died suddenly in a hospital in Zürich, having contracted pneumonia when setting out on a business trip to the Far East.[28] His death evoked a sense of loss amongst co-operators north and south, as intense as Plunkett's death in 1932 or the death of the movement's literary champion, AE, in exile in Bournemouth in 1935. A little over a year earlier, R.A. Anderson and Dermod O'Brien,

25 Early in 1930, following a trip to New Zealand, the Prime Minister, Lord Craigavon, suggested that, in view of the difficulty of producing winter milk in Ulster, the creameries should purchase New Zealand butter to supplement their winter supplies. This was tried but the high colour of New Zealand butter proved unpopular with Ulster housewives.

26 The UAOS also strongly opposed the inclusion of milk haulage in the new Transport Act passed at this time and eventually succeeded in having it exempted. Other UAOS achievements of the period included the exemption of maize from import duty (1932), joint shipping of potatoes by four farmers' associations (1935) and the formation of a co-operative vegetable growers' association (1936).

27 See UAOS Annual Report 1938, p.32.

28 In what was probably his last letter, dated 15 December 1938 and written *en route* to the UAOS secretary, he wrote: "I did not get an opportunity of saying goodbye to Miss Pelan and Miss Beattie, nor to Mr McNeely, will you please do this for me? So now good luck to you and yours, to my fellow workers in the office and my colleagues on the Committee. When I think of it all, my lot has been cast in pleasant places. Good Luck — H.B."

with Dr Henry Kennedy and John Cassidy, general manager of the IAWS, had journeyed north to attend the annual general meeting of the UAOS, when Barbour received a presentation from the Prime Minister of Northern Ireland, Lord Craigavon.[29] Thanking the co-operators for their tribute, Barbour acknowledged the early sources of his inspiration:

> I had the good fortune to have been taught and trained by Sir Horace Plunkett, Father Finlay and R.A. Anderson and the devoted band of workers whom they had attracted around them . . . In 1922, of necessity, the Ulster Agricultural Organisation was formed . . . To the IAOS, our old parent body, I would say we have tried to keep the faith.

Harold Adrian Milne Barbour

Barbour left behind him a co-operative structure that was small and declining but still intact. There were ninety-four societies with a membership of approximately 15,000 and an annual turnover of £1½ million. The level of the members' personal involvement in the matter of share capital was even worse than in the rest of Ireland, an average of £4.75 per member in 1937 compared to £6.53. There were fifty-five creamery societies which had a turnover of almost £1 million in butter sales and a further £93,000 in other goods. Despite better prices, however, the volume of milk handled (18.8 million gallons) was small in comparison to the Republic's total of 157.6 million gallons (123 million in Munster).[30] Forty-one of the fifty-five creameries were in Counties Tyrone and Fermanagh. Killyman Creamery had butter sales of £170,000, one-sixth of the

---

29 Father Tom Finlay, now eighty-nine and seriously ill, sent his apologies and good wishes, as did Harry Norman, Charlie Riddell and Paddy the Cope. The meeting was held at the Clarence Place Hall on 15 April 1937. Harold Barbour's presentation consisted of a beautifully bound album of letters of tribute, plus a cheque for £500.
30 Comparable figures in 1922 were: Ulster — 12.7m. gallons, Munster — 61.8m.

Northern Ireland total, and also had one-third of the total creamery trade in other goods. Agricultural store societies had dwindled to fourteen[31] with a total turnover of £321,000. Only the Antrim societies at Cloughmills and Dervock had a sizeable trade (£70,000 and £58,000 respectively). There were still twenty-two farmer co-operative associations but their dealings were very small; Faughan Valley Association, County Derry, accounted for £9,000 of the total turnover of £23,500 in 1937. All, however, managed to make a profit except the Lecale Association (County Down) which recorded a loss of £1 on the year's trading.[32] Of the five flax societies still extant,[33] only three were working and their total trade was just short of £1,400. Not a single flax society remained of the ten that had been established under the guidance of Frank and Harold Barbour in County Down.

The real watershed came during World War II. Northern Ireland was urged to produce every possible ounce of food to sustain the war effort. The UAOS immediately offered its services and the Ministry of Agriculture, as agents in the province for the Ministry of Food, took over the two UAOS organisers, McNeely and Campbell. In order to avoid any loopholes in the administration of rationing, it was essential that the Ministry have complete control of all food wholesalers. Wages had to be stabilised to maintain a reasonable comparison between the pay of soldiers and that of workers. Effectively, this meant that the price of food would have to be controlled. On the other hand, farmers would have to be given the highest possible incentives to produce the maximum quantities of food. To this end, a system of 'deficiency payments' was conceived which was to remain a common feature of British agriculture for many years afterwards.

Under the Defence of the Realm Act, all co-operative creameries were taken over by the Ministry of Agriculture and their co-operative organisation was suspended. Farmers were now paid for their milk directly by the Ministry. The creamery staffs became civil servants; managers were 'graded' in accordance with civil service ranking and made answerable to a local district milk officer. Many welcomed this in so far as it gave them much better salaries than they had hitherto received. Their work was simplified: no marketing was necessary, quality control was dropped to a minimum,[34] and for a time managers and creamery workers continued to work as they had always done.

However, it was obvious that this arrangement could not continue indefinitely. The northern creamery business was based on buttermaking. This meant that 80 per cent. of the milk supplied by farmers was returned

---

31 Cloughmills, Dervock, East Antrim (County Antrim); Five-lane-ends (County Armagh); Downpatrick (County Down); Lowtherstown, Maguiresbridge, Springfield (County Fermanagh); Kilcronaghan, Magherafelt, Moneymore (County Derry); Ballylurgan, Drumragh and Cappagh, Sixmilecross (County Tyrone).

32 These farmers' associations had an average membership of about 100, with a typical shareholding of 5/- (25 pence) per member.

33 Mullyard (County Armagh), Strule Valley and Arboe (County Tyrone). Camlough and Maydown, County Armagh, did no business in 1937-38.

34 The Butter and Cream Marketing Board, which had effectively controlled the quality and grading of dairy products since 1936, was suspended when the Act was revoked in 1940.

to them in the form of skim milk for animal feeding. Even before the war, the UAOS had been concerned about the creameries' dependence on buttermaking and, in order to stimulate diversification within the industry, had consulted with the creameries about the possibility of producing skim-milk powder. The Tyrone and Fermanagh farmers expressed little interest but a deputation from County Antrim visited Scotland to view some projects there. The price offered to the farmer, little more than 1d per gallon for skim milk, was a disappointment, so the Ulstermen decided to take no further action at that time. They were impressed by the intensity of dairying in the Stranraer area where there was an immense supply of milk produced in a comparatively small region. Yet the Ulster problem was still the same — how to double the milk supply.

During the war people became concerned about the nutritional value of the food they bought. Skim milk was a valuable protein food, suitable for direct human consumption; it was wasteful to feed it to animals. After losses in conversion and a considerable time lapse, the animal could only produce a protein food of little or no biological superiority to milk. This induced the Ministry to invite firms with experience of milk processing to establish plants for the manufacture of milk powder, milk foods, chocolate crumb, and so on. The British Co-operative Wholesale Society set up a factory at Tullygunigan, County Armagh. Bovril established a plant at Magheralin, Moira, County Down, and there was a major controversy when the Nestlé Company set up a major processing centre at Omagh, with subsidiaries later at Castledawson, Ballymoney and Victoria Bridge.

Although the emphasis continued to be on increased production of food-stuffs, the arrival of the Americans led to concern about the quality of food produce. Apart from strategic considerations, American forces were allocated to Northern Ireland primarily because they could best be fed there. All through the war, Allied forces in excess of the defence requirements were quartered in Northern Ireland to effect economy in the shipping of food. The affluent Americans were fastidious about hygiene and what they ate. They complained about the condition of *abattoirs* and the storage and handling of foodstuffs; they were appalled by the bacteri-ological counts of their milk supplies — "more goddam germs than milk". Some commanders threatened to requisition powdered milk from the USA unless the position was immediately remedied. Others were reported to have warned their men that the only safe drink in Ireland was Irish whiskey — "kinda rough but antiseptic". This vociferous American outcry precipitated a Safe Milk Campaign. The Ministry decreed that all milk for human consumption should be bottled and either be pasteurised or pass a tuberculin test. The regulations were rigorously enforced, not only for the sake of the American servicemen but to safeguard the health of mothers, babies and schoolchildren who were being given special priority allocations of free milk under the Ministry scheme.

These stringent requirements led to the closing of a number of creameries where the condition of premises and equipment was regarded as unacceptable. The Ministry decided to build six new creameries. There was considerable disquiet in co-operative circles about these new "Ministry of Agriculture" buildings at Dunman Bridge, Cookstown, County Tyrone, Keady, County Armagh, Lisnaskea, County Fermanagh and Dromona, County Antrim. Killyman Creamery was entirely rebuilt on the original site and Moneymore and Fane Valley were among the larger creameries which were compulsorily closed.

The 'Omagh development' in 1941 caused alarm and resentment amongst co-operators, as James Johnston made clear:

> . . . the President and Committee were very concerned over a report, early in 1941, that officials of the Ministry of Agriculture were, without any consultation, either with the UAOS or the Ulster Farmers' Union, identifying themselves with the introduction of a proprietary concern, viz. Nestlés Milk Products Limited, for the setting up of a dried milk and condensing factory in the Omagh area of County Tyrone. It was said that an official assurance had been given to this company in London of a sufficient milk supply in the area to meet their requirements. Futher, that officials of the Ministry had, after considerable difficulty, secured a site for the proposed factory. The quantity of milk required would mean the diversion of all the milk supplies from some 16 creameries, and as the farmers owned both the creameries and the milk, they could not believe that any official would give such an assurance without previous consultation with them or their representative organisations.[35]

At the meeeting of the UAOS consultative committee on 26 August 1941 Ministry officials were questioned but said they were not free to discuss the matter. However, the rumour soon emerged as an accomplished fact and on 12 September the Ministry conveyed the news to James Fulton Gamble, president of the UAOS. At a conference between the UAOS and the Ministry two weeks later, Dr Scott Robertson, the secretary, stated that his Ministry was not responsible since the decision had been taken by the Ministry of Food. It was later established, in a letter from Lord Woolton,[36] that "the erection of a milk condensing plant in Northern Ireland has been arranged entirely by the Northern Ireland Government. The Ministry of Food are in no way responsible for the arrangement."

Despite all protest, the factory was built and began operating on 1 July 1942. The Ministry, under a sealed order, served notice on over 1,000 farmers to supply their milk from this date to the factory, leaving their own creameries idle. The UAOS opposed the action and, on the recommendation of senior counsel, advised the farmers to continue to send their milk to their own creameries.[37] The Ministry refused to pay the

35 In *Agricultural Co-operation in Northern Ireland*, op. cit., pp.32-33.
36 The private secretary to the Minister of Food in a letter to A.W. Ashy. See Johnston, op. cit., p.34.
37 An offer had already been made to Nestlé to collect the milk at the creameries and deliver in bulk to the factory, as was already being done at their other factory in Ballymoney, but the Ministry refused to sanction such an arrangement. This type of arrangement *was*

farmers full price for the milk delivered to the creameries, although they accepted the resultant butter or cream on behalf of the Ministry of Food. They also withdrew the licences of those farmers who were low-grade producers (Grade C), thereby penalising them by the loss of the greater part of the milk price and the bonus of 2d per gallon. Without a licence, the farmer could not obtain the allocation of feeding ration for his dairy cows. In order to save farmers further loss, the UAOS advised them at the end of August to send their milk to the factory pending a court decision on a test case being taken against the Ministry.

The Nestlé factory was officially opened on 12 August 1942 by the Minister of Agriculture, Lord Glentoran, who stated in his address that the American directors of the firm had subscribed £50,000 to establish the factory so that American troops might be supplied with milk, thus saving the transport across the Atlantic. These observations are interesting; when the site was purchased and the scheme approved, the Americans had not even entered the war, nor was it known that the firm had American directors.[38]

The test case against the Ministry was taken by Orr Kyle of Drumnakelly, Omagh; the UAOS took full responsibility for the plaintiff costs. The trial opened on 25 June 1943 before Mr Justice Megaw in the High Court, Belfast. Early in July judgment was given in favour of the Ministry. An appeal was planned but was never advanced. (The sudden death of James F. Gamble MP, on 11 July, deprived the UAOS of one of its strongest leaders, the Ministry decided not to pursue its claim for costs, and the appeal was never made.)

It had been the unanimous wish of the UAOS committee that Lieutenant James Barbour, son of the late Harold Barbour, should accept the presidency. However, he felt it was vital that the president should be 'a man on the spot' and, since he doubted the possibility of his own release from the Army until 1947, regretfully declined the offer.[39]

The UAOS carried on, appointing a chairman from meeting to meeting, until the unanimous appointment of Alexander Maclean Buller in February 1945. Sandy Buller was an energetic co-operator who had succeeded Harold Barbour as chairman of the Butter and Cream Marketing Board. As manager of the Cloughmills Co-operative Agricultural and Dairy Society, he had created a multipurpose society, active in the business of selling farm supplies and marketing produce.[40] In the first

encouraged in the Republic: when Nestle established a subsidiary in County Donegal, a new co-operative creamery society was founded in Letterkenny in 1954 to be the prime buyer of milk which was then resold to Nestlé.

38 The American forces in Londonderry obtained their supplies of *pasteurised* milk — the only milk approved by their medical authorities — from Leckpatrick Co-operative Society.

39 Because of his youth and inexperience, he had previously declined the invitation to stand for the presidency following his father's death. He was offered the presidency in 1942 but by this time had received a commission in the army. He wrote from his camp in Lanarkshire declining the post and enclosing a cheque for £3,000 towards the general expenses account of the UAOS.

40 A fortunate circumstance, when in 1942 the society's entire milk supply was diverted, principally to the new Ministry creamery at Dromona.

year of his presidency, Buller was also appointed manager of the large co-operative Ulster Creameries Ltd. in Belfast.

The closure of creameries and the establishment of new milk centres was effected under the Ministry of Agriculture's creamery concentration scheme introduced on 1 October 1942. By the end of 1943 the number of co-operative creameries was reduced to fourteen. No compensation was paid to the forty creameries closed under the scheme but the Ministry of Agriculture devised a system of 'care and maintenance' payments which was accepted by the UAOS. These yearly payments were continued until 1952. By this time practically all the premises and their machinery had been disposed of and, apart from some changes of location, the number of co-operative creamery centres never again exceeded the 1943 figure of fourteen. In 1976 there were thirteen milk co-operatives in Northern Ireland. The Armaghdown Creamery came into co-operative ownership in 1963 but in that same year the movement suffered a severe setback when the large Rathkenny Society became a private company.

Little progress was made during the lean war years and it was well into the nineteen fifties before there was any expansion of agricultural stores or service co-ops. Worthy of special mention were the pioneering efforts during the war of the McGuckian family of Cloughmills. Alex (Sandy) McGuckian was vice-president of the IAOS from 1942 to 1949. A comprehensive account of the work of this remarkable family can be found in a memorial tribute[41] published after his death at the early age of fifty-seven in 1952.

In 1954 Winston Churchill scrapped the Ministry of Food and abolished rationing. In that year also the Northern Ireland Ministry of Agriculture set up the Milk Marketing Board which began its work on 1 April 1955. The Board was given full power by statute over the dairy industry and was charged with the purchase and sale of all milk produced in Northern Ireland. It acquired the six Ministry creameries and the full fleet of milk transport lorries, and became a monopoly first-hand buyer of all milk. The Board delegated its milk collection to the creameries at a flat rate. Transport was rationalised and the same collection charge was arranged for all milk suppliers, regardless of distance from the intake point.[42] The events since the establishment of the Ministry of Food, and the subsequent developments under the Milk Marketing Board (NI), radically altered the position of the co-operative creamery societies. Johnston notes the position which had evolved six years after the establishment of the Board:

> It is of interest to record that these 13 creameries in 1961 received and processed 23 million gallons of milk compared with some 15 million gallons received in 1922 by the whole 78 creameries. In that year,

41 A.E. Muskett (ed.), *A.A. McGuckian — A Memorial Volume* (Belfast: McGuckian Memorial Committee, Bryson House, Bedford Street, Belfast, 1956).
42 The 1975 deduction for transport was at the rate of 1.05 pence per gallon. The Board is also empowered to make occasional capital levies, e.g. 0.25 pence per gallon on the two peak months of milk supply. From the foundation of the Board to the year ending 31 March 1975, these capital levies have yielded approximately £2.6 million.

however, they handled practically the whole milk production in the area that went into manufacture but in 1961 their proportion was only a little over 20%.[43]

A.M. Buller retired as president in 1951 and was succeeded by Lieutenant Colonel Robert Henry Todd, a retired army officer and auctioneer, who had returned to his family farm at Fyfin, Castlederg. Colonel Todd was an enthusiastic and energetic newcomer to co-operation and worked untiringly to expand the movement.[44] He ardently urged the expansion of the Society's staff, but without much success. He was keenly interested in the development of co-operative livestock marketing but did not live to see his efforts fructify. In 1952, however, he saw the establishment of the first new co-operatives since before the war, Ulster Wool Growers Ltd. and Northern Ireland Co-operative Canners Ltd. His death after a short illness in 1954 was keenly felt at a time when co-operators were anticipating a great step forward.

Another active co-operator from the Strabane area, Harold William Britton, president of the Leckpatrick Society, was elected president of the UAOS in 1955,[45] but ill-health forced him to retire within a year. The annual meeting in 1956 unanimously elected J.A. (Andy) Gamble, son of the late president, to succeed him.

The first modern co-operative livestock mart in Northern Ireland, the Carrickmore and Gortin Farmers Auction Mart Ltd., was established in 1955, a few months before the pioneer Waterford Mart in the Republic. By the end of 1959 there were ten co-operative marts in operation or ready to commence. This was a hopeful period of diversification which saw the formation of the Ulster Farmers Poultry Packing Co-operative at Moira, County Down, Killyman Apple Packers and Armagh Fruit Growers Ltd. (1961), the Clogher Valley grain drying and milling co-op (1963), and a comprehensive co-operative effort in the Swatragh area of County Londonderry, pioneered by an enterprising Catholic curate, Rev Seamus Shields, in 1963. The first Northern Ireland sea-fishing co-operative was formed at Kilkeel in 1965.

In Northern Ireland today (1976) there are thirteen large milk co-operatives and some forty other societies, mainly marts and stores. The total co-op turnover is of the order of £30 million. The IAWS, with centres at Londonderry and Belfast, does a large trade in agricultural requisites, household supplies and provender milling, which is by no means confined to co-operative societies. The UAOS staff still consists of only the secretary and his assistant. James Johnston retired in 1957 and was succeeded as secretary by his son, George B. Johnston, who resigned in 1962. He was

43 Johnston, op. cit., p.71.
44 His interest in the co-operative movement dated from 1941 when, as an auctioneer, he was approached by the Ministry of Agriculture to secure a site for the Nestlé factory in Omagh. He was impressed by the co-operative spirit and loyalty of the Omagh farmers, not one of whom would sell land for the project.
45 A number of staunch co-operators died in 1955, including A.M. Buller, Andy Crawford, manager of Irvinestown Co-op and, not least, the venerable Miss M.C. McVicker, assistant secretary at the UAOS office for over thirty years.

followed by the present secretary, William Ross, who started work for the UAOS as a development officer in 1961. This gross understaffing is alleviated slightly by occasional appointments for specific projects and the employment by the Milk Marketing Board of a number of fieldmen who act as advisers to the creamery societies. Technical matters are reasonably well catered for but general promotion and development are severely hampered because the UAOS spends a lot of time representing the societies and negotiating with the state marketing boards. Very little educational work at field level can be undertaken. Writing in 1965, James Johnston entered an urgent plea that some of the burden of co-operative education be taken up by the universities and other existing education authorities in the province, but so far there has been little progress.

There is close liaison between the UAOS and the Ulster Farmers' Union. Most of the active co-op members are also members of the UFU and that organisation usually gives strong support to any new co-operative development projects. A proposal was made in 1957, and has been mooted occasionally since then, that the UFU and the UAOS join forces as the National Farmers' Union and Agricultural Co-operative Movement had done in England. Yet it has always been decided that it would not be in the best interests of either organisation to do so. The UFU is predominantly concerned with union matters such as marketing and the prices of farm products. It undertakes very little co-operative educational work and the same is true of the Young Farmers Club movement. The milk co-operatives are fairly large organisations and can solicit advice on their problems from a variety of sources. With an already secure membership, bolstered by the high level of state participation in their particular business, the need for education in co-operation is not so keenly felt. With regard to the small store societies, the IAWS and the Belfast Co-operative have always been ready to give help on specific business matters on an *ad hoc* basis, thus supplementing the efforts of the UAOS. In either case, the broad area of general co-operative education is largely untouched, and the level of 'co-operative consciousness' amongst Ulster farmers is consequently low.

Much of the marketing of agricultural produce is carried on through statutory state boards: the Milk Board, the Pigs Board, the Seed Potato Board and the British Wool Marketing Board. All representational work done by the UAOS with these bodies is paid for by the subscriptions from the co-operative societies, while the work of organisation and co-operative development is paid for by the state grant. In 1975-76 the expenditure was of the order of £13,000 under each heading. The relationship between the state and the co-operative movement, as exemplified in the working of the Milk Marketing Board, is an intriguing one. To some extent it smacks more of socialism than co-operation. From another viewpoint it also incorporates much of Plunkett's ideal of the blending of self-help and state aid. Every milk producer has a vote and producer members are elected democratically to the Board on a county basis, which also has four or five government nominee members. Milk is paid for directly by the Board but the producer is facilitated by being able to sign a voluntary deduction slip to have the cost of his purchases of farm requisites from his co-operative deducted from his monthly milk cheque — in much the same way as civil servants can have insurance and mortgage payments deducted from their salary. The Milk Board's annual general conference differs essentially from a co-operative annual general meeting in that the ordinary milk producer, while he is encouraged to attend and voice his opinions, has no voting rights other than that exercised from his own home to elect producer members to the Board by secret ballot. However, the producers have the ultimate authority to disband the Board. By securing a given number of signatures, they can force a revocation poll and, if a majority were secured, the Board would be disbanded and its assets divided between *existing* producers on a gallonage basis.

The extent to which the ordinary producer can influence current Board policy is arguable and, in practice, the situation is a delicate one since nearly all the authority is vested in the state and much of the industrial infrastructure is state owned. It is a stage in co-operative evolution which is worth the most careful study. It highlights the necessity of more thorough investigation to establish the best type of co-operative structures, taking account of all aspects of organisation, economics, geography and sociology. This is a need that is increasingly compelling, North and South.

Chapter Twelve

The Capitalisation of Honesty: The Village Banks

On the whole, Ireland may be congratulated upon
having forestalled Great Britain in the successful initiation
and development of Co-operation in finance,
as well as in agricultural operations generally.
(Catherine Webb)[1]

Farmers have always had special problems over money. Their business requires a large capital, but the turnover is nearly always slow and frequently uncertain. Therefore their income is often irregular and peaks at certain periods of the year. This has naturally demanded a special approach to their co-operative development. Whereas the Rochdale Pioneers could insist on cash sale, farmer co-operatives found it somewhat unpractical. Thus, it is not surprising that one of the earliest forms of co-operation practised in Europe was the organisation of co-operative credit societies. The Schülze-Delitzsh banks were very successful in Germany, and repeated efforts were made at co-operative congresses during the eighteen seventies to have the system introduced in Britain. These banks were organised co-operatively and conformed to Rochdale concepts: limited liability, limited interest on capital, and surplus funds distributed in proportion to the members' transactions.

The Schülze-Delitzsh credit banks are perhaps best suited to the small businessman and urban worker, but they have many farmer members, particularly in Germany and Italy. Amongst farmers, the most successful type of credit bank was that initiated by Fredrich W. Raiffeisen[2] in Westphalia in 1849. By the turn of the century there were over 2,000 Raiffeisen banks in Germany alone;[3] by 1940 there were over 20,000. The

---

1 In *Industrial Co-operation*, op.cit., p. 174.
2 For a short biographical note, see Arnold Bonner, *British Co-operation* (Manchester: Co-operative Union Ltd., revised edition 1970), p. 510.
3 "... whose boast it is that after 46 years experience that no one, either member or creditor, has lost by them a single penny." (IAOS leaflet no. 2, 1898).

principles on which they are run are more old-fashioned than those of
Schülze-Delitzsh.

(i) The member's liability is unlimited.[4] All members are jointly and
    severally liable for all the debts of the society.
(ii) There is no share capital.
(iii) Membership and activities are limited to a local area, where each
    member will be personally known.
(iv) No dividends are paid. Any surplus is used to form a reserve fund.
(v) The management is not paid.

Agricultural banks of the Raiffeisen type were to be adopted in Ireland.
Plunkett's attempts to establish co-operative shops had come to a standstill
because of the poverty of the rural people and their indebtedness to the
local shopkeeper. Creameries offered an opportunity to get co-operation
working, but a committed reformer could not accept them as being more
than a chance to make a start. It was good to be able to pay 3½d per gallon
for milk, giving the farmer an extra income of 30 shillings per cow,[5] but this
would not solve his financial problems: he was locked in the ruinous
situation of paying excessive prices for his raw materials and interest
between 30 to 60 per cent. or more on his household debts. The basic
problem would have to be tackled: before he could be a useful co-operative
member, the farmer would have to be freed from the vicious economic
cycle wherein his indebtedness compelled him to sell his produce to the
merchant at lowest prices, buy inferior goods at exorbitant cost and suffer a
rate of interest which increased his indebtedness from year to year.
Tragically, it was in the poorest districts that the unscrupulous traders
made the greatest killing. It became proverbial that 'the poorer the district,
the richer the gombeen-man'. Moneylending for funerals, marriages and
family settlements was particularly harrowing since there was no
productive asset to generate money towards repayment.

It is well at this stage to distinguish between the gombeen-man and the
moneylender, who did not combine shopkeeping with his activity. There
were many moneylenders — individuals and companies, native and foreign
— in Dublin and the provincial towns. Their sole business consisted of
lending money, with or without security, but always at an excessive rate of
interest.[6] A contemporary account of the activity of moneylenders
mentions their advertisements, "which fill the columns of newspapers and

4   This pattern of organisation is similar to that of some Danish dairy co-operatives which
    have no share capital and whose members are fully liable. Some Danes argue that limited
    liability dulls the edge of responsibility and is contrary to the 'spirit' of co-operation. See
    Louis P. F. Smith, *The Evolution of Agricultural Co-operation* (Oxford: Basil Blackwell,
    1961), p. 20.
5   Yield per cow: 435 gallons. Price of homemade butter: 8d per lb (3 gallons of milk to
    produce 1 lb butter). See audited returns of the dairy societies in the IAOS Annual Report
    1895.
6   Effective legislation to control moneylending interest rates is comparatively recent. In
    Ireland, Section 11 of the Moneylenders Act 1933 declares as harsh and unconscionable,
    and consequently unenforceable, any rate of interest above 39 per cent.

astonish the reader by their dazzling visions of philanthropy and their casual indifference as to the amount of money to be lent, or the rate of interest to be charged."[7] The pages of the co-operative weekly, *The Irish Homestead*, frequently referred to the moneylenders as "those 60% philanthropists". One such moneylender in Swinford, County Mayo, was reported as having the endearing habit of displaying in his office window a basinful of gold sovereigns. The effect of this glittering gold on the man who needed money to meet some domestic emergency can be imagined; its acceptance, even at a rate of interest (100 per cent. or more) which encompassed the borrower's final ruin, was often a foregone conclusion.

Apart from his availability at the time of a family crisis, the attraction of the moneylender lay in the simplicity and secrecy of the transaction. The people of rural Ireland then, as now, were disinclined to let their neighbours know that they were borrowing money. Consequently they often chose to borrow from the moneylender at unfavourable terms when they could have got cash much more cheaply from other sources.

In contrast to the 'straight' moneylender, the gombeen-man was a combination shopkeeper/produce-buyer/usurer, common to an impoverished rural economy in every country, but with particular Irish connotations. He usually dealt in a wide variety of goods and services and was often a figure of considerable political and social influence, frequently held in high regard in the community. Perhaps one of the best accounts of the gombeen-man, his environment and methods of operation, is in the evidence of Patrick Gallagher of Dungloe before the Departmental Committee on Agricultural Credit in 1914:[8]

> Once a farmer gets into debt with the gombeen man he seldom gets free from the big man's clutches, and the worst feature of it is, while he is in this state he is no better than a slave to the man who gives him the credit. He very often has to leave his home and family and go to America or Scotland to pay the call of the gombeen man. As his family grow up they are sent to service at the early age of from eight years upwards, to help to get their father out of debt, with the result that, I am quite safe in saying, about seventy-five per cent of the people in the gombeen district are illiterate. I have been hired myself at nine years of age in this town [Strabane], and I am quite certain there were younger boys than I hired at the same time.
>
> The 1911 Census shows that the illiterates in the parish which I speak of are as follows, in the several electoral divisions: Dunloe 25.4; Maghery 34.5; Lettermacaward 36.6; Croveogh 38.3; and Doochary 40.* But this in not the true state of affairs, for if a man or woman can only write or spell their own names, they are put down as literates,

7   Lionel Smith-Gordon and Laurence C. Staples, *Rural Reconstruction in Ireland* (London: P. S. King & Son Ltd., 1917), p. 131.
8   This transcript is reproduced by courtesy of Mrs M. MacC. Foley, Cumbernauld, Glasgow. The committee was convened in 1912 and issued its report (C.D. 7375) in June 1914.
*These figures are percentages.

though we would consider these people illiterate for all practical purposes ... amongst such people is the most fertile soil for the gombeen man. The people pay tribute to him to the tune of from fifty to one hundred per cent, according to the grasp he has on his victims. He gives the farmer credit at this enormous rate of interest and if the latter is not able to pay up according to the gombeen man's wishes he takes his victim to the joint-stock bank and sticks him there for the full amount of the account. The farmer here again has to pay the addition to the interest already charged. If, by any misfortune, the farmer should not be able to meet the bills as they become due, here again the gombeen man puts on the screw (as it is he who backs all the bills). He then gets the farmer to put up his land for auction. All the auctioneers in my parish are gombeen men, and here again he gets his five per cent auction fees ... I know of several evictions in my parish by the gombeen man, and I never knew of an eviction in the same parish by the landlord, so of the two evils — landlordism and gombeenism — I have no hesitation in saying that the gombeen man is much worse than the landlord ... the gombeen man is immune from criticism. If any man says a word against him, I can tell you that man will suffer for it, as it is considered anti-national to say a word against him ... he can ruin any man who crosses him, for he is all powerful in his own district.

He is the local magistrate, the man who represents the people on the District and County Councils ... the people are helpless in the matter, as I am quite certain that over fifty per cent of the electorate are tied, through debt, to one gombeener or another and really they look on this matter as the law of nature. Even in a poor parish like ours there are what is known as the upper circle, or society set, and as the gombeen man gets his money easily, he gives dinners and tea parties to this set, and tells his guests about the poverty of his victims and how much he has done to assist them; he gave them credit when times were bad, and many of them would be in the workhouse today only for him.

Talking about the workhouse, I might just mention that the gombeen man's influence there is all-powerful for the purposes of regulating contracts, etc., and so making a further profit out of the pauperisation of his victims. The result of all this is that the few educated who associate with him frequently become demoralised like himself. In fact, the gombeen man is the most prominent on any platform for denouncing landlords and English tyranny, and by these means diverts attention from his own deeds ... There is a transaction of my own with the gombeen man. On the 28th May 1906 my father and I bought seven stone of flour and one cwt of indian meal each. My father paid for his, 17s. I was not in a position to pay for mine until 11th July, 1906, forty-four days later. The gombeen man then presented me with a bill for 21s. 3d. I disputed his right to charge me 4s. 3d. interest and pointed out to him that my father bought the same goods on the same date for 17s. The gombeen man argued that my father paid him 18s. and that he was only charging me 3s. 3d. extra or 144 per cent interest per annum.

During the twenty years my father was bringing up his family he paid interest at this rate.

A different source provides a scathing appraisal of the conditions of economic and social regression consequent on the political and social dominance of gombeenism in the Congested Districts, those highly populated western areas of tiny farms, poor soils, degraded husbandry, appalling rural poverty and inhuman conditions of housing and living:

> In congested Ireland every job which can be filled by the kith and kin of the gombeen kings and queens is filled accordingly and you get every kind of inefficiency and jobbery. They are all publicans, and their friends are all strong drinkers. They beget people of their own character and appoint them lieutenants and non-commissioned officers in their service. All the local appointments are in their gift, and hence you get drunken doctors, drunken rate collectors, drunken J.P.'s, drunken inspectors — in fact, round the gombeen system reels the whole drunken congested world . . .[9]

Although gombeenism was most flagrant in the remote areas of the west, it occurred throughout Ireland. Modern written and verbal accounts of the gombeen-man all tend clearly to identify him as an exploiter of almost satanic wickedness. It is an estimate of character which was not at all self-evident at the time; in fact, the success of the gombeen-man depended on his appearing respectable and philanthropic — a decent man, approachable, helpful, a wise counsellor, often a pillar of the Church and the Party, influential, well-connected, a man one could safely turn to in times of trouble.

The most notorious gombeen-man would perform generous acts on carefully selected occasions. He subscribed handsomely to many good causes; he came to the aid of poor families in unusual distress, so that his generosity would secure wide publicity and future business and goodwill. Sometimes, having quietly brought about the utter destitution of a customer, he would make an outright gift of a fine milch cow to provide milk for the unfortunate children. Frequently, in his roles of undertaker or travel agent, the gombeen-man won the undying gratitude of needy but proud families who did not want the extent of their poverty revealed, by providing the necessaries of Christian burial or advancing passage money to emigrants.

The gombeen-man's usury was selectively applied. His intimate knowledge of different families — their kinship ties, the extent of their education, their financial means, and their reputation and status in the community — defined the areas in which he could effect the severest usury

9   AE, *Co-operation and Nationality* (Dublin: Maunsel, 1912), pp. 13-14.

with the least risk. Where he miscalculated, he was invariably shrewd enough to concede gracefully and avoid a damaging confrontation. One informant from the Cloghaneely district of County Donegal recalls a young man, about the beginning of World War I, asking a gombeen-man for a detailed statement of account. The young man's family had obtained credit from the shopkeeper for many years. The father and his sons went annually as migratory farmworkers to Scotland and during their absence the household provisions for the large family were provided on credit and entered in the 'book'. None of the customers ever saw this book. The money brought home by the father and his sons was paid to clear the account fully or in part each Christmas. There was frequently a balance carried forward, but on the death of the father, and at his request, the book had been cleared. Two years later, however, despite substantial payments on account, it had apparently grown to frightening proportions. When asked to furnish a detailed account, the gombeen-man had first tried to downface one of the sons with abuse and ridicule. However, on learning that the applicant had been to night-school in Scotland and had consulted with the priest and the schoolmaster at home, the usurer's attitude softened considerably. Two days later the intrepid inquirer received a detailed account which was obviously freshly transcribed and which showed a sum substantially less than that previously reported.[10]

Sometimes the merchant adopted a much less rigid stance and the payment of overdue bills was frequently the subject of bargaining; as were the prices allowed by the gombeen-man in counter-account for butter, eggs and farm produce traded to him. Those who bargained longest sometimes came off best. Very often, however, timid customers, and those deeply indebted who had been the recipients of previous concessions, were afraid to question their bills or seek any discounts for fear of incurring the gombeen-man's wrath and having him proceed against them for full recovery of their debts.

When customers did not pay cash for their goods, a common gombeen practice was to enter in the 'book' a credit price often as much as 50 per cent. greater than that asked of cash customers. This system was not only usurious but discriminatory, in that it did not distinguish between the credit customer who paid in a month and the laggard who succeeded in having the account drag on for a year. Some enterprising gombeen-men modified this procedure by initially entering a 'credit price' perhaps 20 per cent. over the cash price and then charging interest of 5 per cent. or more per month, thus achieving an initial bonus of 20 per cent. and thereafter an effective 6 per cent. interest per month on the cash price. When it is considered that the gombeen-man's cash price frequently included an excessive basic profit margin, the real extent of his usury becomes apparent. In cases where the goods were adulterated (as with artificial manures), the accumulated injustice was truly monstrous.

10 My informant could not remember the precise sums in question but he did recall his mother's reaction to the incident: "Sure Mr ———— was always the best in the world . . . Sure, anyone can make a mistake."

Not all merchants, even in remote rural areas, were gombeen-men or usurers; nor did they all adulterate their goods. Some of the larger, well-established firms and small family businesses managed to remain honest and, through good management and diligence, maintained their living in the face of frequently unfair competition from the short-changing gombeen-men.

Rapacious gombeenism did not arise overnight through the moral turpitude and wicked contrivance of a number of merchants. It was a gradual degenerative process dating back at least as far as the latter half of the seventeenth century and the succeeding period, when Irish manufacturing industry was consistently repressed and agriculture became progressively more inefficient and only sporadically profitable. Many Irish towns and villages, denuded of formerly flourishing industries and with decaying rural hinterlands, were left with too many shops and too few customers. Although any rational assessment of the situation could only show the prospects of the distributive trade as hopeless unless there could be a regeneration of primary and secondary industries, the ordinary citizen tended to see it as the only sector in the economy which offered any immediate living. Consequently, and astonishingly, shopkeepers tended to multiply and it was inevitable that in the struggle to survive, many of them would resort to unethical practices.

Gombeenism as a business technique could temporarily enhance the wealth of ruthless individuals but was ultimately self-defeating. As the victims of the system became progressively more impoverished, the exactions of the gombeen-man had to be progressively more severe to maintain the 'yield'. Gombeenism bred only despair, shiftlessness, dishonesty and inefficiency. Plunkett and the early co-operators attempted the daunting task of reversing the pernicious downward spiral, a task comparable to that undertaken by Robert Owen in trying to reverse the degenerative spiral in British industry almost a century earlier. In England there had been an industrial revolution preceded by an agricultural revolution. Despite the social and economic distress of the working-classes, these revolutions generated great wealth which in time achieved some degree of equitable distribution. Owen helped to arrest the deterioration which was leading the industrial system to ultimate self-destruction.

In Ireland there had been no revolution either in agriculture or in the manufacturing industries. Emigration after the Famine had to some extent alleviated the lot of the people who remained and per capita income had been raised by the drastic expedient of halving the population. As land congestion was relieved, there was a slow improvement in agricultural growth but this tended to occur in the already better-off regions of the east and south. In the poorer areas of the country, the reduction in population, though severe, was not sufficient to arrest the wasting of soil fertility, to improve productivity or to provide the smallholder with a tolerable livelihood from the land. In some places in the west, like the Gweedore area of west Donegal, population actually increased in the post-Famine period. The earnings of migratory labourers and the remittances of emigrants were necessary to provide even a subsistence living for many of the small-farm families. There was little investment in local agriculture or industry — the profits of merchants and even the meagre savings of the local population tended to be invested outside the local economy, usually outside Ireland. This was true not only of the poorer western areas but of rural Ireland generally. It is only against this economic background and its disastrous social consequences that the efforts of the early co-operators can be fairly assessed.

One of the main reasons why country people fell into the hands of moneylenders (including gombeen-men) was because they alone provided the countryman with a source of credit. Some better-off farmers availed of the services of the joint-stock banks. Their business, however, was mostly concerned with depositing money in safe-keeping; very few farmers either needed or sought credit for agricultural purposes. Farming was uncertain and fluctuating prices inhibited borrowing for investment in intensive production. Borrowing by farmers was largely confined to the purchase of extra land or dealing in livestock, at which stage the client might often more truthfully be described as a dealer than a farmer.

Some thrifty farmers, and those in receipt of legacies, had deposit accounts in the bank, and few poor families had a few pounds saved against the 'rainy day'; this in spite of the fact that the rainy day was already upon them and the money might be more usefully invested on the farm. This practice was common in the poorer districts. Indeed, to the present day, the joint-stock banks value the west of Ireland as a 'resource area' where they get cheap money by way of deposits.

Up to comparatively recent times, many small farmers entered the august premises of joint-stock banks with considerable awe and trepidation and then only to perform some minor transaction like the discharging of a Land Commission annuity. Few had the courage or even the desire to ask for a loan. In any case, up to the Wyndham Act of 1903 and for a number of years afterwards, the majority of small farmers were still *tenants* and were consequently limited in what they had to offer as security for loans. Another disability was encountered in remote rural districts. Between 1890 and 1910 there was a great expansion of banking services in Ireland and the number of branches almost doubled. Prior to that period, however, and in the poorer counties for a long time afterwards, a bank was often ten or more miles away, and sometimes this was a sub-branch which opened only one or two days a week. The cost of the borrower's travelling expenses and those of his two sureties, whose food and drink he had also to pay for on the journey, was a recurring expense which had to be met every time the three or four months bills required renewing. Added disincentives for the borrower were the unease he experienced in discussing his business with the bank manager and the fact that the interest charged for small sums was deducted before the loan was handed out.

The banks showed little desire to attract small-loan business; sometimes the amounts hardly justified the book-keeping and the tedious task of researching the credit-worthiness of each borrower. The bankers' best friends were usually the traders, publicans and farmers depositing large sums of money. The former class, as a rule, would be hostile to the needs of the poorer people; the latter, more or less indifferent. There was a tacit understanding that the gombeen-man performed a certain moneylending function and the bank manager was often reluctant to solicit, or even to accept, any significant share of that business for fear of losing a valuable client to a competing bank.

In some parts of the country there was still a limited amount of rural credit available through the loan fund system — a moribund survival of eighteenth-century charitable efforts. Jonathan Swift is said to have inaugurated the fund by donating £500 to be loaned by trustees to the workers of Dublin. Various benevolent bodies, notably the Musical Society of Ireland, followed Swift's example and the loan societies thus formed were afforded a measure of protection by the Irish parliament. Following the Act of Union in 1800, a number of associations, known as the 'Irish Reproductive Funds' were established in London to "improve the condition of the Irish peasantry". Loan fund societies were established in many parts of Ireland but, because they were not properly supervised, dishonesty occurred.

In 1836 an Irish Loan Fund Board was established to supervise the system; its members were appointed by the Lord-Lieutenant. No loans of more than £10 were permitted and interest was fixed at a rate of 12 per cent. per annum. A further Act of Parliament in 1843 allowed for low interest rates but there appears to have been no effective deterrent for abuses and irregularities. Although depositors and/or debenture holders often lost their money through the mismanagement or dishonesty of loan fund officers, such occurrences rarely provoked an outcry. Many people continued to make deposits or accept loans from the local loan fund in the mistaken belief that the system was backed by the government. Many loan fund societies disappeared in the eighteen nineties as the joint-stock banks established more branches in the smaller provincial towns, but in some areas loan funds survived well into the new century. Their reputation in official circles is perhaps best indicated by the observation of William L. Micks in his (baseline) report (May 1892) to the Congested Districts Board on the district of the Rosses: ". . . the Northern Banking Company have a branch office in Dungloe; and the district is fortunate in not having any loan funds within or near its limits."

Probably the most ingenious and ruinous method ever devised by farmers for obtaining money on credit was the 'trust auction'. This system prevailed mainly in Ulster where it reportedly first appeared in County Donegal in the late eighteen nineties. A number of men would combine to drive their cattle to an auction where all the animals were offered for sale as the property of one man. The others bid them up to a good price. The auctioneer paid cash to the supposed seller at a discount and the ostensible buyers gave bills for three or four months to the auctioneer at an exorbitant rate of interest for the credit. The cattle were then driven home to their own fields and the syndicate divided the money, less discount for cash, auction fees, interest and the cost of refreshments. Individual farmers also availed of the auction to buy a beast on credit. The animal was subsequently sold for cash.

From his first association with Plunkett and the co-operative movement, the Rev Thomas Aloysius Finlay had expressed his dissatisfaction at the lack of a good system to provide capital for small farmers. He was thoroughly conversant with systems of popular credit, which he had observed working successfully in Germany, and insisted that the establishment of such a system in Ireland must be a priority if the co-operative agricultural movement was to make even minimal progress. No practical steps were taken until the establishment of the IAOS in April 1894, when Father Finlay asked the committee to invite Henry W. Wolff to visit Ireland. Wolff was English born but had lived in Germany for many years. He was an acknowledged expert on agricultural co-operation and particularly on co-operative finance. When the Christian Socialist, Edward Vansittart Neale, died in September 1892, Wolff took his place in the council of the International Co-operative Alliance. He readily accepted the invitation of the IAOS and came to Dublin in June 1894, where his observations convinced him of the prime necessity of establishing rural credit societies. Like Finlay, he deemed the Raiffeisen system to be the one most appropriate to Ireland and discussed its practical application with the IAOS committee and staff.[11]

Henry W. Wolff

Two other English visitors arrived soon afterwards: R.A. Yerburg MP (president) and Thomas Farrow (secretary) of the English Agricultural Banks' Association. Mr Yerburg lectured in Dublin on the subject of

---

11 Henry Wolff's books on co-operative banking were soon acknowledged as classic works on the subject. Details as to how credit societies should be started and worked were given in his book, *Agricultural Credit Societies* (London: P. S. King & Son Ltd., 1895).

agricultural credit[12] and also attended several meetings in County Cavan at the invitation of Thomas Lough, MP for Islington, who lived at Drummully, Killeshandra.[13] Farrow visited many parts of Ireland, observing the commercial banking system and every aspect of provincial trade, and reported regularly to the IAOS.[14]

Having considered a number of different locations, the IAOS committee decided that the first agricultural credit bank should be established in Doneraile, County Cork. Doneraile was a central location in the Munster belt of established co-operative societies, where there were many active co-operators and patrons of the movement who would carefully supervise the venture and ensure its success. The Doneraile Co-operative Agricultural Credit Society was registered on 19 November 1894 but did not start business until the following February. Coroner James Byrne was elected chairman and under his guidance and control the bank committee operated with model efficiency. The business of the society was done with scrupulous care and its accounting was impeccable. James Byrne addressed the first annual general meeting in Doneraile Courthouse on 18 February 1896:

> ... it has now been fully demonstrated that the scheme is practicable and beneficial in the highest degree. The Irishman has shown his honesty, his trustworthiness and his desire to improve his conditions ...
>
> Our operations have extended to every corner of the parish, without the least solicitation, and applications were received by our Secretary (Mr D.L. Roche) from people in neighbouring parishes and places outside our district, which had to be refused, for the working of an Agricultural Bank must be confined to a limited area, so that the members may be known to each other ...
>
> The Doneraile Bank can now be looked upon as the pioneer Agricultural Credit Society of Ireland. It has succeeded beyond our expectations, and from my knowledge of the good done already I believe these associations to be the greatest help to our struggling but honest countrymen.[15]

The IAOS committee appointed the exemplary secretary of the Doneraile bank, David L. Roche, bank organiser for Ireland. An

---

12 In the lecture hall of Leinster House, kindly lent by the Royal Dublin Society, 9 August 1894.

13 Thomas Lough was brother of Arthur Steel Lough, founder member of Killeshandra Co-operative Creamery. Thomas subsequently published a book entitled *England's Wealth, Ireland's Poverty* (London: T. Fisher Unwin, 1896), a well-documented volume with copious tables, illustrations and bar-graphs, which was acknowledged as a devastating exposé of taxation inequalities.

14 From Achill island he wrote enthusiastically to R. A. Anderson that he had found a man named Lynchehaun, "who would make an ideal secretary of a credit Bank". The IAOS committee ruled out Achill as a first venture since it was too far from base. Some time afterwards Lynchehaun was convicted for murder and subsequently passed into legend following his escape from Maryborough and other jails.

15 *The Irish Homestead*, 22 February 1896.

agricultural bank was formed at Kyle, near Roscrea,[16] in October 1895 and another at Belmullet in County Mayo in May 1896. Roche also visited Johnstown, Urlingford, and Mullinahone with a view to forming banks. In Kiltimagh, County Mayo, the parish priest, Rev Denis O'Hara, offered a loan of £200 to start an agricultural bank in his parish. However, no further banks were set up until 1898 and the first three founded in that year (at Ballindaggin, Blackwater and Castledockrell, all in County Wexford) were of a different type.

One cause of the delay was the departure of David Roche, who had been appointed manager of the Irish Co-operative Agency Society Ltd, but there was also a legal problem. The banks at Doneraile, Kyle and Belmullet were Raiffeisen societies with unlimited liability. As the law stood, such banks were not allowed to take deposits except from members, and then only to the extent of two-thirds of their outstanding loans. It was not until the Societies Borrowing Powers Act was passed in 1898[17] that it was possible to accept unlimited loans. The joint stock banks were reluctant to advance money to what seemed to them to be little more than an association of paupers. However, they were ready to lend money where some of the committee of a credit society were persons of substance prepared to enter into joint and several guarantees.

William Lee, The Lord Plunkett

The three Wexford societies were registered as limited liability societies with special rules. They were promoted by the flourishing Enniscorthy

16 The registered address was Ballaghmore, Queen's County. At the annual conference on 3 November 1898, Plunkett commended the efforts of Father John Gleeson of Kyle and Father J. J. Hegarty of Belmullet. Father Gleeson subsequently spoke: "The local gentry did not trust the people enough to deposit money in such a bank and the people were too poor to subscribe any. However, by one means or another — a concert in Nenagh, an athletic sports in Kyle, for which the housekeepers of the locality contributed the refreshments . . . we succeeded in raising a sum quite enough to begin . . . ."

17 A private member's bill was piloted through parliament by Horace Plunkett. The Lord Plunkett steered it through the House of Lords. William Lee Plunkett was the son of a former Archbishop of Dublin. He was an ardent co-operator and member of the IAOS committee from 1896 to 1903. In 1904 he was appointed Governor-General of New Zealand.

Agricultural Society to finance the trade of its branches, but only the Ballindaggin Society ever started work. Wexford was a relatively prosperous tillage county but operated an established system of merchant credit: from the spring to harvest-time, farmers took their seeds and fertilisers on credit from the merchant, even though credit charges equivalent to an interest rate of 30 per cent. or more were common. The farmers believed that this system gave them a certain bargaining advantage when they came to sell produce, such as barley, in the autumn. Towards the end of 1897 the Congested Districts Board voted £100 to the IAOS towards the expenses of organising credit banks. Shortly after Christmas a fresh campaign was launched in the west which resulted in the formation of agricultural credit societies at Kilcommon, Kilmore-Erris, Burriscarra, Enniscoe, Addergoole and Attymass in County Mayo and in Carna, Rosmuc and Spiddal in County Galway.

The ideal method of financing these societies would have been members' deposits, as had been done even in very poor areas of Germany, where the Raiffeisen banks were known as thrift and credit banks (*Spar und Darlehenskassen*).[18] In most parts of Ireland, however, 'pump-priming' from some other source was invariably necessary before members' deposits could provide a reasonable fraction of the finances. In 1898 the Congested Districts Board agreed to provide loans for each society, not exceeding £100, and an interest rate of 3 per cent., to form the nucleus of capital for societies within the board's jurisdiction. On its foundation, the Department of Agriculture followed the Board's example. In 1901 it had loans totalling £1,350 divided between eighteen societies. In the same year the Board loaned £2,980 to thirty-six societies. These advances were made to selected *members* of the bank committees who in turn deposited them in their own names in the credit bank. This put a heavy responsibility on the members, who were mostly poor men, and it took courage to enter into an engagement which made them the only mark in case of failure.

Although farm prices had taken an upward turn since 1896, the condition of the small western congests was not appreciably improved, and apparently all over Ireland the activities of both local gombeen-men and 'foreign' moneylenders seemed to have intensified. Details of their operations were the subject of caustic comment in almost every issue of *The Irish Homestead*. The IAOS Annual Report for 1898 had this to say:

The 60% philanthropist has been reaping a rich reward for his endeavours to relieve distress; and the extraordinary perversions of any system which seemed to afford the needy borrower an opportunity of obtaining money, no matter on what ruinous conditions, as evidenced by the abuses of the 'Trust Auctions' in Donegal, convinced us that not only was a new credit system necessary, but also that an attempt to

18 The German societies attracted considerably more deposits than they could effectively lend to their members and at a later period were able to make substantial investments in *war loans*.

instruct the present generation of farmers in the proper uses of credit ought to be made.

George William Russell (AE) was a prominent IAOS organiser of credit societies. A native of Lurgan, County Armagh, Russell was discovered by Plunkett in 1897 working as a £60-a-year clerk in Pims drapery store in Dublin. Plunkett took him from his unpromising surroundings and trained him as a co-operative organiser. "While he outdreams us all", said Plunkett, "none of us have as shrewd business judgement or as nice a sense of humour."

Whilst organising banks in Connaught and Donegal, AE was also contributing much of the necessary propaganda to *The Irish Homestead*, the weekly co-operative newspaper founded by the movement in 1895. Later he became its full-time editor and the paper became "one of the most distinguished and entertaining agricultural journals ever published, stamped throughout with the impress of his unique personality."[19] In Donegal, AE established firm friendships with Bishop O'Donnell and Hugh Law of Marblehill, O'Donnell's colleague on the Congested Districts Board.[20] The active campaigning of Hugh Law and AE, backed by the Bishop's exhortations to clergy and laity, paid handsome dividends in co-operative development. By the time AE ceased organising work to take over the editorship of *The Irish Homestead* in 1906, County Donegal had twenty credit banks as well as twenty-nine other co-operative societies.[21]

By the turn of the century, the co-operative credit movement was making steady progress. Thirty-three new banks were formed in 1899 and a further twenty-eight in the following year, bringing the total in 1900 to seventy-six societies with a membership of 3,138. The Annual Report of the Department of Agriculture and Technical Instruction for 1904-05 gave details of the procedure by which the Department provided loan capital to the co-operative credit societies; this and subsequent reports indicate how important the provision of this capital (at 3 per cent. interest) was for the working of the village banks. The maximum of these loans was reached in 1907 when the Department had £12,913 outstanding and the Congested Districts Board £5,872. The number of banks availing of the loans was 181, i.e., 96 per cent. of all credit societies making annual returns and thus deemed to be active. The IAOS committee had mixed feelings about these government loans. They welcomed the availability of money on attractive terms but were perturbed by some instances where credit societies had made little effort towards achieving self-sufficiency and seemed to regard

19 M. Digby, op. cit., p.104.
20 Hugh Alexander Law, second son of Hugh Law, the former Lord Chancellor of Ireland. Educated at Rugby and Oxford and a member of the Bar both in England and Ireland, Hugh A. Law was MP for West Donegal 1902-18 and a member of Dáil Eireann 1927-32. The single-roomed cottage deep in untracked woodland on Law's estate at Marblehill, County Donegal, where AE regularly retreated to meditate and paint, is delapidated but still extant.
21 Fourteen creameries, two agricultural societies, four flax co-operatives, and three poultry, home industries and bee-keeping societies.

the Department loan, if not as a permanent gift, at least as a long-term entitlement. There had been at least one emotive outcry, from a society which complained that the Department was "trying to evict us out of our loan".

The peak for credit society members occurred in 1908: 268 societies[22] with a membership of over 17,000. In that year 8,615 loans were made, totalling £52,771.[23] Thereafter the number of societies declined but was over 200 until 1918; their peak coincided more or less with the zenith of total co-operative societies. In 1907 there were over 900 co-ops, so the IAOS could not hope to deal with any but the most urgent problems. To make matters worse, the Department of Agriculture's grant to the IAOS (£3,700 in 1907) was discontinued at the end of 1908. Plunkett made a special appeal to the co-operators to help financially. They made a gallant effort, but the amount fell far short of the £5,000 he needed.[24] In 1909, 103 co-operative societies were dissolved;[25] amongst them were forty-one credit societies. This decline was felt most keenly by struggling banks, particularly in the poorer parishes of the west. In more affluent areas, agricultural banks were making profits and could afford to pay their secretaries. In the typical small bank in the west with capital of a few hundred pounds, lending rarely exceeded £500 per annum and profits were often counted in shillings and pence.[26] It was here that the system was put to the severest test and the unpaid secretary and committee were hard pressed, for applications for loans frequently exceeded the resources of the bank.

The strongest banks, however, were not always in the richest districts nor the weakest in the poorer ones. Among the societies with biggest deposits (i.e., local investments) in 1908 were Mullaghbawn, County Armagh — £1,483; Malin, County Donegal — £1,395; Townacrann, County Mayo — £1,062; Geesala, County Mayo — £870. In contrast, the bank at Oulart, County Wexford, had only £1 on deposit and operated on a loan capital of £150.

During 1910 a fierce correspondence raged between Plunkett and T.W. Russell, vice-president of the Department of Agriculture. Russell declared publicly that the whole system of the agricultural banks was "rotten and indefensible" and that the £24,000 lent by the Department and the Congested Districts Board was not worth more than half-a-crown in the

---

22 Of these 268 banks, 91 were in Connaught, 65 in Ulster, 57 in Munster and 55 in Leinster. County Mayo had 45.

23 See IAOS Annual Report 1909. The figures quoted in report script do not tally with the table of statistical abstracts given at the end of the report. The IAOS committee complained that several societies had failed to send their books for audit.

24 The societies raised an extra £500 along with their annual affiliation fees of £500. Individual subscriptions netted £1,200 including £500 from Plunkett himself, £100 from Harold Barbour and £100 from Andrew Carnegie. Evoking memories of Rochdale was a subscription of £1 from a Mrs M. Sharman Crawford.

25 In most cases their registration was cancelled by the Registrar of Friendly Societies for failure to furnish annual returns in accordance with the Act.

26 Of the forty-five banks in Mayo (1908) average figures were: membership 86, deposits £87, loan capital £140, loans granted 62, total amount of loans £250, net profit £3. (Derived from tables in IAOS Annual Report 1909).

pound.[27] The loans advanced by the Department and the Congested Districts Board were called in, even though the interest had been paid punctually. Russell even questioned the authority of the Congested Districts Board to make its annual grant of £350 to the IAOS for organising and supervising the agricultural banks.[28] This sum, though only a quarter of the money spent by the IAOS on servicing the banks, was very important. The Board ignored Russell's warning and paid the grant a year later. The total amount lost by the Department and the Board on Loans advanced to the credit societies amounted to "approximately ½ of one per cent of one year's interest, the aggregate of the principal was fully recouped."[29]

The recall of this capital did not bring the credit societies tumbling down, as T.W. Russell may have expected. It only hardened the resolve of the more active ones, and won them more support. Regrettably, the real sufferers were again the weak banks in the poor districts which relied almost exclusively on state funds. Many were unable to continue effective service with the meagre capital which had been raised locally.

The little village banks won the respect and affection of the people. The pages of the *Homestead*, and even of the IAOS annual reports, carried numerous and heart-warming accounts of success:

A member of the Burren Bank borrowed £3 for six months and purchased young pigs which he fed on potatoes and meal. The potatoes he did not regard as costing anything, but taking into account 4 cwt of meal at 5s. 6d. per cwt consumed by the pigs, he found he made a profit of £6 on the transaction. This man has a holding of 8 acres of tillage land and a run of mountain grazing but is compelled to go to England every year to earn money to meet his calls. He would be better off if he could stay and work his farm, but he never has sufficient capital to keep going at home for a twelve month.

Bonhams were then selling at 10/- to 12/- each and, even though the husbandry did not always conform to modern concepts of balanced nutrition, the economics often worked out all right. 'W.G.' borrowed £4 from the Innismacsaint Bank, County Donegal, with which he bought bonhams for £3, and for 13/- (65 pence) he procured enough 'refuse' from Finner Military Camp to enable him to fatten the pigs within four months and sell them for £10.

The secretary of Clare Island Bank gave particulars of eight loans

27 At the close of 1908 the amount of capital held by the Raiffeisen banks in Ireland amounted in round figures to £53,000: from depositors £20,000; joint stock banks £15,000; Department of Agriculture £12,000; and the Congested Districts Board £6,000.
28 "His attitude to the self-help' movement was that of the New York saloon-keeper who wrote up over his bar 'God helps the man who helps himself but God help the man who is caught helping himself here!'" (Plunkett, presidential address at the annual general meeting of the IAOS, 14 November 1911).
29 R. A. Anderson, *With Horace Plunkett in Ireland*, p. 257. The net loss to the Department on the fifteen-year experiment was £91. The Board was even more fortunate, recording no loss at all if one discounts a total deficit of three shillings and one penny.

amounting to £19.10s on which the net profit amounted to £58.12.6, and from Claremorris, also in Mayo, the parish priest, Rev P. Kilkenny, wrote:

> The means at its disposal are no doubt slender, still it is easy to point out cases where the loan from the Bank has produced twice or even thrice the amount borrowed ... Greater even than the material advantages of the Bank are the moral effects resulting from it in the district of Murneen; firstly in the education the people are receiving in the true use of credit and again in the gain for the country that can so easily be obtained from mutual co-operation. Heretofore the man who borrowed lost caste in the neighbourhood ... Now the people are learning that it is honourable to borrow, when necessary, for the honest purpose of improving one's position.

The Reverend P. Lyons, Castlebar

Usually, agricultural banks sought to involve the entire community regardless of class or income distinctions. However, there was often an initial reluctance on the part of cottiers and farm workers to participate in a bank which they felt was more designed for the farmers and the better-off. The clergy's influence was helpful in overcoming this hesitation and, thanks to their efforts, most banks succeeded in attracting a cross-section of the community. In the first bank founded near Tipperary town in 1902, Count Arthur Moore reversed the usual procedure. The Lattin Agricultural Bank had an initial membership composed almost entirely of farm labourers who, after they had overcome the initial shock of finding themselves plunged into the world of finance, conducted their business with commendable zeal and took much pleasure in having farmers and gentry join their bank. Another 'exclusive' bank was formed in County Wexford in 1902: the Killurin Agricultural and Fisherman's Bank had a membership of thirty smallholders and cottiers who earned most of their income by net-fishing salmon on the river Slaney.

In the IAOS Annual Report of 1901,[30] the cautious R.A. Anderson was able to say, "we believe we are justified in stating that every pound shown in the statistical sheet as having been lent has brought the borrower another

---

30 Another item of interest in that Report read: "Our Gaelic-speaking Organiser, Mr Lyons, has familiarised many people with Raiffeisenism, whom no English-speaking organiser, however capable, could move. ... we were enabled through the kindness of Dr Douglas Hyde to have the Agricultural Banks explained in a Gaelic leaflet."

pound and more 'lucky money'." Anderson was alluding to the widespread belief that money from the village bank had a special charm — it was 'lucky money'.

Much of the luck could be attributed to the practical rules under which the village banks worked:

(i) The bank operated over a limited geographical area and all members knew each other intimately.

(ii) Applicants for admission had to be 'sober, honest and industrious'.

(iii) Loans were made for productive purposes only.

(iv) Members on admission became jointly and severally liable for the debts of the bank.

(v) Borrowers had to have two sureties.

Mullaghbawn Village Bank Committee, c. 1906

The luckiest item of all was the rate of interest charged. This ranged from a penny to a penny farthing per £ per month, 5 to 6¼ per cent. per annum. The IAOS recommendation was that the bank should try for a margin of two between the borrowing and lending rate, e.g., borrow at 4 per cent. and lend at 6 per cent. The maximum loan permitted was only £50[31] but this rarely posed great difficulties for small-farmer borrowers. It was not a inconsiderable sum in the days when a good cow could be purchased for £15.

31 Credit societies were registered under the old Friendly Societies Act of 1846. "Such a society in common with other Friendly Societies must consist of at least seven members. It must have a registered office and must, through its general meeting, appoint one or more Trustees in whom all property is vested. It may sue and be sued. An annual audit, not necessarily by a public auditor, is compulsory, together with a quinquennial valuation of property. Annual returns to the Registrar must be made and a balance sheet drawn up and displayed in the Society's office. Societies may amalgamate or may be dissolved voluntarily by consent of five-sixths in value of members ('value' being determined by allotting one vote to each member plus one additional vote up to a total of four for every five years of membership) or compulsorily by decision of the Registrar. . . . Special authorised loan societies are in addition exempted from the Money Lenders Act. They are authorised to lend to members only, sums up to £50." (*Agricultural Co-operation in Ireland*, Horace Plunkett Foundation, 1931). Cheques issued by credit societies were exempt from stamp duty and thus did not have to bear the penny stamp required of ordinary cheques at that time.

In 1902 the joint-stock banks, which had hitherto held aloof from these new co-operative credit societies, reviewed their position. Despite the opposition of local merchants, they began to lend money more freely and a short time afterwards agreed to make loans available to societies at a fixed rate of 4 per cent., regardless of fluctuation. A few county councils also voted small sums toward the expenses of organising credit banks, but merchant influence on these councils was generally too strong for the practice to become widespread.

For two years T.W. Russell continued to carp about the conduct of credit societies, bemoaning the difficulties of recovering loans and hinting darkly at the amount of bad debts incurred and the necessity of frequent legal proceedings. Professional etiquette, he said, did not allow him to be more specific or mention any society by name. The IAOS committee repeatedly urged Russell to consult with them, expressing their opinion that any credit society in difficulties would have little objection to conferring with the IAOS. However, Russell steadfastly refused to take the IAOS into his confidence or cast any light on the identity of the "many societies" supposedly causing him so much difficulty.

In January 1912 Russell decided that a formal inquiry into the position of credit societies was necessary and a Departmental Committee on Agricultural Credit was accordingly appointed. There was an outcry in co-operative circles when only one representative of the IAOS, Father Finlay, was appointed. The co-operators accepted the right of the Department to appoint two of its civil servants to the committee but objected to the inclusion of "several gentlemen whose eminence was due to quite other causes than their knowledge of the principles of either co-operation or agricultural credit."[32] The committee's report was finally published in 1914, after a period of two years during which the credit movement remained in abeyance. It was well documented and gave a concise summary of the history of the movement with detailed statistical accounts and the evidence of a number of experts and persons engaged in the provision of agricultural credit. The report clearly showed that the agricultural banks organised by the IAOS had proven a great benefit to the farming community.

The defects of the system were the common organisational shortcomings freely admitted by the IAOS: a general sloppiness in the conduct of meetings and in the recording of minutes and financial transactions, failure to make audited returns in good time, and an apparent reluctance in many cases to solicit local capital by way of deposits. Common faults were the tendency to extend and renew loans to borrowers who failed to complete repayments within the specified period and the consequent slowness on the part of the Society in repaying loans due to the Department or the Congested Districts Board. The finances of the societies (as the ultimate repayment of all loans demonstrated) were generally intact and there was no evidence of misappropriation of funds or other malpractices. The most

32 Smith-Gordon and Staples, op. cit., p. 151.

serious charge was that borrowers sometimes used their loans for purposes other than those represented in their applications.

A sympathetic reading of the main body of the report indicated that, with harmonious co-operation between the state and this voluntary local effort, and the provision of a small subsidy towards organisation and training, the co-operative credit societies could have a very bright future. The committee, however, drew no such conclusions. Ignoring the evidence of the IAOS and of experts such as Henry Wolff, it decided that the co-operative experiment had been a failure, that the IAOS had fallen short of its duty properly to organise and service the system, and that credit societies could not be operated successfully except under more direct government control. To this end, it recommended that a special branch be set up within the Department of Agriculture to organise credit societies and that all credit societies should have the benefit of a free annual audit at the expense of the Treasury.

Understandably, Father Finlay submitted a minority report in total disagreement with these recommendations. No action was taken by the Department and nothing changed. There was, however, an inevitable slackening of effort during the four-year period between the withdrawal of government support and the publication of the Credit Committee Report in 1914. Generally, however, the village banks held their position reasonably well, without any serious decline in numbers, membership or turnover. The lack of expansion was compensated to some extent by the number of creamery and agricultural societies which adopted special rules enabling them to engage in banking business. The conflict with Russell and the Department also resurrected the co-operators' ideas about taking more comprehensive control of the national system of co-operative credit and the establishment of a central credit bank. At the annual general meeting in November 1910, Anderson put forward the following proposal:

> In August last the Farnaught Agricultural Bank (one of the best managed and most successful of these societies in Ireland) passed the following resolution: 'That in the opinion of this Committee, it is most desirable to have a Central Bank established for financing the local banks, and that this project is urgent and that the IAOS be requested to prepare a scheme to this effect.'
>
> We have now 237 societies with a total turnover of £60,000 and it is important that we should consider whether this fact in itself does not go a good way towards proving that our credit movement is ripe for federation. For the present it seems that one federation of the character and scope I shall outline would be sufficient. I suggest that it should perform the following functions:
> (1) It would act as a clearing house for the reception of societies' surplus funds and the re-lending of such funds to societies which could employ profitably more capital than they can secure locally.
> (2) It would attract deposits from people who now prefer to hoard their savings rather than that their neighbours should become

aware that they are possessed of money.

(3) It would act as an intermediary body through which the joint stock banks, the Department of Agriculture and the Congested Districts Board could with safety make advances to the local societies . . .

(4) Finally the central bank would be in a position to lay down the necessary rules . . . There is no body in existence at present which can accept responsibility for loans granted to credit societies except these societies themselves. The IAOS does everything in its power to secure the observance of rules and the fulfilment of obligation, but it has no authority over the local societies.

Anderson's scheme was referred to the IAOS committee and eventually, on 24 February 1913, the Central Co-operative Credit Society was registered. No formal records of the transactions of this Society can be traced. One report mentions that it started business hopefully, with one deposit of £200 and one loan of £50 to an agricultural bank. The IAOS Annual Report for 1914 stated that the Society began business on 12 March 1913 and that it was "working so far on deposit capital from private sources and on shares taken up by friends of the Movement."

But even as the Central Co-operative Credit Society Ltd. was formed, there was a tacit admission that it would hardly prove adequate to handle much of the co-operator's business:

> There has been a good deal of discussion recently, expecially in connection with the Agricultural Credit Committee as to the advisability of forming a central bank and the lines on which a bank should be run, some advising that it should be dependent on the State and others that it should be a private concern.
>
> The experience of Continental countries seems more and more to point to State intervention as economically unsound and politically dangerous . . .
>
> But it seems at all events premature as yet to consider any such proposal. The movement has not yet reached a stage at which definite banking business is needed on a scale large enough to warrant so ambitious an experiment and in the meantime it is hoped that the Central Co-operative Credit Society will suffice for our present needs. It is not anticipated that in the earlier stages this society will do rapid or extensive business, but if it facilitates societies in dealing with surplus deposits and finding additional capital, and helps in the supervision work of the IAOS, it will have justified its existence.[33]

By the end of 1915 the total business of the Society was £400, lent to four village banks: Abbeyleix (£150), Dungloe, Cullamore and Innismacsaint (£50 each), and a short-term loan to Ardagh Creamery. There was a loss of

33 IAOS Annual Report 1913, p. 22.

7 guineas and one penny on two years working. No business whatsoever was recorded for 1916, a year in which the trade turnover of co-operatives jumped by about 33 per cent. in money terms over the previous year, to top the £6 million mark.

In contrast to the boom in business experienced by other types of co-operatives, the agricultural credit societies suffered a steady decline during the years of World War I.

Year	Number of societies	Membership	Loans granted
1913	235	20,211	£55,492
1915	225	20,260	£48,196
1917	171	17,139	£41,993
1919	138	15,914	£33,834

The decline in business came with improved farm prices when people did not need to borrow as before. The commercial (joint stock) banks began lending money more freely to individual farmers, and the co-operative creameries and store societies were also disposed to give credit to their members. Unfortunately, in many cases the local village bank was bypassed, and creameries and store societies advanced loans or extended credit with a minimum of formality and frequently at no interest charge, even though the societies themselves were paying interest on bank overdrafts. There was a general euphoria and a feeling that, with the ever-increasing spiral of farm prices, poor days would never be seen again.

Such elation was not so apparent in the poorer areas of the west. For the most part what happened there was that improved farm prices enabled the smallholders to run their subsistence farming on a cash basis; recourse to the local co-operative village bank was no longer necessary. No ambitious programmes of agricultural expansion were possible, very little land was available for purchase, so that any money in excess of living requirements on small western farms tended to be saved. By 1917 the Irish Post Office Savings Banks held deposits totalling over £18 million and there was £65 million on long-term deposit with the joint-stock banks. A good proportion of this represented the savings of small farmers and much of it was reinvested abroad.[34]

In the more prosperous farming areas, however, the picture was entirely different. There, the farmers were making money and were disposed to reinvest it in their farming business. Unfortunately they favoured land acquisition more than increased productivity, highlighting once again the Irish obsession with land ownership and apparently small regard for improved husbandry or enhanced *per acre* profits. When there was a prospect of acquiring a few additional acres, farmers stretched their credit

34 "As the total value of Irish foreign investment was sometimes estimated as being in the region of £250 million in the early 1920's, it is not unlikely that total Irish investment abroad around 1914 was of the order of £150 million." L. M. Cullen, *Economic History of Ireland since 1660* (London: B. T. Batsford Ltd., 1972), p. 169.

for farm and home supplies with the agricultural store, sought advances against their milk supply and scraped together every possible penny to buy land. Many of them took heavy mortgages with joint-stock banks in order to exchange a small farm for a bigger one, whereupon the co-operative creamery or agricultural store was put under increased pressure to advance more credit for the stocking of this additional acreage or for the provision of equipment, seeds and fertilisers against forthcoming crops. The trading co-operatives, in turn, took maximum credit from the commercial banks and from their wholesale suppliers.

The large amounts of credit extended to co-ops by IAWS Ltd was to have serious consequences for the Wholesale Society when the post-war slump came in 1920. The agricultural credit banks could play only a very limited role in these wartime developments. Their membership of 20,000 was tiny in the context of 500,000 landowners and their lending capacity never developed to the point where they were able to extend the maximum £50 loan to more than a fraction of the membership. Few societies succeeded in procuring any worthwhile capital through local deposits.[35] Very few societies did a volume of business which would justify a full-time paid secretary,[36] and where, as so often happens in Ireland, the officers of the credit society were also the people who were involved in other voluntary parish work, the amount of effort devoted to promoting the village bank was necessarily scant.

By 1922 the number of agricultural banks had fallen to 110; nine of these were in the six-county area of Ulster and due for incorporation in the new state. Of the 101 in the Free State, only about six were doing an annual business exceeding £1,000. The outstanding performance was that of the Columbkille Society in Longford. This bank had a membership of 604; its capital, composed entirely of members' deposits, had grown to over £27,000. In 1921 the Columbkille bank made 335 loans totalling £7,662. The Louisburgh bank in County Mayo made 327 loans totalling £2,684. The Farnaught Society in south Leitrim, under the guidance of Rev J.G. Digges, maintained its reputation for efficiency and good business with a modest £1,504 given out in fifty-two loans, and in south Wicklow another outstanding clergymen co-operator, the Rev John Rothwell Willis, had flourishing credit societies at Moyne and Togher as well as more modest concerns in Tinahely and Newtown. In County Kilkenny there were village banks in Castlecomer and Ballyraggett, well integrated with other co-operative ventures in these areas and contributing to the benefit of workers and small-farmers with loans between £1,000 to £2,000 per annum.

The Agricultural Credit Corporation Ltd., Ireland's first state-

35 A notable exception was the Columbkille society in a small-farming area of north Longford. In 1917 this society was reported to have more than £17,000 in deposits, while its annual business averaged only £4,000 in some 200 loans. See Rev. M. O'Flanagan, *Co-operation*, pp. 12-13.

36 Although the rules of Raiffeisen societies were specific about unpaid management, the payment of a full-time secretary was permitted where the volume of business made the position a necessity.

sponsored company, was founded in September 1927. It was intended to work on co-operative lines, lending money to co-operative societies which in turn would make loans to their members. The Corporation also made loans to finance the foundation of co-operative creameries in the midlands and other areas where dairying was being developed. It was to prove a valuable source of finance for the Co-operative Wholesale IAWS Ltd., still crippled for lack of working capital. A number of creamery societies availed of the Credit Corporation scheme to provide loans to members for the purchase of dairy cows,[37] but the greater part of the ACC's business came to be long- and medium-term loans negotiated with individual farmers. Even here, the volume of business was small and it was not until the nineteen fifties that the ACC came to rank with the commercial banks as a major source of farm credit.

Canon J.R. Willis

By 1930 the number of old Raiffeisen-type agricultural banks had dropped to fifty-two, membership to 3,672 and turnover to a mere £13,269. The IAOS statistics for that year, however, listed an additional sixty-two credit societies of a somewhat different type, under the intriguing title of 'fluke societies'. Their membership of 5,000 and turnover of £27,000 did not provoke great excitement.

These fluke societies originated during a serious outbreak of liver fluke in livestock in the winter of 1924-25, following two very wet grazing seasons. Deaths of cattle and sheep were particularly heavy in low-lying areas along the Shannon and in flat districts of bad drainage and high rainfall. To meet the disaster, the Department of Agriculture voted £100,000, free of interest for three years, to a special loan scheme to enable farmers to restock their holdings. The scheme was to be operated through the existing co-operative credit societies; in areas where no such societies existed, new ones were formed for this specific purpose. They were to operate on the self-same Raiffeisen principles as the older banks. Initially it was arranged that the Department would advance capital to the societies on the basis of £2 for every £1 collected in local deposits. The society was to pay 4 per cent.

37 The maximum loan was £150, at six per cent. interest.

interest to depositors and charge 5 per cent. to borrowers. Organisation of the new societies was undertaken by the IAOS with the help of the county agricultural instructors:

> But a formidable difficulty soon came to light; in the poorest districts where farmers were in greatest need of credit, societies found it impossible to secure deposits. The Department had, therefore, to waive the deposit requirement, and to issue advances at an interest rate of 2½ per cent. in these districts. But despite the agitation for financial help the demand for loans did not come up to expectations; the total amount advanced in 1925-26 and in the three following years reached only £87,495.[38]

Ten fluke societies were formed in 1925, twenty in 1926, seventeen in 1927 and four in 1928. Of these, thirty were in Munster (Kerry 13, Limerick 10), twelve in Connaught, five in Leinster (Longford 3, Louth and Westmeath 1 each), and four in Ulster (Cavan 3, Monaghan 1). The balance of sixty-two was made up of eleven of the older credit societies adapted to a new role. Most of these had practically ceased to function but were resurrected because some organisationsal structure was still extant.

Most credit societies elected not to join the Department's scheme because of the organisational and accounting difficulties: keeping the Department money in a separate account from their other funds, lending it only for livestock purchase, operating two rates of interest, and having to process applications from unknown candidates who lived outside the normal area of the bank's operations. In Leitrim, a county badly hit by the fluke epidemic, the Rev J.G. Digges kept his major Farnaught bank and a few smaller credit societies to their original role but helped to organise separate fluke societies in conjunction with local creameries, as at Eslinbridge, Kiltoghert and Drumshanbo.

In 1940 there were still forty-eight fluke societies extant. They made no loans and remained in existence merely to collect outstanding debts, amounting to £14,500. This had proved a slow process, but by 1944 they had the figure down to £4,075. By that year the ordinary credit societies (thirty-three in 1940) had dwindled to twenty-three. They made loans totalling some £4,000 and had £7,500 in loans outstanding. One of the incidental tasks assigned to Paddy Kelly (later IAOS secretary) on joining the Society in 1942 was to visit these banks, not just to assess the reason for decline but to get some useful information on how they had survived. In every case he found some dedicated local patriot — teacher, farmer, clergyman or official — who would never say die. As long as he lived, so did the village bank.

From 1945 the annual reports of the IAOS ceased to distinguish between fluke societies and the old banks. By this time the total number was down

---

38 D. Hoctor, *The Department's Story* (Dublin: Institute of Public Administration, 1971), p. 159.

to twenty-two. They held at this until 1949, when they lost two of their number. The following year, although there were still nineteen societies[39] with a nominal 3,215 members, business was obviously near an end. Of 204 loans (£3,690) made that year, 100 of them (£2,601) were in Louisburgh. Total loan capital of all nineteen societies was a single sum of £11. 3s. 8d. owed by Togher Agricultural Bank in County Wicklow. Loans outstanding were £4,960. The 1951 Annual Report said briefly and unsentimentally:

Credit Societies

Statistical forms for these societies have been omitted for 1951 as in only a very few societies is any business being done except in regard to the recovery of loans.

There followed a seven-year hiatus until 1958 when Ireland experienced a second wave of Raiffeisenist activity. This time it came not directly from Europe, but after a roundabout 58-year journeying through North America, Jamaica and some seventy other countries throughout the world. In 1900 a French Canadian journalist, Alphonse Desjardins, took up the Raiffeisen idea and sought to put it into action in Quebec. About the same time a wealthy Boston merchant, Edward A. Filene, saw the credit system at work in India and returned to the USA determined to establish credit unions throughout America.

This was the beginning of a thirty year crusade culminating in the passing of the Federal Credit Union Act in 1934 enabling CREDIT UNION to operate under Federal Law in those States where vested interests had frustrated all efforts . . .

In 1921 the first organised plan for the establishment of today's multi-million member CREDIT UNION movement began and in 1935 the CREDIT UNION NATIONAL ASSOCIATION (CUNA) came into being and in the early 1940s the Canadian movement joined forces with the American movement and the stage was set for the development of a programme for a world extension of the CREDIT UNION MOVEMENT.[40]

In 1957, largely because of the efforts of Norah Herlihy,[41] a Dublin

39 Nearly all the survivors were 'old-timers': Belmullet (founded 1896); Enniscoe, County Mayo (1898); Ballyragget (1901); Killeshandra (1902); Louisburgh (Mayo), Gleneely, Tullynaught (Donegal), Ballinode (Monaghan), Lisduff (Laois), Farnaught (Leitrim) all founded in 1903; Lohar (Kerry) 1904; Donaghmore and Lisdoonan (Monaghan), Moyne (Wicklow), Croaghpatrick, Killeen (Mayo), all 1905; Cloone (Leitrim) 1908; Togher (Wicklow) 1909 and Carrigallen (Leitrim) 1910. The 'newcomer' was the Muintir na Tíre Society in Limerick city (1949).
40 *Credit Union Origin and Philosophy*, a pamphlet by the Credit Union League of Ireland.
41 Miss Herlihy was the leader of a small group (aided by a £5 grant from Country Workers Ltd) which met once a week during the summer of 1957 to plan the establishment of a Credit Union movement in Ireland. She was nominated by Country Workers Ltd., through the Irish Countrywomen's Association executive committee, to be a member of the Committee on Co-operative Societies appointed by the Minister of Industry and Commerce, Seán Lemass, on 20 December 1957.

schoolteacher, a small credit union was formed in Dublin and from there the movement has spread successfully throughout Ireland.[42] Operating on the same Raiffeisen principles, the village banks are back again — many of them in tasteful modern offices — in small towns and villages throughout the land. The name has changed, the membership for the time being is more urban than rural, but the function is remarkably similar (cases come to light which suggest that the gombeen-man is not entirely dead). The new credit unions are proving worthy successors of the old Raiffeisen banks which, in poorer days and far less impressive offices, first taught the Irish people to capitalise their honesty, and which, in the words of Horace Plunkett,[43] performed "the apparent miracle of giving solvency to a community composed almost entirely of insolvent individuals."

---

42 In 1975 there were 453 credit unions, including 93 in Northern Ireland, affiliated to the Irish Credit Union League, cf. the peak number of agricultural banks was 268 in 1908.
43 *Ireland in the New Century*, p. 195.

Chapter Thirteen

The Creameries

We want to find our ideal — the synthesis of
all these co-operative efforts. Butter, especially
when it is good, is a pleasant thing to think about;
but you cannot inspire a national movement by calling
out — 'Really choicest butter'.
AE

Co-operative dairying was the main focus of Plunkett's early efforts. It was then and still remains by far the largest sector of Irish agricultural co-operative activity. From a solitary start in Drumcollogher in 1889, to a modest thirty-three at the foundation of the IAOS (1894), the number of creameries soared to a total of 236 at the turn of the century.[1]

In terms of trade, Munster was always the dominant province in creamery development and in 1900 creameries in the province accounted for approximately £250,000 of the total creamery co-operative turnover of £400,000. Ulster, however, had the greatest number of creameries and the highest co-operative membership and maintained that position up to the period of World War I.[2]

The IAOS instructional leaflet number 1, published in December 1894, explained co-operative factory butter-making in great detail and made explicit suggestions for finance, management and farmer participation:

A creamery costs a good deal — perhaps £700 to £1,000. This sum is subscribed in £1 shares, and it is easy to raise this large sum if everybody concerned takes as many shares as he can afford. Farmers generally take a share for every cow, but there is no fixed rule, the main object being to admit everyone who has a cow. Their shares are paid up by four instalments of five shillings each, and interest is paid on them at the rate of five per cent or a shilling in the pound. The first instalment is always paid in cash, so is generally the second, the other two may be paid by the farmer in milk . . .

1 Including 171 central creameries and 65 'auxiliaries'.
2 In 1915 Ulster had 143 societies with a membership of 21,161, compared to Munster's 144 with 9,671 members. Ulster had £61,858 paid-up share capital, Munster £55,506. Munster creameries, however, handled twice as much milk as their Ulster counterparts: 50 m gallons to Ulster's 25 m gallons in 1915 and 20 m lbs of butter made in 1922, compared to Ulster's 10 m.

The Co-operative Creamery — as it is called — is owned and managed entirely by the farmers who have taken shares. They are called 'the members'. They elect a Committee to manage the business, the Committee being formed of the best men in the Society. Every member has a vote in the election of the Committee — the man with one share having the same voting power as a man with two hundred. This Committee appoints the manager, the dairymaid and all the other hands employed in the Creamery. It meets every month, or oftener, to examine the accounts, and to fix the price for milk. The farmers send in their milk, in the summer night and morning, in the spring and autumn once a day and in the winter every alternate day. It is quickly run through the 'Separators' which take out all the cream. When the milk comes in, it is measured; then a sample is taken to be tested. All milk is not equally productive; it would be unfair to pay the same price for poor as for rich milk. There is a testing machine now used in all the Co-operative Creameries which shows exactly how much butter each supplier's milk will yield, and he is paid accordingly. This gives fair play all round, and the man who neglects, or starves his cows, who keeps them till they are too old, or who puts water in his milk, or skims some of the cream off, is punished by getting a low price, while the man who is honest, and who treats his cows well, gets the full value of his produce.

In the Co-operative Creameries every milk-supplier gets back his skim milk (or separated milk as it is called) free, also his share of the buttermilk. For instance, a man supplying ten gallons of new milk gets back eight gallons of separated milk, and about half a gallon of buttermilk. The separated milk is sweet and wholesome.

The members of the earliest co-operative creameries were substantial dairy farmers. In the first thirty such creameries, the average member had thirteen cows and within three years had paid up £9.43 in 'share capital', approximately 15/- (75 pence) per cow.[3] This was a very healthy financial situation since the farmer-members contributed half or more of the capital required for the creamery building and plant. However, this state of affairs deteriorated rapidly as the movement expanded. After 1895, declared cow numbers, always a matter of doubtful veracity, were no longer recorded, but by 1900 the average share capital had fallen to less than £3 per member.[4] Members who joined with four or five cows increased their herds without enlarging their share capital and a great number of milk suppliers never became members at all.

Efforts were made to have suppliers become shareholders but this idea could not be pushed too hard in areas where proprietary creameries already existed[5] and where the newly established co-operative venture needed the

3   1,641 members; 20,714 cows; £15,468 share capital (see IAOS Annual Report 1895).
4   26,577 members; £74,223 share capital (see IAOS Annual Report 1901).
5   By the turn of the century, only 64 of the 250 creameries in Munster were true co-operatives. The others were owned by individuals, joint-stock companies, firms of provision dealers, butter buyers or by the CWS (70 creameries). A number of joint-stock

milk of 800 to 1,000 cows to sustain it. Small farmers and cottiers, if they became members at all (many were excused on the grounds that they could supply only minimal supplies of milk for perhaps two months of the year), were asked to pay perhaps half-a-crown (12½ pence) of their £1 shares. Creamery managers were reluctant to make further deductions of share capital from tiny milk cheques for fear of discouraging the recipients and driving them back to the private creamery or to home butter-making. So a pattern of low share capital developed which has persisted to the present day. Even after the boom period of World War I, the average paid-up shareholding in 1918 was less than £3.50 per *member*.

In the early ventures, where buildings were comparatively cheap and scant expensive equipment was installed, it was still never possible to erect and equip a creamery on the amount of share capital subscribed. Since a wealthy benefactor was a rarity, it was necessary to go to the commercial banks for a big part of the money. The bank always insisted on joint-and-several guarantees of a number of members of satisfactory solvency, but trying to get a representative group of members to make themselves jointly and severally liable for a large sum of money, proved to be one of the IAOS organiser's toughest tasks. Any man who was substantially wealthier than his neighbours usually fought shy of such engagement, knowing that, in case of trouble, he would be an instant and easy mark for the bank. The organiser's task was thus to assemble a group, each member of which had enough capital to satisfy the bank, but none of whom would become an obvious target should difficulties arise.

Christopher Digges la Touche

Anderson and Digges la Touche (managing director of A. Guinness) hatched a scheme that would make every member of the Society liable for a definite amount according to his means, and would ensure that the total guarantees of members would add up to 125 to 130 per cent. of the loan. The scheme also included an undertaking that the loan thus guaranteed would be paid off by instalments over ten years. Each year a deduction would be made from the guarantor's milk payments for which he would be allotted shares in the co-operative; so, at the end of ten years, the Society would be out of debt, the guarantees discharged and the guarantors earning 5 per cent. on their share capital.

creameries were started by groups of 'strong' farmers but did not survive, having "all the disadvantages of proprietary Creameries, without the advantage of the proprietors' business capacity." (IAOS Annual Report 1899, p. 66).

But the banks refused to alter their time-honoured system. They did not savour the idea of having to proceed against a large number of small guarantors instead of against one or a few. However, they were not ungenerous in other respects. One thing that never failed to amaze Anderson was the fact that, even in their joint-and-several arrangements, the banks often failed to stipulate a definite period for repayment or, where they did, rarely insisted on its fulfilment. In his memoirs, written in 1935, he noted that sometimes the banks had lent large sums of money to societies, even larger than Anderson deemed prudent, because they felt that they could rely on the personal guarantees which they held.

Anderson was deeply hurt at the rejection of the IAOS proposal. Christopher Digges la Touche was acknowledged as one of the best financial brains in Ireland at the time and Anderson felt that he should have got a better hearing. Anderson's main worry, however, was the violence which the guarantee system did to the whole co-operative ideal. What at first sight appeared to be a mere financial detail was to have the most disastrous effects on the basic structures of the co-operative movement:

> Quite apart from the unfairness of requiring a small group of members to shoulder a huge burden for the benefit of the community, without even a shadow of advantage to themselves, it was utterly subversive of the co-operative idea. In order to induce men to become guarantors, it was necessary to safeguard their position as far as possible. Accordingly, if they were willing to serve, they were invariably elected on the Committee, even though they might have no special qualifications for the position, and they could not be removed from the Committee while they remained guarantors unless others, acceptable to the Bank, could be found who were willing to take their place on the guarantees. Very often the entire Committee was composed of guarantors who virtually held office in perpetuity; for the guarantees were but rarely discharged, at all events in full, and until the entire debt had been repaid the guarantee remained operative.
>
> Now, one of the most important, if not the most important, functions of a society's general meeting is, or should be, the election of the Committee. In a society whose committee men were guarantors to the bank, and, therefore, fixtures, during the term of their liability, there could be no election and consequently little interest in the proceedings for the ordinary member. As a result, the attendance at these gatherings dwindled until it often became almost impossible to secure a quorum to transact the necessary routine business. This in its turn led to general apathy on the part of the members who left the conduct of the Society's affairs entirely in the hands of the guarantor-committee men. Nothing could have been worse for the co-operative character of the undertaking and nothing could have been more calculated to destroy even its vitality as a trading concern.[6]

6 R.A. Anderson, *With Horace Plunkett in Ireland* (London: Macmillan, 1935) pp 160-61.

It was bad enough having inefficient guarantor-committee men, but local merchants and gombeen-men were admitted frequently as members, by virtue of their owning cows and land, and shouldered their way into dominant positions on the committee. Their main concern was that the creamery should remain as a simple purchaser of milk and maker of butter, not engaging in other forms of trade or activity which might injure the business of 'legitimate' merchants. Thanks to their efforts, the creamery often so remained.

Another unhelpful factor was a hostile press. "It would be hard to say now", said Anderson, "whether the abuse of the Conservative *Cork Constitution* or the Nationalist *Eagle* of Skibbereen was the louder. We were 'killing the calves', we were 'forcing young women to emigrate'; we were 'destroying the industry'." The provincial weeklies were, almost without exception,[7] bitterly opposed to the co-operative movement. The national dailies (at best lukewarm towards Plunkett's efforts) often took up and re-echoed the fanatical outbursts of the 'locals'. In his presidential address at the third annual general conference of co-operators,[8] Plunkett calmly reviewed the onslaught; he ridiculed many of the more outlandish accusations, but gently warned the farmer co-operators against attitudes and actions which might provoke criticism:

> Much of the unfriendly criticisms we have to face dealt with details of our work. Societies here and there can of course be convicted of instances of mismanagement, of shortsighted policy, of business blunders, but those who gloat and those who weep over these shortcomings make no allowance for the wrong-doings incidental to the early steps of all economic changes — in this world at any rate. Give us time and we will satisfy our critics on this score . . .
>
> We are told that it is a SELFISH MOVEMENT, that the farmers are using and will use the power . . . without regard to the interest of any other class . . . The idea is absurd. But those whose peculiar vision only allows them to notice our existence when we go astray, have pointed out that we are organising the farmer as against the agricultural labourer and favouring the large cultivator as against the small. There are no doubt instances where better off farmers have not acted generously to their poorer neighbours . . . I have heard bitter complaints from the neighbourhood of some creameries that since the farmer succeeded in adding by combination to the value of his milk, he sends it all to the creamery, and the poor man can no longer 'get a sup of milk to sweeten his tea' which he formerly obtained in the dairying districts. And this in a country where it has been truly said by Mrs Hartley in her pathetic story of Dublin poverty, 'the charity of the poor to the poor is so boundless as the charity of God.' The spirit of

7 A notable exception was the *Anglo-Celt* which had a large circulation in Counties Cavan and Monaghan and parts of Meath, Leitrim, Longford and Fermanagh, and did much to advance the co-operative idea in that area. The farming press, e.g., *Farmers Gazette* and the *Irish Farming World*, was also usually enthusiastic and helpful.

8 Held in Dublin on 3 November 1898.

our movement may be relied upon to deal with such departures from its principles as these.

Not all the co-operators were as calm and magnanimous as Plunkett in their own defence. They challenged their detractors to state in print that the Irish farmer was the type of man to deprive his own and his neighbour's children in order to send milk to a creamery. Did he have no more humanity or business sense than to starve his calves, or had his daughters so little work to do that the lack of home butter-making would force them, through boredom, to emigrate? The challenge was not met, but the sniping continued for many years.

As late as 1908, Dr John Clancy, Bishop of Elphin, was reported[9] to be reiterating many of the criticisms levelled against the creamery movement from its earliest days:

1. Children who should be at school were employed to bring milk to the creameries.
2. "Morning and evening large numbers assemble in the vicinity of creameries and habits of idleness — if not worse vices — are engendered . . ."
3. Public houses near creameries tempted the farmers and frustrated the Church's efforts to promote temperance.
4. The art of butter-making in the home was endangered.
5. Families, especially children, were deprived of a proper diet in the interest of "cupidity of pecuniary profit".
6. There was a danger of spreading germs of contagious diseases through mixing milk at the creameries.
7. There was no real substitute for whole milk in calf-rearing.
8. Lack of milk in the home led to "inordinate use of tea for domestic purposes — tea without milk and bread without butter; and to the introduction of beer and porter for the agricultural labourer in the field . . ."
9. The destruction of flourishing local butter markets, followed by the "decay of many subsidiary forms of industry . . . . the shipments from our port, the cartage of our quays, the cooperage in a hundred busy workshops . . ."

Despite all criticism, the creameries were becoming commercially successful. This was the Irish farmers' first real attempt at organised marketing; the benefits were tangible and the people were quick to grasp them:

A very pleasing feature in the development of the creamery system is the opportunity it has given to labourers to become cow owners. Numbers of them now have cows and one case has been reported

9 See correspondence in *The Irish Homestead*, 13 June 1908. Also a letter from L. Reynolds, Beechmount, Ballymote, County Sligo in *The Irish Homestead*, 20 June 1908.

where a man living in an ordinary wayside cottage with one acre of land has been enabled to own eight milch cows, from the milk of which he has realised £70 in cash during the past year. This man's case is typical of many others. From grazing one cow by the roadside — on the 'long farm' as it is called in the country — he was enabled to buy additional cows and rent grazing for them through the profits he derived from the Creamery. The gain per cow over the old buttermaking methods is pretty generally estimated at 30 shillings per annum, but in some cases milk suppliers put it down at a much higher figure.

The Co-operative Creameries are gradually taking up other branches of the farmer's business. There is a considerable increase in the number which now transact 'agricultural' business; others have introduced schemes for the improvement of their members' livestock; others again are in the egg and poultry industry; while some are establishing Agricultural Banks to be worked as an adjunct to their ordinary business.[10]

For the year ended December 1898, returns of 125 working co-operative creamery societies show that eighty of them were selling agricultural requirements (seeds, manures, equipment, and so on).[11] The participation of co-operative creameries in other aspects of agricultural business helped to enhance their position in the purely dairying field. Farmers were attracted into dairying by the opportunity of getting cheaper farm requisites in the creamery shop, but there were other important inducements. The annual 'distribution of surplus', although the amounts to individual members were often trivial, had a remarkable psychological impact. To many farmers it was nothing short of fantastic that any buyer of their produce should come back later to share the profit.

Apart from the payment of a bonus, honest trading and good management enabled many co-operative creameries to pay a better base price for milk than their private competitors. Many proprietors of private creameries were gombeen-type merchants who had an innate propensity to adulteration and sharp practice. Many of them mixed margarine with their butter; others cheated their suppliers over the gallonage or butter test. These peccadillos did not always go undetected and sometimes proved costly. The gombeen's answer in almost every case was further exploitation of the milk supplier to recoup lost profits, either by a straightforward reduction of the milk's price or by further shady dealings.

Co-operative creameries may not have prompted suppliers to be remarkably loyal or scrupulous about the quality of the milk which they provided, but it was generally better than that delivered to proprietary

10 IAOS Annual Report 1899, p. 14.
11 Lombardstown had agricultural sales of £7,634; Milford (County Carlow) £5,336; Windgap (County Kilkenny) £3,098 and Killeshandra £2,701. Ardstraw (County Tyrone), an auxiliary of Spamount, was the only society selling liquid milk (£655 worth). Drumlease Society (County Sligo) is included. It was not the usual type of creamery, but a factory which bought butter for blending. It had a small store trade of £284.

concerns. Better, cleaner, fresher milk resulted in fewer losses and in a butter which was of better quality and could command a better price. That the co-operatives could make excellent butter was amply demonstrated at the London Dairy Show in 1904 when Irish co-operatives swept the board in all four commercial classes. Killeshandra won two gold medals, and Coagh and Killyman one each. Aghadowey, Solohead, Leckpatrick and Ballymote won second prizes. Ballintrillick, Derrygonnelly and Sooey gained thirds, while Omagh, Cavan, Loughbrickland, Springfield, Ballyrashane, Longford, Irvinestown, the Harp, Ballinard, Moneymore, Ballinamore, Rathduff, Finn Valley, Castlecaulfield, Lissarda, Glenwilliam and Limavady won lesser prizes. In contrast, a large entry from Irish proprietary creameries gained only two fifth placings.

Finn Valley Dairy Society, County Donegal

Co-operative creameries had an advantage in law which, at least theoretically, could have been significant. A tenant could be compelled to disclose to the Land Court profits from sales of milk to a *proprietary* creamery. This might result in his rent being raised. Co-operative creameries were held in law to be 'tenants' improvements' and thus could not be made the basis for arguing an increase in rent. This point was always stressed by the IAOS but the times were hardly auspicious for landlords seeking increased rents and there is no evidence that co-operatives benefited from this legal nicety.

Many of the creamery buildings were stark, ugly, barn-like structures.[12]

12 An advertisement in *The Irish Homestead*, 18 May 1895: "Harristown Dairy Society . . . invite tenders for the erection of an Iron Creamery, 65 feet long by 25 ft in width; walls 13 ft 6 ins to eaves. The building to be sheeted throughout inside with Norway sheeting

Inside there was often only a flimsy partition dividing the dairy from the engine room. A water tank, about three feet deep, ran the length of the back wall like a miniature but static mill-race. At one end of the building a platform was erected where the supplier could unload milk cans from his cart at floor level. Here the milk had to be measured;[13] it was poured into a measuring drum before being repoured into the receiving vat. The milk was then passed through the separators and the resultant cream, in nine-gallon Schwartz pans, was immersed in the water tank to await churning. The first Peterson separators were heavy, clumsy machines which required four horsepower; in the days before the locomotive-type engine with its horizontal boiler, these called for a vertical boiler and engine which had to have a tall steel chimney stayed with wires, extending above the creamery roof, to give the necessary draught for the firebox and to convey smoke and waste steam upwards. Later types of separator, the Laval and the Alexandra, required only half the horsepower. The Alexandra was installed in some creameries, but Anderson recalls one incident which delayed its widespread acceptance:

> The chief feature was a concave bowl sitting on top of a spindle and revolved by friction . . . the bowl and spindle, owing to imperfect lubrication, had seized and the bowl was hurled, like a high explosive shell, through the wall of the creamery. When it is remembered that both these types of separator had a speed of 6,000 revolutions per minute, the devastating effect of such an accident can easily be understood.

Before the introduction of the simple Babcock tester and the modern Gerber, equipment for testing the butterfat content of milk was primitive. Frequently it meant churning individual sample quantities of suppliers' milk in a small rotary churn. This was laborious work and the dairymaids disliked it. These small churns could easily have been power-driven by gearing them to the shafting which drove the separators and the big barrel churn, but very few 'engineers' had the ingenuity to do this.

The dairymaids and the butter-makers created quite a stir amongst the male rural population.[14] Many of them were good-looking and, as a result of their training in the Cork Model Farm (Munster Institute) and else-where, were businesslike and carried themselves with a certain professional

boards, one inch thick — tongued and grooved — and completed to the satisfaction of the Society's Engineer."

13 "It was before long found necessary to discard the sloppy method of pouring the milk when delivered into a measuring drum . . . so weighing machines were introduced which, more or less accurately, recorded the quantity of milk supplied by each individual." (Anderson, op. cit., p. 235).

14 The IAOS Annual Report of 1900 reported " . . . there are at least 400 dairymaids in Ireland earning on an average £50 a year each." In that year the dairy societies were threatened with prosecution under the Factory and Workshops Act if they worked on Sundays or if the regular working hours laid down were not adhered to on weekdays. A plea was entered on the grounds of the perishability of milk and a special deputation led by Plunkett met the Home Secretary, as a result of which special exemption was granted for creameries in Ireland.

air. Farmers' sons vied with each other for the job of delivering the milk and seeing the dairymaids.[15]

Creamery committees were constantly being urged to improve the appearance of their premises. Members of the IAOS staff who had visited Scandinavia were particularly keen on this. Milk products, they said, should be prepared not only under conditions of scrupulous cleanliness, but in factories which, in their interior and exterior decoration and setting, reflected the fastidiousness and good taste of the manufacturers. The planting of trees, shrubs, flowers and creeping plants, and regular coats of paint to relieve the ugly starkness of exterior walls, were all strongly advocated but all too rarely effected. Particularly offensive objects were "the stark erections for sanitary accommodation of the staff, demanded by the Factory Acts",[16] standing up like badly made sentry boxes at either side of the grounds instead of being decently screened by trees or shrubs.

The disposal of creamery effluent (washing water, spilt milk, and milk or sometimes milk products that had 'gone wrong') was a major problem. Very often the washings went from drain to ditch and found their way into streams and rivers. In dry weather the milk protein rotted with a smell redolent of the flax holes of Ulster and a white flocculent growth developed at the edges of streams. Apart from the smell, the effluent was usually harmless, even to fish, but if cattle in adjoining fields died or got sick for any reason, the creamery was promptly blamed.

There were numerous costly law suits and more often than not the cattle-owner won: "The issue was generally determined", said Anderson, "by the evidence of the expert witness who could swear hardest." The IAOS pestered the Department of Agriculture, from the day of its foundation, to combat the pollution, but it continued to baffle the experts in spite of often heavy expenditure on filtration systems, settling tanks and contact beds. In 1914 one society was involved in a lawsuit costing some £2,000. The IAOS accused the Department of not trying hard enough. No scientific solution was found and the most satisfactory compromise was to reduce milk spillage and dilute the effluent, or as one manager put it, "using a hundred times more washing water than was needed." Creameries which spent money on an extravagant supply of clean water found that their pollution disappeared and with it many other unhygienic difficulties. Managers conceded that hitherto they had, perhaps unconsciously, been too thrifty in the use of this commodity.

The creamery manager was a key man. A good committee was important, but the manager's performance determined whether the society flourished or failed. Hence good committees hired and fired until they got the right man,[17] but good managers were not plentiful. From 1895 special

15 The opening of a creamery was often treated as a public holiday. The clergy officiated at the opening ceremony in the morning, there were sports or other entertainment in the afternoon, and the proceedings continued with a grand dance that night. Pat Courtney, IAOS organiser, mentions such occasions at Aghabulloge, Drumtariffe and Banteer. (See IAOS Annual Report 1917).

16 Anderson, op. cit., p. 240.

17 At IAOS headquarters, and later in the Department of Agriculture, Plunkett was also a

courses for creamery managers were provided at Albert Agricultural College and the Cork Model Farm,[18] but the out-turn could not hope to match the development of creameries at that time. For the most part the training of the manager took place on the creamery floor. In 1897 the Commissioners for National Education appointed Mr A. Poole Wilson as a dairy instructor. They had dairy instructors before that, but in Mr Poole Wilson's case agreement was reached for him to consult with the IAOS regarding visits to creameries and advice on technical matters, allowing the IAOS the opportunity of endorsing his recommendations. The IAOS committee also recommended that

> There is still much needed in the way of practical instruction. The Courses of Training for Creamery Managers at Glasnevin and Cork are certainly valuable; but in addition to these it would be most desirable that a certain number of conveniently situated Co-operative Creameries should be selected and equipped as experimental and training centres. To each such Creamery an expert should be permanently attached, who would be provided with all the necessary apparatus in addition to the plant of the Creamery. Pupils could then be received for training at a moderate fee, who would undergo a course consisting of practical creamery work, simple mechanics, elementary dairy chemistry, the testing, pasteurisation and sterilisation of milk, the ripening of cream, and Creamery book-keeping. At the end of each course — which ought to extend over an entire year — the pupils should be examined and granted diplomas according to the proficiency they displayed. This course would also be available for dairymaids.[19]

A year later the committee induced two of their most efficient creameries, Ardagh and Ballymote, to install equipment for training, but the only help the Board of National Education would give was to permit one of their dairy instructors to lecture in the schools.[20] The co-operators complained bitterly about the government's failure to undertake "The task which Government discharged for its people in every nation in Europe with which we have to compete." The pressure on the IAOS staff was too great and the voluntarily subscribed finances too small to go it alone, so the project had to be abandoned. The newly founded Department of Agriculture was also an organisation under great strain, and was being pressed to implement a myriad of schemes at the same time. Inevitably, dairy instruction, like so many other functions, could only be managed under the supervision and control of the bureaucracy, and so another

great believer in the 'hire and fire' approach. For an otherwise kindly man, he was pretty ruthless in this regard.

18 Later at Ballyhaise and the College of Science. "From 1918 onwards the courses for creamery managers began to take on the shape of the diploma courses which were to be given later at University College, Cork." (Daniel Hoctor, *The Department's Story*, p. 104).

19 IAOS Annual Report 1897.

20 "The Creameries are deriving some benefit from the advice of the two Dairy Instructors, M/s Poole Wilson and Lofmark, and an improvement is noticeable in the quality of their produce this year." (IAOS Annual Report 1898).

worthwhile scheme for the hopeful blending of self-help with state aid was forfeited.

Henry Shaw, Ballymote

The Society's staff of seven accountants did its best to guide the business transactions of 200 creameries as well as some 175 other societies, but the task facing them at the turn of the century was, if anything, more daunting than that of the technical advisors:

> The insufficiency of special technical instruction... is a serious drawback, but it is explicable; what is difficult to understand is the utter failure of the elementary course in our National and other primary schools to provide these young men and women for their struggle in life with one of the most necessary of ordinary requirements of a practical education. Our Accountants, when they visit a new Society to open its accounts, have not merely to induct the Manager and staff into the special mysteries of Creamery and Co-operative book-keeping, but have often to teach them rudiments of simple arithmetic and accounts which they should have learned while they were children at school.

The printers worked overtime to churn out dozens of leaflets[21] and *The Irish Homestead* published explicit instructions on all aspects of dairying in the hope that they would be read. Meanwhile, certain enterprising creameries were taking it on themselves to advertise for pupils and 'apprentices', promising to equip them with a thorough knowledge of creamery management for a fee of £5 for a course which sometimes lasted no more than three weeks. Even the official organ, *The Irish Homestead*, was tricked into carrying some of the advertisements. Usually 'graduates' from such courses were provided with glowing testimonials to their knowledge and outstanding ability. As far as possible, IAOS personnel sat in on

---

21 Titles included Factory Dairying, The Sampling and Testing of Milk and Cream, Pasteurisation, The Use of Ice in Dairying, Cream Separation, Ripening and Churning, Rules for Milk Suppliers, Auxiliary Creameries, and Home Rule in the Dairy.

interviews for the appointment of managers and, where they did, the deficiencies in candidates were soon revealed, but many committees either had to, or in some cases insisted upon, making their own appointments and frequently suffered for their admiration of fine prose. In a few disastrous cases, the manager was selected on compassionate grounds — he was a relative of several committee members and needed the job because the farming or the business had gone against him. Plunkett wryly recalled a comparable case of 'selection by negative qualification' from Wyoming, where a cowboy on his ranch was appointed cook because he had varicose veins.

In some cases neither the manager nor the committee understood the co-operative ethic, and the manager became the overlord, asserting his authority over all and sundry. One manager *directed* the IAOS to rectify matters in a case where "the dairymaid is insubordinate, the engine driver is insubordinate and the Chairman is the most insubordinate of all." There were frequent complaints of managers who engaged in other business to the detriment of their creamery management.[22] The strongest and perhaps the best-founded complaint was that many managers so prized their independence, and so overvalued their own ability to buy and sell, that they sometimes seriously impeded progress towards co-operative solidarity in marketing and purchasing; for example, by failing to support the Co-operative Agency Society's campaign to improve butter sales and the IAWS in the purchase of agricultural goods.

Managers were not without their own grievances. In 1914 the IAOS noted that even some fairly large societies were paying their managers no more than £2 a week.[23] Some were laid off during the winter months. Often there was no suitable dwellings close to the creamery.

Many managers were men of outstanding ability who could have commanded double their salaries in private firms, but chose to give a lifetime of dedicated service to their own co-operatives. Collectively, through their Irish Creamery Managers' Association (founded in 1902), they pushed a sometimes reluctant dairy industry forward to improved technology and business efficiency, while, individually, many of them were outstanding pioneers of agricultural progress in their own districts. Most of the busiest managers nevertheless found time to give often invaluable service on the IAOS national and provincial committees.

No sooner were the co-operative creameries established in Ireland than there was a fiery 'family row' between the Irish and English co-operators — specifically between the IAOS and the English-based Co-operative Wholesale Society. The CWS was established in Manchester in 1864 as a

---

22 In 1901 the IAOS was worried about certain managers accepting illicit commissions and urged that honest officials should supply to the Society a list of firms whose travellers offered such commissions. (IAOS Annual Report 1901, p. 43).

23 In June 1904, the *Sligo Champion* reported (in a five-column spread) wild scenes at a co-operative meeting in Boyle, County Roscommon, involving the brandishing of sticks and fists and the plentiful use of expletives. It appears that the creamery manager, Daniel Aherne, had resigned but agreed to stay on for a salary of £2.5.0. a week — an arrangement which had not been confirmed by the committee which had appointed him at £1.7.6.

federation of consumers associations to act as wholesalers to the co-operative shops. Prominent amongst its promoters were many of the Rochdale Pioneers, including Abraham Greenwood (first president), James Smithies (treasurer), Charlie Howarth, William Cooper and Tom Cheetham. J. T. W. Mitchell,[24] a poor Rochdale boy who joined the Pioneer Society in 1854, became president of the CWS in 1874 and held the position until 1895, making it "the most honourable official position within the movement to which the co-operator may aspire."[25]

The policy of the CWS was almost entirely geared to helping the co-operative consumer with the best quality goods at the lowest possible price. This took it not only into wholesaling, but also into manufacturing and primary production. It owned large farms in Britain and Canada and, later, tea plantations in India and Ceylon but, since its own production could supply only a fraction of their wholesale requirements, it had buying depots in Ireland, France, Denmark, Canada, the USA, Sweden, Spain and Australia. The first depots for the purchase of dairy produce outside England were in Ireland: Tipperary (1866), Kilmallock (1868), Limerick (1869), Armagh (1873), Waterford (1873) and Tralee (1874).

The CWS was a rich and powerful co-operative organisation[26] but its economic interest was a consumer's one and in relation to the farmer / producer very similar to that of the capitalists.[27] Equitable disposition between producer and consumer was then, and indeed still remains, a tricky problem in co-operative ideology and an even trickier one in co-operative practice. The CWS co-operated admirably in the founding of Drumcollogher, but thereafter, relations (and more notably communication) with the Irish co-operators seem to have suffered. At the Co-operative Congress in Lincoln in 1891, Mitchell blandly announced to the assembled delegates that it was the intention of the CWS to acquire land in Ireland, to stock it with cows and to erect and operate creameries. Plunkett and Anderson were on their feet immediately, expressing amazement and indignation. Plunkett made an impassioned plea to be allowed to teach co-operation to the Irish farmer. Dairying was the one fruitful avenue open to him. Only through self-help and personal participation could the Irish farmer come to anything. He was an indifferent producer of home-made butter. Where there were proprietary creameries in Ireland, the farmer was a supplier of indifferent milk. Only

24 John Thomas Whitehead Mitchell (1828-95). His mother was a domestic servant who later kept a small beerhouse. As president of the CWS, he became a prominent figure and was nick-named Baron Wholesale. Despite the fact that throughout his life he continued to live frugally in a Rochdale working man's house, there was much malicious rumour that he had feathered his nest very well during his twenty-one years as president. After his death in 1895, the full extent of his personal estate was established — £350. 17. 6. R. A. Anderson, who disagreed bitterly with Mitchell, nevertheless describes him as "a splendid type of whole-hog co-operator."

25 C. Webb, *Industrial Co-operation*, p. 123.

26 In 1900 it recorded sales of over £16 million and produced £2.6 m worth of its own goods. The Scottish Wholesale Society (SCWS) was founded in 1868. In 1885 it opened a depot at Enniskillen for the collection and distribution of goods and in 1898 established a central creamery there with a number of auxiliaries in the surrounding district.

27 See Louis P. F. Smith, *The Evolution of Agricultural Co-operation* (Oxford: Basil Blackwell, 1961), p. 195.

by taking business and responsibility into his own hands and seeing the benefits of co-operation, could the Irish farmer acquire the qualities of mind and heart, the habits of thrift and industry that would raise him from his position of serfdom. Paternalism, however generous, could not uplift him now; as a policy, it would be no more successful than the coercive treatment which in the past had sought to make him a docile and useful slave.

The delegates did not accept this. Their experience (if any) of farmers was of the sturdy English yeoman or the tough, independent landowner. What could be better than a good price for milk and a strong co-operative organisation to provide the costly infrastructure which would immediately lift Irish co-operative dairying to a position it would otherwise take years to attain?

The Irish continued to protest but the CWS went ahead. It announced its intention to establish twelve creameries in the South of Ireland, mainly in Kerry and Limerick. At the 1895 Congress in Huddersfield, Plunkett moved a resolution condemning the action of the CWS but very few of the 800 delegates supported him.[28] In that same year it came to the notice of the IAOS that the CWS, in contravention of the undertaking given that no district in which a co-operative creamery was operating or about to start would be interfered with, was endeavouring to secure premises in which the Clondrohid Society, County Cork, was planning to erect its creamery. Soon afterwards came the news that the CWS had purchased the co-operative creamery in Castlemahon, County Limerick. The Castlemahon committee had been split over Parnell and their creamery was closed. Father Tom Finlay didn't spare them. "You", he said, "would presume to decide the destinies of your country while you exhibit to the world the miserable spectacle of a divided community which cannot agree to keep the churn in its creamery revolving." Anderson accused Stokes, a CWS agent, of complicity in the sell-out, which Stokes denied, adding that if the CWS hadn't bought it, some unfriendly butter merchant would have done so. Anderson swore that they should have let it rot before they touched it, but his protests were in vain.

The CWS plans had been made and had to be carried through. Castlemahon was taken over[29] and the twelve new creameries were built. Shortly afterwards the CWS invested in about eighty other creameries, some of them disputably too close to existing co-operative ventures. In order to nail down an adequate milk supply, many CWS creameries introduced the unco-operative tactic of giving loans to needy suppliers in winter, provided that they undertook to repay the loans *in milk* throughout the season; cash would not be accepted.

However, the difficulties of a huge 'foreign' creamery organisation, managed by remote control, soon became evident. The creamery buildings

---

28 Notable exceptions included the Christian Socialists, particularly Thomas Hughes, author of *Tom Brown's Schooldays*. Hughes had taken a prominent part in the great debates of the eighteen seventies and eighties on producer versus consumer co-operation.
29 The purchase price, £850, was just sufficient to satisfy the creditors.

were ill-designed for Irish conditions. Similarly, the machinery and equipment were found to be inadequate, but, because their supply and installation were the monopoly of one firm, the local manager was not at liberty to install better types. Other defects, not unknown in co-operative creameries, became apparent. Management was indifferent and sometimes downright dishonest. Anderson takes up the story:

> As time went on, the acid test of price began to operate, and it was found by the suppliers of milk to the CWS creameries that they were not getting as good prices as were the suppliers to the co-operative creameries. Then the fun began ... Ultimately the CWS capitulated and offered to sell *en bloc*. Of course this offer had to be rejected, for they had planted creameries in places where the milk supply was insufficient to begin with and these were, therefore, worthless. Further, the IAOS could not create out of a horde of unorganised farmers, in close on a hundred localities, one compact organisation to take over all the creameries simultaneously ... there were conferences between the CWS and the IAOS ... in which the Irish Section of the Co-operative Union acted as an intermediary. At the Conference held in Newry[30]Father Finlay and I attended to represent the IAOS. At this conference an agreement was reached mainly through the good offices of Mr W. J. McGuffin, President of the Belfast Co-operative Society, whereby the CWS undertook to negotiate with co-operative societies, to be organised by the IAOS for the purchase of individual creameries at a price to be fixed by the arbitrator.[31]

The negotiations were drawn out. The farmers of Boherbue and Greybridge sought to buy immediately but could not meet the CWS demands. The first purchases — Herbertstown, Ballymacelligott, Ballinlohane, Garryduff and Hollyford — were not achieved until 1903. Boherbue did not buy until 1909, Greybridge not until 1911. By the time disposal was completed, the CWS is estimated to have dropped £100,000, not to mention their trading losses.[32] The IAOS took no pleasure in this nor in the fact that it was the groups of unco-operative farmers, who had been the first to invite the CWS into their areas, who held out unreasonably at the end in order to force it into selling the creameries to them at scrap prices.

It took a long time to allay the lingering rancour in the minds of the English co-operators, and the Co-operative Union felt compelled to cease its contribution to the IAOS. The CWS claimed that it had been singled out for attack, rather than the proprietary creameries.[33] The IAOS

---

30 Probably on 6 May 1900.
31 Anderson, *With Horace Plunkett in Ireland*, pp. 80-81.
32 In 1902 the CWS in Ireland owned forty-one main creameries and fifty-two auxiliaries, with a milk intake of approximately 16 million gallons. The CWS had reputedly advanced up to £500,000 to farmers by way of loans against their milk.
33 "Extreme Republicans, it is said, are logically bound to hate a good king much more than a bad one." (Percy Redfern). In fact, about that time proprietary creameries were also being

countered that it had attacked nobody: the CWS had been repeatedly warned and, if resistance to the Society was strong, it was because its members were supposed to be *co-operators* but showed little signs of it in Ireland. The CWS claimed that it was animated solely by a desire to help Irish farmers. The IAOS gave them full credit for worthy motivation but regretted that, despite advice, they persisted in operating on such utterly wrong lines that they ultimately "suffered the common experience of those Englishmen who seek to pave the bogs of Ireland with good intentions."[34]

Dowdall Brothers Creamery, Charleville, County Cork

One major technical problem dogged creamery development from the beginning: the breakdown of the whole dairying system during the winter months:

> The most universal habit in the rich dairying districts of Ireland is to feed the cows almost entirely on grass and to abandon any attempt to

taken over by co-operatives in a fairly constant pattern: in 1902 Castletown, Effin, Templebredin and Cappamore from the Maypole Company; Rathnaveen, Donoughmore and Berrings from J. & J. Lonsdale Ltd.; and in the North, Moylough and Rathkenny from the Northern Creamery Company and Mr J.W. McKillop. Millowen in County Cork was purchased from a Mr Ellis.

34 See Percy Redfern, *The Story of the CWS 1863-1913* (Manchester: CWS Ltd., 1913).

produce milk between October and May. As a result the creameries are hardly working during this period . . . Naturally the market falls into the hands of the Danes, who continue to produce butter uniform in quality throughout the year. Every Spring, therefore, Irish producers have to buy their way back to the market. The remedy evidently is to institute a system of winter dairying . . . and this in turn will depend on a considerable extension of tillage.[35]

At the 1898 annual general conference, Arthur S. Lough of Killeshandra called on the IAOS to issue a pamphlet on the subject of winter dairying. He said it paid him a great deal better than summer dairying and he detailed his methods of feeding. R. P. Gill of Ballywilliam formally seconded Lough's resolution, but promptly went on to explain a scheme they were about to carry out in Tipperary, whereby three societies would combine to make into butter what little winter milk there was amongst their members, sending it all to one creamery. Other speakers were dismayed at the prospect of ploughing up the rich grasslands of Limerick for such a doubtful venture, even though Lord Monteagle mildly suggested that even in Limerick there were farms where it might be profitable. The discussion developed into an argument about the best breeds of dairy cattle, whereupon the irascible Lough avowed that he cared not one goddam what make of a cow she was so long as she gave 600 gallons of milk!

The IAOS noted at an early stage that farmers in Ulster produced much more of their milk supply in the winter months and many Ulster creameries paid significantly better prices and end-of-year dividends. It was suggested that the Ulster farmer's industry and thrift was attributable in some measure to the security which he had long enjoyed under the 'Ulster custom' and that, given time and proper direction, the newly liberated tenants in other parts of Ireland would apply themselves with equal vigour. Yet there were misgivings and differences of opinion as to whether they could be induced to undertake the amount of intensive tillage required for profitable full-year dairying. In 1898, when the proposal for a separate Department of Agriculture and Technical Instruction for Ireland was being strongly pressed, John Dillon made an impassioned plea in the House of Commons. The western peasantry, he claimed, understood agriculture and, given fair land and proper guidance, would create capital out of the land and become sturdy, independent citizens. Mitchell Henry,[36] however, had a somewhat different view:

The Irish peasant hates agriculture — meaning the cultivation of the soil — and is utterly ignorant of all its principles. He detests to dig, and

35 Lionel Smith-Gordon and Francis Cruise O'Brien, *Co-operation in Ireland* (Manchester: Co-operative Union Ltd., 1921), p.33.
36 Mitchell Henry (1826-1910) was a wealthy London surgeon who in 1862 acquired an estate of 9,000 acres at Kylemore, Connemara and later built a castle there (now Kylemore Abbey). He was a benevolent landlord and expert farmer, MP for Galway (1871-75) and Glasgow (1885-86). See *Who Was Who (1897-1916)* (London: Adam and Charles Black, 1929).

has not the patience to see things grow, as he himself expresses it. He is by nature a trader and a quick-witted one, and delights in cattle-jobbing and in taking the turn of the market. He wants extensive grazing farms to raise his stock and his greatest pleasure is to drive them from market to market and partake of the pleasures of the outing and the indulgence in hilarity, to use a mild term, which attends all these gatherings.

As it happened, Mitchell Henry's assessment was not only more hilarious but nearer the mark. Ten years later more than half the year's butter was still being produced in three or four months.[37] Ned Gallen of Urney Dairy & Flax Society,[38] strongly backed by Rev E.F. Campbell of Killyman, was urging that the Department of Agriculture should finance a deputation of members and creamery managers to go to Denmark to see how year-round dairying was carried out. The resolution was carried[39] but the excursion never took place. The IAOS reported sorrowfully:

> The old system of summer production . . . is dying hard; creamery butter is never heavily salted nor often cold stored. It is essentially a produce for quick sale and quick consumption, for its delicate flavour forbids any lengthened period of storage. But while the system of manufacture has undergone a revolution, the system of milk production stands still and many creameries in Ireland are idle during the winter months when they might be working profitably. The creameries are in some degree to blame for this state of things, for investigation of their transactions has gone to show that in the great majority of cases the summer suppliers are paid more than their milk is worth, while those who are energetic and enterprising enough to arrange for a winter supply of milk, are not paid a price which will make their industry remunerative.[40]

The lack of winter dairying precipitated a host of difficulties. In many areas, April-calving cows had a very short lactation and many were dry by October. This was particularly true in places new to dairying, where cows tended to have a beef strain in their breeding. It was common everywhere in poor soils of low fertility where liming and manuring were minimal. In 1913, when creamery coverage had become widespread, it looked as if the previously accepted average milk yield per cow of 450 was too high. Indications were that the figure was more like 350 to 400 and in Connaught

---

37 Particulars of monthly milk supplies to creameries in 1907 indicated that "our creameries receive less than one-fifth of their total milk supply during the six months from November to April." (IAOS Annual Report 1909, p.29).

38 A townland near Strabane, County Tyrone, Urney was later to lend its name to a large chocolate factory at Tallaght, County Dublin.

39 But not before John McKay (Clonduff) and William Scully (Roscrea) had observed that it had been known for deputations to go away and come back, not only unable to recount what they had seen, but in some cases apparently unable to recall where they had been!

40 IAOS Annual Report 1907, p.6.

100 gallons less! Cow-testing associations were introduced to help farmers identify good cows and cull bad ones, but their development was limited and they never had much influence.[41]

The scarcity of winter milk in 1911 gave rise to the old accusation of 'starving the children' and the IAOS committee referred the matter to the newly-formed society of United Irishwomen (renamed the Irish Country-women's Association in 1935) for investigation:

> The Committee believes that there are no grounds for the belief that Creameries deprive the public of the quantity of milk necessary for rearing young children. There is not a Creamery in Ireland which would not gladly dispose of its entire milk supply at 8d per gallon, at which price milk would probably be the cheapest food procurable. Wherever there is evidence of a local demand for milk, the IAOS is prepared to advise the local Creamery to organise a system of milk supply . . . The matter is in good hands. The United Irishwomen will organise the demand: the Creameries may be counted on to arrange for the supply.[42]

The United Irishwomen reported back that there was indeed a scarcity of milk but mostly in areas where there were *no* creameries! This was corroborated by a Vice-Regal Commission which inquired into the milk supply at that time: "the need for a milk supply in rural districts (to say nothing at all about urban districts) is very great, and the health of the children is suffering accordingly."[43]

The United Irishwomen were of the opinion that small quantities of milk were consumed in the homes of farm labourers and others, not because milk was scarce, but because people did not realise its nutritional value: many country people did not like milk and children were sometimes not given enough of it.[44] The organisation set up a number of milk depots and nearly 42,000 gallons of milk were sold through them in 1914.

41 Beltrim Society in County Tyrone was very active in this development, as was Silvermines (County Tipperary) whose manager, Jeremiah Ryan, adopted a realistic approach to butter costing which enabled him to pay an incentive price for winter milk. By 1917 there were still only thirty-seven cow-testing associations in all Ireland: nineteen in Cork, five in Limerick, three in Tyrone, two each in Fermanagh and Kerry and one each in Counties Antrim, Donegal, Derry, Tipperary, Waterford and Wicklow. At the peak period of cow-testing in 1929, there was still only 6.8 per cent. of the total cow population under test and a year later this figure had dropped to 4.5 per cent.

42 IAOS Annual Report 1911, p.12.

43 IAOS Annual Report 1912, p.12.

44 Ten years later the complaints were coming from the co-operative camp. *The Irish Homestead* (15 April 1922) complained about Dublin's non-participation in co-operation: "Dublin likes being bled; it is always complaining, but it will not do anything to enable it to live in decency. Other cities, even Belfast, which is so much abused in the South, could build up a gigantic co-operative store with about thirty branches and keep down prices. There is hardly a town in Great Britain or Scotland where there is not a flourishing co-operative store. But Dublin people will do nothing to ease their own burdens. There is their milk supply. They have been told over and over again that it is the impure milk that is largely responsible for the high infant mortality. Would they try to organise a co-operative milk supply like Belfast or Plymouth or other big cities? No! It is less trouble to let the children die."

For years the IAOS had been making gallant efforts to improve butter quality. In 1909 Anderson reported the tribulations of the Earl of Carrick, representing the IAOS in London, who was contriving to sell Irish butter in competition with the professional trio, Faber, Bagge and Van Rijn — special commissioners representing Denmark, Sweden and Holland. He recommended the creation of an 'Irish butter control'.[45] This was implemented in June 1910 with ten creameries. The control involved (i) permitting creameries which produced butter of suitable quality to use a national brand or trade mark; (ii) a system of inspection, testing and 'surprise' butter competitions, to ensure that standards were maintained; (iii) providing cultures to standardise the ripening of cream and consequent butter quality, and imparting advice to creameries to help them maintain or reach the required standard. The wrapper upon which the trademark was printed also bore a guarantee that the butter in the package was made solely from pasteurised cream, skimmed centrifugally and artificially ripened by pure culture, and contained no margarine or other foreign fat. The preservative, other than common salt (in stated proportions) was $\frac{1}{2}$ per cent. of a preparation of pure borax, and the water content did not exceed 16 per cent.

Before the scheme was launched, the IAOS had tried to involve the Department of Agriculture — in the first instance to administer it, but failing this, at least to provide technical and scientific help on the bacteriological aspects. Anderson was frustrated and embittered by the lack of response:

> I personally made every effort to get the Department to father it, but I was met with all manner of objections, most of which appeared to me frivolous. I will not go so far as to say that the officials of the Department opposed it, though some of them appeared to sneer at it. The fact is that in all the huge staff of the Department, there was not a single individual who possessed vision enough to see how vitally important and necessary was our scheme to the creameries, for I cannot recall a single instance in which any of the Department's scientific staff evinced the smallest interest in our new departure.

Were it not for an enthusiastic pensioner operating from a tiny laboratory in the Plunkett House, the control would not have been possible. Professor David Houston had just retired from the Royal College

45 "The object of the scheme is to establish a national brand of Irish creamery butter of guaranteed purity and uniform excellence of quality for the exclusive use of selected co-operative creameries affiliated to the IAOS which are prepared to comply with the rules and conditions hereinafter set forth, which have been laid down by the creameries themselves and have been approved by the Control Committee, in order that the produce of creameries participating in the control may realise its full market value and ultimately obtain such recognition as will secure special classification in the markets of the United Kingdom. To attain these objects it is proposed to admit to participation in the Control only those creameries whose standard of equipment, cleanliness and general business methods fulfil the condition of the Control Scheme."

of Science. He was an outstanding bacteriologist, full of boyish enthusiasm and idealism. His pension enabled him to accept a modest salary from the IAOS and from his strange little sorcerer's den to perform his modern dairy magic, with pure cultures of the proper bacteria: hundreds of tubes, flasks and petri dishes, identifying the bad germs causing trouble in the creameries' milk, cream, butter and water supplies.

There was no magical way of having Houston's remedies applied at the creameries. It took a lot of hard slogging, visits, inspections, committee meetings, staff selection and training, better equipment, improved water supplies and better buildings. Where really bad butter resulted from a single cause, the solution was comparatively simple. The greatest problem was butter rendered indifferent by a combination of defects and faulty practices. Sometimes the trouble was so diffuse and endemic that even the phlegmatic James Fant was moved to recommend a suitable charge of dynamite and a fresh start.

Yet the picture was not entirely black. Nearly all the best creameries joined the control scheme, as did a number of creameries which had serious butter-making problems. Many of these applied themselves so actively that they produced excellent butter. The overall effect was a significant raising of standards which, if it did not always result in first-class butter, was often significantly better than it had been. Anderson was happy to report that the participants in the scheme behaved honourably at all times:

> It was left to the honour of their managers not to affix the control brand to any butter which failed to reach the required high standard of quality. In no single instance was this honourable behaviour departed from. Professor Houston was invariably advised by telegram that the use of the brand has been discontinued until he was able to detect and lay by the heels the offending microbe. It should be borne in mind that, unlike the Department (which in such cases as this might have been reasonably expected to co-operate) the IAOS had no staff of inspectors or experts at its command, one of whom could be dispatched instantly to the creamery in trouble. We had to rely on the honour of the managers and they did not let us down.

· The failure to back up the control scheme with a proper marketing system inevitably led to a decline. Creameries which had an established reputation for their butter could command a reasonable price for their product and no longer saw much advantage in going through the elaborate control procedures of testing and labelling.

By 1914 the butter control was almost a dead letter.[46] An attempt to revive it brought a temporary response and in 1916 some forty-five central creameries and forty independent auxiliaries were operating the scheme. The war-time disregard of quality took its toll, as did the post-war slump, the civil war and the internal troubles of the IAOS. By the time Irish

46 IAOS Annual Report 1914, p.10.

Associated Creameries Ltd. was formed in 1928, nothing remained of the butter control scheme but the 'surprise' butter competitions run by the Department of Agriculture. Houston had departed and the spiders wove webs to cover his glassware in the Plunkett House.

With the multiplicity of creameries and a limited supply of milk, there was cut-throat competition not only between co-ops and proprietary creameries, but, regrettably, between co-ops themselves — the stronger often tending to encroach on the supply area of the weaker societies. Auxiliary creameries and separating stations were sometimes set up for little more reason than a doubtful hope of garnering an adequate milk supply to guarantee the employment of staff in a central creamery where a dwindling supply threatened redundancies.[47] Although many auxiliaries provided a useful service and facility for suppliers, others were located with scant regard for economic realities. Only rarely did supplier members subscribe worthwhile share capital and in some instances the majority of suppliers were not members at all.

Anderson ranted against 'milk grabbing' creameries and the notorious 'outlanders' — farmers living equidistant from two or more creameries but with membership in none, who played one creamery against the other for a price for milk often regardlesss of its butter-fat content or quality. He condemned the consequent chaos of paying too much for summer milk and too little for winter supply as "a premium on sloth and a penalty on enterprise". Some courageous societies sought to insist on supplier membership[48] and tried to agree demarcation of supply areas with adjoining creameries. Attempts were made to enforce the 'binding rule' whereby the milk supplier was committed in his co-operative membership not to sell milk to "any creamery other than the creamery of the society, or to any company, society person or persons who sells milk or manufactures butter for sale." These remedial efforts were rarely successful and occasionally involved the co-ops in heavy litigation.

Famous cases were those of *Hanley* v. *Tipperary CDS* in 1912, in which the decision against the co-op led to a revision of the rule; *Coolmoyne and Fethard* v. *Thomas Bulfin* (1916), which was decided in favour of the Society; and the spectacular case of *Ballymacelligott CDS* v *Richard McEllestrim*. This County Kerry Society sued McEllestrim, a defaulting member. By supplying milk to another source, McEllestrim, as per membership agreement with his co-op, had made himself liable for a penalty (described as liquidated damages!) of one shilling per cow per day for every cow's milk sold contrary to the rule. The County Court awarded a decree in the amount sought, which was later affirmed by the Judge of Assize and confirmed by a Court of Appeal. Realising the crucial

---

47 By 1921 there were 104 auxiliaries to 336 central creameries.
48 A reversal of the situation in earlier days when some smug, unenterprising societies were 'carpeted' by the IAOS for illegally refusing to take on new members because it would involve them in expensive and troublesome investment in expansion, new building and equipment.

importance of the issue, the IAOS had stood behind the Ballymacelligot Society.[49]

McEllestrim, aided by opponents of the co-operative movement, brought the case to the House of Lords in 1919, where by a majority decision the appeal was allowed. The Lords deemed that the co-op rule was "in restraint of trade". The rule seemed to bind the member indefinitely, i.e., to supply his milk to the Ballymacelligot Creamery *for all time* and this, understandably, was deemed unreasonable. If it had been limited to a definite period, there is little doubt that the appeal would have been dismissed.[50] The rule was immediately modified to allow for a time clause, but the exercise had cost the IAOS £3,850 in costs discharged.

If faulty husbandry had directly or indirectly involved the co-operative movement in difficulties, Thomas Wibberley was not to blame. As organiser with the IAOS and, before that, as agricultural instructor in County Limerick, his efforts to promote his system of 'continuous cropping' were little less than heroic. The system entailed the use of catch crops to enable the farmer to distribute his work and his crops (including grass) throughout the year. Farmers, Wibberley maintained, were continually complaining that they could not get labour, but they did not have enough profitable employment all year round, and yet hoped to be able to recruit big numbers of casual labourers at peak periods. The labourers were not enamoured of this and chose to migrate to England and Scotland for lengthier seasonal work rather than hang about for short spells of gruelling, long-houred, part-time work at home. Wibberley was an ardent advocate of machinery to improve the productivity of labour, to smooth out the peaks and valleys of farm work, thus allowing the farmer to diversify his production both in intensive tillage and livestock husbandry and so build up a full-time labour force of skilled workers. Horace Plunkett was impressed:

> Under the prevailing system, agricultural labour may be, as it is in many parts of Ireland, miserably paid and yet extremely dear. A man employed digging potatoes with a spade at 6d per day is, Mr Wibberley tells me, dearer than a man carrying out the same operation at 5s per day with a mechanical potato digger. Apply the same calculation to cutting corn with a scythe and with a reaper and binder, to working land with a wooden harrow and disc harrow or to threshing with a flail

49 A legal defence fund was launched in 1917 to fight this and finance any further cases. "The larger the Movement grows the more likely it is to be assailed. Few Societies can afford the expenses of higher Court litigation and in any case it is not right or just that any one Society should be allowed to fight at its own expense any principle for which all Societies should equally contend." (IAOS Annual Report 1917, p.34).

50 In 1904 the Greenane Society, an auxiliary of Solohead (County Tipperary), was in contention with a number of its members who had defaulted because a proprietary creamery had offered them a better price for milk. The interesting thing in Greenane was that the members had devised their own binding rule which had been accepted by the Registrar of Friendly Societies. It bound the member to supply milk to his own creamery *for a given period* and listed a penalty of ten shillings for every cow which the defaulting member grazed in the year of his default.

or with a power thresher, and a similar conclusion will be reached . . .

We have not attempted to develop intensive cultivation on a large scale for the double reason that we [the IAOS] have not the means and that the greater part of the work . . . belongs more properly to the Department. But the matter being extremely urgent, we have conducted experiments . . . some creameries and agricultural societies and some implement societies, founded for this special purpose, have used their organisation for providing their members with the necessary implements and doing co-operatively other things upon which the profits of their enterprise will depend. Here I speak from experience in my capacity as milkman at Foxrock. I confess I too had looked forward to a leisurely old age knee-deep in grass. Mr Wibberley organised me and I now walk erect waist-deep in giant rape and hardy greens.[51]

Dr E. E. McLysaght recalls something of the strange goings-on at Kilteragh and the Sunday influx of odd-looking countrymen to the sedate suburb of Foxrock:

It is the object of the IAOS to enable the small farmer to buy and sell to advantage, to command, as he should, the terms proper to a manufacturer. It should be the object of the Department of Agriculture to assist him in the other aspect which makes for better business: economical production. It has made sporadic attempts to do so, but on lines which did not appeal to the people and which have had little effect. Here again Sir Horace Plunkett has shown himself a man both of wisdom and discrimination; wisdom in that he saw the necessity of practical example; discrimination in that not being a farmer, he chose an agriculturalist with imagination to make a practical demonstration . . . But there are few progressive farmers in any part of Ireland who will not acknowledge a debt of gratitude to Sir Horace Plunkett and Mr Wibberley. During the three years the experiment lasted, almost every Sunday the South-Eastern Railway discharged a cargo from one train after another at Foxrock station, of farmers large and small, who had come from every county in the country to see for themselves the Kilteragh farm and hear Mr Wibberley expounding his ideas on production of farm foods, with actual practise of them at hand to illustrate his words. The fairy tales which Mr Wibberley seems to tell in his writings on continuous cropping appear true when one visits Kilteragh. Of course his methods are not applicable in their entirety to all parts of the country. But even with a rainfall of almost fifty inches, I have found from my own experience that by modifying them to suit my own circumstances they are practical . . . It is, however, a commentary on what the Department might have been, had Sir Horace Plunkett remained in office, to think of the numbers of farmers who have travelled from Clare and Kerry, from Wexford and Donegal,

51 President's address at the annual general meeting, 4 December 1914.

losing their time and paying their own expenses, to see a new idea put into practice.[52]

Wibberley's work[53] was soon to be overshadowed by political events, civil disorder and recurring periods of economic difficulty for the industry. It was almost half a century before anything on the same scale of practical demonstration and down-to-earth reality was to make a comparable impact on the ordinary dairy farmers — this time in large-scale pilgrimage to the Agricultural Institute's dairy-farm and research centre at Moorepark near Fermoy. But the message had got across and many dairy farmers who had observed Wibberley's findings went on to a successful career in liquid milk supply where they realised a better return for their winter milk. Unfortunately, very few butter-making creameries ever achieved a volume of winter milk to enable them adequately to compensate farmers for their higher costs and year-round hard work.

Wibberley's major difficulty (apart from the Irish peasant's alleged hatred of tillage) was that he was advocating a system of intensive, integrated, year-round farming in an era before there was adequate mechanisation. Although Harry Ferguson and a number of other manufacturers were ardently advertising the merits of their farm tractors, the majority of farmers still had to depend on horses and in many districts on spade labour. The full implementation of the Wibberley system thus called for a degree of dedication and hard work far beyond the norm. Although the number of farmers who persevered with the system could be reckoned in hundreds rather than thousands, by their example they improved the general standard of husbandry in their districts and it is to Wibberley's undying credit that, under such difficult circumstances, he won so many active adherents.

By 1915 some 248 creameries out of a total of 344 were trading in other goods[54] and the total of such sales was almost £285,000. This was in addition to the turnover of £310,000 in agricultural goods recorded by the 219 co-operative agricultural societies especially set up for that purpose.

Nineteen-fifteen was a great year for the creamery societies. Butter sales topped £3 million and total sales were estimated at over £3¾ million. As always, Anderson fretted and fumed about the slowness of societies in sending in their annual returns, about those who sent in incomplete returns and the really worrisome ones who sent in none at all. He had equipped his organisers with motor cars[55] and dispersed them to provincial offices.

52 Edward E. Lysaght, *Sir Horace Plunkett*, Irishmen of Today Series (Dublin: Maunsel, 1916), p.84 et seq.

53 In Ulster in 1916 Harold Barbour paid for an extra organiser to promote tillage. In 1917 Mrs Barbour employed Mr P. McGee to operate the co-operative implement hire scheme in County Cavan for twelve months. At the end of the year she offered to continue her assistance and McGee was placed on the staff of the IAOS.

54 In Munster 109 out of 144 creameries did an 'agricultural trade'; in Ulster 94 out of 143; in Leinster 27 out of 31, and in Connaught 18 out of 26. Of Limerick's 54 creameries, 44 did a store trade, as did 40 out of 50 in Tipperary and 24 out of 39 in Tyrone.

55 Plunkett was enthusiastic about speedy transport and communications. As early as 1901 he had his own motor car. By all accounts he was a furious (Jehu-like) driver. During Easter

James Adams was in Dunmurray, County Antrim; Charlie Riddell was ensconced in Limerick and James Moore was still looking for suitable accommodation in Connaught. Paul Gregan, who covered Leinster, still operated from the Plunkett House headquarters, as did special creamery organiser, James Fant, a knowledgeable and versatile expert in all aspects of dairy science, organisation, engineering and technology. The audit department had audited the accounts of nearly 400 societies that year (including 112 creameries), but returns were still slow and often incomplete. However, with the creameries about which he had full details, Anderson was able to make a revealing comparison with the previous year.[56]

	1914	1915
Number of creameries (with full returns)	283	278
Number of members	40,723	41,612
Total turnover	£2,731,628	£3,499,264
Average per society	£9,652	£12,542
Average per member	£67	£84

Even allowing for a measure of wartime inflation, this was very healthy progress. Other good news was that:

> Almost all the 'creamery' areas in Ireland have been occupied. In the South and in a few cases in the West proprietary creameries are still in existence. In the North, with the exception of those owned by the SCWS, proprietary creameries are non-existant ... The newly established creameries are a fine example to the whole country. They do credit alike to their designers, architects and builders, and to the enlightened enterprise of the Societies to which they belong, whose Committees, in spite of war prices, have determined on having the best possible buildings and equipment.[57]

Despite the difficulties occasioned by the shortage of supplies and raw materials during World War I, farming prosperity continued. As mentioned previously, 1913-1920 were the seven years of plenty for the co-operative movement. Turnover of the co-operative creameries more than trebled (£2½m to £8¼m). By 1916 creameries were paying from 6d to 7½d per gallon for milk.[58] Three years later, few creameries were paying less

week 1916 he was driving recklessly through Dublin, with total disregard for his own safety, to attend to food distribution (Digby, p.209). In 1929, at the age of seventy-five, he learned to fly (ibid., pp.286-87).

56 Nineteen-fourteen was a very sad year for Anderson and the IAOS. Amongst the friends who died (some of them comparatively young) were Alexis Roche, Digges la Touche, Coroner James Byrne, Colonel Pilkington, Thomas Mee, T.J. Griffin and Thomas Sinclair. Two weeks before Christmas, Anderson got word that his youngest son, Alan, had been killed on the Western front. Alan, a graduate of Oxford and an enthusiastic co-operator, was a great favourite at the Plunkett House, where he had worked before joining the British Army at the outbreak of World War I.

57 IAOS Annual Reports 1914, p. 9, and 1915, p. 12.

58 In 1913 prices ranged from 3½d to 5½d. In 1916 the top price for milk was 8¼d paid by the new co-op creamery of Brandonvale, County Kilkenny.

than a shilling and many were paying 14 (old) pence.

Co-operative creameries in the Republic today have a £408 million turnover and a milk supply of nearly 555 million gallons.[59] In 1920, when turnover was only £8¼ million, the creameries still had a very important place in the economy and, in the general poverty of the times, were even more crucial to the farmer's existence. In Munster, where more than half the milk was produced, many farmers were dependent on the monthly creamery cheque. As the War of Independence hotted up, undisciplined British troops (auxiliaries and the notorious Black and Tans) began a systematic burning of co-operative creameries as a suitable method of reprisal for 'outrages' and a hurtful way of getting back at a rebellious population. Beginning on the 9 April with an attack on Rearcross Creamery, County Tipperary, over fifty attacks were made on co-operative premises (including thirty-five creameries) in 1920,[60] over sixty, if fourteen separate raids on one society are accounted. Value of property destroyed was estimated at more than £¼ million and in the attack on Ballymacelligot, a society member, John McMahon, a young, newly-married man, was shot dead. Another member, Tim Walsh, was very seriously wounded.[61]

From the outset the IAOS brought all attacks to the notice of the governments in Dublin and London, indicating that available evidence pointed to the Forces of the Crown "acting in some cases seemingly with and in others seemingly without orders." No charges were made but an investigation was demanded and the Society sought protection of co-operative property. In London the Parliamentary Committee of the

59 Latest statistics available (1974): dairy produce turnover £315,345,005; agricultural goods and services, £92,276,805. In 1920 turnover was £8,274,836 and milk supply 77,732,423 gallons, of which 44,809,402 gallons were produced in Munster.

60 Creameries attacked were Rearcross (9 April), Reiska (10 April, 10 August), Knockfune (10 April, 10 August), Kilcommon (10 April, 16 December), Killonan (14 April), Newport (23 July), Garryspillane (25 July), Upperchurch (31 July), Loughmore (6 August), Templeree and Castleiney (16 August), Killea (17 August), Shanagolden (27 August), Newcastlewest (8 September), Silvermines (15 September), Devon Road (19 September), Tubbercurry, Achonry (1 October), Banteer (8 October), Kildimo, Grange (9 October), Hospital (11 October), Abbeydorney (18 October, 11 November), Lixnaw (25 October), Ballintrillick (27 October), Littleton (31 October), Ballymote (3 November), Nenagh (4 November), Ardfert (5 November), Milford (8 and 27 November), Ballymacelligott (12 and 13 November), Duharra (21 November), Carnadoe (27 November), Mountcollins (28 November), Collooney (30 November, 1 and 7 December), Swanlinbar (19 December), and Atha (23 December).

Agricultural stores attacked were Foynes (6 August), New Ross (7 October), Moycullen (18 October), Maryboro (9 November), and Cloghaneely (18 November). The Co-operative Village Hall at Kilmallock was burned down on 27 May. Fourteen separate attacks were reported on the small store operated by the Raheen Workers' Society, Tuamgraney, County Clare, beginning on 26 November 1920.

61 British forces admitted the attack on this creamery, claiming that they had been shot at from the premises. The manager, John Byrne, was threatened by the military and the assistant manager was arrested in court when he was about to give evidence. He was released a few days later without any charge being preferred against him. The British authorities had sent to the press a photographic reproduction of the alleged ambush. Its propaganda value was considerably diminished when the scene of the photographs was recognised by hundreds of people to be at the Vico Road, Dalkey, County Dublin, where a number of persons came forward who had witnessed the official faking. See *The Irish Homestead*, 28 April 1921.

Co-operative Congress arranged for a deputation of British and Irish co-operators to wait on Sir Hamar Greenwood, Secretary of State for Ireland, on 22 October 1920. Greenwood gave them a courteous hearing and promised protection for co-operative property. He also promised to consider compensation by the Crown where evidence showed that the attacks could not be fairly charged on the locality itself. He would not consider the possibility that these attacks in any way involved the forces of law and order or were other than the work of murderers, rebels and lawless elements. He refused to set up an inquiry in cases where there was a conflict of testimony between Crown forces and civilian eye-witnesses who had given their account on oath.

The sympathy and support of the co-operative movement in Britain was outstanding. Numerous meetings under the auspices of the Co-operative Union were held throughout England and Wales. 'Co-operative' members of both Houses of Parliament, irrespective of party, focused attention on the tragic occurrences in Ireland and many successful protest meetings were held.[62] Plunkett himself personally investigated the famous Newport, County Tipperary case:

> We implored the Government, where the evidence implicated the forces of the Crown, to take whatever steps were necessary to have compensation paid not as provided by the Malicious Injuries Acts, by the ratepayers, many of whom would be actual victims, but by the British Treasury.
>
> I am bound here to state that we were not fairly met by the authorities. They suggested that the perpetrators of the outrages might be Irish Republicans disguised in stolen British uniforms, travelling in stolen British motor-lorries, filled with stolen incendiary material from the arsenals of the preservers of Irish peace. Another suggestion was that the traders of the country towns were taking advantage of the state of the country to wreak their vengeance upon a movement which was interfering with their profits . . . Then it was asserted that the buildings of our societies were occupied by the Irish Republican Army, who fired at the forces of the Crown. Now there are only two cases in which, either in public or in private, have we heard the suggestion of any actual firing. The first was the Newport case, which I personally investigated, because the military called upon me to substantiate statements I had made in the Press. As the case was about to be brought into Court, I asked the Military Authorities to be represented, to produce their own evidence and cross-examine our witnesses; this they declined to do. The Judge appointed by the Crown, and not, remember, a local jury, awarded over £12,000 damages to the Society

62 An American relief committee also did much useful work and arranged to advance funds to affected creameries recommended by the IAOS. It is noteworthy that the CWS also put aside all memories of its quarrel with the Irish movement and was actively associated in the work of the Parliamentary Committee of the Co-operative Congress. The CWS had, of course, previously sent a shipload of food to Dublin during the Lock-out of 1913 and had also participated in arrangements to have children of Dublin workers evacuated to Britain.

upon evidence every bit of which consistently proved that the incendiarism was the work of soldiers as a reprisal for the cutting off of a girl's hair, and that not a shot was fired by anyone except the Military![63]

Attacks on co-operatives abated towards the end of 1920 but isolated assaults continued in many parts of the country until the end of April 1921. Creameries affected included Bridgetown, Newtownsandes, Garryduff, Inver, Kiltoghert, Kilmactranny, Fermoy, Aghadillane, Ballyhahill, Monaghan, Boherbue and Cahir. Ballintrillick, Tubbercurry, Garryspillane and Ballymacelligott were also invaded. Agricultural co-operative stores at Bonniconlon, Castleplunkett and St Maolins (Galway) were also attacked. In many cases the burning and looting of co-ops were accompanied by great brutality and grievous bodily harm to co-operative personnel who had tried to protect their property.

In May 1921, as milk supplies were moving towards their peak, a different tactic was adopted. This was the compulsory closing of creameries by military order, intended as a form of military reprisal for 'occurrences' in the area. Over thirty creameries were affected[64] and suffered serious financial loss. It would be difficult to imagine any more successful expedient to ensure the complete alienation of a people's sympathies and drive them to total rebellion. The burning and closing of creameries must rate as a major factor leading to British admission of the ungovernability of Ireland and the forcing of a truce on 8 July 1921.

During 1921 the White Cross Association came to the aid of the movement by advancing monies to the societies most seriously affected by attacks on their premises. Loans totalling £15,500 were made to seven societies in 1921 and in the first quarter of 1922 an additional £20,000 was advanced to nine societies. The advances were made by way of indentures at nominal interest rates and in some cases no interest at all was charged for the first two years. The Association also made loans totalling some £2,000 (free of interest for the first year) to the IAOS, which enabled the Society to organise and supervise the speedy reconstruction of creamery premises. The destruction of the creameries came within the scope of the Compensation (Ireland) Commission and the British government agreed to pay compensation on the issue of awards by the Commission. The claims for compensation for compulsory closure were still unresolved in 1924 when the terms of reference of the Wood-Renton Commission were amended to allow these claims to be investigated.

No destruction of co-operative property arose during the Civil War, but the societies were inconvenienced by the disruption of communications

---

63 President's address at the IAOS annual general meeting, 23 March 1921.
64 Ballyclough, Lombardstown, Boherbue, Bansha (four auxiliaries were also affected), Collard and Ballyconry, Lixnaw, Glenmore, Mullinavat (plus one auxiliary), Tournafulla, Meenahela Bridge, Coolmoyne, Kilmanagh, Tullaroan, Garryspillane, Kilvilcarris, Castlehale, Clodia, Berrings, Athea, Ballywilliam, Toomevara, Silvermines, Suirvale, Cratloe, Kilflyn (auxiliary to Abbeydorney), Glenpipe (auxiliary to Ida) and Gortatlea and Potalley (auxiliaries to Ballymacelligott).

and the frequent commandeering of transport vehicles. *The Irish Homestead* of 15 July 1922 commented acidly that it appeared that "no civilian had any right to possess motor lorry, motor car or motor cycle until the numerous Generals operating in Ireland had satisfied their insatiable appetite for means of pursuit or flight."

Ireland had now entered a period of serious economic depression. In 1916 creameries had been paying from 6d to 7½d a gallon for milk. By 1919 few creameries were paying less than a shilling and many were paying up to 14d, but in 1921 they were back to between 7d to 8d for a milk supply that had dwindled from 102 million gallons in 1916 to 76 million in 1921. The latter year was exceptional in its combination of a very dry summer and a slump in butter prices, because of the cessation of price control and the unloading of a vast store of 'colonial' butter onto the British market. The situation in Ireland was worsened by the government's decision to hold up the export of butter for a higher price, which could not be realised. During the autumn of 1921 and early in the following year there was serious congestion and dumping of Irish butter in Britain. In Liverpool the problem was aggravated by a serious outbreak of black mould in butter that had lain too long. Some societies had up to twenty tons of butter at a time in Liverpool, Manchester and London.

Milk supplies to co-operative creameries increased to 100 million gallons in 1922 but thereafter grew by no more than 5 per cent. a year until the latter years of the nineteen twenties. The butter market showed little improvement and the dairying industry disintegrated. Because of low milk prices, some farmers reverted to home butter-making. For farmers in outlying areas the economics of transporting milk to a creamery became critical. At the same time there were too many creameries for too little milk: the competition for the available milk supply was intense and this often led to a further proliferation of creameries. Co-operative creamery managers, under pressure from their members, were often forced to provide additional auxiliary intake points at convenient locations. This no doubt reduced transport costs and in the short term improved the economics of milk production for the farmer-supplier but increased the overhead and running costs of the central society. If milk supplies failed to expand, this could ultimately result in a reduced milk price or a trading deficit. In the area of the Golden Vale there was already a density of creamery units which would require the productivity and efficiency of Danish dairy farming to make them all profitable — but still they continued to increase in number.

A popular mythology is promulgated even to the present day that the proliferation of creameries was almost entirely due to the 'co-operators' who (i) behaved less than honourably or (ii) were starry-eyed idealists with little business sense. There were indeed many cases where a co-operative society stretched its financial budget to the limit in an attempt to provide a service to satisfy its members. Nevertheless, by far the greatest economic stupidities were perpetrated by the supposedly hard-headed businessmen who operated the private proprietary creameries. From the earliest days many of these believed that the co-operatives must be beaten by hook or by crook; and the economic realities were ignored.

In its initial development the co-operative movement exercised good economic sense in establishing creameries only in workable locations. The immediate supply area of the proprietary creamery was avoided and the co-operative was set up only where a sufficient number of farmers, who promised to supply a certain amount of milk to make the venture profitable, desired to undertake business on their own account. Invariably it was private enterprise that planted a creamery in the heartland of an area where the majority of farmers had already pledged their support in honour of their own combination, and where the success of the private creamery depended not on the minority of farmers who had freely and legitimately chosen not to partake of co-operation, but on the number of committed farmers who might be persuaded to break their word. There is no evidence of a single instance where the early co-operators ever approached a farmer to break a prior business contract, or where they were the initial intruders into an area that was already adequately serviced.

In remote, thinly-populated mountain areas, the wartime price of a shilling a gallon induced many farmers to take their milk to a creamery. Where family labour was plentiful, a number of neighbours often found it worthwhile to club together and take turns at transporting their limited supply of milk to a creamery ten or more miles away. The fall in milk prices after 1920 disrupted this custom, since one or more members of the group discontinued his supply. The ostensible reason for this was economic, for dairying under such circumstances was rarely more than marginally profitable. However, the psychological factors of resentment and apathy, induced by the price decline, cannot be discounted. In many cases labour was still available since there was rarely any alternative employment. The creamery supply frequently consisted of the summer surplus of the three or more cows, kept originally to supply the household (remote from a purchasing source) in milk and home-made butter. These cows were retained of necessity, but such was the conservatism of the people and the pattern of cattle-raising, that where larger herds had grown (maybe six or more cows), these also tended to be kept on. A further opportunity was presented to the gombeen-man.

Butter-buyers were quickly in the field encouraging the production of home-made butter. The higgler's cart traversed the mountain roads exchanging the farmers' butter and eggs for shop goods. In the nineteen twenties the price offered for home-made butter was rarely more than a shilling a pound, frequently less, representing at best a price of 5d per gallon for milk. The farmers sometimes clubbed together to market a weekly or fortnightly supply of home-made 'fresh' butter by carting it to some town where a reputedly more favourable price was available. Another gombeen refinement was to set up so-called 'dairies' in remote areas. These were often no more than sheds, crudely and cheaply constructed of corrugated iron and slab timbers — sometimes with only an earthen floor. The principal item of equipment was a hand separator operated by the milk supplier to separate the cream from the milk. In some better appointed places there was also a barrel (end-over-end) churn which enabled the butter to be made on the premises; otherwise, the cream was transported for churning at a central base. Usually the cream separators were large and required two men to turn them by hand. The normal arrangement was that the man whose milk was being separated and the man next in line operated the machine together. Thus each supplier had to do two 'separatings' before he was free to return home with his skim milk, unless of course some neighbour had sent a girl or small boy with the milk supply, in which case he might have to do an additional turn. There were a number of these 'dairies' operating in west Cork in the nineteen twenties; eight or ten of them in the neighbourhood of Skibbereen were reported as paying 3¾d per gallon for milk in 1920 — a time when all co-operative creameries in County Cork were paying twice that amount.[65]

The payment for milk in such establishments was determined by gallonage measurement with little regard for milk quality or butter-fat content. The 'dairies' had the advantage of being under the supervision of the buyer or his agent (sometimes generously accorded the title of 'creamery manager'). Gross dirt in the milk would be detected as the separator bowl emptied and adulteration could only be practised on a limited scale.[66] If he considered the flow from the cream pipe to be inadequate, the supervisor delivered a reprimand, privately in the first instance, but openly before the neighbours for any subsequent shortcoming.

The Dairy Produce Act 1924 was a comprehensive piece of legislation relating to the production and manufacture of dairy produce. All creameries had to be registered and had to adhere to strict standards regarding the suitability of their premises and equipment, and the employment of properly trained staff.[67] The regulations had some inhibiting effect on the operation of the 'dairy' depots. They had little if any effect on the haphazard proliferation of larger-sized creameries and auxiliary separating stations in the lowland areas of Munster, or on the war of attrition that was developing between proprietary and co-operative concerns.

By 1926 there were some 580 central and auxiliary creameries in the Irish Free State, 400 of which were co-operatives. Of the 180 proprietary creameries, 114 were now controlled by the Condensed Milk Company which had recently acquired the creameries of the Newmarket Dairy Company and a number of smaller proprietary concerns. The Condensed

65 See Irish Folklore Commission, May 1949, MS. 1306, J. Barry and S. O'Coileain. The average price range amongst Cork co-operative creameries for the year 1920 was from 11.57d to 14.58d. The informant might have been mistaken about the exact year. If he was thinking of 1921, the co-op prices ranged from 7. 36d to 9. 45d.

66 There is an apocryphal story told of a supplier suspected of watering his milk who was finally betrayed by a minnow found flapping in the empty separator bowl!

67 A previous piece of legislation, the Dairies, Cowsheds and Milk-Shops Order 1908, had caused an outcry from the co-operators: "... it appears to discriminate unfairly against Creamery milk suppliers to whom it applies, while it does not extend to farmers making butter in their home dairies." (IAOS Annual Report 1908, p. 9).

Milk Company had a powerful advantage over the co-operative creameries in its development of a range of products and valuable retail outlets in Britain.[68] This diversification and marketing enabled the Company to pay a marginally higher price for milk, an advantage which it hoped to exploit to acquire more of the limited milk supply and achieve better economies of scale in the processing and marketing of its products. The co-operative creameries, largely because of their own failure to combine, were left with a single product, butter, for which the price was frequently declining. The German economist Moritz Bonn had once remarked to Anderson, "But you Irish — you can *conspire*, but you cannot combine." The aptness of his observation would soon be confirmed once more, but in the meantime there were many co-operative creameries forced by competition to maintain a price of 7d to 8d per gallon for milk, a figure which left them losing money on their butter sales:

> ... many creamery societies found themselves going deeper and deeper into debt, and when refused credit by the banks, they appealed to the Government for aid. Towards the end of 1926 the trade war reached its climax and the outlook for co-operative dairying was dismal indeed ... A decision had to be taken as to whether the law of the jungle should be allowed to prevail. If allowed, the result might well be the extinction of co-operative creameries and the transfer of the industry to British capitalist concerns.[69]

By 1926 the Condensed Milk Company was also becoming disenchanted with the milk price war. Profits were being drastically reduced but the price factor was not evoking the required response from the farmers. Co-operative creameries seemed intent on ruining themselves by paying prices which butter production could not justify; but even where the Company had a clear-cut price advantage and was offering a penny more than the local co-operative, the capitalist response was often niggardly. There was a measure of co-operative loyalty and an inertia and conservatism amongst farmers, the same inertia which thirty years previously had kept many of them dealing with gombeen-men long after there was a co-operative advantage in leaving them. The hoped-for extra volume of milk for the condenseries was not readily forthcoming.

In 1926 Dr Henry Kennedy was appointed secretary of the IAOS. His interest in the co-operative movement was heightened by his experience as a director of the White Cross in which he was responsible for channelling aid to a number of stricken societies in 1921-22. Physically, as well as intellectually, Henry Kennedy was a very big man, a giant-sized figure whose apparel had to be specially made. He always reminded Plunkett of the Nebraskan farmer's description of President Howard Taft, "a gentleman of great personal magnitude". Kennedy was destined to be the

---

68 A large shareholding in the Irish Condensed Milk Company was held by the firm of Lovell and Christmas, one of the largest wholesale grocers in Britain.
69 Daniel Hoctor, *The Department's Story*, pp. 153-54.

chief architect of legislation which would resolve the struggle between co-operative and proprietary creameries, a conflict which would result in economic degradation for the whole dairying industry.

At the prompting of Kennedy and the IAOS, the Department of Agriculture undertook negotiations with the Condensed Milk Company with a view to purchasing their creameries, condenseries and toffee plant. Agreement was reached and in 1927 the government set up a state-sponsored company, The Dairy Disposal Company Ltd., to manage the newly acquired creameries until arrangements could be made for their integration into the co-operative system. Those creameries which were too close to co-operative creameries in areas of limited milk supply, were closed down. Attempts were made to transfer the non-redundant ones to existing co-operatives or to form new co-operative societies to take them over — in either case, at purchase prices repayable by instalments. Many transfers were soon arranged but in a great many places no deals could be made, so The Dairy Disposal Company was obliged to stay in business.

In the period up to 1931 The Dairy Disposal Company purchased 170 proprietary creameries. Seventy-nine of these were closed, forty-four were transferred to co-operative ownership and the remaining forty-seven were held by the DDC. The Company also took over seventeen co-operative creameries, of which they closed four and retained thirteen. They also built four new creameries. Toames Co-operative Creamery was transferred to the DDC in 1932 and, two years later, eleven creameries were similarly transferred. Ownership of two famous Kerry creameries, Ballymacelligott and Rathmore, went to the DDC a year later.

The Dairy Disposal Company managed the creameries left in its hands and also took over and rehabilitated the creameries which got into difficulties at a later stage. Later the Company also extended the creamery system, by means of auxiliaries or mobile separating plants, into areas not previously served where the organisation of co-operatives was unpracticable. This was done partly to improve the profitability of their existing creameries and partly as a social aspect of the government's policy to help poor areas.

The Creamery Act of 1928 introduced a system of licensing, empowering the Minister for Agriculture to control the establishment of new creameries, thereby preventing the future erection of new creameries in unsuitable locations. The reorganisation proved a life-saver for the co-operatives, although this was not always appreciated by the milk-supplier members whose immediate benefit was often a reduction in the milk price. There was much grumbling when local creameries were closed and farmers were redirected to a creamery some miles away. Republicans and others who opposed the Cosgrave government contrived to make political issue of the hardships inflicted by the closing of creameries and the suppression of the backcountry 'dairies'. R. A. Anderson listened to the parochial lamentations and recalled the man who had made a flying visit to the IAOS offices in Dublin in 1902 — a Mr Nissley, who collected milk at some 200 creameries in the State of Kansas but only made butter in one (the milk and cream were sometimes transported up to 300 miles).

Henry Kennedy now sought to reduce the congestion of creamery units in the developed areas and to extend the creamery system to districts which seemed admirably suited for dairying but which so far had made little development in that direction. Between 1927 and 1929 about a dozen new centrals and some eighteen independent auxiliary creameries were established (in many cases with the help of loans from the newly-formed Agricultural Credit Corporation) serving areas in the midlands, the west and other undeveloped dairying areas.[70] Increased productivity would solve many problems both in the old areas and the new. At the opening of Scariff Creamery in 1927, the Bishop of Killaloe, Dr Fogarty, gave such a pragmatic discourse on agricultural development that the IAOS subsequently published his speech in pamphlet form:

> I myself have only four cows. They were not specially selected; they came on to me haphazard from neighbouring farmers around Ennis. Now one of these cows ... milked in 45 weeks last year over 1,200 gallons. How many cows in Clare bring in £45 a year? or rather, how many cows could we not have in Clare yielding that return if we only got into the business with a full heart? My second cow gave 1,198 gallons, and the other two, which were heifers of the first calf, very nearly 1,000 gallons each, with proportionate butter values. There is no four-leaf shamrock about the Bishop's house; there is no earthly reason why the ordinary farmer's herd, be it big or little, would not reach the same level, instead of crawling on the 400 gallon line. Therefore, I say there is money running idle on the land.

Concurrent with the rationalisation of production and processing, Kennedy's economist's eye was on the organisation of a real market for Irish butter. The role of the Co-operative Agency Society (1893) in butter-making had declined until, by 1923, the Agency with its thirty-four societies, sold only £500,000 worth of the co-operative £5 million butter sales in the Free State. Anderson, who had been making gallant efforts to establish an effective butter control, had serious misgivings when, in 1928, the co-operatives were brought together to launch the Irish Associated Creameries Ltd., a new central organisation for the marketing of dairy produce. He felt that Kennedy and his satellites were pushing the matter too hard and that the lessons of the past were being ignored:

> The chief lesson which ought to have been learned by the failure of the Agency Society was that it is perfectly futile to attempt to centralise the sale of any produce so variable in quality as butter without first standardising it and providing a machinery that will maintain that

---

70 Centrals at Scariff, Askeaton, Donaghmore, Rathscanlon (1927); Annagelliffee, North Cork, Clonmel and Newcastle, Roscrea, Midlands, South Leitrim (1928); Slaney Valley (1929) and West Clare (1930). The independent auxiliaries served areas in Counties Carlow, Cavan, Clare, Cork, Kildare, Kilkenny, Laois, Leitrim, Longford, Mayo, Offaly, Tipperary and Wexford.

standard. I personally urged that view on the promoters, who agreed that standardisation, plus a Government brand or mark which could only be used on butter of the required high quality was eminently desirable. But, they argued, the need for centralised marketing was so very urgent and the number of creameries which could qualify to use such a brand was, relatively, so small, that unless the admittedly chaotic condition of individual marketing was to be allowed to continue there was nothing for it but to launch the project . . .[71]

Anderson continued to urge some form of product standardisation for the new marketing organisation. Failing a revival of the butter control, he asked that only those creameries with consistently high marks in the 'surprise butter' competitions should be admitted initially. When this request was turned down, he continued to plead that at least this 'gilt-edged' butter from the best societies should be placed in a class by itself and sold under a brand indicative of its high quality:

> I argued that if this were done and it could be shown that butter sold under this special brand realised a definitely higher price than that obtainable for unbranded butter, all the creameries would strive to gain admission to the 'inner circle'.

The only creameries which derived any great benefit from the IAC were the small concerns whose managers had little experience or salesmanship. Nearly all the creameries joined in the venture,[72] but very soon complaints were voiced that the price obtained through joint marketing did not match those obtainable by individual efforts. The irrepressible Anderson made a final effort:

> . . . I tried very hard to bring about an amalgamation with the [Co-operative] Agency Society, which although it had become an ordinary butter-merchant business or, at best, a sort of friendly broker, was well and carefully managed by two men of great experience in the butter trade. I foresaw that as long as the Agency Society lay athwart of the path of the IAC it must be a really formidable competitor. The Agency Society had numerous friends among the creameries. It had been in existence for nearly forty years and it had retained this much of its original co-operative character — its directors were appointed by its federated societies . . . Its services in selling these large consignments of butter, which the creameries themselves could not dispose of,

---

71 R. A. Anderson, *With Horace Plunkett in Ireland*, p. 209.
72 "About 80 per cent of co-operative creameries joined the new organisation and bound themselves to deliver the bulk of their output to it. Unfortunately, the 20 per cent of creameries which remained aloof included some of the most important concerns in the country." (Hoctor, op. cit., p. 156). In the details of each co-operative creamery given in *Agricultural Co-operation in Ireland* — a survey by the Horace Plunkett Foundation (London: George Routledge & Sons Ltd., 1931) — membership of the IAC is noted.

earned for it their gratitude. In return, they bought their creamery requisites from the Agency, sometimes at higher prices than they could procure them elsewhere. I have had unmistakeable evidence of this loyalty and of the extent to which the Agency had created for itself a real goodwill, and I was more than ever convinced that unless it were amalgamated with the IAC it would prove a thorn in the side of that body.

Financially, the Agency Society was embarrassed, but not to so great an extent as to present an absolute bar to amalgamation. Its bankers, the Munster & Leinster Bank, were also the bankers of the IAC and it is almost inconceivable that the bank directors would not have gone a long way to assist in bringing about the amalgamation of the two bodies. I was assured that the Agency was quite willing, but after prolonged negotiations, the directors of the IAC declined to take the step.

The ill-fated Irish Associated Creameries Ltd. did not last long. Some of the best creameries stood by loyally in the hope of better things, even though they could get a higher price on their own. The major defection came from the less efficient societies (some of them big enough to know better) whose managers fancied themselves as salesmen. Some of these sold their best butter privately, unloaded the inferior stuff on the IAC, and applauded their own salesmanship by pointing out the disparity in price. In 1929 the IAC handled less than half the total output of creamery butter. This, coupled with a disastrous fall in export butter prices,[73] forced the organisation into liquidation at the end of 1930. Anderson commented bitterly:

The blood of the huxter seems to be so much in us that we hate to surrender the sale of what we produce, even to a man whom we know to be a better salesman than we are ourselves. We were born with the instinct of the fair and the market deeply implanted in us. And we have apparently inherited the secretiveness of the old people who would never reveal what they got for a beast or for their farm produce.

The IAC affair was the one really disgraceful episode in the co-operative story. The débâcle took place when there were few extenuating circumstances. The co-operators should have learned from the history of the Agency Society. Their recent retrieval from their trade war with the proprietary creameries should have taught them a salutary lesson in co-operative solidarity. There was a Minister and a Department of Agriculture very favourably disposed to them. But most of all, co-operative idealists took it particularly hard that the creameries showed such disloyalty and disarray in the face of falling markets and the tough times that were so obviously ahead.

73 The average price of Irish butter exported in 1929 was 164/9d per cwt. This dropped to 127/6d in 1930. Worse was still to come. The 1932 price was down to 95/4d.

The dairying industry sank into a deep slough of despond. In the post-war period, the low level of winter milk production had compelled Saorstát Eireann to import up to 30,000 cwts of butter annually. The government's first reaction to falling butter prices was to impose a customs duty of 4d per lb on imported butter in 1931. A year later, under the Dairy Produce (Price Stabilisation) Act, imports of dairy produce were prohibited except under licence, duties were imposed and levies collected on all creamery-made butter[74] and the proceeds were paid out in bounties on exports. When an economic war broke out in 1933, the new Irish government withheld the land annuities payable to Britain and the UK government retaliated with penal import duties on Irish goods. Dairy produce suffered like the rest — 20 per cent. *ad valorem* duty, which was later raised to 40 per cent. Bounty payments were no longer adequate and a special export subsidy was introduced. A further Act in 1935, the Dairy Produce Price Stabilisation Act, empowered the Minister for Agriculture to fix a minimum price for butter sold on the home market. Creameries were encouraged to diversify their production and special export subsidies were paid on cheese, condensed milk, dried milk and cream. The prohibition of cheese imports gave an impetus to cheese manufacture.

Previous efforts at cheese-making (mainly with a view to fuller utilisation of skim milk and more home-produced food) during World War I had been reasonably successful,[75] but total output was comparatively small and in most of Munster, as the war progressed, skim milk came to be more highly valued for pig-feeding than for cheese-making. The IAOS Annual Report of 1917 noted that skim milk "at the present time is regarded in many places as being worth 6d to 8d per gallon."

By the mid-nineteen thirties there were fewer inhibitions about cheese-making. Whole milk was fetching 3d to 4½d per gallon. Calves were being slaughtered in an effort to limit the population of unsaleable cattle and in many fairs and markets small farmers with creeled carts sought to seduce town housewives into accepting free gifts of unsaleable bonhams.[76]

In 1936, Dr James Ryan, the Minister for Agriculture, suggested that a butter marketing committee be set up to enable individual Irish butter exporters to link up with British importers of their own choice who would agree to pay a fixed price for a steady supply of Irish butter. Several British importers had been interviewed and many of them had agreed that there

---

74 Also on certain factory and farm butters exported. In 1933 the Department of Agriculture encouraged cold storage of butter, so that imports during the winter months were largely avoided. The price of creamery butter in 1932 was stabilised at 117/- per cwt.

75 Caerphilly was the main type of cheese made during World War I. The IAOS asked creameries to consider a full-cream cheese more akin to Cheddar and called by a name which would at once reveal its origin, like the 'Ardagh cheese', a distinctive product pioneered by Mabel, wife of artist Dermod O'Brien, then farming at Cahirmoyle. The first co-op to undertake cheese production on a large scale was Mitchelstown and by 1937 some 40,000 cwts of processed cheese were being produced, almost half of which was exported.

76 In a survey of 98 dairy farms in the Limerick-Cork border area in 1937-38, Michael Murphy from Universtiy College Cork calculated that if the farmer were to get 4 per cent. on his capital plus a standard agricultural wage per labour unit, the average cost of milk production would be 6.47d per gallon. Average prices paid by co-ops in those years ranged from 4.55 to 6.77d, the latter being paid by Lombardstown in 1938.

was much Irish butter of excellent quality which did not realise anything like its full market value because of ineffective marketing. At this time the price paid for milk was averaging about 4d per gallon and the price of butter ex-creamery was less than 1/- per lb. Because of considerable wrangling and difficulties about representation, the initial butter marketing committee had no representative of the industry and consisted solely of three officers from the Department of Agriculture. Shortly after, a marketing advisory council from the industry was appointed to advise and assist the committee. Later, in 1939, the chairman of the Dairy Disposal Company and three representatives of co-operative creameries were appointed by the Minister to replace the three original members of the committee who had resigned. The committee was just getting into its stride when the outbreak of World War II altered the whole marketing strategy.

The most grievous marketing defect highlighted by British importers in 1936 was the failure of Irish butter suppliers to keep up regular week by week deliveries. This was no new problem but the same old trouble of the breakdown of the whole Irish dairying system in the winter months because of the lack of winter feed.

The Dairy Disposal Company had been incorporated in 1927 as a temporary expedient to help reorganise the dairying industry and settle it rationally in co-operative hands. The years went by, however, without the rationalisation taking place and the DDC seemed to become more and more a fixture. The major limitation on this state-sponsored company was that in every season it was expected to pay its way and provide its own capital investment for expansion. It was thus inhibited from undertaking any courageous schemes of reorganisation or re-equipment that would give it a true developmental role. Inevitably the management became entrenched and showed little enterprise. As time went by, the DDC began to show considerable reluctance to yield either its assets or its territories to co-operative takeover.

In 1937, after what was reported as an "exhaustive discussion", the IAOS unanimously passed a resolution calling on the Minister for Agriculture to declare his Department's policy on the disposition of the Dairy Disposal Company. The matter was pursued by the Society's officers but annual general meetings in 1939 and 1940 were unable to report any progress. In 1943 the powers of the DDC were actually increased by the Creamery (Acquisition) Act to enable it to purchase compulsorily the small number of proprietary creameries which remained. The chairman of the DDC was designated Controller of Creamery Development. The co-operators felt as uneasy about the state's intervention over the creameries as they had about the butter committee, the establishment of the Dublin and Cork Milk Boards, the Regulation of Supply and Price of Milk Act 1936, and the regimentation of the Dublin District Milk Board under the Emergency Powers Order in 1942. They felt that the government was encroaching too much and consulting too little.[77]

77 In 1909 the Departmental bill affecting the butter trade was introduced without consulation with the IAOS.

The government's policy of strict neutrality spared the country's participation in World War II.[78] Nevertheless, scarcity of supplies, transport and fuel shortages and a serious outbreak of foot and mouth disease in 1941 made the war years difficult for the co-operative movement. Butter was rationed and prices were controlled. Despite compulsory tillage, or perhaps because of it, the milk supply to creameries remained low, fluctuating around the 130 million gallon mark for most of the decade. Not until four years after the war did it show signs of taking off; 153 million in 1949 and a further jump to 172 million gallons in 1950.[79]

A separating station, County Kilkenny, 1940.

Resumption of butter exports became possible in the early nineteen fifties but the amounts exported were small — mostly summer surplus for which there was no storage because the bulk of manufacture was now more than ever a summer operation. Despite the continuation of a mild form of rationing, some New Zealand or Danish butter had to be imported for winter use. Soil fertility had suffered over the years of shortage and

78 In the first year of the war, however, an unidentified bomber flying off course jettisoned its load and destroyed the premises of Shelburne Co-operative Agricultural and Dairy Society at Campile, County Wexford. Three people lost their lives.
79 Creamery turnover rose from £8 m in 1940, to £20 m in 1949 and to approximately £23 m in 1950.

economic depression. A New Zealand grassland expert, Holmes, reported in 1948 that the country's grasslands were producing the minimum possible under an Irish sky. With the return to normal trading after the war, things gradually began to improve. One of the most important technical developments was the emergence of ground limestone as a suitable and economical soil conditioner. Previously, liming had depended on the expensive and laborious burning of limestone in primitive kilns or the almost equally laborious extraction of natural calcareous materials, shell sands and marls. The provision of Marshall aid[80] enabled many agricultural improvement schemes to be undertaken. The Land Project for drainage and land reclamation was begun in 1949 and its ancillary Fertiliser Credit Scheme a year later. A transport subsidy scheme in March 1951 enabled farmers everywhere to obtain ground limestone at 16/- per ton. Under the influence of price supports for milk, improved fertility and cattle stocks (Friesians became popular), milk supplies increased rapidly.[81] Home butter-making, which had experienced a resurgence during the rationing period of the war and post-war years, now declined once more, particularly where creameries extended their influence into the west and other non-dairying areas.[82] Even the tardy figure of milk-yield-per-cow began to rise to a hopeful (but still disgraceful) 500 gallons by the late nineteen fifties. Hand labour had long been a serious limiting factor in dairying expansion. The conservative (and self-esteemed perfectionist) Irish farmer had always been suspicious of mechanical milking machines.[83] Now, machine-milking tended to be more acceptable to him as improved machines came on the market and the scheme of rural electrification initiated in 1948 brought a convenient source of power to the countryside. This was a very important factor in increasing the size of dairy herds.

Newmarket Co-operative Creameries Ltd. succeeded in purchasing a number of creameries held by the Dairy Disposal Company in the Newmarket area of County Cork in 1944. Failure to made further acquisitions precipitated another strongly worded resolution at the IAOS annual meeting in 1948 calling on the Minister for Agriculture "to hand over all the creameries and milk supplies belonging to the Dairy Disposal Company to co-operative control and ownership." A year later the Society negotiated with the DDC to acquire creamery groups owned by the Company at Coachford and Terelton, County Cork, but without any

---

80 Ireland obtained a loan of $128.2 million and a grant of $18 m.

81 Much of the enthusiasm for improvement and change was generated by Macra na Feirme, a voluntary organisation (with an educational emphasis) for young farmers, founded in 1944. Expanded agricultural advisory services were needed to meet the farmer's demand for technical advice. The Parish Plan of providing an agricultural advisor to every three parishes was initiated in a few areas in 1955, whereupon most of the County Committees of Agriculture bestirred themselves to retain their local control of the advisory service by appointing additional staff.

82 From 20 per cent. of the nation's butter production in 1950, home butter dropped to less than 6 per cent. in 1965.

83 Some progressive farmers, however, had milking machines from very early times. The O'Briens of Churfield, Clarina, had a milking machine as early as 1907. Patrick O'Sullivan of Colncrippe House, Feenagh, Rathluirc was reported to have a Moreton milking machine working successfully in 1916.

prospect of success. Meanwhile, the DDC was building a new creamery at Milltown-Croagh between Adare and Rathkeale, County Limerick, an addition which would deplete the milk supply of four neighbouring co-operatives. A year later, Charlie Riddell, assistant secretary to the IAOS, wrote whimsically in the *Year Book of Agricultural Co-operation in the British Empire 1950*, the annual international publication of the Plunkett Foundation: "The Government Holding Body, the Dairy Disposal Company Ltd., continues to occupy an anomalous position in relation to the co-operative movement."

In 1951 the Dairy Disposal Company confessed that the debts owed by its milk suppliers and customers were a serious problem. It wanted the co-operative movement to take over responsibility for the collection of these debts, but the IAOS would not accede to this request. It was usually a big undertaking to prepare the DDC milk suppliers in these areas to accept even the basic responsibilities of co-operative ownership. The fact that the district was still under DDC fosterage often indicated a long-standing lack of co-operative zeal. An attempt was made to arrange the transfer of the Dicksgrove group of DDC creameries to the local co-operative society but negotiations became bogged down. There was a growing realisation on both sides that the transfer of creameries could not be handled adequately in local isolation. What was needed was a new approach and an overall plan for total takeover. The physical and economic logistics of the transference were critical to ensure viability and equity at all stages; there would have to be a transitional period of co-operative education during which good committees would be established for each group to take over management. The IAOS submitted such a plan to the Department of Agriculture on 26 April 1954, but no action resulted.

After the setting up of a separate Organisation Society in Northern Ireland in 1922, there remained some 260 co-operative creameries in the South. By 1929 the number was up to 274 but thereafter a gradual process of attrition and some rationalisation set in. Henry Kennedy disapproved of the idea of creameries at every crossroads and set out to build on the foundations of existing strong societies, encouraging the big to absorb the smaller, weaker units and achieve a size where they could be really effective in processing and marketing. By 1951 the number of creamery societies had been reduced to 193 but turnover had increased from £4.7 million in 1931 to £23.8 million. However, forty-six creameries, of the total 193, accounted for £14.3 million of the total turnover.[84] In fact, the five largest creameries — Mitchelstown, Ballyclough, Dungarvan, Killeshandra and Drinagh — accounted for more than 20 per cent. of the total turnover. The larger creamery societies had tended to expand at a much faster rate than their smaller counterparts.

The year 1951 also gave a portent of the shape of things to come. A type of federal society, Miloko Co-operative Society Ltd., was established at

---

84 Forty-six creameries had dairy turnover in excess of £100,000 each and they made up £10,420,501 of the total dairy produce turnover of £16,861,645. They also accounted for £3,845,113 of the total creamery trade in other goods of £6,929,914.

Carrick-on-Suir. This was a new concept in co-operative development, in which thirty-eight co-operative creameries in the region joined forces with a number of English capitalist stockholders for the purpose of manufacturing chocolate crumb. Golden Vale Food Products Ltd. in Rathluirc, County Cork, was also getting well underway; this was a consortium of twelve cheese-producing creameries (registered in 1948), processing and marketing their whole output of cheese.

As production and exports increased, so too did marketing problems. Butter was still exported in half cwt wooden boxes which, when emptied and upholstered, made pleasant fireside 'creepies'. Their usefulness as export packaging was much less obvious. In 1957 the Minister for Agriculture set up an advisory committee on the Marketing of Agricultural Produce.[85] As a result of the recommendations of that committee, An Bord Bainne (The Irish Dairy Board) was set up in 1961. The Board, which comprised representatives of milk producers, manufacturers and the Department, took over the responsibilities of the old Butter Marketing Committee (1936) and, from 1 March 1964, the additional responsibility for export marketing, with certain exceptions,[86] of all other Irish dairy products. The Board's terms of reference were broadly defined under Section 4, subsection 3, of the Dairy Produce Marketing Act of 1963:

> It shall be the general duty of the Board to endeavour to improve the marketing of milk products outside the State and achieve such flexibility in the marketing aforesaid and in its development as will ensure that the producers of milk obtain reasonable returns thereon.

Any loss or subsidy incurred by the Board was made good by a government subvention of two-thirds and by a levy on all milk delivered to creameries of one-third. The Board's administrative expenses were also being met from this levy.

Towards the end of 1961 Britain introduced a heavy, so-called 'anti-dumping' duty on imports of Irish butter.[87] A few months latter this duty was removed and quantity control of imports was introduced; Ireland was allocated a very low quota of 12,000 tons for the year 1962-63. The Irish government protested strongly but without much success. There were some slight increases granted in subsequent years, but there was no worthwhile relief until the Anglo-Irish Free Trade Agreement of 1965. This agreement almost doubled the original quota and gave the industry a chance to grow. Bord Bainne inherited many problems but achieved a measure of success: marketed under the brand name of 'Kerrygold' in a distinctive wrapper, Irish creamery butter began to edge its way upwards towards a more appropriate place in the British price league table.

85 Its chairman was Dr Juan Greene, the first president of the National Farmers' Association (now the Irish Farmers' Association).

86 These were chocolate crumb, milk powder for baby foods and some cheeses supplied by proprietary manufacturers to branches of their firms in Britain.

87 In its customary place near the bottom of the price table, Irish butter was open to the accusation of being dumped.

The IAOS Report for 1960 indicated that fourteen co-operative societies were engaged in the liquid milk trade, selling pasteurised bottled milk. It was an area of co-operative development in which the movement had hitherto made remarkably little progress. A meeting was convened in Thurles in November 1960 and a committee was set up to liaise with the participating societies and to coordinate development.[88] In 1959 a small co-operative marketing agency, Irish Milk Powder Exports Ltd., was set up by the co-operative creameries engaged in milk powder manufacture. The founder societies were Ballyclough, Dungarvan and Mitchelstown. The Dairy Disposal Company was also admitted to the group and when Golden Vale began manufacturing milk powder in 1962, it too joined. The volume of output was then large enough to enable Irish Milk Powder Exports Ltd. to arrange the orderly marketing of Irish milk powder in Britain through Unigate (Milk Products) Ltd.[89]

The report of the inter-departmental committee on the problems of small western farms[90] advocated the expansion of dairying in the western counties. It was envisaged that existing creameries would extend their areas of operation to embrace new dairying areas in the west. There was some disquiet when it was learned that the Taoiseach, Seán Lemass, had also invited the Dairy Disposal Company to participate in this new development. The matter was resolved, however, when the Minister for Agriculture, Patrick Smith, stated that there was "never any intention of setting up the Dairy Disposal Company in competition with the co-operative effort in the West of Ireland and if the Co-operative Societies were willing to undertake the work of developing the West and prepared to accept the bad areas from the point of view of milk production with the good areas, there was nothing to prevent the societies from going ahead."

Arrangements were made for dairy co-operatives already in the west to extend their area of operation. Achonry, Gurteen and Kiltoghert received industrial grants to enable them to provide new separating stations. Kilnaleck Society, based in County Cavan, established a new central creamery at Kilconnell, with separating stations at Athlone, Athenry and Cloonbeirne. The Nenagh Society established a separating station at Killimor, County Clare. The agricultural advisory officers, notably in Counties Roscommon, Mayo and Galway, displayed great enthusiasm for the new development and put in a great deal of hard work in organising and instructing farmers in what was for many of them a new farm enterprise. A fair indication of the success of the venture was the increase in creamery milk production in Connaught from 12.3 million gallons in 1960 to 26.13 million gallons in 1970. National milk supply also doubled during that period.

88 The committee comprised J. Deasy (Clonmel & Newcastle Society), W. P. Sugrue (Newtownsandes), J. O'Donnell (Town of Monaghan), N. Norris (Kilkenny) and a representative of the IAOS.
89 A subsidiary company formed as a result of the amalgamation of the two giant British companies, United Dairies Ltd. and Cow and Gate Ltd.
90 *Report of the Interdepartmental Committee on the Problems of Small Western Farms* (Dublin: Stationery Office, 1963), Pr. 6540.

In retrospect, the most significant event in the nineteen sixties affecting the future of the dairying industry appears to be one which evoked little comment at the time. This was the appointment by the Minister for Agriculture, Paddy Smith, in 1962 of a team of experts to examine the industry and recommend any changes necessary in preparation for Ireland's entry into the European Community. The team's principal finding[91] was that there were too many small inefficient creameries. They recommended amalgamation, by compulsion if necessary, and the formation of larger units to effect economies of scale and allow diversification in production and marketing. There were then 606 creamery premises (156 centrals and 450 other units, auxiliaries and separating stations).[92] The survey team recommended groupings which would reduce the total number to about 150. The Knapp Report[93] dealt with the co-operative movement as a whole and, although it was critical of the report of the survey team, it endorsed many of its recommendations. Having discussed both reports with the interested parties, the Minister for Agriculture urged the IAOS to encourage its creamery societies to "form such consolidations and mergers as were necessary to put their businesses on a sound footing." Also, the perennial problem of trying to dispose of the Dairy Disposal Company was taken up afresh. In 1965 there were still seventeen central creameries and several auxiliaries in the hands of the DDC, which handled 25 per cent. of all milk for manufacturing. Dr Knapp, in his *Appraisement*, complained of the apparent reluctance to get to grips with the problem:

> The decision must be made whether the Dairy Disposal Company is to be liquidated and its components converted to co-operative operation or whether it be continued as a competitive Government organisation. It cannot be looked upon as a self-directed co-operative organisation. If it is going to continue as a Government operation it would seem reasonable that it should be required to provide full information to the public in the same way that a co-operative is required to provide information to the members and to the public on its operations. There should be a basis provided for measuring the effectiveness of the two forms of enterprise. Up to this time very little information has been made available to the public on the operations of the Dairy Disposal Company. If full information were available it would be possible to better determine what might be done.

No such forthright procedure proved possible since the DDC continued obdurately to keep its own counsel. There was a considerable amount of politicking and bargaining as suggestion after suggestion was put forward, but the negotiating ended in stalemate. It was not until 1972 that there was any further progress, when four DDC creamery groups were transferred to

91 See *Report of Survey Team on Dairying Products* (Dublin: Stationery Office, 1963).
92 The IAOS Annual Report for 1963 lists 141 central co-operative creamery societies and 46 auxiliary societies in 1962.
93 See Joseph G. Knapp, *An Appraisement of Agricultural Co-operation in Ireland* (Dublin: Stationery Office, 1964), Pr. 7467.

be supplied by a number of creameries which would comprise the Avonmore group. During 1968 also, extensions were made to the Miloko plant in Carrick-on-Suir and to the Glaxo factory attached to Lough Egish. Other ventures into milk processing were mooted and many co-operatives were anxious lest too much of the processing might fall into the hands of non-national organisations. When the matter was discussed by the Society in 1964, it recommended that the Department of Agriculture should ensure that, wherever possible, all the manufacturing stages should be under the control of Irish creameries and, if this were not possible, that the participation of non-national organisations should be limited to a maximum 20 per cent. of the capital of any undertaking.

In December 1971 the law providing for a 75 per cent. majority vote for amalgamation was changed to a 51 per cent. requirement, at each of two special general meetings of shareholders. Even in the short period during which the new regulation has been operative, it has considerably speeded up the rate of progress. In October 1972, the IAOS published revised proposals for creamery reorganisation in the southern counties, where over 80 per cent. of creamery milk supplies are now concentrated. Considerable regroupings had already taken place in the north and west and were still continuing in, for example, Lough Egish, North Connaught Farmers, and Donegal Co-operative Creameries Ltd. The new proposals for the south were based on expanding the production facilities of existing co-operatives rather than the establishment of new ones. They also in some measure embody AE's long cherished dream of a comprehensive co-operation rather than a single purpose one.[97]

> The revised proposals envisage the development of *seven* major multi-purpose co-operative creamery groups for the area in place of the *thirteen* groups proposed in 1966. Although there is room for argument about the disposition of some creameries between the new groupings, the scheme provides that all creameries in the south of Ireland can now come under the influence of one or other of the proposed new groups, each creamery having the right to supply milk to the processing co-operative to which it is allocated and also the right to amalgamate with it if it so desires .. [98]

Six of the major groupings are centred on: Avonmore Farmers Ltd., Ballyragget, County Kilkenny; Ballyclough C. C. Ltd., Mallow, County Cork; Golden Vale Creameries Ltd., Rathluirc, County Cork;

97 "It is not enough to organise farmers in a district for one purpose only ... in a credit society, a dairy society, a fruit society, a bacon factory or a co-operative store. All these may be and must be beginnings, but if they do not develop and absorb all rural business into their organisation they will have little effect on character. The specialised society only effects economic efficiency. The evolution of humanity beyond its present level depends absolutely on its power to unite and create true social organisms." For an account of the 'all-purpose' creamery society at Rathmore, County Kerry, established in 1919, see the IAOS Annual Report 1920, p. 10. Billis, County Cavan, tackled the problem differently, having five different co-operative societies established as early as 1900.
98 IAOS Annual Report 1972, p. 6.

Mitchelstown C.A.S. Ltd., County Cork; Waterford C.S. Ltd., Dungarvan, County Waterford; North Kerry Creameries Ltd., Listowel, County Kerry. The seventh group comprises all creameries in Counties Clare and Galway, together with that at Nenagh, County Tipperary.

> By comparison with the 1966 proposals the smallest of the new groups would have an intake of *40 million* gallons of milk, whereas the *maximum* intake under the 1966 proposals was 38 m gallons. The largest of the new groups on the basis of 1971 figures would have a milk intake of over *90 m gallons*. In drafting the new proposals, although the major concern has been with milk supplies and milk processing facilities, the growing importance of the non-dairy trade, which today accounts for over one-third of the total trade of these groups, has also been taken into account. In this whole exercise the primary concern has been to develop a small number of large multi-purpose co-operative concerns, each capable of supporting a full range of modern milk processing facilities as well as providing an efficient and effective farm supply and marketing service to its farmers.[99]

Of all the various types of co-operative society, the creameries have proved consistently the most successful. Their success, however, was not achieved without a great deal of effort, and the struggle is a continuing one. Today's task of unifying the major co-operative groups and welding an effective overall movement calls for as much sacrifice and generosity as in the past. The history of many creameries has been a proud and generous one. For others, regrettably, it has been a story of fairly continuous shame, even from the earliest days: the failure to support the Agency Society, the IAWS or the IAC, the failure of members to agree or to provide worthwhile services, the failure to co-operate with neighbouring co-operatives and, above all, a miserly failure to really identify with the national co-operative movement through support of their Organisation Society.

Yet few creameries were without some period of glory or worthwhile service. One of Horace Plunkett's proudest moments concerned a none-too-affluent creamery in the west of Ireland in 1911, when the Department's Council of Agriculture had refused to support the IAOS application for funds from the Development Commissioners:

> I never felt prouder of the Movement than when one day last year shortly after that fateful meeting of the Council, the Secretary of a Connaught Creamery which had paid its affiliation fee and a special subscription besides, put down on Mr Anderson's table £20 as an extra subscription to help us through our immediate difficulties.[100]

The co-operative creameries have come a long way since Drumcollogher

99 ibid., p. 6.
100 IAOS Annual Report 1912, p. 48.

in 1889; a long way since a model creamery, the Daffodil Dairy, was built on the grounds of the great Cork International Exhibition in 1902. This full working creamery was the object of tremendous interest to overseas visitors but, (symbolic perhaps of the travail of co-operative dairying) lost a lot of money since it was not allowed to sell liquid refreshment to its numerous admirers. At Cork, too, was a striking exhibit using statistical cubes to represent the growth of the co-operative movement in each year,[101] starting with a tiny one-inch cube representing the state of movement in 1889 and twelve progressions later, looking up at an enormous cube of seven feet. Considering the one-inch cube as representing the total turnover of £4,363 of fifty dairy members in Drumcollogher, we leave the reader to contemplate today's cube for 80,000 co-operative members with a turnover in dairy produce of £315 million.

101 "A cubical box for each year, painted green, with the year, the number of Societies, their membership and their trade painted in white on one side was constructed, the dimensions for each year being determined by multiplying the number of members by the total volume of trade in pounds sterling, dividing the result by a common factor, and extracting the cube root." (IAOS Annual Report 1901, p. 44).

Chapter Fourteen

The Co-operative Agricultural Societies

*It does not readily appear why there should be a legitimate trader
any more than there should be a legitimate farmer . . .
As for the combination in these trading operations, are not the
Irish farmers just as free to combine as a railway company, or a
brewing company or a mining company? The privileges of the law
are open to them as to their richer neighbours, and the fact that
they are, as a rule, poor men is no reason why they should not use
any advantage which the law creates while they are pursuing their
industry honestly. In the fullness of this liberty we have acted hitherto:
IN THE EXERCISE OF THIS SAME FREEDOM WE
PROPOSE TO CONTINUE.*
(Rev T.A. Finlay, SJ, at the Sixth Annual Conference
of Co-operative Societies, Cork, 10 July 1902).

At the first general conference of Irish co-operatives in 1895,[1] Horace
Plunkett was happy to report: "There are thirteen Societies on the model of
the *Syndicats Agricoles* of France, five of which in Kilkenny and Tipperary
jointly effected this Spring saving of over £6,000 on the purchase of their
manures, besides securing an even more valuable advantage in an effective
guarantee of analysis."

Although some creameries had already begun to supply farm requisites
(as had some of the dozen retail stores affiliated to the Co-operative Union),
these *syndicats*, or co-operative agricultural societies, were entrusted with
the major responsibility of providing agricultural requirements and
disposing of agricultural produce other than dairy products.

In the early days of the IAOS, these agricultural societies, in addition to
purchase and sale, were concerned with the improvement of livestock:
providing pure-bred sire animals, rams, boars, bulls and even stallions.
This activity was inspired by the existence in many European countries,
especially Switzerland, of special 'breeders' societies' which proved that a
co-operative group was the most economical and effective vehicle for
effecting livestock improvement. These societies were able to convince
central government of the efficiency of their organisation and thus procure

1 Held in the Leinster Hall, Dublin, 25 September 1895.

234

the government subsidy and allocation of skilled livestock personnel which enabled them to speed up their improvement work. This was particularly fortunate for the farmer, since it was unlikely that most governments or state departments would be willing to face the financial and human cost of establishing nation-wide schemes which would have to be administered by personal dealing with individual farmers.

The early co-operators hoped that this situation would evolve in Ireland but it was not to be. The Department of Agriculture effectively took over and Plunkett could not point to co-operatives with sufficient achievement in this field to resist the pressures of so-called 'democracy' from his Council of Agriculture and vested interests bent on retaining the spurious independence of the individual farmer — the backbone of the country! Livestock improvement schemes, like most Department projects, were mainly administered on an individual basis.[2]

Few freedoms were preserved apart from the freedom to be individually poor; but the system did retain the role of the jobbing politician in making 'representations at the highest level' on behalf of the individual farmer. In this peculiar political ethos, the working farmer was indulgently agreed to be a reluctant letter-writer, poorly equipped for talking or dealing with official agents. Not much immediate political effort was devoted to making him a better letter-writer or a better talker, if such was indeed required.

The main business of the agricultural societies was the purchase of seed, fertiliser and animal (mostly cattle) feeding-stuffs. An early IAOS leaflet (no. 4) gave explicit instructions and cautionary advice:

The success of this co-operation will depend upon these things —
(1) A code of rules which ensures fair play all round
(2) A sufficient trading capital
(3) A capable and trustworthy committee and secretary
(4 The strictest honesty, punctuality, unselfishness and loyalty among the members
(5) The exclusion of all questions except such as affect the business of the society, and above all things, a clear understanding of the true meaning of co-operation.

The shares are £1 each. Only a small sum is usually paid as a first instalment and if the committee discharge their duties faithfully it is unlikely that any further call will ever be made. Generally speaking, the following advice may be followed with advantage:
(1) The area of the Society's operation should be confined to a parish or at all events to a district where every member's character and reputation may be known to the Committee . . .
(2) No applicant for admission should be accepted whose reputation for honesty or industry is doubtful.
(3) The Committee men should, as far as possible, be elected so as to

---

2 For the most part, group work was limited to dealings with breed societies — clubs' of individuals specialising in the propagation of one breed of one particular species of farm animal, e.g., shorthorn cattle, large white pigs, Suffolk sheep.

secure due representation of the various townlands or districts comprised in the Society's area . . .

The first Agricultural Society was in Kilmessan, County Meath, and was registered on 17 December 1894. This society (in Plunkett's home parish) had an enthusiastic first committee and secretary, Joe Kelly, but thereafter never aspired to greatness. The annual turnover rarely exceeded £2,000 but the society continued in business up to the mid-nineteen sixties. Ten societies were registered in a four-month period[3] and all did their first effective business in the spring of 1895.

A group of small co-ops near Thurles caused the first excitement and saved £6,000 by their joint purchase of manures. The first societies were Urlingford, Johnstown, Galmoy, Crosspatrick (County Kilkenny) and Moyne (County Tipperary); a number of farmers in the Thurles area formed another society, Two Mile Borris, in July 1895. The farmers of the area knew that they were being fleeced by the local traders who supplied their manures. They also soon learned that the fertiliser manufacturers were bound firmly in a ring; small orders by the individual co-operatives were steadfastly refused in polite letters pointing out that "supplies of our fertilisers can be purchased from Mr _____ of _____, who is our agent in your area." No manufacturer was going to risk the goodwill and custom of the established traders by supplying a few tons of manure to an unpromising handful of co-operators.

Yet the Tipperary-Kilkenny neighbours did not give up easily. They went from farm to farm, ascertained their total requirements and inserted advertisements inviting tenders for the supply of a modest 2,000 tons. The traders individually and collectively put pressure on the manufacturers[4] to stand firm for a month, by which time the farmers would have quarrelled over the non-arrival of manures and would be hurrying back to the shops to get their requirements in time for sowing. But, miraculously, it was not the farmers who split. One Morgan Mooney, who felt that his fellow manufacturers had never done much for him, secretly broke away from the ring and tendered unbeknownst.[5] "Ye may all go to hell now", he said, "for

---

3 Urlingford, Johnstown, and Galmoy were registered on 6 February 1895; Bohola, County Mayo, 15 February 1895; Ballinagore, County Westmeath, 6 March 1895; Killasser, County Mayo, 11 March 1895; Moyne, County Tipperary, 18 April 1895; Crosspatrick, County Kilkenny and Enniscorthy, County Wexford, 23 April 1895. Bringing the number up to the thirteen mentioned by Plunkett, were Two Mile Borris, County Tipperary (July 1895), the County of Cork Co-operative Farmers Society and Donaghpatrick, County Meath, registered in October of that year. In 1894 the Congested Districts Board voted a sum of £200 for the purpose of organising agricultural co-operative societies in the Congested Districts. Major W.P. Gaskell was appointed organiser and, after great difficulties, he succeeded in forming two societies at Bohola and Killasser.
4 A private circular issued by the Mercantile Traders Association, Thurles branch, fell into co-operative hands and was published in full in *The Irish Homestead* on 23 March 1895.
5 The co-operatives effected savings of from £1.10.0 to £2.0.0 per ton on superphosphate, which was selling in the shops for £5.0.0 to £5.15.0; £3.0.0 to £4.10.0 on potato manure, selling for £9.0.0 to £10.10.0, and £2.5.0 to £2.15.0 approximately on turnip manure selling for £6.10.0 to £7.0.0. The overall saving was about forty per cent. Subsequently Edward O'Keeffe supplied bone manure and both Mooney and O'Keeffe gave prizes the following year for the best roots grown with their manures.

I have the co-operative contract in my pocket."

A very big occasion was at hand:

> The arrival of the consignment in a special train to Thurles was treated as a great occasion, as indeed it was. On arrival I had taken care to see that the superphosphate and other fertilisers were properly sampled in accordance with the Fertilisers and Feeding Stuffs Act, hitherto a dead letter. This preliminary having been duly carried out at the railway station, the concourse of co-operating farmers, with the horses drawing their carts gaily decorated with ribbons, headed by a local band playing national airs, loaded up their lots and dispersed, cheering vociferously through the town of Thurles.[6]

What impressed the Thurles farmers almost as much as the 40 per cent. saving in price was the guaranteed analysis of the fertilisers supplied. One batch of dissolved bone compound was found to be marginally lower in phosphate content than stated and some farmers received small refund cheques by post:

> Never in all the history of Thurles had a farmer been refunded one bob for a deficiency in the value of fertilisers. The refund was insignificant in £.s.d. but its payment made almost a deeper impression than had the newly acquired power to purchase at wholesale rather than retail prices. It was a revelation of the power inherent in co-operative organisation which they had not hitherto understood or appreciated . . . Rightly or wrongly I have always regarded this almost parochial transaction as one of the biggest things ever accomplished by our movement.[7]

Meanwhile, in County Westmeath, the Ballinagore Society, under the dynamic leadership of George de Belle Ball, had written to several Irish manufacturers. Only one firm deigned to reply — if it could be deemed a reply to return the Society's letter with a curt "All Sold" scrawled underneath. Ball and his friends decided that they had done their best to support home industry and now felt free to try further afield. English manufacturers were far from indifferent and a short time afterwards a train pulled into Kilbeggan with fifty-six tons of superphosphate at £3.12.9 per ton free on rail — one shilling and ten pence per ton cheaper than the Irish cargo into Thurles! Ballinagore also purchased twenty-one tons of seed potatoes and seven tons of seed oats and barley.

In accord with the Rochdale principle of selling only pure, unadulterated goods, these cereals and all subsequent purchases of seeds were bought subject to guaranteed purity and germination. It was remarkable that in those days, despite the numerous bodies (like the Royal Dublin Society and

---

6   R.A. Anderson, *With Horace Plunkett in Ireland*, p.90.
7   ibid., p.91.

the universities) purporting to foster agriculture, no one seemed disposed to provide the simple facilities required to carry out the elementary purity and germination tests which today are within the competence of every rural vocational school. The Irish farmers' seeds had to be sent to Switzerland for testing,[8] a condition which pertained until the establishment of the Department of Agriculture and Technical Instruction in 1900.

This quality control, strictly observed henceforth by the IAWS and insisted upon in co-operative dealings with other suppliers, proved a boon to tillage farmers and brought many into the ranks who were otherwise but poorly disposed to co-operation. Farmers, accustomed to purchasing seeds from local merchants who were none too scrupulous about disposing of last year's seeds, began to find a double saving: (i) cheaper seeds; (ii) far less seed required. Until they adapted to the change, many grain growers complained that their crops, grown from co-op seed, were far too thick and suffered great loss through 'lodging'. The nutrient value of some of the 'fertilisers' being sold by local merchants was extremely doubtful. One fairly common commodity being imported into Ireland was *guano*, a product consisting of the dried and powdered excreta of sea-birds from South America.[9]

On one occasion, in the early eighteen nineties, Robin Anderson suffered a great loss of face whilst addressing a farmers' meeting in Skibbereen. A few years later Anderson would have been able to speak knowledgeably about percentages of ammonia and soluble phosphates, but as yet he knew nothing of such technical matters. He made a compelling case for co-operation among farmers, which was going down very well until:

> . . . up rose a stalwart and evidently gombeen critic. 'Tell me', he yelled in his high-pitched West Cork voice, 'did ye ever pierce mingures?' I had to confess my ignorance. 'There now', he said, 'an I piercing mingures for ye min all me life; this fella doesn't even know what it manes.' The curtain was rung down and I made the best exit I could. I learned subsequently that cargoes of Peruvian guano used to be brought into Irish ports, and though the Fertilisers and Feeding Stuffs Act was a dead letter at the time, the importer used to test the value of the cargo, carried in bulk, by thrusting into the hold of the vessel an immense auger which brought out a sample of the stuff. I doubt if it was ever analysed, but I suppose the importer satisfied himself through the evidence of his nose, and even of his palate . . . The value of fertilisers was, often as not, determined by their horrible stench and sometimes by their hue.

Some of the 'special' manures were exotic and of doubtful content when they left the factory. Frequently their varied composition was added to on the merchant's premises; it was not uncommon for merchants to dispose of

8 The testing of seeds for the IAOS and IAWS was carried out by Dr Stebler in Zürich until 1900 when samples were sent both to Dr Stebler *and* to the Department of Agriculture.
9 There was a temporary revival of this trade during the years of World War II.

various waste materials — loft sweepings, spent cement, lime, salt and oddments of broken bags of spoiled mealstuffs — by a mild admixture, stretching a ton of manure to 22 or 23 cwts. This compounding was usually effected, after hours, by merchant family labour. Its justification within the family circle was that it did nobody much harm and helped to keep the place tidy. Large-scale adulteration with salt, lime or sea-sand was not very common but it sometimes did occur. The practice moved Cornelius Creed of Toames CDS to suggest at an early IAOS meeting "that if a man were to take a bag of sand and put a herring with it and call it an artificial manure, he would be doing nothing more extraordinary than many of the traders were in the habit of doing!"[10]

Once Plunkett had settled on his best approach to co-operative development, he decided on a policy of 'no more grocery shops' like Dunsany or Doneraile. Agriculture was the fruitful area, and the creameries and agricultural stores would be well advised to avoid 'controversial trading' and antagonising the powerful merchant interests by competing in household goods. Not everyone agreed with him. Whole-hog co-operators like Anderson, Monteagle and the fiery Loftus Bryan from Enniscorthy, together with many of the tough Ulstermen, saw little virtue in appeasement or the avoidance of activities which might arouse trade or political opposition: "They could not hate us any more than they already do." After much discussion (and certain reservations), the IAOS committee decided, however, to pursue the line of least resistance.

It has been frequently urged upon the Committee to include organisation of Distributive Societies on the English model as part of its programme. The matter has been under discussion at several meetings and it has been unanimously resolved that while it is essential to the welfare of the Agricultural Industry that farmers should be enabled through co-operation to acquire upon the best terms the requisites of agricultural production, it has not been, and is not, the policy of this Society to promote, or assist, in the organisation of Co-operative Stores for the sale of the general commodities consumed in rural districts.[11]

As the whole-hog men had suspected, this announcement did little to appease the traders. The gombeen-men were not bound by any code of high principles, but they showed great scope and flexibility in their continued assault on the co-operative movement. The approach varied to suit the circumstances — switching from a play on the customer's lack of moral courage to open economic blackmail. Sometimes a merchant sold

10 See Lionel Smith Gordon and Francis Cruise O'Brien, *Co-operation in Ireland* (Manchester: Co-operative Union Ltd., 1921), p.40. There were some major frauds of adulteration during the nineteen forties, this time by mobile black marketeers who sold, direct to farmers, sulphate of ammonia richly laced with common salt and fine quartz sand.

11 IAOS Annual Report 1898, p.20.

seeds and manures at little more than cost and made his profit on other sales. Alternatively, it might be a straight ultimatum: "If you don't buy your agricultural requirements from me, I will not give you tea, sugar, candles and bacon."[12]

A constant campaign of misrepresentation and vilification was pursued. Sometimes it went too far. The following apology, inserted in nine different newspapers in June 1895, demonstrated the need for caution on the part of certain critics of the movement:

> I, James Maloney, of Clooncagh, Ballinagore, in the County of Westmeath, do hereby unreservedly withdraw all the statements circulated by me to the effect —
> 1. That Mr G. de B. Ball, President of the Ballinagore Co-operative Agricultural Society Limited, had falsely represented the liability of shareholders as being only £1 for each £1 share held.
> 2. That I had the authority of Mr Nooney, Solicitor, Mullingar, and of Mr Lucas, Manager of the Hibernian Bank, Mullingar, for stating that every holder of £1 share is liable for £5.
> 3. That Mr G. de B. Ball had been to every bank in Mullingar endeavouring to raise money to the amount of £4 10s per share, and every other statement made by me of a nature injurious to the prosperity of the Society or reflecting on the honesty of its management, and calculated to deter members from joining it. And I hereby publicly state that all such statements are absolutely without foundation, and I express my apology to the President and Committee of the Ballinagore Co-operative Society Ltd.
>
> Signed this 18 June 1895.
> James Maloney

Although the IAOS could state policy and make recommendations, they could exercise little control on the activities of a co-operative society. They could refuse on principle to register a society whose avowed purpose was consumer retail trading, but once registered and a legal entity, the co-op and its members were free to do as they pleased. Some societies, like Enniscorthy, went the whole hog and suffered little in consequence.[13] At the other end of the country, and indeed the other end of the agricultural scale, in west Donegal, where the bare bones protruded through the starved skin of earth, Patrick Gallagher of Dungloe (Paddy the Cope) had not only little compunction about grocery trading, but little option!

The twenty-eight poor weavers of Rochdale may have felt somewhat undercapitalised with their £28. Sixty-two years later, in 1906, in Cleendra near Dungloe, the Templecrone Co-operative Agricultural Society had its

12 Report of Paul Gregan (organiser) to the IAOS, 1917.
13 The Enniscorthy turnover in 1897 was £8,030. Ten years later it had more than doubled and by 1917 it had grown to £61,000, the second highest turnover of any agricultural society in Ireland. Lisburn topped the league with a turnover of £86,000 in that year.

beginning with fourteen farmers, each contributing half a crown (12½ pence). By the time the society was registered, the membership had risen to sixty-five with a total share capital of £10. The story of the Templecrone Society is told with appealing simplicity in Mr Gallagher's autobiography.[14] Patrick Gallagher was a resourceful man. He had some experience of dealing with a consumer co-operative when he worked as a labourer in Scotland. On his return to Ireland he was an early member of a credit society in the town of Dungloe in 1903. He interested himself in the farming leaflets which the Department of Agriculture sent regularly to the secretary of the agricultural credit society. Gallagher's farm was very small and his orders of five and ten cwts of the 'new' fertilisers being recommended by the Department were not indulged by the local merchants — he could take what they had or leave it — manure was just manure! Somewhat illegally, he contrived to have a tiny cargo of superphosphate from the IAWS shipped into Burtonport, a few cwts for himself and some neighbours for their small patches of potatoes and oats. The price attracted them to buy twice as much as they had bought previously; 7s 5d per two cwt bag compared to the merchants' price of 12s 6d.

A few tons of fertilisers once a year, however, would not provide much commercial activity. Gallagher's memory increasingly harked back to the little co-op store in Pumperstown, Scotland, where his wife, Sally, bought everything she wanted, collected a quarterly dividend on purchases, and banked, at 5 per cent. interest, the money they were saving to buy the Cleendra farm. This is what they should have in Dungloe instead of a village bank which got leaflets and IAWS price lists it could do nothing about. Gallagher wrote to Dublin and was advised by return that Mr Shaw, IAOS organiser, would visit him soon.

'I am sorry', said Mr Shaw, 'we cannot organise a Society for that purpose; we can only organise a Society for agricultural purposes.'
'What purpose is that for?', I asked.
'Dealing in seed, manures and agricultural implements, also eggs and butter', he said.
'Can you deal in spades and shovels?', I said.
'Yes, you can, that comes under agricultural work.'
'All right, Mr Shaw', said I, 'that is what we want, we want nothing else.'
That was the first deliberate lie I told in my life.[15]

Once registered, the Templecrone Society made open warfare on the gombeen-men. The country people paid in advance for their tea, sugar and household goods and waited on delivery; they contributed their eggs and

14 Patrick Gallagher, *My Story — Paddy the Cope* (London: Jonathan Cape, 1927). A revised paperback edition, published by Templecrone Co-operative Society Ltd., is currently in print.
15 ibid., p.75.

waited to be paid. No rumour or slander could shake their faith in Paddy Pat Bawn. The Londonderry wholesalers refused to supply goods, but the Scottish Co-operative Wholesale Society (SCWS) in Glasgow did so readily, and after the first few transactions no longer sought cash in advance. Gallagher revelled in the fight and for every trick the gombeen-men pulled, the simple country boy was a jump ahead. Within a short time the Cope (Co-op) was transferred from Mrs Gallagher's kitchen to more spacious premises in Dungloe town, thus carrying the fight to the gombeen-men's door. The society subsequently affiliated with the Co-operative Union in Manchester, as did the Lisburn and Enniscorthy societies. This affiliation legitimated the society's trading in groceries, putting it on a similar footing as all Rochdale-style retail shops in Britain. The arrangement saved the IAOS some embarrassment since Gallagher continued to claim IAOS support and guidance for the 'agricultural' side of his business. The opposition of local traders continued unabated but neither slander, obstruction, fist fights nor jail sentences made much impression on Gallagher. It was more subtle social pressures which at one stage nearly forced him to quit.

> Imagine our surprise the following Sunday when we heard the priest denouncing us from the altar. He declared that no dance could be held in the parish in future without the consent of the priests ... At this time I was living in Dungloe and the following day my mother came in from Cleendra and appealed to me not to fall out with the priests.
>
> I met the curate a few days later and I saluted him as usual, but he did not acknowledge me. I told Sally and she was very hurt, and put her head in her lap. I went out again and I was very sorry for telling her. After about half-an-hour I went in, and I was sure she was crying.
>
> I said, 'Sally, I have made up my mind that we will go back to Scotland. We cannot live here with so many people against us ... I will commence to sell out, and pay every penny that we owe. If I have not enough I will sell the Cleendra land.'
>
> She looked up at me, but with no sign of tears, and I shall never forget that look.
>
> 'Paddy', she said, 'you are a coward.'

By 1917 the humble co-op in the Rosses was the third biggest agricultural society in Ireland. Its turnover of £56,000 was exceeded only by Lisburn and Enniscorthy. Today Templecrone's turnover exceeds £1 million.

Anderson was outspokenly in favour of the Gallagher approach and on the question of 'controversial trading' saw no point in trying to be all things to all men. Even as the IAOS declared its policy, Anderson in the same report contrived to publicise a legitimate tactic:

> It is pleasing to note that the feeling in Societies is against adopting an aggressive attitude towards the traders. Where they are dissatisfied

with the prevailing methods of doing business, they in many cases make use of a very simple but effective expedient. The members agree among themselves to purchase for cash large quantities of their ordinary household requirements, such as flour, etc. They invite tenders for the supply of such articles to be delivered to each member in such quantities as may be required ... This system works admirably; the co-operating farmers secure their goods at reduced prices. .... The trader who secures the business is also well satisfied.[16]

Anderson, with tongue in cheek, foresaw this strategy as effecting a marked improvement in the business methods of Irish traders. It certainly kept the controversial pot boiling. The trader who got the contract might be happy, but automatically there were a dozen others who were not, and their hatred and distrust of the co-operative system intensified.

However much we might curtail our programme, we were hated and feared by a large section of the traders who always perceived the danger of the co-operative store lurking in the shadow of the creameries and the credit societies... The politicians were equally distrustful and apprehensive. They feared, and even stated repeatedly on public platforms, that co-operation was nothing more or less than an insidious attempt to frustrate their efforts to obtain Home Rule.[17]

As head of a Department of Agriculture which was devoted to the ideal of farmer self-help, Plunkett had to tread warily with a Council of Agriculture composed largely of politicians with strong merchant connections. It was a role he could not sustain and he resigned in 1907. Under his successor, T. W. Russell, the trader influence, in patriotic guise, branding the IAOS as covertly political and anti-Home Rule, succeeded in having government help for the organisation withdrawn. When, after much difficulty, a grant-in-aid was procured from the Development Commission, it was on condition that the Society did not support or encourage trading in non-agricultural goods.[18] At the annual general meeting of 1912, Plunkett referred to the controversy that had raged within the IAOS before that condition was reluctantly accepted:

We do not, and in my judgement, ought not to organise societies for non-agricultural business, or assist them in it. My associates in this work, I am bound to tell you, are not all agreed with me in this. Some of them say that no work we can do is more important than that of enabling the farmer's family to spend their none too ample means to

16 IAOS Annual Report 1898, pp.20-21.
17 *With Horace Plunkett in Ireland*, pp.87-88.
18 The grant carried four conditions: (i) the IAOS should co-opt onto their committee eleven persons nominated by the Council of Agriculture and the Congested Districts Board, (ii) the IAOS should assist only affiliated societies, (iii) any society 'carrying out non-agricultural business should cease to be affiliated, (iv) the IAOS should avoid political partisanship.

the best advantage, and that the farmers, and more especially the farm labourers, ought to follow the example of the Rochdale Pioneers. However that may be in general principle, it is quite clear that the money provided by Parliament for the 'organisation of co-operation' as a means of 'aiding and developing agriculture' cannot go outside the farmers' business. . . So I think the Committee did right to accept the Development Commission's chief condition, and I am sure you will support us in loyally adhering to it. Even those who felt strongly on the necessity of the larger programme saw that they could not justly handicap the organised farmers of Ireland, in comparison with those of England, Scotland and Wales, by withholding the means of giving them instruction in the principles and working methods of agricultural co-operation.

Plunkett went on to suggest that, even if the grant had been refused, he should deplore any change in general policy. The movement had been built up as a purely agricultural one and many of its most generous supporters subscribed money on the understanding that it was to remain so. Co-operation would demonstrate its worth and gradually win acceptance. It would be tragic at this stage to embroil the Irish people in a futile class war which was not just a simple ideological conflict of good versus bad.

Moreover, the traders of the country districts are not wholly responsible for the defects in their service to the community. Many of them are in trade simply as an alternative to emigration and most of the class suffer from defective commercial education, as the farmers have suffered from lack of agricultural education.

Plunkett wanted individual societies to work out local solutions, having due regard for the interests of the country traders which were so closely interwoven with those of their relatives and kinsmen on the land. He conceded the possible usefulness of the tactic of bulk purchasing proposed by Anderson fourteen years previously:

If compromise is possible, why should not members of our societies collectively offer to purchase their domestic requirements for cash from local traders, provided the latter would agree to give a reasonable reduction in price and a guarantee of quality?

It might work in some places but not everywhere. Thinking no doubt of Paddy Pat Bawn in the Rosses, Plunkett still pleaded for goodwill and compromise but had to admit the apparent hopelessness of the situation in some western districts:

There are some poor Western districts where, I fear, this would be no remedy, for there the existing relations between the peasantry and the traders and the demoralised condition of the retail trade seem almost incapable of reform. I confess that, in such cases, most of the objections to general trading fall to the ground.

The first purchases of the agricultural societies were made through the Irish Co-operative Agency Society and the short-lived Irish Co-operative Agricultural Agency to which we have referred in chapter seven. In 1897 a central federation was founded[19] to act as a wholesale purchasing agency for the entire co-operative movement in Ireland. This was the Irish Agricultural Wholesale Society Ltd. The membership of the forty-six agricultural societies then established was a mere 4,000 but many of them were active; the start of IAWS operations followed closely on the breaking of the Manure Manufacturing Alliance. In 1897 the turnover of agricultural societies totalled £43,000 but the creameries also had an agricultural trade of £31,500. In its first year (1897), IAWS trading amounted to only £14,500, but rose to £30,000 in the full year 1898. The first premises were at 35 Dame Street, Dublin, but within a year, despite many difficulties, the Society had secured "new and commodious premises" at 151 Thomas Street, Dublin, where the wholesale operated efficiently under Alfred O. Watkins. The breaking of the manure ring provided an auspicious start, with admirable publicity:

> These manures are now to be bought at 20 per cent. less than their former cost, and the reduction is general all over Ireland. The home trade in artificial manures amounts annually to about £400,000. . . . A reduction of 20 per cent. would, therefore, mean a gain to the farmers of £80,000 per annum. The reduction in reality is considerably more, especially as a large quantity of manures to which the reduced price also applies is annually imported from England, but we prefer to adopt the lower estimate. If to this be added the saving effected in the price of seeds and other agricultural requirements, the total for two years would amount in all probability to close on £250,000.[20]

The IAWS immediately faced three major difficulties: (i) the Society was opposed by the manufacturers; (ii) it was undercapitalised, and (iii) it was poorly appreciated by many of its constituent societies. To gain membership, a society was asked to take a £1 share for each of its own members, with 5/- paid up. Individuals could become preference shareholders by taking ten £5 shares.[21] At the end of 1898 the IAWS

19 Registered as a co-operative society on 15 January 1898. The first manager, A.O. Watkins, resigned in 1903 and P.M. Smith was appointed manager in 1904, a position which he held until the society was reorganised in 1922.
20 IAOS Annual Report 1897, p.10. Continuing in this vein, adding accumulated 'profits' of the creameries (£181,353) and allowing the organising expenses of the co-operative movement from its inception in 1889 (£8,000), the *Report* demonstrated that every £1,000 spent on organisation work had produced over £50,000 of actual cash benefit to Irish farmers.
21 Provision was also made for deposit order accounts whereby sums not exceeding £1,000 might be deposited with the society, bearing interest at 3½ per cent. per annum. See L.P. Byrne, *Twenty One Years of IAWS 1897 — 1918* (Dublin: IAWS Ltd., 1919).

comprised seventy-four members, including twenty-five societies with a membership of 2,986 members and forty-nine preference shareholders. The paid-up share capital totalled £1,861, of which the societies subscribed less than £200. A pattern of low share capital was set which has dogged the IAWS[22] throughout its entire life. This persistent and dangerous under-capitalisation must temper any criticism that might be offered of IAWS activities. In view of this, the survival of the federation is little short of miraculous.[23] Nevertheless, after a very slow start, the IAWS forged ahead to build up a trade of impressive dimensions. Up to 1905 the Society had been compelled to operate mainly on an agency basis but in that year (not without some disagreement amongst its members) it became a wholesale society in fact as well as in name, stocking goods in its own warehouses and supplying customers direct. Its turnover increased from £54,000 in 1905 to top the £1 million mark by its twenty-first birthday in 1918 and reached £1.3 million a year later.[24]

'Compounding' manures, Ballysakeery Co-operative Agricultural Society, c. 1902.

Despite the fact that the manure ring had been effectively broken, a few niggles remained. In 1901 the IAWS discovered that the terms which it obtained from the manure manufacturers were less favourable by 2½ per cent. than the terms given to ordinary merchants. By patient negotiations,

22 The first chairman was Horace Plunkett. The directors (preference) were Sir Henry Grattan Bellew, Lt. Col. M.W. Biddulph, R.S. Lamb, George de Belle Ball. Ordinary directors were Loftus Bryan, Hugh Ryan, John Molumby and Henry McCarrick.
23 As recently as 1966, when the IAWS had sales of over £7½ million, the paid-up share capital was only £53,579. In that year a bonus issue was made of three £1 shares for every £1 of paid-up capital. This issue, paid entirely from the society's reserves, produced a more respectable figure of paid-up capital of approximately £200,000, including some £8,000 in preference shares. The IAWS Annual Report 1966 also displayed an interesting graph showing the heavy burden of loan interest, £184,000 between 1957 and 1966.
24 In 1919 the total capital (including reserve funds) employed by the IAWS was £75,982, of which only £16,150 represented capital invested by the affiliated societies.

full trade terms were achieved a year later.[25] The determination of the Irish manufacturers of machinery was more overt. Under the jealous influence of the established agents, they boycotted the IAWS, refusing point blank to supply agricultural machinery or dairy equipment to any co-operative society. By this action, the machine- and implement-makers did themselves a great disservice, since the co-operators promptly turned to the American market where they had no trouble in getting machinery for less money.[26] Having thus inadvertently introduced a powerful and dangerous competitor, the Irish manufacturers were eventually forced to participate and lower their prices by an average of 20 per cent.

The unkindest cut of all for the struggling young federation was the behaviour of some of its members: societies were very slow to commit themselves to full formal membership. Thirty-two societies joined the IAWS in 1906. This was the year of the founding of the Templecrone Co-op and the reported 'warfare' from west Donegal, which stimulated this sympathetic reaction, but even at the end of that year the total number of societies in full membership of the wholesale federation was only seventy. Two years later the IAOS reported with gratification that the agricultural societies (166, membership 13,000, turnover £87,000) were "almost all supporting the IAWS with their trade and finding it greatly to their advantage to do so."

Yet the quality of the support varied considerably. Subscribed share capital was invariably low, many societies were slow to settle their bills and several were reported as employing the most unco-operative stratagem of using the IAWS estimates to beat down the quotations of private agents and merchants and then giving their trade to the outsiders.

This betrayal of the co-operative principle was particularly reprehensible in the light of the continuing campaign of slander and vilification being carried on by many of these same merchants. As well as attacking the local agricultural societies, they undertook a persistent campaign of rumour aimed at creating doubts about the stability and financial condition of the IAWS. The detractors and rumour-mongers were usually careful not to commit themselves in public statements. In 1912 however, Mr McCowan, a prominent Tralee merchant, came into the open and stated that the IAWS was "a bankrupt institution bolstered up by Government grants and subsidies".[27] This was the first opportunity afforded to the IAWS of challenging the charges and insinuations which were being made against it. A libel action was promptly taken. After a lengthy hearing, Mr Justice Dodd summed up strongly in favour of a verdict for the IAWS but, to everyone's amazement, the jury found for the defendant and awarded costs

25 In 1902 also the attitude of the banks towards the co-operative movement underwent a dramatic change. With most of the joint-stock banks, co-operative societies were able to negotiate overdrafts at 4 per cent., compared to 4½ to 5 per cent. previously.

26 In 1900 Enniscorthy Society on its own account placed a series of large orders for machinery with an American company. By July of that year the society's consignment of forty Osborne corn binders had all been sold to members and the manager had orders for ten more.

27 See L.P. Byrne, op. cit., p.69 et seq.

of one farthing! There was little doubt that the decision would be reversed in the Court of Appeal but the IAWS chose not to take any further action, being satisfied that the widespread newspaper publicity given to the case was sufficient for their purpose.

In the early days, particularly before the founding of the Department of Agriculture, a number of the agricultural societies took their 'agricultural' development role very seriously. Some of them had demonstration farms on which to carry out experiments on barley and potatoes and to test the suitability of various manures to certain soil types.

There was great to-do about 'sweated' barley and various crops were manured with single substances, ranging from dissolved bones to common salt. The experimenters learned fast and soon their methods became more refined. In 1899 barley trials, sponsored by Messrs A. Guinness, Son & Co. were conducted at eight centres[28] under the supervision of H.C. Sheringham, the IAOS agricultural expert, and a number of valuable points were proven. The top yield of $28\frac{1}{2}$ cwts of barley per statute acre recorded on Captain Wolfe's farm would not entirely disgrace a modern farmer, though the price of thirteen shillings per barrel would hardly be acceptable. The lessons driven home by results from all centres were:

(i)   Complete manuring
(ii) Clean (weedfree) land achieved by autumn cultivation
(iii) Early sowing
(iv) Light seeding — 9 stone per statute acre was deemed sufficient.

There was also a foretaste of modern selective weedkilling when it was demonstrated at three of the centres[29] that a 3 per cent solution of copper sulphate "applied at the rate of 50 to 60 gallons per acre with a cart-sprayer effectually destroyed every trace of charlock without injuring the barley." In 1900 also, the Enniscorthy Society sponsored tobacco trials on Mr Rudd's farm at Monfin and an experimental plot of sugar beet on the farm of H.A. Lett at Kilgibbon.

"Nothing can be more misleading", said Plunkett, "than to suggest that there is any antagonism between the interest of the rural and urban communities." Quoting an American presidential candidate, he postulated[30] the simple truism that burned and ruined cities would always be rebuilt so long as the countryside remained green and flourishing; but if you destroyed the crops on the farms and burned the grass on the plains,

28 On the farms of J. Willington, St Kierans, Parsonstown; T.A. Rudd, Monfin, Ballycarney; H.H. O'Neill, Clonroche; Captain Wolfe, Rockford, Nenagh; W.S. Hunt, Dromdiach, Killeagh; Mr Flynn, Ballybrittas; J. Mullany, Shanagarry and on the Asylum farm at Maryborough. Mr Sheringham came to the IAOS from South Creake, Fakenham, Norfolk. Irish farmers were intrigued by his accent and took some pleasure in having him repeat where he came from.

29 St Kierans, Monfin and Ballybrittas. Iron sulphate was also tried but with negative results. At both the County Wexford centres certain plots were sown in October, grew very well and were ready for harvesting in the third week of July. Unfortunately these early-sown plots were severely damaged by rooks both at sowing time and harvest.

30 In his presidential address at the annual general meeting 1896.

then grass would very soon grow on the city streets: "In cheapening and increasing the volume of agricultural production we are benefiting every class in the community and every interest."[31]

In this spirit, some of the early agricultural societies set about the task of agricultural development with commendable zeal. Ballinagore and Drumcliffe Societies were amongst the first to advocate local agricultural shows and livestock breed improvement. As early as 1896 the societies at Milford (County Carlow) and Edenderry (Count Offaly) were anticipating modern mart development in arranging joint marketing of sheep and cattle — an idea which was followed up by a number of societies from Tipperary to Mayo which arranged group deliveries of pigs to a Limerick bacon factory, gaining from 10/- to 15/- per pig in so doing. Greencrop experiments featured in the Tullamore and the Nenagh areas, while Killasser (County Mayo) and the Donaghpatrick Society, near Navan, pioneered the manuring of grassland. A very interesting development in the growing of early potatoes was successfully carried out by the Kilronan Society (Aran Islands) in 1899. The potatoes were sold on the Dublin market for the very attractive price of 3d per lb.

Co-operative grazing, an arrangement whereby the society rented grazing land for the use of its members, was successfully initiated by the Donaghpatrick Society and was soon emulated by the Killaroran Society near Ballygar, County Galway,[32] under the direction of Willie Holmes, a landlord's agent. This development was welcomed by the small farmers in the societies, for it enabled them, by paying a headage charge per beast, collectively to graze lands which were previously beyond their competence to acquire as individuals, since they were let only in large acreage lots which greatly exceeded the grazing requirements of a single small farmer. If, as a result of manuring, the land was able to carry more stock than was estimated when calculating the headage charge, the surplus was distributed and the grazier member could look forward to a 'discount' at the end of the grazing season.[33]

The guiding light in the Donaghpatrick Society was Nugent T. Everard.[34] An extensive landowner, Everard (*Virtus in actione consistit*) farmed at Randlestown with great zeal and unbounded enthusiasm for progress. Colonel Sir Nugent Talbot Everard was later, as president, to guide the IAOS through a very difficult three years (1905-07) before Plunkett returned from the Department of Agriculture. "His good temper, tact and sound common sense", said Anderson, "saved many an ugly

31 Some years later in 1909, AE was to expound his hopes of a rural civilisation: "The thoughts of the world have been too much with their cities ... Civilisation, in historical times, has been a flare-up on a few square miles of bricks and mortar. Outside the cities there have always been the same countrysides of little houses, the same neglect of culture, the same want of education, the lack of *organised* intellectual, political and economic power which set up a barrier between the countryman and his access to the finer things in life."
32 On farms at Cartron, Castlepark and Hermitage on the Bagot estate. See *The Irish Homestead*, 20 October 1900, p.683.
33 Tissara Society (Four Roads, County Roscommon) also rented two large farms from a local landlord for five years and made grazing available to sixteen small farmers. The 'bonus' achieved was 3/6d in the £.
34 See Burke's Peerage.

situation ... at a time when relations between the Department and ourselves were strained almost to breaking point." These qualities were evident when he persuaded a local farmer to make his smallholding available for use as an experimental farm:

> It is hardly necessary to point out the great advantage from an educational point of view farmers in the neighbourhood must derive from object lessons such as these carried out under their own supervision by one of themselves on land very similar to their own. The situation chosen for this experiment farm was (as advised in the Recess Committee's Report on France) by the side of the high road so that the largest number of passers-by could see it. This choice of situation had the desired effect, bringing the lesson of the farm under the direct notice of the farmers of practically the entire locality. A series of experiments on a somewhat larger scale on my own farm confirmed the results arrived at on the DACS farm.[35]

Many societies began spraying potatoes to prevent blight and, by 1900, nearly all the 106 societies owned an efficient horse-drawn sprayer.[36]

> Potato spraying has become universal among the societies and their Committee take much pains not merely to secure for the farmers genuine spraying materials but also to spread among them the most accurate information concerning the process and the manner in which it ought to be carried out. Besides, the spraying machines are carefully stored at the headquarters of the Society and are in proper order for use when the season arrives at which they are called into use.[37]

In that same year Ballycarney Agricultural Society (Ferns, County Wexford) pioneered another agricultural development when it purchased a threshing machine which did such good business that the members promised themselves a second one as soon as funds would permit.[38] Later,

35 Report of Nugent T. Everard (November 1897), later published as IAOS leaflet no. 8.
36 Bordeaux and Burgundy mixtures (copper sulphate with lime or washing soda) were first discovered to be effective against fungus infection in the vineyards of France, where legend has it that a farmer sprayed his grapes with a mixture of lime and bluestone to deter marauding schoolboys and so accidentally discovered its fungicidal properties. This method of blight prevention was well-known in Ireland and was advocated by various agricultural bodies for many years. It was only with the advent of co-operatively owned spraying machines that the practice won large-scale acceptance, for in most cases the only spraying equipment available to the small farmer was a bucket and 'besom', or white wash brush, with which he laboriously and not very effectively applied the spray mixture to the leaves of his potatoes. Numerous ineffective folk remedies for the cure and prevention of blight were also in use. Materials used varied from animal and even human urine to common salt and peat ashes.
37 IAOS Annual Report 1900, p.8.
38 Later, in 1915, this society, which had only nine members, was in very bad odour with the IAOS when it dissolved, distributed its large accumulated profit between its members and proposed to start again with an enlarged membership. The nine original members, who had contributed £154 share capital and taken a loan of over £1,000 to start the venture, felt entitled to a capitalist return on their risk capital. The IAOS condemned it as blatant profiteering.

many agricultural societies (as well as creameries) owned threshing machines, motor tractors, grinding mills, reapers and binders, as well as ploughs, harrows, horse and hand sprayers, manure distributors, potato diggers and weighing machines for pigs and cattle. This activity gained impetus with the drive for increased tillage in World War I. The IAOS Report for 1915 observed that "most progress would appear to have been made in certain districts in Connaught and Munster, where the farmers seem to have realised more fully than elsewhere the advantage of possessing up-to-date machinery and the great economy effected by purchasing and owning it co-operatively." Special 'implement societies', which devoted their efforts entirely to machinery, sprang up in many areas.[39] In his presidential address to the annual general meeting in 1914, Plunkett described the progress of one of them:

> At Meenahala Bridge in County Limerick, where the land is poor and agriculture was in an extremely backward state, our organisers induced seventeen farmers to form themselves into an implement society in March last year. Through the courtesy of the Secretary of the Society, I am able to tell you what these seventeen men have done to increase their tillage. These seventeen small farmers have in that time increased their area under tillage from 39¼ acres to 91 acres. In 1912 there was only half an acre of catch crops, and now they have 45 acres under the continuous cropping system recommended by Mr Wibberley and the Department. The milk supply to the creamery in the district has also increased in these two years from 188,000 to 317,000 gallons.

By the turn of the century there were 106 agricultural societies established in nineteen of the thirty-two counties. Connaught was strongly to the fore with fifty-four societies, twenty-four of them in County Galway and twenty in County Mayo.[40] County Roscommon had nine and Tipperary had eleven. Many of these early societies 'compounded' their own manures. In 1902 the IAOS employed A.T.S. Magan of Tisara Society and later George Enraght Moony of Ballinahown to supervise this

39 In 1910, 51 farmers around Kilmallock (Kilmallock Farmers' Association), with a paid-up share capital of £7 and a loan of £26, bought a corn binder. With the money earned by the binder, they bought a potato digger which was hired out at 10/- per acre, enabling the society to buy a horse sprayer and spray their potatoes at one-tenth of the former cost. Another interesting item was reported by Plunkett in 1912. In his presidential address, he claimed that experiments conducted by the Kilmallock society under the direction of Thomas Wibberley, county instructor, had shown that "co-operatively purchased seeds produced better results than those obtained from selected wholesale merchants and enormously better results than those provided locally. Mr Wibberley was, however, forbidden by the Department to make known these facts, and to this we owe it that he has now joined us as our organiser . . ."
40 Ulster 9, Munster 18, Leinster 25, Connaught 54. In Ulster, only Cavan, Down and Derry were represented at this stage but there were a number of very active creameries in the province and also some retail stores affiliated to the Co-operative Union in Britain. Carlow, Clare, Dublin, Kerry, Leitrim, Longford and Wicklow had no agricultural society in 1900. By 1913 there were agricultural societies in every county except Carlow, where the Milford society, established in the early days by John Alexander, had ceased to function before 1900.

activity. Manure compounding was particularly popular in Connaught where in 1904 twelve societies compounded a total of 338 tons of special manures; a year later this had risen to 450 tons at fifteen different centres. However, the lack of storage space seriously hampered this work. Most new societies were dependent initially on the good offices of some generous members and it took time and money to build their own stores. Among the first to do so were Dunamaise, Kilcormac and Killoughy, Ardrahan, Ballysakeery, Clonbur and Templecrone. Many societies excused their lack of progress on the lack of storage facilities. Diplomats in the IAOS, like Monteagle and Everard, suggested a correlation between co-operative spirit and store ownership. Count Arthur Moore of the Giving Hand put it more succinctly: "They do not lack success because they have no stores, rather they lack stores because they are not working to be successful."

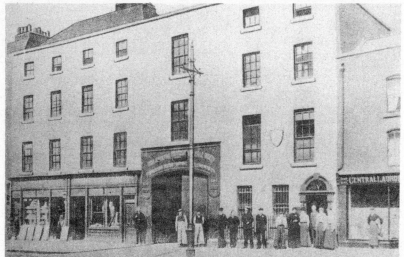

Early premises of the IAWS in Thomas Street, Dublin, 1898.

The IAWS was trading successfully in manures, seeds, feeding stuffs, coal, machinery, implements, dairy requisites and even peat moss litter, in which it pioneered a small export business to Wales. In 1906 the IAWS established a depot at Limerick[41] for the importation of basic slag, initiated a successful grass seed business with Ulster farmers and was contemplating the export possibilities of seed potatoes. As a result of an amalgamation in 1909, the IAWS took over Irish Producers Ltd., a Dublin co-operative founded in 1902, which was doing a £40,000 per annum business in marketing eggs, poultry and honey. The IAWS turnover topped the £100,000 mark.

A joint board of trade for agricultural co-operative trade had been inaugurated,[42] which envisaged united action between co-operatives in

41 Later in 1911, the IAWS had depots at Belfast, Sligo, Foynes, Thurles, Cahirciveen, Cork and Waterford.
42 The boards were constituted in 1908: The Joint Board for Agricultural Organisation and The Joint Board for Agricultural Co-operative Trade. See IAOS Annual Report 1908, p.31.

England, Ireland and Scotland, but the condition of many of the Irish agricultural societies was far from satisfactory:

> Agricultural societies are, in some respects, the least satisfactory of all the forms of co-operation which the IAOS has introduced. In most cases, they still remain small parish associations of farmers whose system of doing business has undergone little if any change since they joined the movement. Long credit is still looked for and given. Scarcely anything is done except to purchase seeds and manures. The purchase of feeding stuffs and coal is extremely rare and during the greater part of the year the majority of these societies may be said to be non-existent.[43]

In an effort to eliminate some of the deadwood, the IAOS dissolved twenty-four agricultural societies in 1910 and urged the remaining laggards to "extend their scope and enlarge their trade by catering more satisfactorily for the needs of their members." They should:

(i) Secure premises
(ii) Employ an active, paid secretary
(iii) Trade in agricultural machinery and coal
(iv) Arrange sales of livestock and farm produce, including wool
(v) Incorporate a credit bank
(vi) Provide ancillary services, such as implement hire, corn grinding, sheep dipping, spraying and threshing
(vii) As an aid to new membership and to protect the farmer-employer members, actively promote the IAOS scheme for workmen's compensation.[44]

Other advice included combining with neighbouring societies for bulk deliveries, using the same railway station and requesting bank overdrafts rather than term loans.

Two years later, however, the IAOS regretfully had to report that "The agricultural society, as a rule, continues its annual hibernation with irritating regularity", coming alive for a short period in the spring to transact some business in seeds and manures and then lapsing into its usual condition of suspended animation.

Something of the bashfulness of the poor weavers of Rochdale affected the farmers of Ireland when it came to opening a store. The idea of "clodhoppers of farmers with no knowledge of the world of business — opening a shop — to deal with the public — to buy and sell — to talk to the

43 IAOS Annual Report 1910, p.10.
44 Under the Workmen's Compensation Act 1900, from 1 July 1901 farmers became liable for (i) a sum of not less than £150 and not more than £300 to be paid as compensation to those dependent on the deceased labourer; (ii) in case of injury, to pay the injured man a weekly sum equal to half his wages not exceeding £1 per week. By arrangement with the Yorkshire Insurance Company, the IAOS devised a scheme enabling co-operative societies to provide coverage at the premium rate of 8 shillings per £100 of annual wages.

commercial travellers" — was widely ridiculed by publicans and gombeen-men. Ballads and doggerel verse, derisive of the co-op store and its management, were much applauded:

Oh, me name is Mister Dooner and me age is sixty-four;
I live six miles from Longford, and a quarter from the Store;
I have meadows in Clooncumber, the finest ever seen;
And me daughter, Mary Ellen, is the makins of a Queen.

The exasperating slowness in making financial returns to the IAOS was common to all societies, but seems to have been particularly bad in the case of short-season agricultural societies. Some of these returns, made after repeated requests and dire threats from headquarters, were truly remarkable in their content and layout. As Anderson pointed out in 1907, "the system of account keeping followed by many of the agricultural societies is, to say the least of it, *primitive.*"

If there could be a problem more fundamental than account-keeping, it was perhaps in the very basic requirement of the social process of co-operation — getting the members to meet! A co-operative expert from India noted:

Nearly all store societies find it difficult to get their members to come to general meetings. In Italy absentees and indifference are common and in Ireland at only one of the five meetings I attended were more than 12 per cent of the members present. It is a serious drawback to the co-operative store, and one which should be considered by those who would subordinate everything to it, that it is a bad medium for drawing people together. The importance of this is that if people do not meet the co-operative spirit cannot be developed. It was a dim perception of this that made a member at a thinly attended meeting to suggest a tea-party as a remedy, and it was doubtless a clear perception of Irish character which made the President reply — 'You'll never get 'em in for tay'. Education in co-operative principle is probably the only true remedy. Meanwhile, 'thou shalt not live by bread alone' might well be written up in every store.[45]

With the establishment of the Department of Agriculture, direct participation in livestock-breeding schemes by agricultural co-ops was diminished. The keeping of sire animals, bulls, boars, rams and stallions in group co-operative ownership posed certain problems and sometimes more than a little friction, so it was deemed more advisable in many cases to arrange to have these animals kept in individual ownership by co-op members, thus obviating the necessity to keep a hired groom and also

45 M.L. Darling, *Some Aspects of Co-operation in Germany, Italy and Ireland* (Lahore: —, 1922) pp.153-54. The exceptional Irish society was Templecrone. The same author gives a graphic account of the jailing of Patrick Gallagher, his release and triumphal return to the Rosses, ibid., p.155.

ensuring better and more economical maintenance.[46] Several people complained that under the malevolent anti-co-operative influence of Russell, the Department of Agriculture tended to locate sire animals in competition and in proximity to the co-op with farmers who were themselves anti-co-operative. Co-operative marketing of livestock was spasmodic and generally failed to achieve steady success until the establishment of the co-operative livestock marts.[47] The co-operative marketing of pigs was not sustained and until 1912 Roscrea was still the only co-operative bacon-curing factory in Ireland.[48]

The need for organised co-operative marketing was constantly urged by the IAOS. A concerted effort was made between 1910 and 1912 when some fifty pig and cattle supply societies (registered separately) were formed. Most of these were in County Wexford and adjoining counties, with a small number also concentrated in the vicinity of Roscrea Bacon Factory. The immediate task was to provide an outlet for fat cattle which could not be exported to Britain because of an outbreak of foot and mouth disease in Ireland. The long-term aim was the establishment of an Irish meat industry to save the cost of transport to Britain[49] and provide employment at home. The function of the pig and cattle supply societies was to try to organise at local level the purchase and despatch of fat animals for slaughter to the co-op factories at Wexford and Roscrea or to any other *abattoir* with which business could be transacted. It was an *ad hoc* arrangement and, with the passing of the foot and mouth epidemic and the ready sale of livestock in the war years, the pig and cattle societies disbanded — by 1916 not a single one remained. A few societies struggled gallantly. Cavan Central Creamery (Ballyhaise) successfully initiated the marketing of fresh pork; Achonry and Belleek extended their business in home-cured bacon, but the organisation of dealers and shippers proved too strong for any co-operative breakthrough in cattle and sheep marketing.

The IAOS continued to press the agricultural societies to diversify their activity. In 1912, when the number of agricultural societies had risen to 175, but trade per member[50] was still only £8 per annum, the IAOS urged every agricultural society to show some concern for its members' needs:

> To take one instance as an example. The custom all over Ireland is to sell livestock in fairs and markets without ever applying the test of the

46 At Ballinagore, George de Belle Ball kept a sizeable stud for the benefit of co-op members and local farmers. The boast of the groom's wife is still recalled: "My Jim is the best man to bull cows or any other thing in the whole country."

47 These marts were not established until the late nineteen fifties at which stage they were registered as separate societies.

48 Wexford Co-operative Bacon Factory Ltd., registered as a 'miscellaneous' society in 1909, began operating in 1912 when it had a turnover of £34,256. Some agricultural and certain dairy societies killed and cured pigs for their members' use. In 1918, under the impetus of wartime shortages in certain areas, about twenty-five societies were reported as killing an average of two to eight pigs per week.

49 Apart from transport costs, the loss attributable to injury and weight reduction in the shipping of fat cattle was at the time estimated at £1 per head.

50 The average trade per member was approximately £5 in 1902, £7 in 1907 and £8 in 1912. In 1912 the total turnover of 947 co-operative societies was £878,043, of which the 175 agricultural societies accounted for £157,775.

scales to the animals sold — assuredly the best and truest test of value. The individual farmer brings his stock to the fair and there endeavours to sell them at a profit to a man whose whole life has been spent in gauging the weight and value of what he buys. Nothing is more deceptive than the live weight of an animal. The inexperienced farmer is hopelessly at a disadvantage when he is dealing with an experienced buyer who, almost daily, is in a position to correct his estimate of weights by the actual results shown by the scales ... Every agricultural society ... ought to be equipped with either a fixed or portable weigh-bridge. Its secretary should further be in touch with the principal markets and he should be in a position to advise as to what prices should be demanded or paid and when it was advisable to buy and when and where to sell. That one service would, by itself, justify the existence of an agricultural society in every parish in Ireland.[51]

Another imaginative and useful idea put forward was the establishment of a 'veterinary dispensary' in each society premises. It was hopefully suggested that, for a moderate retaining fee, the services of the local veterinary surgeon could be secured to the members on payment of a nominal sum for services rendered; ordinary animal medicines could be procured at much reduced prices in the society's dispensary. The same report expressed some amazement that no agricultural society in Ireland had attempted to sell wool for its members; with proper grading and classi-fication it seemed an obviously profitable venture.[52]

On the outbreak of the Great War, the government called for an increase in food production and earnestly exhorted the farmers to increase the area under tillage crops. Increased tillage had long been a basic aim of the co-operators who saw it as essential for the well-being of the dairying industry through the development of year-round milk production. Also, as the redoubtable Thomas Wibberley had so ardently emphasised, intensive tillage was not only the obvious prerequisite of intensive livestock production, but also the only practical means by which Irish agriculture could develop a stable and efficient labour force. Since 1900 the Department of Agriculture had spent large sums of money in efforts to promote more intensive cultivation but, despite its best efforts, Irish farming was showing an exasperating tendency to become more, rather

---

51 The 1912 Annual Report also carried some pungent comment on the typical Irish cattle fair: "Cattle hustled into a fair in the small hours of the morning, often under pitiless showers of sleet or rain, cannot look their best. The long stand in the filthy street ... and all the time the men in charge are tempted to leave ... for the public house and such 'comforts' as it can provide. Cattle fairs are, beyond doubt, responsible for more drunkenness than any other institution in the country. The all-powerful publican sees to it that the fair is held, if possible, in the street of the town. No more disgusting spectacle presents itself in Ireland than the fairs held under such conditions and until the holding of fairs in the streets of towns and villages is made illegal and the law is rigidly enforced, the Irish country town and village must remain as it generally is, an eyesore and an exhibition of sordid squalor."

52 This was emphasised in 1914 when, at the outbreak of World War I, Australian wool was no longer available in Britain. In that year the societies in County Wicklow, meeting in Rathdrum, called on the IAOS to assist a scheme establishing wool sales in the county.

than less, *pastoral*. Agricultural instruction and exhortation, the establishment of agricultural stations, or any of the various official schemes, appeared to make remarkably little progress towards the changing of the farmers' conservative attitudes.

The only evidence of real progress towards acceptance of 'better farming' seemed to come from the organised group efforts of farmers in co-operative societies. Although these local achievements were not yet large enough to show up in the national statistics, Plunkett was satisfied that the value of co-operative effort was already amply demonstrated:

> The Society had already proved in several instances that this problem which had hitherto baffled agricultural reformers in Ireland — which the efforts of the Department had been powerless even to mitigate — could be solved through co-operative organisation. By this means, and by this means alone, the efficient and labour-economising implements and machinery, necessary for a more intensive cultivation but too costly to be individually acquired, can be jointly owned and, what is more important, jointly used and cared for by groups of small farmers of which our societies mostly consist. Several societies had demonstrated the ease with which a rapid and substantial increase in the area under tillage could thus be effected.[53]

Plunkett now saw hopes of putting an end to the friction that existed between the Department and the IAOS. He appealed to the Department to allow its technical advisers to work in collaboration with the Society organisers in promoting schemes of agricultural production at local level through the co-op societies. The IAOS made an outline proposal on these lines to the Departmental Committee on Food Production[54] but the committee rejected reconciliation with the IAOS by eleven votes to four.

Plunkett was deeply grieved at this blank refusal, which also angered certain prominent personalities in agricultural and industrial circles. Yet the Department was unmoved and the official answer to those who questioned the propriety of the decision was that "the IAOS has no grievance because the members of the local societies can, as individuals, obtain the services of the Department and the County Committees of Agriculture's experts upon the same terms as any other ratepayers." The IAOS Report commented sadly:

> This, no doubt, on paper sounds reasonable enough. But in practice the Department's refusal to recognise and work either with the co-operative societies, in their corporate capacity, or with the IAOS makes all the difference both to their work and ours.
>
> The most elementary knowledge of the agricultural industry and of Irish conditions shows that a considerable change in the methods of farmers, such as is now required, is not easily brought about . . .

53 IAOS Annual Report, 1914-15.
54 First convened on 21 July 1915.

> Instruction and exhortation addressed to an organised body animated by a common spirit . . . have an efficacy and a range which they lack when addressed to unorganised individuals . . . Moreover, the knowledge that the Department . . . is hostile to the IAOS must obviously have a disturbing, if not a paralysing, effect upon the scattered working farmers throughout the country. In their embarrassment they get what help they can, sometimes from one body, sometimes from the other and sometimes from both. But the immensely greater advantage enjoyed by continental farmers, whose industry is developed by an efficient and economical co-ordination of the governmental and voluntary agencies concerned, is denied to ours.

Departmental cold-shouldering, however, did not deter the co-operators from energetic participation in the Grow More Food campaign. Plunkett exhorted them to greater efforts, both on economic and patriotic grounds, and although his offhand references to "our country at war" and "our boys in the trenches" did not evoke sympathy in every breast, the general tenor of his arguments was accepted. Anderson, who was even more ultra-loyalist and intransigent in his politics,[55] was much more discreet in his conversations and stuck to the practicalities of better farming.

In 1914 twenty-one new agricultural societies were registered, of which two (Killany, County Louth and Pallaskenry, County Limerick) were exclusively implement societies. Milling (provender, flour and oatmeal) became a popular activity, particularly with creamery societies, many of which were able to gear a grinding mill to their existing creamery engines.

By 1918 some sixty-one creameries were engaged in milling, together with nine societies formed exclusively for the purpose[56] (registered as miscellaneous societies). Only nine regular agricultural societies were reported as engaged in milling. Nevertheless, these societies were enterprising and it was hoped that the good example shown by the best would inevitably make its impact on the less active.

Agricultural societies generally made good progress during the war years. By 1918 the trade per member, at £24, was treble that of 1912.

55 Anderson lost two sons, Alan and Philip, in the trenches in France. He himself was a member of the home guard regiment of veterans named after King George (Georgius Rex) and colloquially known as the 'Gorgeous Wrecks'. He sustained a flesh wound in one of the first encounters of the Easter Rebellion when his contingent marched on Mount Street bridge.

56 Ardara, Athleague, Drumcliffe, Effin, Enniskillen, Erris, Killeedy, Killucan, Milltowr (County Wicklow) and Tipperary. The agricultural societies engaged in milling were Blackwater Valley (County Waterford), Geesala, Iverk, Lisburn, Menlough, Monivea, Mountbellew, Tisara and Turin. A controversy arose in Ardara (County Donegal) where the Congested Districts Board, after agreeing to lease a site to the newly-formed co-op, later, under pressure from merchant interests, changed its mind and declined to complete the deed "owing to the conflicting views prevailing in the Ardara district about the proposed mill." The co-operative's secretary, Hugh Melley, wrote: "Having waited patiently for nigh twelve months to have this site handed over, they are now told that they cannot get it, after all the expense and trouble which the promoters have incurred . . . No wonder poor farmers listen with disdain to the clap-trap of public speakers from pulpit and platform, urging them to grow more crops. This is the help they get from public departments when they put their spouting to the test." (*The Irish Homestead*, 9 December 1916, p.777).

Allowing for an element of war-time inflation, this was still promising and the Society was hopeful. Forty-two new societies, with 5,500 new members, were added in 1918 and another thirty new ones increased the number of agricultural co-operative societies to 300 in 1919.

> Indications continue that the functions of these societies will become more and more varied as time goes on; thus we find them running stores, working flour and oatmeal mills, owning machinery for hire to members and curing bacon. There is a wide field for development in such direction, and it is possible that out of the agricultural will be evolved 'the general purpose' society to rival in importance, if not surpass, the co-operative creamery. It should not be forgotten that many of the creamery societies do a large business in goods which, strictly speaking, come more properly within the sphere of the agricultural societies.[57]

The distinction between different types of co-operative society was becoming less clear. The IAOS generally designated store societies as 'agricultural' and creameries as 'dairy societies', with special purpose societies in separate categories, but frequently a society's business relationships properly called for a reclassification. Some agricultural societies found that their store business dwindled and their participation in other functions flourished. Some, which started as single purpose (implement, milling, flax, poultry or miscellaneous) societies, developed a store trade in agricultural requisites. The IAOS, struggling to service 1,000 co-ops throughout Ireland, was not always able to keep track.

The co-operative stores were flourishing and beginning to feel proud of themselves. At the 1919 annual general meeting, vice-president Father Tom Finlay moved a resolution demanding that the restrictions on the organisation of co-op stores by the IAOS, as imposed by the Development Commission, be withdrawn and that the Society be allowed the same liberty in its work as kindred organisations in England and Scotland. The motion, seconded by Nugent T. Everard and with strong support from Father Michael O'Flanagan and the Rev E. F. Campbell, was carried unanimously. Later in 1919 the Development Commissioners agreed[58] and the agricultural societies rejoiced in their new-found freedom, even though many of them had long since ceased to observe the restrictions. A factor which had made it impossible to pin down 'illegal trading' was the difficulty in distinguishing between what constituted grocery trading and what sale of agricultural produce. During the war years many co-operative societies sold home-produced foodstuffs — bacon, meal, flour, potatoes, vegetables, eggs — and because of their efforts in encouraging food

57 IAOS Annual Report 1918, p.10.
58 T.W. Russell, implacable enemy of the IAOS, retired early in 1919 because of ill-health and was replaced as vice-president by Hugh T. Barrie, a prominent Unionist and practical farmer from Coleraine. From April 1919, when Dáil Eireann set up its own Department, there were two Departments of Agriculture in Ireland.

production, the government was happy enough to have them do so. At one stage in 1916 it was contemplated that co-operative societies and the IAWS might arrange food supplies to British garrisons, thus abolishing the unsatisfactory system of military contractors.

Despite shortages of certain goods, the trade of agricultural societies topped £1¼ million in 1919 — an increase of over 40 per cent. since 1917.[59] Share capital was more readily forthcoming. "Farmers for the first time since the movement started are thinking rather of how much they can spare to invest than of how small a contribution will procure admission to their society." Enthusiasm was growing for a big store under competent, well-paid management where the farmer could purchase *all* his requirements at prices competitive with those of the new private general stores which were then, even in the small towns, rapidly eroding the livelihood of shopkeepers who traded only in one or two lines. Nineteen-twenty saw the spectacular addition of seventy-one agricultural societies, now more popularly referred to as 'general purpose societies'.[60]

One of the reasons given for this quick increase in numbers was that shortages were becoming very acute in the immediate post-war years:

> ...the discovery of Irish farmers that without the check upon profiteering ... they would quickly relapse into the relation to the village shop and country town 'store' from which the combined agency of the creamery and the agricultural bank in some cases, and of the agricultural society and the agricultural bank in others, had provided a way of escape a decade or so ago. Above all, however, the progress of this branch of the movement is due to the discovery that the same device which saved the farmer in the earlier years of the movement from 'seeds which would not germinate and manures that would not fertilise' offers him in his home the same control over his interests as a consumer that he obtains over the raw materials of his industry on the farm — so vital to his success as a producer. As yet, of course, he is only at the beginning of this discovery. He is still in the experimental stage and has not learnt the necessity for using his co-operative stores for procuring all he needs in both capacities.[61]

The growth in numbers and trade of agricultural societies during the war years is all the more remarkable in view of the fact that it was practically impossible for societies established since 1916 to increase the volume of their business in rationed articles. The IAWS was even unable to supply more than a fraction of the quantities of unrationed goods.[62]

Apart from shortages, the overall picture continued to be one of

---

59 And an increase of 159 per cent. on the turnover in 1914, allowing for the variation in purchasing power. See IAOS Annual Report 1920, p.7.
60 The peak number (on paper at any event) was reached in the following year when there were 389 agricultural societies on the books of the IAOS. There were 440 creameries in 1921.
61 IAOS Annual Report 1920, p.15.
62 Mainly due to a shortage of shipping.

comparative affluence. But, as Anderson had warned, "the farming industry is passing through a period of great, though brief and fictitious prosperity". The IAWS, now well patronised by the societies,[63] had its share of the boom. It had depots at Limerick, Belfast and Foynes, for the convenience of the societies, and turnover in 1920 was over £1.6 million. However, over £140,000 due by debtors represented goods purchased by societies on extended credit.

Towards the end of 1920 the bubble burst. An economic slump, coupled with civil disorder in Ireland (roads blocked, transport services dislocated and martial law regulations being imposed), left trade in disarray. Even though much of 1920 had been a period of increasing trade, by the year's end the profits made by the successful agricultural co-ops (£32,895) were almost matched by the losses made by others. Some ninety societies incurred aggregate losses of £28,377.[64] In 1920 the IAWS made a modest profit of £9,218 but the following year witnessed a disastrous deficit of almost £51,000. Nineteen twenty-two was little better. Trade turnover dropped from £1,118,718 in 1921 to £686,486 the following year and there was a further loss of £21,617 on the year's trading. The drop in turnover, though partly attributable to the rapid fall in prices, was mainly due to the stagnation in trade all over Ireland because of the disturbed condition of the country and the general depression.[65] Early in 1922, the board of the IAWS, deciding that desperate diseases call for desperate remedies, took drastic action. The banking department was discontinued and the business of the produce department was suspended. It was hoped that this suspension would be only temporary and that a complete reorganisation would enable it to resume its business of marketing graded and standardised farm produce. Unfortunately this was never really successfully effected and from this moment the Society's operations became almost entirely one-sided.

The Rochdale principle of selling only "pure, unadulterated goods" was especially relevant in the early years of the Irish co-operative movement. The co-operators worked not only to eliminate this fundamental abuse, but also to extend the concept. They were the first people in Ireland honestly to face up to economic realities. It was not enough that butter should be unmixed with margarine, that honey should not contain added glucose, that tea, sugar, pepper and meal should be the genuine dust-free commodities, that fertilisers should actually contain plant food! Henceforth, the emphasis would be increasingly on quality and grade, particularly for the goods which the farmer had to sell.

The efforts of the IAWS and the co-operative societies to achieve grading and standardisation were limited in scope and not very successful. Nevertheless, they were praiseworthy and courageous, in that they chose to

63 491 federated societies in 1920.
64 In forty, the loss exceeded £100, in thirty — £250, in fourteen — £500 and in six societies the loss exceeded £1,000: Adare £3,940; Foynes £3,099; Kilkelly (County Mayo) £1,720; Deele Valley (County Donegal) £1,589; Maryborough £1,202 and Headford £1,096.
65 The Index of Agricultural Prices (1913 = 100) fell from 288 in 1920 to 160 in 1924. Later, between 1932-36, the index averaged 88!

run directly against the trend of contemporary merchant and peasant feeling.

Farmers who were prepared to work like slaves at the rough toil of agricultural production considered the task of selecting and grading their produce as a soft, childish exercise unfitted for strong men. Where co-ops sought to establish grading standards, farmers frequently sabotaged the venture by concealing in the package items of substandard quality; the bottoms of potato sacks often contained stones and clay, as well as potatoes which did not compare to the excellent quality of the tubers visible at the top. Such malpractices were encouraged by traders who did everything in their power to ensure that grading should not become the accepted norm. Governments tended to fight shy of regulations to establish quality standards and, where such were imposed, their implementation was rarely pursued vigorously.

Gombeen propaganda subtly cast the co-operators in a variety of villainous roles — not least as the dupes of foreign trading interests. By pioneering quality standards, the co-operatives had given the British housewife fanciful ideas and unreasonable expectations. This (reputedly) suited the British trading combines admirably. They could now cream off only the produce of outstanding quality from every country. When this was finally established, more than half the farmers' produce as ordinarily produced would be unsaleable!

In 1922, however, the produce department of the IAWS saw the problem differently. For years they had struggled vainly to get fair and orderly marketing of Irish produce. In the early years of the century the Society had tried to establish a reputation for its graded exports to a British market that had long (and with some justification) held all Irish produce in disdain. Some measure of success was being achieved when war-time shortages and inflated prices enabled Irish shippers to ignore quality standards with impunity. The IAWS had ample evidence that, even in wartime, quality still paid, even though the margin was often a tiny one.

In 1922 the IAOS called on the new Saorstát Eireann government as a matter of urgency to enforce "strict regulations regarding the marketing of agricultural produce which will compel shippers to grade and standardise the products which they handle in accordance with the requirements of present-day markets." It was felt that unless this was done the best efforts of the IAWS would be frustrated. The mere tag of 'Irish' was often sufficient to relegate produce to the rubbishy tailend of any British market. The response of the Saorstát government was sympathetic but it would have been indiscreet to impose drastic regulations overnight on powerful merchant interests.[66]

The IAWS organisation was in trouble. A special general meeting of the Society was held on 25 October 1922, at which changes in the entire

---

66 Regulations for the export of eggs were introduced under the Agricultural Produce (Eggs) Act 1924, but little progress was made on other commodities until the Agricultural Produce (Fresh Meat) Act 1930 (mainly concerned with pork) and the Agricultural Produce (Potatoes) Act 1932.

structure and management were endorsed and the following resolutions adopted:

(1) That all societies now indebted to the IAWS for goods supplied be required to take immediate steps to provide for a substantial payment in reduction of such debts, and further, at the earliest possible date to make arrangements for the remaining balances ascertained to be due.

(2) That in cases of default the IAWS Board be urged to collect all such accounts by any and every means available.

(3) That henceforth the business of the IAWS shall be conducted on a system of monthly accounts.

(4) That we pledge ourselves and our Societies as far as it lies in our power to give practical effect to these resolutions.

After the solemn resolutions had been passed, came the high point of the doleful drama. In a subdued and anxious atmosphere the rules of the Federation were formally amended to allow for the appointment of a managing director. There was no competition for the post — just a single, rather reluctant volunteer, Robert Andrew Anderson, sixty-two, former court clerk, landlord's agent, co-operative organiser, and then secretary of the IAOS. He would be available on loan from that organisation for a period of five years. His formal appointment was ratified by a solemn nodding of heads and a ragged round of applause which he politely acknowledged, showing little elation and feeling less. He knew the extent of his impossible assignment. His own story, more than any historical or financial record, conveys in vivid terms the appalling situation which he faced:

Utterly demoralised by the huge profits of the War years, by hitherto unknown extravagance, which had become a habit of life long after the War profits ceased, we were quite unprepared for the post-War slump... Its effect on many of the Societies, especially those formed during the War, was disastrous. Those that had carried considerable stocks saw their value shrink to one-third of what they had cost. Those that had given extended credit could not recover from the debtors.

The business for which milling and implement societies were formed was no longer necessary. The whole country was strewn with the wrecks of hastily formed War-time societies. The most numerous fatalities were to be found in the General Purpose or Consumers' societies... Their organisation had been defective; there was little or no supervision over them and their business methods had been slipshod... On the Irish Agricultural Wholesale Society, the chief trade federation of the movement, its full violence was felt... It carried stocks valued at £150,000, had accepted money on deposit (mainly withdrawable at call) to an even greater amount, had given credit to societies to the extent of almost a quarter of a million sterling,

and owed to trade creditors and its bankers a like amount ... trade
creditors pressed as they had never done before for payment and writs
were as 'thick as leaves on Vallombrosa'. The quarter of a million outstanding debts could not be collected, for on the strength of the credit
so lavishly given to the societies by the IAWS they had in their turn
been encouraged to give undue credit to their members who were now
being hard pressed by their bankers and other creditors.[67]

Anderson's action in standing forth in apparently hopeless defiance of
the onsweeping disaster was in the tradition of foolhardy gallantry which
had come to characterise the co-operative movement. There is hardly a
single successful co-operative in Ireland today but owes its existence to the
fact that, at some hopeless moment in its history, one man, or a very few,
stood forth, risking everything.

In 1922, Anderson was no longer a young man. In 1894 he narrowly
survived a bout of typhoid fever[68] which had him hovering between life
and death for ten weeks, reducing his weight from a normal twelve stone to
less than eight. He was a man of iron constitution and normally robust
health but, in 1917, following a bad attack of flu, he had a serious heart
attack which kept him confined for thirteen weeks until he rose from his
sickbed, again "a creature of skin and bone but likely to live and recover".
His home life had proved unhappy. For years he had been living alone,
estranged and separated from his wife. Two of his four sons were killed in
the Great War. He sought consolation in his work, but as a meticulous man
was constantly oppressed by the slovenliness displayed by so many co-op
societies and their recurring financial crises. On his sixtieth birthday in
June 1920, a time at which Ireland, although politically disturbed, was still
enjoying a good measure of agricultural prosperity, Anderson had looked
forward to happier, better and quieter times. Shortly afterwards he knew
that he would have no rest, no peaceful retirement. The co-operative
movement would have to fight for its life once more.

But I knew I could not rest while all I valued most was crashing down
on all sides. With many misgivings I agreed to join the board of
directors, misgivings as to my own ability and my lack of business
experience, and fears that it was too late to save the Society. Before
long I realised that the management of the Society was inefficient and
that unless drastic reforms were at once introduced, the IAWS would
bleed to death. I therefore stipulated that I should be appointed
Managing Director and given unlimited powers. This was agreed to. It
was not a pleasant experience, nor one that I shall easily forget, for I
had to be perfectly ruthless and relentless.[69]

67 *With Horace Plunkett in Ireland*, pp.198-99.
68 He was stricken down in Stranorlar on a tour of Donegal with Plunkett and Bishop
O'Donnell. He made his way to Timoneys Hotel in Donegal town, from where, after two
days of raging fever and against the entreaties of Dr Warnock, the local physician, he
undertook a 'suicidal' seven-hour train journey to Dublin.
69 *With Horace Plunkett in Ireland*, p.200.

Where payments were not forthcoming, he issued decrees and forced into liquidation societies which he himself had founded and spent arduous years in building. Yet, in dealing with any society which showed true co-operative spirit and determination, the hard aggressive line of his jaw softened considerably.

> If you were less than honest with him he hammered you without mercy. But if you honestly acknowledged and faced up to your debt, and showed your determination to fight, work hard to build up your society and pay your way . . . then, even if you were only giving him £5 against a debt of £500 he shook your hand as a gentleman and there was no one better to help you.[70]

Such magnanimity did not come easily. The trading year of 1923 showed another disastrous loss, £26,000 on a turnover down to £353,000 — less than half the 1922 figure. The bad harvests of 1923 and 1924 left many farmers in dire straits. The banks refused to consider any reduction of interest rates to co-operatives,[71] and for many societies bank interest remained a crippling overhead — the interest on a £1,000 overdraft was the equivalent of a labourer's wages.

Slowly and methodically, by weeding out the bad customers and encouraging the good, Anderson brought the IAWS back on its feet. He was ruthless and relentless in building up the business efficiency of the Wholesale. He gave short shrift to any worker who did not show incentive and obvious belief in what he was doing. Anderson's stay with the IAWS stretched to more than twice its allocated span, but by 1935, although he continued to attend at the office daily, he was happy to relinquish the entire management to his former secretary, John Cassidy.[72]

Neither the heroism of Anderson nor the devotion of his staff could have won the battle had it not been for the wise forbearance of their bankers and other creditors. The Co-operative Wholesale Society — the same English CWS which had quarrelled so bitterly over creameries — was very generous about credit and continued to supply the goods. Anderson paid what he could.

In 1937 the CWS made a magnificent gesture to their Irish counterpart when they wrote off almost £¼ million as a bad debt. In the mid-thirties this was an enormous amount of money and IAWS personnel still speak of the event in reverential tones. The wiping out of this liability enabled the

70 Spoken by a retired co-op manager who wishes to remain anonymous.
71 The Irish Banks Standing Committee on 20 June 1920 had rescinded the arrangement which enabled co-operative societies to obtain overdrafts at a special rate, usually 4 per cent., regardless of the current bank rate. Approached by the IAOS in September 1923, the committee refused to revoke its resolution. Many societies had fallen into serious arrears in the payment of unemployment insurance contributions. In January 1924 it was agreed by the Minister for Industry and Commerce and the Minister for Finance that the arrears due for any period before 6 December 1921 would not be pressed for and that arrangements might be made for payment by instalments.
72 Characteristically, Anderson gave most of the credit to Cassidy: "In him we found what is so very rare — a combination of great business ability, integrity, courage, loyalty and amazing energy."

Society to obtain some £200,000 (in two debentures) from the Agricultural Credit Corporation, which provided badly needed working capital.

In 1920 total co-operative turnover for all societies had reached a record £14½ million, a figure not to be reached again until 1944. In 1922 the figure fell short of £9 million. The agricultural societies had held their own better than creameries or other societies in 1921 and the IAOS was urging all agricultural societies to seek a turnover of not less than £10,000 each in order to operate successfully.

In 1922, however, the agricultural and miscellaneous societies were the hardest hit of all. Of the 250 agricultural societies which made financial returns for that year,[73] only eighty made a profit. The total profits of these came to £12,000, while the remainder made losses of £41,000. The average turnover was £6,442, and only forty societies topped the recommended turnover of £10,000. The decline continued and by 1930 the total turnover of agricultural societies had fallen by almost a million pounds in eight years (from £1,610,625 in 1922 to £628,495). Of 180 registered societies, only about 120 were believed to be trading. The fine hopes of diversified general purposes societies were forgotten and many small societies had withdrawn into a very restricted shell, but frequently without any great improvement in their business methods:

In most of the small co-operative agricultural societies artificial manure is the main business. It is usually bought through the IAWS and is paid for by the 30th June. The members, however, as a rule get credit until the end of the year. To enable the society to do this, it becomes necessary to obtain a bank overdraft, as the share capital in almost all cases would be quite inadequate to finance the business. The overdraft is usually obtained on the joint guarantee of a number of the members, usually the Committee. At the end of the year the audited balance sheet will probably show 'sundry debtors' to an amount almost equal to the total trade turnover. All these accounts are, however, cleared off before the process is repeated in the ensuing Spring. This system of business is hard to defend, but so rooted has it become that it is not likely to be eradicated in the very near future . . .

The formation in future of societies of this kind is scarcely practicable unless their organisation is both more broadly and more deeply based . . . more broadly in that they should grow out of the definite needs known to exist in the locality they are designed to serve and more deeply through drawing the necessary financial nutriment from the soil through adequate capitalisation . . .

In no department of the movement is there greater necessity for co-operative propaganda than in the 'stores'. Too often members of an agricultural society merely use it as a lever to bear down the prices of the local traders . . .

Credit is demanded as a right from the co-operative society by

73 Of 392 registered societies, 142 published no returns. Belmullet Society showed an intriguing return of: Total Sales £1, Loss £20.

members who know perfectly well that rival traders would refuse to grant it to them. Goods that bear a very slender margin of profit are bought at the 'store' while other and more profitable lines are reserved for the competing traders . . .[74]

By this time, however, the agricultural distributive sector was passing rapidly from the purely agricultural societies to the creameries. Most creamery vehicles (and official documents) now bore the initials CA & DS (Co-operative Agricultural and Dairy Society). By 1932 creameries were reported as doing more than half the agricultural business. Although 180 agricultural societies still appeared on the official list, the IAOS annual report indicated that only eighty did any significant trade; these were estimated to have a total turnover of approximately £600,000 in 1932, an average of £7,500 per society. The 1933 Annual Report also indicated that there were about twenty other societies whose yearly transactions ranged from £100 to £300, and noted that while these tiny societies "may seem to superficial observers to be of small importance, they are regarded quite otherwise by their members, who cling tenaciously to them, as affording them their only protection against profiteering."

By 1935 the creamery trade in agricultural and consumer goods was more than double that of the store societies[75] and for the remainder of the decade 'store' turnover stagnated around the £600,000 mark.

By 1940 'agricultural' sales by creameries totalled £2.6 million, while sales by the agricultural societies still dawdled at £724,000. It is revealing to note that in 1940 the turnover of the IAWS was only £838,000, indicating that the bulk of co-operative business was being transferred elsewhere. The above figures are merely a crude indication of the lack of co-operative support for the IAWS. It must be remembered that the £838,000 sales of IAWS is an all-Ireland figure. There is no breakdown available but IAWS trade in Northern Ireland, from the depots at Londonderry and Belfast, was certainly sizeable. Also, within the Republic, by no means all the IAWS trade was done with co-operatives.

The passage of time has brought little improvement in this situation. Co-operatives still fail to identify with their wholesale federation and seem to regard it merely as one of a number of possible wholesale suppliers rather than as an integral sector of the co-operative movement. In 1972 the all-Ireland turnover of the IAWS was less than one-third of the total agricultural trade done by creameries and agricultural societies in the Republic.[76] Many co-ops accept the concept of co-operative integration, but spend their time complaining bitterly of the shortcomings of the IAWS, rather than organising their immense power to improve it and build it to a size that would make it into an Irish equivalent of the CWS.

74 IAOS Annual Report 1931, pp. 20-22.
75 £1,142,012 by creamery, compared to £551,515 by agricultural societies. Of 234 creameries, 209 did store trade, an average of £5,416 per creamery.
76 IAWS turnover £19.3m, agricultural goods sold by creameries £49.1m, and by agricultural societies £9.4m.

From the early nineteen thirties, the co-operative agricultural supply trade moved rapidly and inevitably away from the agricultural societies into the creameries with their greater resources of capital and management. By the Jubilee Year of 1944,[77] of 208 creamery societies, all but thirty-one were engaged in some agricultural trade[78] and their total turnover in 'agricultural and other goods' was £2.8 million, compared to the £1.6 million turnover of seventy agricultural societies.[79] This seems to indicate a strengthening of the store societies, but when we consider that over a million pounds of this total turnover was achieved by four societies,[80] we see the weak position of the others. Of these, only sixteen exceeded[81] the £10,000 turnover recommended in 1922, despite the fact that the 1922 pound sterling had a purchasing power greater[82] than that of thirty shillings in 1944.

The mortality rate among agricultural societies is difficult to assess. Some which disappeared through amalgamation represent progress rather than failure, whereas many others which were cited as extant on the records, were so only in name. However, it is significant that of the ninety-four societies registered before 1900, only eighteen were extant in the Jubilee Year 1944.[83]

Reasons for failure are not hard to find. The agricultural societies tackled the most difficult sectors of co-operative development, got the least help and evoked the strongest and most widespread opposition. Father Michael O'Flanagan[84] said: "The Co-operative creamery came into a new field. The Co-operative shop has come into a field already fully occupied." So pervasive was the merchant propaganda against farmers and workers going into trade that it took a strong-willed man to withstand it. Many

77 Fifty years since the founding of the IAOS and 100 years since the opening of the little Toad Lane store in Rochdale.
78 Of these, eighteen were auxiliary creameries. Only thirteen central creameries failed to engage in store business.
79 There were ninety-seven societies, of which seven failed to make returns for that year. The average turnover for the seventy societies was £22,800.
80 Shelburne (County Wexford) £387,000; Midlands (County Offaly) £385,000; Templecrone £154,000 and North Offaly £141,000.
81 Buncrana, Corkey, Doe, Gartan, Inniskeel, Moville (County Donegal); Duhallow (County Cork); Killarney, Ardfinnan (County Tipperary); Adare, Rathgormack (County Waterford); Iverk (County Kilkenny); Clara (County Offaly); Enniscorthy, Loch Garmain (County Wexford) and Mount Bellew.
82 See Department of Local Government Circular H.14/73, 30 July 1973.
83 Of the ninety-nine societies registered, five were now in Northern Ireland. The survivors in the twenty-six counties were:

Moycarkey		Ahascragh & Fohena	
Moyne	County Tipperary	Ardrahan	County Galway
Lower Ormond		Mountbellew	
Two Mile Borris		Tynagh & Killimor	
Ballysakeery		Carn	
Burriscarra	County Mayo	Kiltoom	County Roscommon
Mayo Abbey		St John's	

Also the original Kilmessan and Donaghpatrick (County Meath); Enniscorthy (County Wexford) and Iverk (County Kilkenny).
84 See Rev M. O'Flanagan, *Co-operation*, a booklet published by Cumann Leigheact an Phobail, Series B, No 9 (1922).

professional people — doctors, lawyers, teachers, clergy, as well as local officials, auctioneers and farmers — came of merchant stock and, if they were not openly opposed to the co-operative movement, their attitudes and thinking (as William Thompson had pointed out many years previously) were inevitably influenced by their environment and upbringing. They rarely assumed the role of positive leadership which was required for the co-operative movement to flourish locally.

The controversy brought forth some belligerent advocates of co-operation, who knew little of what it was all about but were notably ready to use the fist or stick to emphasise a point of argument. On the other side, it was not unknown for merchants' bullyboys to beset known co-operators at the fair, or in the dance or public house to convince them of the error of their ways. In a country where secrets are hard to keep, it was only rarely that these attacks were carried out on the express orders of the gombeen-man. Rather were they subtly indicated, tacitly approved and quietly rewarded by a sufficiency of drink or the bestowing of other minor favours.

It was also a favourite trick of the opponents of co-operation to incite violence against the co-operators by invoking political antipathies: they were against Parnell, against Home Rule, against the Church, the Kaiser, Sinn Féin, the Treaty, or whatever 'anti' was most appropriate to the particular case. It is not surprising that a great number of mild-mannered, 'respectable' people steered clear of the controversy and the co-operative store.

The most violent era of opposition passed, or was rather superseded, by a period of much more serious political and military violence — the War of Independence and the Civil War — but the undertones of anti-co-operative feeling persisted for a long time. In his presidential address at the annual general meeting of 1937, R. A. Anderson was as forthright as ever:

> Committees need not think to placate the opponents of the Movement by refraining from consumers' co-operation. The 'hymn of hate' will be sung, perhaps, rather more lustily than before, but that will be all there is to it. When your opponents begin to look on your society with favour, it is time for you, too, to look critically into its affairs for your own sake. The surest sign that a society is doing real good is when it becomes the object of attack. The surest sign that it is either little use or is going downhill is when the lying dogs remain soundly asleep.

Anderson had always been an ardent advocate of full-blooded co-operation. He believed that by backing down on the issue of 'non-controversial trading', the movement lost the spirit and fire which would have carried its agricultural societies forward to free-trading business success. Many doubted this, but both Anderson and his milder colleagues would have appreciated more energetic efforts by local societies to make themselves more successful within the constraints of purely agricultural trading.

The real problem was lack of good management: so few agricultural societies did enough business to justify the employment of a good manager; indeed, many of them could not afford a full-time manager. Of those that did, the special requirements of *co-operative*, as distinct from proprietary, management was a major problem. In spite of the availability of large numbers of men who had valuable experience in the retail trade, it proved remarkably difficult to find one who made a really good co-op manager. Padraic Colum, the poet and playwright, reports[85] on a visit to Dungloe in the mid-twenties and his discussions with a highly successful co-operator (Paddy the Cope):

> He was of the opinion that the stores failed in the main because the co-operative societies went for their management to young men trained in shops; it was a management that was used to taking orders. He convinced me that it was the executive that really counted in the success or failure of a co-op enterprise in the Irish countryside. Why was it that the co-op movement by this time had not got a grip on the distributing business in the Irish countryside, definitely and completely replacing the gombeen men? It is because the societies have not been able to draw on an executive ability. Before the War a managing class was beginning to emerge; now there are less signs of such an emergence, I am told. The destruction of co-operative plants in many parts of the country by the Black and Tans in their campaign of reprisals, and the general slump in agricultural business following the war, have made people listless about co-operative effort.
>
> Ireland exports her executive ability, chiefly to America; the man who had created a chain of co-operative businesses in this little village is of the same type as the couple of Irishmen who have created the chain-store grocery business in America. . .

For the most part, the problems of management were tackled successfully from 1950 onwards, at least amongst the agricultural societies which survived. A number of new store societies[86] were formed which today have a turnover of from £500,000 to £1 million or more per annum. While the formation of these new store societies in the nineteen fifties reflected a welcome reawakening of interest in co-operation, it is regrettable that in every case their foundation should have been unnecessary. In each location there were already long-established societies which should have long since expanded to meet the co-operative needs of the district. However, such was the intransigence and lack of initiative of local managers (remembering that the major responsibility for management lies with the committee), that there was little alternative for the rising generation of progressive farmers but to form a new society, even though in so doing there was inevitably

---

85 Padraic Colum, *The Road Round Ireland* (New York: Macmillan, 1926), p.193.
86 Including Bunclody (County Wexford); Mullagh, Tara (County Meath); Clonleigh, Tirconaill, Inishowen (County Donegal); Cloghan (County Offaly) and Ballydangan (County Roscommon).

some fragmentation of the co-operative effort. Reorganisation did, however, revitalise many of the older societies in other areas and a number of these have already merged with the creameries in the new comprehensive co-op groupings. It is expected that most of the remaining forty-two independent co-operative agricultural stores will find their place in similar association with the creameries, marts, pig-fattening, farm service and other miscellaneous co-op societies.

There is still an unfortunate tendency to form small, vulnerable, independent societies with minimal resources of capital and management, rather than place them under the umbrella of an existing co-operative. Sometimes this reflects a narrow parochialism where one village community will not trust another village five miles away to give it a fair deal. Historically, however, it has been more often a case of the established society proving intractable and lacking the initiative or expertise to provide for the varied needs of the wider community.

That is not to say that small, independent co-operative societies should not be formed. On the contrary, there is a variety and a dynamic in human living which does not always permit of organisation being implemented in neat, unchanging geometric (or econometric) patterns. Often it will be found that small societies, set up for a specific purpose, are best initiated independently by the small group of real enthusiasts who first came up with the idea. The major constraints are those of finance, management, co-operative loyalty and, above all, commonsense. Co-operation, like politics, is the art of the possible. The human dynamic should never be stifled by trying to impose rigid patterns which do not allow for regional and local peculiarities. We can hardly prevent people from forming small co-ops of any kind. We can, however, reasonably request that the understanding be a sensible one which takes account of the human, the technical and the economic facts of life. The structure of a new co-operative should be carefully planned and, while its future must be projected, it should not be rigidly predetermined. Some small ventures will remain small. In spite of all the so-called 'economic' propaganda, it is not *always* necessary to grow to mammoth size in order to survive; big organisations are not *ipso facto* more efficient than small ones. Conversely, small units are not necessarily efficient. All we can say from experience is that bigger enterprises can sometimes afford to make bigger mistakes. There are certain specialised activities best suited to small, efficient units, yet it will always be necessary for them to adapt, develop and keep in step with improved technology.

Ranging from specialised 'hair trigger' crop spraying (which is probably not at all amenable to co-operative effort but best done by individuals), there is a progression of specialised services in agriculture, industry and trade most efficiently and economically done co-operatively by groups, whose varying sizes allow of little variation to achieve optimum results in their particular function. Outside of this, some small co-operatives may grow in a particular line in which they continue to have the edge in efficiency and economy. Others will grow and emerge in something entirely different from what they first undertook. Some co-ops will continue to be autonomous, others may amalgamate or integrate with other bigger or smaller co-op units. The possibilities of varying degrees of association between co-ops at varying stages of evolution and development are as numerous as the possibilities for diversification, departmentalisation, devolution and delegation within a major regional co-op. Co-operation hitherto has been confined within restricted limits of size, scope and function. There is a need for more co-operative penetration. This will entail the emergence of a lusty co-operative diversity, found in other countries with co-ops of all sorts, shapes and sizes, in varying stages of evolution and at every level from national and provincial federations to small townland 'syndicates'.

In 1966 a new co-operative wholesale society emerged, Co-operative Agricultural Purchases Ltd. By that year the IAWS had declined as a supplier to co-operative societies: although co-op creameries had a turnover in agricultural goods of almost £20 million and the sixty-five agricultural societies[87] had total sales of another £4m, the total trade of IAWS Ltd. stood at £6.6 million. Nearly every creamery manager in Munster dairy societies was a separate trading entity, doing all his own purchasing, usually from a great number of different suppliers. They regarded the IAWS as another wholesale company which occasionally provided good value in certain lines, but was undercut more often than not by some other supplier. Piecemeal buying from a wide variety of sources absorbed a great deal of the manager's time and energy, often to little financial advantage. There were *ad hoc* ventures in collective bargaining but, for the most part, as Robin Anderson had noted years previously, "the blood of the huckster" had ensured that managers kept their own counsel and kept on trying to beat the system.

The IAWS was singularly unsuccessful in any of its attempts to secure the combined custom of the co-operatives. Many co-op managers felt that, even if the societies subscribed the necessary share capital, the IAWS, with its conservative board of directors, would not be able to measure up to requirements. Other societies proudly felt that they were too big and too diversified to ever have all their requirements supplied from a single source.

Little happened until 1966, when an initiative was taken by James D. Hegarty, manager of Kilcorney Creamery, County Cork.[88] Hegarty was a well-respected and experienced manager whose advice was sparingly offered but invariably heeded. His proposal was that co-ops should get together, set up a central office and arrange bulk buying. He visualised many ancillary developments: the supply of current information on market

87 More than three-quarters of the trade of these societies was done by the twenty-two store co-ops in Leinster and the twelve in Ulster. The thirteen societies in Munster had a total trade of only £185,000.
88 Kilcorney Co-operative Agricultural and Dairy Society was a small society serving the area between Banteer and Millstreet. In 1966 it handled 1.3 million gallons of milk, giving a turnover in dairy produce of £152,000 and an almost equal trade in agricultural goods of £132,000.

trends and on new materials and techniques being developed in the agricultural industry; better communication and regular meetings between co-ops to exchange information; group negotiations with government agencies on import licences, quotas and other important and complex items of bureaucracy.

Hegarty had many ideas but, with that "shrewd blending of idealism with immediate and practical utility" which characterised the Rochdale Pioneers, his judgement of what could be done, when and how, was unerring. His first approach to the co-operative societies was a simple request for £10 each to cover the cost of setting up an office and investigating the idea. One hundred and ten co-operatives paid up and the trial got underway. It proved difficult to arrange any conclusive testing of the system, but, following a few ventures (mainly in fertilisers), involving a trade of £326,000 in 1966, it was agreed that the idea was sound and worth developing. Progress was slow and three years passed before turnover was doubled.[89] In 1969 Hegarty projected that, all being well, they should top the £1 million mark in the following year and that Co-operative Agricultural Purchases Ltd. (familiarly CAP) would achieve a turnover of £6 million by 1974.

The IAOS was in principle opposed to the idea of another co-operative wholesale and would naturally have preferred to see the development of a thoroughly comprehensive service through the existing agencies. The IAWS was the established wholesale federation with an 1966 turnover of more than £7½ million. The Irish Co-operative Agency Society continued its modest business with a turnover of £½ million, mainly in the supply of dairy requisites.

The initial efforts of CAP were to achieve economic bulk purchasing of fertilisers. In the summer of 1969 the IAOS set up a study group "to investigate the possibility of centralised purchasing of fertilisers for co-operatives or, if feasible, the involvement of co-operatives in the manufacture of fertilisers." At that period it was estimated that co-ops were handling 40 per cent. of the fertiliser trade and that one-sixth of the farmer's total expenditure was spent on fertilisers. A special sub-committee investigated the possibility of the co-ops becoming shareholders in a fertiliser company, either as a group or through the IAWS. It reported that a number of factors, including the high cost of buying a shareholding in such a concern, outweighed any advantage that might be gained. It was decided that the IAWS would undertake a survey of the needs of co-operatives and of the price structure obtaining, since it was generally agreed that, to make bulk purchasing worthwhile, there would need to be a guaranteed order in excess of 150,000 tons of fertilisers. The survey was completed by the end of 1970 and IAWS Ltd submitted a scheme outlining the way in which the wholesale would organise the purchase of fertilisers and enable co-operatives to participate.

By this time, however, a great number of societies were making their

---

89 The society was registered with an office in Limerick in 1967. The 1967 turnover was £371,000; 1968 — £551,000; 1969 — £648,000; 1970 — £1,093,000.

own decisions in the matter. They were attracted by the success of the aggressive new federation and many of them took shareholdings of £1,000 or more in CAP and gave it their business. In October 1973 CAP opened a large fertiliser blending plant in Waterford. The directors also declared their intention of taking a majority shareholding in a new £9 million plant at Whitegate, County Cork, to manufacture ammonia, urea and other nitrogenous fertilisers. Besides its involvement in the fertiliser trade, CAP was also supplying its participant co-ops with a wide variety of other farm requirements, from galvanised iron to polythene and binder twine. A subsidiary co-operative, Capmec Ltd, established around a small engineering factory at Cloghan, County Offaly, was operating as a base for the marketing of imported agricultural machinery and for the fabrication and manufacture of certain items of farm equipment.

In 1974, operating from new headquarters in Cork city, CAP achieved a turnover of £6.5 million. In that year CAP had supplied some 96,000 tons of fertilisers to co-operative societies and at the year's end claimed to have a committed share capital of £450,000. Plans were going ahead for the major development in fertiliser manufacture.[90]

Nineteen seventy-four, however, had been a year of disastrous cattle prices. Beef cattle were sold in many areas for less than half the 1973 prices and by year's end store cattle were practically unsaleable. Coupled with this was a galloping inflation which drove the costs of farm inputs to record levels. In springtime, credit had been freely available to farmers wishing to increase their cattle stocks in prospect of the high cattle prices which Ireland's participation in the enlarged European Community seemed to offer.

In the spring of 1975, the farmers' reaction was drastic. Many farmers purchased less than half of their usual annual supply of fertilisers and severely curtailed their purchases of other farm requisites. CAP, with large supplies of unsold fertilisers on hand, was soon in financial trouble. Considerable quantities of blended fertilisers deteriorated in storage. The Society was involved in huge extra costs of labour, rehandling, storage and bank charges, for no return. Management was overstretched. The engineering unit, Capmec Ltd, was sold, but the financial situation was irretrievable and CAP went into receivership in the autumn of 1975. Various attempts have been made to rescue the organisation. Hopes were expressed that the IAWS might effect a takeover, with financial backing from the co-operative societies, but at the time of writing the general indications are that liquidation is inevitable.

In this chapter we have considered those societies which were registered

---

90 Co-operative leaders, concerned for solidarity in the movement, had watched the evolution of CAP with some misgivings but were now hopeful that CAP would emerge as a *manufacturing* co-operative and have its major commitment in that area, rather than as a competing wholesale federation. Many, however, had doubts as to the wisdom of going into fertiliser manufacture, in view of the plans of Nitrigin Eireann Teo. to establish a plant in Cork and the plentiful supply of manufactured nitrogen throughout the world. Concern was also expressed about the high financial gearing of CAP and the capabilities of management to control a many-sided enterprise going so far and so fast.

as agricultural societies and appear as such in the annual reports and returns of the IAOS. To a greater or lesser degree, the store societies have always had a complementary association, and function with all other co-ops — credit societies, creameries, poultry produce and the many miscellaneous groups with their myriad agricultural, business or industrial aims.

The co-operative agricultural societies were conceived on the pattern of the French *syndicats agricoles* and the Italian *consorzio agrario,* with far-reaching objectives over the whole field of agricultural development. In the early days, Plunkett and his associates had hoped that the co-operative store would provide the nucleus around which the whole diversity of local co-operative effort would be co-ordinated and integrated, in accordance with the lofty co-operative ideal enunciated by George William Russell:

> It is not enough to organise farmers in a district for one purpose only . . . in a credit society, a dairy society, a fruit society, a bacon factory or a co-operative store. All these may be and must be beginnings; but if they do not develop and absorb all rural business into their organisation, they will have little effect on character. The specialised society only affects economic efficiency. The evolution of humanity depends absolutely on its power to unite and create true social organisms.

In the eighteen nineties it seemed a sanguine hope that the generalised agricultural society should be the one which would play the leading role in co-operative achievement. The peculiar economic, political and social conditions obtaining in rural Ireland, however, ordained differently. The story of the agricultural societies is largely one of ignorant men in remote rural communities grasping for a poorly understood and ill-defined ideal. They stumbled forward blindly, with little planning, seeking what was possible, learning by hard experience and constantly facing ruin in the process. They fought the dishonest dealer, but were not without sympathy for his predicament in a country with too many shopkeepers and too little trade.

> The struggle for existence sometimes produces the hero, but a more usual product is the petty rogue. I have always felt it was a forlorn hope preaching honesty to the grocer in a society where his neighbour sands his sugar, dusts his pepper, adulterates his butter, sells cheaper, and gets the trade. We should aim at creating a social order where the struggle for existence will give way to a brotherhood of workers; where men dependent on the success of their united endeavours for their own prosperity will instinctively think first of the community and secondly of themselves.[91]

91 George W. Russell, "The Building up of a Rural Civilisation", an address to the Annual General Meeting of the IAOS, 10 December 1909.

Very few of the early farmer/storekeepers had revolutionary thoughts of a new social order. They were conservative and individualistic, banding together to relieve obvious hardships or trying to right blatant wrongs. They discovered profitable areas of activity, failed to pursue them, but their pioneering efforts often came to fruition at a later date: cattle marts, cattle-breeding societies (AI), pig-fattening stations, veterinary supply, machinery syndicates, farm services, co-operative insurance, compounding units — are all modern co-operative developments based on the initiatives of the early co-operators.

One could rightly complain of the delay. Directions were lost, and, perhaps, it is only now that it is feasible to seek to embody the many co-operative activities in an integrated, comprehensive co-operation such as AE dreamed of. The implementation of this ideal is still a major task, but the main thing is that after many wanderings the direction has been fixed once more, and we have the consoling thought of an early co-operator[92] that "direction is more important than speed."

92 Fred Hall, adviser of studies and first principal of the Co-operative College, which was set up in co-operative headquarters, Holyoake House, Manchester, in 1922. At the age of thirteen, Hall started work as an office boy with the firm of John Bright & Bros., Rochdale. Later he became assistant manager of a textile firm and manager of an eyelet manufacturing company, while teaching classes in co-operation for the Rochdale Pioneers Society. In 1913 he was Professor of Commerce in The Queen's University, Belfast.

Chapter Fifteen

Co-operative Poultry Societies

The Report of the Recess Committee bore the following comment.

Poultry and eggs are an important form of agricultural produce to which the attention of Ireland ought to be specially directed. Foreign competition cannot affect us here as in the case of cereals. . . Moreover, eggs and poultry are a poor man's or rather a poor woman's industry. The humblest labourer's wife or 'widow-woman' by the roadside can directly participate in its extension. It is impossible, we regret to say, owing to our unsatisfactory statistical system, to obtain reliable figures as to the present position of this industry in Ireland. Having applied to the Agricultural Department of the Land Commission for figures . . . we were informed that the Department collected no such statistics. It is true that Thom's Directory, which contains the best collection of Irish statistics published, shows that the number of poultry kept in Ireland has been increasing in recent years and their value in 1891 was £381,309. But there are no figures as to eggs or other items.

The total value of eggs imported into the United Kingdom, however, is ascertainable. In 1894 this was £3,786,329 — an enormous sum, when we consider it is paid for foreign eggs alone and does not include the price of those supplied by the United Kingdom. These eggs come chiefly from France . . . and from Hungary, Germany, Belgium, Denmark and even Russia. There is no reason why every penny of this £3,786,329 might not be earned in Ireland, if the suppliers learn the secret of getting their eggs to market fresh, if they are helped to do so by railway and steamboat facilities and if good breeds of poultry be introduced and proper principles of rearing and keeping inculcated. It is gratifying to know that in certain localities in the west, the Congested Districts Board and co-operative societies are making promising efforts in this direction.[1]

The prospect of land ownership for the Irish small-tenant farmer would, it was alleged, turn sand into gold.

Yet the market prospects for his traditional farm produce were somewhat less exciting. His basket of home-laid eggs evoked even less

1 *Report of the Recess Committee* (Dublin: Browne & Nolan Ltd., 1896), p.21.

enthusiasm than his firkin of home-made butter. "The Irish egg", said Plunkett, "has acted as a depreciated currency. In its too long life it became as dirty as a one pound note, and the process of securing for it its proper place in the English wholesale trade aroused the wrath of those who profited by its humble place in Irish retail trade." With unconscious humour Catherine Webb wrote of the trade in Irish eggs in the eighteen nineties as a decaying one, principally because of the system — or lack of a system — upon which the industry was based:

> The practice amongst farmers' wives all over Ireland had been to hold their eggs until they had a·sufficient quantity to make it worthwhile taking them to market, particularly when prices were going up. The injury done to the trade by this abominable system of 'holding up' eggs was enormous. The Irish egg — under proper conditions the best in the world — was sold at the lowest price and was difficult to sell at all.[2]

The trouble came to a head in 1897 when the Liverpool and Glasgow egg merchants issued a circular stating that they would in future refuse to buy Irish eggs unless they were clean, fresh and properly packed. The IAOS had been campaigning for proper instruction in poultry-keeping and the agency society had made earlier efforts to ensure the proper marketing of eggs. At the annual general meeting of 1897, Dr Wallace Taylor of Aughnacloy and Mr McNamara from Ennistymon berated their co-operative colleagues for putting too much emphasis on butter. In some parts of Ireland, they said, the land was too poor to support dairying and "the people had to depend to a very great extent on the raising of poultry and eggs". Co-operative societies, dealing exclusively with the poultry business, were set up in that year at Nenagh (County Tipperary), Cratloe (County Clare) and Moneygall.[3] Several creamery and agricultural societies also took up the business. The following year saw the establishment of special poultry co-operatives at Mallow, at three centres in County Galway (Kinvara, Pallas, Clonbrock and Ahascaragh), and at Glasson, County Westmeath. In 1899 were added eight more,[4] six of which were in County Donegal. In 1898 the IAOS appointed Henry de Courcy as their poultry expert, a man with long practical experience of poultry-keeping, who was a graduate of the University Extension College, Reading. They also 'imported' from Denmark Mr Viggo Schwartz, who achieved immediate success in teaching the societies how to select and pack eggs for the British market.[5]

2 *Industrial Co-operation*, op. cit., p.162.
3 Cloughjordan, Moneygall and Toomevara Co-operative Poultry Society, County Tipperary.
4 Clonmany, Carrigart, Kincasslagh, Lettermacaward, Bunlin, Cratlagh and Milford, Glenvar and Killygarvan (County Donegal), Desertmartin (County Antrim) and Newmarket (County Cork).
5 Along with de Courcy and William Domville Rowland (organiser of poultry societies — based in Lifford), Schwartz was a charming and popular visitor to poultry societies throughout Ireland until he returned, still a bachelor, to take up a remunerative post in his own country in 1906.

By the turn of the century there were twenty-one special poultry societies with 2,569 members, but turnover totalled a mere £9,475. Although by 1902 (thirty-one societies),[6] turnover had trebled (£29,914), it was becoming obvious that small, independent poultry societies were rather impractical. Some of the earliest ones had already disappeared and more were being absorbed into larger creamery and agricultural societies as their trade (still almost entirely in eggs) fitted in better with the agricultural store business.[7] The financing of these societies depended on 5/- shares, only half of which were paid up, but even the half-crowns were not subscribed with particular speed. Despite the fact that the co-op was paying up to 50 per cent. more for eggs than the local merchant, in the early days it took three-dozen eggs or more to pay the half-crown shareholding. Despite the efforts of the new Department of Agriculture and the poultry experts, and the hen-wife's undoubted enthusiasm for higher prices, the job was proving extraordinarily difficult. The small-farm poultry flock mostly comprised poorly fed mongrel hens. Egg production virtually ceased for the winter months and the co-ops consequently found it very difficult to maintain steady supplies. They got too many eggs which had been hoarded in the autumn weeks in expectation of the increased winter prices. Few of the small poultry societies could afford expert management and other constant dangers, like breakages,[8] returns with heavy freight charges, and bad debts, threatened their existence daily.

A persistent problem facing the early efforts to improve the quality of the Irish egg was that cheap, low-grade, foreign eggs were sold in England as 'Irish', whilst the good Irish eggs supplied by Irish co-operatives were passed as English or French. One Welsh egg buyer flatly refused to believe that a consignment of eggs from the Mallow Co-operative Poultry Society were Irish; he insisted that they must be foreign and regarded the transaction as a practical joke. "I ordered Irish eggs", he wrote, "Why have you sent me Danish eggs?"[9] In an attempt to overcome the frauds and the

6   Newcomers were Dervock, Cloughmills, Ulster Egg Exporters (County Antrim); Toames, Codrum, Mossgrove (County Cork); Desertlyn, Dunboe (County Derry); Erne, Kinawley (County Fermanagh); Dunbreen (County Tyrone); Tamney (County Donegal); Collooney (County Sligo); Moyne (County Tipperary); Rathnure (County Wexford); Burriscarra (County Mayo); Shanagolden & Foynes (County Limerick); Doohamlet (County Monaghan); Whitecross (County Armagh) and Athlone. An attempt was made in 1900 to establish a large poultry enterprise (North West Poultry Society) at Strabane with a poultry-fattening station at Lifford and several egg-collecting depots at various centres along the Donegal and Great Northern railway systems.
7   Windgap Dairy Society (County Kilkenny), which had also a considerable store trade, reported £1,300 trade in eggs in 1902. In 1900 the following agricultural and creamery societies were selling eggs for their members: Lombardstown, Doneraile, East Muskerry, Drumcliffe, Lagan, Killeshandra, Barndarrig, Collooney, Doons, North Cappagh, Kilmactranny, Toames, Boyle, Croghan, Ferrymount, Mossgrove, Great Northern, Castledawson and Enniscorthy.
8   It took some time to design an egg case to withstand the rough handling of the railway porters. Another problem arose because the wood-wool supplied by Irish manufacturers for packing eggs was sometimes damp and contained a good deal of turpentine which infected the eggs and gave them a terrible flavour. At an IAOS annual general meeting (20 October 1903), Lady Clonbrock (Clonbrock and Castlegar Poultry Society) reported some anomalies in freight charges. The carriage of a box of eggs from Galway to London cost 3/10d, to Birmingham 5/1d and to Sheffield 5/-.
9   IAOS Annual Report 1899, p.25.

deep-rooted prejudice against Irish eggs, the IAOS introduced a trade mark — a diamond shape with an odd-looking shamrock and the letters IAOS. In 1910 this logo was superseded by the more distinctive trade mark KARKA, a phonetic rendering of the Gaelic word for 'hens'.

As with all other forms of co-operation, there was active opposition from the established traders. It was the local shopkeeper's system of bartering eggs for groceries that had led to the crisis of dirty, stale, ungraded eggs being refused by the British merchants. The co-operative approach was startlingly different: eggs were bought by weight rather than by number. Instead of holding eggs for days or even weeks, the hen-wife was encouraged to sell her eggs as freshly as possible. In some cases it was arranged that children would take the day's laying of eggs to the poultry co-op on their way to school. Payment was spot cash and the eggs were graded and packed on the continental plan and despatched in non-returnable cases. Dividends were paid twice yearly and often came to sizeable sums.[10] At average prices being paid by co-op societies for eggs, the IAOS calculated that in 1899 forty hens gave as much profit as one cow. (By 1906 the Society had revised the figure to twenty hens.)

The local trader would not be outdone. He did not want to lose the barter system of exchange of eggs for household goods — a system which, as the co-operators pointed out, "gave two profits to the trader and none to the hen-wife". The trader's tactic — to pay an excessive price for ungraded eggs until the poultry co-op would be put out of business — was not entirely successful, since some co-ops were quick to apprise their suppliers that good eggs would get a premium price at the co-op, while the merchant was prepared to pay an almost equal price for the rest. Frequently the merchant who had operated a barter system with a farmer's wife, of egg exchange for groceries, raised the price of his provisions when she sold her eggs to the co-op and arrived at her friendly grocers to purchase her goods for cash. It was the unfriendly attitude of a grocer's clerk in Dungloe which precipitated the formation of the Templecrone Co-op:

> A few days after the manures were landed, Sally went with her basket of eggs to the local shop. The boy behind the counter used to say when she would come in: 'Now how are you today, Mrs Gallagher? How is wee Annie and Mr Gallagher? I suppose he is killed working — tell him not to work so hard, there will be plenty of work after he is dead . . .' This day when she went in, he did not speak.
>
> Sally put her basket of eggs on the counter and said: 'Are you going to take my eggs?'
>
> After some time he lifted the basket and counted the eggs and said: 'What do you want?'
>
> Sally said: 'Half a pound of tea, quarter a stone of sugar, two pound

10 No dividend was paid until shares were fully paid up. Interest on capital was paid at 5 per cent. and, of the remaining surplus, 5 per cent. was carried to the reserve fund and the remainder distributed to the members in proportion to the value of eggs or poultry supplied.

of soap, pennyworth of thread, pennyworth of blue and the rest in cakes.' He gave her the goods. When she came home she made the tea and called me in for a drop and told me of the boy's attitude . . .

Sally said: 'I am not going back to that shop, Paddy, should we starve.'[11]

Merchant and co-operative had eventually to submit to the same discipline of proper grading and marketing.

It is of historical interest that at one time Ireland had a considerable export trade in 'store' chickens. The IAOS Annual Report of 1897 gives an interesting detail of this trade, and the proposed alternative:

> Large numbers of Irish fowls — drawn mainly from districts where improved breeds exist, such as in County Wexford — are annually bought by 'Crammers' in Surrey and Sussex at very low prices. These 'store' fowls are then crammed for the London market, and realise on an average 3s 6d apiece (*vide* the Report of Mr R. Henry Row to the Royal Commission on Agriculture). Numbers of these fowls bought at a very low price, die in transit, and the Irish producer pays for all such risks in the low price he has to accept . . . Attention to breeding, feeding, killing, plucking, trussing and packing for market will enable us here to turn our 'store' chickens into 'Surrey fowls' and reap the profits ourselves instead of having to send them across the water to be 'hall-marked'.

Experiments in fattening were carried out by the poultry society at Dunboe, County Derry,[12] and at Windgap creamery in 1902, but most of the separate poultry societies were too small to provide premises for this and lacked the necessary working capital. In 1905 an attempt was made to federate the poultry societies but it met with only limited success. It did, however, lead to some regrouping and the formation of bigger societies covering larger areas. Thus the North Kilkenny Poultry Society (established in 1905) served an area of seven parishes, whilst the Longford Society covered some twenty parishes. Sizeable societies were also emerging at Dervock and Cloughmills (County Antrim), Desertmartin, Dunboe, Limavady, Sessiagh O'Neill (Ballybofey, County Donegal), Rathkeale, Mallow and Athlone, but of these only Rathkeale reported any trade in poultry (£400 in 1904). Soon, however, the Longford Society and the Forth Society, Tagoat, County Wexford, were fattening poultry, as to a lesser extent were North Kilkenny and some of the northern societies. The trend towards incorporation into agricultural or creamery co-ops continued and only the bigger poultry societies were capable of independence.[13] The egg and poultry business was an important section of the Irish economy

11 P. Gallagher, *My Story* (London: Jonathan Cape, 1927), p.74.
12 It is likely that it was to the Dunboe Society near Castlerock, County Derry, that Paddy the Cope went to acquire a training in testing, grading and packing eggs — an event humorously recounted in *My Story*, pp.83-84.
13 Eleven small poultry societies were dissolved in 1904.

(accounting for exports of £2.8 million in 1905, compared to butter exports of £3.2 million) and many efficient traders made good profits. In 1905 the Department of Agriculture established a poultry-fattening station at Avondale, County Wicklow, Parnell's former home and estate which had been taken over by the Department as a research and experimental station for forestry.

The Dunboe Poultry Society, c. 1902

A profitable table poultry trade emerged, which was the forerunner of the modern broiler chicken industry; although the co-operative share of the trade was relatively small, it had a significant controlling influence on the whole industry. The Department of Agriculture and the county committees of agriculture played an important role in improving poultry breeds and management, and Irish eggs and poultry began to win a better reputation.[14]

That chicken was a luxury food, on which only the affluent could afford to dine with any regularity, was underlined by the complaints of many of the societies about the slump which invariably occurred in the game season.[15] Domestic fowl was dropped from the menu when the master took

14 Poultry numbers also increased, especially during the war years, which prompted Plunkett to congratulate his successor, Russell, for having "made two cocks crow where only one had crowed before." (On the subject of cock-crowing, *The Irish Homestead* (23 July 1904) carried an interesting snippet on a cock-crowing competition held in Devonshire. The winning bird crowed 51 times in 17 minutes!).

15 See IAOS Annual Report 1906, p.11. The importance of chicken as a delicacy and as a food for invalids was emphasised when the Department of Agriculture and the IAOS advised poultry-keepers to refrain from selling their pullets and to hatch out all available eggs to maintain the supply of poultry: "the hospitals of the United Kindom will be full of sick and wounded soldiers and the demand for fowls and eggs will be very great." (IAOS Annual Report 1914, p.22).

his gun to pot pheasant, partridge, plover or grouse, or when Cook could buy a few brace cheaply on the market. The working classes had not yet aspired to chicken and chips as standard fare or as a 'take away' from café or public house. The egg enjoyed broader popularity but even here there was an élite trade which was worthy of special attention. The 1907 Annual Report urged each poultry society to go after this select market:

> ...to select from among its members a limited number who will undertake to supply their eggs daily in an absolutely spotless condition. These eggs could then be specially packed to suit the requirements of the highest class retail trade, e.g., clubs, private houses, etc. Eggs so handled would in a very short time realise prices sufficiently high to pay, not only for the extra expenses involved, but also a handsome profit ...

By 1908 the number of poultry societies had fallen to twenty-four. There had been no increase in membership and their total trade (home and export) of £72,000 was an unsatisfactory fraction in an industry which was now approaching £4 million in export sales. It was conceded that the egg trade was more appropriate to agricultural and creamery societies stores, but the co-operators had hoped that there would be at least a few specialised poultry societies in each county, to fatten, breed and give impetus to general poultry improvement.[16]

In fact only half the counties had any poultry society at all and there was much soul-searching as to why this profitable field of co-operative endeavour was not being penetrated. Plunkett said: "I have come to a conclusion which I hardly dare to express ... The member, in the case of poultry societies, is not a mere man, but an entirely superior being and with all her other excellencies, I am afraid she is not a good co-operator!" He conceded, however, that the poultry societies were neglected: "I doubt whether there is any branch of agricultural industry the workers in which have suffered more from the lack of organisation." The IAOS regretfully agreed; the organisers were overwhelmed by bigger societies with more pressing problems, the skills of the poultry business were woefully lacking and difficult to supply, the competition from merchant interests was intense. Most intractable of all was the firmly established 'barter' system of exchanging eggs for groceries and household requisites. Many housewives regarded the change of system as an intrusion on their own jealously guarded domain. Besides, it was much more convenient to trade as always with the grocer or the higgler's cart which called to the door exchanging eggs for household necessities:

> A passive, but most determined resistance ... exists throughout the

16 In 1904 Isaac Varian of Stillorgan, County Dublin, exhibited at the Royal Dublin Society a new dual-purpose breed — the Hibernia — which reputedly had taken nine years of intensive work to establish as a distinctive breed: "an excellent layer of large brown eggs and a large shapely fowl which can readily be fattened." (*The Irish Homestead*, 17 December 1904).

country. The prices paid by the society are compared unfavourably with those paid by the local dealer. All kinds of difficulties are raised which feminine wit can devise, and the farmer whose money had been invested in the society finds to his chagrin that he cannot control the supply of eggs, but is simply a partner in an amateur higgler's concern which is forced into competition with rivals who are unscrupulous enough to bribe his wife and daughters to give them the preference.[17]

The ban on grocery trading was a sore restriction on many poultry societies. Some northern societies, like Cloughmills, Dunboe and Limavady, defied the ban and flourished, but, for the most part, the hen-wife found the co-op a cold, uninviting place where her eggs were often criticised and, even if she got good money, she was denied the satisfaction of filling her empty egg basket with household necessities and comforts.

In 1908 The IAOS organised a number of special poultry conferences throughout the country, which culminated in a major conference under the auspices of the Department of Agriculture in 1909. Yet little co-operative progress resulted, apart from the amalgamation of Irish Producers Ltd.[18] with the IAWS and the establishment of IAWS egg-packing depots at Sligo and Enniskillen, which helped co-ops in the north-west to market eggs more effectively.

The co-op poultry trade was in the doldrums in the years preceding the outbreak of the Great War. There was no further development in the production or marketing of table fowl and even in the egg trade there was a tendency to let standards slip and to revert to the old system of buying eggs by 'count' rather than by weight. Great hopes were expressed that the newly-formed United Irishwomen would work wonders in the organisation and management of poultry societies but, despite some heroic work (e.g., Alice and Mary Spring-Rice in Foynes), their efforts went largely unrewarded. The number of poultry societies declined to eighteen in 1913 and in that latter year turnover declined by a drastic 25 per cent. to £48,000. The war brought a sudden upswing in trade[19] and in 1914 the poultry societies' turnover was back to £65,000. As the war continued, the prices of eggs and poultry rose to unheard-of levels and, even though feedstuffs were scarce and dear, the producers were enthusiastic. Most of the increased business went to the traders but certain creameries and store societies also enjoyed a greatly increased egg trade. Of the separate poultry

17 IAOS Annual Report 1910, p.15.
18 The Dublin-based federation founded in 1902, which in 1908 had a £24,000 turnover in poultry, eggs and honey.
19 Father Tom Finlay presaged a dramatic change in the outlook of the British consumer towards the agricultural industry. Hitherto he had been very indifferent: "Enough for him that his bread comes from the baker, his meat from the butcher and his vegetables from the greengrocer. His still more intelligent housewife knows that these purveyors of domestic commodities are able to sell them at moderate prices because they are not dependent on the stupid and inefficient rustics of the islands. Irish eggs are cheap because they can be got from Russia and the best of Irish butter can avail itself of the Danish label." (IAOS committee meeting, 12 October 1915).

societies, however, only the twelve strong ones survived,[20] in nearly all cases by adding grocery supply to their business:

> They state frankly that they could not otherwise compete with the huxters. This provides an additional argument for liberty to include the co-operative store in the programme of the IAOS. Where the business is left in the hands of the ordinary trader or huxter; groceries are exchanged as a matter of course for eggs, no money changing hands. In the case of the co-operative society, both transactions — the purchase of the eggs and the sale of the groceries — are for cash and bartering is eliminated.[21]

Even with eggs selling at fourpence and fivepence each, it was necessary to warn against hoarding because of the likelihood of still higher prices. Anderson considered that the sale of bad eggs at such a price was deplorable and the sellers deserved to be punished.

On the positive side, there was good news reflecting credit on the work done years previously by Mr Schwartz:

> The average size of eggs (in certain societies) has been raised to a degree that it has been found impossible in practice to realise on the market prices for eggs, weighing 18 lbs per long hundred and upwards, which would enable the societies to buy them at the current price per lb without loss. However, the societies still continue to buy these extra large eggs, and the public gets the benefit.[22]

The trade turnover of the poultry societies soared from £118,000 in 1916 to £165,000 in 1917 and in the following year Plunkett commended the North Kilkenny Society on its record turnover of £59,550.[23] In 1919 the Shanagolden & Foynes Society and the society at Newmarket disbanded. The Sessiagh O'Neill Society, Ballybofey, was taken over by the IAWS. The number was maintained at ten by the addition of a small society in Dublin,[24] still a notoriously unco-operative county. Although the unsettled state of the country posed special difficulties — disrupted transport, delays[25] and pilferages — the turnover of the ten poultry societies for 1920 totalled £253,462.[26] An Egyptian visitor[27] to Ireland in 1920 was loud in his praise of the North Kilkenny Society at Ballyragget and of Dean Michael Barry "head of the church as well as the co-operative enterprises." The

20 Cloughmills, Dervock, Dunboe, Limavady, Sessiagh O'Neill, Newmarket, Rathkeale, Shanagolden & Foynes, Borris, North Kilkenny, Clonbrock & Castlegar, and Athlone.
21 IAOS Annual Report 1917, pp.14-15.
22 ibid., p.14.
23 A remarkable achievement in view of the fact that the North Kilkenny Society had no store trade.
24 Irish Poultry Keepers: membership eight, share capital £24 and turnover of £481 in 1921.
25 One English customer reported that his eggs arrived "unsuitable even for election purposes."
26 Creamery turnover was £8¼m and agricultural societies £2½m in that year.
27 Ibrahim Rashad, *An Egyptian in Ireland* (Privately printed, 1920), pp.33-34.

same observer admirably illustrated the whole *raison d'être* of co-operative poultry societies:

> Poultry and eggs are the great industries of the small farmer, and lend themselves admirably to co-operative methods. Before these were adopted, the trade was conducted by a host of middle-men, who delayed the egg in its transit to the consumer. The following lines might be supposed to be addressed to them by an infuriated customer who was suffering from the aroma of the eggs served to him at the breakfast table —

> What the deuce is your use? You nothing produce,
> You never lay eggs. Oh, you're a transmitter,
> If A has an egg intended for me
> He hands it to B, B to C, C to D
> D to E, E to me — who pay after A
> B, C, D and E, for stopping the way;

> For surely 'twere fitter A's egg and my penny
> Changed hands without paying a toll to so many,
> Which terribly docks Farmer A of his gain,
> While of eggs far from fresh I often complain.

All co-ops took a hammering in 1921 and the independent poultry societies were hardest hit of all. Turnover dropped by 30 per cent. to £177,282. Although egg prices were still relatively high, marketing was exceptionally difficult because of mass unemployment in Britain and guerilla warfare at home. Miraculously, eight of the ten poultry societies managed to make a small profit;[28] the North Kilkenny Society held its sales up to £40,000 and scraped a profit of £279.

In 1922 trade was, if anything, more difficult: prices were down and turnover dropped to £151,750. Some of the societies, like Cloughmills, Dunboe and North Kilkenny, had built up reserves of around £5,000 each which helped them to weather the storm.[29] The Northern societies were still making their returns to Dublin in 1923. Limavady folded but the remaining three (Cloughmills, Dervock and Dunboe) accounted for £90,000 of the total all-Ireland turnover of £138,000 in that year. Although there were still ten societies including Limavady on the books, the end was in sight for Rathkeale, Borris and the tiny Dublin society with its eight members. In 1924 the poultry co-ops ceased to be registered as separate societies. At Foynes the co-operator and nationalist gun-runner, Mary Spring-Rice, lay dying. Her father, Monteagle, would live for nine years more to lament the decline of what had promised to be a great co-operative community.[30]

---

28 Borris, County Carlow, had a loss of £671 and Irish Poultry Keepers, Dublin of £19.
29 In 1922 Athlone had a reserve fund of £1,420, Dervock £670 and Clonbrock & Castlegar £450.
30 Besides Monteagle's sawmills, there were an industry society, poultry society, credit

The co-operators, and particularly the IAWS, had for a long time been seeking compulsory grading and standardisation of agricultural produce for export. Their efforts were belatedly rewarded in 1924 when the Agricultural Produce (Eggs) Act, which laid down definite standards for grading and packing export eggs, insisted that each package be marked so as to identify the exporter and indicate the grade of eggs contained in it. It also required registration of egg-dealers' premises and made it a punishable offence to sell dirty or bad eggs on the home market. Eggs continued to be an important item in the economy, with a crucial role in the farm household budget, during the years of economic depression, when the egg reverted very much to its 'depreciated currency' function in exchange for the weekly groceries. Many agencies, including co-ops, dealt in eggs, but by 1940 only three specifically poultry co-ops had survived — North Kilkenny, Athlone and Clonbrock & Castlegar. The County Cork Co-operative Egg & Poultry Society was formed in 1931 but failed. The affairs of the Athlone Society were wound up in 1942. Clonbrock & Castlegar shut down in 1952. The Muskerry Hatcheries Ltd. was founded in 1948, at a time when the poultry industry was making a tremendous leap forward into the modern intensive system, but survived only until 1951.

Lady Clonbrock

North Kilkenny continued as a co-operative although, in practice, it had long since become a proprietary concern in the hands of its manager, Mr Carey, whose outstanding business ability had made it prosper through thick and thin. Although there were a number of co-ops engaged, the marketing of eggs and poultry had become very much an 'every man for himself' effort, with no central marketing agency. The IAWS, beset with numerous financial difficulties, had ceased since the early nineteen twenties to be an effective selling agency. In 1954 the hoped-for breakthrough on

society, a co-operative wheat-growing society, an IAWS depot, very active branches of the Gaelic League and the United Irishwomen, and a workman's club.

the British market had not materialised and there was a serious slump in the egg trade. The IAOS committee carried out investigations to establish the extent of co-operative trade in eggs and poultry but concluded that centralised co-operative marketing would not be feasible or remunerative.

A group in the Cavan/Monaghan area, however, saw the need to tackle the marketing problem and in 1956 founded Co-operative Poultry Products Ltd. in Cootehill. It proved to be a difficult struggle but the society has survived and, although its turnover (£933,507 in 1974) is small in the context of the large poultry output from the Cavan/Monaghan area, it has played a very important part in the development of modern intensive poultry-keeping; just as across the border the first poultry co-ops (Dervock, Dunboe, Cloughmills) set the pattern and established the tradition which led to the adoption of large-scale, intensive poultry-keeping in Northern Ireland.

A number of co-operative societies continue to trade in poultry and eggs. In the Republic the co-operative market share[31] of the poultry trade is almost 40 per cent. The really big commitment, however, is on the part of the famous Castlemahon Co-op in County Limerick — the same dairy society which caused such consternation in the early days by selling out to CWS. The creamery came back into co-operative ownership in 1907 and since the depression years has been developing and expanding trade in processing and marketing poultry and eggs for its members. Later the society built its own hatchery and established broiler units, laying farms and experimental growing stations. In 1970 a new processing plant was opened, producing vacuum-packed and deep-frozen birds for retail. Castlemahon supplies some 120,000 turkeys annually for the Christmas trade and the total annual turnover of their poultry division is of the order of £4 million.

31 See *The Agricultural Co-operation in the European Economic Community* (Brussels: COGECA, 1974), p.48.

Chapter Sixteen

Flax Societies

In the eighteen sixties the Irish linen industry had enjoyed a boom as a result of the cotton famine caused by the American Civil War. In 1864 there were over 300,000 acres of flax grown in Ireland and the linen industry was flourishing. Later, for various reasons, including foreign competition, the trade declined: by 1880 acreage of flax was halved and by 1893 it was down to less than 68,000 acres, most of which was grown in Ulster.[1] Four years later it had dropped to 46,000 acres.

The spinners were considerably frustrated because the problem was not merely one of foreign competition — the demand for Irish flax was still about four times the supply. The Belgians and the Dutch were superior in linen manufacture; their farmers grew the best quality flax to which the spinners and weavers added refined manufacturing techniques. Yet the knowledgeable Ulster businessmen would be loth to admit that they were backward in manufacturing skill (although some machinery might be a little outdated) and were convinced of the necessity of a supply of good quality Irish flax.

The decline in flax acreage was ascribed to two main causes: shortage of labour and lack of technical skill.

> The scarcity of labour ... is plainly one of the results of emigration, and is an indication that emigration from non-congested districts of Ireland has now reached a point beyond which it cannot go without serious detriment to the country. For the decline in the production of flax is but a part of the general decrease of tillage throughout Ireland ... which seems due to the same cause — the diminution in the amount of labour available for application to the land.[2]

Every year, 50,000 people emigrated and the labour shortage would soon be aggravated by many adventurous ploughboys going off to fight in the Boer War.

1   The total acreage under flax in 1893 was 67,487, of which Ulster grew 67,047, Leinster 247, Connaught 101 and Munster 49 acres.
2   Report of Recess Committee, p. 15.

The question of technical skill, however, was a bigger and tougher problem. Experts were satisfied that the land of Ireland could grow flax as good as anywhere in the world, but the farmers were not getting the quality or the yields which would make flax-growing an attractive financial proposition. Frank Barbour, head of a firm of flax spinners in Lisburn (who with his younger brother, Harold, was destined to play a worthy role in the Irish co-operative movement) was excited by some experiments which he had carried out in the Ballina area of County Mayo, which confirmed the possibilities already shown in the Report of the Flax Supply Association (1893).[3] The latter report gave details of a statistical survey which Sir William Ewart subsequently simplified in a statement that flax yields in Leinster and Connaught were from 50 to 75 per cent. greater than in Ulster.[4] The Belgians were doubtless amused to learn of the typically Irish discovery that their flax was grown in the wrong place. The Irish had grown used to this kind of thing, but with the textile infrastructure and tradition based almost entirely in Ulster, it would prove difficult to do much about it.

The Barbour brothers and other co-operators were exceedingly willing to try. If Connaught could be persuaded to take up flax-growing, not only would there be excellent flax produced at home (Belfast was importing some £3 million worth per annum) but the small congested farmers of Connaught would have an ideal crop, utilising their surplus labour and providing incomes hitherto undreamed of.

This was not a new idea. The Flax Association had been set up in Ulster in 1863— the linen boom days of the American Civil War. In Dublin, the Joint Flax Committee, a state-aided body drawn from the Royal Dublin Society and the Royal Agricultural Society, was established in the same year. The government granted monies[5] for the employment of flax instructors who were sent afield to teach the best methods of growing and saving flax. The experiment was not successful and, in another typically Irish denouement, the Royal Commission on Technical Instruction advanced the opinion that the failure of this effort to introduce flax-growing in the South was "largely due to the ignorance of the home instructors employed."[6]

In 1898 the position continued to deteriorate. The price differential between Belgian and Irish flax widened (£63 compared to £38 per ton) as quality differences became more marked. Farmers complained that they could not grow as good a fibre as formerly. Some blamed the land, others the seed; nearly everyone blamed the government. Labour grew scarcer, prices of livestock and other crops made flax less inviting and, at the third annual conference of co-operative societies in November 1898, J.J. Crilly of Dunleer complained of the high freight charges and the unhelpful

3   Barbour wrote an exhaustive report on flax-growing possibilities, with detailed costings on processing and so on, which was later incorporated in an IAOS instructional leaflet.
4   Yields in stones per acre: Ulster 34.30, Munster 38.80, Leinster 56.33, Connaught 64.42.
5   £2,000 in 1864, £3,000 in each of the two succeeding years, £2,000 in 1867, £4,000 in 1868, £3,000 in 1869, £2,000 in 1870 and a final £1,000 in 1871.
6   Second Report, Vol. 1, p. 535.

attitudes of the Irish railway companies. Crilly noted that flax could be carried from Riga on the Baltic to Belfast for just twopence (2d) per cwt more than it would cost from Dunleer.[7]

Undismayed by former failures or present difficulties, the co-operators resolved to *do* something. Frank Barbour employed a travelling instructor in County Mayo, worked personally with a number of farmers in County Down, and got excellent results. He also visited the Tullamore area to guide some interested farmers there whose interest had been aroused by master-farmer, George de Belle Ball, founder of the Ballinagore Co-op. On 7 June 1900, a great conference of flax-growers and spinners was held in the boardroom of the Chamber of Commerce in Belfast where every aspect of the industry was debated in exhaustive detail.[8]

As a result of this conference, four co-operative flax societies were formed and an organiser, John Hull, was appointed. The rules adopted by the co-operative agricultural societies were deemed to meet the requirements of the flax societies and it was hoped that many of them would also engage in agricultural business. The new societies at Broughshane (County Antrim), Dromara (County Down), and Boghill and Dunboe (County Londonderry) went into action in the autumn of 1900. This extract from the report of the Dunboe Society (fifty members) illustrates the methods of approach.

At the commencement of the scutching season 1900-01 a scutch mill was rented by the Dunboe Co-operative Flax Society and workmen engaged to scutch the flax grown by the members of the Society and work was commenced on September 3rd, 1900. From that date until March 9th 1901, the mill was kept fully occupied; 47 tons of flax were scutched producing 25 tons 15 cwts of flax, which was sold in the public market, and realised £1,719 9s 7d. The highest price obtained was 74/- per cwt. and lowest 54/-; the average for all was 66s 10d per cwt. The above flax was the produce of 75 bags of flax seed, the yield per bag being 6 cwts 3 qrs 13 lbs. The amount spent on wages was £185 15s 5d.

The tow made in scutching was bulked together and sold by tender; £82 7s 6d, being the highest, was accepted.

After deducting the expenses of saving the tow, the balance was divided up amongst the members whose flax was scutched in the mill and the division came to 17/- per bag of flax seed sown.

Arrangements have been concluded with the Department of Agriculture and Technical Instruction to carry out a series of trials of flax seeds and manures, and a field belonging to Mr George Kane was selected and approved of by the Department's Inspector and has been

---

7 See Lionel Smith-Gordon and F. Cruise O'Brien, *Co-operation in Ireland*, op. cit., p. 68: "One linen spinning firm in Belfast stated that flax could be brought from Belgium for 26/- to 28/- per ton whilst the carriage from some places in Ireland to Belfast costs 45/- per ton."
8 See Annual Report of IAOS 1900, pp. 83-108.

laid out into nine different plots — four for seed trials and five for manure trials. Arrangements have been made with the Department to allow one of their Flax experts, Mr de Zeeuw, to remain in the district for another season.

The Dunboe co-operators declared that imported Dutch seed had proved to be significantly better than the seed obtainable locally. The IAWS undertook to stock and provide seed of the finest quality but many farmers were reluctant to pay a higher price. There was nothing against the saving of home-grown seed provided that it was of good origin and had been cleaned and stored properly to ensure purity and germination at sowing time. The Flax Association strongly advocated this approach, noting that farmers were losing up to £200,000 per annum by not saving the seed before processing the fibre.

Despite the propaganda of the Association, the IAOS and the Department, flax-growing was hard to popularise. Farmers said it was all very fine for academic gentlemen to talk and write about it, but *who* had to do the back-breaking work of sowing, weeding and pulling? Who had the stinking work of retting and the 101 laborious chores before they had a few stone of fibre and tow for sale? And then, who made the money but the buyers and the spinners? — that was why they urged the farmers to grow it! The farmers saw many snags. Flax was hard on land;[9] it could only be grown successfully in an eight- or nine-year rotation, and was subject to diseases and very susceptible to the weather. The big trouble was the strenuous labour and, even if one could employ help, it was difficult to get labourers who were skilled and careful (an immense amount of damage was done by careless pulling). E.T. Herdman said: "A large scutch millowner told me lately it was impossible for him to get his flax properly pulled, the people were so careless. Flax should be pulled in small handfuls, and the retts kept perfectly straight; the class of people who pull the crop won't take the trouble to do this; consequently there is great loss in the value of the flax."[10]

Farmers were annoyed because the Ulster tradition of sowing down land to grass and clover with the flax crop was now being deplored as a "most injurious practice" and the experts were recommending that "clover must precede the flax by two seasons, that is clover followed by barley and flax gives the best flax fibre."[11] Indeed some authorities were suggesting an

9 Despite Professor Johnson's (of the Science and Art Museum, Dublin) assurance that, since flax fibre and flax oil were mostly carbohydrate, they built up their substance from air and water and took very little from the soil. Nitrogen manuring was very important to induce growth, as was potash to avoid yellowing of the stalks. There would be a loss of plant foods from the soil by drainage and leaching but the growing of flax did not impoverish the soil. Some farmers were of the opinion that if they top-dressed their land with 'flax water' from the retting dams, they would restore some of its strength. E. T. Herdman said that this was nonsense: flax water contained nothing but decaying proteins and fermented gum, but, presumably because it smelled so badly, farmers felt that it was bound to be beneficial!

10 A verbatim report of the Flax Conference in Belfast, 7 June 1900.

11 ibid., Professor Johnson.

even more revolutionary change: that the farmer should merely provide the land to grow flax. In Belgium the flax was bought while growing, and persons other than the growers carried on the subsequent processes; this produced a good quality standard product. In Ireland, however, where each individual farmer did his own pulling, retting, grassing and drying, there were as many variations in home-grown flax as there were in home-made butter.[12]

If progress in flax-growing was slow, the development of co-operativisation was even slower. The Broughshane and Boghill Societies disbanded, Dromora and Dunboe grew slowly and no new societies were set up until 1904 when small operations started at Macosquin and Glens of Antrim. The following year saw a cluster of four new societies in the Lagan area of County Donegal — Castlefin, River Finn, Stranorlar and Letterkenny — with another adjacent at Urney, County Tyrone. Societies began to see the need for a federation, and an agent was employed in Belfast to sell on behalf of the flax societies. It was hoped that they would federate with the IAWS and that that body would establish a special department to deal with their business. Unfortunately this never happened. The co-op societies scutched 5,238 cwts of flax in 1906-07 and had a total turnover of £14,667. Statistical returns for 1906 show that 55,171 acres of flax were grown in Ireland, giving an estimated fibre yield of 11,812 tons — an average of some 34½ stones per acre. Growing was largely concentrated in Ulster: Counties Antrim, Down, Derry and Tyrone averaged approximately 10,000 acres each. Donegal grew 6,000 acres, Armagh 5,300, Monaghan 2,500 and Cavan 1,200; Fermanagh, a county of little tillage, grew only 209 acres, yet this exceeded the total acreage outside Ulster. Cork was the only Munster county which grew an appreciable amount of flax — 76 acres, chiefly in the Rosscarbery district. Leinster also totalled 76 acres, mostly in Louth and Meath, whilst Mayo grew 40 of Connaught's 50 acres. The Mayo acreage was concentrated in the area from Ballina to Kilalla. Of the country's 682 scutch mills in 1906, only nine were co-operatively worked and only eight of the total number were outside Ulster — two each in Counties Louth, Meath, Cork and Mayo. Six new societies were formed in 1907, two in Donegal, one in Tyrone, two in Armagh and one close by in County Monaghan.[13]

A depression in the spinning trade in 1908 set matters back considerably. The promising Dunboe Society was forced into liquidation and total trade turnover of the flax societies was a mere £17,000, representing the sale of only 6,000 cwts of flax. Acreage of flax was down in 1909 and a bad season of poor yields did not help matters. The agency in Belfast was discontinued but the newly-established Belfast Co-operative Flax Growers Society later

12 "Whether the introduction of co-operative methods will ever restore this branch of the farmers' industry to its former position remains to be seen; but the conditions which have brought about the decline in flax growing appear to resemble very closely those which led to the decline in home buttermaking." (R. A. Anderson, in a paper on "Co-operative Agriculture", read at the International Co-operative Congress in Hamburg, 1910).

13 Pluck and Swilly Valley (County Donegal), Ardstraw (County Tyrone), Tassagh (County Armagh), and Fane Valley (County Monaghan).

took on some of its functions. In 1910, however, there was an encouraging upswing both in the price and acreage of flax.

The Urney Society's mill was burned down. There was no insurance cover, but the members won praise and fame for coming forward with money and voluntary labour to restore their assets. Other societies also were finding it difficult to survive and felt the need to be involved in other business, for co-operative spirits were inclined to sag during the inactivity of the off-season. Castlefin was fortunate that it had a profitable sideline in corn milling, but it was clear that most societies would have to engage in agricultural trading if they were to be able to retain and pay good management and staff. The IAOS suggested that, if it supplied seeds, manures, feeding-stuffs and machinery to its members, this would be a beneficial service, and it was making inquiries about a flax-pulling machine of American invention. Many societies expressed dissatisfaction with the Department of Agriculture's slowness in providing training for mill managers. A limited number had been trained under the extended scheme of the Department's advisory committee on flax, but it was felt increasingly that with Plunkett gone, his successor, vice-president Russell, was dragging his heels on this and other schemes which might help the co-operative sector.

Some farmers saw Russell in a more sinister role, setting his departmental inspectors to harass co-operative flax-growers over flax-water prosecutions. It was forbidden by law to release water from a flax dam into a river or stream in such a manner as to cause pollution and endanger fish life. The strict letter of the law forbade any discharge of flax water into a river even when the dilution factor was large enough to render the effluent completely harmless. In fact, legal action was rarely taken except in cases where there was gross and obvious pollution and evidence of dead fish, but many farmers claimed that, since the accession of Russell, an unduly severe line was being taken. Whether by coincidence or otherwise, there were a large number of flax-water prosecutions in Ulster in 1908 and 1909. Undoubtedly there were many instances of extensive pollution but, on the other hand, there were claims that people were being brought to court on tenuous evidence and for trivial infringements. Many also maintained that water bailiffs and owners of fishing rights were being moved to act differentially against members of co-operative flax societies.

The flax co-operators were frustrated because they had still made no progress in marketing. Buyers and jobbers hung around the scutch mills buying individual parcels of flax in much the same way as the butter buyers and egg higglers operated at the crossroads and country pubs. It was obvious that a good deal of high quality flax was not getting anything near its true price by being sold in this fashion, but the dealers were always able to purchase enough flax from non-members (and even many Society members) to frustrate any attempt at organised co-operation in open marketing or even local auction sales.

The period of stagnation continued well into the years of World War I. No new society was formed until Garvagh (County Derry) was established in 1914, but flax acreage continued to decline and the shortage of labour was considered a major limiting factor. Four flax societies — River Finn, Stranorlar, Pluck (County Donegal) and Fyfin (County Armagh) — were discontinued in 1915 but in that same year a new flax society at Avoca, County Wicklow, was looked on as a hopeful pioneering effort in a new area.[14] Wartime scarcities were beginning to tell and the acreage of flax increased spectacularly in 1916. It was reported that the Avoca Society and five others in the North[15] owned their own scutch mills. Labour problems were accentuated, particularly in Ulster, by the large numbers joining the Army, but the price of flax rose to unprecedented heights which, despite all difficulties, ensured an increasing acreage. There was an insatiable demand for flax and linen fabric for the building of aeroplane bodies. Aircraft technology was still in its infancy and the development of spotter and fighter planes demanded a fabric which was at once extremely light and tremendously durable, to improve speed and load capacity in planes which had to be powered by fairly primitive engines. Ten new flax societies were founded in 1917-18, including one at Ballinacarriga (County Cork), and by the end of 1918 there were twenty-nine co-operative flax societies in business.[16] The government had made an order that seed should be saved from one-eighth of the flax crop. This was regarded as a necessary and sensible decision. The IAOS regretted that the seed from the remaining seven-eighths, value for at least £500,000, should be allowed to go into the flax dams, a total waste in a country grievously short of protein feeding-stuffs. Linseed meal was excellent stuff for calves, cattle and dairy cows and could do much to enhance winter milk production.

A conference of delegates, representing twenty-five flax societies,[17] expressed considerable dissatisfaction with the workings of the regulations governing the grading and sale of flax. The co-operators called on the government to advance the price of all flax by 10/- per stone and set a minimum price of 45/- per stone. This was felt necessary because, despite the already high price of flax, the growing of the crop was so difficult that farmers were becoming increasingly interested in the inflated prices being offered for oats and potatoes. To overcome some local irregularities, it was recommended that government flax-graders not be employed in their home districts and that producers as well as spinners have some say in the selection of graders. It was strongly argued that the retaining of tow by

---

14 This co-operative was founded on the initiative of a local farmer, Joseph A. Crammond, who held office as secretary and treasurer of the society. Some seventy acres of flax were grown in the district and scutching was in charge of John Gowan from the Omagh area of County Tyrone. The original scutch mill, operated by an oil engine, was erected in the townland of Ballamurtagh but was transferred later to Avoca village where the machinery was driven by water power.

15 Castlefin, Garvagh, Letterkenny, Swilly Valley and Urney.

16 Newcomers included Annahilt, Drumgooland, Draperhill, Loughislandreevy, Rosconnor, Silverford (County Down); Omagh (County Tyrone) in 1917; Camlough, Diamond, Hilltown, Mayobridge (County Down); Ballinderry, Tullyinkesay (County Derry); Convoy, Raymockey (County Donegal); Seskinore, Caulfield (County Tyrone); Castleblayney, Clones (County Monaghan) and Killylea (County Armagh) in 1918. With the exception of the Wicklow and Cork societies, all twenty-nine societies were in Ulster.

17 Held in Belfast on 14 December 1917.

scutch mill-owners, as part payment for scutching, should be made illegal and the government was asked to fix a fair price for scutching and advise on the best methods "of handling and dealing with tow at the scutch mills and the marketing of the finished article."[18]

The flax societies gained representation in 1918 on both the Flax Supplies Committee and the Department of Agriculture Flax Advisory Committee and efforts were made to remedy many of the organisational defects. Unfortunately, in 1918 some crops failed completely and generally there were poor yields. The next was a better year and co-op turnover jumped from £21,300 to £47,791. Two new societies[19] brought the total to thirty-one with a membership of 2,531 and paid-up share capital of approximately £10 per man (£26,581). This proved to be the peak year of activity for the co-operative flax societies. In 1920 — a year of bad flax and economic depression — although there were six more flax societies registered,[20] turnover was down to £34,126 and nineteen societies suffered a loss on the year's working. The others made only tiny profits. Castleblayney, the society with the largest membership (308), recorded a loss of £1,175 on a turnover of £1,467. In contrast the biggest profit was Urney's £218. There was a further disastrous drop of 35 per cent. in trade turnover in 1921. Along with depressed prices, the quality of the flax was poor — attributable partly to a poor season and in many cases to the use of inferior seed. Indicative of the scale of price decline was flax tow: at the height of the market it had been making up to £220 per ton; now it was being disposed of at £25. The prices being offered for flax fibre were so poor that many farmers chose to hold on and not sell at all. This created difficulties for the mills since it proved very hard to collect scutching and cleaning fees from clients who had not succeeded in selling their produce.

Turnover dropped again to £18,234 in 1922 and the IAOS (itself in serious financial trouble) was distraught with the problems of insolvent flax societies, many of which had been formed in 1919 and 1920 and were now discovered to have committed themselves to contracts before they registered.[21] By 1923 turnover was down to £12,165. This total was made up from the seventeen societies out of twenty-five in Northern Ireland which made returns of £9,054, and five out of nine in Saorstát Eireann which made £3,111 (Avoca's trade was the £111). Ballinacarriga,

---

18 Other resolutions called for the control of the price and distribution of flax seed, proper arrangements for weighing, and the exemption of small growers (sowing one bushel or less of seed) from the seed-saving ordinance — this latter because the threshing caused some deterioration in the value of the flax straw.

19 Foreglen (County Derry) and Strule Valley (County Tyrone).

20 Carnteel (County Tyrone), Clough (County Antrim), Dernaflow & Dungiven (County Derry), Millvale (County Down) and Mullyard (County Armagh). The sixth society was a historically notable but short-lived venture at Easkey, County Sligo — the only co-operative flax society in Connaught. In 1920 the thirty-seven societies (membership 3,504) owned buildings and plant worth approximately £60,000 and held reserves totalling £8,822.

21 "The fosterage was no doubt unavoidable but it attached a nominal responsibility where neither power to direct the future of the societies nor any legal authority to see that they were properly capitalised and adequately equipped for their functions existed, and it was to that extent inexpedient." (IAOS Annual Report 1923, p. 18).

Castleblayney, Clones and Swilly Valley made no returns and disappeared. The Donegal societies struggled on for a number of years but gradually folded up or passed into private ownership.[22]

In 1924 there was a slightly larger acreage of flax grown (53,000) but it was noticeably retracted into the strongest traditional flax-growing areas. The principal drawback facing co-operative development at this period seems to have been the impossibility of insuring flax mills against fire. Linen goods were now selling at little more than the price of cotton and it was hoped that this might favour the flax-growers if only co-operative production and marketing could be organised. Alex Hasslett of Glaslough and others made trojan efforts to resurrect the industry in the Free State but the political border made an already difficult task more formidable and the activity inexorably tightened into Ulster and the manufacturing hinterland. Even there co-operative flax-growing made little impact. In 1926, of sixteen flax societies in Northern Ireland, only nine were working and no more than three of these showed a profit. The UAOS reported that it was "hopeless to expect any improvement in these societies so long as the depression in the linen trade continues."[23] Good flax was selling for as little as 10/- per stone and flax acreage in Northern Ireland in 1927 was the lowest for twenty years.[24] It rose somewhat in 1928 as prices hardened, but the recovery was short-lived and by 1931 it was down to 7,000 acres. In Saorstát Eireann the decline was even steeper — from 10,000 acres in 1925 to 647 acres in 1931. By 1932 only seven flax co-ops survived — Camlough, Maydown and Mullyard (County Armagh), Millvale and Silverford (County Down), and Arboe and Strule Valley in Tyrone, the county of the forty co-operative creameries.

In the desperate years of the Economic War, farmers in Donegal, Cavan, Monaghan and west Cork turned once more to try their hand at flax-growing and by 1936 acreage had expanded to 5,118. In that year the Flax Act fixed a standard price for flax and the Minister for Agriculture was enabled to pay a bounty to cover any disparity between the average price obtained by growers and the standard price. After 1936, however, the flax acreage went into decline once more. The price obtained by growers never dropped below the standard price and, when the Act was suspended in 1939, there had been no expenditure on bounties. There was some upsurge in flax-growing during the war years but, largely because of the shortage of labour and the compulsory tillage orders, which compelled farmers to till up to three-eighths of their arable acreage[25] with the emphasis on food crops, little attention could be given to flax-growing. Nevertheless, flax acreage in the Free State expanded from 4,000 acres in 1939 to a peak

22 The Raymockey and Convoy societies, however, survived until the late nineteen forties. Although the Avoca society ceased to operate in 1923, its affairs were not wound up until 1935.
23 UAOS Annual Report 1926, p.19.
24 32,322 acres. The average acreage in Northern Ireland for the years 1904-1914 was 50,000.
25 The requirements were gradually raised from one-eighth of the arable land of ten acres and over in 1940 to three-eighths in 1944, with an allowance for tillage land newly laid down to grass. From 1944 also it became compulsory to grow wheat, the quota varying from one-tenth to one-twenty-fifth of the arable land.

of almost 33,000 acres in 1945, and in Northern Ireland increased from 21,000 in 1939 to a spectacular 124,000 in 1946. North or South, very little of the war-time flax was handled co-operatively. The co-operative creameries at Barryroe, Drinagh and Lisavaird (County Cork) and Lough Egish (County Monaghan) made arrangements for scutching flax. The old co-operative scutch mills at Convoy and Raymockey in Donegal were briefly revived. The far-seeing manager of the Lough Egish society, John Daly, acquired a large quantity of flax seed in Britain immediately before the outbreak of war and the profits acquired from its flax venture helped the society to instigate larger-scale developments in other fields in the post-war period. The last mention of co-operative flax societies in Northern Ireland is in the 1940 Annual Report of the UAOS, which showed that Mullyard and Arboe did business and made a small profit.[26]

After the war, the acreage of flax dwindled as continental and Russian flax became cheaply available. Many people are now concerned that the Northern Ireland linen industry should at least have some skeleton organisation of mechanised flax-growing which could be expanded in the event of this imported fibre becoming unavailable. Researches during the nineteen sixties by An Foras Talúntais (The Agricultural Institute) indicated that County Cork was probably the optimum location for producing the biggest yields of best quality flax.

The initiative to revive flax-growing, however, was taken by Bunclody Co-operative Agricultural Society in County Wexford. Pulling was done by machines and the flax mechanically laid in swaths to dew-ret (ret in the dew by the action of fungi from the soil on the plant).[27] Field work was fully mechanised, even to the extent of using an ordinary farm baler rather than the traditional sheaf or bundle in which all straws were kept parallel.

A modern scutching plant was erected at Bunclody to scutch the flax straw on the 'Lin-Total' system. Previous systems had been on the 'Line Fibre' principle, where parallelisation of the fibres was essential. In the Lin-Total system there was no division between 'Line' and 'Tow', just the total processing of the fibre into one mass.

A good start was made. Two-hundred and fifty acres were grown in 1969, 400 in 1970, 650 in 1971. Then a decline set in because of the inability of the processing plant to handle the crop quickly enough. Growers got restive about having a crop on their hands beyond the normally expected span. Farm storage was inadequate and poor, and storage provision at the processing plant was not available.

It all need not have occurred. Revival was hampered at a time when market outlets were abundant. The produce of thousands of acres could be used and at prices which were sufficiently attractive to be interesting for a much bigger development. It would be a pity if the shortage of capital for investment in the project should be the impeding factor, just as new

---

26 Mullyard: turnover £656, profit £141; Arboe: turnover £565, profit £53.
27 Dew-retting is often looked upon as a very modern technique but the late Professor J. B. Ruane of University College Dublin gave me clear evidence of its use by the well-known co-operator, Lord Cloncurry, in the early days of the century, at Lyons estate, Celbridge.

methods, new markets and new uses were emerging.

The crop is still being grown and processed. Yet the quantity of it available is a contentious subject. It has become a large and mechanised enterprise for the bigger farmer. Today's competitors are not the cotton-pickers of Alabama but the multi-national combines who produce synthetic fibres for an international market. At the time of writing, the future of Bunclody flax-growing is one of considerable doubt.

The impact of co-operative ventures on the industry was never more than minimal and there was an almost complete failure to popularise the growing of flax outside the traditional flax areas of the North, particularly in Connaught where it was most needed. The efforts in Wicklow and Cork were heroic but ill-fated. Even in the midlands where, in the later half of the nineteenth century, Perrys, the flourmillers, had a flax mill on the Brosna, the revival of flax-growing failed to materialise. Perhaps if the dynamic George de Belle Ball had not moved to Dublin (Lissan Hall, Swords) and died soon afterwards, things might have been different. As it is, the only memory is that in the ballad[28] of the redoubtable women of Ballinagore and Cloonagh who sallied forth to pull the Perrys' flax — the contrived rivalry traditionally exploited by employers in the interests of high productivity but which perhaps for everyone concerned helped to bring some light-relief to the back-breaking chore of pulling flax by hand:

It was on a Monday morning, we left our own abode;
We travelled on together, along the King's High Road;
We travelled on together, although 'twas some way round;
That brought us to the flax that grew on Thomas Cowley's ground.
Just as we entered in the field, ould Hughes to us did say,
'Come on my girls and hurry up or you'll be bet today;
Last night I met the women, and those Cloonagh women swore;
They'd send you home disgraceful, to the street of Ballinagore'.

28 Courtesy of Mr Matt Daly, Ballinagore, per Miss K. Flynn, Kilbeggan.

Chapter Seventeen

Home Industries Societies

As a consequence of the industrial revolution and the factory system, cottage industries and crafts were in serious decline in the eighteen nineties. The quality of many handcrafted articles was deteriorating and some of the more artistic Irish crafts were in danger of extinction. Benevolent ladies, such as Lady Aberdeen and Lady Beatrix Cadogan, sought to remedy the decline through associations like the Irish Industries League and the Royal Irish Industries Association.[1] The nationalists for the most part regarded these genteel organisations as 'society playthings'[2] but, concurrent with the Gaelic and the literary revivals, there was a rising nationalist feeling for the revival of native Irish industry and crafts. Plunkett found Lady Aberdeen an enthusiastic and formidable ally — rather scatter-brained and requiring tactful handling but influential.[3]

For the co-operative movement there was a double incentive to organise societies for the promotion of cottage industries and home crafts: many small farms were moribund and in sore need of additional income, and the creamery movement was being blamed for taking away employment from farmers wives and 'forcing' their daughters to emigrate.

In 1896 two co-operative home industries societies were established — in totally different environs: one in Ballinagleragh, County Leitrim, and the other attached to the Loreto Convent, Dalkey, County Dublin.[4] M.D. Flynn, who with the local curate, Rev M. McTernan, had helped to

1 Also deeply concerned in the RIIA were the Countess of Dudley, the Countess of Mayo, Lady Arnott, Madame de Bunsen, Lady Jaffe, Mrs John Jameson, Miss Goodbody, Mrs C.L. Loftus Townshend, Mrs D.S. Bolger and Colonel and Mrs Nugent T. Everard.
2 "Just as Mr Bung may like to put a little ointment on his troubled conscience by subscribing a sovereign to a charity, a great many of the landlord class in this country . . . like to toy with the 'royal' Irish Industry Society . . . and, of course, where a countess is, there shall mesdames, on the climb, be gathered together. Lady Aberdeen takes a great interest in this industrial plaything. We freely give her the credit of meaning well." (D.P. Moran, *Leader* magazine, September 1905).
3 Irreverently known as 'Blowsy Bella', Lady Aberdeen played a leading role in organising the Irish Village at the Chicago World Fair (See Digby, *Horace Plunkett*, pp.58,74). In England the Womens' Co-operative Guild had been founded in 1883 with the object of organising women as co-operators. A Scottish Guild was established in 1892 with an associated Irish Guild. The Irish Guild became independent in 1907 and received an annual grant of £15 from the Co-operative Union.
4 Lady Betty Balfour, wife of the Chief Secretary, published an article on the Dalkey Society in *The Irish Homestead*, 27 February 1897.

organise the Ballinagleragh Society, gave an interesting outline of its works and hopes:

> My Society has already taken up one branch, that of lace-making, and ... the Irish Industries Association have very opportunely come to our assistance in the beginning... I consider that it would be very desirable if the skill already possessed in crochet, sewing and knitting could be turned to account while awaiting higher things. What is wanted is some plan to bring remote districts into touch with a market for the articles thus produced; and in this connection I think it should be possible to further educate the public taste to recognise the superiority, in many cases, of handmade goods. Another industry which would be very suitable in our district is wickerwork and basket making and, in reference to this and woodcarving, a resolution was passed at the district conference asking for the appointment of instructors in this... In my district, a congested one, owing to the poverty of the soil and the smallness of the holdings, the earnings from cottage industries are very much needed to supplement the returns from the land, which alone is quite inadequate to afford a living to the people.[5]

In 1898 five further home industries societies were formed — at Leighlinbridge (County Carlow), Youghal (County Cork), Carrickmacross (County Monaghan), Kilmuckridge (County Wexford) and Crossmaglen (County Armagh). "The object of these Societies", wrote Anderson, "is not so much to provide a living wage for the workers, but to find them pleasant and profitable employment in their own homes, and to supplement such scanty and precarious earnings or income as the population in poor districts have hitherto been forced to subsist upon."[6] The membership was composed mainly of women and girls, especially in the societies which concerned themselves with feminine crafts, lace, crochet and knitting, but in those Victorian days the ladies still considered it advisable to have some men on the committee of management, particularly to guide them in organisational and business matters. Membership was made as easy as possible, the taking of one five shillings share, of which only one-fourth had to be paid. The rules were generally the same as those governing agricultural societies, with a number of special ones in addition:

> The special rules of these societies state that 'the objects of the society shall be to develop and improve among the members of the society home industries, such as poultry and egg production, pig rearing, knitting, lacemaking and needlework of all kinds, weaving,

5　Second Annual Conference, Dublin, 10 November 1896.
6　IAOS Annual Report 1898, p.15. Population density in the Congested Districts was still extremely high in some places, despite the considerable emigration which was taking place — 413,516 persons during the ten years ended 1902.

woodcarving or any other industry which may be suitably carried on in the homes of the members; to provide them with the material and appliances for them; to obtain a market for their produce, and to save for them the profits derived from its sale. One half of the net profits of the societies, after paying 5 per cent upon capital, is to be carried to a reserve fund until this equals the share capital, and the remaining profit is to be divided amongst the members in proportion to their wages earned, their sales through or purchases from the society. No proportion of the net profits, however, except interest on share and loan capital, is to be allotted in cash until such time as the available cash surplus of the society is in excess of its liabilities'.[7]

The inclusion of pig and poultry enterprises is legally significant in that it permitted home industries societies to engage in these activities. In practice very few societies did, although, for a time, a number of poultry societies did incorporate a home industry society. Members were encouraged to engage in poultry and pig-keeping (then very much woman's work) on an individual basis.

The early promoters of home industries had misgivings that overemphasis on the production of craft work for sale might lead to a deterioration in the standard of housekeeping and general domestic economy. With this in mind the Congested Districts Board and the Department of Agriculture incorporated instruction in domestic economy in their training of female craftworkers. There were some complaints that the training in cookery and housework only 'spoiled the hands' of trainee lacemakers. However, most good lacemakers were good homemakers also.

In the co-operative home industries societies, Plunkett hoped that there would be a sensible balance between the production of articles produced for home needs and those produced to earn income. Of the goods produced for sale, he pointed out the distinction between articles which relied on their artistic merit (lace, crochet, embroidery) and those which would have to compete with the commercial machine-made equivalent,[8] and carefully explained the marketing difficulties that would be encountered in each case.

Such problems arose almost immediately. In 1898 the Irish Lace Depot in Dublin co-operated with the IAOS to purchase all the lace available but, since the number of societies grew to seventeen a year later[9] and products were diversified, the problem became severe. The Irish Industries Association furnished a depot in the shop and basement of 21 Lincoln Place[10] and also undertook to establish a wholesale agency to dispose of

---

7 Catherine Webb, *Industrial Co-operation*, op.cit., p.163.
8 See also an article by George Fletcher [FGS], "Rural Industries and Home Life" in *Rural Life and Industry* (Dublin: Hely Ltd, 1907) in connection with the Irish International Exhibition 1907.
9 New societies were Killian, Clifden, Rosmuc, Carna, Carraroe (County Galway); Pullathomas (County Mayo); Moan Cross, Brookeboro' (County Fermanagh); and Coonian (County Tyrone).
10 The premises were shared by *The Irish Homestead*, then registered as the Irish Co-operative Newspaper Society Ltd. The IAOS had just moved its headquarters from 2

craft goods. They were not outstandingly successful despite the fact that much embroidery and lace was being imported and it should have been possible to replace some of these by comparable Irish products. The Irish Co-operative Needlework Depot at 33 Dawson Street was somewhat more successful, at least in the short term. This society was formed in 1898 expressly for the purpose of instructing home industry societies in needlework, crochet and lacemaking and subsequently for disposing of the goods on the societies' behalf. It continued to provide a useful service until it was forced into liquidation in 1908.

In addition to the marketing difficulty, there was a critical need for technical training. Without qualified instructors, the work produced was necessarily of very elementary technique and uninspiring design; even when it was saleable, the price was low and the hours of work comparatively ill-rewarded. As new societies continued to spring up, [11] the IAOS appointed Miss L. Reynolds as organiser of home industries, who did valuable work in training the new recruits, with the aid of some elderly ladies who were already experts in traditional lace and crochet work (at Limerick, Carrickmacross and Innismacsaint). The newly-formed Department of Agriculture and Technical Instruction was besieged with requests for the necessary technical instruction. The Department expressed its readiness to help to finance instruction for societies which could show that their enterprise was worthy and likely to prove economically successful. In most cases it was impossible to present any such proof, for in many places the home industry society had been founded on nothing more definite than "a vague desire for employment on the part of the would-be workers".[12] With the best will in the world, the amount of instruction and organisation was always much less than required, and there were other equally intractable problems:

> There is no department of the work of the IAOS which is more important or indeed so difficult as the organisation of Home Industries ... Every new district entered has its own problem. The creameries over Ireland vary little in their construction and the organiser with little differences repeats in one district the work

St Stephen's Green to 22 Lincoln Place, after a short period of temporary accommodation in 29 South Frederick Street. The very first offices of the IAOS had been two small rooms on an upper floor at the corner of Trinity Street and College Green. The Lincoln Place premises were commodious but suffered from being next door to the Dental Hospital and backing on the Pathology Laboratory of Trinity College. Anderson commented on the harrowing shrieks of dental patients recovering from anaesthesia and the gruesome sights of corpses being dissected in the Pathology Lab.

11 Beechmount (County Sligo) and Monaghan in 1899. Tissara, Castlebellingham, Clogherhead, Dunleer, St Raphael's (Galway), Loughrea, St Josephs (County Tipperary), Mullafarry (County Mayo), Gort, Manorhamilton, Kildallon, Bundoran, Ballyshannon, Derrylin, Clones, Dartry (County Leitrim) and Cruagh Home Industry Society (County Dublin) in 1900. Mourne Abbey, Carrigeen, Achonry, Augher, Ballinanard and Crumlin in 1901.

12 IAOS Annual Report 1902, p.23. Switzer's, Arnott's and Clery's, Dublin, as well as Morton-White's Belfast, were fairly sizeable buyers of good quality lace and crochet at this time, but their biggest demand was for more intricate designs. Consequently, it often proved difficult to sell the simpler work of trainee lacemakers.

accomplished in another. But this is impossible with Home Industries. The multiplication of Societies with identical products would defeat the purpose and lower the price obtainable. There is no such continuous market for lace, crochet, embroidery, knitted work and other like product as there is for butter and poultry, and a very little increase in the number of workers in lace or embroidery will cause over-production and a fall in price. Again the varied character of the products is rather a bar to the federation of Home Industries Societies for the purpose of joint sale . . . Yet without a federation, the local Societies are continually at a loss for the means of disposal of their work. The shops afford only an intermittent means of sale . . . While this is so, it is yet out of the question to start a Federation without a large capital of several thousands of pounds, which could never be supplied by the workers themselves. The workers require to be paid cash, for they cannot afford to wait months for the returns from sale and up to the present it is impossible to find any source from which capital could be drawn to finance such a Federation. A great part of the time of the IAOS industries organiser is spent in trying to find markets . . . It is comparatively easy to get workers . . . but it is much more difficult to find industries which can be successfully established in a country without the habits of industrial life, where the workers have no technical or manual training, nor the instruction in drawing or design which is so important in all industries into which art or taste enter; and if these difficulties are surmounted the all-important problem of market cries for solution.

Nothing is more heartbreaking than to educate workers in an industry with the hope of bettering their condition and then to find the product unsaleable, not because there is no demand for it, but because there is no channel by which the workers can get into contact with those who might purchase.[13]

Yet, despite these difficulties, some progress was made. By 1901 there were thirty-eight home industries societies and a year later the number had risen to fifty,[14] with almost 3,000 members and a trade turnover of nearly £12,000. Earnings of women and girls ranged from 5 to 15 shillings per week from such activities as embroidery, sprigging, knitting and weaving (which also employed some men). The products ranged from small articles in crochet lace, point lace and drawn thread-work, to clerical vestments, underclothing, hats, rugs and dolls. On the initiative of Sir Josslyn Gore-Booth and his enthusiastic sisters, a co-operative shirt factory was started in Sligo in 1901 and in August of the following year a co-operative boot factory opened in Ballina. Although the money seems tiny in present-day

13 IAOS Annual Report 1902, p.24.
14 Castlecomer, Carrick-on-Suir, Lough Egish, Dundalk, Bawnboy, St Macartans (County Tyrone) and St Brigids (County Leitrim) were founded in 1901; Ramelton, Boyle, Ballyconnell (County Cavan), Drumkeeran (County Leitrim), Mullabawn (County Louth), Donard (County Wicklow), Kinvara, Killanley (County Mayo), Stewartstown, Meath County (Navan), Naas and Bray in 1902.

terms, the weekly earnings were much appreciated at the time. There was a heartening story in the Annual Report of 1901 of a girl who earned £9 at lacemaking which enabled her to buy a cow for her father who was a small farmer in very poor circumstances.

> Some of the Societies pay several hundreds yearly to their workers, and though the total appears small, yet when a girl is enabled to earn seven or eight shillings weekly, it means often the difference between comfort and poverty in the small farmer's home. The work itself has a refining effect on the character; the production of a beautiful piece of lace or embroidery marks an epoch in the ordinary country girl's ideas and tastes. The disorder, slovenliness and squalor, too often met with in the Irish homestead, and hitherto accepted as a matter of course, become recognised as defects capable of remedy and the desire for neatness, order and cleanliness, insisted upon in the workroom, extends to the home. Here as in other branches of the IAOS work the indirect results, the reflex action upon character, are as important as the direct material gain for which the Societies are ostensibly organised. In former Reports reference was made to the effect of these little industries upon emigration, and the IAOS still continue to get cheering accounts of the way in which even a little employment here is preferred to the glittering lure and rush of life in the United States.[15]

Home industries societies reached their peak number[16] of fifty-five in 1904. They could have gone much higher but the IAOS exercised selectivity in registering new societies, seeking rather to improve the condition of the established ones. There was a fall in demand and price for Irish lace, and the IAOS professed itself scarcely equal to the job of organisation, but totally unfitted in funds or personnel for the task of investigating markets. The Society felt that market research abroad should best be undertaken by the Department of Agriculture and Technical Instruction, particularly since this Ministry, through its schemes with the county councils, was providing instruction in home-crafts which resulted in increasing demands on the IAOS to organise and register more home industries societies. There was no doubt but that a spirit had been awakened which could lead to a grand nation-wide revival of rural industries but, unless this enthusiasm was properly harnessed, the last condition of rural Ireland would be worse than the first.

Serious defects in these home industries societies were manifest. Standards tended to drop: inferior lace fetched a lower price but the

15 IAOS Annual Report 1902, p.25.
16 Societies formed in 1903 were Breffni (County Cavan), Lissan (County Tyrone), Moneyguyneen (County Offaly), Skreen and Dromard (County Sligo), New Ross, and an Art Furniture Guild in Dublin comprising eight members, previously registered (1901) as a miscellaneous society. 1904 saw the foundation in Dundrum of the Dun Emer Guild and the Dun Emer Art Industries Society, later to be renamed the Cuala Home Industries Society (1908) and to become famous in the world of art printing. Societies were also formed at Belleek and at Raferagh (County Monaghan), plus the Bray Co-operative Art Furniture Supply Company.

reaction of the home worker was often to turn out worse lace in less time to try to meet her weekly earning target. Many home workers also tended to work at their own convenience, so that the society often failed to deliver orders on time — a damning shortcoming which put many otherwise excellent societies out of business. Trying to raise the standard of workmanship was frustrating and teachers were often discouraged not only by the deficiencies of their pupils but by the fact that their own remuneration was often unsatisfactorily arranged:

> Under the county schemes, instruction in lace making is provided dependent on the attendance for instruction in cookery and other subjects, which is given free. The payment of the lace or other teacher being dependent on such instruction and certain conditions, the teacher often cannot get one penny of salary until after many months when the result of cookery instruction is known. If the conditions are not fulfilled, she gets no salary at all, unless it is provided out of the private purse of individuals or religious communities. It is to be hoped that a better system may be devised, which while dependent on attendance, and thereby forcing the local committees to see after the matter, will not leave the teacher in pecuniary difficulties and debt on account of her lodging.[17]

Father Matt Maguire, Dromore, (St McCartan's Home Industries Society), complained[18] that the county technical committee had not given his society (which employed from 160 to 200 girls at lace and crochet) the assistance they had expected. It was impossible to train girls in lacemaking within the designated period of eighteen months. "If it was possible", he stated, "they would have done it in the district of Dromore, where they had had good teaching and worked very assiduously."

For a while in 1905-06 prospects brightened. It was felt that the slump had passed, as crochet and, to lesser extent, lace sold steadily at greatly improved prices. Everybody spoke hopefully of the interest being aroused in France and America.[19] Orders from abroad were eagerly and quickly supplied with excellent goods but a few societies were none too scrupulous about unloading inferior work on the home market. Some societies urged their workers to great haste to fulfil large orders, yet, just as slump prices had formerly induced workers to lower standards and to turn out more

17 IAOS Annual Report 1904, p.22.
18 At the annual general meeting on 27 September 1904.
19 A number of societies sent exhibits to the International Exposition (World Fair) in St Louis, which opened on 11 June 1904. An exhibit of lace made by the Donard Home Industries Society won a silver medal. Highly commended was the work of Moneyguyneen Home Industries Society (Kinnity, County Offaly) which, like Donard, was a newly-formed society still at the learning stage: "About 30 young women, some of whom came five, six and seven miles, are in daily attendance from ten to three except on Saturdays when the classes close at one and they are turning out Clare embroidery and other articles for which there is an ever-open and ready market. A visit to the classrooms, with the bright and happy faces of the girls, the subdued hum of work being executed quickly and well and the prosperous air which pervades the place is indeed an inspiring sight." (Kings County Chronicle, quoted in The Irish Homestead, 31 December 1904).

goods to maintain the weekly income, some women now got greedy and rushed their work to make lace while the price shone!

Lace and crochet predominated and efforts at diversification met with tremendous difficulties. Simple articles in wood, metal and leather were saleable in small quantities, but anything of artistic quality had great difficulty in making a price which would reasonably remunerate the hours spent in producing it.

> The greatest difficulty is for the Art Industries, where work in copper, wood-carving, costly embroidery, rugs and products akin to these are produced, to find a market. Not enough work of each particular kind is produced in any of these Industries to make them well known, or make it worthwhile for any firm to push them or create any general demand. At a sale the exceptional beauty of the work may enable the industry to dispose temporarily of work at good prices, but these industries cannot afford to advertise themselves, or bring their products before the class of people who would gladly buy if they had knowledge of the excellent work done.[20]

Yet another helpful organisation was formed: the Irish Art Industries Association, registered as a co-operative society in 1905 to help the art industries to bring their work before the public. Through the kindly aid of Mr Gatty of the Irish Art Companions, the Association secured premises in Clare Street, Dublin. A counterpart association was founded in Belfast about the same time: the Irish Decorative Art Association, also registered as a co-operative in 1905 with a membership of nine and paid-up share capital of £280. Nevertheless, not a great deal of art work was produced nor was there any great diversification of crafts. Complementary to their lace and crochet production, a number of societies essayed dressmaking; the Queen purchased a beautiful silk frock made by the Moneyguyneen Society,[21] but dressmaking tended to become an individual rather than a co-operative enterprise and in the years preceding World War I rural Ireland had, if anything, too many dressmakers (and tailors) doing too little business in a country that had already too many small shopkeepers.

Good quality art furniture was produced by the Dublin and Bray furniture societies but output was small, as was that of the Kilkenny Co-operative Guild of Woodworkers,[22] a 'miscellaneous' society registered in 1905. The Dun Emer Guild under Miss Gleeson gained distinction in

---

20 IAOS Annual Report 1905, p.10.
21 See *The Irish Homestead*, 13 February 1904, p.133.
22 The Kilkenny Woodworkers Society was one of the many developments sponsored by Lady Desart, who also built a hospital (still retained as the Ait Aoibhinn hospital), a small village on the English style with its own water supply, a village hall, a ball-alley and later a hosiery factory. Lady Desart's benevolence was little appreciated. The local clergy denounced her and her brother-in-law as proselytisers and later in the nineteen twenties her house and the woodwork factory and sawmill were maliciously burned. The reasons for this latter "outburst of patriotic fever" are obscure. Although she was an ardent Gaelic Leaguer, Lady Desart was no politician. She wasn't even English, but an Austrian Jewess.

carpet weaving as did the Misses Yeats and their artistic companions with refined embroidery and art printing by Dun Emer (later Cuala) Art Industries. The Skreen and Dromard Society, County Sligo, showed good promise of producing a wide range of craft articles until it was incorporated in an agricultural store society in 1912 and the emphasis switched to male rather than female pursuits.[23] Very few societies developed worthwhile factory units of production, and of those which did, few lasted long. Although Youghal Society had sales of over £4,000 in 1910, its production was largely home based. The Breffni Society started work with twelve knitting machines in a small factory and for a few years provided full-time employment for up to thirty workers. The Ballina Co-operative Boot Manufacturing Society commenced operations in August 1902 but lasted for little more than two years.[24] At the end of the first year it was reported to be turning out 140 pairs of finished boots per week and providing employment for fifteen skilled workers and sixteen apprentices. The Sligo Manufacturing Society employed over seventy female workers at shirt-making, some of them earning up to 15 shillings per week, a considerable wage in 1902. The shirts were of first-class quality and were much admired at the exhibition of co-operative products at the Co-operative Congress in Doncaster in 1903. The society had a traveller in Dublin and sales hit a peak of £5,500 in 1905 but thereafter declined and the society was liquidated in 1907.

A few agricultural and dairies societies were fairly successful with manufacturing sidelines. Enniscorthy Co-operative Agricultural Society in the early days had often as many as thirty male workers on manufacturing projects: brass and nickel-mounted harness, saddles, bridles, pole-mountings, as well as simple farm equipment, wheelbarrows and feeding troughs. They also produced quality rugs from wool obtained locally from Clohamon Mills. As early as 1897 the Ballinagore Society (County Westmeath) was sending wool to Foxford and getting back finished products.[25] The Providence Woollen Mill at Foxford, founded by the Irish Sisters of Charity, although not a formal co-operative society, was largely co-operative in character and very much influenced by the personal help and guidance given by Father Tom Finlay.[26] It did excellent work in one of the poorest districts of the west and, as a soundly based rural industry, survives happily to the present day.

As the total number of co-operative societies approached 1,000 in 1907, the IAOS, beset by financial difficulties and short-staffed, could devote

23 This society subsequently went in for implement hire in a fairly big way during the war years.
24 The whole of the rate for technical instruction available in 1902 from the Urban District of Ballina was voted for instruction in boot-making. The Department of Agriculture and Technical Instruction encouraged and assisted the project.
25 There was a good co-operative community (poultry society, credit bank and so on) at Tagoat, County Wexford, which ran an agricultural show and sponsored needlework, weaving and all kinds of homecrafts.
26 The Congested Districts Board gave financial help to start the Foxford venture, as it did to the Ballinagleragh Home Industries Society and many other home industry societies throughout the congested districts.

little time to the problems of its womenfolk. Only one new home industries society was formed, Carrickmore in 1906, but many fell away so that by 1910 there were twenty societies left of which only seven made returns.[27] In that year Miss Reynolds went to work for the United Irishwomen and the general suggestion was that the home industries societies should follow her. No action was taken on the matter, presumably because the newly-founded United Irishwomen were extremely busy setting up their organisation. By 1913 the IAOS was showing some anxiety.[28]

> While reluctant to cut off from their programme of work ... the Committee feel that they are no longer justified in including the organisation and supervision of Home Industries Societies ... They wish, however, to repeat the suggestion that the supervision and organisation of these societies should be taken over by the United Irishwomen, in whose capable hands they feel confident that this branch of rural and co-operative organisation would be adequately provided for and rendered really fruitful. They are prepared by every means in their power to assist the United Irishwomen in the necessary work.[29]

The United Irishwomen, however, had even less money than the IAOS and as yet had not the prestige or the air of 'central authority' which would enable local ladies (often of the nobility) to organise other ladies of lesser rank who felt they knew at least as much as their advisers.[30] The IAOS Report of 1914 noted regretfully: "It was hoped that the United Irishwomen might have seen their way to take these societies over and infuse some life into them, but they seem to have regarded the task as hopeless."

The real death blow, however, came not from lack of organisation or guidance, but from rising prosperity. As farm prices improved, the womenfolk no longer felt the pressing need to supplement the farm income. Lace- and crochet-making was demanding work, hard on the eyes, and, because of its previous association with grinding poverty, many were glad to be rid of it. Beautiful craftwork still continued to evoke fine feelings in the female breast — but in genuine leisure time, as a hobby.

As previously noted, few home industries societies were financially or organisationally strong enough to put their industry on a really business-like footing. The major success story was Templecrone, where the astute

27 Total sales of these seven (excluding the Youghal Society) were £4,815.
28 In 1913, although there were still eighteen societies on the books, only four, Belfast, Moneyguyneen, New Ross and Bray Co-op Art Furniture, made financial returns.
29 IAOS Annual Report 1913, pp.25-26.
30 This superficial resentment, however, must be noted against a deeper contrary historical experience. In many areas during the famine years of the eighteen forties, the practice of lacemaking, crochet and embroidery, organised by the ladies of the Big House (wives, sisters and daughters of landlords) to alleviate distress, not only improved the condition of the people but helped to form lasting bonds of affection across the barriers of class and creed. The horrors of famine and pestilence drove women, more quickly than men, to find common cause and work together. See Mrs Meredith, *The Lacemakers* (London: Jackson, Walford and Hodder, 1865).

manager of a thriving agricultural co-op saw the potential of the female craft workers and took them in hand. Dungloe never had a formal home industries society but for generations the women in nearly every farm household in the Rosses were engaged in the production of knitted articles and other homecrafts for private firms. "These poor people", said Finlay, "were hitherto dependent upon home industries under conditions which it would not be unduly severe to describe as one of the worst forms of 'sweating'." Paddy the Cope had a hard look at the co-operative village hall which his society had won from the Pembroke Charities Trust[31] and which subsequently got him into 'dancing' trouble with the clergy. He persuaded his committee to equip the hall as a knitwear factory. At the IAOS annual general meeting on 12 December 1916, Finlay (vice-president) reported on progress and hammered home the co-operative moral:

They have shaken off that yoke and using their own efforts they have set up a factory, built and equipped by themselves where ninety-six girls are employed finishing the work, and hundreds more in the homes round about. Instead of the 5/- or 6/- a week which they had formerly earned under trying circumstances, these ninety-six girls now receive, as I saw by the pay-sheet, £101 per week. And they have succeeded because they do honest work. One of the men representing these workers went over to London lately and brought over an order for 5,000 dozen pairs of gloves. These workers in Dungloe are now invading the British market and are able to supply goods which

31 In 1908 the Pembroke Irish Charities Trustees decided to grant to the IAOS the sum of £1,500 towards the erection of six village halls in districts where co-operative societies had been instrumental in improving the social as well as the material well-being of the people. The offer of the Trustees was published in *The Irish Homestead* and, out of twenty-nine applicants, the IAOS selected six societies to receive grants of £200 each: Templecrone, Effin (County Limerick), Columbkille (County Longford), Kilskeery (County Tyrone), Whitecross (County Armagh) and Cushinstown (County Wexford).

formerly came from Germany. These people in the North have succeeded because they are imbued with the co-operative spirit. That society is affiliated to the IAOS and, considering the circumstances of the locality, the amount they subscribe[32] is perfectly amazing.

By 1917, although there were still nine home industries societies on the register, none made returns and three were definitely known to have ceased working. The survivors were Irish Decorative Art Association (County Antrim), Derrylin, Cuala, Dun Emer, Moneyguyneen and the County Meath Home Industries Society (Navan). Thereafter these societies were no longer reported upon. The United Irishwomen[33] (Bantracht na Tuaithe or Irish Countrywomen's Association after 1935) maintained interest in homecrafts and nearly every guild was able to present a commendable display of crafts on the appropriate occasion. Some individual members engaged in limited business transactions but, because of its designation as a charity, the Association's craft activities remain at educational level, reaching a standard of excellence at its Termonfechin residential college of adult education.[34] Many religious communities (St Louis Convent, Carrickmacross and Banada Abbey, County Sligo) continued to promote interest in lace and crochet, as did private enterprise firms in some of the traditional craft districts. As fine lace became scarcer, it inevitably became dearer, but this did not evoke any great increase in production — the fine arts in rural areas were now very markedly a leisure occupation typically pursued by the benevolent grandmother who had a teenage favourite granddaughter with 'a great pair of hands'. It was good to hear stories of the fun they had in the old days, at the classes with Miss Reynolds, Miss McCormack, Miss Kelly, Miss O'Brien, or whoever — of all the fine ladies and gentlemen — of Lady Fingall, Mrs Pilkington, Mary Spring-Rice, Susan Mitchell, Father Finlay, AE — and the day that Sir Horace Plunkett himself looked in!

From 1926 onwards the Royal Dublin Society granted space at its shows for the United Irishwomen to organise exhibitions and demonstrations of country crafts. In 1929 some United Irishwomen, led by dedicated co-operator, Muriel Gahan, formed a private non-profit company, Country Workers Ltd, and opened the Country Shop on St Stephen's Green, Dublin. No further co-operative venture was made until 1946 and the formation of Country Markets Ltd — an all-Ireland society of craft

---

32 In 1915 Templecrone Society paid £7 affiliation fees and £7.10.0 subscription, a total exceeded by only one other agricultural society, Enniscorthy (£12 plus £5). Best creamery contributions in that year came from Kantoher (£15 plus £20) and Clones (£10 plus £25). The little poultry society, Dervock & District (County Antrim), gave £5 plus £10. None of the nine surviving home industries societies made any contribution in 1915.

33 In 1935 the ICA ceased to be a co-operative society because of a technicality relating to a change in its constitution.

34 An Grianan, adult education college at Termonfechin, County Louth, was given to the ICA in 1954 by the W.H. Kellogg Foundation of America in trust "for the health, recreation and welfare of the people of Ireland". It is open to all comers the year round. The Kellogg Foundation gave a further grant to the ICA in 1967 towards the building and equipping of a horticultural college for girls, also at An Grianan. This grant was supplemented by one from the Department of Agriculture.

workers and small producers (men and women) to promote the production and sale of rural crafts, and also to organise weekly sales of farm and garden produce. In 1975 Country Markets Ltd had forty-eight local produce markets, the members of each market organising the co-operative retail sale of their farm, garden and home products on one or more days each week in a nearby town or other centre. Increasing numbers of markets also sell their members' crafts but the greater part of the Society's work for craft development is in co-operation with the ICA, organising local courses and tests to raise the standard of home crafts production.

The next significant co-operative happening was in the area of Strokestown, County Roscommon, where from the early nineteen sixties a guild of ICA workers with their president, Patsy Deignan, wife of a local vet, had been working for the revival of rural crafts in Roscommon and adjoining counties. They formed a society to organise the production and sale of a wide variety of craft articles. Trading first under the Country Markets umbrella as Strokestown Handicraft Market Ltd, they became a co-operative society in their own right in 1966 when they registered as Slieve Bawn Co-operative Handcraft Market Ltd. This Strokestown centre today provides an outlet for a great number of individual craftworkers and groups all over the west.[35] The example was emulated by Kinturk Homecrafts Co-op, Kinvara Handcraft Co-op and the short-lived Birrcrafts Ltd, all registered in 1968.

Meanwhile in south-west Donegal, Father James McDyer, along with his many other co-operative commitments, struggled on to create a distinct artistic and craft milieu in Glencolumbkille. His many co-operatives include Glencolumbkille Hand Knitting Co-op, Glencolumbkille Knitting Co-op and Glencolumbkille Metalcraft Society. Father McDyer is also keen to encourage smaller units of private enterprise production in specialised crafts such as pottery, weaving and jewellery. The craft shop in his Folk Village affords a market for many craft workers throughout Donegal, as does his Glencolumbkille Shop in South Anne Street, Dublin. At the time of writing, there are hopeful signs that some of the major co-operative groups, already showing increased interest in the social and cultural pursuits of their members, may also be inclined to promote and foster local crafts.

---

35 The published turnover of home produce and handcraft co-operatives in 1974 was £217,109. Of this Country Markets Ltd accounted for an estimated £128,000, Slieve Bawn £47,179, Kinvara Handcrafts £25,705, Glencolumbkille £12,636, Kinturk Homecrafts (County Clare) £3,589. (IAOS Annual Report 1975).

Chapter Eighteen

Co-operative Meat Processing

Prompted by the decision of the British Co-operative Wholesale Society (CWS) in 1900 to establish a bacon factory in Tralee, the IAOS District Conference in Athlone sought guidance from headquarters on the feasibility of a similar venture.[1] At that time efforts were being made in many places throughout Ireland to organise the orderly production and marketing of pigs, but little success was achieved. The national committee of the IAOS considered the project, but thought it inadvisable, at least for the time being:

> The Committee regret that they cannot afford, at the present time, any encouragement to Societies in establishing Co-operative Bacon Curing Factories, owing to the great risk and expense entailed, which could not safely be faced without a much more perfect and widespread organisation among Pig Feeders than now exists.[2]

Yet the idea was kept in mind and interest was shown in various centres throughout the country. In 1904, around Tipperary town, a beginning was made at collecting share capital but the promoters dropped the idea because of the major campaign started in Roscrea about the same time.[3] Roscrea Bacon Curing Factory was registered as a 'miscellaneous' society with the IAOS in 1905 and arrangements were made for building a factory. The society started with a membership of 3,182 and share capital of £10,171, on which a first call of 5 shillings per £1 share had been collected. The board of directors was appointed from the general committee representing the twenty parishes which the society proposed to serve. Its organisation was similar to that of the Danish societies, binding the members to supply all their bacon pigs for a period of five years, under penalty of a fine of 10 shillings per pig in case of default. Meetings and

1 This request was coupled with one for a co-operative fertiliser factory.
2 IAOS Annual Report 1900, p.22.
3 A co-operative bacon factory was also planned for Rathkeale, County Limerick, following a large meeting held there on 22 April 1904 and addressed by R.A. Anderson. Although the project did not materialise, it was doubtlessly a happier occasion for Anderson than that some years previously when a worthy solicitor avowed that any pound of butter made in Rathkeale would be made in accordance with Irish nationalist principles — or it would not be made at all!

instructional classes were held throughout the area to introduce members to an improved system of pig husbandry and to impress on them the necessity for maintaining a regular supply of pigs at all seasons of the year. A modern factory, on the Danish model with the most up-to-date equipment, was speedily provided and began operating in 1908. The society had a flying start, excellent prices for pigs and a turnover of £33,759 in the first year. The despatch with which this project got under way was a reflection of the organising ability of the chairman, Rev John Cunningham, and the wholehearted backing of the clergy.

Arthur Moore

Arthur Moore of the Giving Hand had died on 5 January 1904 but his influence was still strongly felt. Throughout his life his generosity to the Catholic clergy had been magnificent, so that when a major co-operative industrial project was mooted for Roscrea (near where, in 1878, he had established a Cistercian Monastery in Mount Heaton)[4] clerical help was generously given. One is left to speculate on the difference it would have made to the early co-operative movement if the Roscrea experience of intensive support by a large number of clergy had been repeated elsewhere.[5] Despite the excellent organisation, the Roscrea enterprise was not spared the common co-operative experience of staring failure in the face. Roscrea was then a poor town in a poor countryside. To raise £10,000 was a remarkable achievement, but it was not enough. The promoters

4 Renamed Mount St Joseph Abbey. Moore donated £10,000 of the £15,000 purchase price and lent the remaining £5,000 until the monks raised it by mortgage.
5 Clergymen provided outstanding leadership and immense personal effort in other places: Dean Barry in Ballyragget, Archdeacon Phelan in Piltown, Rev E.F. Campbell in Killyman, Father O'Grady in Bohola, Father O'Donovan in Loughrea, Father Hegarty and Father Quinn in Belmullet, Canon J.R. Willis in Wicklow, Father T.C. Connolly in Sligo/Leitrim, Father P. Lyons in Castlebar, Rev J.R. Perdue in Killala, Rev H. de Vere Hunt in Roscommon / Galway and many others. Yet their efforts rarely drew more than nominal support from their superiors and clerical colleagues. Even today the efforts of co-operators like Father McDyer in Glencolumbkille, and Father Shields (Swatragh and Magilligan), do not seem to evoke any exceptional support from or emulation by neighbouring clergy.

started business owing the building contractor £1,400. There was practically no provision for working capital and a factory which was capable of killing 600 to 700 pigs a week had at first to be content with 50 — they had no money to buy any more. Matters were considerably improved, however, when Sir Horace Plunkett donated a further £3,000.

The Roscrea experiment was keenly observed throughout Ireland. During the winter of 1908 a series of meetings was held in the neighbourhood of Enniskillen, but when the Fermanagh farmers compared Danish pig prices with those obtainable at their local pork markets, enthusiasm was dampened. It became apparent that the Irish farmer was faced with a major task in selection and breeding to produce a pig meat and provide bacon of a consistent quality and type to please the British housewife.[6] Wisely, perhaps, the Roscrea factory did not set its sights so much on the 'quality' market but was content to handle pigs of all types, shapes and sizes and provide an Irish alternative to the considerable imports of American bacon then coming into Ireland. The American bacon was cheap but most of it, in Ireland at least, was of very inferior quality. Many Irish landowners purchased it for feeding their labourers as a supplement to Irish cabbage and potatoes. The labourers in turn conjured many colourful names for this tough fatty, yellow American product, the most charitable (and printable) being "Yallagh End". The Roscrea co-op developed a lucrative home trade in bacon by diverting some of the lowest quality meat to sausages and cooked products; it sold bacon of better than American standard to the farmers and was able to establish a small export trade in quality bacon. One of the problems confronting bacon curers at that time was the difficulty of dealing with female pigs which were in heat when they arrived at the factory. If pigs were slaughtered in this condition, the bacon would be of poor quality and easily tainted.[7] Despite repeated

M.J. Hickey

6   In 1908 the main suppliers of bacon to the British market were the USA (2½ million cwts), Canada (1 million) and Denmark (2 million). Ireland, however, produced some bacon of excellent quality. Quality Limerick bacon and ham had an international reputation and at an earlier date some Danish experts had come to Limerick to study techniques of bacon-curing. In an exchange arrangement, some superior Irish bacon was sent to the USA and inferior American bacon imported.

7   A letter from M.J. Hickey, Enniscorthy ('The Little Master') to *The Irish Homestead,* 4 June 1904, deals extensively with this problem.

warnings to suppliers, the problem persisted because pigs were often eight to ten months old before they reached slaughter weight, at which age the onset of sexual activity in sows was natural and inevitable.

Today the problem is a limited one; because of improved breeding and feeding, and lower weight requirements, the great majority of pigs are ready for slaughter before they are six months old. Pig quality improved slowly; factory techniques and co-operative organisation at a much faster rate. As early as 1910 J. W. Walsh, the Roscrea factory manager, was engaged by a group of farmers in Bedfordshire to advise them on the setting up of a co-operative bacon factory. In the same year Achonry Creamery Society, at a cost of less than £100, equipped a suitable premises for the killing and curing of a limited number of pigs for local consumption — an initiative later followed by Belleek and the Cavan Central Creamery. There were stirrings too in Wexford and in Omagh where a full-scale bacon factory was planned in 1911. These were years in which pig prices were particularly good and the Roscrea turnover climbed to £47,000 in 1911 and £55,500 a year later.

A group of co-operators in the Wexford area, who had registered a society in 1909, finally went into business in 1912 and achieved a modest turnover of £34,256 in their first year.[8] Strangely enough, the bulk of this turnover was from the slaughter of cattle — a departure occasioned by an outbreak of foot and mouth disease which prevented the export of fat cattle to Britain from this part of Wexford, where in the winter months feeding of cattle on barley meal, oats and turnips, was traditional. It was not until 1914 that the Wexford factory was curing bacon on a large scale.[9] In 1913 the liveweight price of pigs was abnormally high — 57 shillings per cwt — but . . .

> The price of lard and other by-products fluctuates but little . . . the margin of profit earned on bacon is not sufficient to make up for the loss sustained by buying the whole pig at a high price and disposing of the offals under cost. Moreover the fluctuations of the pig market do not always appear to bear any true relation to the condition of the bacon market, for it often happens that a fall in the price of bacon is accompanied by a rise in the price of pigs. This condition of things would seem to point to the necessity of greater improvements in the processes employed in dealing with the by-products . . . and also the desirability of working bacon curing factories on the system which is universally followed in the creameries — that of *paying for the raw material by results*. It must be admitted that the introduction of such a system would be extremely difficult in the case of Roscrea where the society is obliged to buy pigs, even from its own members, in competition with other curers . . . If members of a co-operative factory force their society to pay them competition prices they can not only

8 Membership 2,031; paid-up share capital, £3,617; loan capital £1,267.
9 Wexford turnover in 1914 was £116,602; share capital had risen to almost £10,000 and loan capital to £4,330.

expect no dividend, but may actually wreck their society by obliging it to trade at a loss. If, on the other hand, they are convinced that they are ultimately going to get from their society all that their pigs are worth, it matters very little to them that their selling price is comparatively low for they will participate in whatever profit may be made when their pigs are turned into bacon and sold. The difficulty of securing acceptance of this plan is mainly due to the custom prevalent in most parts of the country of selling pigs for 'cash down'. The same difficulty was encountered in the early days of creamery organisation and there are still some co-operative dairy societies whose suppliers insist on the expensive and troublesome system of fortnightly payments for milk.[10]

The need to eliminate speculation in pig buying — by dead weight selling, quality grading and a general acceptance of the idea of payment by results — is a constant theme throughout co-operative literature. But even today, while most larger-scale pig producers take their pig directly to the factory and accept payment on the scale of dead weight and grade, in some places the bacon industry still largely depends for its supply of pigs on 'middlemen' who buy pigs by hand and by liveweight throughout the country districts.

In 1913 the Templecrone Society, as a further service to its members, established a co-operative butcher's shop for slaughtering cattle and sheep. Creamery societies like Achonry, Belleek, Cavan, Urlingford and Lombardstown were killing pigs for home consumption and interesting their members in the merits of skim milk and buttermilk for pig-feeding. The Lombardstown Society was killing on average six sheep, ten to fifteen pigs and three or four fat cattle per week. The co-operators were beginning to recognise the advisability of combining the butchering of dressed meat with bacon-curing rather than concentrating on bacon alone. Besides improving production and factory profits, it was being noticed in Wexford[11] that even a small weekly draw-off of cattle and sheep to the co-operative factory was considerably enhancing the farmer's selling position.

A motion at the 1913 annual general meeting, proposed by Sir John Keane and seconded by Ernest Brown from O'Brien's Bridge, called on the IAOS to "consider carefully the possibility of organising the Irish dressed meat industry upon co-operative lines and if found practicable to prepare a scheme." The Wexford and Roscrea Societies were doing well. Roscrea expanded and re-equipped for bigger business, incidentally providing an electric light supply for the town of Roscrea.[12] Omagh, however, had failed

10 IAOS Annual Report 1913, p.26.
11 The Wexford factory had a very efficient by-product department, producing blood and bonemeal fertilisers, refined beef suet, oleo oil, stearine and soap. The guts were made into sausage casings for export, and other manufactures included pork pies, brawn, polonies, puddings, sausages and tongue.
12 Templecrone Co-op similarly supplied electric light to the town of Dungloe from 1922 to 1956.

to start, and a co-operative bacon factory for Castlebar was still at the talking stage.[13]

An attempt was made during 1913 to establish the meat industry on semi-co-operative lines and the promoters of the scheme formed themselves into a society called Irish Meat Limited, with the object of forming a company to erect and equip *abattoirs* in Dublin and elsewhere. About £1,000 was subscribed and a company called Irish Abattoirs Ltd was registered. Yet the shares were never allotted because the amount subscribed was not nearly sufficient. The promoters were unable to get a site in Dublin city since the Dublin Corporation sought to restrict the company from selling to anyone except individuals or firms in the meat trade. An option secured on a piece of ground outside the city boundary lapsed when the required capital was not forthcoming.

It was this failure to make progress on semi-co-operative lines that prompted Sir John Keane's motion at the annual general meeting. Plunkett, in hospital at Battle Creek, Michigan, saw the need for entry into the meat industry but he was aware of the need for organised production to sustain it. He wrote:[14]

> The backwardness of our business organisation, owing to the difficulties under which we have had to work the last few years, has recently been well illustrated by our failure to secure for the farmers their due share in the profits of the sale and manufacture of the products of which cattle, sheep and swine are the raw material. I have no doubt this subject will come up for discussion at the meeting. I just want to give it as my own personal conviction that the basic factor in the success of all such projects is a guaranteed supply from well organised farmers. To attempt to compete with those long in the business without the certainty of being able to count on the great advantage which organised farmers enjoy is simply to court disaster.

The pig business continued to flourish throughout the war years. A bacon factory was established in Castlebar in 1917 but was not affiliated to the IAOS. In 1917 Roscrea and Wexford achieved turnovers of £150,000 and £140,000 respectively. A year later the Wexford Society outpaced Roscrea, which had not shown the same diversification.[15] A big expansion of the bacon and pork trade was taking place at the Cavan Central Creamery and over twenty-five societies throughout the country were reported as killing limited numbers of pigs for their members. So

---

13 Several creameries and store societies lost money on the sale of pork in 1913-14 because of incautious buying and ignorance of the trade.
14 The letter, dated 30 November 1913, was read at the annual general meeting held on 10 December that year. Plunkett also wrote an open letter to Thomas Dooley, chairman of Roscrea, on 6 May 1914, urging farmer members to greater efforts and consolidation of the co-operative structure.
15 In 1918 the turnover at Wexford was £235,221 and at Roscrea £162,713. Roscrea's progress was somewhat retarded because of a government restriction on the allocation of pig numbers for slaughtering at different centres.

important had this business become that the IAOS appointed Mr A. Hinchliff (formerly of the Department of Agriculture) as its consulting expert, and his advice was eagerly sought and acted upon by a great number of societies.

The IAOS sought a general permission for societies to kill and cure pigs for their own members. This was refused by the Ministry of Food which insisted on individual applications. Large numbers of pigs were being exported live to Britain and the Ministry was concerned that proprietary bacon factories should not suffer too severely. In 1918 the co-operators revived their ambitions for a large-scale meat plant and a decision was made to locate a £200,000 factory in Waterford. Within a year, mainly as a result of the vigorous campaign organised by IAOS official Paddy Courtney, £150,000 of share capital had been subscribed. The subscription of such a large amount reflected (apart from a change in money values) the growing prosperity of the farming community and its increased willingness to invest in the co-operative effort. It also confirmed the Roscrea experience of the value of wholehearted participation by the clergy, of whom there were many dedicated co-operators in the Waterford hinterland. However, it was by no means smooth sailing. In the unsettled state of the country in 1920, opposition came not only from private enterprise but from the undisciplined forces of the Crown:

> The Society's canvassers have been held up, threatened and interfered with in their work, and farmers, although convinced of the soundness and the great importance of the project to them, are for the present refusing to come forward and put money into buildings and plant which, to use their own expression, 'may go up in smoke and flames'. So far it has not been found possible to obtain any guarantee of protection for those who are working on the organising of the society . . . [16]

The post-war slump hit the Wexford Society very hard. Turnover dropped from £411,000 in 1920 to £288,000 in 1921 and to £158,000 in 1922. Roscrea was less seriously hit (£257,000 to £202,000 to £193,000), since the fall was in prices rather than volume output. Both societies continued to make marginal profits through the years of the civil war. One factory manager observed that their transport lorries were less likely to be hijacked or commandeered if they had pigs in them — and arranged accordingly. Apparently the opposing forces were reluctant to incur the wrath of local farmers by letting pigs loose throughout the country.[17] The Waterford project, Irish Co-operative Meat Ltd, further delayed by an agricultural labour dispute in Counties Kilkenny and Waterford in 1923,

16 IAOS Annual Report 1920, p.22.
17 There is an apocryphal story from the same period of a patient who could only get to hospital by travelling in a factory lorry with the pigs. Before disembarking outside the hospital, he addressed his travelling companions: "Well, me poor fellas, ye'll be cured, anyway — whatever about me!"

finally got under way in 1924.[18] It had facilities to handle 150 cattle and 1,000 pigs per week and also had extensive cold storage accommodation to serve its owns needs and room to store up to twenty tons of butter (or equivalent produce) on a rental system.

Progress was slow in the latter half of the nineteen twenties but by 1929 the Waterford factory had a turnover of £360,000, compared to Roscrea's £223,000. The Wexford Society was doing badly. On a turnover of £118,000 in 1929, it lost over £16,000. It rallied later and suffered various changes of fortune until it was taken over by the Waterford Co-op (renamed Clover Meats Ltd) in August 1946. Ireland could not escape from the effects of world depression following the Wall Street crash and prices tumbled in 1930 and subsequent years.[19] The government intervened with custom duties on butter, oats and bacon in 1931 and eventually heavy duties were imposed on imports of all kinds. In the USA Henry Wallace (son of Plunkett's close friend), now Secretary of State for Agriculture, provoked an emotional outcry from the American public when, in an effort to correct disastrous farm prices, he approved the ploughing up of ten million acres of cotton and the slaughter of six million young pigs in 1933. Simultaneously Britain prohibited the import of beef and fixed import quotas for live cattle. In Ireland this led to the slaughter of calves and a scheme was devised for the supply of free beef to persons entitled to welfare payments.

Pigs were also a major problem. Bacon, which made a top price of 67 shillings per cwt in March 1931, had dropped to 33 shillings by November 1932. When the British imposed heavy import duties on pigs and bacon, the Irish government sought to alleviate matters by paying export subsidies, but in 1933 Britain introduced quota restrictions which made it very difficult for the Department of Agriculture to organise the equitable allocation of exports. There was large-scale dumping of bacon on the British market by Denmark, Poland, the Netherlands and even the Argentine. In the South of Ireland bonhams were often completely unsaleable and farmers gave them away rather than prolong the financial fantasy by buying meal to feed them. Further North along the Border there was intense activity and ingenious movements of livestock, since Northern Ireland produce had freer access to mainland Britain.

A gradual improvement set in from 1935: Britain granted substantial increases in the import quota for cattle, and trade agreements with Germany and Belgium provided small but significant outlets for some Irish cattle. The Pigs and Bacon Act 1935 established the Bacon Marketing Board and the Pigs Marketing Board. The former board sought to organise the marketing of bacon, the latter established a fund to stabilise pig prices

18 Irish Co-operative Meat Ltd had a small turnover from butchering in 1923 — £8,154 — on which it showed a profit of £2,270. Roscrea (turnover £180,000) and Wexford (£107,000) also continued to make small profits. In 1923 there was a different kind of co-operative effort when a shipping strike stopped the export of live pigs from Cork. Father John Crowley and Drinagh Creamery Society organised the farmers and chartered ships to take pigs to Britain from Bantry Bay.
19 Exports valued at £46.2m in 1929 dropped to £35.5m in 1931 and to £17.5m in 1934.

and took the first tentative steps towards the introduction of a grading system. With these improvements and a world reduction in pig numbers, by 1939 the price of bacon gradually improved to 65 to 70 shillings.

The co-operative factories at Roscrea and Waterford were assigned special roles in implementing two government schemes in 1935. Roscrea established a special department to cater for a government scheme to eliminate old cows and thus improve the nation's dairy herd. Officers of the Department of Agriculture purchased old cows at 50 shillings each and despatched them to Roscrea for slaughter and processing,[20] mainly into meat-and-bone meal which was the common protein supplement used in animal feeding-stuffs at that time. Irish Co-operative Meat Ltd in Waterford undertook the canning of beef from Kerry bullocks. The Kerry cow is a hardy native breed which was much prized as a 'poor man's cow' (particularly in Kerry and Cork) because of her ability to yield a reasonable quantity of milk even under the poorest conditions in mountainous areas. Her male progeny, however, like the offspring of other purely milk breeds such as the Jersey and Ayrshire, were singularly unattractive as beef animals and during the slump period were almost unsaleable either as stores or fat — if the latter condition was at length attained. Department officers attended fairs and purchased these Kerry bullocks for prices not otherwise attainable. From November 1935 to February 1937 some 5,000 bullocks were purchased under this scheme. Under the Anglo-Irish Trade Agreement of 1938, the penal duties on Irish meat and livestock[21] entering Britain were discontinued and trade was getting back to normal by the outbreak of World War II. The Wexford Society had languished[22] but Waterford had a turnover in 1938 of £413,000. Roscrea and the Cork Factory (Cork Farmers Union Abattoir and Marketing Co-operative Ltd, which had been founded in 1934) were both approaching the quarter of a million mark. Imports of animal feeding-stuffs and maize practically ceased during the war years. Increased tillage reduced the grazing area by about a million acres, but, strangely enough, cattle numbers increased, although the growth was largely offset by a substantial decline in sheep.[23]

In general, the war caused very little disruption or change in grazing livestock. Pig numbers, however, dropped spectacularly, since it was forbidden to feed pigs on cereal foods which might be made available for human use. By 1945 pig numbers were more than halved (from 931,000 in 1939 to 426,000 in 1945). Their relative dependence on different types of livestock is shown in the trade returns of the meat processing co-ops for 1942. Although Waterford reached a record turnover of £1,325,088, the

20 Arising from this, 'Roscrea' became the destination suggested for mothers-in-law and other vintage females by comedians in stage patter and sketches enacted in village halls and by travelling shows in rural Ireland.
21 Sheep had been subject to import duties but was free of quantitative restrictions. Export bounties were paid for a time on sheep and mutton. Poor prices brought a decline in numbers and, when trade improved a little, the bounties were discontinued early in 1935.
22 Turnover in 1938 was £124,977 compared to £235,221 in 1918.
23 Between 1939 and 1945 cattle numbers increased by 188,000, but sheep declined by 466,000. The number of horses increased by 19,000, only to decline spectacularly in the post-war period because of rapid farm mechanisation.

others had dropped significantly: CFU £173,000, Roscrea £132,000 and Wexford £99,000. There was keen competition for the limited number of pigs being fattened and, in order to maintain a reasonable output, some bacon factories undertook the processing of sheep. A new product, 'Macon' — salt-cured mutton — appeared for a while on the grocery counters but was not greeted enthusiastically by housewives.

Just as the creamery business was affected by an increase in home butter-making, the bacon shortage was aggravated by the fact that many farmers revived the custom of killing and salting a pig 'for the house'. Grave dis-satisfaction was being expressed at the failure of the Pigs and Bacon Commission[24] to conjure up enough pigs for everybody. As a co-operative contribution toward improving pig supply, an interesting development was undertaken in 1941 by the Knockmeal CA & DS in Waterford. Their Ballymacarberry branch undertook the fattening of bonhams on potatoes and skim milk, plus a small amount of mealstuffs. The pigs, potatoes and skim were bought from the members and a house was erected to fatten 240 pigs. In this development the society had the encouragement of veteran Northern co-operator, A.A. (Sandy) McGuckian of Cloughmills, who shortly afterwards became vice-president of the IAOS. Mitchelstown followed suit, with fattening houses for 2,000 pigs on a farm which they purchased near the town. Feeding here was largely based on whey, a by-product available in large quantities from the society's cheese factory. McGuckian provided house-plans, advised on the site and erection, and trained the Waterford and Cork pigmen at Cloughmills, where for many years the McGuckians had developed large-scale pig production with outstanding success.[25] Dungarvan Creamery and Roscrea Bacon Factory purchased farms for similar developments, as did Lough Egish (County Monaghan) and Milford and Ballyclough (County Cork) in 1943. It was the Ballyclough Society, again at the insistence of Sandy McGuckian, which pioneered the introduction of artificial insemination of cattle in Ireland.[26]

Clover Meats Ltd took over the Wexford factory in 1946, purchased Shaws of Limerick in 1949, Donnellys in 1967 and Clonmel Foods in 1968. At the end of that year they had an annual turnover of £12,607,000, a figure only marginally short of the combined total trade in that year of the three co-operative wholesale societies, IAWS, ICASL, and the CAP. In comparison, Roscrea turned a modest £2.7 million and Cork Farmers

---

24 The Commission was made a statutory corporation in 1940 under the Pigs and Bacon (Amendment) Act 1939. A motion from Herbertstown CA & DS, to the annual general meeting in 1942, moved that the Pigs and Bacon Commission be abolished and that the bacon industry be reorganised on co-operative lines. See IAOS Annual Report 1942, p.30.

25 See A.E. Muskett (ed.), *A.A. McGuckian Memorial Book* (Belfast: McGuckian Memorial Committee, 1956).

26 This development was pioneered in Britain by Dr John Hammond at the School of Agri-culture in Cambridge. At the invitation of Dr Henry Kennedy, Hammond visited the Plunkett House in 1944 and shortly afterwards the Ballyclough Society arranged for some inseminations. They were followed soon afterwards by Mitchelstown and Dungarvan. The Livestock (Artificial Insemination) Act 1947 controlled the licensing of artificial insemination stations.

Union £1.4 million. Many things had happened in the meantime. Livestock numbers had increased in nearly every category, pig numbers were more than double the wartime figure. The system of selling cattle in marts[27] was now widespread and, in 1968, the thirty co-operative marts sold livestock valued at £46 million. This development had been met at its inception by an outcry from vested interests and tactics no less inhibited than those employed against the early co-operators sixty years previously. The IAOS Annual Report for 1956 was, however, less expansive than when the late R.A. Anderson had fulminated against the merchants and the gombeen-men. It dismissed the matter in a single sentence: "The lack of support from professional buyers amounts to a virtual boycott of the Co-operative Marts." Nevertheless, the practical advantages of organised selling proved so popular with the farmers that today the biggest problem facing the livestock trade is the growing multiplicity of marts, both co-operative and privately owned — a tendency reminiscent of the disastrous proliferation of creameries in the eighteen nineties.

Some semblance of organised production and marketing was also belatedly brought to the pig industry. After Knockmeal, Mitchelstown and a number of other creamery societies in the South, such as Castlelyons, had popularised large-scale pig fattening, the first unattached co-operative pig society (dealing initially only in pigs and feeding-stuffs) was established at Rath in south Wicklow[28] in 1959. It was set up on the initiative of local farmers led by James Joyce, a young agricultural advisor with the Irish Sugar Company in Carlow, who was encouraged by his general manager, Michael J. Costello, the inspirational figure behind so many co-operative developments. The strategy was to have the small farmer keep the sows to produce bonhams which would be sent in for fattening at a central station. The station also manufactured pig feed and, by organised recording at station and farm, selection of pigs and provision of improved breeding stock, sought to improve pig quality.[29] Many misgivings were expressed in official circles but, by 1968, after much travail, the pig-fattening stations had demonstrated their possibilities and there were some thirty co-operative pig societies throughout the Republic (twelve independent[30] and the remainder attached to creamery and other societies), fattening close on 10 per cent. of the nation's pigs. The Rath experiment and subsequent developments have undoubtedly helped the pig industry to get away from the haphazard situation, wherein each farmer kept one or two sows (often

27 Pioneered by Waterford Co-operative Sales Mart Ltd, which held its first sale on 10 April 1956, and followed soon after by Kilkenny Co-operative Mart Ltd and Bunclody Co-operative Agricultural Society.
28 The townland of Rath, famous for its system of ring forts which are allegedly inhabited by fairies, is in the extreme south of County Wicklow but, because of its proximity to the town of Tullow, is commonly attributed to County Carlow.
29 In 1960 and subsequent years it was the turn of the sons of the late Sandy McGuckian to provide guidance and help (including a number of excellent breeding stock) to the co-operative pig producers in Rath Co-operative Enterprises Ltd and elsewhere.
30 The free-standing pig co-ops are (1975) Carbery, Clonaslee, East Cork, East Galway, Glen of Aherlow, Rath, Premier Pigs (Tipperary), Balla, Wexford, Roughty Valley, Maine Valley and Ballinamoney. Total turnover in 1974 was just over £5 million.

poorly attended to) and whereby production was an unpredictable succession of scarcity and glut reminiscent of the days when the nation's poultry industry consisted almost entirely of farmyard scavenger flocks of twenty to thirty hens. Today's pig production (both co-operative and private enterprise) is becoming increasingly one of organised (albeit small) units which allow the farmer to specialise or at least to pay adequate attention to all aspects of pig husbandry as well as breeding, feeding and organised marketing.

Today, when Clover Meats (£45.5m) and Roscrea (£4.5m) are making their way,[31] when other societies like Golden Vale, Mitchelstown and Castlemahon are developing rapidly in meat technology, when co-operative developments in the meat-processing field are happening with bewildering speed, it is appropriate to close this chapter with a brief reference to a momentous happening in 1968. In that year Cork Marts Ltd, a composite of co-operative livestock marts in Munster, in conjunction with the CFU and actively aided by co-operative societies, farming organisations and individuals throughout Ireland, took over the huge meat packing company, International Meat Packers Ltd. International Meat Packers Ltd was then employing up to 2,000 people. In 1967 it had throughput of some 265,000 cattle and over 100,000 sheep, and a trade turnover of some £21 million.[32] It would surely have gladdened the heart of Horace Plunkett, cowboy and rancher of Powder River Valley, Wyoming, to see his co-operators take on a packing plant of real Chicago size, particularly since, in so doing, they handsomely oversubscribed the £3,000,000 share capital required. Thus in ten short weeks the farmers of Ireland subscribed possibly more share capital to the agricultural co-operative movement than they had done in all their previous history.[33]

---

31 The figures are for 1974.
32 In 1971 turnover reached £31,800,000 and the mart division sold livestock valued at £56,200,000.
33 At the end of 1967 the total paid-up share capital of the 333 extant co-operative societies was £2,999,216.

Chapter Nineteen

Co-operative Fishing

The Aran Isles Co-operative Fishing Society Ltd was registered in 1915 and started business in September of that year. It had a membership of 140, consisting mainly of the crews of thirty boats fishing out of Kilmurvey (four men per boat) for the autumn mackerel. The boats and the fishing gear had been supplied on loan by the Congested Districts Board in one of its earliest development projects.[1] The arrangement whereby the Congested Districts Board provided boats and gear, marketed the fish by auction and paid the proceeds of sales minus deductions to the fishermen, worked reasonably well for a while until the fish buyers, who had previously held the islanders in their grip, also succeeded in forming a ring against the Board.[2] The prime movers behind the formation of a fisherman's co-op were Padraic Mac an Iomaire, fisherman, and the Rev Murtagh Farragher, who in Kilronan some years previously had pioneered the co-operative growing of early potatoes. In a letter in English to AE on 12 December 1916, Father Farragher gave the financial facts and the measure of their co-operative success:

> In the autumns of 1913-14 the men got prices ranging from 2/6 to 5/- per 126 fish (mackerel). The buyers cured the fish, each barrel containing an average of 350, equal to 12/- paid to the fisherman, and the buyers got £2 15s 6d per barrel, leaving 28/- net profit on 12/- worth of fish, thus receiving over 9/- (not including cost of fish) for every 126. . . .
>
> I had often thought of co-operation, but hesitated, knowing the many difficulties to be met with and not the least among them the necessary trouble to myself, want of funds, difficulty of getting the people themselves to understand, and especially to get them to wait for the money until the fish was disposed of and, last though not the least, the opposition of buyers and their local representatives.

1 Fishery development in Aran suffered a severe setback in 1899 when, in a bad storm on 28 December, four fishermen lost their lives and five boats, valued at £1,200, were destroyed. A public appeal was launched to assist the forty families thus deprived of their livelihood.

2 An interesting account of the work of the Congested Districts Board in fisheries development is given by W.L. Micks in his *History of Congested Districts Board 1891-1923* (Dublin: Eason & Son, 1925).

325

Then it was the Congested Districts Board was again to be our salvation... They agreed to lend money on the security of our Committee, to pay our expenses, procure salt and barrels, and lend us their stores and curing plant on very easy terms... All things in readiness we started at Kilmurvey with 28 canoes and after paying all expenses were able to pay the fishermen 12/- per 126, or practically three times what they had been receiving previously. Facts are stubborn things, and the facts here set down convinced the Aran fisherman what co-operation meant to him.

Rev Murtagh Farragher, with some of the Aran Island's Choir, 1904

The crews of the Kilmurvey boats earned £12 per man for three months fishing and the Kilronan men who joined the co-op earned sums varying from £10 to £26 per man.[3] The herring fishing was equally remunerative. The first balance sheet of the society showed a net profit of £94, after repaying £214 of a £300 loan from the Congested Districts Board. The acquisition of the Board store as a curing centre (purchase price £50) was a great boon to the shore workers — men and women who initially had to work in an open yard by the shore. In bad weather, after a heavy catch, the cleaners and curers often had to work all night exposed to the wind and the rain — a fair test of co-operative determination.

The co-op was able to sell some prime quality fresh fish at good prices as far afield as Liverpool and Manchester but the bulk of its trade was in barrels of cured fish mainly to a firm in Boston.[4] The barrels were marked

3   The intriguing figure of 126 fish, mentioned in reports, had its origin in the 'hand' (*lámh*) of fish, viz. three fish. Twenty hands made a score (*scór*) and it was customary when selling fish by the score to give an extra hand for luck. The long hundred (120) was two score and merited two hands for luck, thus making a total of 126 fish.
4   Pickarts of Pickarts Wharf, Boston (proprietor, Mr Les Pickart). The firm of J.J. Bankin of Liverpool acted as buyer and shipper for the American market.

with a distinctive 'Shamrock' brand which soon earned itself a good reputation abroad. The society, registered in the 'miscellaneous' category, had a special binding rule forbidding members to sell their catch outside the society, with a scale of penalties for disloyalty. In the first year of operation there was only one defaulter and within a very short time he was glad to cry *peccavi* or the Gaelic equivalent, pay his fine and beg for readmission. When the cost of barrels increased from 4/2 to 6/6 each, the co-op undertook its own coopering.[5] In 1917, when the Congested Districts Board discontinued its service of supplying ice at 30 shillings per ton, the Aran men contemplated building an ice plant of their own, but this was not technically feasible. As the war continued, the price of salt rose from 32 to 60 shillings and eventually to 90 shillings per ton and freight charges increased by 50 per cent., but the Aran Isles Co-operative Fishing Society Ltd continued to flourish. Turnover climbed from £762 in 1915 to £6,098 in 1916, in which year the society showed a profit of £614 and a reserve fund of £708.

The following year was also good. Membership had risen to 184 and subscribed share capital totalled £150. The fleet had grown to forty canoes (currachs) and 11 'nobbies'.[6] Members were realising from 17/- to 22/- per long hundred for mackerel and the co-op's sales for the year totalled £21,507, leaving a profit of £611, building the reserve fund to over £1,300. In 1918, the last year of the war, increased prices and a bigger catch almost doubled the turnover (£36,748) but the society took only a modest profit of £709, for by the year's end trade had started to dwindle. When the fighting stopped and the seas were safe again there was an influx of food products from the British colonies, causing a drastic fall in fish prices. The British housewife straightaway decided she could do with less fish than had of necessity to be included in the wartime fare. The disastrous slump came just as Irish fishermen, hardbitten and slow to react, had recognised the co-operative experiment in Aran.

Even as the Aran men were incurring a disastrous loss of £3,000 on their £10,000 turnover in 1919, five new fishing societies were planned: Gorumna (County Galway), Tory Sound, and West Donegal (Kincasslagh) Fishing Societies (County Donegal), West Carbery (Baltimore) and West Kerry.[7] All were registered in 1920 but succeeded only in losing their

---

5   This did not prove very successful, even when the price of barrels rose to 9/6 each in 1917. There was better success with fish boxes (returnable but seldom returned) when the shop price rose from 2 to 5 shillings.

6   The nobby was a two-masted drifter, typical dimensions 40′ × 13′ × 7½′, with a six- or seven-man crew fishing forty nets of 32 fathoms length each. It is said to have originated in the Isle of Man and was introduced to Ireland by the Congested Districts Board.

7   The formation of these societies was encouraged by the then underground parliament, Dáil Eireann, which in June 1919 voted up to £10,000 for the assistance of sea fisheries. A year later the Dáil set up its own Department of Fisheries with Seán Etchingham, the diminutive but lively Sinn Féin deputy from Courtown Harbour, County Wexford, as its first director. At a Dáil session held on 11 March 1921, Michael Collins, Minister for Finance, indicated that all fishing schemes should be held in abeyance since it would require at least £1½ millions to tackle the fisheries problem on a proper scale. See Minutes of First Dáil 1919-21 (Dublin: Stationery Office), p.275. The West Donegal Fishing Society was formed on the initiative of P. Gallagher (Paddy the Cope).

meagre initial capital. Baltimore was forced into liquidation within a year and none did any business in 1921. The Donegal men had long been keen to try co-operative fishing, or indeed fishing of any kind, but had been compelled to sit out the war years watching the fine prices of fish being gleaned by their Galway, Cork and Kerry counterparts. At the outbreak of the war, the British Admiralty had made an order prohibiting fishing off the Donegal coast because of the presence of German submarines: fishing boats would clutter up the likely naval battleground and make submarine spotting difficult. It was further suspected that disloyal Donegal fishing crews might inform the enemy of the disposition of the British fleet in Lough Swilly, sell food and provisions to submarines, or even facilitate a German invasion of Ireland! Some of the larger fishing boats were commandeered by the Admiralty for coast-watching and minesweeping.

Low prices were disastrous in themselves, but the real death blow came in 1920 when a 120 per cent. increase was imposed in through rates of transport on fish from Irish ports. The Congested Districts Board made all possible efforts to persuade the Ministry of Transport in London to modify the order or schedule, but to no avail. The Aran Fishing Co-op turnover in 1920 was down to £2,471 but this drastic restriction of trade did nothing to avoid a further disastrous loss of £486 which left the unfortunate society £1,110 in the red. Equally unfortunate was the Tory Co-op whose thirty-seven members had subscribed a handsome share capital of £833. The Tory men, nine miles out in the rude Atlantic, had purchased a boat, the "Ferry Bank", to carry their catches to the market. The "Ferry Bank" was burned, allegedly by British forces. The IAOS non-committally reported it as having been "lost through burning during the war conditions then prevailing". Yet the consequence was well substantiated — a loss to the society of £520 on sales of £2,327 for 1920. It was the end for all the newly formed fishing co-operatives.

The Aran venture struggled on for two years longer, partly reducing its debts through the members taking tiny prices for fish, but the co-op finally closed its doors in 1922 when the Rev Murtagh Farragher, committed to surviving and fighting back, was suddenly transferred to a mainland parish. By that time the British market was unprofitable. The American market for cured mackerel was difficult, declining and a long and costly shipping distance away. Germany, which in pre-war years had been a reasonable market for herring, had its own troubles. The financial situation there reached farcical proportions when a suitcase of devalued currency notes would no longer buy a pickled herring — the only acceptable media of exchange being gold, diamonds or cigarettes![8]

The nineteen twenties saw a continuing decline in fish prices but the cost of engines and fishing gear rose steeply, a double disincentive to the Irish fisherman. Activity dwindled to spasmodic forays by small boats on herring and mackerel shoals which in inshore waters were usually erratic. There

8   In 1928-29 the American market for mackerel and the limited European market for herring collapsed completely. By this time too the small home market for demersal fish had been largely filled by imports from Britain.

was also a part-time effort at small inshore fishing of white fish — plaice, cod, haddock and whiting — but Irish cities were coming increasingly to rely on the more regular supply of such fish from Britain. Salmon and shellfish might have been reasonably profitable, but merchant interests, never seriously challenged except in Aran, had now an undisputed sway. The Congested Districts Board wound up its activities in 1922 and, apart from the feeble efforts of the Department of Fisheries[9] and some marine works provided by the Board of Works, there was no source of direct help for fishery development until the establishment of the Sea Fisheries Association of Saorstát Eireann Ltd in November 1930 to

(i) encourage fishing for demersal species
(ii) provide boats and gear to fishermen on hire-purchase terms
(iii) provide for the co-operative marketing of catches.

The problems facing the Association in trying to resurrect and re-orientate the fishing industry were immense. All through the nineteen twenties there were numerous fishermen who had bought motor boats and gear at high prices during the boom years (1916-1919) and were now struggling to repay the outstanding loans. Morale was at a low ebb. The Departments of Agriculture, of Fisheries, and of Lands and Fisheries had continued to offer loans for boats and gear, but they got few takers. Even if there had been, the finances available were small,[10] and terms could not be generous since the repayment of existing loans was doing little to augment the finances. Eventually a great amount of arrears had to be written off — a step provided for in the Revision of Loans Act 1931. Even with a fresh start, there were few fishermen prepared to commit themselves for larger boats while the price of fish went from bad to worse. The attempts at 'co-operative' marketing were minimal and, at best, informal. No co-operative society was registered from 1920 to 1955. However, some progress was being made and fish landings were beginning to rise when World War II interrupted the programme.

The war brought an increase in fish prices but, because of shortages of fuel and materials, it inhibited the development of fishing by larger boats. Yet the nation's 10,000 fishermen (most of whom were part-timers fishing with tiny craft in inshore waters) were active. By 1941 fish landings had increased by 46 per cent. in volume and 155 per cent. in cash value above the 1939 figures.

Inevitably, fishing so close to shore was unpredictable. Some years the big shoals of pelagic fish came in; some years they didn't. But, despite the

---

9 The Department of Fisheries (1923) was later incorporated with the Land Commission in the Department of Lands and Fisheries (1928), before being transferred back to the Department of Agriculture in 1934.

10 Shortage of finance had long been a chronic trouble with Departments seeking to develop fisheries. Even in 1908, T.W. Russell, Plunkett's successor in the Department of Agriculture, complained of the impossibility of tackling any realistic scheme for fishery development when £6,000 of the £10,000 annual endowment for fisheries had to be spent on policing the coast.

annual variations of fortune between different regions and ports, the total national landings were always well above those of the immediate pre-war years. For the most part, marketing posed very few problems.

In 1952 Bord Iascaigh Mhara took over the functions of the Irish Fisheries Association and directed the main effort towards an increase in catching power. The Board established four boatyards[11] to build larger fishing boats which were supplied to fishermen on attractive terms — generous grants and low interest (4 per cent.) repayments of loans. The grant and loans scheme also applied to the purchase of good secondhand trawlers of foreign origin — the speedy post-war development of Killybegs as a major fishing port was sparked off by the purchase of some very good second-hand trawlers in Scotland. Within a short period, although the number of fishermen had been halved, the value of landings had been doubled,[12] principally because of larger, more efficient boats and modern locating and catching techniques.

With the increase in fish landings, the need for the producer to participate in marketing was becoming increasingly obvious by the mid-nineteen fifties. Yet the organisation of fishermen for business purposes was still as difficult as it had always been. The typical fisherman is possessed of great physical courage and vitality, which enable him to face the hazards of the elements and endure long periods of physical and mental endeavour at sea. Ashore, he is notably reluctant to involve himself in the dull chores and minutiae of business. Apart from the fact that his work of fishing and caring for his boat is exhausting, one also detects in his attitude towards land people and their book-keeping a quaint mixture of arrogance and *naïveté*: "Pay me a good price for my fish and let me get on with it."

The first of the modern fishermens' co-ops was formed in 1955 at Kilmore Quay, County Wexford.[13] It had an uninspiring existence for over a decade with a turnover rarely in excess of £2,000, until it established a firmer foothold with a turnover of £23,000 in 1967, jumping to almost £42,000 a year later. The Coshen and Feale Society, registered in 1960, failed to get underway successfully.[14] It was only with the formation of the Donegal Co-op Fisheries Ltd in 1963, and the down-to-earth discussions between the IAOS and Bord Iascaigh Mhara, that the need for co-operative organisation was recognised. The Galway Bay Society was formed in 1964, and the North Mayo Coast Fishermen in 1965. There

11 At Killybegs, Meevagh (Downings), Dingle and Baltimore.
12 Total national landings grew from 124,000 cwts in 1934 to 600,000 in 1961. Bord Iascaigh Mhara estimated the value of landings to have increased from £680,000 in 1945 to £1,700,000 in 1965. The cumulative tonnage of fishing vessels, issued under official arrangements from the inception of the Sea Fisheries Association in 1931 until 1961, was 5,500. State investments — grants and repayable advances — amounted to £1,772,238.
13 Comharchumann Iascairi Rosgoill (County Donegal), founded in the same year, and the Cromane Society (Killorglin, County Kerry), set up in 1957, both failed after a few years. The Cromane Society was based on a Sea Fisheries Association development which set up a purification plant for mussels in 1940.
14 This society (eighteen members, £44 share capital) made only two financial returns, showing turnover at £66 in 1961 and £61 in the following year. It was succeeded by Cashen Fisherman's Co-operative Society Ltd in 1971, a society which to date has not made much progress.

followed a fairly steady stream: Achill, Greencastle and Foyleside in 1966, Ballycotton, Burtonport, Castlemaine and Dingle in 1967, and Castletownbere, Conamara and Dublin Bay in 1968. Not all survived, but those based in good fishing ports achieved almost instant success in turnover and profits, although the service they provided at this stage was almost exclusively the auctioning of the fishing catch. The Donegal societies, Killybegs[15] and Burtonport, had the advantage of a fishmeal factory located at Killybegs which enabled their fishermen to fish in the knowledge that, even if the fresh fish market were glutted, there was an outlet for their catch and a reasonable factory price.[16] In its first year of operation (1968), Burtonport Fisherman's Co-op had a turnover of £132,633; the society sold every fish (salmon, pelagic, demersal or shellfish) landed at the port.[17] Killybegs had in that year a turnover of £214,525 and the South and East Coast Fishermen's Co-op, based in Dunmore East,[18] had an almost equal turnover (£213,432). Others showed more modest returns[19] — from Kilmore's £41,663 down to Achill's £2,881. The newly formed (salmon) co-op at Porthall, County Donegal, was not yet working nor was the Tralee Bay Shellfish Society, but it was ruefully noted that several co-ops, after a few years in business, had quickly acquired the habit of making no returns.

The notable event in 1968 was the formation of the Federation of Irish Fishing Co-operatives, which brought together all fourteen societies engaged in sea-fishing. In contrast to the previous reticence of the press concerning co-operative happenings, this development received widespread and favourable reporting, one correspondent observing that this "could prove the most significant development for Irish fishing since the launching of An Bord Iascaigh Mhara." Some fishermen with a twinkle of malicious humour asked "Oh! is that all?"

The Federation developed after a hard-fought organisational struggle and much of the credit for its formation is due to the IAOS and the promotional efforts of the ICDT (Irish Co-operative Development Trust), an organisation formed in 1966 to promote and assist in the expansion and development of co-operative enterprises, especially in the underdeveloped areas.[20] Particularly praiseworthy were the voluntary efforts of Ethna Viney (nee McManus), pioneer of some notable co-operative developments in Killala, County Mayo, Seamus Rickard and Seamus McLoughlin of Howth Fisherman's Co-op, Seán Brosnan of Dingle and ICDT secretary, Denis Ryan.

The Federation adopted a statement of policy and principles, outlining

15 Donegal Co-operative Fisheries Ltd (1963).
16 This factory, established in 1958 by private enterprise, was acquired by the IAWS in 1968.
17 A position which fortunately still obtains because of the unwavering co-operative loyalty of all the Burtonport fishermen.
18 This society was registered as early as 1962.
19 Castlemaine £40,000, Dingle £37,565, Conamara £14,498, Greencastle £7,945, Dublin Bay £3,902.
20 It is a matter of much regret that the ICDT and Dochas (an organisation with broadly similar aims, inspired by Peadar O'Donnell) failed to become effective vehicles for promoting co-operative education and publicity and for supplementing the organisational efforts of the IAOS at regional and local level.

their proposals for development and incorporating many of the recommendations of the American survey team[21] which had reported on the Irish fishing industry in 1964; the statement dealt with co-operative structures, marketing, state assistance, education, training, social development, and representation on public bodies whose activities affect the interests of the fishermen. The Federation endorsed the American opinion that the existing Dublin fish auction system was inadequate and should be replaced by a single auction agency. Little has been done about this.[22] Considerable success has been achieved on the political level and the Federation is now represented on all state bodies concerned with fishing and is recognised as the body to be consulted on all matters concerning co-operative fishing and the interests of individual fishermen. Federation representatives played a prominent part in the negotiations preceding Ireland's entry into the European Community.

As far as development is concerned, co-operative activity is still rather restricted.[23] Fish processing is largely in the hands of private enterprise but co-ops are now entering this field. There is a need for much deeper and more comprehensive penetration into catching, marketing, the provision of fisherman's requirements, insurance, and so on. The future of co-operative fishing is in some doubt. There is the world-wide question of conservation, with many continental waters now over-fished. There is as yet insufficient knowledge of the extent of Irish fish resources or how they can be adequately conserved and efficiently harvested. Since the total Irish fishing catch is as yet not much greater than that of a single Scandinavian fishing port and, in European terms, fishing as an industry in Ireland hardly exists, these questions need to be answered. If the portents are auspicious, we might look hopefully beyond the present situation, which to date has been little more than the *ad hoc* servicing of an existing fishing activity. With definite planning and commitment by all concerned — the government, the statutory body, Bord Iascaigh Mhara, and the fishermen — we could undertake the development of a fishing *industry*.

21 See *Recommendations for Improvement of the Sea Fisheries* (Dublin: Stationery Office, 1964, Pr. 7983). In 1958 a Swedish expert, Carl G. Bjuke, had been commissioned by the government to advise on the improvement of fishing ports. See *Report on the Project of Improvement of Fishing Harbour Facilities in Ireland* (Dublin: Stationery Office, 1960, Pr. 5669).

22 The fishermen did set up their own auctioneering business in the Dublin Fish Market in 1963 with the formation of the National Fisherman's Marketing Co-operative Ltd. This society made a small profit (£2,856 on a turnover of £217,000) in its first year but subsequently, through lack of organisation and support, accumulated losses of over £10,000 and was wound up in November 1966.

23 For a comprehensive review of the fishing industry in the Republic, see J.F. Doyle, *Co-operation and Concerted Action in the Irish Fishing Industry* (Dublin: IAOS Ltd, 1973).

Chapter Twenty

Co-operative Bee-keeping

The Reverend Joseph Robert Garvan Digges was the very model of a learned country clergyman. He had a range of knowledge, skills and lore which made his parishioners and neighbours in south Leitrim extremely proud of him. This versatile and slightly eccentric rector of Mohill loved honey and bees and knew all there was to know about them. His *Irish Bee Guide — A Manual of Modern Bee-Keeping*[1] is still a standard work on apiculture. A man of insatiable scientific curiosity, he dabbled in everything but excelled at bee-keeping. For many years he was the bee expert for *The Irish Homestead*, giving weekly advice on bee culture and frequently digressing to comment on other matters of scientific interest.[2] He was also a member of the examining board of the Irish Bee-Keeper's Association, as well as editor and major contributor to the *Irish Bee Journal*, which he printed and published (at 2d monthly) from his home at Lough Rynn, Dromod, County Leitrim.

It was entirely predictable that the industrious Digges, extolling the co-operative habits of his winged friends, should prevail on some seventy human associates to form the South Leitrim Co-operative Bee-Keepers Society in 1902. Their example was quickly followed by groups of bee-keepers in Magheravealy (County Fermanagh) and Ahascragh (County Galway). Fourteen more societies[3] were registered by the end of the year,

---

1 Published in 1904 at the modest price of two shillings per copy by the Irish Bee Journal Office, Lough Rynn, County Leitrim, Eason & Son Ltd, Dublin and Belfast, and also Simpkin, Marshall, Hamilton Kent and Co Ltd, London.

2 In 1903 Rev Digges produced a pamphlet on "The Cure for Inebriety", in which he dealt with alcoholism, not as an incurable vice, but as a disease which was amenable to scientific treatment and cure. He outlined an American method of treatment by which, allegedly, more than 7,000 drunkards had been cured: "Bichloride of gold and sodium are used to act upon the seat of the disease, and after a few days, desire for the drink or drug gives place to a positive loathing. A month generally is sufficient to completely cure the patient." Having lived as a boy in Belgium, Digges was keenly interested in racing pigeons and the farming of 'Belgian hares' (broiler rabbits). A brief sketch of his life and work is given in an article by Mrs Thornton in *The Irish Beekeeper*, February 1972.

3 Inishowen, Glenties and Milford (County Donegal), Cootehill and Crossdoney (County Cavan), Mid-Tyrone and Drumquin (County Tyrone), West Cork and Sugar Loaf (County Cork), Mullaghroe (County Roscommon), Westport (County Mayo), Tullaroan (County Kilkenny), Kilflyn (County Kerry) and Kilmessan (County Meath), seat of the first agricultural society.

so that seventeen bee-keeper co-operatives were dispersed through twelve counties from extreme North to extreme South. Wexford, a traditional and reputedly model bee-keeping county, was not represented until a small society at Ferns was affiliated in 1903, but the *Irish Bee-Keepers Journal* (March 1902) carried the uplifting story of a Wexford farmer, starting with a vagrant swarm which had cost him nothing, who had built up his apiary to the point where he could sell 4,000 sections of honey in 1901 and make a profit of £100.

The Reverend J.G. Digges

Bee-keeping was a project to appeal to the thrifty, industrious mind inbued with the co-operative ethic, and a practical venture whereby the humblest labourer might raise himself to a position of virtuous economic well-being. The IAOS leaflet, *Co-operation in Bee-keeping*,[4] outlined the possibilities. Ireland could be producing £200,000 worth of honey per annum, instead of a meagre few thousand pounds' worth. England was importing between £40,000 to £50,000 worth of honey every year — much of it of inferior quality and frequently adulterated with artificial glucose:

> There is, therefore, a splendid opportunity for Irishmen to compete with the foreigners by placing pure Irish Honey on the English market which is at our own doors, as against the less excellent honey raised six thousand miles away.
>
> Every farmer and cottager should have one or more stocks of bees attached to his home. During five months of the year they require little or no time for management, and during the remaining seven months an average of one hour per week is sufficient to devote to each stock . . . no one can plead lack of time as an excuse for not undertaking the industry. There is not a farmer, or labourer, rural postman, or even an intelligent schoolboy or schoolgirl in the country, who could not, with

4 IAOS leaflet No 24, published in 1902.

a little trouble and with instruction — which can always be obtained easily — add a goodly number of pounds to the family purse every year. The capital required in order to start the industry may be roughly stated at about 30s 0d; 18s 0d will provide hive and accessories and the balance will be sufficient to purchase an early swarm; while stocks of driven bees at the end of the season may frequently be secured at the cost of one shilling each, and these commonly make the most profitable stock for the coming season.

The preliminary outlay can be recouped in one year with ordinary careful management, and there may be a little extra profit. After this the expenses will average about five shillings per stock and the proceeds may amount from £1 to £2 per stock according to locality and suitability of season.

The year 1901 was an excellent one for honey. Despite the fact that even a bumper Irish crop of honey was still a trivial commercial quantity, it was an opportunity which the buyers were not slow to seize. When the individual producers simultaneously unloaded their relatively large outputs on the market in August and September, they were in an untenable position. The middleman, with a well-studied show of reluctance, bought top quality honey for as little as 2d per section. This was passed on at 4d to 4½d to the main Dublin buyers who had facilities to store it and realise a further 100 per cent. mark-up in January and February. It was this market experience which precipitated the formation of the primary bee-keepers' co-operatives in 1902 and their simultaneous affiliation to the Irish Bee-keepers Federation Ltd, which undertook the marketing of all the honey produced by its member societies.

The Federation also undertook to supply hives and bee-keeping requisites. The traditional, round 'bee-skep', made of twisted straw rope (sugawn), looked picturesque and had the virtue of being home-made at little or no cost, but it could only produce natural combs, which had to be bled to produce jars of run honey. This run honey, however excellent or genuine, was difficult to market and inevitably fetched a lower price, partly because of the ease with which it could be adulterated. The 'skep' hive did not lend itself to winter feeding of bee stocks and, although traditionalists (who required only a little honey for home use) persevered with it, it had no place in modern commercial bee-keeping. Trading informally as the Irish Honey Company before the formation of the bee co-operatives, the Federation (before it was a federation) under the guidance of the Rev Mr Digges and his friend M.H. Read, honorary secretary of the Irish Bee-keepers Association,[5] was able to pay 6½d per section for honey in 1901. In subsequent years, from their premises at 44 Temple Bar, Dublin, the Association was able to pay prices for honey some 70 to 100 per cent. above

5 The Bee-Keepers Association was principally concerned with providing education in the technical aspects of bee-keeping. Mr Read stayed on as honorary secretary of the Irish Bee-keepers Federation Ltd. At the Cork Exhibition of 1902 and the Royal Dublin Society Spring Show in 1903, the beehives and appliances exhibited by the Federation were awarded silver and bronze medals for inventiveness.

previous levels and sell modern wooden hives and appliances at 25 to 50 per cent. below the merchants' price.

Yet, unhappily, just when co-operative bee-keeping was getting under-way, the honey season of 1902 turned out to be the worst in living memory. The average bee-keeper was lucky if he had enough honey for his own family. South Leitrim, the society with the biggest membership, sold a mere £50 worth of honey.[6] The next season was little better. Ten new societies were formed but by the season's end six (including all three Donegal societies) decided to abandon the co-operative effort.[7] The. Federation was in financial difficulties. Some blame was attached to a few societies and a number of private members who, although they used the Federation for the sale of their produce, bought their hives and appliances elsewhere, using the Federation's price list as a weapon to beat down the merchants' price — the same unco-operative tactic used by certain agri-cultural societies in their dealings with the IAWS.[8] Much more serious, however, was the fact that there was not enough honey. Future market possibilities were jeopardised when the Federation was unable to supply all its Scottish and English customers, just as they were coming to appreciate the purity and quality of Irish co-operative honey and acknowledge it with top prices.

However, the co-operators were still superbly optimistic. There were still twenty-one bee-keeping societies with a membership of over 400. T. W. H. Banfield was appointed IAOS organiser — to be guide, philosopher and friend to the patient bee-men. Unfortunately, against the law of averages, 1904 was another deplorably bad year.[9]

> We have often heard it remarked — and observed it ourselves — that it is very unusual to have two bad honey seasons in succession; therefore 1904, being the third consecutive season of this description, must have broken the record. This should be very discouraging, and may be enough to turn ordinary people away from their pursuit, but the average bee-keeper is not like an ordinary individual; instead of being dismayed by an occasional reverse, he will gird himself up for the next season's work and in a sportsmanlike fashion say 'better luck next time'. Nothing of the pessimist about the genuine beekeeper; he has too much grit to 'cry over spilt milk'. And really, the beekeeper has no

6 The turnover of the Federation, including sales of equipment with payment for honey and bees-wax, totalled only £675. The Federation in that year comprised sixteen bee-keeping societies. One hundred and ten individuals also took some of the five-shilling shares, bringing the total paid-up share capital to £203.

7 New societies were Armagh, Newtownards, South Fermanagh, Mountshannon, Ferns, Roughty (County Kerry), Fethard (County Tipperary), Glynwood (County Westmeath), Athenry, Lough Derg (County Galway) and Crossboyne (County Mayo). Along with the Inishowen, Glenties and Milford societies which wound up, were Armagh, Mullaghroe and Lough Derg. Of these, only the latter had done any business.

8 Occasionally, freight charges and convenience were mitigating factors, as well as the endemic Irish problems of social ties and kinship with merchants.

9 Honey yields varied from 74 lbs per stock in Offaly to 'no surplus at all' in other places, leaving the average for all Ireland at 34¼ lbs, "an exceedingly poor yield under modern bee-keeping".

reason to complain under any circumstances — unless that dread disease, foul brood, gets into his apiary — as even in the worst seasons, bee-keeping, under careful and intelligent management, will pay its way; though the profits may not be a quarter of what they should be in a good season.[10]

These were brave encouraging words, but they were not enough. The year 1905 was fair but the fine weather did not come in the honey time. Seven societies had to be wound up, only one new society was formed (Kilmeague and District, County Kildare) and few had any honey to sell. The genuine bee-keepers stuck to their bees in the hope that a good season would put them in business again, but yet another bad season in 1906 saw their co-operative structures fall apart through lack of use.

The Irish Beekeepers Federation was incorporated with Irish Producers Ltd, the Dublin based co-operative (1902) which was trading in eggs and poultry, but there was little to amalgamate since only four bee-keepers co-operatives had survived.[11] Of these, only the Athenry Society had any honey for sale (£10 worth). In 1909 Irish Producers Ltd was in turn taken over by the IAWS Ltd and independently registered bee-keeping societies practically ceased to exist.[12] Most bee-keepers who continued, did their business with agricultural co-ops or creameries. A rather informal group, Wexford Beekeepers Association, continued to pay an annual 10 shillings affiliation fee for associate membership of the IAOS and many of its members marketed their honey and bought requisites through the Enniscorthy CAS. In other parts, co-operatively minded bee-keepers kept in touch with their co-operatives but few had more honey than could be conveniently sold at the farm gate. All down the years local enthusiasts sought to enlist their friends and initiate them in the magical arts of bee-keeping, but with little success. As recently as 1950 a group of enthusiasts in County Wexford[13] tried once again to formalise the organisation of individual bee-keepers in that county by founding the County Wexford Beekeepers Co-operative Society Ltd. They made an auspicious start with a membership of 233 and sales of nearly £4,000 worth of honey in 1950. The society (typical shareholding £5) did useful work and survived up to 1968, but unfortunately achieved little growth. Its peak sales were £9,364 in 1960.

Every year there are even fewer and fewer individual bee-keepers.

10 J. G. Digges in *The Irish Homestead*, 15 October 1904, p.872.
11 South Leitrim, Ahascragh, Crossboyne, and Athenry. Some ten others had still a nominal existence.
12 The society at Ahascragh (twenty-five members) maintained its distinct identity up to 1914 in an area of County Galway where Lady Clonbrock and her fellow co-operators had succeeded in establishing a milieu of rural industry and craft, with home industries and poultry societies. The poultry society of Clonbrock & Castlegar survived to comparatively recent times.
13 Notably John Richards-Orpen, scion of a family which had long associations with the co-operative movement in County Wexford. Evocative of the doughty Enniscorthy co-operators of earlier days, Richards-Orpen, at the IAOS annual general meeting in 1953, urged societies to double their subscriptions and make themselves independent of government grants.

Perhaps the Rev Mr Digges made it seem all too simple and under-estimated the ability of the Irish to learn the art and to persevere in the face of difficulties. The average hours he allocated as necessary to attend to the bees were not unreasonable but he laboured against the prevailing system where farmers and their workers had to spend arduous hours from early morning until dark, six days a week, at their ordinary agricultural pursuits. The young people still seemed to reserve plenty of vigour for games and sport, but many of the more mature men had little time or energy left for active hobbies like bee-keeping.[14] The busiest time with the bees also coincided with the busiest time on the farms and few farmers relished the idea of their labourers rushing off from the haymaking to track and recapture a swarm.

Some prejudices (such as that against feeding the bees with syrup in wintertime) were difficult to overcome. There were also the 'purists' who, despising clover as a source of honey, sought the greater part of their produce from heather. Heather undoubtedly gave excellent flavour but yield was not so good and bee-keeping only proved profitable in districts where tillage and clover abounded.[15] In the west where people (and heather) were plentiful, climate, lack of clover and the spread of disease unfortunately combined to make bee-keeping very difficult. It is regrettable that in recent times the decline in the number of small individual bee enterprises has not been offset to any great degree by the development of large-scale apiaries.[16] The creamery societies, which have achieved such success in making Ireland 'a land flowing with milk', could contribute greatly to making it flow with co-operative honey.

14 Even today, although mechanisation has undoubtedly alleviated the fatigue, farm labourers still work a fifty-hour official week in summer. Farm proprietors often work much longer.
15 In the east and south of Ireland and some tillage districts such as east Galway, east Donegal, Tyrone and Derry.
16 Consumption of honey in the Republic is currently (1975) about 1,250 tons per annum, of which only some 250 tons is home-produced.

Chapter Twenty-One

Co-operation in Horticulture

The Report of the Recess Committee was eloquent on the possibilities for Irish horticulture. Britain was importing £1 million worth of vegetables and £6 million worth of fruit annually. Even allowing £2 million for oranges from Spain and a further £1 million for lemons, grapes and more exotic fruits from warmer climates, there was still a profitable margin left for produce that might be grown in Irish orchards and gardens. There was exciting evidence that certain Irish locations were pre-eminently suited for certain desirable and profitable crops:

> A gentleman of considerable experience . . . Mr W.B. Hartland of Ardcairn, Cork, holds that the sheltered bays of the South of Ireland afford an unrivalled ground for the cultivation of early vegetables and fruit . . . He is of the opinion that employment in these operations might be provided for twenty thousand people in the County Cork alone. Mr Alfred Harris, of Kirkby Lonsdale, a well known English authority, thinks that in such climates as those of Glengarriff and Bantry Bay — where he was struck with the luxuriant growth of many tender plants which will not survive the winter in England — a valuable business in cauliflowers, early potatoes, peas, gooseberries, asparagus, etc. might be established with English markets if the same methods were pursued as in Cornwall and the Scilly and Channel Islands.[1]

Nobody was under any illusions that success would be instant. It would be a long, hard struggle to achieve even moderate husbandry amongst a small-farm people, tenants or new peasant proprietors notwithstanding, whose system of farming even the rougher agricultural crops was primitive and barbarous by European standards. William Hartland was growing tulips and daffodils in Cork, Mr Mitchell Henry[2] was growing fifteen to twenty tons of potatoes per acre on reclaimed land in Connemara, but the

1 Report of Recess Committee, pp.22-23.
2 The same Mitchell Henry who in 1898 asserted the Irish peasant's hatred of tillage and his preference for cattle-jobbing.

average yield of potatoes for all Ireland was a mere two-and-a-half tons.[3] Individual landlords could demonstrate outstanding success with farm and garden crops; yet, although they merited some measure of imitation, their impact on the small farmer was remarkably little.

Such had been the conditioning of the peasant mind that many things which were done on landlord estates were of a world apart — somewhat on a par with the esoteric rites performed in churches and schools, to effect which required men of unusual ability and high station.[4] If the small tenant farmer alloted any part of his potato patch to vegetable-growing, he rarely experimented with anything more exotic than cabbages or swede turnips.[5] Any suggestion that he should try peas, beans, or carrots, of which he had ample experience in milady's kitchen garden, was frequently countered with the irrefutable "It's all right for *them*. They have the *money!*"

Some benevolent landlords and landed gentry took positive steps to enlighten their tenant and cottier neighbours. The Reverend William Hickey, the progressive clergyman who started the first agricultural school at Carrick-on-Bannow, County Wexford in 1821, testified to the good work of a few landlords throughout Ireland who awarded prizes for the best-kept farmhouses and kitchen gardens.[6] In the light of this admirable, if limited, tradition, it is not surprising that the first co-operative gardening societies should have been set up under the guidance of progressive gentry. The very first was the Castlehaven Gardening Society, County Cork, founded in 1900 with thirty members under the supervision of the knowledgeable Hartland. Within a year, Arthur Steel Lough of Killeshandra Co-operative Creamery had organised some 170 Cavan cottiers and small-holders to form the Drummully Farm and Garden Society. This society (named after the townland where Mr Lough and his brother Thomas, Liberal MP for Islington, lived, close to the town of Killeshandra) was designed not for trading purposes but to instruct its members in methods of farm and garden husbandry and, by practical project work on their own holdings, to ensure that they grew enough fruit and vegetables for their own requirements, with possibly a small surplus for local shops.[7]

---

3 2.6 tons per statute acre to be exact: see Report of Recess Committee, p.11. The ten-year average yield, 1885-94, was 3.5 tons. For an analysis of Irish crop yields 1847-1939, see B. R. Mitchell and Phyllis Deane, *Abstract of British Historical Statistics* (Cambridge: Cambridge University Press, 1971).

4 The agencies to which the miracles were attributed were often different — the landlord being the more likely one to be in league with the devil!

5 It was conceded that some greens were necessary, especially in early spring when impure blood caused boils, pimples and skin disorders. Nettles which grew in profusion and required no cultivation (but thrived on neglect) were deemed an admirable tonic when plucked young and boiled.

6 The Reverend Hickey, who later ministered in historic Boolavogue, wrote extensively on farming subjects under the pen-name of 'Martin Doyle'. A copy of the *Collected Works of Martin Doyle* is available in the National Library, Dublin.

7 The gardens of Drummully are now tended by the Sisters of the Holy Rosary who have their headquarters in the big house. It is historically appropriate that in later years Killeshandra Co-operative Creamery should be in the forefront with schemes to benefit its farmer members. In the years after 1948 it imported and sold large quantities of phosphate to its members at cost price — a scheme which greatly enhanced the milk supply from the small drumlin farms of Cavan, impoverished after the war years. Later, in the nineteen fifties, under

In the west of Ireland, where benevolent landlords were somewhat thinner on the ground, the Congested Districts Board had been vigorously experimenting with new crops and attempting improvements with old ones. It was with the assistance of the Board and its instructor, Mr P. Lawrey, a Cornish market-gardening expert, that the Kilronan Agricultural Co-op undertook the growing of early potatoes in the Aran Islands in 1899. The Department of Agriculture, from its foundation, pursued this experiment at likely locations along the coasts of Cork, Kerry and Clare, where severe frosts were unlikely. By 1904 early potato-growing was firmly established in County Cork, particularly in the Clonakilty area.[8] Certain areas of Clare were also doing well: crops were disposed of by early June and gross returns of up to £50 per statute acre were reported.

Cottage gardening had an economic and aesthetic appeal for Horace Plunkett. He saw in it a valuable training of character and "one of the primary means of elevating the tone of the people generally, and training their minds for the adoption of other forms of minor industry." Consequently the IAOS was quickly in the field with the publication of leaflets[9] and the appointment of a horticultural expert and organiser, Thomas Shaw, FRHS, in 1899.

> The IAOS has realised the fact that one of the first steps towards the development of the various branches of Cottage Industry in which our people living in rural districts could profitably engage, should be the concentration of their attention on their own homes and the rendering of these homes more attractive and comfortable. The primitive state in which the majority of the people in some portions of the country existed, the glaring contrast between the condition of their lives and homes and those of the people of other countries, where the cultivation of simple fruits, vegetables and flowers is understood by the people, and the appreciation of the great possibilities of Ireland in the matter of supplying our home markets with those garden products for which our country is so eminently suited — all pointed to the establishment of a general system of Cottage Gardening . . .[10]

For all his qualifications, Shaw was no dilettante academic. He preferred to do his lecturing in the field with a horticultural implement in his hand, giving practical instruction in planting, pruning, grafting, preparing soil and sowing seeds of various garden crops. He was a man of Anderson-like energy: during his first year as organiser he lectured extensively throughout Louth, Dublin, Tipperary, Limerick, Sligo, Cavan, Leitrim, Mayo and Roscommon. He was not at all averse to sleeping in a different bed each

---

the guidance of manager John O'Neill and pilot area advisor, Paddy Keenan, the Killeshandra society pioneered a farm prize scheme, giving awards under a number of headings to the best-kept and most efficiently managed farms.

8 *The Irish Homestead*, 4 June 1904, p.467.
9 *Growth of Garden Vegetables on Small Farms, Fruit Farming, Instructions for Establishing Experimental Plots* and, equally relevant, *Co-operation and Social Life in Ireland*.
10 IAOS Annual Report 1901, p.35.

night but always rose early to view the flora of each new district before getting down to the specifics of gardening. In the tradition of Johnny Appleseed, he sought everywhere to leave something growing behind him — but in the organisational as well as the horticultural sense.

The most exciting prospect for co-operative organisational success was in the district of Drogheda, where a total of some 400 acres of fruit was already grown for the Dublin market. However, middlemen were reaping the richest harvest and the costs of packaging, freight and sale commissions were oppressive for the individual grower.[11] In 1900 some 200 Louth and Dublin growers subscribed a capital of £2,000 to form a co-operative society in Drogheda — Drogheda Fruit Ltd. The aim was collective marketing of fruit, either as the fresh product carefully selected, or in the form of jam or other preserves. For this latter purpose a factory was necessary. Suitable temporary premises were secured and, with the blessing of the mayor and the active support of the citizens of Drogheda (over a hundred of whom were numbered amongst the co-op membership of 298), the project was enthusiastically undertaken. The IAOS appointed as its fruit expert Mr Willie Orr from the traditional apple-growing area of Loughgall, County Armagh.[12] About 700 tons of fruit (raspberries, gooseberries, currants, damsons, plums and apples) were produced annually in the Drogheda area and the greater part was exported and made into jam in England.

The Drogheda co-operators[13] were interested not only in jam manufacture but also the most modern techniques of fruit and vegetable processing. There was a demand for dried fruit and vegetables for army rations, for the last of the 'gentlemen's wars' was being waged against the farming Boers of South Africa. The Drogheda men had the help and advice of James Harper of Ebley, Stroud, Gloucestershire, a practical expert in these matters, who came to Drogheda to plan the factory layout and install suitable equipment:

> Work was commenced in September with damsons grown locally . . . These were purchased at 5/- per cwt, were quite successfully dried and finished and were ultimately sold at a very considerable profit. Local apples were also dried; these were bought at 3/- per cwt and 7/- per cwt, the former were turned into rings and cored apples, the latter into

11 The IAOS calculated these as more than £11 per acre on average — equivalent to the total cost of planting and maintaining (first year) an acre of strawberries. See *The Irish Homestead*, 2 February 1900, p. 351.

12 The Society had previously commissioned Edward Luckhurst, fruit expert of Derbyshire County Council, who was recommended by the English Board of Agriculture, to inspect the districts of Balbriggan, the Naul, Gormanstown, Slane, Duleek and Drogheda and report on their fruit-growing possibilities. The local police (Royal Irish Constabulary) co-operated by gathering statistics — names and addresses of fruit-growers, farm size, acreage of fruit, and so on.

13 Notable amongst them were Arthur Mitchell and Thomas McCourt of Stamullen, Miss Weir of Weir Hall Drogheda, Michael McKeown of Julianstown, Captain Nicholson of Glenmor, Colonel Coddington of Oldbridge, Joe English of Smithstown and a Mr Arnold and a Mr Tiernan, both "extensive fruit-growers in the Gormanstown district". The largest plot of fruit was seven acres and the smallest just ⅛ acre.

pippins. Owing to the fruit being much too ripe when dried, this part of the work did not yield a profit, the dried product being too 'brown' to fetch the highest prices. A good quality apple, not so ripe, sent from Carrick-on-Suir, was most successfully dried, being equal when finished to the best imported from abroad. Potatoes, cabbages, parsnips, carrots, turnips, beetroot, onions, herbs, etc., were also evaporated and when mixed in the usual proportions made a most excellent soup. All this has not been sold but such as has been disposed of has been sold at a very satisfactory profit.

The workers were drawn from the district; three girls, a domestic servant, a factory employee and a farm worker, learnt the art very quickly and really showed remarkable aptitude in carrying on the work.[14]

The products — jams, dried vegetables and fruit — produced at Drogheda, and models of the machinery used, were exhibited at the RDS Winter Show and at the Great Exhibition in Cork in 1902. Mr Harper averred that fruit and vegetable processing had a great future in Ireland — a much-repeated and familiar prediction ever since! At the IAOS annual general meeting of 1901, Charles McCann of Drogheda illustrated the success of his society not only in manufacture but in the fresh fruit market — a package of fruit which formerly fetched only 12 shillings now brought 37/6, mainly because of better grading, packing and marketing. Amid much merriment, he sought to exact guarantees from delegates 'jointly or severally' to eat nothing but Drogheda jam.

Guarantees, if given, would have proved difficult to keep, for little more jam was made by the Drogheda society. When all the excitement and experimentation was accounted, the total turnover of Drogheda Fruit Ltd was only £733 in 1901 and £2,530 for the full year of 1902. Fruit merchants paid inflated prices in the short-term to starve the Drogheda factory, the disloyalty of the member growers was outstanding, and consequent committee and management squabbles soon brought the venture to an end.

Three more co-operative horticulture societies were formed in 1902: Carrick-on-Suir, Bray, and County Kerry Fruit Growers Ltd. All were short-lived, despite the fact that the consumer continued to pay more for fruit and vegetables in Dublin than he would have had to pay in London. Ireland continued to import large quantities of apples from Canada, the USA and Australia, unit freight costs from these foreign parts to Dublin being considerably less than on small quantities dispatched from Armagh, Dungarvan, Kerry or Cork.

... there is not much use in organising Societies of fruit-growers on a large scale until the Railway Companies are prepared to make very substantial reductions in the rates charged for the conveyance of garden produce. At present, by the time the Railway charges and marketing expenses are paid, the fruit and vegetable grower has very

14 IAOS Annual Report 1901, p.36.

little left. Of course these expenses can be considerably reduced if large areas are organised and depots provided at convenient centres . . . but the carriage on small lots is prohibitive.[15]

It was a vicious circle and the railway companies would do nothing to break it. The people who had money invested in the Irish railway companies were generally not of co-operative stock and were notably ill-disposed to make concessions which might promote the movement. As early as 1896 the co-operators were complaining bitterly of the refusal of all but the Waterford-Limerick and the Dublin, Wicklow and Wexford companies to give cheap fares for delegates attending the IAOS annual conference — a concession freely granted on the occasion of even the most trivial football match or 'any £4.19.0. race meeting'. Later in 1909 some railway companies withdrew the facility of single fare travel for IAOS organisers — a concession which they had grudgingly granted in 1904. The co-operators, for their part, had from the earliest days sought a generous co-operation with the railway boards — Plunkett, Digges la Touche, Coroner Byrne and others projecting the prosperity which would ensue from agricultural growth. So unyielding was the response and so great the frustrations of the rural societies that, although the national committee sought to pursue its policy of sweet reasonableness and continuing representations, from 1895 onwards there were very few conferences at which a resolution was not put forward calling for nationalisation of the railways. These proposals, as Plunkett wryly observed, had as much political potential as a snowball in the nether regions and only served to reinforce the smug stockholders in their already inbred conviction that Plunkett and his co-operators were liberal subversives and socialists of the most dangerous type.[16]

Freight charges also militated against the early potato-growers: only in the Cork area did they produce a sufficient volume to reduce unit costs. The Aran growers and those in the seaside areas of Clare and Kerry were never big enough to afford suitable premises or good managers. Local buyers nibbled so successfully at the small total of produce that organisation or forward planning became impossible: orders solemnly promised could not be fulfilled because grower members sold for short-term advantage to the local merchant, who gave a higher price for small lots only because he knew of the co-op contract and was determined that it should not be met, or repeated. Growers consistently resisted the idea of quality control and grading, arguing with vehement business ignorance that merchants paid a good price for everything when trade was good — grading was merely an elaborate way of cheating the grower still further in a time of poor markets! No co-operative became strong enough to under-take local processing, which ostensibly would obviate freight charges and

15 IAOS Annual Report 1902, p.28.
16 One old gentleman in a country club said to Anderson, "It's a pity Mr Plunkett was an Oxford man. Tom—, my neighbour, sent his boy there — a clever young fellow — and back he comes, an out-and-out Socialist. I believe he even wears a red tie!" See *With Horace Plunkett in Ireland*, pp.41–42.

also enable a price to be paid for misshapen, odd-size fruit, or fruit of good but second-rate quality. The IAOS suggested the local manufacture of cider, a pleasant wholesome drink and an Irish national beverage in former times. It would provide a suitable local outlet for apples. The idea was taken up by private enterprise in Clonmel but co-operators generally looked on it as a desirable but rather remote possibility, like the growing of flowers (for table decoration) — advocated for Cork and Kerry to supply Dublin, Cork and English cities, then getting their flowers from the Channel Islands.

After the establishment of the Department of Agriculture and Technical Instruction, several county councils appointed horticultural instructors, most of whom, after a few frustrating essays at organisation for commercial production, confined their efforts to technical instruction, to help the rural family to provide a range of fruit and vegetables sufficient for home needs.[17] Even this limited objective was rarely achieved. Apart from the few (usually better-off, better educated and predominantly of the methodical and industrious Protestant ethic), the work habits of most farmers were but poorly attuned to the needs of the kitchen garden.

In the horse-and-buggy days, work hours were long and the labour was manual and strenuous. It required great stamina, after a hard day's toil, to take a spade after supper for more work in the garden, especially if, apart from potatoes, cabbages and onions, you did not know the best way of doing things! There were a host of other difficulties facing the would-be horticulturalist / farmer. The axiom that good fences make good neighbours was accepted, but little acted upon. Irish farm fences seventy years ago were even worse than they are now.[18] Today the open-plan or badly fenced garden is at risk from tinkers' horses, but up to recent times when motor traffic was still light, many farmers were none too worried if their livestock strayed along the roadsides or into neighbour's fields. Even fences that were to rancher Plunkett's specification, "horse-high, bull-strong and hog-tight", were not proof against rabbits.[19]

The overriding difficulty was marketing. In the case of horticulture, the indirect problem occasioned by a chaotic marketing system was even more intractable than the obvious ones. All down the years the lack of market stability for any specific agricultural product deterred farmers from specialising, concentrating their production on one particular crop or one type of livestock. It is significant that the co-operative development of dairying provided the first (and for a long time the only) opportunity for

17 The energetic Thomas Shaw resigned in 1904 to go as trade organiser to the IAWS.
18 In his baseline report to the Congested Districts Board on the district of the Rosses, W. L. Micks refers repeatedly to the inadequacy of fencing: "Exceedingly few fences are proof against sheep . . . just before sowing of potatoes and oats all the sheep are driven off to the mountains and moors, to which uninviting pasturages they are restricted only by the unremitting vigilance of children and well-trained mongrel dogs; and very frequently the frontier patches of the cultivated land suffer severely from the incursions of sheep."
19 From 1935 onwards, many co-operative societies in Northern Ireland purchased equipment for poison gassing rabbits and other vermin in their burrows, since rabbits were causing havoc not only among vegetables, but among cereals and ordinary farm crops. President Harold Barbour commented on the problem at the UAOS annual general meeting in 1936.

the small farmer to specialise in one aspect of husbandry.[20] The farmers' answer to price uncertainty was to 'have a little bit of everything'. This frequently gave rise to a system of so-called mixed farming which was very 'mixed' indeed. It was not unusual to find a farmer with wheat, barley and oats, potatoes, sugar-beet, turnips and mangels, cows, cattle, sheep and horses. For farmyard enterprises he would have pigs, hens, ducks, geese, turkeys and guinea fowl. This was particularly true in the better tillage areas most suitable for horticultural enterprises. Horticultural crops, if they are to be successful, require dedication and constant care.

Even today, with modern techniques of seeding, weed-killing and disease prevention, horticultural crops are still very labour intensive, time-consuming and have hair-trigger demands for the application of timely skills. It is never a simple matter of substituting an acre of fruit or vegetables for an acre or more of some previously-grown crop. Even a small plot of fruit may demand a complete overhaul and readjustment of the farming programme. Enthusiastic promoters, though they are immensely skilled and knowledgeable on their own horticultural items, are still astoundingly ill-conversant with or heedless of the farmer's daily routine. Thus, in a district-wide campaign to promote a new crop, processors and advisory experts adopt a hard-sell technique which enthuses farmers with the prospects of monetary gain but frequently presumes too much of the farmer's own ability to allocate the new project efficiently into his farming programme. They concentrate on informing and training the farmer in the finest details of cultivation but are often blissfully unaware of the wider farm-management implications. Farmers, like school-children, are a prey to the enthusiast / expert / teacher who unconsciously presumes that the student can devote his whole thought and energy to one particular subject in the curriculum. The superimposition of an horticultural enterprise upon an already overcrowded farm work schedule is inevitably disastrous. It continues to happen because the myth still persists that 'the small farmer is a shrewd business operator although he may not look it'. The reality is very different.

Farming in Ireland is still very much a traditional occupation which is *inherited* rather than entered into after consideration of economic criteria. The typical small Irish farm is farmed because it is there. The way it is farmed this year is to a great extent determined by how it was farmed last year. It is possible to plant a different crop in the tillage ground, but rarely is there a scientific appraisal to allocate land, labour, capital and management to maximum advantage in a well-planned, coordinated programme. Irish peasant farming in the early days sought to compensate for the low input of capital by a maximum input of labour. This was a sensible if not always effective stratagem. It did, however, fix patterns and habits which became enshrined as 'traditional' and did not always respond and adapt effectively when labour (as well as capital) began to be a scarce resource.

20 Even in dairying, although the price per gallon of milk was to some extent steady and/or predictable, there were still wild fluctuations in farmers' incomes because of weather, fodder supply, the suitability of milking season and the price of calves.

The development of horticulture, or rather its failure to develop, must be viewed against this socio-economic backcloth. The failure then appears less incomprehensible and the difficulties outlined, none of them insuperable but collectively very formidable, offer some explanation to the town-dweller who may have come to view the problem simply as one of lazy farmers reluctant to grow crops.

The fruit-growers of Armagh formed a co-operative in 1911 — Ulster Fruit Growers Association. Again the buyers conspired and, within a few years, the membership had been whittled down from 143 to 37. The financial commitment of £12 paid-up share capital by 143 growers was less than wholehearted. The society retained a formal existence for a number of years but did very little trade. It was much the same story with the Piltown Co-operative Fruit Growers Society in County Kilkenny. This was a small society of fifteen fruit-growers who subscribed 5 shilling shares. It was founded in 1914, wound up in 1917 and reformed shortly afterwards. The society was still on the books in 1924 but did little effective business. Generally, horticulture persisted only in places which were close to large markets or else were so pre-eminently suitable in soil and climate that horticulture could hardly be avoided, as in the apple-growing areas of Armagh and Dungarvan. During the years of World War I a number of small co-ops registered: the Lisburn Garden Plots Association, the North Antrim Agricultural Association and the Foynes Tillage Society (all established in 1917) and the Food Conservation Societies at Navan and Tipperary (1918). These were mostly inspired by the 'Grow More Food' campaign and disappeared at the war's end.

In the lean years of the nineteen twenties and thirties very little happened in the co-operative field or garden. Creameries and store societies sometimes helped groups of growers in a small way to market some of their produce. This was often a useful deterrent against exploitation — a warning to commercial buyers not to become too greedy. The horticultural co-ops, even where they were moribund, had also a useful function in this regard.

Following the outbreak of the economic war, the Free State government imposed import duties on all classes of fruit and vegetables, fresh or processed, that could be successfully grown within the country. The Department of Agriculture sought to encourage home production of a wide variety of fruit and vegetables, and thousands of demonstration plots were laid down throughout the country. Onions and tomatoes received particular attention and strawberry-growing in County Wexford proved so promising that its large-scale adoption in the nineteen fifties was inevitable.[21] Even by the late nineteen thirties, commercial onion-growing had taken root in the Castlegregory area of County Kerry. Special efforts were made to encourage tomato-growing in the remote Gaeltacht areas and

21 During the early years of World War II, the Wexford county manager, T. D. Sinnott, inspired a scheme for planting apple trees on the roadsides. Despite many misgivings, the project succeeded. The quantity of fruit which survives is perhaps rather small, but the trees beautify and distinguish the Wexford roadways and are particularly attractive in blossom-time.

between 1933 and 1940 the Department gave loans to over 200 small-holders in these Gaelic-speaking areas for the erection of small glass-houses. The benefits of co-operation were extolled but no formal steps were taken to establish suitable co-operative structures to help the growers. Even the advisory service of technical instruction for the growers was far too thinly spread and many individual ventures failed for lack of proper know-how. As with many government schemes before and since, the small schemes for the encouragement of horticulture could be suggested, perhaps uncharitably, to be more of a publicity effort and a series of impressively sounding, modestly costed projects on the politicians' record, than an earnest attempt to get a worthwhile job done.

The Northern Ireland co-operators tried to form a co-operative vegetable association in 1935 but were not successful. South of the border, there was very little stirring until 1938:

> An effort was made in the Clonmel District to organise the sale of apples according to approved modern methods. It is regretted that, owing to the scarcity of varieties of apples suitable for the trade and to the results of neglect in cultivation over many years, it could not be hoped for some time to come to organise the sale of apples to compete successfully with imported apples. Generally, much attention to orchards is needed, and several years must elapse before success can be expected in the organised sale of apples on a large scale. The Committee are grateful to Mr George Scott, Annaclare, Armagh, one of the most successful apple growers in the North, for the advice on the growing and preparation of apples for market he gave so freely to the Society.[22]

Despite daunting obstacles, the project was pursued. It was the out-break of World War II and the shortage of foreign supplies that gave the real impetus. By 1940 the Department of Agriculture was deeply involved and gave valuable assistance in organising apple-growers and arranging marketing through a number of co-operative societies — Ardfinnan Agricultural Society (County Tipperary), Askeaton Creamery (County Limerick), Castlelyons Creamery (County Cork) all responded energetically, and in the Waterford / South Kilkenny area, Piltown CA & DS took up where Piltown Horticultural Society had left off. Success attended their efforts and they were soon joined in a combined marketing scheme by an association of growers at Killorglin, County Kerry. The IAOS expressed hopes that there would be a revival of apple-growing to an acreage comparable to that grown on landlord estates in the early nineteenth century, "when Irish-grown apples were generally in high repute and when Irish-made cider was second to none."

Everyone became more conscious of his kitchen garden during the war years. Town and parish councils provided allotments for those eager to 'dig

22 IAOS Annual Report 1938, p.8.

for victory' or at least for food. However, farmers were too involved in the production of the more basic crops: without cereals and potatoes the island could starve if war continued and shipping failed. These was no possibility of large-scale horticultural innovations until the Emergency had passed. However, many existing orchards were rehabilitated and well cared for. Apples met ready sales and good profits. By 1950 the Waterford apple-growers were confident and willing to face post-war competition. Ninety-seven growers formed the Co-operative Fruit Growers Society Ltd in Dungarvan, subscribing modest £10 shares but committing themselves to loans of £95,000 for building and the most modern equipment for apple-grading, packing and refrigerated storage.²³ From a modest £9,000 turnover in the first year, the society has continued to grow despite seasonal fluctuations of fortune; membership has more than doubled and turnover topped the £100,000 mark in 1969. Share capital is now over £14,000 and loan capital has been reduced. Onion-growing in Castlegregory was co-operativised in 1955; it was named St Brendan's Co-operative, after Brendan the Navigator, and was capably steered by manager, John Mark Egan, a disciple of the community development movement, Muintir na Tíre.²⁴ Within five years the output of onions in the area had been quadrupled and the Irish home-grown onion had redeemed its previously bad reputation.

There was a speedier development of horticultural co-ops in the nineteen sixties with Wexford Growers (1960) and Kerry Foods (1962). In 1965 Kilcrohane took up the bulb-growing for which Cork had long been recommended. It now has some sixty growers. A small number of early potato-growers in Cork formed a co-op in the same year. Fane Valley in Monaghan and Portumna Packers went into the processing and packing of vegetables, as did Clare Vegetable Co-op in Ballyvaughan a year later. A large-scale fruit and vegetable co-op, grading and packing for the fresh market, was established at Blakes Cross, north County Dublin in 1963, as North Dublin Growers Ltd. The Dublin horticulturalists again proved notably disloyal for a period²⁵ and the co-op was soon in trouble. The Department of Agriculture came to the rescue and further loan capital was provided after IAOS and Department experts had planned to reorganise the venture. North Dublin Growers Ltd is now trading profitably, has a membership of 620 growers and a turnover in 1974 of £2 million.

During this period private companies were making rapid strides in getting farmers to grow fruit and vegetables on contract for processing. Strawberries became quite an important crop in County Wexford and in many parts of the country farmers grew peas, carrots and other vegetables

23 The society also provided high-pressure sprayers and other orchard equipment for the use of growers. The Department of Agriculture, as well as underwriting the Agricultural Credit Corporation loan, provided the services of three horticultural advisors and financed a special scheme for planting an additional 500 acres of dessert apples in the district.
24 Founded in 1931 as a voluntary association for the promotion, by the application of Christian principles, of the cultural and material welfare of the Irish people.
25 It should be noted, however, that in this notoriously unco-operative county, there were always a few steadfast co-operators whose efforts were truly heroic.

for canning, drying or freezing. The semi-state company, Comhlucht Siúicre Eireann Teoranta (Irish Sugar Company Ltd) and its associate, Erin Foods, entered the processing field with an eye to the export market. Perhaps of all the experts it was their general manager, Michael J. Costello, who saw most clearly the necessity for Ireland to develop a fitting horticultural industry, the scale on which the problem should be tackled and the resources required for proper development. He had brought a decrepit and inefficient beet-sugar industry to life and had developed it to play a major role in the national life, benefiting farmers, workers, native industry and the national economy. An ardent believer in the benefits of co-operation, Costello had continually sought to encourage co-operative developments in both the agricultural and industrial fields. He actively associated himself with the horticultural developments in Kerry and Cork (Fastnet Co-op, 1963) and Glencolumbkille, County Donegal.[26] He had established vegetable processing plants for Erin Foods at Carlow, Thurles and Tuam and pioneered the new development of accelerated freeze drying of all kinds of food products. It soon became evident, however, that a large, nation-wide horticultural development would not receive the measure of financial commitment that was necessary and, amid considerable controversy, Costello departed in 1966. Erin Foods Ltd was subsequently taken over by the international food processing firm of Heinz. "A sell out", said the forthright Costello, "hardly conceivable in the worst banana Republic!"

It is inconceivable but that in the modern world Ireland must have a future in horticulture. The departure of General Costello and subsequent events may have inevitably delayed matters, but recent indications are that the future for the industry is promising. The main concern is that it should be an Irish future in Irish hands. Whilst Irish co-ops handle over 30 per cent. of fruit and vegetables for the fresh market, they have as yet but 10 per cent. of the processing side.

---

26 The Glencolumbkille society, Coras an Eargail Teo, established in 1961 in association with the Irish Sugar Company and Erin Foods, had only limited success in vegetable-processing (mainly celery). It has since scaled down its vegetable enterprise and has a successful fish-processing business.

Chapter Twenty-Two

Co-operative Insurance

The concept of insurance and communal protection is near the core of the co-operative ethic. The labourers in Ralahine operated a simple form of sickness and unemployment benefit scheme based on a premium payment of ½d for every shilling earned in wages. In Britain, on a more formal basis, the Co-operative Insurance Company was established in Rochdale in 1867, housed in the premises of the Equitable Pioneers.[1] The types of insurance provided by the English movement were, however, of only limited advantage to the agriculturally-based producer societies in Ireland. The IAOS reported in 1899:

> The question of Co-operative Insurance of Live Stock is one which has been for long in our minds. The premiums charged by the large . . . companies in England are prohibitive, and practically there is no system of Live Stock Insurance in operation in Ireland. This is not a matter which is of so much importance to the large farmer with whom the loss of a cow is an incident to be occasionally expected and which is provided for in the ordinary wear and tear of stock; but it is quite otherwise with our small holders who form so large a part of our agricultural population and who have only a few animals, perhaps only a single cow and two or three pigs, with whom the loss of part of their stock creates a serious financial difficulty . . .

Father Tom Finlay saw insurance as a necessary ancillary service to that provided by the co-operative agricultural banks; with Anderson and Digges la Touche, he hammered out a detailed set of rules for the establishment and running of special co-operative livestock insurance societies. The envisaged constitution of these societies was very similar to that of the agricultural banks and comparable societies on the Continent. Under the Friendly Societies Act, the societies would be exempt from stamp duty on insurance policies, and the principle of unlimited liability would operate as

---

1 This enterprise had to be registered as a joint-stock company because insurance was outside the authorised functions of co-operative societies, under the Industrial and Provident Societies Acts, until 1893. The Co-operative Insurance Company did not become a full co-operative — the Co-operative Insurance Society — until 1899. It was taken over by the CWS and the SCWS in 1912.

in the case of the co-op banks. Provision was made for the insuring of cattle, horses, sheep and pigs, but only for established herds or flocks kept permanently in the area of the society's operations. There was a recommendation for the exclusion from membership of livestock dealers, and due provision was made against the insurance of "animals ill-fed, over-worked, unhealthy or incapacitated by age or other cause". It was hoped that annual premiums could be arranged at an initial payment of 2 per cent. of the market value of the animal insured and, if all went well, this percentage would be sufficient to meet claims and build up a respectable reserve fund.

The matter of insurance was discussed at IAOS meetings throughout the country and the principle of co-operative insurance everywhere met with undisputed approval. But after everybody had nodded their approval and even spoken at some length on the merits of the scheme, there was a remarkable slowness in implementing it. A year passed with more discussion and local canvassing, but no group actually registered. It was hoped that insurance societies would be established to handle not only livestock but general farm and farm-household insurances. In particular, it was hoped that they would be operating in good time to embrace the provision for insurance under the Workman's Compensation Act 1900, due to become law on 18 July 1901. As the months slipped by, the IAOS saw little hope of local organisation being ready in time and hastened to make arrangements for local societies and their members to effect insurance through the IAOS headquarters. A satisfactory arrangement was made with the Ocean Accident and Guarantee Corporation, whereby farmers who were members of co-op societies could effect workman's compensation insurance at premium payments as low as one shilling per £25 wages paid. A farmer paying £100 a year in wages[2] could cover his liability for 3 shillings, whereas, up to then, no insurance company had been offering any policy at a lower premium than 5 shillings per £100.

Very good concessions were also negotiated with Ocean and with the Norwich Union regarding fire, life and other classes of insurance. It was never envisaged that local co-operative insurance societies would, of their own resources, be able to give coverage to farmers at premium rates comparable to the large commercial companies, but it was hoped that they would provide the local organisation for collecting premiums and, by popularising insurance among farmers, would build up a volume of business which would enable them, either directly or through IAOS head-quarters, to exact the best terms from the commercial firms. The provision of livestock insurance would be their own exclusive venture, which, with the benefit of local knowledge and selectivity regarding membership, could be operated as successfully as the credit banks.

However, the IAOS soon began to see that the field of operations could not be too local. While the local society would be the unit, it would be necessary concurrently to establish a sizeable number of local societies all

---

2 At the turn of the century, £100 per annum represented the wages of four or five adult males in agriculture in most areas.

linked in a nation-wide federation, offlaying some portion of the risk through reinsurance and, most important, giving the large statistical spread, on which forecasts of claims could be assured without fluctuations from year to year:

> While it would have been easy to start local societies, it would not be good policy to do so, as an epidemic or even an unusually high death rate among the animals insured would be certain to break up the association. To ensure a normal premium the losses must be spread over a wide area and a large number of members, and no one county has become co-operative enough in spirit up to the present to ensure the union of thousands of farmers in a new enterprise... The federation of Societies which is rapidly being effected for various purposes will, in a little time, afford the basis on which such developments as livestock insurance can take place, as it will give the connection between districts widely apart which is necessary for a beginning to be made.[3]

There was a dichotomy in IAOS thinking. At the turn of the century, societies were springing up at a bewildering pace. The IAOS committee and overwrought staff could not hope to do everything; they must clearly apply their limited efforts to best advantage to exercise some control on the booming movement. It was natural, they thought, that 'productive' co-operation should appeal more strongly than conservative co-operation which sought to preserve resources, minimise individual losses and effect economies. On the other hand, it was glaringly obvious that certain risks had to be minimised before the small farmer could confidently undertake the necessary expanded production. There could be no 'better living' unless there was better farming and better business. The dilemma was to reconcile what was necessary and what was feasible.

In 1902 the IAOS calculated that the co-operative movement had insurable risks of more than £9 million which should have insurance coverage. Insurance was required for co-operative buildings and plant, creamery boilers, fidelity guarantees and wages, farm buildings and produce, personal life and livestock. The £9 million was a minimum figure; Father Finlay, a man loth to speculate, was sure that the total insurable risks connected with the movement were nearer to £20 million than they were to £10 million. Even a fraction of this business was, for the time being, beyond the financial competence of the co-operators themselves. Indeed, some thought that there had to be excessive dependence on the commercial banks to provide even fixed capital for creameries, not to mention working capital for co-operative stores. The IAOS committee published the facts and offered the co-operative movement's insurance business to "some really enterprising and forward looking Company" which was eager to take it on. There were no takers.

Comparatively good concessions were negotiated piecemeal with

3   IAOS Annual Report 1901, p.37.

individual companies like the Ocean, the Norwich, and the Railway Passengers Insurance Company on policies of life assurance, fidelity bonds, fire, accident, workman's compensation, and so on. At local level the effort was patchy and in some places less than wholeheartedly co-operative. Some of the stronger societies, whether through local connection or their unyielding addiction to huckstering — as evinced in their marketing of butter and eggs — tended to give their insurance to local agents. The consequent failure of IAOS headquarters to deliver the volume of insurance business that had been anticipated, seriously dampened the enthusiasm of insurers and left them less disposed to tickle the market with more expansionary offers.

The concept of insurance was new and strange to the Irish peasant farmers, a fact not surprising in a rural community that for generations had the expectation of little and the assurance of nothing, not even the short-term assurance of a roof overhead. For many families on the fretful borderline of subsistence, the loss of a cow could mean disaster. Yet in this situation there tended to be more dependence on the spiritual power of prayer than on the temporal safeguard of insurance. The cost of an insurance premium might be small but it always represented the price of some article of foodstuff or clothing for which there was invariably a more immediate and pressing need. Many beliefs and superstitions in the folk culture ran contrary to the insurance ideology. These varied from the feeling that insurance would somewhat dull the edge of husbandry to the fear that the taking of a life policy, like the making of a will, would tempt providence and shorten the life of the 'victim'. Some looked on indemnity insurance as a game of chance or at least were inclined to regret the waste of money if, after paying several annual premiums, some little misfortune had not struck to entitle them to a payment.[4] It was also widely held that farming was such a risky business — a prey to weather, disease and scores of other natural and man-made hazards — that it would be impossible to insure against everything. Farm profits at their best could not justify such expenditure. While it was agreed that certain risks like fire should be covered, the gloomy contemplation of the whole risk-riddled enterprise tended to excuse a certain inertia. As for farm livestock, the chances of establishing a comprehensive system of monetary insurance must be viewed in the context of the times when literally thousands of farmers were reluctant to incur the small expenditure involved in necessary 'husbandry' insurance, such as the dosing of animals to eliminate parasites like fluke or worms, or to prevent diseases.

Near Ballyhaunis in County Mayo the first Co-operative Livestock Insurance Society was formed at Aughmore in the early days of 1903. No information is available, apart from the listing of the society in the IAOS

---

4 The mixed feelings on this score are I think admirably illustrated by one farmer's reported comment on renewing his premiums: "God bless the mark, and spare us from harm but if something bad doesn't happen to me soon I will have wasted a lot of fine insurance money for nothing!"

reports, which continued until 1905. Apparently the venture never got off the ground since no returns, financial or otherwise, were ever made.[5] Livestock insurance was a lively topic discussed at all the IAOS district conferences in 1904 but the only positive outcome was a Livestock Insurance Society at Billis, County Cavan, in 1905. Before any business was undertaken, the Billis committee, whose previous success with dairy, store and credit societies suggested that they were not easily daunted, were forced to have second thoughts. The provision of a comprehensive scheme of livestock insurance was just not possible for the time being. There were local men — excellent judges of livestock — whom the society had hoped might do the leg work of visiting farms to select and record details of animals to be insured.[6] Unfortunately, by the time plans were ready, the ranks of the livestock experts were depleted by the loss of two of their best men. Those remaining were hard-working farmers, already involved in 'co-operative overtime'. The few men who were available for some voluntary work were deemed to be insufficiently skilled and the society (even the whole co-op group) lacked money to employ anyone on a full-time basis.

The IAOS came to recognise the difficulties and urged its members to forego attempts at comprehensive insurance co-ops and concentrate for the moment on the insurance of dairy cows. With this in view, the IAOS formulated its own scheme of milch cow insurance in 1908. It was envisaged that initially the scheme would operate through the creameries but that agricultural societies and credit banks would become centres in due course.[7] The creamery would form a local insurance group with an admission fee of 1 shilling per farmer. All the groups would be federated in a national union serviced by the IAOS, which undertook to organise the groups, teach the methods, supervise the system and audit the accounts for a small fee. It was hoped that the creamery manager would act as secretary to the group, keep the insurance registers and generally manage the scheme locally. For this he should be appropriately paid, as should the 'valuers' — local members elected at each annual general meeting. It was recommended that two valuers should be elected and employed for each quarter of the creamery area, i.e., a minimum of eight valuers covering the entire milk-collection district. By this time the IAOS had the benefit of some livestock statistics from co-operative societies on the Continent, which indicated that mortality in milch cows ranged from 1 to 3 per cent.

5　It is understood that this society shared the same personnel as Aughmore Co-operative Agricultural Society, founded earlier that year: chairman, Rev Pat Molloy; treasurer, John Egan; secretary, James Drudy. When Drudy fell ill shortly afterwards, the job of secretary was performed by thirteen year-old Andrew Patrick Waldron (acting for his father, John A. Waldron, the local schoolteacher). Young Waldron subsequently emigrated to Canada and became editor (1951-58) of a co-operative newspaper in Saskatoon, *The Western Producer*.

6　The identification of individual cattle, which because of the eartagging under the bovine tuberculosis eradication scheme is today a simple matter, used to be a formidable task. The 'insurers' would need to fill in comprehensive details of colour markings and so on, or else resort to a laborious system of branding.

7　For precise details, see IAOS Reports for 1908, p.41, and for 1910, p.103. The scheme was largely devised by E.A. Stopford.

The Irish scheme was devised so that premium payments were calculated to cover losses up to 4 per cent. The scheme made provision for timely compulsory slaughter of animals[8] and it was hoped that with an efficient system of dealing with carcases, good management and such supervision as is possible in a limited local area ("where everything goes on under the eye of the neighbours"), the system would operate so successfully that the premium could be reduced. The premiums that were initially envisaged worked out on average at something more than 2 per cent. of the market value of the animal when insured, for an indemnity of two-thirds of the agreed or arbitrated value at time of loss. For an animal valued at £16, the premium payable was 6/8 (33 pence); for a heifer valued at £5, the premium was 2 shillings. At the discretion of the creamery manager, a certain proportion of the premium could be paid by deductions from a member's milk account. Cattle under six months or over twelve years were not insurable. In 1910 the upper value limit was set at £16. The committee could, however, insure cows of greater value by special permission, but purely on the proven commercial value of the beast — her 'farm and dairy value', rather than any notional figure of her value as a pure-bred or show animal.

The co-operators had always a pragmatic approach in such matters,[9] not always emulated by livestock breeders or those in charge of formulating national livestock policies. The IAOS leaflet no 24, *Cattle Insurance*, (April 1910) makes the pointed comment "Prize cattle, pure breds and fancy breeds are not wanted." The scheme was taken up and operated more or less successfully by a number of creameries. The society stated to have achieved the greatest success was the Whitecross CDS in the County Armagh, whose manager, John McDermott, seems to have operated his own modified system so well that it became a significant factor in ensuring milk supply to his creamery in the face of keen and sometimes unfair competition from proprietary creameries in his area.

The premium payments were at the rate of 6d in the £ on the value of milk supplied. All the members' cows were covered and premiums were deducted entirely from the milk account. The society paid half of the vet's fee in all cases but claimed the hide of all dead cows. Compensation was two-thirds of the average value of milk per cow, on the owner's milk supply during the previous year, multiplied by two. Thus, if a farmer had ten cows and supplied £100 worth of milk, the amount paid on the death of any cow was two-thirds of £20, i.e., £13.6.8. This ingenious scheme was the subject

8   Those disabled by accident or on point of death from non-infectious disorders such as tetany and bloat. Societies were advised to retain a veterinary surgeon on a yearly fee and, where called in by the valuers, the society paid half the vet's fee if the animal died. If it recovered, the owner paid the full fee. Because of the retainer from the creamery, the vet's fee to members was usually somewhat less than the regular fee to non-members, and in areas where the scheme operated it played a significant role in bringing vets and farmers to work together, particularly in demonstrating the importance of seeking veterinary advice in good time.

9   Recall Mr A.S. Lough's comment in 1898: "I don't care . . . what make of cow she is as long as she gives 600 gallons of milk."

of a leading article in *The Irish Homestead* on 23 September 1916. Mr McDermott also arranged the speedy replacement of cows through the credit society incorporated in his creamery.[10]

In 1911 Lloyd George was promulgating his National Health Insurance Bill in Britain. The IAOS had hopes that they might secure considerable benefits for co-op members, but having considered the matter, they came to the conclusion that it would be neither desirable nor practicable to participate as an 'approved society' under the Act:

> In arriving at this decision they were actuated mainly by two considerations, the first being that a very small percentage of the members of societies belong to the class which come within the scope of the Act and, in the second place, that to put forward the claims of the IAOS to be recognised as an 'approved society' would in all probability bring it into conflict with other organisations having a similar object in view, but having, also, a political or sectarian complexion, and who would unquestionably regard the IAOS as a rival. Apart from these considerations, the Committee were of the opinion that the suggested new departure did not properly belong to the work of the Society and would necessitate the employment of extra office hands having a special knowledge of the work.[11]

In 1911 also, the Essex and Suffolk Equitable Insurance Society, which for some years previously had offered the best terms and obtained the co-operative workman's compensation insurance business, intimated that they could not continue because of lack of support from the societies. It was anticipated that premiums might be raised as high as 15 shillings in the near future. The IAOS looked again at the prospects of 'going it alone' but it was little more than wishful thinking.[12]

A new possibility emerged in 1912 when the Co-operative Insurance Society in Manchester was taken over jointly by the CWS and the SCWS. The IAOS showed considerable business astuteness: anticipating the takeover, they whipped up as much workman's compensation insurance as they could and gave this business to the CIS before the takeover.[13] This gave them a lever for negotiating with the wholesale societies to have the Irish wholesale federation, IAWS, included in the deal so that "the Irish co-operative insurance business be properly provided for." However, the

10 An agricultural bank was established in Whitecross in 1899 but from 1903 it ceased to be registered separately, having been absorbed in modified form into the creamery society, as too was a poultry society founded in 1902.
11 IAOS Annual Report 1912, p.29.
12 The volume of support from societies was small and offered little hope of the scheme being operated profitably. The IAOS was in very straitened circumstances following the withdrawal of a government grant. Had the prospects been better and the necessary capital obtainable, some members of the IAOS committee felt that the insurance business could make a valuable contribution to IAOS overheads and even cover the employment of a few co-op organisers, while still being able to offer better insurance terms than those obtainable from commercial companies.
13 Previously a small amount of fire and general insurance business was done with the CIS.

memory of the CWS débâcle in creamery development still rankled and the British, though by no means unfriendly, were considerably chary about getting bogged down in Ireland once more. The feeling was that the Irishmen had been 'rather too clever' in the past and there was a notable reluctance to be involved too intimately in business with them again. The Irish contention was that once again the British approach was raising doubts in the minds of all true co-operators — they would need to demonstrate to Ireland and the world that they really were a *co-operative* movement! The moral leverage was considerable; the CWS valued its international co-operative prestige and was prepared to compromise. They agreed to co-operate, but at arms length. The IAWS was not to be admitted but it was agreed that the Co-operative Insurance Society would establish an office in Dublin.[14] The takeover by the wholesale societies would not prejudice previous arrangements. On the contrary, the Dublin office would do "all kinds of insurance business which is common to societies on exceedingly favourable terms."

Some 200 co-operative societies took out workman's compensation insurance with the CIS. It was a poor enough response in view of the 1,000 co-operatives in the country, over half of which (creameries and agricultural stores) presumably had some employees and all of which had farmer members (106,000 in 1914) who were to be encouraged to effect their insurances through the co-operative. The high point of participation was 6,000 workman's compensation policies effected through 225 societies in 1917.[15] The IAOS committee was perplexed that so many societies should continue paying premiums of 15 shillings to outside companies, when co-op coverage could be had for 8 shillings. For other insurances — fire, fidelity guarantee, war and marine risks — IAOS organisers were frequently horrified to find societies exposing themselves to unpardonable risks through inadequate or non-existant coverage. 'Economy' in payment of insurance was most common on the part of poorly financed societies which could least afford losses.

The more idealistic co-operators constantly sought to promulgate the concept of insurance as mutual protection. Their aim was a national co-operative insurance society, self-owned, self-operated, non-profit-making, wherein the concept could be truly demonstrated with facts and figures. Insurance as it was practised was more evocative of gambling and the bookmaker's craft — the statistical odds were nicely calculated to yield a handsome profit to the capitalist insurance companies. The CIS was but poorly appreciated. Extreme nationalists view it as a foreign company. Others, while readily admitting that it was largely co-operative in character (return on investment was limited to the 5 per cent. allowed under co-operative law),[16] felt that it was too big and impersonal and not visibly

14 At 3 Commercial Buildings, Dame Street.
15 Prior to this, the CIS issued through the local society a combined policy covering a number of members jointly. In 1917 the change to issuing single policies was deemed to be more easily managed, more conducive to participation and gave the individual member a greater sense of involvement.
16 The General Co-operative Survey Committee, appointed at the Dublin Congress in 1914,

different from the commercial companies with which it competed for business. Still others complained that it accumulated excessive reserves, some of which should be distributed in end-of-year dividends, according to the co-operative principle of distribution of surplus, or by the way of individual and local no-claim bonuses to enhance the feeling of co-operative participation and responsibility.

The criticisms of the CIS were often less than fair and few of the suggestions were practicable. Much of the niggling could perhaps be attributed to resentment at the exclusion of the IAWS from the CIS reorganisation. The CIS introduced many useful insurance schemes but these met with comparatively little enthusiasm.[17] Nor was there any notable effort to encourage co-operators to back the CIS effort by investment. On the contrary, some co-operators were prepared to dissipate the co-operative solidarity by playing the CIS against the commercial companies: the IAOS committee was constantly having its attention drawn to specific instances where private companies had offered better deals on particular items — a not unfamiliar anti-co-op tactic. Nevertheless, the IAOS stood firm, demonstrating that, despite the increased premiums necessitated by the Workmen's Compensation (War Addition) Act 1917, the CIS premiums were still 33⅓ per cent. less than those of any other first-class office, giving an estimated saving to farmer-members of between £3,000 and £4,000 per annum. In 1919 the committee had a particularly hard fight to persuade the creameries to give their boiler and electrical plant insurance to the CIS which was offering attractive terms, following a new agreement with the Vulcan Boiler & General Insurance Company.[18]

Little progress was made on the question of livestock insurance. When the IAOS regained a measure of financial stability from the Development Commissioners grant (max. £4,000) in 1913, there were hopes that organisers might be recruited to initiate local schemes. However, the pressures of other work were so great that no organisers could be spared specifically for this purpose. It was soon conceded that a comprehensive scheme, which would cover all types of livestock, was impracticable and the limited organisational time available was devoted to trying to implement a nation-wide scheme for insuring dairy cows. Even this proved to be an intractable problem: the CIS could not see its way to help, the scheme

recommended the removal of limitations on individual investments and loans and the launching of a campaign to seek more deposits from co-op members.

17 Enniscorthy Society was the first (in 1917) to participate in the CIS scheme of collective life insurance. For a premium of 1d in the £ of annual turnover, the lives of all members were insured to the extent of 4 shillings in the £ of the members' annual purchases. The Society reported that the scheme was a great incentive to members' loyalty and an encouragement to business. The scheme, which gave insurance without any inquiry as to the age or health of members, was introduced in England in 1904 and in 1910 was extended to cover also the wife or husband of a member. William Thompson would not have been amused by the wrangling that went on for many years over the status of women in co-operative societies and their entitlement to savings and dividends. See G.D.H. Cole, *A Century of Co-operation*, pp. 183-84, 270.

18 There was a long-standing association between the CIS and the Vulcan Company dating back to 1901. The Vulcan is of historic interest, being the first insurance company to offer third-party insurance on motor vehicles in 1912. Their system was remarkable in that premiums were calculated on a mileage basis.

devolved on local effort and, after a few years of non-progress, the IAOS reluctantly conceded that, unless the creamery had a manager of the calibre and enthusiasm of a John McDermott (Whitecross), plans were best left in abeyance. By this stage the wartime emphasis was switching from livestock to tillage and, although livestock — particularly dairy cows — were important in the 'Produce More Food' campaign, livestock insurance had a low priority.

We have read how the 'spurious prosperity' of the war and immediate post-war years (notably 1916-19) was a major factor in the undoing of the co-operative credit societies. It did similar violence to the concept of livestock insurance. Creamery managers, who were reluctant to undertake the paperwork of a livestock insurance society, were very ready to extend credit (often interest-free) for the purchase or replacement of dairy cows. When, at the IAOS annual general meeting of 1919, the Hon. A. Broderick, supported by Sir Henry Grattan-Bellew, urged the formation of a national co-operative insurance society to cover all kinds of insurance risks, including "the poor man's cow", he got scant hearing. The tide of new-found affluence was drowning all thought of protection or caution. A general attitude was being engendered of 'get on with the business and to hell with the risks'. In the flood-tide of profitable trading, societies forgot the buildings constructed and the equipment installed on borrowed money, the debtors owing and creditors owed — the urge was to make hay while the sun shone and "with a bit of luck we will avoid serious accident. Anyway, we are now a *strong* society and well able to carry a few risks on our own."[19]

The euphoria was short-lived. However, the slump of 1920, although it doubtlessly taught sharp lessons to those unfortunate enough to suffer uninsured losses coinciding with business disaster, did not cause any rush on the insurance offices. In many cases it had the reverse effect. Societies in parlous financial straits chose the last desperate gamble of paying no insurance. Many farmers with incomes reduced by 50 per cent. or more, chose to gamble with workman's compensation and let their employees go temporarily uninsured. This default was aggravated by an extra war addition of 50 per cent. under the 1920 Act, which compelled the CIS, in common with other insurance companies, to increase their premium charges by 10 per cent. In 1919 the CIS had contemplated the opening of district offices in order to compete more effectively with the agents of other companies, who although their premiums were up to 50 per cent. dearer, were stealing a lot of insurance business because of their local contacts and farm-to-farm canvassing. The all-round reduction in business a year later killed the idea.

The widespread civil disorder of the War of Independence created additional problems:

> In consequence of the destruction of co-operative property in the Spring of 1920, it became necessary for societies to consider the advisability of

19 Private account.

insuring against the risks of civil commotion. At the commencement, societies could insure against these risks at the rate of about 25/- per £100 for six months, or 40/- per £100 for twelve months. These premium rates were increased from time to time, and at present the rates are so high as to be almost prohibitive. Recently the premium rate quoted for a period of six months was £6.15.0 per £100. It is understood that the premium rates at present are somewhat higher . . . attacks on co-operative property have become of such frequency that . . . [insurance] became a business necessity and societies were obliged to go out of their way financially in finding the money necessary for the purpose. In the case of many of the smaller and weaker societies the insurance risks which attacks imposed on them were out of all proportion to their financial resources.[20]

The crippling cost and also the conditions imposed[21] to effect 'commotion insurance' were such as to cause many societies to forego the idea of financial insurance and either seek physical protection from the Sinn Féin forces or establish their own vigilante system. Another discouraging factor was the delay in the settlement of claims. The first claim under a policy of this type was made by Shanagolden CDS in August 1920, but was not settled for nearly a year. Nineteen twenty-one saw a reduction in insurance[22] but a considerable growth in the number and size of claims. There was an alarming increase in the number of burglaries. Hitherto, burglary was an infrequent occurrence in rural Ireland but, in a time of civil disorder, many co-operative societies presented a soft target, particularly some of the smaller societies which did not even have a safe to protect their cash. Some dishonest employees availed of the unsettled state of the country to help themselves and abscond with a single haul. Others fled only when closer examination of the society's records, consequent on financial difficulties, revealed a system of more regular 'withdrawals' over a period. The number of claims on fidelity guarantee policies became so numerous that the CIS, which did a great deal of this type of insurance, seriously considered declining such new business:

> This arises in part out of the fact that the check exercised by the committees of creameries and agricultural societies on their officials is frequently exceedingly lax. It is clear that in the interests of societies a rigid check is necessary, and the last few years have proved this conclusively. Societies, in furnishing the information asked for in fidelity guarantee proposal forms, do not always give correct answers to the questions or fill the forms up properly and as these forms are the basis of the contract between the insurers and the insured, any laxity in

20 IAOS Annual Report 1920, p.25.
21 In early policies of this type, the underwriters insisted on the inclusion of a clause to which many prospective insurers took exception. After considerable negotiation, the wording was altered to a form acceptable to some: "Warranted that the Principals of the Assured Firm shall not take part in any meetings antagonistic to the Government of Great Britain and Ireland or take part or assist in any disturbances except to uphold law and order."
22 The CIS, however, did increased business in fire insurance and also increased its percentage of the workman's compensation business.

dealing with them is likely to reduce the liability . . . if not actually to vitiate the contract altogether.[23,]

In 1921 there was also a considerable increase in the number of claims on fire insurance. The number of fires in flax mills were so numerous that the CIS refused to offer insurance on these premises. Although the vast majority of fires occurred in privately-owned mills, no exception was made in the blanket refusal of insurance,[24] a fact which contributed to the decision to wind up the affairs of many co-operative ventures. Most of the fire claims were for farms. Very few fires occurred in agricultural co-op stores during this period of unrest and none of them were attributable to arson. Suggestions, jocose and otherwise, were frequently made to store committees to the effect that 'a good fire' would solve some of the problems occasioned by stocks of goods which could not be sold for more than one-third of their purchase cost. It is to the credit of store managers and committees that they refused such ignoble solutions and, however great their collective or individual liabilities, elected honourably to live or to die.

The Co-operative Insurance Society also behaved honestly and generously and won itself an increasing share of the fire and workman's compensation insurance business because of the reputation* it had established for prompt and satisfactory settlement of claims. Only in very few cases did they repudiate liability and in many cases made *ex-gratia* payments where no valid claim could be sustained. For two fire claims in 1922 they paid out over £15,000, in addition to paying a large number of smaller claims. All this was done without any increase in the rate of premium charged. In a number of instances, both the CIS and the victim co-op societies felt justly aggrieved when fires which were obviously malicious[25] were not accepted as such by the courts. In every case the CIS paid up. The IAOS spoke openly in praise of the CIS in 1922, urging co-operators to be mindful of the honourable treatment accorded to them, which should be well-remembered when choosing insurers in future:

> With possibly one exception, the Co-operative Insurance Society is, it is believed, the only really first-class non-tariff office operating in the Free State. There are, of course, always a number of companies which are willing to accept business at specially low premiums in order to attempt to build up a large premium income, particularly since the termination of the European War, but neither has their experience of this kind of business been satisfactory nor can their clients have found the business satisfactory to them.[26]

23 IAOS Annual Report 1921, p.27.
24 Whilst refusing to insure flax mill premises, the CIS still gave workman's compensation coverage to mill employers. The refusal of premises, said the CIS, was purely on the grounds of obvious fire risk and inadequate prevention methods, a discrimination exercised for all types of premises during that period.
25 Under ordinary insurance policies, insurance agencies are not liable for malicious burning, claims on which, when proven, are paid by the local authority out of charges on local taxation.
26 IAOS Annual Report 1922, p.25.

By 1923 claims had abated on all fronts except with regard to fidelity guarantee. Here the position was so bad, both in the private and in the co-operative sector, that the CIS decided not to accept any further business in the Free State. It continued to do so, however, in the new state of Northern Ireland where the Society had established premises at 10 Royal Avenue, Belfast. The following year the CIS reviewed its decision and resumed its fidelity guarantee insurance of co-operative societies, on condition that there should be a tighter financial check on their affairs, specifically half-yearly audit of creameries and quarterly audit of general-purpose societies.[27] The CIS continued to do considerable business with the co-op societies North and South but by no means all of the societies participated, despite the attractive inducement of low premiums and special bonuses on premiums paid yearly — 10 per cent. to societies which were shareholder members of the CIS and 5 per cent. to other societies.

Thereafter, the IAOS took little interest in insurance, apart from dealing with specific problems of co-operative societies.[28] Because of the depressed state of agriculture, there was no suggestion of launching new exciting co-operative schemes. Indicative of the agricultural depression and disillusionment were the CIS endeavours to penetrate the non-agricultural sector, offering keen terms for life insurance, general accident, motor-car, plate-glass and householder policies. Their efforts were not particularly successful. They continued to cover a fairly wide range of agricultural risks — fire, workman's compensation, motor, tractor and threshing machine insurance. The only venture into livestock insurance was to cover foaling risk and horse insurance at high premium charges, as was done by numerous commercial companies. Business was so slack, however, that in 1932 the CIS decided that they could no longer justify expensive offices in Dublin,[29] but they continued to do a small volume of business in the Free State through their offices in Belfast and Manchester.

On the departure of the CIS, what were described as particularly favourable terms for workman's compensation insurance (22 shillings per £100 wages) were negotiated by the IAOS with Messrs. A.R. Brassington & Co of 14 Fleet Street, Dublin. In the years afterwards there were no new developments and co-op insurance business became dispersed over a large number of commercial companies. No mention of insurance is recorded in any succeeding IAOS Annual Report until the year after the cessation of World War II, and this was only an admonition to societies to ensure that their fire insurance was adequate:

Societies should examine their policies at least once a year ... The value of everything appreciated very considerably during the war, and

---

27 Including creameries which did a store trade.
28 In 1924 it negotiated the reduction of transit and marine risks for produce in transit to Britain, with Messrs. Lionel Sage & Company Ltd, a firm of Lloyds brokers.
29 The closure of the Dublin office meant a loss of only £25,000 a year in premiums. See R.G. Garnett, *A Century of Co-operative Insurance* (London: George Allen & Unwin Ltd, 1968), p.208 et seq.

the value in terms of money of all building materials and machinery equipment is very much higher today ... indeed, machines that were purchased before the war are still, in many cases, worth more than what they cost originally.[30]

It was thirteen years later when the subject emerged once more. At the annual general meeting of 1959 the following resolution from Milford Co-operative Creamery was passed unanimously:[31]

That we are of the opinion that the time is opportune for the Co-operative Societies of this country to contribute to and form an Insurance Company that will embrace all the various risks in their Societies.

The IAOS committee pondered the problem and decided that the first requirement was some up-to-date information on the nature and extent of insurance in force in the societies. A questionnaire to over 300 societies elicited only 87 replies. Indications from the completed questionnaires were that slightly over two-thirds of the premiums pertained to cover for fire, motor and workmans' compensation. In view of the poor response and apparent lack of interest, the committee decided to defer the matter. There it remained until 1967 when Mr Herlihy of Milford bounced back with a similar resolution, this time coupled with a proposal for a co-operative bank. The committee was dubious about the possibility of a bank but much more hopeful of the prospects for a co-operative insurance service, on which matter they consulted specialists from the International Co-operative Alliance, three of whom visited Ireland in 1968.[32] They recommended a survey which was undertaken by the IAOS but which again proved abortive: by September 1969 replies had been received from 102 societies, of which only 47 submitted details of insurance claims. Following further consultations with societies[33] and interpolation from available data, it was found possible to make an appraisal and projections. The IAOS secretary, Patrick Kelly, was able to tell the annual general meeting that the likely capital requirement would be of the order of £250,000.

A new impetus came from the interest of FBD (Farm Business Developments Ltd), a company promoted by a number of progressive agriculturalists active in the National Farmers' Association (later named the Irish Farmers' Association) and other farming organisations. The company had the energetic support of the influential *Irish Farmers' Journal* and its editor, Patrick O'Keeffe. FBD had for some time been planning to launch an insurance company specialising in farmer insurance[34] and had

---

30 IAOS Annual Report 1946, p.17.
31 Proposed by Mr M. Herlihy (Milford) and seconded by Mr D. Keohane (Imokilly).
32 Klas Back (Folksam Insurance, Sweden), H.H. Knighton, deputy general manager of CIS Manchester, and Berno Kalns of the Raiffeisen movement in Germany (Raiffeisen und Volksbanken Versicherungs Gesellschaften).
33 The IAOS was also at this time investigating the possibility of establishing a pension scheme for co-operative society employees.
34 One of the most active proponents of a farm insurance system was NFA president, Rickard Deasy.

registered as a co-operative society in 1968.

The IAOS appointed a special insurance committee[35] in October 1969, which undertook lengthy discussions and planning sessions with FBD. By May 1970 they had reached agreement and were able to put detailed proposals to the annual general meeting of the IAOS. Meanwhile, FBD had gathered sufficient financial resources to secure a licence to go into the insurance business. A substantial part of the share capital was to come from the huge Belgian bank co-operative, Boerenbond Belge.

The licence granted to FBD Insurance Company Ltd in May 1970 was the first general insurance licence granted by an Irish government since the 1936 Insurance Act had been passed. The Department of Industry and Commerce laid down exacting standards regarding capital structure, ownership of the capital, quality of reinsurance and standard of policies, before agreeing to issue the licence.

FBD Insurance Company Ltd has a paid-up share capital of £250,000. Seventy-two per cent. of this capital is owned by 2,764 Irish farmer and co-operative shareholders. Twenty-eight per cent. of the capital was subscribed by Assurances Du Boerenbond Belge. Four representatives of shareholding agricultural co-operative societies were elected to the board and this representation will increase as the societies' volume of business grows. An excellent relationship exists with the IAOS.

The structure of FBD had to be designed to fit in with the Insurance Acts since, under existing legislation, a co-operative cannot engage in insurance business. The other developments undertaken by FBD, which do not legally require a specific type of structure, will, where suitable, be carried out by FBD Co-operative Society Ltd. Individual farmers and up to fifty farmer co-operative societies have invested in both FBD Insurance Company Ltd and FBD Co-operative Society Ltd.

The declaration of the former president of the Irish Farmers' Association, T.J. Maher, at the launching of FBD, holds good today:

> The history of Irish agriculture is one of a people trying desperately to shake off economic shackles and look after their own business. Each step forward is uphill, requiring effort and sacrifice, but this sacrifice is not unrewarded.
>
> We have moved into the insurance business and our greatest assurance of success is that we stand together. I exhort the farmers in every county to join with their fellow farmers in supporting FBD and giving FBD an opportunity of quoting for their insurance business. The success of FBD depends on your loyalty and support in the long term.

Steady progress is being made. The FBD Insurance Company has now (1975) over 25,000 clients and a premium income of approximately £2 million.

---

35 The committee comprised six representatives of co-op societies and three members of the IAOS national committee.

Chapter Twenty-Three

Co-operative Turf Societies

The *Journal of the Department of Agriculture* for March 1904 carried a series of three communications dealing with "The Manufacture of Peat Fuel in Ireland", with interesting detail of the work done by J. Tissington Tatlow, an expert brought over from Schleswig by Plunkett to investigate the possibility of mechanised turf production. Mr Tatlow's conclusions were that the project was one which could best be undertaken on a co-operative basis because of the size of enterprise required to effect economies of scale in the use of expensive machinery and the marketing of the finished product. Arthur Steel Lough of Killeshandra Creamery was the moving spirit of the scheme and the initial experimental work was undertaken in his area of County Cavan. Plunkett publicly commended him for his enthusiasm, his commonsense approach, and his untiring efforts in organising the work.[1]

Arthur Steel Lough

I think that Mr Arthur Lough deserves the gratitude of his countrymen for having brought into clear light the too little regarded importance of the more prosaic use of this great national asset. While

---

1   At a meeting of the Council of Agriculture held in the Royal University Buildings on 12 April 1904.

many have been dreaming of a peat age, when our bogs would supply many of the necessaries and not a few of the luxuries of an advanced civilisation, Mr Lough has been largely instrumental in calling attention to one of the prime uses for which Providence probably intended this resource, namely to keep us warm and dry without having to go abroad for our fuel.

The *Anglo-Celt,* a provincial newspaper long sympathetic to the co-operative cause, was hopeful that by the following year small co-operative societies would exist to ensure that the farmer's fuel supply could be "stacked in the haggard ready for burning, with greater ease, with much more economy, and with the saving of ten weeks labour." It was stated that at the end of ten days the Cavan farmers who were working at Mr Tatlow's experiments would have secured for themselves the year's supply of fuel free, Mr Tatlow undertaking to send it for them to their nearest railway station.

These experiments undertaken on Killybandrick bog[2] near Killeshandra in June 1903 evoked considerable local interest, and are remarkable in the extent to which they presaged modern development in mechanical peat harvesting. County Cavan was a traditional area for the production of hand-won 'mud' turf, a primitive but effective arrangement whereby wet turf mould from every layer of the turf bank is thoroughly mixed by hand (and foot) before being spread in a large sloppy mass to a depth of nine to twelve inches. The individual runs and 'sods' are then cut out by the flat of the hand and the product is left to dry.

Mr Tatlow mechanised this laborious process by two items of plant which he operated with the help of a German machinist: a machine for cutting and lifting the peat from the bog; and the masticating and shaping machinery which formed the turf into individual blocks.

> The former was planted on rails on the edge of the bog, and worked much like a piledriver, a heavy three-bladed cutter being windlassed up a framework about twelve feet high, and then allowed to drop suddenly into the bog. When raised to the surface again it was full of 'mud', which was dug out and wheeled to the chopper of a shaping and mixing machine resembling nothing so much as a large mincing machine; the peat was thoroughly mixed and continuously pressed out through a nozzle, being, as it passed out, cut by a lad with a blunt knife into blocks which then measured about ten inches by four inches by four inches, and received on boards. These loaded boards were carried to the drying ground, where the blocks were slipped to the ground, and the boards brought back to the mixer. Two horses were required to drive the mixing machine, and ten men and boys to attend to the two machines. The output was about fourteen thousand peats per day and

2 Turbary was owned by Mr James Harman, with organisational arrangements under a local committee including A.S. Lough, P. McManus, J.P. Gannon, E.T. Hanlon and county agricultural instructor A. Teevan.

these, when dry, weighed nearly one pound each, or say, six and a half tons.[3]

The experiments were conducted under extremely unfavourable conditions. The bog was too small and very shallow, the weather was bad, the horses literally 'bogged' down[4] and the haulage of the raw material from the cutter to the mill was too slow. The organisers were of the unanimous opinion that the use of steam power would be much more satisfactory and would practically double the output. Nevertheless, the results were inspiring. The 'mechanical peats' were ready for footing in less than a week, of excellent quality, and "the only dry turf in the country" landed home at a total cost of six shillings and fourpence per ton, compared to ten shillings per ton for conventional harvesting. The Cavan pioneers also saw great possibilities in the marketing of peat moss and the Cavan Co-operative Turf-Making and Peat Moss Litter Company was formed in 1903 to undertake large-scale developments in the coming year.[5]

Unfortunately, the hoped-for national development was never realised. Plunkett was increasingly criticised for the expense of his Department, his employment of foreign experts and his allegedly indiscriminate readiness to embark on all kinds of fanciful schemes. Besides, the technology of mechanised turf production was at a very early stage, the railways were unhelpful about transport charges and the whole operation required a capital investment and an organisational structure which no co-operative group could attain at that time. A number of agricultural and creamery co-ops dabbled spasmodically in organising the cutting and marketing of turf by conventional methods; the IAWS even developed a modest market for peat moss in Wales but no co-ordinated national effort emerged until thirty years later.

The de Valera government, which came to power in 1932-33, strongly urged the concept of national self-sufficiency. In the spring of 1933, the IAOS, by arrangement with the Department of Industry and Commerce, undertook to organise co-operative societies in turf-yielding areas to enable owners of peat bogs to "find a market at a minimum price for all turf of approved quality and sold under approved conditions." Early in 1934 the Department asked the IAOS to undertake the formation, registration and supervision of societies in certain approved areas over a period of one year commencing on 1 April 1934.

Seán Lemass, the Minister for Industry and Commerce and then the youngest cabinet minister in Europe, attended a conference on co-operative turf production at the Plunkett House on 7 March 1934, at which R.A. Anderson presided. Tactics were discussed and arrangements got underway. The Department would reimburse the costs, provided that these did not exceed £3,000. Three additional organisers were appointed

---

3 *Journal of the Department of Agriculture and Technical Instruction,* March 1904, pp.446-47.
4 An illustrated description of the experiments was published in the *Anglo-Celt* in June 1903.
5 I have been unable to trace the registration of this co-operative.

for the sole purpose of organising and supervising co-operative turf societies. Much of the time of the existing staff was also taken up with organisational and administrative work to do with these new co-ops, and the IAOS staff played a major role in the successful organisation of national turf-cutting competitions at Allenwood, County Kildare (21 April 1934) and at Moonavan Bog, Walsh Island, Portarlington (4 May 1935).[6]

The turf societies, of which thirty-three were registered in 1933 and 124 in 1934, performed a very useful function and constituted an effective build-up towards the establishment of the state-sponsored Turf Development Board in 1934.[7] However, their co-operative nature was very limited. Membership was available on the acquisition of even a single one-shilling share. The turf cutting was done entirely by hand and the typical turf-cutting society consisted of some fifty to a hundred farmers who cut and won turf on their own farms or turbary holdings and then brought it to a central place. This was usually a rented store or yard, sometimes a large rick on the roadside or railway siding where the individual member's turf was bought by weight or measure and became the property of the co-operative society. From there, through the agency of the Turf Development Board, the turf was sold to wholesalers, merchants or institutions and carried away by rail or purchasers' lorries. To buy and sell effectively, it was important to have a good secretary who knew the trade. There were frequent wrangles over the moisture content of some of the turf supplied. Although the rules provided for distribution of profits in proportion to the value of turf supplied by each member, this distribution was rarely carried out — the profits being either tiny, non-existent, or else allocated to a reserve fund, with the long-term view of buying a lorry or acquiring premises. The remuneration of the secretary/manager was commonly at the rate of 6d per ton of turf marketed. This system rarely elicited full-time managers of great expertise or dedication.

Contacts were made by the Turf Board and the orders were sent to the societies, which forwarded the turf by road or rail as directed. The price fixed by the Board was 11/6d per ton, in sacks supplied by the Board. Some societies were fortunate to have a sizeable local market, and frequently defaulted on orders received through the Board in order to supply local customers at a better profit.

Transport costs were always a difficulty. In the early days of the scheme, the Board had negotiated with the railways a flat rate of six shillings per ton and this enabled some less-favoured societies to dispose of their surplus

---

6 On both occasions Major H.E. de Courcy Wheeler, chairman of the national turf-cutting competition committee, thanked the IAOS for the great assistance given by the members of its staff.

7 The Turf Development Board (with offices at 10 Hume Street, Dublin) was incorporated as a joint-stock company with a nominal capital of five £1 shares held by directors, who were nominees of the Minister for Industry and Commerce. They were not selected on any representative basis and the managing director was always a civil servant. The object of the Board was "to develop the turf industry by improving methods of selling turf and its by-products". It received grants-in-aid for administrative costs and repayable grants for development work. Expenditure in the five years up to 1939 totalled approximately £¼ million.

turf to distant customers. The withdrawal of this concession brought about the demise of a number of societies in remote areas, which had operated successfully, even though the money earned by their producer members was very small. In those days of economic depression, many farmers were glad of a market for turf which paid even a minimal margin.

Many suppliers of turf to the societies, although they had paid their shilling, were no more than vaguely aware of belonging to a co-operative. Committee meetings (a mandatory minimum of twelve per year) were often perfunctory and badly attended. Some societies were better than others and possibly some co-operative benefits did accrue,[8] but for the most part registration as a co-operative society did little more than provide the group with the legal existence necessary to trade and perhaps acquire some measure of working capital by a loan or bank overdraft.

Altogether 168 co-operative turf societies were organised, with a membership of about 10,000. It was apparently deemed that, once the initial establishment had been effected, the operation was so simple that there was little need for development or supervision. The financial arrangements with the IAOS were discontinued and on 1 April 1935 the turf societies were handed over to the supervision of the Turf Development Board. The IAOS never received statistical returns for these societies and, although some continued to serve a useful function until the Turf Board, and subsequently Bord na Mona,[9] put turf production on a more centralised footing, they were effectively 'deco-operativised'.

Many societies were shortlived. A total of 134 societies had their registrations cancelled by 1940, mainly through their failure to make statutory returns to the Registrar.[10] By 1940, also, the Turf Development Board felt that the producers of hand-won turf could, without the infliction of hardship, be left to their own initiative to find markets. The reasons quoted for this decision were:

1. Members of many societies which benefited from large grants for development works to enable them to produce turf received payment for their labour on these works throughout the Autumn, Winter and Spring and then failed to produce any turf during the Summer months for sale subsequently.
2. Some societies refused to continue to produce turf and supply it to the Board unless particular development works, in which they were interested, were sanctioned and carried out. When these societies failed to force the Board's hand, they disposed of their turf locally and to the detriment of the contracts into which the Board had entered on the societies' behalf.

8   Some societies successfully arranged with landlords to rent turbary to their members on favourable terms. They also succeeded in having extensive schemes of bog drainage and road construction undertaken. Generally speaking, however, the co-operative activity of the societies was mostly in marketing, with very little co-operative organisation of the basic production process.
9   The Irish Peat Development Authority, established by the Turf Development Act 1964.
10 Cancellations were as follows: 1935 — 1; 1937 — 48; 1938 — 37; 1939 — 36; 1940 — 12.

3. Societies tended to withhold supplies from the Board and marketed their turf locally at higher prices than those contracted for with the Board whenever there happened to be a local shortage of fuel.

4. The Board were no longer able to guarantee fulfilment of contracts.

5. Institutions and barracks which had been receiving supplies of turf through the Board of Works were compelled to revert to coal because of the failure of hand-won turf supplies. In some cases, special turf-burning apparatus had been installed as a result of representations made by the Turf Board.

6. The production of hand-won turf does not lend itself to rationalisation, division of labour or any of the normal processes by which the costs of manufacture can be reduced or the quality of the product improved. Its transport is excessively costly and its fuel value low in comparison with the machined variety.[11]

The parish councils, set up on an *ad hoc* basis during the Emergency to look after general community welfare, played a notable part in turf production at a time when supplies of imported coal were practically cut off. Despite the fact that the task of keeping the home fires burning during those difficult years probably evoked more genuine co-operative spirit and involved more people in earnest co-operative partnership than the nation had witnessed for many years, very few of these parish councils registered as formal co-operatives.

Although the good words of co-operation as a manifestation of true christian charity were constantly invoked, the organisational harnessing of the co-operative idealism which was generated left much to be desired. The ordinary parishioner could achieve a good feeling of co-operative togetherness working shoulder to barrow with his neighbour at the turf bank,[12] but his role in the organisation and decision-making was limited. Strong appeals from the pulpit and through the village media (bellringers, handbills, posters and housecalls), coupled with the general sense of urgency of the Emergency, often assured large attendances at parish council meetings, yet participative democracy was often absent. Parliamentary procedures were not always adhered to, discussion was often minimal and decisions were frequently taken on the say-so of one or more strong men or institutional figures.

On policy matters — where and when the turf was to be cut, and on problems such as disposal or storage of turf in excess of the local community's need — the parish council had an arrangement (often ill-defined) with the local authority. The county surveyor was delegated the task of co-ordinating the efforts of the turf producers, including the county

11 Memorandum from Turf Development Board to Commission on Vocational Organisation, July 1940.
12 For many town-dwellers and non-manual workers in rural areas, this was a novel and exhilarating experience.

council itself, which, availing of its emergency powers to acquire bogland, was often a major turf producer in its own right, providing (or at least offering) employment for large numbers of people who registered as unemployed. The surveyor took his guidance from the Department of Local Government and Public Health about the amount of turf which could be cut for assured sale. There were many unpredictable difficulties of weather and labour supply,[13] transport was a perpetual headache and the almost inevitable addition of a measure of bureaucratic bungling created some wild fluctuations of under- and over-supply in particular areas.

In some cases the superb co-operative efforts of parish councils in organising voluntary work teams saved thousands of pounds by retrieving turf which was lying exposed on the bogs. Many of these councils came out of the war years unscathed and sometimes with small financial profits. Others were less fortunate and, although the government had agreed to reimburse many local authorities for losses incurred on turf production, some parish groups were unable to substantiate their claims and for one reason or another ended the Emergency with financial deficits — and, more tragically, with a burden of local acrimony and ill-will.

Even though the formal co-operative movement was not involved, the legacy of these parish councils had an important effect on every type of co-operative effort in the post-war era. In some places the feeling was very good; in others the word 'co-operation' had undeservedly acquired unfortunate connotations.

After the war came the big developments in mechanised turf production. Machines were constantly adapted and improved and Bord na Mona embarked on turf production on a very large scale, acquiring over 130,000 acres of bogland, producing machine-won turf which, because of the mixing and compression involved in its production, proved much easier to save and superior in fuel value to the traditional hand-cut product.[14] The evolving peat technology in Ireland was watched with interest in many parts of the world but at home particular attention was focussed on the large turf-cutting machines operating on Bord na Mona's big bogs. If these machines could be successfully miniaturised, it would open up the possibility of mechanising the smaller bogs, particularly in the blanket peat turbaries of the West where traditionally the small farmers relied on turf for fuel and had to devote excessive time and manual effort to the winning of it.

Again, much credit must to to the Irish Sugar Company's general manager, Michael J. Costello, for his pioneering work, which resulted in a modified 'Lilliput' machine being made available by the Sugar Company

13 From Donegal in 1941 the county surveyor complained that he needed an extra 1,000 men for turf-cutting. The committee of Herbertstown CA & DS, County Limerick, called on the government to ease up on turf production because large numbers of 'milkers' were taking work on the turf schemes, and creameries were facing a drastic reduction of their milk supplies.

14 The Board now produces large quantities of milled peat for electricity generating plants, peat briquettes as a convenient solid fuel, and baled peat moss for horticultural and other purposes. Over four million tons of peat products are produced at twenty-two centres throughout the country and capital investment totals some £30 million.

on hire to farmers in the vicinity of Tuam sugar factory in 1957. Success was instant and within two years the company was operating four additional machines, one working as far afield as Killasser[15] in County Mayo, some fifty miles from base. Costello sought to encourage co-operative groups and syndicates to acquire their own machines, but with little success. Ironically the very success of the Sugar Company's hire system militated against such a development: it was much easier to hire the machine than have the responsibility of ownership, particularly since these machines required major overhauling (almost rebuilding) during the off-season. The sugar factory personnel had well-equipped workshops and superior mechanical skills. A number of skilled private operators, with workshop facilities, were the first to avail of the new development and are operating profitably in various parts of the country.

The problems of establishing machinery co-operatives have always been notoriously difficult, particularly if they have to be free-standing co-ops with no other business, starting from scratch with small resources. Ideally, such ventures should be undertaken by existing co-ops which have adequate management, money and expertise. Unfortunately, the locations of turf bogs rarely coincide with those of strong co-operatives. However, some turf-cutting co-ops have been formed,[16] one of the most recent being the Rostrim Turf Cutting Co-operative Society, registered on 9 March 1972 and operating on neighbouring boglands in Roscommon and Leitrim.[17] The co-op has a membership of 106 with paid-up share capital of £1,200, including a shareholding by Kiltoghert CADS, a long-established creamery society in the area. The principal item of equipment is a 'miniput' turf-cutting machine which cost £8,500 in 1972 and earned £4,500 in member payments for the work done in 1973. Co-operative turf-cutting has also been successfully undertaken by the Iveragh Co-op in Kerry (1969), West Clare Turf Producers (1970) and Kilmactigue Co-operative, County Sligo.

15 The scene of one of Ireland's first agricultural societies (1895).
16 A turf-cutting co-op was established at Four Roads, County Roscommon in 1965 and another at Drumlish, County Longford, a year later; both, incidentally, in the heartlands of former co-operative communities, Tissara and Columbkille.
17 The name Rostrim incorporating the first syllable of Roscommon and the last syllable of Leitrim.

Chapter Twenty-Four

Other Miscellaneous Societies

Tobacco

Some interesting historical facts were presented by Colonel Nugent Talbot Everard at the annual general conference of societies in 1903. Ireland, he said, was probably the first country in Europe to grow tobacco. The statute of the fifteenth year (1674) of Charles II prohibited its growth in Ireland, expressly to protect the industry in the colonies and plantations of America. The prohibition was removed in 1799, "to encourage the produce and manufactures of Ireland, which did not materially interfere with the commercial interests of Great Britain." The sixth article of the Act of Union 1800 expressly provided for tobacco-growing in Ireland but, despite this provision, the cultivation of tobacco was again absolutely forbidden by Act of Parliament in 1830. E.T. Craig in Ralahine was probably not aggrieved by this prohibition for he was opposed to the use of tobacco and snuff and anyway may have considered the crop unlikely to be successful in the damper western climate. In County Wexford, however, it was different. There, in the eighteen thirties, there were 1,000 acres of tobacco providing employment for more than 1,500 people.

The injustice of prohibition rankled with the Wexford men for many years. More for perversity than profit, small patches of the illegal weed were grown, hidden in Wexford gardens, and some of the traditional skills were thus preserved. It was Everard, however, in County Meath, who took practical steps to redress the grievance and who sought to have the almost forgotten industry restored. Both he and Lady Everard[1] were enthusiastic members of the Royal Irish Industries Association, so anything which offered prospects of industrial development or rural regeneration was of immediate interest to them. In 1898 they obtained permission to grow plots of tobacco for experimental purposes and undertook an ambitious programme of field trials. After 1900 the Department of Agriculture and Technical Instruction lent a hand and grew experimental plots at a number of centres in County Wexford. In the barony of Forth in South Wexford an association of tobacco growers was formed, the Forth Association, which

1 Colonel Everard was knighted in 1911 but his wife Sylvia (Humphries) had long since been known locally as 'Lady' Everard. Later Everard was nominated a Senator by the Saorstát government, whereupon he had the impressive designation Senator Colonel Sir Nugent Talbot Everard, Bart DL.

374

was not a co-operative society but was strongly influenced by the Rev Luke Doyle, enthusiastic promoter of a number of co-operative ventures in the parish of Tagoat. Some members of the IAOS committee and other active co-op supporters established small trials in their own areas.[2] In 1900 the Department secured the services of a French expert, M. Le Cornet, to advise on the management of the crop from the planting-out stage to the harvesting and drying. In that year also, Colonel Everard's report on his experiments in the previous two seasons was made the basis of an IAOS leaflet on tobacco-growing. Although he was experimenting with only a few plots of forty square yards each, of different soil types and under different manurial treatments, his average yield of over a ton (2,640 lbs) of manu-factured tobacco was calculated to leave a gross margin of £132 per Irish acre (1.6 statute acres). This would be considerably greater were it not for the sum of £352 payable in excise duty.[3]

By 1904 the Colonel was no longer dabbling in small experimental plots but growing a full twenty acres. He was in good humour at the annual general meeting in September, with a bumper crop of tobacco safely harvested, and was happy to report to his co-operative colleagues that as a result of their resolution of the previous year the ban on tobacco-growing had been lifted and the excise duty substantially reduced.[4] "Further-more", he said, "it is established beyond doubt that a very good type of tobacco can be grown in this country. I give this not as my own opinion but that of the chief expert of a station in Kentucky, who was over here, not looking for employment but on a holiday. That gentleman having seen what had been grown in Ireland, gave it as his opinion that good tobacco of a certain type could be grown in Ireland as well as it could be in Kentucky, and that given proper conditions for curing it would be an undoubted and unqualified success." Mr G.E. Moony of Ballinahown Agricultural Society (County Westmeath) contributed to the general good cheer with a humorous reminiscence of his own experiences. To begin with, he had been granted permission to grow only three plants — which, however, had grown to a fantastic size! The experiment so far was a success, but he had been worried by an excise officer who rode fifteen miles almost every other day to see how he was behaving. Finally he sent the leaves to Dublin to be cured but from that day to this he had never heard any more about them. "Seriously though", he had smoked the tobacco grown by Colonel Everard and found it very fine indeed. Colonel Everard had earned their gratitude for his plucky enterprise and the results had shown that tobacco could be grown advantageously in Ireland.

In Wexford the tobacco-growers had an ardent advocate in Captain

2 P.J. (later Sir Patrick) Hannon, IAOS organiser, supervised a number of small experi-ments in the west. Henry McCarrick grew some in Enniscrone, as did veterinarian Michael Cleary in Mullingar. William Julian took on special responsibility to establish trials in the Freshford area and Mr J. Willington (see p.248) carried out trials on his own farm and on those of a few other members of the Lower Ormonde Society, County Tipperary.
3 Excise duty at 2/8 per lb payable on tobacco sold at four shillings per lb.
4 By agreement with the Chancellor of the Exchequer, one-third of the tax was refunded to the growers.

Willie Redmond,[5] who worked hard as a member of the IAOS to promote the cultivation of the crop and as an MP to win a better deal for the industry. So impressed were the Wexfordmen by their visit to Colonel Everard's estate at Randlestown in 1904 that they arranged to have Mr N. Harpur of the Forth Association travel to Meath and spend an entire season under Everard's tutelage, after which he would be able to return confidently to instruct the farmers of Tagoat and other areas of Wexford.[6] This he did and the Wexford Co-operative Tobacco Growers' Society was duly registered on 8 May 1906, consisting of twelve Wexford farmers, each of whom had engaged to grow an acre of tobacco. The nominal share capital was £48, each member being required to hold one £1 share for every rood or fraction of a rood of tobacco grown. The Department of Agriculture was extremely helpful and erected a barn in which the tobacco was cured. The society, under the expert part-time management of Mr Harpur and with the help of the Department's tobacco expert G. N. Keller,[7] ensured that everything went smoothly for the growers, although some of them decided at planting-out time not to hazard a full acre in their first year. The turnover was enhanced by the purchase of a very fine crop of tobacco grown by Mr J. Farrell on the lands of Rosslare House. The Board of Inland Revenue offered no objection to this procedure.

The Wexford Tobacco Growers' Society, however, was to remain a very limited success and it worked effectively for no more than a decade. Turnover was never more than £1,000 per annum — usually around £700 to £800 — and by 1915 the number of growers was down to six and turnover a mere £300. A few interested landowners in County Wexford grew plots of the weed and experimented endlessly with varieties, manurial treatments and the blending of home-grown with foreign leaf to produce a smokeable product to the public's taste. At Mount St Benedict near Gorey, The Rev Dom Sweetman, who ran a school for young gentlemen, was a life-long enthusiast.

In Meath, the master grower Everard went to considerable lengths to promote the industry. He provided the facilities of his drying sheds to his neighbours and personally guaranteed a net profit of at least £20 per statute acre to any prospective grower who would join him. In the decade before World War I a net profit of £20 per acre (labour paid at standard rates) was a considerable sum but Everard could guarantee it as a 'disaster' figure, whatever the weather or the level of the grower's husbandry. Despite this, he rarely had more than five or six participants. Everard was very aware that tobacco-growing could never really succeed unless it was fully co-operativised: individual growers, unless they grew hundreds of

5 Younger brother of John Redmond MP, the leader of the Parnellites. William replaced his brother on the IAOS committee in 1897 and retained this position until 1905.
6 The author has been unable to pursue the suggestion that Everard's inspiration for tobacco-growing may have come from the sons and grandsons of Wexford pikemen. Isolated in Meath at the end of the 1798 Rebellion, the Wexford rebels hid their arms and took employment with Meath farmers, some of them eventually becoming tenants and small landowners.
7 Mr Keller came to the Department from Kentucky and for many years was its expert on tobacco and sugar beet.

acres, could not justify the capital expense and overhead of buildings and drying facilities. Both growing and curing could be improved by better machines and equipment, but Everard hesitated while his existing 'primitive' but effective facilities were still so grossly underutilised.

By 1908, when Plunkett was calling on the Irish gentry to take their proper place as democratic leaders amongst their liberated tenantry in advancing the economic and social progress of the countryside,[8] the amiable Everard was already a shining example. His Donaghpatrick Co-operative Agricultural Society was both an economic and a social catalyst in the district, while on his own estate he was developing the farming resources to their fullest and providing full-time employment for a large and increasingly skilful workforce. Unfortunately, the majority of Irish landowners and farmers did not see their way to rally to Plunkett's call or to emulate Everard's example. The morale of the tenant and labouring classes was extremely low. Farmers generally did little to plan year-round employment for their workers or the improvement of their skills. They chose rather to continue farming in the traditional, mainly pastoral, fashion, relying on the casual employment of labourers for the peak work periods at spring and harvest. It was a condition of dis-equilibrium: workers emigrated or joined the army, rather than waited about in the expectation of employment, and, inevitably, labour became scarce.

Everard, as a lone employer at Randlestown, was not proof against the general malaise and his tobacco enterprise could be expanded only gradually. He was in a similar position as Mr Herdman in Tyrone with the flax:[9] people available for such work were neither properly skilled nor properly motivated to exercise the care necessary in handling a new crop. Even if they were, available workers could not be recruited *en masse* but only in small numbers, consistent with the employer's ability to train and supervise them. Failing to enthuse the neighbouring farmers, Everard sought to interest his own workers in a co-operative effort to grow small plots of tobacco in their own cottage gardens or smallholdings, but with limited success.

Elsewhere little progress was made.[10] No sooner was the IAOS beginning to recover from its financial difficulties after the withdrawal of government help in 1908, than world war broke out. It was not until the nineteen thirties that there was a renewed interest in tobacco-growing. With farm prices in a ruinous state, nearly every farmer was prepared at least to consider an alternative source of income. In the economic war with Britain, emotions ran high and, allied to the determination "to burn everything British but their coal", was the self-sufficient ideal of Irishmen to

8   Horace Plunkett, *Noblesse Oblige — An Irish Rendering* (Dublin: Maunsel & Company, 1908).
9   See p.292.
10 There was, however, a notable development of tobacco-growing and processing in Adare, County Limerick, pioneered by Lord Dunraven. Although not a formal co-operative, the scheme was to some extent run on co-operative lines. See Edward E. Lysaght, *Sir Horace Plunkett* (Dublin: Maunsel & Company Ltd, 1916), pp.100 et seq.

produce and smoke their own tobacco. The government sought to organise the growing and processing of the crop. The Tobacco Act 1934 arranged for the licensing of growers by the Revenue Commissioners and the rehandling of tobacco leaf at licensed stations under the supervision of the Department of Agriculture. As an inducement to growers, the duty on home-grown tobacco was reduced[11] and the old Kentuckian G.N. Keller was in demand once more to advise a new generation of tobacco-growers. In 1934 licenses were issued to some 1,500 growers to grow a total of more than 1,000 acres of tobacco. It was very much an individualistic effort, with each farmer tending his own small plot. Drying was mostly done in improvised sheds on individual farms, and, despite the attentions of Keller and other devoted departmental officials, it was often performed inexpertly and improperly by growers who had their own ideas and were reluctant to follow the experts' advice. Marketing was arranged through the Department's station, which was usually a rented farmer's barn or merchant's store, conveniently located but frequently less than ideal in its structure and layout.

The IAOS took comparatively little interest in the tobacco revival. Henry Kennedy, secretary and chief executive, was a technical man but his faith was firmly pinned on the potential of Irish grassland. For politico-economic reasons, Irish farming was in utter chaos but the practical economist Kennedy could not pretend that there was any macro-economic substitute for grass — or that Ireland could really live without a flourishing livestock and dairy industry. The reality was borne out when, as livestock prices improved, tillage declined and 'exotic' crops such as flax and tobacco disappeared. By 1939, although the Revenue Commissioners were prepared to license 1,500 acres, only 300 acres of tobacco were sown. Nor did the scarcity of tobacco during World War II lead to a revival. On the contrary, the industry disappeared almost overnight and all that remained was an occasional enthusiast who illicitly grew a few plants of tobacco and processed them for his personal use.

During this period only two co-operative efforts at tobacco-growing were undertaken. One was the Munster Co-operative Tobacco Growers' Society Ltd at Kilnap, County Cork, the other the Meath CTGS, predictably at Navan. The South Leinster Tobacco Society in County Wexford was registered in 1933 but, with the intervention of the Department to provide storage depots, the organisation was dropped. The Cork and Navan societies, also formed in 1933, were both small and short-lived.

Nugent Talbot Everard lived for eighty years but died without realising his ambition of even a small formal tobacco co-operative. He passed away quietly on 11 July 1929, and his son Richard William, aged fifty-five, who had followed his father's dream, died suddenly ten days later. For thirty years through thick and thin the Colonel had stuck to his guns. Throughout the hungry twenties he continued to provide full employment on his

11 In 1934 it was fixed at 10d per lb below that on imported tobacco.

estate, farming with determination and intensity. His accounting was meticulous and no one was more sensitive to the economic climate; yet his planning was always long-term and he refused to be deflected by short-term vicissitudes. He had the Owenite conviction that capital should be satisfied with a limited return and, unlike many of his class, he never sought to save money by temporarily laying off labour during rough patches or slack periods. As with Robert Owen, the philanthropic formula was in the main financially successful. Everard was a versatile farmer and livestock breeder and made money from a wide variety of farming enterprises, but in tobacco culture, as his close friend R.A. Anderson commented, "I fear he lost a fortune". Of English ancestry, Unionist upbringing and steeped in the Anglo-Irish tradition, Nugent T. Everard was essentially an outstanding exponent of the true philosophy of Sinn Féin; not the narrow, restricted perversion of "Ourselves Alone" but the full gallant co-operative concept of "We, Ourselves". "There is nothing", he said, "that Irishmen cannot do!" Of himself, it may fairly be suggested that Ireland can have raised few more practical patriots and, even if Irish tobacco is one of Ireland's many lost causes, perhaps all the more reason that Navan, Royal Meath and Ireland should remember him with pride.

Nugent T. Everard

Co-operative Land Ownership

From New Harmony, Indiana (1825) and Ralahine (1831) to the present-day Israeli *kibbutzim*, there have always been co-operative experiments which testify to the undying appeal of Robert Owen's concept of villages of co-operation. Long before the beginnings of modern formal co-operation, people were working out co-operative systems of living together and working the land. Communal living is as old as man and communal agriculture probably started as soon as man began to be a cultivator as well as a hunter. In the old Irish clan system, which predates history, the land belonged neither to chief nor commoner but to the clan, and the Brehon Laws were based on the communal ownership of land. All through history, whatever the majority system of government, there were in nearly every country examples of minorities and small groups who sought to establish co-operative communities to live and work their own land. The monasteries of the feudal Middle Ages were not in themselves self-sustaining communities, but occasionally a monastery established a working relationship with the local village (which either existed previously or grew up outside the monastery walls) from which together they eventually evolved as a self-governing, largely democratic and co-operative community. The post-Reformation period has more numerous examples of religious sects who sought a serene and separate existence and established themselves in full family communities which were largely co-operative in structure.

Such was the Quaker settlement established near Timahoe in County Kildare in 1704. Six wealthy Quaker families from Ulster leased two large townlands and proceeded to farm the land on a co-operative basis. The area was subsequently partitioned into separate farms in 1709 but the community retained much of its co-operative character.[12] Another co-operative colony was established at Prosperous, County Kildare, about 1780 by Robert Brooke, ancestral kinsman of the Brooke family of Brookeborough, County Fermanagh. This commune was an industrial one, based on cotton, and was set up with the aid of a government grant. Weaving was done in the homes, which had very large kitchens to accommodate the weaving looms. At one stage it was reported that some 1,200 looms were working but by 1786 the commune was in financial difficulty and, when Mr Brooke was refused further government aid, the business collapsed, causing great poverty to its members.[13]

Of course, long before that, the old farming systems of English land tenure were partly co-operative. In the three-field system, introduced to Ireland by the Normans, the tillage and grazing land was held in common. In later times many well-disposed landlords and larger landowners, notably in Leinster, combined to provide certain services to their tenants. For this purpose they formed farming societies which in an informally co-operative fashion arranged for the interchange of labour and farm machinery and for the education of the tenantry in better farming methods. There is a report that the Fingal Farming Society held an agricultural show of wheat and barley in 1839 which concluded with a sale of the exhibits.[14] A system prevalent in the west of Ireland about that time, whereby a group of people, rather than an individual, leased and worked an area of land, is well

12 One of the striking features of this commune was the large windmill, a novelty on the Leinster landscape. One of the original Quaker settlers was a John Milhous, whose son emigrated to America and became the maternal ancestor of Richard Milhous Nixon, 37th President of the USA.

13 Unemployment and destitution bred subversion and it was at Prosperous that the Rebellion of 1798 (later largely centred on Wexford) first broke out.

14 I am indebted to Martin Kelly of Celbridge for this report and for much of the research and information in this section.

described in Weld's *Survey of County Roscommon* (1832) and persisted in certain areas up to the eighteen seventies.

It is not surprising, therefore, that when co-operation in Ireland became a formal movement, the questions of co-operative land ownership and co-operative land use should emerge. In the aftermath of the land war, land ownership was an emotive subject and one which the IAOS had to handle warily. The Irish tenant's approach was entirely individualistic: he wanted his own farm for himself and himself alone. Given a sufficiently large private holding (and it might prove difficult to satisfy him on this point), he might consider co-operative usage of other lands but, meanwhile, would be inordinately cautious of any co-operative device or landlord trick which might occasion an amendment of the Land Acts to put him off with anything less than absolute ownership and control of his own holding. Landlords, too, had their own sensitivities and fears. The first co-operative activities in this field were therefore advisedly non-controversial and centred on the co-operative usage of rented grazing land[15] on the eleven months system pioneered by the Donaghpatrick Society in Meath and by William Holmes in the west. This latter development in the Galway / South Roscommon area near Ballygar was doubtlessly facilitated by the tradition of similar leasing arrangements which had persisted in the area up to the eighteen seventies.

A different development in 1898, however, was to impel co-operatives to participate more forthrightly in the question of land ownership. This was the foundation of the United Irish League and the consequent agrarian unrest which portended a renewal of the Land War.[16] The League was originally established because of the land problems in the west, the existence of large grazing ranches and the delays and shortcomings of the previous Land Acts, but it grew and spread very quickly: by 1901 it was nationwide and had a membership of nearly 100,000. Although for the most part it did not create as much violence as did the Land League, it entailed a considerable amount of boycotting and intimidation and influenced the new Chief Secretary, George Wyndham, to introduce his new Land Bill. As the Bill was being drafted, the co-operators were concerned that provision should be made for co-operative societies to buy land. The existing land purchase laws did not permit the Land Commission to sell to anyone but an occupying tenant. In 1899, while Arthur Balfour was still Chief Secretary, the IAOS had proposed that co-operative societies should be enabled to obtain advances from the Land Commission for the purchase of land, either for joint use or for *distribution* amongst *members*. In 1902 the difficulties that would beset the latter objective were reconsidered in the light of the existing agitation, and the request was modified:

> . . . it may be urged that Co-operative Societies should be qualified as

15 See p.249.
16 See F.S.L. Lyons, *Ireland Since the Famine* (London: Weidenfeld & Nicolson, 1971), p.216 et seq.

trustees and enabled to purchase untenanted land for the benefit of their members who in such cases would be free to cultivate more of their own holdings. In many cases it will be far more profitable that grazing lands should be held in this way than that universal 'striping' should be encouraged. In many districts water cannot possibly be made available on all small 'stripes' and the difficulty of access to the holdings themselves, as well as the inconveniences of the lack of turbary and shelter, will make division into small holdings a work of great difficulty indeed. Again, where tenants and sons of tenants are reinstated, the small farms which having regard to their limited capital would only be possible for them to stock would be made much more valuable to them if grazing accommodation were provided in this way.[17]

On September 2 1902, Captain John Shawe-Taylor, an enterprising but comparatively unknown young man of a Protestant landlord family (who was a nephew of Lady Gregory and equally unconventional), took an initiative reminiscent of Horace Plunkett and the Recess Committee. Shawe-Taylor wrote a letter to the newspapers inviting certain named representatives of landlords and tenants to meet in conference and settle their differences.[18] The letter would certainly have been ignored, had not Wyndham remarkably acclaimed it as soon as it appeared. The tenants' representatives readily agreed but the landlords refused. Other representatives were found to take their place: Dunraven, famous yachtsman and model landlord of Adare, the Earl of Mayo, Colonel Hutcheson-Poe and the ever helpful Nugent Talbot Everard. After only a fortnight's discussion, the conference produced an agreement, embodied in a report that became the basis of the Wyndham Act which passed triumphantly through Parliament in 1903. It was the most far-reaching and generous Land Act to date, allocating an extra £100 million for land purchase, and it greatly accelerated the speed of land transfer.[19] Everard could report with pleasure that the co-operative request had been met; at the annual general conference of co-operative societies[20] he proposed the following motion with supporting comment:

That we recommend dairy and agricultural co-operative societies to take advantage of the provision of the new Land Act, which empowers the Land Commission on the sale of an estate comprising untenanted lands to vest such land in trustees for the accommodation of its members.

17 IAOS Annual Report 1902, p.43.
18 For the landlords, he invited the Duke of Abercorn, Lord Barrymore, The O'Connor Don and Colonel E.J. Saunderson. For the tenants, John Redmond, William O'Brien, T.C. Harrington and T.W. Russell.
19 Between 1903 and 1920 nearly nine million acres changed hands and two million acres more were in the process of sale. Under the Wyndham Act alone, some 200,000 tenants purchased their holdings.
20 21 October 1903.

The new Land Act offers unique opportunities for reviving an ancient Irish tribal custom and a system of land tenure which obtains even now in other countries. The system of the co-operative tenure of land has passed beyond the experimental stage. It was initiated by the Donaghpatrick Society five years ago. Small farmers and labourers were enabled to get grazing for their cattle, and, although they had to pay a competitive rent for the land, they were able to return their members a bonus of 15 per cent. on their money. The system was carried out by two societies, who had been able to rent over 100 acres whereby additional accommodation was provided them for their cattle, the result being a large increase in tillage on their own small holdings. Legislation will do much but this movement of self-help will do more.

Arthur Tilson Shaen Magan, the IAOS organiser with the beautiful sisters,[21] seconded the motion and reported that as recently as four days ago a number of farmers around Four Roads, County Roscommon, had formed themselves into a society for the purpose of buying a farm of 100 acres under the new Wyndham Act. The agreement to purchase had been entered into and now only awaited the approval of the Estate Commissioners.

Violet Magan   *Rachel Magan*

Co-operative leasing, even co-operative ownership, could not hope to assuage the peasants' yearning for full title and private possession. After centuries of the fearful system of tenancy-at-will, there was no substitute for "the deeds in your hand" — the untrammelled ownership of ten acres of bog would be grasped more eagerly than a 10 per cent. shareholding in 1,000 acres of prime land; not that such a striking alternative was ever patently offered, but such was the feeling of the newly liberated tenants of the time. 'Striping' went on unabated, regardless of the waste. Miles and

21 The Misses Rachel and Violet Magan worked actively with their brother, "Tat", organising co-operatives in Counties Roscommon and Westmeath. They played a big part in the establishment of the Athlone Poultry Federation and were personally responsible for a home industry society and a village library at Tissara, the first of its kind in Ireland.

miles of laboriously constructed stone and sod fences were willingly built through long hours of oppressive toil to demarcate tiny, impoverished holdings which seemed to have been designed for maximum inconvenience. Parnell's admonition to "keep a firm grip of your homesteads" was being psychologically implemented and reinforced with physical barricades of stone walls.[22] Exchanges of plots, which on badly fragmented holdings would have eased matters considerably, were seldom effected satisfactorily. An acre of land was an acre of land and new owners were rarely able to agree on monetary adjustments to balance disputed variations in land quality, any more than they could agree that an acre of good land, which rationalised the layout at the farm itself, would be a fair exchange for two acres of poorer land a mile away.[23]

The co-operative ideal could make little headway against this obsessive urge to possess land anywhere, regardless of its viability or convenience. In 1912 Dermod O'Brien, lifelong co-operator and gentleman farmer of Cahirmoyle, produced a well-researched memorandum on co-operative ownership and co-partnership on large farms. It was well received and enthusiastically applauded by the IAOS committee[24] but made little general impact. Ireland was moving into a period of comparative prosperity. The hovels of the tenant farmers were being replaced by substantial stone dwellings. Even the lot of the agricultural labourer was being improved with better housing and wages which had almost doubled since the days of the first Land Act. Agricultural prosperity increased during the war years and, as farming came to be more remunerative, more land was acquired for private ownership. Some farmers seemed disposed co-operatively to use machinery in crudely organised co-operative crop production but, by and large, the idea of group farming made little headway and the principle of individual land ownership remained sacrosanct. Land prices almost doubled within a few years but this only seemed to make farmers more anxious to buy more. This preoccupation with land buying undoubtedly impelled farmers to seek and obtain excessive credit from their co-operative societies. Many farmers invested every penny of their sales in land purchases, leaving the creamery and co-op store to supply them with goods on credit.

Meanwhile a interesting situation was developing in certain areas of the west, and indeed in congested areas in parts of the midlands and south. Land congestion was severe but transfer and division tended to be slow. Coincidental with this was a growth in population as emigration to Britain practically ceased during the war. Migratory workers were afraid to make their seasonal trips for farmwork to England and Scotland lest they be conscripted into the British Army. The lack of these seasonal earnings, which had helped to underpin the precarious income of many smallholders,

22 Nowhere perhaps more so than in the Dillon country around Ballaghaderreen, where Mitchell Henry, a man of expansive and co-operative ideas, observed that there would soon be more area under stone walls than in total arable land.
23 The legal profession, with its ponderous and expensive procedures, did little to facilitate the sensible exchange of small parcels of land between owners of fragmented holdings.
24 At the IAOS annual general meeting, 19 November 1912.

caused considerable distress at a time when shop prices for household goods and groceries were increasing almost daily. As Mitchell Henry had previously noted, there was little taste for intensive tillage and little knowledge of husbandry methods for new crops. Even if there had been, there was frequently no marketing agent; transport costs of farm produce to centres of consumer population were prohibitive. Even with optimum marketing, there was a very restricted technical limit to the quantity of farm produce which five- and ten-acre holdings could produce — not that this limit was very often tested. Large numbers of young men congregated at country crossroads in idleness, deprivation and boredom.[25]

The outcome was predictable. In these areas, what can be best described in modern parlance as gangs of agrarian skinheads effectively terrorised the countryside. Under the judicious direction of land-hungry elders, these gangs vied with each other in the takeover and arbitrary reallocation of untenanted holdings and the farms of absentee landowners. Intimidation of 'people with too much land' was rife and a number fled their holdings under threat to their lives.[26] So rapidly had this trouble escalated that by 1919 it offered a serious threat to the provisional Sinn Fein government which was trying to maintain law and order in the countryside while conducting a tough guerilla war with the forces of the Crown. The Sinn Féin courts were establishing a reputation for fair dealing and wise judgments but their efforts, both in the administration of justice and in the apprehension of criminals, were being jeopardised by the growing volume of agrarian strife. Even summary 'justice' administered outside the courts, often at gunpoint, did little to contain the problem.

In January 1919, Dáil Eireann established the National Land Bank. This institution was organised under the direction of co-operator Robert Barton, an active member of the IAOS national committee since 1910, Dáil deputy for West Wicklow, and Director of the Department of Agriculture in the first Dáil. The Land Bank was a co-operative society affiliated to the IAOS, whose primary object was the "redistribution of untenanted land through the medium of co-operative Farming Societies to which loans on mortgage would be made." Lionel Smith-Gordon, assistant secretary of the IAOS,[27] was appointed general manager of the Bank. The 'Minister for Finance', Michael Collins, had been successful with his Dáil Eireann national loan which was supported by the public to the extent of almost £358,000. Part of these funds was allocated on an 'as required' basis to the National Land

25 This was a complete reversal of the social conditions which obtained previously. In 1880, for example, it was reported from the Tubbercurry area of County Sligo that "the tillage has to be carried on during a great part of the year by feeble old men, women, boys and girls owing to the absence of most of the young men in England and Scotland . . ." See L.M. Cullen, *An Economic History of Ireland since 1660* (London: B.T. Batsford Ltd, 1972).

26 "Big ranches and little farms were invaded indiscriminately until no holder felt his title of possession secure": (Report of Art O'Connor, Tuairisc Oifiguil, Lunasa, 1921). Art O'Connor, Dáil deputy for South Kildare, replaced Robert Barton as Director of the Department of Agriculture when Barton was arrested in January 1920.

27 Smith-Gordon had played a major role in the establishment (1914) and running of the Co-operative Reference Library. He was the author of a number of co-operative publications.

Bank which, for its own part, was also to seek public support by way of share capital and deposits. Within a year Dáil Eireann had contributed £203,000 as share capital, representing 406,000 £1 shares on which 10 shillings had been paid up. The difficulties were enormous. Dáil Eireann was an illegal and essentially fugitive parliament[28] and the members of the cabinet were all wanted men who could meet only rarely and with great difficulty. The Bank, which set up its headquarters at 10 College Green, Dublin,[29] ran the risk of being closed down and having its funds confiscated if their Dáil origin was discovered. The co-operative structure and appropriate share certificates were a useful cover. Land prices were running abnormally high and the greatest difficulty (and physical danger) was encountered in trying to sort out the rightful ownership of 'confiscated' lands. One official had to pose as a pedlar, selling skin ointment, revealing his true identity only to clergy and reliable persons, in order to gain the information he required.

Despite the almost insuperable difficulties, progress was made. By the end of 1920 the Bank had facilitated the purchases of some 16,500 statute acres (at an average price of £22.40 per acre) for thirty-nine co-operative farming societies. These societies contributed 25 per cent. of the purchase price in the form of fixed security deposits to the Bank.

> An average annuity of less than £1 15s 0d per acre enables the purchasers to repay capital and interest within a period of 31 years.
>
> The number of estates purchased is 53 and they are held by 39 societies with a combined membership of approximately 850 persons. In sixteen cases lands totalling 3,100 acres have been subdivided; eight other societies holding 3,750 acres are now in the process of subdividing; six societies with 2,220 have taken the preliminary steps for this purpose while in 9 cases, totalling 7,430 acres, the land is being still held in common.[30]

Sixty-four co-operative farming societies were registered in 1920. Of these twenty-eight were in Connaught, twenty-five in Leinster and eleven in Munster.[31] A year later the number had risen to seventy-one but only forty of these had succeeded in acquiring land (valued at approximately £320,000). Dáil Eireann had set up special land courts for the settlement of land disputes. The first of these was held in Ballinrobe in May 1920 and presided over by the then Director of the Department of Agriculture, Art O'Connor. Subsequently Kevin O'Shiel, who had been appointed a special commissioner, held land courts in several counties and in September 1920 the Dáil set up its own Land Commission which, despite incessant harrassment, operated fairly successfully.

28 See F.S.L. Lyons, *Ireland Since the Famine*, op. cit., p.406 et seq.
29 Branches were subsequently established at 68 Lower Leeson Street, Dublin and at Cork, Limerick, Waterford, Enniscorthy, Ennis, Athlone and Tralee.
30 IAOS Annual Report for the year ending 31 March 1921.
31 Again I am indebted to Martin Kelly of Celbridge for a detailed account of the co-operative farming society at Straffan in 1920.

Neither 'state' nor co-operative effort, however, was enough to quell the agrarian trouble. The real solution of the problem came suddenly and in an entirely unexpected fashion. Just as Dáil Eireann and the National Land Bank directors were beginning to panic because funds were nearing exhaustion and land trouble was increasing, the general slump which struck at the end of 1920 altered the whole picture. Almost overnight land became a liability rather than an asset — very much so if it were purchased with 50 per cent. borrowed money, as through the commercial banks. Even with the more favourable interest rates and long-term payments arranged through the National Land Bank, the number of customers was greatly reduced. The Land Bank and the farming societies for the most part emerged without financial loss but their activities had almost ceased by the time the new Saorstát Eireann government took over in 1922 and abandoned the co-operative experiment.

The general slump in farm prices also put paid to an interesting experiment conceived by a farmer in Clare, which evoked memories of Ralahine and John Scott Vandaleur.[32] In 1919 Sidney Royse Lysaght of Raheen, Tuamgraney, proposed to his workers a generous and advanced concept in agricultural democracy. While Mr Lysaght was to retain owner- ship of the land (at least for the time being), the profits were to be divided between him and his fifty workers. This division of profit would initially be effected so as to give a return to the workers equal to twice, if not three times, their present agricultural wage — allowing, of course, for improved productivity. The workers were more than a little dubious of the scheme but agreed to do a pilot experiment before committing themselves to participate. They contributed a total of £20 share capital to form the Raheen Workers' Co-operative Society. In almost exact imitation of the Rochdale Pioneers, they decided that their first venture would be a small shop selling household goods and some agricultural requisites. From there they would undertake small-scale bacon-curing and expand into lime- burning and other agricultural services, so that within five years they would have sufficient capital to expand their initial venture of small-scale co-operative crop-growing on the farm and enter into full co-operative partnership with the landowner.

Unfortunately ·1919 was a very bad season: with a small loss on the field experiment and a small turnover in the shop, the total profit came to a mere £4. In 1920, however, they went ahead with an increased acreage and the help of a £500 bank loan. This time they had to contend not only with bad weather but with a disastrous economic situation: they bought dear goods in spring only to find by the year's end that their shop stocks and farm produce could command less than half the previous year's prices. Profitability was not enhanced by repeated attacks on the premises by forces of the Crown who seemed to regard the Raheen Workers'

32 In 1908 Constance Markievicz, greatly enthused on reading Craig's *History of Ralahine*, was inspired to attempt a co-operative commune at Belcamp, Raheny, County Dublin. It was an ill-conceived venture which bore little similarity to the Ralahine experiment and did not last long. See Seán O'Faoláin, *Countess Markievicz* (London: Jonathan Cape, 1934) and Anne Marreco, *The Rebel Countess* (London: Weidenfeld and Nicolson, 1967).

Co-operative Society as a hot bed of subversion.[33] Shortly after the first raid in November 1920, when the store was looted, the manager was shot dead in the Exchange police station in Dublin.

When a turnover of £1,960 produced a net loss of £58, the Raheen Workers decided that the managerial and financial worries should best be borne by Mr Lysaght and voted unanimously in favour of a standard weekly wage. Despite his disappointment, Lysaght[34] diversified and the Raheen farm developed as one of Ireland's most successful horticultural nurseries.

The National Land Bank had also made a gallant effort to establish itself as a democratic national banking institution for ordinary banking business. It was beginning to succeed in this when its land purchasing operations were suspended in 1923, pending the implementation of the Land Purchase Act which transferred all land purchase functions to the Land Commission. In one move the chances both of a co-operative land structure and of a co-operative banking system were lost. The farming societies divided their lands and disbanded; no real attempts at full co-operative ownership and group working had been made.

> . . . it must be admitted that, aside from the actual purchase and reclamation of land, the co-operative idea does not appear to have made much progress among the members of the societies, and there has not, of course, been any opportunity for an intensive campaign of organisation. It is doubtful whether co-operative farming, as practised in some parts of Italy, will make any appeal to the Irish farmer; so far there has been no successful experiment of this nature, and the estates have, in most cases, been divided among individual members.[35]

Readers are by now well accustomed to the recurring pattern in the co-operative story, the yawning twenty-year inactivity between the two world wars. 'Striping' and subdivision of lands under the Land Commission continued. Much useful work was done to help achieve equitable land distribution in a small-farm pattern but the Commission's work almost invariably failed to keep pace with the economic trend. Holdings which were doubtfully viable, even at the time of their establishment, rarely managed to provide, under traditional farming practice, a full-time living for the small-farm families. The standard of farming on many smallholdings declined as the owners sought supplementary income

---

33 A brief report in *The Irish Homestead* (30 April 1921) stated: "This Society has been raided in or about thirteen times . . . money taken; all papers torn and littered about the floor. All doors broken open and floors torn up. Workmen held up, beaten with sticks, rifle butts, and fists, kicked and otherwise ill-treated. Society's turnover reduced . . . from £30 to £8 weekly. All new developments stopped. Damage estimated at over £2,000."

34 About this time, at the suggestion of Sidney's son, Dr E.A. MacLysaght, the family formally resumed the earlier form of their name, *viz* MacLysaght. This was done simultaneously with eleven other families of the name in Counties Clare and Limerick. This rather unusual, concerted action was promoted by William MacLysaght of Doon, County Limerick.

35 IAOS Annual Report 1922, p.21.

elsewhere. Social problems 'sometimes acute and persistent' occasionally arose where small-farm families were 'migrated' from the poor-land congested districts of the west to the east and midlands and a completely different social and cultural environment.[36]

Government policy over much of the period was concerned with providing a living on the land for the greatest possible number of small farmers. Continual controversy raged as to what acreage constituted a workable small-farm unit; there were too many variables to allow for a positive answer. Many families of exceptional industry and ability succeeded in living in comfort on tiny holdings[37] — which caused many observers to argue the case of the 'economic farmer' rather than the 'economic farm'. Yet it was only comparatively recently that measurement of farm size in terms of capital investment, rather than acreage, gained much credence. Although the Land Commission's concept of viability rose successively from twenty to thirty-three and then to forty acres, the necessary equilibrium between the various factors of production — land, labour, capital and management — got scant consideration. The consequence was that most Land Commission holdings (either those created anew from divided estates or reconstituted by added acres) were too small.

Perhaps the greatest damage was done unwittingly by failure to observe the structural pattern necessary for healthy agricultural development. In agriculture, as in other industries, the natural growth structure is a hierarchical one with big, medium and small-sized enterprises side by side in complementary arrangement. This is particularly so in Irish mixed farming. Little agricultural development takes place in areas where there are large numbers of smallholdings without any intervening large and medium-sized farms. Similarly, in areas exclusively under large farms, the range of farming activity is limited — in Ireland mainly non-intensive, low-profit, pastoral farming. A judicious admixture of large, medium and small farms is the one best adapted to allow farming flexibility and change by overcoming the 'factor indivisibilities' with which the business of farming is constantly beset. Thus small farms can provide some of the permanent and much of the casual labour force required on large farms. Smallholders can (by co-operation or contract) avail of the machinery and equipment which the big farmer can afford. Medium-sized family farms can have satisfactory working arrangements with large and small.

Much theory has been expounded on the benefits of co-operation between small farmers and the possibilities are indeed considerable, but, in practice, unless there is a good admixture of different-sized farmers, co-operation can be exceedingly difficult. The socio-political situation in the days of the landlord often greatly inhibited the agricultural development

36 One hopeful experiment by the Irish Land Commission in the nineteen thirties involved the transference of some twelve small-farm families from the coastal area of Cois Fhairrge to form what was hoped would prove to be a close-knit farming community, suffering minimal 'culture shock' on an area of reclaimed bogland not too far away in the Cloosh valley in inland Connemara. Unfortunately the experiment did not work and the land went to state forestry.

37 Usually, however, in fairly favoured locations with specialised enterprises and some capital.

pattern but, where benevolent landlords encouraged the complementary working of their estates with small and medium-sized farms in their locality, the results were beneficial. The Land Commission's division of large estates and the trend towards equalisation of farm sizes were contrary to the desirable type of farm structuring. This might have been corrected by the development of larger farms under co-operative ownership in small farming districts but unfortunately this never happened.

It was not until the years of World War II that a number of the stronger trading societies acquired farms. The IAOS Annual Report of 1943 carried the following commendation:

> The Committee commend highly the enterprise of a number of societies which have purchased farms for practical demonstration purposes. No more interesting and useful extension of co-operative work has been undertaken for a very long time and from its results already apparent, it is probable that other Societies will follow their example. The Societies that have engaged in Farming are: Ballyclough CC Ltd, Co Cork; Dungarvan CC Ltd, Co Waterford; Knockmeal CADS Ltd, Co Waterford; Lough Egish CA & DS Ltd, Co Monaghan; Milford CC Ltd, Co Cork; Mitchelstown CAS Ltd, Co Cork, and Roscrea Bacon Factory Ltd, Co Tipperary.

The farms acquired by these societies carried out useful demonstration and pioneering work but the example was not followed by other co-ops to anything like the desired extent. Some of these farms formed convenient centres for cattle-breeding societies and other such societies (AI stations) also acquired farms. The development of pig-fattening societies in the nineteen sixties also required that each such unit acquire a sizeable area of land, if only to dispose of the accumulated pig slurry. In the mid-nineteen seventies, considerable interest is being evinced in pilot schemes in group and co-operative farming organised by the Irish Land Commission with migrant farmers in the midlands. These experiments are worthy of the most careful management, until procedures and pitfalls have been thoroughly charted and a readily workable system has been evolved. The concept should not be abandoned because of initial failures.

Throughout the country small groups of farmers are pooling their resources and working their farms jointly. Such amalgamation is most frequent between large and medium-sized holdings which conveniently adjoin.[38] Numerous formal and informal syndicate ventures have been evolved for co-operative machinery use, cattle-rearing, group milking, silage-making, and so on. In Northern Ireland for a time in the nineteen sixties government grant schemes encouraged the pooling of farm buildings, machinery and equipment to achieve maximum utilisation and

---

38 The usual procedure is to form a limited company, since the number of proprietors is usually no more than two to four people. Sometimes the inclusion of relatives or others with small shareholdings provides the mandatory seven members to enable registration as a co-operative society.

efficiency. Perhaps the greatest opportunity that exists is for the large con- solidated co-op groups to encourage 'vertical integration' in the production and marketing of their members' produce. Lough Egish Co-op in County Monaghan has already made a start with a scheme to collectively rear and fatten the calves of the small-farm milk suppliers, thus enabling the small farmer to stock his holding more intensively with high-yielding dairy cows — the most profitable end of the business.[39] This necessitates co-operative ownership or leasing of land. Co-operative ownership could also play a major role in the restructuring of small and fragmented holdings, a prerequisite of successful farming and marketing in the European Community.

Other Miscellaneous Co-operatives

It is not proposed to dwell at length on other types of co-operative societies which were founded for specific purposes. There were many of these and they varied greatly in their co-operative content, usefulness and length of survival. Some were registered as co-operative societies mainly to give them a legal existence — a convenient arrangement where the particular business, social or cultural activity, although limited and non- expansionary, requires legal status for the organisation to operate. Registration as a co-operative society or as a friendly society was often an arbitrary choice, some groups allowing themselves the added scope of engaging in trade as provided in the rules of a co-operative, even though they did not engage in such nor were likely to do so in future. From time to time small groups registered as housing co-operatives but the co-op often became obsolete when the requisite number of houses was built. It is regrettable that, as yet, co-operative house-building has not developed as an integral part of the co-operative effort. The same can be said of other co-operative ventures such as printing, taxi and other service societies, which tend to be localised and slow to develop.

Many of the earlier miscellaneous co-operative societies, although separately registered, were intimately connected with other local co-ops; often, committee members were largely the same people and in some cases even management was shared. Most of these societies have already been mentioned in preceding chapters. Agricultural show societies, particularly those sponsored or supported by neighbourhood co-ops, tended to register as co-operative societies.

The dissimilar procedures of co-operators in different areas was remarkable. Whilst Templecrone Society embraced a multitude of activities under one co-op registration — store, factory, bakery, shipping,

39 The present cattle mart system may have to be superseded. A survey in the nineteen sixties demonstrated that, although the present system fulfilled a need in so far as it effected the transfer of cattle to farmer customers, it was laborious and expensive, since as many as five different auction fees were paid on a beast. The disastrous slump in cattle prices in 1974 demonstrated the weakness of a cattle mart system which merely effects the sale of store cattle from farmer to dealer or from one dealer to another. A more orderly marketing system would probably require mart societies or other co-operatives to acquire land to assemble, market and transport cattle in required grades and numbers and especially to acquire, retain and feed cattle to avoid market gluts.

fishing, butcher's shop and even a co-operative hotel — other co-operative communities founded a number of separate co-ops. One which springs to mind is Urlingford, County Kilkenny, which had, in addition to the usual creamery and co-op store, banks, poultry societies and home industries societies in the vicinity. Urlingford also had a co-operative trade and labour association (1910) and the Urlingford Motor Co-operative (1916).

Of historical interest are the co-operative lime-burning societies: Tynan & Middletown, County Armagh (1906); Columbkille, County Longford (1910); Moydristan, (Mountnugent), County Cavan (1912) and the Tyrone Lime Burners' Society founded in 1918 near Pomeroy. These efforts represent only a minute co-operative involvement in the business of lime-burning which at the turn of the century was a widespread local activity for the production of burnt lime and slaked lime for agricultural purposes, building and whitewashing. It is possible that some agricultural or creamery societies may have engaged in this trade but no references have been noted. The small scale and very localised nature of this activity,[40] which required very little capital, can explain the lack of formal co-operative participation. What is surprising is that, when lime-burning was superseded by the large-scale milling of ground limestone, co-operative societies took little part in the action. The nearest approach to co-operative participation in production was on the part of Comhlucht Siúicre Eireann Teo (again, the co-operative instinct of M.J. Costello) in establishing a large plant at Ballybeg Quarry, County Cork in 1948, which effectively dictated the scale of lime prices, at least in that region.[41]

Amongst the more exotic co-operative societies formed in recent times were the Duhallow Mineral Exploration Society (1942) and the Muintir na Tíre Co-operative Film Society, Tipperary (1944). There are doubtlessly some others in those and previous times[42] which have eluded my researches, and readers are invited to communicate.

A more recent phenomenon is the emergence of 'common ownership' co-operation in manufacturing industry at places like Navan, Dundalk and a number of centres in Northern Ireland. The progress of these societies will be followed with much interest. The common-ownership concept has also been implemented in the Bewley Community Ltd, Dublin (cafés, bakery and a farm). The owners of this family business in 1972 handed over assets of some £2 million to a common trust. Information on the Industrial Common Ownership Movement can be had from the Secretary, ICOM, 31 Hare Street, Woolwich, London SE18 6JN.

40 There is hardly a parish in Ireland without the ruins of several stone-built lime-burning kilns. The lime-burning process often involved a considerable amount of *informal* co-operation between neighbours.

41 When the Ballybeg plant was first opened, there was a conference of co-operative societies in Mallow to discuss participation in distribution. The idea of storage hoppers at creamery premises was mooted but a study of costs revealed that this would not be economic. It was decided that the best way for the societies to help was by ordering lime for farmers and collecting the accounts. The creamery society, Feale Bridge and Headleys Bridge CDS, County Limerick, initiated a scheme whereby its milk suppliers could obtain lime at a reduced price in the off-peak (summer) months.

42 In practically every town in Ireland there have been radical idealists whose co-operative ventures, though rarely successful, deserve to be recorded.

Of the retail grocery stores in the Republic which were affiliated to the Co-operative Union, only the small shop at Lucan, County Dublin, remains. There are, however, a number of co-ops (of various kinds) affiliated to the Co-operative Development Council (see p.132) for the organisation and guidance of non-agricultural societies.

Village Libraries

Although village libraries were never registered separately as co-operative societies, they were a prominent part of the co-operative ethos. Education of the members was (and still is) a basic Rochdale principle. In the days of the Pioneers, the major educational effort was focussed on the bottom rung of the ladder — members had to be taught to read, write and count! Even fifty years later Plunkett and friends were to realise with considerable shock that in Ireland the level of literacy was far from satisfactory. We have noted Paddy the Cope's evidence on the situation in west Donegal and Anderson's frequent despair at the inability of co-operative management staff properly to write reports or keep accounts. Privately, the forthright Anderson fumed at the futility of the whole educational system, but in public he held his tongue, for few of his colleagues were prepared to provoke more controversy and many were loth to believe that things were as bad as they appeared. It was felt that the establishment of local libraries would do much to improve the cultural life of the nation. In 1900 the IAOS produced a leaflet entitled *Village Libraries* which urged every co-operative society to spend £10 on books to form the nucleus of a library. Several sources had been requested to suggest a list of a hundred suitable books and, after some deliberation and amendments, the IAOS approved the selection chosen by the Rev Jeremiah O'Donovan, the curate of Loughrea, County Galway:[43]

Rev Jeremiah O'Donovan

43 Father O'Donovan left the church about 1905 and went to live in England where he married in 1910. In subsequent years he achieved considerable fame as a novelist writing under the name Gerald O'Donovan. His novels include: *Father Ralph* (Macmillan, 1913), *Waiting* (Macmillan, 1914), *Conquest* (Constable, 1920), *How They Did It* (Methuen, 1920), *Vocations* (Martin Secker, 1921), and *The Holy Tree* (Heinemann, 1922).

> . . . farmers are as a rule not in a position to acquire information about the best books, and the list, which contains numerous works dealing with Agriculture, Industries, Care of Livestock, etc., is one eminently adapted for Irish farmers. The books of a more general literary character have been selected with great care, so that no possible controversy could arise over their introduction on any religious or moral ground.[44]

Over seventy of the books listed were of a literary or historical nature and there were many works by Irish authors.[45] Anderson was doubtful if there would be widespread interest in W.B. Yeats's *Celtic Twilight*, Boswell's *Life of Johnson* or even Prescott's *Conquest of Mexico.* He was slightly dubious of the *Publications of the Royal Agricultural Society of England*, the *Primer of Geology* and Devas's *Political Economy*. He had relayed to Father O'Donovan the urgent warning of Alexis Roche that Plunkett would amend an order for a bag of coal. Still there were many good and readable books; both Anderson and O'Donovan warmly agreed that *Alice in Wonderland* was an excellent choice.

The rules for the conduct of village libraries were fairly straightforward. Membership was available to everyone living within the parish boundary for a membership fee of 3d, with a charge of one penny per month for each volume taken out. The books were to be kept in a bookcase under lock and key at some central place and handed out on a fixed day and hour every week. The scheme was administered by a library committee, comprising a sub-committee of the sponsoring co-op together with clergymen of all denominations in the parish. No book was to be lent for longer than one month and the committee controlled the membership, the selection of books, exacting fines for overborrowing, damage or loss of books, and the expulsion of members for violation of the rules.

Village libraries were established early in Enniscorthy and in Tissara and in Caltra, County Galway. The Enniscorthy library, with a strong co-op behind it, was outstandingly affluent: it had a reading room and between 200 and 300 books. From the active Roscommon committee[46] came the report that

> The Tissara Library has seventy-five members. The number of books borrowed and exchanged during 1900 was 689. Irish books are very popular, and some of the members have learned much ballad poetry by heart, and recite it to their neighbours of an evening. They also tell each other stories from Carleton and other Irish writers, and so brighten their home-lives a little.

44 IAOS Annual Report 1900, p.25.
45 The full list is extant in *The Irish Homestead* of 20 January 1900.
46 A prime mover in this development, along with the Magan family, was Thomas Mee (1850-1914), chairman of Tissara Co-op Agricultural Society. At the age of twenty Mee had emigrated to England where he became a successful businessman. On medical advice he returned to Roscommon about 1887, bought a 350-acre farm and became a progressive farmer who saw the lack of education (even more than the lack of sufficient land or capital) as the major stumbling-block to Irish farming progress.

A year later there was the heartening account of a farmers' circulating library established by the Dromahair Dairy Society at Creevelea, County Leitrim. This library not only lent books but also sold "scores of books" at cost price.

Plunkett's Rural Life competition in 1901, in which he gave prizes totalling £50 to the societies which had done most to brighten rural living and make their parish a better place to live in, was a fillip to the library movement. By the end of 1901 some thirty societies were reported to have libraries, many of them availing of the Department of Agriculture's offer to give books on economic and industrial subjects, valued at £3, to libraries and associations which formed a committee to manage and take care of the books. There were excellent libraries established at Drumully (Killeshandra), Spiddal, Foynes, Carrickmacross and Bekan (County Mayo). All these societies, as well as Dromahair, Tissara, Enniscorthy and Clarina (County Limerick) were winners[47] in Plunkett's competition (sometimes known as the 'Stop Emigration' Scheme) which continued during 1902.

The village libraries, like the village banks, succeeded or failed according to the measure of devotion applied by the management. In some places they continued to operate successfully for several years until they were absorbed into the County Council Library structure.

The Co-operative Reference Library was set up in the Plunkett House Dublin in January 1914. The initiative again came mainly from Plunkett and Father Tom Finlay who put in many books from their own personal collections to give the library a start. The generous grant of £2,000 from the Carnegie United Kingdom Trustees in July enabled the co-operators to purchase many more useful volumes. Lionel Smith-Gordon and Francis Cruise O'Brien (the father of the present Conor Cruise O'Brien) were employed as librarians and did an excellent job. The object of the Co-operative Reference Library was "to supply accurate information as to the progress and distinctive features of co-operative organisation in *all countries* to genuine inquirers and more especially to the field workers of the three Agricultural Organisation Societies of the British Isles."[48] In 1917 an Education and Publicity Bureau was instituted with its head-quarters in the *Irish Homestead* office at 18 South Frederick Street. This bureau was controlled by a committee representing the IAOS, the IAWS, *The Irish Homestead* and the Co-operative Reference Library. Under the direction of its acting secretary, P.J. Gillespie, the Bureau took over the publicity work initiated by the Reference Library and informed the press

---

47 The Creevelea group were major prizewinners for an "amazing record of social activity in a poor country parish". See IAOS Annual Report 1901, p.39 et seq. At Clarina the assiduous work of Lord and Lady Emly was praised for the way in which it assuaged the effects of the class warfare between farmers and labourers.

48 Membership was available to suitable persons for a subscription of not less than one guinea per annum (£1.05) which entitled the member to one copy of each of the library's publications. Associate membership cost 7/6 (37½ pence) and special terms were given to co-operative societies and federations. Consultations and the ordinary supply of information were free but special research was charged for on the basis of the labour and expense involved.

and co-operative societies of co-operative news through circular letters, reprints of technical articles and topical talks.[49] The Co-operative Reference Library became world famous in a short time, its services being extensively used by co-operative organisations in every continent despite the difficulties caused by the Great War; a great deal of business was done with India and the USA. From October 1915, the Reference Library published a quarterly business bulletin, *Better Business* (price 1/-), which drew subscriptions and contributors from all over the world. However, in 1917 the IAOS reported that its circulation in Ireland still remained lamentably small. Yet, for many, it remained a popular and informative magazine and continued to appear regularly until 1923 when, because of lack of support and despite having changed its name to the *Irish Economist*, it finally gave up the unequal struggle.[50]

The Co-operative Reference Library suffered a similar fate. After his home at Kilteragh was blown up by armed men on the night of 30 January 1923, Plunkett, who had been studying and lecturing in Washington, returned to England homeless and disconsolate. The location of the Horace Plunkett Foundation (a trust for the promotion of rural social development, endowed with £20,000 by Plunkett) was inevitably drawn to mainland, more settled, Britain. Plunkett had hoped that, in a happier Ireland, it would have been possible to house the Foundation in Kilteragh while still securing foreign support and patronage from wealthy benefactors, even far in excess of what he himself had given. The Foundation was moved to London where it was housed at 10 Doughty Street. With it went the Co-operative Reference Library. There was nothing anyone in Ireland could do.

Farm Service Co-ops

Ideally, one would like to think that the work of a co-operative society and the notion of 'service' to the community were synonymous, and that its reiteration would be superfluous. We have witnessed the aspirations of the early co-operators and their dreams of a co-operative commonwealth. We harken back once more to AE's ideal that co-operative societies should "develop and absorb all rural business into their organisation". The concept of 'service' motivated the pioneers during the early years of the century to establish up to five or six different types of co-operative society to seek to establish a total co-operative service organisation — a co-operative community. There was, in addition, the hopeful trend toward general purpose societies in the euphoric latter years of World War I. Soon afterwards came the tragic recurring pattern — hope, disaster, depression. Just as the labourers of Ralahine returned with quiet fatalism to their old

---

49 Material sent to co-ops was always dispatched with a covering letter from the local IAOS organiser. Some 7,000 farmer members of co-operative societies were on the mailing list in 1918.

50 *The Irish Statesman*, a business and political weekly first published in July 1919 and sponsored by Plunkett and wealthy supporter Dr James Ashe, had a considerable foreign readership. *The Irish Homestead* became incorporated in the *Statesman* in 1923 under the editorship of AE.

subservience, the shattered co-operative movement in the nineteen twenties retired to lick its wounds and regret that it had all been 'too good to be true'. Societies became introspective and parochial — even modest proposals for progress were viewed with the 'poor man's' horror of speculation. Soon the majority of creameries were doing little more than paying a poor price for milk. Co-operative stores were little trading posts which did an uninspiring (and often apparently reluctant) trade in the commonest farm requisites. Traces of the co-operative character of many of these institutions became increasingly elusive and, if the Irish peasantry had learned regrettably little of co-operation in the first thirty years,[51] they learned exceedingly little in the thirty years that followed. Traditions establish themselves rather easily in Ireland — particularly traditions of doing nothing. As late as 1967 we find the IAOS noting with regret the inactivity of societies in the service field and their failure to emerge from their 'traditional' shell:

> Traditionally the development of agricultural co-operation has concerned itself mainly with transactions on behalf of the farmer 'beyond the farm gate' ... The Local Co-operative geared itself to market as efficiently as possible what the farmer produced. It provided him with his raw materials ... It did not consider that it had a function within the farm gates.[52]

From the mid-nineteen fifties, farmers had become increasingly discontented at the failure of their co-operatives to help them make their way in the new and confusing post-war era of rapidly developing farm mechanisation and new agricultural technology. Demands were made on the local· co-op committees to involve themselves in their members' problems. They varied from demands for more credit facilities, provision of machinery hire services, advice and help to provide better milking machines or better farm buildings, to establish milking relief organisations, to introduce better breeds of livestock, seeds, manures, fertilisers, and a wider range of farm requisites and gadgetry. Many farmers required help in dealing with government and other official agencies, not only in the implementation of field work (land drainage, reclamation, farm building) but also with the extensive paperwork — seeking grants, planning permissions, farm accounting and negotiations for loan capital. Certain reactionary managers and committees who, through successful penny-pinching and frugal housekeeping over a generation, had accumulated capital,[53] found themselves increasingly under pressure from the progressive young bloods of the better educated generation of farmers emerging

---

51 From the founding of the IAOS in 1894 to 1924.
52 IAOS Annual Report 1967, p.7.
53 A number of societies had accumulated substantial reserves. One creamery society in the west, far from engaging in development work in its own small-farm area, had a large sum invested at very low interest in Dublin Corporation!

from the ranks of Macra na Feirme and other rural organisations.[54]

In many cases, particularly in the western counties, the frustrations of the progressively-minded farmer were matched by those of his agricultural advisor, who found that his farmer client was often unable to act on scientific advice given to him because of the lack of adequate agricultural infrastructure in the pioneer farmer's district.

The new farming frequently called for the use of machinery which, though comparatively simple and cheap, was uneconomic for individual ownership; the small farmer's priorities for profitable investment were usually the acquisition of an extra cow or the fertilising of an additional area of grassland.[55] The use of fertilisers in many western areas remained minimal for many years after fertiliser usage in better farming areas had trebled. One major inhibition was the lack of proper spreaders. Farmers might be persuaded to *purchase* fertilisers but many balked at the prospect of spreading them by hand from a bucket or a sack-apron:

> The gap between what we know has to be done and what is actually being done is very great. The Agricultural Adviser must feel very frustrated in his work when he realises that in spite of the best advice he can give to the individual farmer, the latter is very often not in a position to put it into practice . . . To follow in an adequate way the scientific advice which is available to him, the farmer requires what might be termed a practical field service operating on his behalf.
> It is suggested that the local Co-operative Society should be the link between the advisory service and the local field services . . . A broad division of function . . . might be that it is the advisor's job to condition farmers to make use of the services . . . It is the Co-operative Society's job to enable the physical work to be done.[56]

Although it was in the 'post-Knapp' period (from 1964 oward) that the big push was made for the provision of co-operative field services, much useful pioneering had been undertaken before this time. The enthusiasm of Killeshandra to extend the scope of its services has already been noted. Also worthy of special mention were the efforts of the small but highly efficient dairy society at Mullinahone, County Tipperary. Other societies participated and some of them achieved notable results with specific services. Some of the larger societies employed their own agricultural graduates to supplement the local advisory service provided by the committees of agriculture. Others had agricultural advisors, appointed under the parish plan, based in the area, with office facilities provided on

54 Let it be said also that some committees successfully resisted these pressures for a long time — sometimes through the illegal expedient of closing their share registers and refusing to transfer shares or admit new members.

55 Private contractors usually emerged only when the new farm practices had been adopted by a sufficient number of farmers to make contracting a profitable venture. In western areas, much of the contract work was undertaken by men who were themselves small farmers operating part-time and thus unable to budget for the period of low or non-existent profits until demand for the services increased.

56 IAOS Annual Report 1967, p.7.

the co-op premises. Yet the most striking example of a society providing a comprehensive service, covering almost all the farmer's requirements, is that of the Lough Egish Society. In the difficult drumlin area of County Monaghan, so typical of many small-farm areas of the underdeveloped counties, this progressive, long-established society, which has grown from a crossroad creamery (1902) to a major multi-purpose co-operative,[57] is effectively demonstrating how the West is won.

In other areas different circumstances prevailed. In some places, either through the intransigence of the local co-operative committee or the total absence of any society within operating distance, the local people were compelled to establish completely new societies to meet the demand for vital services. The ideal arrangement is that service operations of this nature are best undertaken by an existing strong society with adequate capital, efficient organisation and proven resources of management.[58] Undercapitalised, pioneering ventures with inexperienced personnel are particularly vulnerable. This would seem to be borne out by the fact that of the six farm services co-ops formed between 1966 and 1968,[59] only two have achieved success. The survival and notable success of Comhar Iorrais Teo (County Mayo) and Comhar Chumann Forbartha Chorca Duibhne (County Kerry) bear heartening witness that, even in the most difficult circumstances, the truly heroic effort rarely goes unrewarded.

---

57 Its membership in 1974 was 1,894. Turnover was £7.4 million.
58 This presumes, of course, an honest enthusiasm, the desire to provide a good service and assiduous 'nursing' over the critical period until the inevitable teething troubles are overcome.
59 Corca Duibhne (1966), Iorrais (1967), Clarinbridge, Dunmore, Glencolumbkille, Graneyside (1968).

Author to Reader Again

This narrative ends here, but the story continues. Some of the major developments in the last decade have already been revealed in the previous sectoral chapters of this book. Many others are either incomplete or else too recent to be viewed in an historical perspective. Perusal of the most recent IAOS Annual Reports, followed by a visit to your local co-operative society or credit union, will quickly apprise you of the most recent co-operative happenings. A visit to the Plunkett House in Dublin is also recommended. Here, under one roof, there is much of the bustle of the present and the shape of things to come, set against the background of a not inglorious past and an aura of history that is almost palpable.

In writing this book I set out initially to do nothing more than uncover the historical happenings and present them in a sensible perspective. However, readers are conditioned to expect something more — facts revealed, evaluated, conclusions reached and recommendations made. As it happened, I found it impossible in revealing 'facts' to refrain from comment and comparison (I trust not always odious). Some of my remarks may qualify as evaluation and, even if they do, not everyone will agree with them. In any case I am little inclined to summarise them here as a formal evaluation. Evaluation belongs more properly to the immediate rather than the distant past. The really important evaluation of past performance is the one which is done by the individual society and the individual co-op member as to how well they have lived up to the co-operative ideal.

The historian's job would be an easy one if historical 'facts' were as solid and as discrete as individual pounds of butter. What teaches the historian humility is the realisation that there are no well-defined limits to a so-called historical fact. In even the smallest quantity of sand we can never grasp, encompass, retain and analyse every grain. In history, happenings result from previous happenings and in turn contribute to future ones. We can only hope to capture enough to indicate the general substance and its likely uses and consequences. All is not gold that glitters and gold mixed with baser materials does not always glitter; so we are sometimes abashed to find out later that some once tarnished nuggets have been overlooked or some glittering material of great promise has proved worthless. However, when the research is adequate and conscientious and the separate findings can be reconciled, the historical blunders are rarely major ones. But even where the historical picture is essentially true and comparatively clear, deductions

and conclusions are notoriously difficult. The citizen is little concerned with the minor deductions which historians make in the context of what did or did not happen. He is more concerned with how validly the actions and experiences of the past can effect and influence the future.

History has some hopeful pointers and some cautionary tales. The important thing is not to be overenthused or overawed by either, but to weigh them soberly in the balance with the other data which the wise manager collects to guide him in his decisions. This principle applies equally to the policy decisions of committees as to the strategies of managers. History can guide our decision-making but it should never be considered in isolation or presented as the sole basis for doing this or not doing that. It should never be used to condone inaction or absolve us from making decisions.

It would be folly, therefore, for me to offer any deductions or conclusions other than in the rigid historical context of looking back at what happened in the past and contriving to see things more clearly. Many of these conclusions are facile and you will have reached them long before now:

(1) The Irish co-operative movement has *succeeded* — certainly by ordinary commercial criteria. The movement comprises some 200,000 families and has an annual turnover rapidly approaching the magic figure of a billion £'s.

(2) Its success has been largely (indeed, almost exclusively) in the agricultural field. Outside the sphere of influence of the Belfast Co-operative Society, there has been little formal co-operation in the towns — certainly none which has coalesced as a 'movement'.

(3) The success of the agricultural co-operative movement emerges as something almost *fortuitous*. One is prompted to evaluate it as an 'economic miracle' — and in a much more literal context than the loose phrase commonly employed to describe remarkable economic growth.

The 'miracle' is the business success of an association which has always contained in strong measure all the ingredients of business failure. In every generation the co-operators have been, in overwhelming majority, a body of men, none of whom individually would (or could) ever embark successfully on a commercial venture of any sizeable scale. A co-operative society has been more than once cynically defined to me as "a business association of losers". It was a definition which, in the context of Irish agricultural co-operation up to recent times, one could offer little to gainsay.

What if a patient suffering from several fatal ailments reluctantly and imperfectly undertakes treatment and survives? We look to a combination of factors to explain his recovery — perhaps some slight exaggeration of the symptoms, the skill of physicians, the care of nurses, the encouragement of family and friends, the faith, courage and resilience of the patient. The analogy in the case of the Irish co-operative movement seems straightforward — pointing fairly conclusively to the inherent faith, heroism and resilience of the men concerned — leaders, policy-makers, organisers, managers and ordinary co-op members.

On the matter of recommendations, myriads of them, major and minor ones, spring to mind. Every page of our history cries forth the need for co-operative education and participation. It is time for progress towards industrial democracy — the identity of interest of workers and employers — in a movement providing direct employment for more than 10,000 employees! One would equally wish for a better career structure for co-operative employees which would enhance the talents of workers and reward their merit; where the lowliest apprentice entering the smallest co-op shop could aspire to be, one day, general manager of a major group or federation.

Many of J.G. Knapp's recommendations and suggestions are still valid — and still unfulfilled.

The IAOS, overwhelmed with the volume of co-operative progress, has been unable to employ and retain sufficient suitable personnel to build up strong divisions on the recommended pattern. In fact it has had to forego some areas of service in order to maintain other more immediately essential services. Some of the major co-op groups employed private consultants to undertake work which should have been done by appropriate sections within the IAOS, had such been available and adequately equipped for the job.[1] There is as yet no full commitment on the part of the societies about the future role and structures of the IAOS. Accession to the European Community has put additional strain both on the finances and the man-hours of the organisation society, and progress is meantime halted whilst the co-ops withhold money and fail to agree on structural details.

There are some who favour a policy of 'decentralisation'. They suggest that the IAOS be a smaller organisation and that the bulk of the services hitherto provided by the IAOS be made available at local level by the major co-op groups. There are undoubtedly many basic functions and services which properly should devolve to some extent but in this writer's opinion they must be "in addition to" rather than "instead of" a strengthening of the parent body. Decentralisation increases rather than diminishes the need for a strong co-ordinating organisation to provide more specialised services which local participation will surely bring out. The need for co-ordination and supplementation of services will undoubtedly increase. Above all, the IAOS must remain strong in the role conceived for the original Co-operative Union — "the co-operative conscience".[2]

One can go on endlessly discussing details of policy and management. All management, they say, is merely the expression of a great idea.[3] What is the great *co-operative* idea? For George Russsell and the founder fathers it was a limitless concept of pursuing the "golden heresy of truth". Father

---

1 Some of the business consultancy work was so shallow and costly as to evoke memories of Robert Townsend's cynical definition of a consultant: "A gentleman who takes the loan of your watch to tell you the time; and then walks off with the watch."
2 See Joseph Clayton, *Co-operation* (London: T.C. & E.C. Jack, n.d.).
3 See Robert Heller, *The Naked Manager* (London: Barrie & Jenkins, 1972).

Tom Finlay did not deal in fantasies; but, as a Christian, he must necessarily believe in an achievable Utopia (as did St Thomas More, four centuries previously) — attainable by applying "the familiar magic of commonsense".[4] AE urged a synthesis of all the co-operative efforts to achieve the great co-operative ideal. He conceived of "carving an Attica out of Ireland"[5] and creating an even wider co-operative commonwealth. But the essence of the ideal was to create, at every level, "true social organisms".

The key word is "organism". A community is organic but unfortunately the outlook of the 'experts' dealing with it is often mechanical. It is vitally important that the organic concept be appreciated when we are almost daily devising new groupings and better organisational structures for our co-operatives. "How big should a co-op be?" As well as questioning the size of the economic unit, we must ask, "How many people?" The structure of a living organism, however flabby it may appear, is still far more delicately geared than is the most elaborate machine. An 'organism' has also a capacity for accommodation and spontaneous adaptation which a machine lacks — and which often the most complex machine lacks most! A co-operative community built on proper organic lines has vital advantages. It has the ability to heal its own wounds; it may be partially or temporarily disabled but it does not grind to a halt when some of the parts fall out, and it does not carry the threat of explosive self-destruction inherent in the machine.

Co-operative solidarity is an ideal, but an ideal which should never be artificially contrived in the face of co-operative inefficiency or indolent monopoly. Co-ops should compete with each other in the efficiency and 'style' with which they do their business — but competition in its full capitalist context is anathema to co-operators. It should rather be hoped that neighbouring co-ops would work together, guiding and helping each other and, where possible, contriving better mutual efficiencies. Territorial intrusions should never be done by stealth but by agreement. There is a vital role here for a strong central body (IAOS) representing majority co-operative opinion, armed with the facts, and thus able to exercise the strongest moral persuasion.

It is worth reflecting also whether we have not so far been pursuing co-operative development in a rather unbalanced, two-dimensional way — with perhaps too much emphasis on length and breadth rather than *depth*. There is undoubted need for the major co-operative consortia to meet the challenge of the capitalist multi-nationals. There is equal need, however, for co-operative penetration, with the development of co-operatives at every level from the national and provincial federations to the small townland syndicate. There is room for all kinds and sizes of co-operatives pursuing all kinds of appropriately diverse aims. All truly natural (organic) development is diverse but complementary, hierarchical in unit size, but in function co-ordinated and symbiotic.

4   Vice-president's speech at sixth annual conference, Cork, 10 July 1902.
5   See G.W. Russell, *The National Being* (Dublin: Maunsel and Company, 1916).

For all our faults,[7] great things, even heroic things, have been accomplished. But, as ever, a great deal is waiting to be done. Plunkett liked to quote Walt Whitman:

> It is provided in the essence of things, that from any fruition of success, no matter what, shall come forth something to make a greater struggle necessary.

7   A favourite phrase of Dr Henry Kennedy was "For all our faults; and they're neither few nor small."

Index

Note: The method of alphabetisation used is word-by-word. References in bold characters denote illustrations.

ACC, *see* Agricultural Credit Corporation Ltd
AE, *see* Russell, George William
Abbeydorney Co-operative Dairy Society, 210*n*, 212*n*
Abbeyleix, agricultural bank, 176
Abercorn, James Hamilton, 2nd Duke of, 382*n*
Aberdeen, Lady, 69, 300
Achill, co-operative fishing society, 331
Achonry, co-operative creamery society, 210*n*, 227, 255, 316, 317; co-operative home industries society, 303*n*
Act of Union 1800, 164, 374
Adams, James, 140, 142, 143, 144, 209
Adams, W.G.S., 112
Adare (Limerick), co-operative agricultural society, 261*n*, 268*n*; tobacco-growing, 377*n*
Addergoole Agricultural Credit Society, 168
Advisory Committee on Marketing of Agricultural Produce 1957, 226
Aghabulloge, creamery, 192*n*
Aghadillane, creamery, 212
Aghadowey, co-operative creamery society, 190
agrarian outrages, 13-15, 18, 46, 50, 52
agricultural affairs, administration of, prior to 1899, 83-84
Agricultural and Horticultural Association, 66*n*
Agricultural and Technical Instruction Act 1899, 84-85, 97
Agricultural Co-operative Association of England, 121*n*
agricultural co-operative movement, *see* co-operative movement (Ireland); co-operative movement (Northern Ireland)
Agricultural Co-operative Movement (England), 154
agricultural co-operative societies, *see* co-operative societies (Ireland);

co-operative societies (Northern Ireland)
Agricultural Credit Committee 1912, 158-60, 174-75, 176
Agricultural Credit Corporation Ltd (ACC), 114, 178-79, 218, 266, 349*n*
agricultural credit societies: financing and government loans, 91, 167-71, 174-76, 179-80; legislation, 167, 173*n*; loans, 170, 171-72, 177, 180; numbers and membership, 170, 172, 175, 177, 178; organisation of, by IAOS, 165-81; rate of interest, 173; rules, 173; decline in business during World War I and 1920s, 177-78; establishment of central credit bank, 175-77; fluke societies, 179-81; *see also individual societies*
agricultural crisis of 1870s, 48-50
agricultural goods, co-operative trading in, *see* agricultural societies; creameries
Agricultural Institute (An Foras Talúntais), 208, 298
Agricultural Ireland, 122-23
agricultural policy, post-Emergency, committee of inquiry on, 125
Agricultural Produce (Eggs) Act 1924, 262*n*, 287
Agricultural Produce (Fresh Meat) Act 1930, 262*n*
Agricultural Produce (Potatoes) Act 1932, 262*n*
agricultural societies: administration and management, 235-36, 253-54, 260, 266, 270, 271; creamery involvement in agricultural trading, 125, 189, 208, 234, 245, 267, 268, 272; finance, 126, 235, 260, 266; formation of, 234, 236, 240-42, 247, 255, 258, 259, 260, 270; insurance, 362; membership, 126, 245; numbers, 126, 245, 251, 259, 260, 266, 268; opposition of traders to, 63*n*, 236, 239-40, 242-43, 247-48, 262, 268-69; organisation of, by IAOS, 120, 235-45, 247-48, 251-59, 262, 273; prosperity of,